Lecture Notes in Computer Science

Lecture Notes in Computer Science

Edited by G. Goos and J. Hartmanis

259

PARLE
Parallel Architectures
and Languages Europe

Volume II: Parallel Languages
Eindhoven, The Netherlands, June 15–19, 1987
Proceedings

Edited by
J. W. de Bakker, A. J. Nijman and P. C. Treleaven

Springer-Verlag

Berlin Heidelberg New York London Paris Tokyo

CR Subject Classification (1987): C.1-4, D.1, D.3-4, F.1, F.3-4

ISBN 3-540-17945-3 Springer-Verlag Berlin Heidelberg New York
ISBN 0-387-17945-3 Springer-Verlag New York Berlin Heidelberg

Printing and binding: Druckhaus Beltz, Hemsbach/Bergstr.
2145/3140-543210

Preface

PARLE, the conference on Parallel Architectures and Languages Europe, was organized as a meeting place for researchers in the field of theory, design and applications of parallel computer systems. The initiative for the conference was taken by project 415 of ESPRIT (the European Strategic Programme for Research and Development in Information Technology). The scope of the conference covered central themes in the area of parallel architectures and languages including topics such as concurrent, object-oriented, logic and functional programming, MIMD and reduction machines, process theory, design and verification of parallel systems, performance evaluation, interconnection networks, systolic arrays, VLSI and RISC architectures, applications and special purpose architectures.

The scientific programme of PARLE consisted firstly of five invited lectures devoted to overviews of major recent research areas. Moreover, 44 papers were selected for presentation from 156 submitted ones. The program committee for PARLE was constituted as follows:

S. Abramsky (Imperial College)*
J.W. de Bakker (chairman,Amsterdam)*
J.P. Banâtre (Rennes)*
H. Barendregt (Nijmegen)*
W. Bibel (Munich)*
M. Broy (Passau)
W. Damm (Aachen)*
J. Gurd (Manchester)*
D. Harel (Weizmann and CMU)*
P. Henderson (Stirling)
L.O. Hertzberger (Amsterdam)*
T. Johnsson (Gøteborg)*
N.D. Jones (Copenhagen)
Ph. Jorrand (Grenoble)*
W. Kluge (Kiel)*

V.E. Kotov (Novosibirsk)
H.T. Kung (CMU)
H.W. Lawson (Linköping)*
G. Levi (Pisa).
D. May (INMOS)*
C. Moser (Orsay)
E.-R. Olderog (Kiel)*
W.P. de Roever (Eindhoven)
G. Roucairol (Bull)
G. Rozenberg (Leiden)*
L. Steels (Brussels)
J.-C. Syre (ECRC)*
P.C. Treleaven (chairman,
Univ.Coll.London)*
M. Vanneschi (Pisa)*

Members of the Program Committee who were present at the selection meeting are marked by a *.

We wish to extend our sincere thanks to the members of the Program Committee for their invaluable contributions to the shaping of the PARLE programme. We also express our gratitude to the PARLE referees for their assistance in this process.

The programme of PARLE furthermore comprised presentations on the subprojects which together constitute ESPRIT project 415. Parallel architectures based on a variety of programming styles (object-oriented, logic, functional, dataflow) were represented in these overviews.

The Proceedings of PARLE are collected in two volumes, the first one containing the papers in which the emphasis is more on Parallel Architectures, together with ESPRIT project 415 overviews, and the second one containing the papers which fall under the heading of Parallel Languages.

PARLE has received substantial sponsorship from the ESPRIT program, and from the companies which together form the consortium for ESPRIT project 415: AEG, West Germany; Nixdorf (Stollmann), West Germany; Bull, France; CSELT, Italy; GEC, UK; Philips, the Netherlands.

Philips Research Eindhoven was responsible for the local organization of PARLE. A special tribute is due to Frank Stoots for his skilful, cheerful and meticulous handling of all organizational details. Hans Oerlemans provided valuable help at crucial moments in the PARLE preparations. The Dutch National Concurrency Project assisted at various points in the organization. Technical support has been provided by the Centre for Mathematics and Computer Science, in particular by Ms. L. Vasmel-Kaarsemaker, and by University College London.

Thanks to the contributions of all the above listed persons and institutions, we have been able to collect in these two volumes a wealth of material on the theme of PARLE. The editors would be amply rewarded for their efforts if these results were to prove instrumental for the further advancement of European research on Parallel Architectures and Languages.

March 1987   The Editors,

                                                             J.W. de Bakker
                                                             A.J. Nijman
                                                             P.C. Treleaven

Contents Volume II

Contents Volume I

List of Referees

Alfons
Ambriova, V.
America, P.
Amjone, M.
Andersen, J.D.
Asirelli, P.
Aspetsberger, K.
Augustsson, L.
Baiardi, F.
Balbo, G.
Balsamo, S.
Bandman, O.L.
Barahona, P.M.
Barbuti, R.
Barringer, H.
Bayerl, S.
Beer, J.
Behr, P.
Benker, H.
Best, E.
Bistrov, A.V.
Bloedorn, H.
Bohm, A.P.W.
Brookes, S.
Bulyonkov, M.A.
Bush, V.J.
Capon, P.C.
Carlstedt, G.
Chassin de Kergommeaux, J. de
Cherkasova, L.A.
Cindio, F. de
Clausen, J.
Corsini, P.
Courcelle, B.
Cunningham, R.S.
Danvy, O.
Danulutto, M.
Dekkers, W.
Dencker, P.

Dill, D.L.
Dittrich, G.
Donatelli, L.
Duinker, W.
Eder, E.
Edwards, D.A.
Eekelen, M.C.J.D. van
Einarsson, B.
Emde Boas-Lubsen, G. van
Enjalbert, P.
Fagerstrom, J.
Fantechi, A.
Fehr, E.
Feijen, W.H.J.
Field, A.J.
Fischer, K.
Fjellborg, B.
Foley, J.F.
Francesco, N. de
Francoise, A.
Fronhofer, B.
Frosini, G.
Furbach, U.
Gamatie, B.
Gerth, R.
Glaser, H.W.
Goeman, H.J.M.
Goltz, U.
Graziano, F.
Groenewegen, L.
Grumberg, O.
Gruntz,
Hahn, W.
Halbwachs, N.
Hankin, C.L.
Hartel, P.H.
Harvills, P.
Hattem, M. van
Haverkort, B.R.H.M.

Held, A.J.

Holldobler, S.

Hommel, G.

Hooman, J.J.M.

HuBmann, H.

Janssens, D.

Jones, K.D.

Jonckers, V.

Josko, B.

Kaplan, S.

Keesmaat, N.W.

Kirkham, C.C.

Klint, P.

Klop, J.W.

Konrad, W.

Koymans, R.

Kramer, T.

Kreitz, C.

Kreowski, H.J.

Kroger, F.

Kuchcinski, K.

Kuchen, H.

Kucherov, G.A.

Kusche, K.D.

Laforenza, D.

Laurent, K.

Lange, O.

Lehmann, F.

Lelchuk, T.I.

Leoni, G.

Levin, D.Y.

Letz, R.

Lightner, J.M.

Lingas, A.

Lodi, E.

Loogen, R.

Lopriore, L.

Lotti, G.

Ljulyakov, A.V.

Main, M.

Maluzijnski, J.

Mancareua, P.

Marchuk, A.G.

Marcke, K. v.

Martinelli, E.

Marwedel, P.

Mazare, G.

Meijer, E.

Meinen, P.

Merceron, A.

Meurant, G.

Moiso, C.

Mooy, W.

Muntean, T.

Nepomnyashchy, V.A.

Nett, E.

Neugebauer, G.

Nickl, R.

Nicola, R. de

Nielsen, M.

Nocker, E.G.

Panzieri, F.

Paredis, J.

Park, D.

Pedreschi, D.

Pehrson, B.

Pepels, B.

Perrin, G.R.

Persson, M.

Peug, Z.

Philips, L.H.

Pinegger, T.

Plasmeyer, R.

Quinton, P.

Radig, B.

Rannov, R.

Ratiliffe, M.J.

Raynal, M.

Reisig, W.

Rezus, A.

Ribas, H.

Ricci, L.

Ringwood, G.A.

Robert, P.

Roscoe, A.W.

Rosenfeld, A.

Sadler, M.R.

Sardu, G.

Saubra, A.

Scheperes, J.

Schmeck, H.

Schnittgen, C.

Schneeberger, J.

Schumann, J.

Sedukhin, S.G.

Sestoft, P.

Seznec, A.

Simi, M.

Sleator, D.

Sofi, G.

Sondergaard, H.

Song, S.W.

Sralas, A.

Starreveld, A.G.

Stavridou, V.

Steen, M.R. van

Stoyan, H.

Swierstra, S.D.

Tanenbaum, A.

Tarini, F.

Taubner, D.

Tel, G.

Teugvald, E.

Thiagarajan, P.S.

Thorelli, L.E.

Tijgar, D.

Tomasi, A.

Tucci, S.

Vaglini, G.

Valkovsky, V.A.

Vautherin, J.

Vree, W.G.

Waning, E. van

Wanhammar, L.

Watson, I.

Westphal, H.

Yvon, J.

Executing a Program on the MIT Tagged-Token Dataflow Architecture

Arvind

Rishiyur S. Nikhil

Laboratory for Computer Science

Massachusetts Institute of Technology

545 Technology Square, Cambridge, MA 02139, USA

Abstract

The MIT Tagged-Token Dataflow project has a radical, but integrated approach to high-performance parallel computing. We study high-level languages that have fine-grained parallelism implicitly in their operational semantics, rather than extending conventional sequential languages. Programs are compiled to *dataflow graphs* which may be regarded as a parallel machine language. Dataflow graphs are executed on the MIT Tagged-Token Dataflow Architecture, which is a multiprocessor architecture. In this paper we provide an overview of this approach.

1   Introduction

There are several commercial and research efforts currently underway to build parallel computers with the intent of achieving performance far beyond what is possible today. Most of the approaches that can be classified as general-purpose, MIMD (Multiple Instruction Multiple Data stream) approaches are evolutionary in nature. At the architectural level, they involve interconnections of conventional von Neumann machines, and at the programming level they involve taking a conventional sequential language (such as FORTRAN or C) and augmenting it with a few "parallel" primitives which are usually interpreted as operating system calls.

In contrast, the dataflow approach that we are pursuing is a radical one. We believe that von Neumann architectures have fundamental characteristics that preclude extending them to the parallel environment. First, they exhibit an intolerance for high memory latencies which are inevitable in a parallel machine, and second, they do not provide fast synchronization mechanisms. We also believe that basing the parallel programming model on sequential languages significantly complicates the compiling process and will not lead to efficient utilization of parallel machines. Our detailed and technical justifications for abandoning the von Neumann approach are explored in [5].

In our approach, we begin with *Id*, a high-level language with enormous parallelism *implicit* in its operational semantics. Programs in Id are compiled into *Dataflow Graphs*, which constitute

This research was done at the MIT Laboratory for Computer Science. Funding for this project is provided in part by the Advanced Research Projects Agency of the Department of Defense under the Office of Naval Research contract N00014-84-K-0099.

a parallel machine language. Finally, dataflow graphs are encoded and executed on the *Tagged-Token Dataflow Architecture* (TTDA), a machine that abandons completely the Program Counter-based sequential scheduling of instructions in von Neumann machines in favor of purely data-driven scheduling.

In this paper we attempt to demystify the dataflow approach by providing a fairly detailed explanation of the compilation and execution of Id programs. Because of the expanse of topics, our coverage of neither the language and compiler nor the architecture can be comprehensive; we provide pointers to relevant literature throughout for the interested reader.

In Section 2 we present the program examples, taking the opportunity to explain Id, our high-level parallel language, and to state our philosophy about parallel languages in general. In Section 3 we explain Dataflow Graphs as a parallel machine language and show how to compile the example programs. In Section 4 we describe the MIT Tagged-Token Dataflow Architecture and show how to encode and execute dataflow graphs. Finally, in Section 5 we discuss some characteristics of the machine, compare it with other approaches, and outline our current and planned research.

Before we plunge in, a word about our program examples. First, we are not concerned here with algorithmic cleverness. Improving the algorithm is always a possibility, but is outside the scope of this paper— we concentrate here on efficient execution of a given algorithm. Second, our examples are necessarily small because of limitations of space. (In our research we are concerned primarily with large programs.) However, even these small examples will reveal an abundance of issues in parallelism.

2   The Language Id and Program Examples

In our approach to parallelism we believe it is necessary to begin with a programming language with the following characteristics:

- It must insulate the programmer from details of the machine such as the number and speed of processors, topology and speed of the communication network, *etc.*

- The parallelism should be implicit in the operational semantics, thus freeing the programmer from having to identify parallelism explicitly.

- It must be *determinate*, thus freeing the programmer from details of scheduling and synchronization of parallel activities.

The last point deserves elaboration. Implicit parallelism in the language, varying machine configurations and machine load can cause the particular choice of schedule for parallel activities in a program to be non-deterministic. However, the *result* computed should not vary with the schedule. For example, Functional Programming languages, because of the Church-Rosser property, are determinate in this sense.

Id is a high-level language which may be considered to be a functional programming language augmented with a data-structuring mechanism called *I-structures*. I-structures are array-like data structures related to *terms* in logic programming languages, and were introduced into Id to overcome deficiencies in purely functional data structures (see [6] for a detailed discussion of this topic).

The exposition here relies heavily on the intuition of the reader. The precise syntax and operational semantics of Id (in terms of rewrite rules) may be found in [17] and [18].

2.1 Example 1: Inner Product

The inner-product of two vectors of size n may be written in Id as follows:

```
Def ip A B = {  aux j s = If j > n Then s
                         Else aux (j + 1) (s + A[j] * B[j])
            In
              aux 1 0 } ;
```

This defines a function ip that takes two vectors A and B as arguments and returns a number as its result. The body of the function is a Block which contains one local function definition aux. The value of the block (and the function) is the value of the expression following the In keyword. aux is a tail-recursive function that iterates on index j and carries a running total in s.

To simplify the exposition, we assume n to be a constant. In practice n would be extracted from A or B using the *bounds* function.

We follow the usual static scoping rules for functions and blocks. For example, the variables A and B are free in aux and refer to their definition in the immediately surrounding scope (*i.e.*, the formal parameters). The expression following the In keyword may use variables defined in the block and variables from the surrounding scope. For example, an equivalent definition of ip is:

```
Def ip_aux A B j s = If j > n Then s
                     Else ip_aux A B (j + 1) (s + A[j] * B[j]) ;

Def ip A B = ip_aux A B 1 0 ;
```

In fact this transformation is performed automatically by our compiler and is called *lambda-lifting* [14] in the functional programming literature.

Tail-recursion is a special case of general recursion which is amenable to significant optimization (equivalent to iteration). Id provides a special syntax for iterative loops, and the inner-product program would more likely be written as follows:

```
Def ip A B = {  s = 0
            In
              {For j From 1 To n Do
                   Next s = s + A[j] * B[j]
                   Finally s }} ;
```

In the outer block, the value of the running sum s is bound to zero for the first iteration of the loop. During the j'th iteration of the loop, the s for the $j + 1$'st iteration is bound to the sum of s for the current iteration and the product of the j'th elements of the vectors. The value of s after the n'th iteration is returned as the value of the loop, block and function.

The semantics of Id loops differs radically from that of loops in conventional languages (like Pascal). All iterations execute in parallel (after some initial unfolding), except where constrained by data dependencies. Thus all $2n$ array-selections and n multiplications may proceed in parallel, but the n additions are sequentialized.[1] Thus, s is not a *location* in the Pascal sense, which is updated at each iteration; rather, every iteration has its own copy of s.

---

[1] Of course, a different definition could use a divide-and-conquer method to parallelize the additions also.

2.2   Example 2: Vector Sum

The vector-sum of two vectors of size n may be written in Id as follows:

```
Def vsum A B = {  C = array (1,n) ;
                  {For j From 1 To n Do
                      C[j] = A[j] + B[j]}
              In
                  C }
```

This defines a function *vsum* that takes two vector arguments A and B and returns a vector result C. In the first statement in the block, C is bound to a *new* array (an I-structure) whose index-bounds are 1 and n inclusive. The expression $(1, n)$ denotes a 2-tuple containing the values 1 and n. The array is initially empty. Meanwhile, the second statement in the block, executing in parallel with the first, unfolds into a loop of n iterations. All n iterations execute in parallel. In the j'th iteration, the j'th components of A and B are summed and stored as the j'th component of C. Meanwhile, C may be returned immediately by the *In* clause of the block, even though it is still fully or partially empty.

The last point needs some elaboration. It demonstrates the synchronization and "pipelined" parallelism implicit in the use of I-structures. Suppose we were to compose our two functions as follows:

```
ip (vsum X Y) Z
```

vsum may return its vector result to *ip* even before it has filled in the components. If a sub-expression in *ip* tries to read such an empty component, that sub-expression suspends; when the component is written by *vsum*, the sub-expression in *ip* is automatically resumed (see Section 3.8.4).

To preserve determinacy, we decree that a component of an array may be assigned only if it is empty— it is a run-time error if multiple assignments are attempted. Thus arrays in Id are not like arrays in, say, Pascal; they are called *I-structures*. I-structure components are like logical variables which get instantiated when assigned.

2.3   Higher-Order Functions

Id also supports the powerful programming tool of higher-order functions. Consider:

```
Def map_array f A = {   l,u = bounds A ;
                        B = array (l,u) ;
                        {For j From 1 To u Do
                            B[j] = f A[j]}
                    In
                        B }
```

map_array takes a *function* f and array A as arguments, and returns an array B which is the pointwise image of A under f. Some examples of its use:

```
map_array negate A
```

returns a "reversed" version of vector A by negating all its components, and

```
map_array (vsum A) Bs
```

adds vector A to each vector in Bs (an array of vectors). The expression ($vsum\ A$) is a *partial application* of the function $vsum$ to one argument A (where it expects two), and represents the function that when given another argument B, will return the vector sum of A and B. In the usual functional programming parlance, $vsum$ is said to be "curried".

3 Dataflow Graphs as a Target for Compilation

In this section we describe *Dataflow Graphs* and show why they are an excellent parallel machine language and a suitable target for programs written in high-level languages like Id. This idea was first expressed by Jack B. Dennis in a seminal paper in 1974 [10]. The version we present here reflects a) an augmentation from "static" to "dynamic" dataflow graphs that significantly increases the available parallelism [4,3], and b) numerous significant details and optimizations due to several past and present members of our group.

3.1 Basics

A dataflow graph consists of *Operators* (or instructions) connected by directed *Arcs* that represent data-dependencies between the operators. Each operator may have one or more input and output arcs. Arcs may be named— the names correspond to program variables. Figure 1 shows a graph for the simple expression "s + A[j] * B[j]". The fork for j can be considered a separate one-input, two-output operator, but since any operator can have more than one output, forks are usually incorporated into the preceding operator.

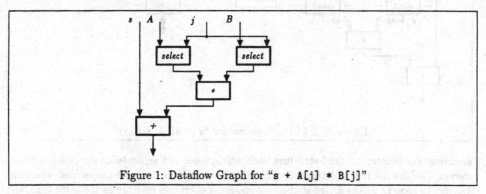

Figure 1: Dataflow Graph for "s + A[j] * B[j]"

Data values between operators are carried on *Tokens* which are said to flow along the arcs. In a dataflow machine, this is represented by including a *destination* in the token, that is, the address of the instruction (operator) at the end of the arc. (So, except in special signal-processing machines, one should never think of the dataflow graph as representing physical wiring between function modules.)

An operator is ready to *fire*, *i.e.*, execute, when there are tokens on all its input arcs. Firing an operator involves consuming all its input tokens, performing the designated operation on the values carried on the tokens, and producing a result token on each output arc. Figure 2 shows a possible firing sequence for our simple expression. Tokens on the A and B arcs carry only a

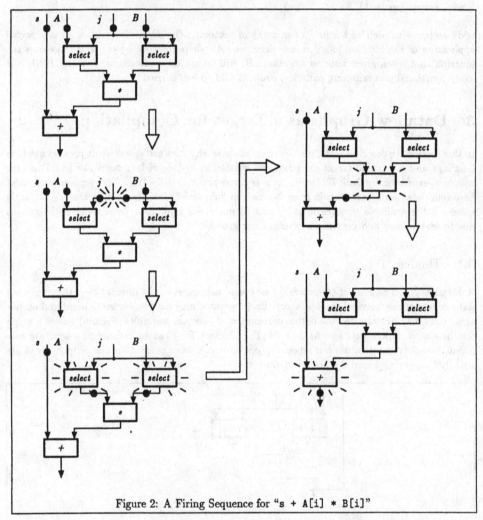

Figure 2: A Firing Sequence for "s + A[i] * B[i]"

descriptor (or pointer) to the I-structure itself which reside in a separate area called *I-structure storage*. (We discuss this in detail in Section 3.8). Note that the timing is unspecified: operators may fire as soon as tokens arrive at their inputs, many operators may fire at the same time, and the latencies of operators may vary.

The compilation of constants requires some care. In many cases such as the 1 in the expression $j + 1$ the constant is incorporated as a literal into the + instruction itself, making it a unary operator. However, in general, a constant can be compiled as an operator with one *Trigger* input and one output. Whenever an input token arrives, an output token carrying the constant is emitted. The data value on a trigger token is irrelevant (see Figure 3). In Section 3.4 we will discuss where trigger tokens originate.

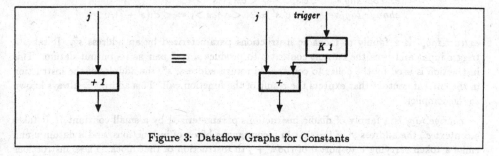

Figure 3: Dataflow Graphs for Constants

3.2 Functions

The body of a function-definition is an expression; its dataflow graph will have as many input arcs as there are formal parameters, and one output arc for the result value. There are two major issues to be addressed: a) how a corresponding function call should be linked to this graph, and b) how to handle multiple invocations of a function that overlap temporally. We address the latter issue first.

Because of parallelism and recursion, a function may have many simultaneous activations. A way to handle this might be to *copy* the entire graph of the function body for each activation. However, in the TTDA we avoid this overhead by keeping a single copy of the function body, and by *tagging* each token with a *context* identifier that specifies which activation it belongs to.[2]

The format of a token can now be revealed:

$$< c.s, v >_p$$

Here c is the context (simply a unique identifier), s is the address of the destination instruction, v is the datum, and p is the *port number* identifying which input of an n-ary instruction this token is meant for. The value $c.s$ is called the *Tag*. We have written p as a subscript for convenience; we will drop it wherever it is obvious from the graph.

Tokens corresponding to many activations may flow simultaneously through a graph. The normal firing rule for operators must therefore be changed so that tokens from different activations are not confused:

- An operator is ready to fire when a *matched* set of input tokens arrive, *i.e.*, a set of tokens for all its input ports that have the same tag $c.s$.

- The output value produced by that firing is tagged with $c.s'$, *i.e.*, the instruction in the same context that is to receive this token.

In order to handle function calls, it is necessary for a new context to be allocated for the callee,[3] for the caller to send argument tokens to the new context and for the callee to send result tokens back to the caller's context.

---

[2]Of course, this does not preclude also making copies of the function body across processors to avoid congestion.
[3]Analogous to allocating a new activation record or stack frame in conventional machines.

Two instructions $extract\_tag_s$ and $change\_tag_j$ manipulate contexts on tokens:

$$extract\_tag_{s''} : \quad < c.s, \_ > \Rightarrow < c.s', c.s'' >$$
$$change\_tag_j : \quad < c.s, c'.s' >_0 \times < c.s, v >_1 \Rightarrow < c'.(s' + j), v >$$

$extract\_tag_{s''}$ is a family of monadic instructions parameterized by an address s''. It takes a trigger input and uses the current context c to produce a $c.s''$ pair as its output datum. This instruction is used by the caller to construct a return address, s'', the address of the instruction in the current context that expects the result of the function call. This address is always known to the compiler.

$change\_tag_j$ is a family of diadic instructions parameterized by a small constant j. It takes a context c', the address s' of the first in a contiguous block of instructions, and a datum v and emits a token carrying v to port 0 of the $s' + j$'th instruction of that block. These instructions are used by the caller to send arguments to the callee, and by the callee to send results back to the caller.

It is difficult to depict the output arc of $change\_tag$ graphically, because the destination of its output token is not determined statically— it depends on the left input data value. We call such arcs *dynamic arcs* and show them in figures using dashed lines.

To allocate a new context for the callee, we use the operator $get\_context$:

$$get\_context : < c.s, s'' > \Rightarrow < c.s', new\_c.s'' >$$

$get\_context$ takes a destination address s'' (the callee's entry point), and produces $new\_c.s''$, where new_c is a new, unique context identifier.

The astute reader will immediately realize that $get\_context$ is unlike all the other operators seen thus far. Whereas all other operators were purely functional (outputs depended only on the inputs), it appears that this one needs some internal state so that it can produce a new unique identifier each time it is called. The way this is done is discussed in Section 3.9— $get\_context$ is actually an abbreviation for a call to a special dataflow graph called a *Manager*.

We now have enough machinery to specify the linkage for function calls and returns. The graph for this function call:

ip *arg1 arg2*

is shown in Figure 4, where s is the address of the operator expecting the result. By convention, the return-address and the arguments are sent to the callee at offsets 0, 1, 2, ... *etc.* where they are received at I (identity) instructions. The final result token is sent back to the instruction at s. (The identity instructions can usually be optimized away). An important point is that the call/return scheme supports *non-strict* functions. The function can execute and return a result before *any* of its arguments arrive. Our experiments show this to be a significant source of additional parallelism.

What we have shown here is only one of a number of possible linkage mechanisms for function calls that we have investigated. The reader should recognize that the mechanism also supports multiple results.

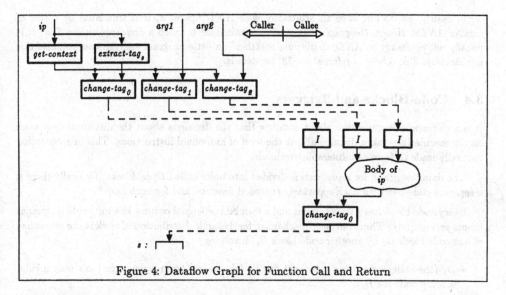

Figure 4: Dataflow Graph for Function Call and Return

3.3 Well-Behaved Graphs and Signals

When a function is invoked, some machine resources must be dynamically allocated for that invocation. On a conventional machine such resources include activation records, registers, *etc.* As we shall see later, resources in our machine include code-block registers, constant areas, *etc.* For now, we will treat them as if they were embodied in *contexts*; the reader should regard their allocation as synonymous with obtaining a new context.

Because machine resources are finite, they must be reclaimed when a function invocation terminates. This termination is *not* synonymous with the return of the result token. Because function calls are non-strict, a result may be returned while operators are still executing within the function body. How then can we determine when it is safe to reclaim the resources for that function instance? We need a separate *signal* indicating that all activities within the function have completed.

As a first step to solving this problem, we insist that all dataflow graphs are *well-behaved*, that is,

1. Initially, there are no tokens in the graph.

2. Given exactly one token on every input, ultimately exactly one token is produced on every output.

3. When all output tokens have been produced, there are no tokens left in the graph, that is, the graph is *self-cleaning*.

The reader is invited to check that all the dataflow graphs we have seen so far have this property.

We can now see a simple way to produce the termination signal. All output arcs from the code-block are also routed to a strict *AND* operator. When tokens are produced on all these arcs, the *AND* operator fires, producing a token (a copy of any input token will do) which is the termination signal.

In reality, we do not have an arbitrarily wide *AND* operator; it is simulated by a tree of smaller *AND*s. Hence, the graph that detects termination is called a *Synchronization Tree*. It is usually not necessary to *AND* all outputs together— a little program analysis can optimize this significantly. The reader is referred to [23] for details.

3.4 Code-Blocks and Triggers

It is a common misconception about dataflow that the decisions about the distribution of work on the machine are taken dynamically at the level of individual instructions. This misconception naturally leads to fears of intolerable overheads.

The dataflow graph for a program is divided into units called *Code-Blocks*. Typically there is a separate code-block for each separately compiled function and for each loop.[4]

Every code-block has a trigger input and a termination-signal output, in addition to its regular inputs and outputs. Thus, the basic mechanism for dynamic distribution of work is the *invocation* of one code-block B_2 by another code-block B_1, involving

- B_1 (the caller) acquiring a context for B_2 (the callee) from a manager (this may involve loading code for B_2),

- B_1 sending a trigger token to B_2,

- B_1 sending input tokens to B_2 (and continuing its own execution),

- B_2 returning results to B_1 (and perhaps continuing execution)

- B_2 returning a termination signal to B_1

- B_1 deallocating the context for B_2

The work *within* a code block is distributed automatically with some hardware support, as described in Section 4.4.

3.5 Higher-Order Functions

Every function has an *arity* (≥ 1) which is the number of arguments it must receive before the body can be evaluated. The arity of a function is a syntactic property, based on its definition. For example, *vsum* has arity 2.

The call/return scheme described in Section 3.2 is used when a function is applied to all its expected arguments. However, a function may also be applied to fewer arguments than its arity as in the expression (*vsum A*). In this case, we use a general *apply* schema (Figure 5).

The *apply* operator receives a new kind of token on its left input called a *closure*, containing a function name, a partial set of arguments, and a count of the number of remaining arguments expected, called the *remaining-arity*. A function-name by itself is a trivial case of a closure.

The *apply* checks if the remaining-arity is 1. If not, it produces a new closure with decremented remaining-arity and incorporating this argument. If the remaining-arity is 1, this argument is

---

[4]Our compiler also creates a code-block for each nested function by "lambda-lifting" [14] them out to the top-level. It may also split large code-blocks, or substitute small code-blocks in-line.

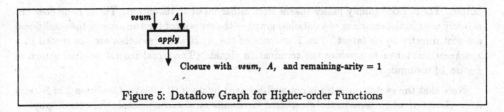

Figure 5: Dataflow Graph for Higher-order Functions

the final argument; *apply* performs the function call (gets a context, sends the arguments to the function body, and passes on the result).

The *apply* operator is an abbreviation for a more detailed schema in which closures are actually implemented using I-structures (Section 3.8). This allows the *apply* schema to return a closure (as an I-structure) even before the token carrying the function's argument has arrived (when it arrives, it is stored in the I-structure). Thus the *apply* schema is consistent with the non-strict semantics of full function calls. The reader is referred to [23] for further details.

3.6 Conditionals

The graph for the conditional part of

```
If j > n Then s
Else aux (j + 1) (s + A[j] * B[j])
```

is shown in Figure 6. The output of the $> n$ operator is actually forked four ways to the side inputs of the four switches; the pictorial abbreviation is meant for clarity only.

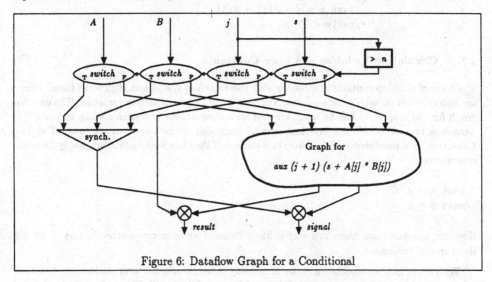

Figure 6: Dataflow Graph for a Conditional

A *true* token at the side input of a switch copies the token from the top input to the *T* output. A *false* token at the top input of a switch copies the token from the top input to the *F* output. The ⊗ node simply passes tokens from either input to its output. The ⊗ node does not actually exist in the encoding of a dataflow graph— the outputs of the two arms of the conditional are sent directly to its target. The T outputs of the A, B and j switches are are routed to a *synchronization tree* to produce the termination signal. (The signal output was not shown in Figure 4 for simplicity).

Note that the switch operator is not well-behaved by itself (it violates Condition 2 of Section 3.3). However, when used in the structured environment of a conditional, the overall graph is well-behaved. The reader should convince himself that after a token has appeared on each of the output arcs no token could remain in the graph.

3.7 Loops

As mentioned before, tail-recursive functions are better expressed in terms of loops, which are amenable to much more efficient implementation. In Id, the programmer may express his computation directly as a loop, or the compiler may recognize tail-recursive forms and transform them to loops. (The impatient reader may safely skip to Section 3.8; but we invite you to scan the intermediate subsection headings, hoping that you will be tempted to come back!).

We will discuss only *while*-loops here, using this version of the function *ip* which is equivalent to the *for*-loop version:

```
Def ip A B = {   s = 0 ;
                 j = 1
            In
                {While (j <= n) Do
                    Next j = j + 1 ;
                    Next s = s + A[j] * B[j]
                 Finally s }} ;
```

3.7.1 Circulating Variables and Loop Constants

The body of the loop contains expressions with free variables j, s, A and B. Two of them, j and s are also rebound on each iteration using *Next*— we call these *circulating* variables. The dataflow graph for the loop body has an input arc and an output arc for every circulating variable. The remaining two, A and B, are invariant over all iterations of the loop, and are thus called *Loop Constants*. It is possible to think of loop constants as if they too were circulating, using the trivial statements

```
next A = A ;
next B = B
```

However, implementing them this way is likely to incur unnecessary overheads, and so we give them special treatment.

With every loop we associate a region of memory called its *constant area*. In fact, the "context" in which the loop runs may be regarded as incorporating this area. Before the loop body executes, there is a *Loop Prelude* that stores the loop constants in the constant area. Within the loop body, every reference to a loop constant is translated into a simple fetch from the constant area.

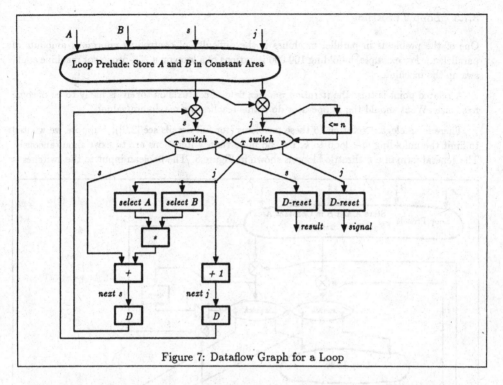

Figure 7: Dataflow Graph for a Loop

The dataflow graph for our loop is shown in Figure 7. For the moment, ignore the operators labelled D and D_reset. The Loop Prelude stores A and B in the constant area. j and s circulate around the loop as long as the $j \leq n$ output is true.

3.7.2 Loop Iteration Context

Because of the asynchronous nature of execution, it is possible that the j tokens circulate much faster than the s tokens. This means that since the loop-condition depends only on j, many j tokens corresponding to different iterations may pile up on the right inputs of the *select* operators. Thus, we need a mechanism to distinguish the tokens corresponding to different iterations. This is performed by the D and D_reset operators. The D operator merely changes the *context* of its input token to a new context; the D_reset operator resets the context of its input token to the original context of the entire loop.

We could use the general *get_context* mechanism for this, but this is likely to be expensive. Instead, we assume that *get_context* returns C_0, the first unique identifier in a contiguous block of unique identifers $C_0, C_1, \ldots$. The D operator simply increments the context from C_i to C_{i+1}, the D_reset operator simply resets the context to C_0. The i part of context field is called the *iteration number*.

The astute reader will recognize that the loop-iteration-context mechanism is not sufficient to handle nested loops— tokens can still get confused. For this reason, every loop is packaged like a procedure call and given its own unique context when executed.

3.7.3 Loop Throttling

One of the problems in parallel machines is the difficulty of controlling enormous amounts of parallelism. For example, unfolding 100 000 iterations of a loop on a 256-processor machine could swamp the machine.

A related point is this: the *iteration number* field of contexts on tokens is likely to be of some fixed size. What should the D operator do if this reaches the maximum value?

There is an elegant solution to these problems (for full details see [2,9]). Suppose we wanted to limit the unfolding of a loop to k, *i.e.*, no more than k iterations are to exist simultaneously. The general form of a k-throttled loop is shown in Figure 8. The boolean input to the switches is

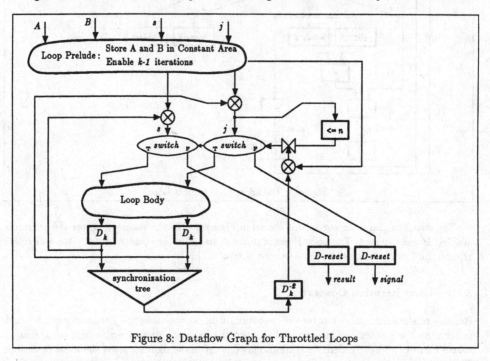

Figure 8: Dataflow Graph for Throttled Loops

now *gated* using ⋈, a two-input operator that fires when both inputs arrive, copying one of them to its output. Any particular iteration of the loop can proceed only if the corresponding boolean token arrives at the switches. By gating this token, we can hold back an iteration of the loop.

The loop prelude primes the gate with the first $k - 1$ loop iteration contexts C_0, ..., C_{k-2}, which allows the first $k - 1$ booleans to go through, which allows the first $k - 1$ iterations to proceed. At the bottom of the loop, each circulating variable goes through a D_k operator which increments the loop iteration context from i to $i + 1$, *modulo* k. Thus the loop iteration context is the same for the i'th and the $i + k$'th iteration.

The reader should convince himself that tokens with contexts C_0 through C_{k-1} inclusive may now be sitting at the inputs to the switches. In order to prevent mixing tokens up, we must allow the C_{k-1} iteration to proceed only after the C_0 iteration is over.

The outputs of all the D_k operators are combined using a synchronization tree. When a signal token appears here with context C_1, we know that the C_0 iteration has terminated completely, and that there are no more C_0 tokens extant. When triggered by such a token, the D_k^{-2} box enables the gate with a token carrying context C_{k-1} (hence the "-2" in the name, since $(k-1) = (1-2) \bmod k$).

The value k may be specified as a compile-time or load-time pragma, or may be dynamically generated based on the load of the machine. We have glossed over the code generated by the compiler to consume the k extra tokens left at the gate when the loop terminates.

The astute reader will recognize that the semantics of throttled loops differs from those of general loops. In particular, loops that have backward data-dependencies from the $j+l$'th iteration to the j'th iteration will deadlock if $l \geq k$.

Even though a loop is semantically equivalent to a tail-recursive function call, the former can be executed much more efficiently than the latter, because of the cheaper allocation of contexts (using D_k), the treatment of loop constants, and loop throttling.

3.8   I-structures

In discussing the dataflow graph for ip in Section 3.1, we mentioned that I-structure tokens actually carry *descriptors* of (*i.e.*, pointers to) I-structures which reside in a memory area called *I-structure storage*. The reason was not merely pragmatic but also semantic: when an I-structure token moves through a fork, it is duplicated. This duplication must be "by reference" because one arm of the fork may assign a value into a location of the I-structure, and this must be visible in the other arm. Duplicating the token at a fork merely duplicates the descriptor, and thus makes a copy "by reference".

3.8.1   I-structure Allocation

I-structure allocation is performed by the expression

```
array (l,u)
```

which translates into a dataflow graph as shown in Figure 9. The *allocate* operator sends a token of the form $< \textit{"allocate"}, c.s, (l, u) >$ to the storage allocator. The $c.s$ part specifies the

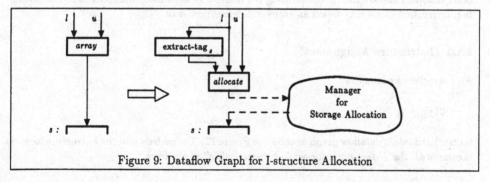

Figure 9: Dataflow Graph for I-structure Allocation

forwarding address to which the manager must send the descriptor. The storage allocator (which is a *manager*, see Section 3.9) simply allocates a free area of I-structure memory, initializes all locations to the "empty" state, and sends the descriptor (pointer) to the operator at *c.s*.

The allocation request and the reply are not synchronous. During the round-trip journey to the manager and back, the prcessor is free to execute any number of other enabled dataflow instructions. In fact, the destination instruction at *c.s* may be on an entirely different processor.

3.8.2 I-structure *select* operation

The details of the *select* operation are shown in Figure 10. First the address *a* to be read is computed, based on the bounds and on the index. The *I-fetch* operator then sends a "read-token" of the form

$$< address, \text{``}read\text{''}, destination\_tag >$$

to I-structure memory asking for the contents at the address.

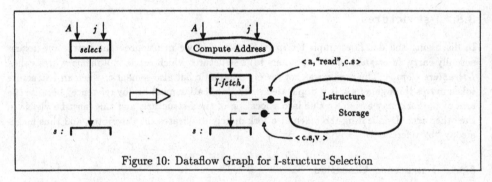

Figure 10: Dataflow Graph for I-structure Selection

At the I-structure memory, if the location is not empty, *i.e.*, it contains a value *v*, it is sent in a token $< c.s, v >$ to the instruction at *c.s*. If the location is empty, the *c.s* destination address is simply *queued* at that location.

Thus, all memory-reads are so-called *split-phase* reads. As in the allocation discussed above, the request and the reply are not synchronous— the processor is free to execute any number of other enabled dataflow instructions during the round-trip to memory and back, and the destination instruction at *c.s* may be on an entirely different processor.

3.8.3 I-structure Assignment

An I-structure assignment

$$C[j] = v$$

is translated into a dataflow graph as shown in Figure 11. The address *a* of the I-structure location is computed; the *I-store* operator sends a "write-token" of the form

$$< address, \text{``}write\text{''}, data >$$

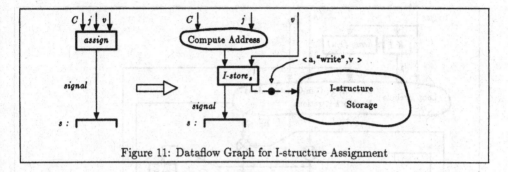

Figure 11: Dataflow Graph for I-structure Assignment

to I-structure memory.

The *I-store* operator also generates a signal; this does not imply that the value has been stored in the I-structure, only that the *I-store* operator itself has fired, and a write-token has been dispatched to I-structure memory (it may still be on its way).

At the I-structure memory, if location a is empty, the value v is written there and the location is marked "non-empty". If any destinations *c.s* were queued there (from prior memory-reads), a copy of v is also sent to all those instructions. If a write-token arrives at a non-empty location, it is treated as a run-time error.

3.8.4 Discussion

The dataflow graph for the vector-sum program *vsum* is shown in Figure 12. The array C may be allocated (by the $array(1, n)$ operator at the top) and returned as the result as soon as the trigger arrives. This may occur before anything is stored in C, even before either A or B arrives. A consumer of C (as in ip (vsum A B) Z) may try to read elements of C without any possibility of time-dependent errors. The reader may want to examine Figure 12 and see that the loop itself produces nothing but a signal indicating that all activities of the loop body have completed.

Our memory-writes are unacknowledged writes. A different possibility would be to include a destination tag *c.s* into the token sent to the I-structure memory, which in turn would send an acknowledgement to the instruction at *c.s*. This may in fact be necessary for certain resource management-related operations.

The write-once semantics that we have described supports the Id language I-structure semantics. However, dataflow graphs can just as easily allow multiple writes into a location, thus supporting other source-language semantics. But this introduces non-determinism into the memory-reads and it is not clear how to manage this effectively in the source-language. In fact, architecturally it is not difficult to include a small ALU in the I-structure controller to perform the *fetch-and-add* type of instructions [12,22,15].

3.9 Managers

In any machine supporting general-purpose programming, various resources need to be allocated and deallocated dynamically. We call the entities that perform these services resource *Managers*. In a conventional machine, examples of resources include memory, working set pages, devices, *etc.*, and the resource managers are services in the operating system.

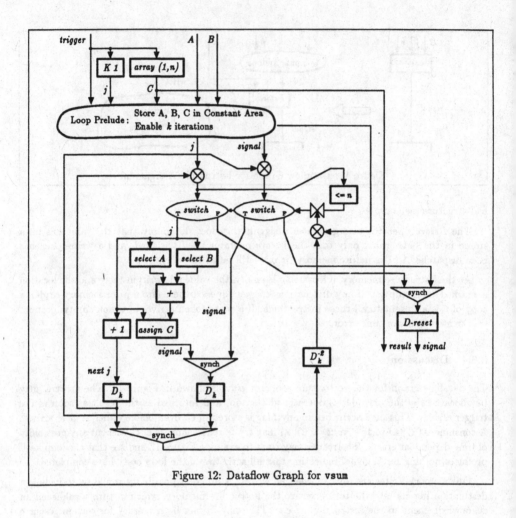

Figure 12: Dataflow Graph for vsum

Even though the bulk of a resource manager may be written as an ordinary procedure, the entry and exit are handled quite differently from ordinary procedure calls. First, unlike procedures that get a new context for each invocation, managers run in pre-assigned, *well-known* contexts. Second, because all executions of a manager share the same context, multiple entries into a manager must be *serialized*. Typically, this serialization is performed in the non-deterministic order in which requests arrive.

On a conventional machine, the manager context is either well-known directly or transitively through some other well-known entity such as a global service name, or a trap vector. Serialized entry is ensured by disabling interrupts, setting semaphore locks, *etc.* This area of programming is notorious for its difficulty and high probability of errors.

The dataflow approach offers a much cleaner and more elegant solution to these problems, allowing significant internal parallelism in the manager itself. The body of a manager looks like just another dataflow graph. A very simple (and simplistic) scheme for the context manager called by *get_context* is shown in Figure 13. The manager is initialized with an *initial state*

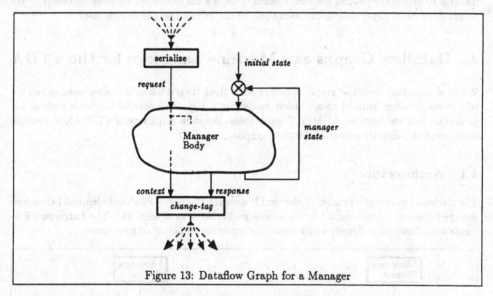

Figure 13: Dataflow Graph for a Manager

containing data structures holding available contexts. Requests arrive at the *serializer* which lets them through one at a time. An input— either a *get_context* or a *release_context*— and the current *state* enter the manager body (which can be an ordinary dataflow graph). The manager may be able to respond immediately to the request, or it may decide to store it internally in its state variable (*e.g.,* because it has run out of contexts). The manager produces a *next state* which is fed back, ready to be combined with the next request.

When the manager responds to a request, it is sent to the forwarding address that accompanied the request using the *change_tag* operator.

A call to a manager such as this is expanded like a function call, except that the destination context is well-known, either directly, or transitively *via* some other well-known object like an I-structure (which behaves like a trap vector).

There are several possible implementations for the serializer. One possibility is to borrow the "throttling" idea from loops. Another possibility is to use I-structure queueing. The details are beyond the scope of this paper.

Dataflow managers permit *all* the flexibility one normally expects in resource managers, such as priority queues, pre-emptive resource allocation, *etc.* Further, managers do not have to be a bottlenecks: there may be many copies of a manager, each managing its own pool of resources, perhaps negotiating with each other for balancing the pools. Managers may be heirarchical— a manager can allocate a sub-pool of resources that is then managed by a local manager.

Functional programmers will recognize that a manager entry-point performs a "non-deterministic" merge. However, managers are significantly more powerful than merely adding a non-deterministic merge to the language, which cannot adequately cope with systems in which the users of a manager are dynamically determined. The reader is invited to see [1] for more details, including programming methodology for managers.

Dataflow graphs provide all the *mechanisms* necessary to implement managers; all that remains is to decide the *policies* encoded therein. This is a major subject for research (see [8]). We do not have much experience in this area (nor, to our knowledge, has anyone else).

4 Dataflow Graphs as a Machine Language for the TTDA

We have seen that dataflow graphs together with their tagged-token execution semantics constitute an excellent parallel computation model for a high-level parallel language such as Id. In this section we describe the MIT Tagged-Token Dataflow Architecture (TTDA), a machine architecture for directly executing dataflow graphs.

4.1 Architecture

The machine consists of a number of identical Processing Elements (PEs) and identical I-structure storage Elements interconnected by an n-cube packet network (Figure 14). The I-structure Elements are addressed uniformly and collectively implement a global address space.

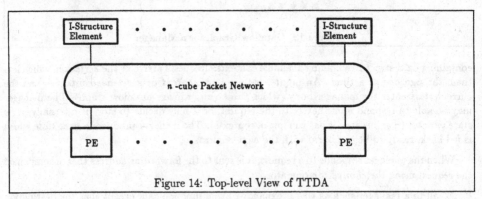

Figure 14: Top-level View of TTDA

A single PE and a single I-structure element constitute a complete dataflow computer. To simplify the exposition, we will first describe the operation of the machine as if it had only one PE and I-structure module; in Section 4.4 we discuss multi-processor operation.

4.2 A Processing Element

The architecture of a single Processing Element is shown in Figure 15. A PE has two main components: the *Compute Section* and the *Control Section*. Input tokens arrive at the top and are routed to one of the two main components based on their contents. Output tokens at the bottom of these sections are routed back to the top of the PE or to the I-structure Element (in a multi-processor they may go to other PEs or I-structure elements).

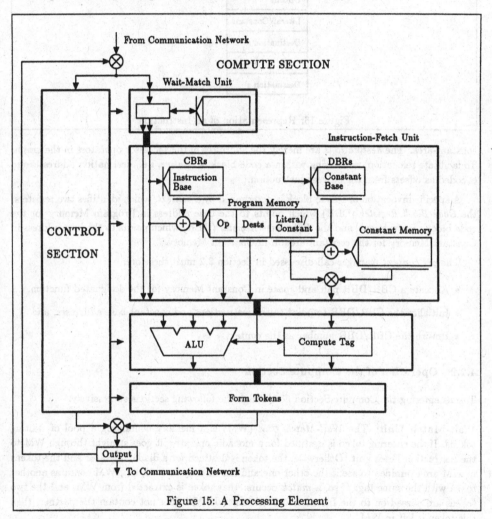

Figure 15: A Processing Element

4.2.1 Representation of Dataflow Graphs and Contexts

Recall that a dataflow program is translated into a set of *code-blocks*, where a code-block is a dataflow graph with some number of inputs and outputs including a trigger input and a signal output. The graph for the code-block is encoded as a linear sequence of instructions in Program Memory. The address for each operator in the linear sequence is chosen arbitrarily, except for certain conventions as to where input tokens are received. As an engineering decision, we decree that every operator has no more than two inputs. Thus, every operator in the graph is encoded as shown in Figure 16. The *literal/constant* field may be a literal value or an offset into the

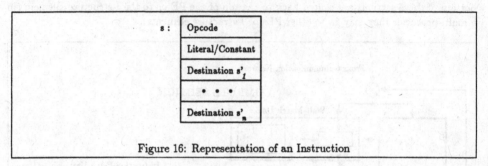

Figure 16: Representation of an Instruction

constant-area. The *destinations* are merely the addresses of the successor operators in the graph. To facilitate relocation, addressing within a code-block is *relative, i.e.*, destination addresses are encoded as offsets from the current instruction.

A specific invocation of a code-block is determined by a *context*, which identifies two registers: the *Code-Block Register* (CBR) which points to the base address in Program Memory for the code-block's instructions, and the *Data Base Register* (DBR) which points to the base address in Constant Memory for the constant area in in Constant Memory.

The *get_context* manager-call discussed in Section 3.2 must therefore:

- Allocate a CBR/DBR pair and space in Constant Memory for the designated function,
- Initialize the CBR/DBR to point to the instruction- and constant-base addresses, and
- Return the CBR/DBR number as the context.

4.2.2 Operation of the Compute Section

Tokens entering the Compute Section go through the following sections successively.

Wait-Match Unit: The *Wait-Match Unit* (WM) is a memory containing a pool of waiting tokens. If the entering token is destined for a monadic operator, it goes straight through WM to the Instruction-Fetch unit. Otherwise, the token is destined for a diadic operator and the tokens in WM are examined to see if the other operand has already arrived, *i.e.*, WM contains another token with the same tag. If so, a *match* occurs: that token is extracted from WM, and the two tokens are passed on to the Instruction-Fetch unit. If WM does not contain the partner, then this token is left in WM.

The Wait-Match unit is thus the *rendezvous* point for pairs of arguments for diadic operators. It has the semantics of an associative memory, but is implemented by hashing methods.

Instruction-Fetch Unit: The tag on the operand tokens entering the Instruction-Fetch unit identifies an instruction to be fetched from Program Memory (*via* a CBR). The fetched instruction may include a literal or offset into the constant area, and a list of destination instruction offsets. The tag also specifies a DBR; using the constant base address found there and the constant offset in the instruction, any required constants from the constant area are now fetched from Constant Memory.

The data from the tokens, constant from the constant area or literal from the instruction (if any), opcode from the instruction, destination offsets from the instruction and the context itself are all passed on to the next stage (ALU and Compute-Tag unit).

ALU and Compute-Tag Unit: The ALU and Compute-Tag units are actually two ALUs operating in parallel. The ALU unit itself is a conventional ALU that takes the operand/literal/constant data values and the opcode and produces a result.

The Compute-Tag unit takes the CBR and DBR numbers from the context and the instruction offsets for the destinations, and computes the tags for the output of the operator. Recall that the tag for two instructions in the same code-block invocation will differ only in the instruction offset.

The ALU result and the destination tags are passed to the Form-Tokens unit .

Form-Tokens Unit: The Form-Tokens unit takes the data value from the ALU and the tags from the Compute-Tag unit and combines them into result tokens.

The Compute Section can be viewed as two simple pipelines— the Wait-Match unit, and everything below it. Once tokens enter the lower pipeline, there is nothing further to block it. Pipeline stages do not share any state, so there are no complications such as reservation bits, *etc.*

4.2.3 The Control Section

The Control Section receives special tokens that can manipulate any part of the PE's state— for example, tokens that initialize Code-Block Registers, store values into Constant Memory and Program Memory, *etc.* These tokens are typically produced by various managers such as the context manager.

The Control Section also contains any connection to the outside world, such as input-output channels.

4.3 I-structure storage

An I-structure Element is a memory module with a controller that handles I-structure read and write requests, as well as requests to initialize the storage. The structure of the memory is shown in Figure 17. In the Data Storage area each location has some extra *Presence Bits* that specify its state: *Present*, *Absent* or *Waiting*. When an I-structure is allocated in this area, all its locations are initialized to the Absent state.

When a read-token arrives it contains the address of the location to be read and the tag for the instruction that is waiting for the value. If the designated location's state is Present, the datum is read and sent to that instruction. If the state is Absent or Waiting, the read is *deferred*,

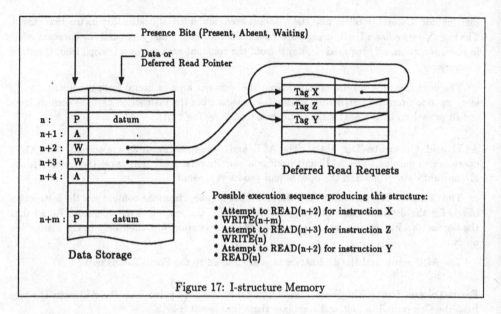

Figure 17: I-structure Memory

i.e., the tag is *queued* at that location. The queue is simply a linked list of tags in the *Deferred Read Requests* area.

When a write-token arrives it contains the address of the location to be written and the datum to be written there. If the location's state is Absent, the value is written there and the state changed to Present. If the location's state is Waiting, the value is written there, the state changed to Present, and the value is also sent to all the destinations queued at the location. If the location's state is already Present, it is an error.

4.4 Multi-Processor Operation

In a multi-processor machine, all memories are globally addressed. Thus one can implement any desired form of interleaving on I-structure Elements.

The simplest form of distribution of code on the TTDA is to allocate an entire code-block to a PE. However, the TTDA has a sophisticated *mapping* mechanism that also allows a code-block to be allocated *across* a group of PEs, thereby exploiting the internal parallelism within them. For example, it is possible to load a copy of a loop procedure on several PE's, and distribute different iterations of the loop on different PE's according to some prespecified hash function on the tags. The hash function to be used is stored in a MAP register which like the CBR and DBR is loaded at the time of procedure activation. In fact it is also possible to execute a code-block on several PE's by loading only parts of it on different PE's. When a token is produced at the output of either a PE or an I-structure Element, its tag specifies exactly which PE or I-structure Element it must go to. The token is sent there *directly* (there is no broadcasting).

It is important to note that the program does not have to be recompiled for different mapping schemes. The number of instructions executed in a TTDA program is *independent* of the number of PEs it is executed on. This is in contrast to von Neumann-based multi-processors, where the multi-processor version of a program would typically execute many more instructions than the single-processor version because of synchronization and process-switching overheads.

4.5 Discussion

Any parallel machine must support mechanisms for very fast synchronization and process-switching. The TTDA supports these at the *lowest* level of the architecture, without any busy-waiting. Every Wait-Match operation and every I-structure read and write operation is a synchronization event directly supported in hardware. Sequential threads may be interleaved at the level of individual instructions. Unlike von Neumann machines, switching between threads does not involve any overheads of saving and restoring registers, loading and flushing caches, *etc.* All memory reads are *split-phase*, *i.e.*, between the request-to-read and the·datum-reply there may be an arbitrary number of other instructions executed. Thus, the latency (round-trip time) of memory reads, which is bound to be high in a parallel machine, is less critical than the overall throughput of the interconnection network.

5 Conclusion

5.1 Project Status

The MIT Tagged-Token Dataflow Project bases its approach to the problem of high-speed, general-purpose parallel computing on the belief that it cannot be solved at any single level. We believe that the goal will be achieved only with synergy between the language, the compiler and the architecture (the recent publicity on RISC machines has belatedly made people aware of this tight coupling even on sequential machines). We believe that this synergy cannot be achieved simply by extending conventional sequential languages and architectures— the problems of determinacy, cost of synchronization and context switches and intolerance of memory latency are insurmountable in the von Neumann framework.

In this connection we must point out that neither dataflow graphs nor the TTDA are wedded to programming languages such as Id or functional programming languages. With trivial changes to graphs and the I-structure memory controller, they could support other programming languages, such as a parallel C or FORTRAN. However, we are skeptical about the ease of programming and amount of parallelism available in such languages.

Our research on languages is constrained only by the two requirements of *implicitly* parallel semantics and *determinacy*. Our language Id began as a functional language, was augmented with I-structures to address deficiencies in functional data structures, and continues to evolve [4,6,20,17,18]. Issues we are looking at include further improvement of the data-structuring facilities, types and automatic type-checking, abstraction mechanisms and debugging.

The showpiece of our research on compilers is the Id compiler written by Traub [23]. Issues we are currently investigating all revolve around optimization techniques: use of type-information, code motion and transformation, fast function calls and loops, reducing dynamic resource management requirements, and the efficient execution of dataflow graphs on sequential machines (and parallel machines based on sequential machines).

To support this research, we have constructed *Id World*, an integrated programming environment for Id and the TTDA [16,19] running on workstations such as Lisp machines. In addition to sophisticated edit-compile-debug-run support, Id World measures and plots parallelism profiles, instruction counts and other emulated TTDA machine statistics. We are also releasing Id World publicly on April 15, 1987.

At our location the same Id programs (identical object code) can also be run on two other facilities. Our Multi-Processor Emulation Facility (MEF) is a collection of 32 TI Explorer Lisp Machines interconnected by a high-speed network that we built, and has been operational since January 1986. Our event-driven Simulator provides the detailed timing information essential for designing a real dataflow machine.

We are so encouraged by the dataflow experiments conducted to date that we are proceeding with the plans to build a 256-board 1 BIPs (billion instructions per second) machine to be completed by 1990. The achitecture of this machine is a significant variation of the TTDA proposed by Papadopoulos and Culler [21]. The idea is basically to make the wait-match store *directly addressable* to facilitate very fast token-matching. A chunk of *token store* in the Wait-Match memory is allocated at the time of a code-block invocation. This chunk may be regarded as the "activation record" for that invocation. A "context" is then merely the pointer to that chunk of store. Tokens now have the following format:

$$< S, R, v >_p$$

where S is a pointer to an instruction in Program Memory, R is a pointer to the activation record, v is the datum and p, as before, the port. The *instruction* now contains the offset of a location in its activation record where its input tokens are to wait.

When a token arrives, S is used first to fetch the instruction. The offset r encoded in the instruction, together with R is used to interrogate exactly one location, $R + r$, in Wait-Match memory. If empty, this token is left there to wait. If full, the partner token is extracted, and the instruction is dispatched.

It is also possible to view R as an I-structure address and specify fancy I-structure operations using S which can point to any instruction. With minor modification to the empty/full states associated with the token-store elements, I-stuctures can be implemented on the same PE hardware.

This new architecture eliminates the registers of the TTDA and thus simplifies one of its resource management problems. By combining PE's and I-structures it reduces the engineering work. Most importantly, our current software will run on this machine with minimal changes in the Id compiler.

5.2 Future: Macro-Dataflow or Pure Dataflow

We have often been urged to take a less "fine-grained" approach to dataflow by using a hybrid computation model which may be termed *Macro-Dataflow*. Rather than adopting dataflow scheduling at the individual instruction level, one considers larger chunks or "grains" of conventional von Neumann instructions that are scheduled using a program counter, the grains themselves being scheduled in dataflow fashion.

We do not think this approach is any more viable than our pure approach. To begin with, the compilation problem for Macro-Dataflow is significantly harder. Choosing an appropriate grain size and partitioning a program into such grains is non-trivial to say the least. Second, this approach requires very fast von Neumann-style context switching between grains, and we have yet to see good solutions to this problem. However, the appeal of such a dataflow machine, which can be regarded as an *evolutionary* step away from a von Neumann machine, is undeniable. Such a "von Neumann-Dataflow" machine is currently under investigation by Iannucci, another member of our group [13].

Many researchers are studying architectures based on *Parallel Reduction*, and these approaches are similar to our own with respect to abandoning sequential languages ([11,7] and others). These projects are mostly based on functional programming languages and inspired by the graph-reduction approach [24]. Their focus thus far has been more on language issues and less on architectural issues. Many of their implementations are currently targeted to von Neumann-based multiprocessors and consequently may face the same problems as other parallel machines based on conventional processors. We think that *latency* and *synchronization* problems have no satisfactory solution in the conventional frame-work [5].

The connection between dataflow and reduction is often not recognized. We invite the reader to examine the parallel rewrite-rule semantics of Id [6,18] to be convinced that dataflow and graph-reduction are just two different ways of implementing the *same* abstract concept of *reduction*. The operational semantics of Id are written using rewrite-rules in a style immediately familiar to anyone who has looked at graph-reduction, and yet the technical details of the reduction *strategy* are chosen to capture exactly the behavior of dataflow graphs.

Acknowledgements

The ideas presented in this paper are due to the efforts of the very talented students and research staff of the Computation Structures Group of the Laboratory for Computer Science at MIT. While every member of the group is typically interested in, and contributes to several aspects of the project, we mention here only some rough areas of specialization: Languages and Reduction: Keshav Pingali and Vinod Kathail; Demand-driven evaluation: Pingali and Steve Heller; Compilers: Kathail originally, and now Ken Traub; Architecture: David Culler, Bob Iannucci and Grep Papadopoulos; Resource Management: Culler; Id World: Dinarte Morais and Richard Soley; Simulator: Steve Brobst, Andrew Chien and Gino Maa; Emulator: Culler, Morais and Traub; MEF: Papadopoulos, Soley and Andy Boughton.

Still, for criticisms of style or substance in this paper, brickbats should be thrown only at the authors.

References

[1] Arvind and J. Dean Brock. Resource managers in functional programming. *Journal of Parallel and Distributed Computing*, 1(1), January 1984.

[2] Arvind and David Ethan Culler. Managing resources in a parallel machine. In *Fifth Generation Computer Architectures, 1986*, pages 103–121, Elsevier Science Publishers, B.V., 1986.

[3] Arvind and K.P. Gostelow. The u-interpreter. *Computer*, 15(2), February 1982.

[4] Arvind, K.P. Gostelow, and W. Plouffe. *An Asynchronous Programming Language and Computing Machine*. Technical Report TR-114a, Dept.of Information and Computer Science, University of California, Irvine, CA, December 1978.

[5] Arvind and Robert A. Iannucci. *Two Fundamental Issues in Multi-Processing*. Technical Report CSG 226-5, Computation Structures Group, MIT Lab. for Computer Science, Cambridge, MA 02139, July 1986.

[6] Arvind, Rishiyur S. Nikhil, and Keshav K. Pingali. I-structures: data structures for parallel computing. In *Proc. Workshop on Graph Reduction, Los Alamos NM, September 28-October 1, 1986, Fasel, J. and Keller, R.M. (eds.)*, Springer-Verlag, Berlin, 1987.

[7] C. Clack and Simon Peyton-Jones. The four-stroke reduction engine. In *Proceedings of the 1986 ACM Conference on Lisp and Functional Programming*, pages 220–232, August 1986.

[8] David Ethan Culler. *Effective Dataflow Execution of Scientific Applications*. PhD thesis, Laboratory for Computer Science, Massachusetts Institute of Technology, Cambridge, MA 02139, December 1987 (expected).

[9] David Ethan Culler. *Resource Management for the Tagged Token Dataflow Architecture*. Technical Report TR-332, MIT Lab. for Computer Science, 545 Technology Square, Cambridge, MA 02139, 1985.

[10] Jack B. Dennis. First version of a data flow procedure language. In G. Goos and J. Hartmanis, editors, *Proc. Programming Symposium, Paris 1974*, Springer-Verlag, Berlin, 1974.

[11] Benjamin Goldberg and Paul Hudak. *Alfalfa: Distributed Graph Reduction on a Hypercube Multiprocessor*. Technical Report, Department of Computer Science, Yale University, New Haven, Connecticut, November 1986.

[12] Allan Gottlieb, R. Grishman, C.P. Kruskal, K.P. McAuliffe, L. Rudolph, and Marc Snir. The nyu ultracomputer— designing an mimd shared memory parallel computer. *IEEE Transactions on Computers*, C-32(2):175–189, February 1983.

[13] Robert A. Iannucci. *A Dataflow/von Neumann Hybrid Architecture*. PhD thesis, Laboratory for Computer Science, Massachusetts Institute of Technology, Cambridge, MA 02139, August 1987 (expected).

[14] Thomas Johnsson. Lambda lifting: transforming programs to recursive equations. In *Springer-Verlag LNCS 201 (Proc. Functional Programming Languages and Computer Architecture, Nancy, France)*, September 1985.

[15] David J. Kuck, Duncan Lawrie, Ron Cytron, Ahmed Sameh, and Daniel Gajski. *The Architecture and Programming of the Cedar System*. Technical Report Cedar No.21, Lab. for Advanced Supercomputers, Dept. of Computer Science, University of Illinois at Urbana-Champaign, August 12 1983.

[16] Dinarte R. Morais. *ID WORLD: An Environment for the Development of Dataflow Programs Written in Id*. Technical Report MIT/LCS/TR-365 (Bachelor's Thesis), MIT Laboratory for Computer Science, 545 Technology Square, Cambridge, MA 02139, May 1986.

[17] Rishiyur S. Nikhil. *Id Nouveau Quick Reference Guide*. Technical Report (Forthcoming), Computation Structures Group, MIT Lab. for Computer Science, Cambridge, MA 02139, April 1987.

[18] Rishiyur S. Nikhil. *Id Nouveau Reference Manual.* Technical Report (Forthcoming), Computation Structures Group, MIT Lab. for Computer Science, Cambridge, MA 02139, April 1987.

[19] Rishiyur S. Nikhil. *Id World Reference Manual.* Technical Report (Forthcoming), Computation Structures Group, MIT Lab. for Computer Science, Cambridge, MA 02139, April 1987.

[20] Rishiyur S. Nikhil, Keshav Pingali, and Arvind. *Id Nouveau.* Technical Report CSG Memo 265, Computation Structures Group, MIT Lab. for Computer Science, Cambridge, MA 02139, July 1986.

[21] Gregory M. Papadopoulos. *Implementation of a General-Purpose Dataflow Multiprocessor.* PhD thesis, Laboratory for Computer Science, Massachusetts Institute of Technology, Cambridge, MA 02139, August 1987 (expected).

[22] Peiyi Tang, Chuan-Qi Zhu, and Pen-Chung Yew. *An Implementation of Cedar Synchronization Primitives.* Technical Report Cedar No.32, Lab. for Advanced Supercomputers, Dept. of Computer Science, University of Illinois at Urbana-Champaign, April 3 1984.

[23] Kenneth R. Traub. *A Compiler for the MIT Tagged Token Dataflow Architecture.* Master's thesis, Technical Report TR-370, MIT Lab. for Computer Science, Cambridge, MA 02139, August 1986.

[24] David A. Turner. A new implementation technique for applicative languages. *Software: Practice and Experience,* 9(1):31–49, 1979.

PARLOG: THE LANGUAGE AND ITS APPLICATIONS

Keith L. Clark
Dept. of Computing, Imperial College
London SW7 2BZ

Abstract

The key concepts of the parallel logic programming language PARLOG are introduced by comparing the language with Prolog. Some familiarity with Prolog and the concept of logic programming is assumed. Two major application areas of PARLOG, systems programming and object oriented programming are illustrated. Other applications are briefly surveyed. Some comparison is made between PARLOG and the related parallel logic languages Concurrent Prolog and GHC.

1. PARLOG versus Prolog

PARLOG is one of a family of parallel logic programming languages characterised by the use of the concept of guards and committed choice nondeterminism as in Dijkstra's procedural language of guarded commands [Dijkstra 1976]. The family comprises three main languages: Concurrent Prolog [Shapiro 1983], GHC [Ueda 1985] and PARLOG [Clark & Gregory 1984a]. All three can be viewed as descendants of the Relational Language [Clark & Gregory 1981], which was the first parallel logic programming language to incorporate the concept of committed choice.

The use of committed choice makes programming in PARLOG and its sister languages very different from programming in Prolog. Given a conjunction of conditions

$a(X),b(X,Y),c(Y)$

only one solution to the conjunction can be found because PARLOG will commit to using just one clause to solve each condition/call in the conjunction. If the clause that is selected to solve the $a(X)$ call ultimately fails, or if the use of the clause generates a binding for X for which there is no solution to the $b(X,Y)$ call, then the whole conjuction fails. There will be *no* backtracking on the choice of the clause.

Shallow backtracking as search for a candidate clause

At first sight this may seem to be overly restrictive and to be throwing away much of the power of Prolog. However, there are many applications of Prolog which only make use of very shallow backtracking to search for a matching clause, or to search for a matching clause for which some initial sequence of test calls in the body of the clause succeeds. A cut after the sequences of test calls is then used to prevent backtracking - to *commit* to the use of this clause. For these programs the deep search capability of Prolog is not needed.

An example of this type of program is the following Prolog program for partitioning a list into two sublists comprising respectively all the elements greater than and all the elements less than or equal to some partition element **PE**. The program is written in Edinburgh syntax. Names beginning with an uppercase letter are variables.

```
partition(PE,[],[],[]).
partition(PE,[H|T],[H|G],L) :-  PE < H,!,  partition(PE,T,G,L).
partition(PE,[H|U],G,[H|L]) :-   partition(PE,T,G,L).
```

Given some call **partition(2,[1,4,-1,-7,9],Gr,Ls)** the Prolog backtracking search will first try to unify the call with the head of the first clause **partition(PE,[],[],[])**. This will fail. Prolog will backtrack to try to unify with the head of the second clause **partition(PE,[H|T],[H|G],L)**. This unification will succeed with **H** bound to **1** and **Gr** bound to **[1|G]**. The evaluation will continue with the test condition 2<1, which will fail. A shallow backtrack will cause Prolog to undo the bindings to **H** and **Gr** and to try the last clause. This will bind **H** to **1** and **Ls** to **[1|L]**.

In PARLOG, the search for a *candidate* clause, a clause to which the evaluation can commit to in the attempt to solve some call, can either be done sequentially, as in Prolog, or in parallel. That is, all the clauses for the relation of a call can be tried in parallel to find a matching clause for which some initial sequence of test calls succeeds. The unification with the head of the clause and the evaluation of the test calls is the *guard* computation of the clause, so the test calls are the *guard* calls. Successful completion of the guard computation of a clause makes the clause a candidate clause. When a candidate clause is found the evaluation commits to the use of that clause. It will commit to the first candidate clause to be found.

The PARLOG program for partition is:

partition(PE,[],[],[]).
partition(PE,[H|T],[H|G],L) <- PE < H : partition(PE,T,G,L).
partition(PE,[H|T],G,[H|L]) <- H =< PE : partition(PE,T,G,L).

where the **:** separates the *guard* calls from the *body* calls. Given the call **partition(2,[1,4,-1,-7,9],Gr,Ls)** PARLOG will try the three clauses in parallel. The second and third clauses will unify with the call, but only the third clause will have a succeeding guard call. This is the only candidate clause. Notice that because of the parallel search we need to have an explicit **H =< PE** test in the last clause. In Prolog, because of the sequential search, we can 'cheat' and drop the test because it is the complement of the test **PE < H** of the second clause which must have failed if Prolog ever tries the last clause. The parallel search for a candidate clause of PARLOG forces a more declarative style.

Delaying the output bindings until commitment

In Prolog, during the sequential search for a candidate clause for a call **G**, provisional partial bindings may be made to variables in **G** as a clause **C** is being tested. These provisional partial bindings are then undone if it is found that the head of **C** does not fully unify with **G** or if one of the guard calls of **C** fails. This happens with the **partition(2,[1,4,-1,-7,9],Gr,Ls)** call when the second clause is being tested. The provisional bindings **H=1,Gr=[1|G]** are undone when Prolog bactracks to try the third clause.

In PARLOG, because clauses may be tried in parallel, no clause is allowed to generate bindings for variables in the call until the evaluation commits to the use of some candidate clause. This is achieved by associating with each relation **R** a mode of use, a specification of which argument positions are *input* and which *output*. During the guard evaluation of a clause for **R** only the terms in the input argument positions of the call and the clause are unified and the unification must be an *input match* in which only variables in the clause are bound. Unification between the terms in the output argument positions is delayed until after the commitment to use the clause.

The mode declaration for the **partition** program is:

mode partition(PE?,L?,Gr^,Ls^).

The **?** signals an input argument position, the **^** an output argument position. Because the third argument and fourth arguments are specified as output arguments, the variables **Gr** and **Ls** of the call **partition(2,[1,4,-1,-7,9],Gr,Ls)** will not be unified with the head arguments whilst the three **partition** clauses are being tested. For example, during the guard evaluation of the third clause, only the first two arguments **PE** and **[H|T]** of the clause will be unified with the first two arguments of the call generating input bindings **PE=2,H=1,T=[4,-1,7,9]** for variables of the clause. The unification for the third and fourth arguments will be delayed pending the result of the test **1=<2**. Only when this guard test has succeeded, and the evaluation has committed to the use of this clause, will the unification of the third and fourth arguments be attempted, resulting in the bindings **Ls=[1|L], G=Gr**.

Communication on commitment

This delaying of the binding of call variables until after commitment has a double benefit. It means that local copies of the arguments of the call do not need to be created for use by each clause that is being tested in parallel. The second and more significant benefit is that it allows for efficient parallel execution of a conjunction of calls. Suppose that we have two calls **G** and **G'** being evaluated in parallel with a shared variable **X** that will be bound by **G**. By delaying the binding of any variable in **G** until the evaluation of this call commits to the use of some clause, we are also delaying the communication of that binding to the concurrent call **G'**. Since provisional bindings during the search for a candidate clause are not made, and there is no backtracking after commitment, there is never any need to rescind a binding communicated between parallel calls. Commitment to a clause for **G** means that the programmer *guarantees* the communicated binding. This concept of delaying communication between parallel processes until commitment was derived from CSP [Hoare 1978].

As an example, suppose that we have a parallel conjunction:

partition(2,[1,4,-1,-7,9],Gr,Ls),process(Gr,Ls,Sl)

The **process(Gr,LS,Sl)** call will only get access to the binding for **Gr** when the evaluation of the **partition** call commits to the use of the third clause. It will not see the tentative binding to **Ls** that would have been made by the test for candidacy of the second clause if unification on the output argument positions was allowed before commitment.

Data flow versus control flow

In Prolog, because of the sequential evaluation, the first call in which a shared variable **X** appears usually generates the first partial binding, say binding **X** to a list pattern term of the form **[A|X1]**. This first call will also usually generate the complete and final binding for **X** by subsequently generating a list structure binding for the variable **X1** and some term binding for the variable **A**. (Of course, it is not essential that the first Prolog call generates the complete binding for a variable. A very useful Prolog programming feature has the first call generate only a partial binding that is completed by later calls. We shall see that the generalisation of this, where the calls are evaluating concurrently, is an exceedingly powerful feature of PARLOG.)

In PARLOG, the fact that the input argument matches are not allowed to bind a variable in the call is usually what determines which call binds a shared variable. This is because the attempt to bind a call variable during an input match will result in a *suspension* of the guard evaluation of the clause.

Suppose that we have three calls

a(X),b(X,Y),c(Y)

being concurrently evaluated. Assume also that **c** has been declared as input on its single argument and that all the clauses for **c** try to match the argument **Y** of the call with some non-variable term. Then each clause for **c** must suspend until **b(X,Y)** generates a non-variable binding for **Y**. The evaluation of **b(X,Y)** will generate this binding providing **b** has an output mode declaration for its second argument position and some clause for **b** generates a non-variable binding for **Y** by an output unification, performed *after* the commitment to use the clause. Whether the **a** or **b** call is the first to bind **X** will similarly depend on the mode declarations for **a** and **b**. If **b** is declared as input on its first argument, and all the clauses for **b** attempt to match the first agument of the call with non-variable terms in their guards, then the **b** call will suspend until supplied with a non-variable binding by **a**. The **b** clause that is selected will be determined by the partial binding for **X** that is supplied by **a**. Similarly, the **c** clause that is selected will be determined by the partial binding for **Y** that is supplied by the selected candidate clause for **b**.

Suppose that **partition** is invoked within a parallel conjunction:

feeder(List),partition(0,List,X,Y),c1(X),c2(Y)

Because of the read only constraint on the input matching for the second argument, the **partition** call will suspend until the **feeder** call generates at least the first element of the list to be partitioned by binding the variable **List** to a term such as **[2|Rest]**. Now each of the second and third clauses for **partition** pass the input match part of the guard and the alternative guard calls **0 < 2, 2 =< 0** will be tried concurrently. Only when the first guard call succeeds, will the second clause be selected to reduce the **partition** call to **partition(0,Rest,G,Y)**. At this point, the output unification of **X** with output term **[H|G]** of the head of the second clause will be effected binding **X** to **[2|G]**. This is also the act of communication of this partial binding for **X** to the parallel call **c1(X)**, which we will assume was suspended waiting for the binding to be made available. The **partition** call will again suspend if **feeder** has not yet generated a partial binding for the variable **Rest**.

Suspension of input matching until a variable is bound is the process synchronisation mechanism of PARLOG. Shared variables are communication channels between processes, a process being the evaluation of some call of a parallel conjunction.

The communciation can be two way; processes can cooperate in the construction of the complete binding for a shared variable. A call **G** may generate the first partial binding **[m(A)|X1]** for some shared variable **X**, which is the sending of the partial message **m(A)** down the channel **X**. But **A** can now be bound by some other call, as can the variable **X1** representing the remainder of the message sequence. By suitable programming, the call **G** can be made to suspend until either

A or **X1** or both are bound to some non-variable terms. The binding of **A** by some other process can be viewed as a *back communication* via a variable in a message, whilst the binding of **X1** to a term of the form **[t|Z]** is a *reverse communication* of the message term **t** down the channel **X**. Back communciation is the usual form of two way communication used in PARLOG programs. It is an exceedingly powerful programming technique enabling one to emulate lazy evaluation in what is an eager evaluation language, as first shown in [Takeuchi & Furakawa 1984]. The PARLOG emulation of bounded buffers and lazy evaluation is discussed in [Clark & Gregory 1984a].

2. Programming in PARLOG

A PARLOG program for a relation **r** comprises a *mode* declaration and a sequence of clauses separated by "." or ";". The mode declaration is of the form $r(m_1, m_2, .., m_k)$ where each m_i is an optional argument identifier followed by "?" or "^". A "?" specifies an input argument position and a "^" an output argument position.

In the search for a candidate clause, each group of "." separated clauses is tried in parallel. The clauses following a ";" are only tried if all the preceeding clauses are found to be non-candidate clauses. That is, if each of the preceeding clauses has a failed input match or a failed guard call. Suspension of an input match waiting for the binding of a variable does not make a clause a non-candidate clause.

As an example, suppose that a relation is defined by a sequence of clauses:

C1. C2; C3.

The clauses **C1** and **C2** will be tested for candidacy in parallel but the clause **C3** will be tested only if both **C1** and **C2** fail the candidacy test. If **C1** and **C2** were separated by a ";" instead of a ".", then the search for a candidate clause would be entirely sequential, as in Prolog.

Each PARLOG clause is of the form

$r(t_1, t_2, .., t_n)$ <- <guard calls> : <body calls>

where the ":" separates the guard calls from the body calls. The guard calls are the calls that must succeed before the clause can be selected as a candidate clause. The body calls of a clause are only executed if the evaluation of some **r** call commits to using the clause.

Both the **<guard calls>** and the **<body calls>** are conjuctions of calls. There two types of conjunction: the parallel conjunction **(G1,G2)** in which the calls are evaluated in parallel, and the sequential conjunction **(G1 & G2)** in which the calls are evaluated sequentially, as in Prolog.

Example program

```
mode  queue(Messages?),aux_queue(Messages?,List^,Tail^).
queue(M) <- aux_queue(M,L,L).
aux_queue([],L,T).
aux_queue([insert(U)|More_M],L,[U|Rest_T])<-
          aux_queue(More_M,L,Rest_T).
aux_queue([remove(U)|More_M],[U|Rest_L],T) <-
          aux_queue(More_M,Rest_L,T).
```

This is a PARLOG program which represents a queue as a process that receives messages to insert and delete elements from the queue. The messages are of the form **insert(U)**, where **U** is some given element to insert, and **remove(U)** where **U** is a variable or element. If it is an element, the program checks that this is the head of the queue before removing it. Usually **U** will be a variable, in which case there is a back communication. The queue is represented as a *difference list*, a much used data structure of logic programming. Conceptually, the queue is the difference between the two lists **L** and **T** held as the second and third arguments of the auxiliary relation **aux_queue**. The queue is all the elements on **L** that precede the tail list **T** of **L**. Thus, the pairs

L	T	
[2,5,9]	[]	
[2,5,9,4]	[4]	
[2,5,9|X]	X	X a variable

all represent the queue **[2,5,9]**. The empty queue is represented by any pair **L L**, where **L** is a list or a variable. Hence, the initialising call **aux_queue(M,L,L)** of the **queue** clause, which initialises the queue to a pair of identical variables, the most general representation of the empty queue. Note that the second clause inserts the element **U** at the back of the queue by removing it from the head of the tail. To insert

4 into the queue represented by the pair **[2,5,9,4] [4]** we can remove **4** from the head of the tail list **[4]** to produce the new pair **[2,5,9,4] []**. Finally, a pair **L [U|L]** represents a 'negative' queue, an empty queue from which some element **U** has been removed. This is a queue into which only **U** can now be inserted as a first element.

Let us examine the behaviour of a call

queue([insert(7),remove(U),remove(V),insert(3)])   (1)

The call immediately reduces to

aux_queue([insert(7),,remove(U),remove(V),insert(3)],L,L)   (2)

The second clause is the only candidate clause since the call unifies with

aux_queue([insert(U)|More_M],L,[U|Rest_T])

on its input argument position. There are no guard calls. The output unifications will bind the **L** of the call to the **L** of the clause, and then bind this to the term **[7|Rest_T]**. This transforms the most general representation **L L** of the empty queue into the slightly more specific representation **[7|Rest_T] [7|Rest_T]**. Removing the **7** from the tail list will now have the effect of inserting it as the first element of the queue. The call (2) reduces to

aux_queue([remove(U),remove(V),insert(3)],[7|Rest_T],Rest_T) (3)

Now, the third clause is the candidate. The output unification of **[U|Rest_L]** with the **[7|Rest_T]** of the call will bind **U** to **7** and the call is reduced to

aux_queue([remove(V),insert(3)], Rest_T,Rest_T)   (4)

to which the third **aux_queue** clause is again applied. This time the output unifications will produce the bindings **T=Rest_T=[V|Rest_L]** leaving **V** unbound. Call (4) is reduced to

aux_queue(insert(3)], Rest_L,[V|Rest_T])   (5)

in which the **Rest_L [V|Rest_T]** pair represents a 'negative' queue into which the first inserted item must be **V**. Now clause 2 can be used and the output unification with this clause will bind **V** to **3**. So the back communiciation via the variable in the preceeding **remove(V)** message only takes place when an element is inserted into what was an empty queue when the **remove(V)** message was received.

Kernel form

The mode declaration and a program with non-variable terms in the head of a clause are just syntactic sugar for a program with no mode declaration but with only variables in the head of each clause. The input matching is performed by explict calls to a one way unification primitive **<=** in the guard sequence, and the output unification by explicit calls to a full unification primitive **=** in the body sequence of the clause. Such a program is said to be in *kernel form*. The **partition** program has the kernel form

    partition(PE,I,G,L) <- [] <= I : G = [], L=[].
    partition(PE,I,G,L) <- [H|T] <= I , PE < H :
                    G = [H|G1] , partition(PE,T,G1,L).
    partition (PE,I,G,L) <- [H|T] <= I , H =< PE :
                    L = [H|L1] , partition(PE,T,G,L1).

In the kernel form the distinction between input and output unification is quite explicit, as is the time at which the unification occurs. A call

    t1 <= t2

succeeds only if **t1** and **t2** unify *without* binding any variables in **t2**. The call suspends if it can only continue by binding a variable in **t2**.

Safe guard calls

    The input unification cannot bind a variable in a call. However, the input unification can give a guard call access to a variable in a call. In the **partition** program, the unification with the head term **[H|T]** gives the guard calls of the second and third clauses access to the head of the input list, which could be an unbound variable at the time of the input match. In this case of the **partition** program, the guard calls are test primitives which will suspend if either argument is an unbound variable. PARLOG has a primitive **data(X)** which can be used to explicitly delay an evaluation until the variable **X** is bound. It is used to implement suspending primitives such as **<** and **<=**.

    An attempt by a guard call to bind a call variable to which it has been given access is an error. A safe guard is a guard which cannot bind a call variable.

Runtime versus compile time safety check

The mode declarations of PARLOG can be used to implement a crude compile time test for guard safety of a program. Details are given in [Gregory 1987]. It is crude in the sense that it declares as unsafe some programs that are actually safe. However a safety analysis of a program using the test is a useful programmers aid. In our current sequential implementations of PARLOG [Foster et alia 1986, Gregory et alia 1987], the programmer is responsible for ensuring that his guards are safe. This is not onerous. The natural PARLOG style is to use test only, safe guards.

An alternative to a compile time certification of safety is a runtime test. At runtime the attempt by a guard call to bind a variable in the call can be trapped and reported as an error. Unfortunately, the run time test for safety of the guard calls does impose a quite costly overhead. The implementation must be able to distinguish between call variables and variables in terms constructed during the guard evaluation, because the latter variables can be bound by other calls in the guard. The language GHC *must* make this distinction, because the attempt to bind a call variable during the guard, either during input unification *or* a guard call, is the GHC suspension mechanism.

In PARLOG, it is only the attempt to bind a call variable during input matching that leads to suspension. The PARLOG suspension mechanism can be cheaply implemented by compiling the one way unifications of the kernel form programs into unification code that uses the **data** primitive [see Clark & Gregory 1985 or Gregory 1987]. In PARLOG guard calls *must not* try to bind call variables, and this property has to be guaranteed by the programmer, perhaps by using a compile time safety check. Interestingly, current GHC implemention effort is directed towards implementing flat GHC (FGHC), a variant of the language in which guard calls must be test only primitives; they cannot be calls to program defined relations. This is also true of the Concurrent Prolog implementation work, which is focusing on flat CP. For FGHC and FCP suspension only occurs during unification, as in PARLOG.

Time dependent behaviour

Consider the program

```
mode merge(In1?,In2?,Out^).
merge([],In2,In2).
merge(In1,[],In1).
merge([X|M_In1],In2,[X|M_Out]) <- merge(M_In1,In2,M_Out).
merge(In1, [Y|M_In2],[Y|M_Out]) <- merge(In1,M_In2,M_Out).
```

which has the kernel form

```
merge(In1,In2,Out) <- In1 <= [] : Out = In2.
merge(In1,In2,Out) <- In2 <= [] : Out = In1.
merge(In1,In2,Out) <- In1 <= [X|M_In1] :
                            Out= [X|M_Out] ,
                               merge(M_In1,In2,M_Out).
merge(In1,In2,Out) <- In2 <= [Y|M_In2] :
                            Out= [Y|M_Out] ,
                               merge(M_In1,In2,M_Out).
```

Suppose that it is called from a parallel conjunction

```
gen1(L1),gen2(L2),merge(L1,L2,L).
```

The merging of the two lists **L1**, **L2** that will be generated on **L** will partly depend upon the rate at which **gen1** and **gen2** generate their output lists. This is because the merge call will invoke a parallel attempt to find a candidate clause from amongst its four clauses. They will all be suspended until **L1** or **L2** is given a non-variable value by one of the other processes. Suppose **L1** is the first to be bound, to the partial list value **[2|MoreL1]** by **gen1**. Then the third clause for **merge** will immediately become a candidate clause and the **merge** evaluation will commit to using this clause, binding **L** to a partial list **[2|MoreL]** and reducing the **merge** call to the recursive call **merge(MoreL1,L2,MoreL)**. If **gen2** now binds **L2** to a partial list before **gen1** binds **MoreL1** then the fourth clause will be the one used to reduce the recursive **merge** call. Only when both **gen1** and **gen2** have generated output at the same time will the **merge** evaluation have more than one candidate clause from which to select the clause to which it commits. Which clause is then selected is not determined by the program.

Time dependent merging of message streams from one or more sources is what one wants for many applications. It is exactly what one wants for an operating system where a communal resource is shared and accesed by sending messages. The messages from the different clients can be merged and passed through to the resource as and when they arrive.

The above **merge** program is not a fair merge because, when messages are always waiting on both input streams, the program may repeatedly select the third clause. However, fair and efficient merge programs can be written in the parallel languages. We refer the reader to [Clark & Gregory 1984a] and [Shapiro & Mierowsky 1984] for details.

Example use of merge

Consider the parallel conjunction
printer(Remove_reqs),user1(Insert_reqs1),user2(Insert_reqs2)
merge(Remove_reqs,Insert_reqs1,Insert_reqs2,Queue_reqs),
queue(Queue_reqs)
in which **printer** generates a stream of **remove(U)** requests, with **U** a variable, and **user1** and **user2** each generate a sequence of **insert(Text)** requests, with **Text** some ASCII text to be printed. The four argument **merge** is the obvious generalisation of the three argument **merge** to allow merging of three streams.

The **merge** and **queue** calls together implement a spooler for a printer control process. **user1** and **user2** send print requests as **insert** messages. These are merged in the order that they arrive and placed on the queue. The **printer** controler sends **remove** requests when it is ready to print. If there is no item in the queue when the request is received the back communcation of the text to be printed, via the message variable, is delayed until either **user1** or **user2** sends an **insert** request.

3. Meta level programming

Prolog has a meta call facility which enables a term to be evaluated as a call. This is done using a Prolog primitive **call(G)**. This can be used to write a user supervisor, even a programming environment for Prolog in Prolog.

PARLOG also has such a meta call facility, but the PARLOG metacall is much more powerful than its Prolog cousin. In its current implementation, in addition to the term to be evaluated as a call, it has the name of a data base (or module) in which the call is to be evaluated, and two extra arguments that respectively carry control and status messages. It has the form:

call(Db?,G?,Status^,Control?)

The **Control** argument is an input stream of messages that can be used by a supervisor or monitoring program to control the evaluation of the goal **G**. The meta call accepts the control messages **stop, suspend** and **continue**.

The **Status** argument, which must be a variable at the time of the call, will be instantiated to a stream of messages reporting key states of the evaluation of the call. For example, on termination, the last message sent will be **failed, succeeded** or **stopped** indicating the form of termination. **stopped** indicates a premature termination due to an input control message **stop** sent on the **Control** stream. Before termination, messages **suspend, continue** may be output on the **Status** stream when the same messages are received on the control stream. Finally, **exception** messages may also be output on the status stream, signaling program exceptions such as deadlock, overflow or a call to a relation undefined in the data base **Db**. A monitoring program can then handle the exceptions. For the undefined relation exception, the exception message is of the form

exception(Undef_call,undefined,Var)

with an unbound variable **Var** for a back communication. The meta call suspends waiting for this variable to be bound. When it is, the meta call evaluation continues, with the term to which the variable is bound used in place of the undefined call. This enables the monitoring program to substitute some other call for the undefined call. By binding **Var** to **call(OtherDb,Undef_call)** it can even cause the call to the relation that was undefined in **Db** to be evaluated in another data base **OtherDb**.

The meta call plays a crucial role in the implementaion of the PPS, a PARLOG programming system implemented in PARLOG [Foster 1986]. For details of how the PPS uses this powerful meta call primitive we refer the reader to [Clark & Foster 1987]. Here we give the flavour of its use in the PPS by showing how it can be used to implement a Unix style shell that accepts a stream of user commands to call programs in a pariticular data base. The shell program is a slight modification of one given in [Clark & Gregory 1984b]. The user programs are to be executed as either background commands (a command term of the **bg(Db,Call)**) or foreground commands (**fg(Db,Call)**). Whenever, a foreground command arrives, the shell suspends all the current background processes until the foreground command terminates. Priority is given to foreground processes. The second argument of the **pri-shell** program is a control message stream into each of the meta calls running a background process.

```
mode  pri-shell(?,^).
pri-shell([],Control).
pri-shell([bg(Db,Call)|Commands],Control)  <-
        call(Db,Call,Status,Control),
        pri-shell(Commands).
pri-shell([fg(Db,Call)|Commands],[suspend|Control])  <-
        call(Db,Call,Status,NControl)  &
        (Control = [continue|Ncontrol]) ,
        pri-shell(Commands,NControl)  ).
```

Notice the essential use of the sequential conjuction in the last clause. This delays the sending of the **continue** message to the suspended background calls, and the concurrent accepting of more commands, until the foreground evaluation terminates.

Defining the meta call in PARLOG

The meta call is a primitive of PARLOG which simply makes available to a PARLOG program the facilties of the underlying machine that is evaluating that program. We have found it quite straightforward to implement it on the sequential PARLOG machine [Gregory et al. 1987]. It can also be implemented as an interpreter program in PARLOG [Foster 1987].

To give a flavour of its definition, we give here a definition of **call** for program defined relation but without the control and status streams. We assume a primitive

program(Db?,Call?,Program^)

which retrieves the program for the relation of **Call** in a data base **Db.** The returned program is in kernel form, with any empty body or guard sequence represented by a call to **true.** We also need to assume a single argument meta call **call(G)** as a primitive for executing calls to PARLOG primitives, such as the unification primitives of the kernel form programs.

```
mode  call(Db?,Goal?).
call(Db,true).
call(Db,(G1,G2) ) <- call(Db,G1) , call(Db,G2).
call(Db,(G1 & G2) ) <- call(Db,G1) & call(Db,G2).
call(Db,G) <-
        program(Db,G,P) : % G a call to a program defined relation
        select_body(Db,G,P,B),
        call(Db,B);
call(Db,G) <- call(G).    % else G is a call to a primitive. This is
                          % directly executed using the single
                          % argument meta call for primitives

mode  select_body(Db?,Goal?,Program?,Body^).
select_body(Db,G, (Clgr1 . Clgr2),B) <-
        select_body(Db,G,Clgr1,B) : true.
select_body(Db,G, (Clgr1 . Clgr2),B) <-
        select_body(Db,G,Clgr2,B) : true.
select_body(Db,G, (Clgr1 ; Clgr2),B) <-
        select_body(Db,G,Clgr1,B) : true;
select_body(Db,G, (Clgr1 ; Clgr2),B) <-
        select_body(Db,G,Clgr2,B) : true;
select_body(Db,G,Clause, B) <-
        copy(Clause,Copy) &
        Copy=(G <- GCalls : BCalls) &
        call(Db,GCalls)  &
        B = BCalls.
```

The above program has safe guard calls providing the programs in the data base **Db** all have safe guard calls. Under this condition, the **select_body** calls in the guards will not bind any variable in input argument **G**. The unification **Copy=(G <- GCalls : BCalls)** in the last clause will simply bind the argument variables of the head of the copied clause to the argument terms of **G** because the clause is in kernel form.

4. Object oriented programming

The parallel logic programming languages lead themselves naturally to the object oriented style of programming in which data is encapsulated in an object and can only be accessed or updated by sending a message to the object. A computation becomes a network of communciating objects.

An object can be represented in PARLOG as a tail recursive process which accepts the an input stream of messages sent by other objects. The data stored in the object is recorded by the values of unshared arguments of the process which will be updated for the recursive call when an update message is received. Communicating objects are other processes that access and update the state of the object by putting messages on the message stream. Messages with variables are used to retrieve information about the state of the object by back communication.

This way of representing objects in a parallel logic language was first explored in [Shapiro and Takeuchi 1983]. It has been further developed in [Kahn et al. 1986] and [Davison 1987].

The program given above for **queue** is an example of an object represented as a process. For a more complex example, let us consider the representation of an object which is, in Smalltalk terms, a counter class object which can spawn and kill counter objects. Counter class can accept messages to create a new counter object with some initial value, and messages to retrieve or check the number of counter objects that are currently active. When a counter object **C** is created, as a result of a message sent by some other object **O**, **O** is given the identity of **C** and subsequently can send messages directly to **C**. The *identity* of **C** is a variable that is the input message stream to **C**.

Let us assume that a counter object **C** can accept messages to:

(1) increase or decrease its count value - with messages **up** and **down**,

(2) to retrieve or check the current count value - with a message of the form **retrieve(Count)** where **Count** is a variable for the back communication of the current value of the counter, or it is a count value to be checked,

(3) to display the value - with a **display** message,

(4) to kill itself - with a **kill** message.

The **kill** message, which will be the last message, must be relayed up to the counter class object for it has to know that a counter has been killed in order to decrement its recorded value of the number of current counter objects. We shall also assume that the **display** message has to be handled by counter class, so it must also be relayed to counter class by any counter object that receives the message. Because of the need to relay messages to counter class, each counter object must 'know' the identity of the counter class that created it, in our terms, it must have access to the counter class input message stream.

We can implement a counter object as a PARLOG program with the mode

counter(Inmessages?,Value?,Outmessages^)

Inmessages is its input message stream. Any other object that can place messages on this message stream, knows about the counter object. **Value** is the unshared local argument that is the current value of the counter. **Outmessages** is the message stream that will link the counter to the counter class object that created it. Any message **Mess** that the counter object cannot handle for itself, such as the **display** message, is relayed to counter class on this message stream as a message **handle_for_me(Mess,Me)** where **Me** is the 'identity' of the counter object, i.e. it is an unbound variable which can be used by the counter class to send a messages back to the counter object that has passed up the **handle_for_me** message.

The program for **counter** is:

```
mode  counter(Inmesages?,Value?,Outmessages^).
counter([up|Inmess],Value,Outmess) <-  % up message
        NValue is Value+1,  % causes Value to be incremented
        counter(Inmess,NValue,Outmess).
counter([down|Inmess],Value,Outmess) <- % down message
        NValue is Value-1,  % causes Value to be decremented
        counter(Inmess,NValue,Outmess).
counter([retrieve(Count)|Inmess],Value,Outmess) <-
        Count = Value ,  % Back communication or check
        counter(Inmess,Value,Outmess).
counter([kill],Value,[kill]);  % counter is terminated
                % and kill message is relayed to counter class
counter([Other|In],V,[handle_for_me(Other,Me)|Out) <-
        merge(Me,In,NewIn),  % Me stream is merged with In
        counter(NewIn,V,Out).
```

The last clause deals with all the messages that **counter** cannot handle for itself. It puts these out on its output stream linking it to counter class. **Me** is a communication channel through which the counter class can send back a message to the counter object. Note that this message stream is merged with the regular input message stream.

The program for **counter_class** is given below. The **counter_class** object will be invoked with a call of the form

counter_class(Inmess,0,Outmess)

where **Inmess** will be a shared variable link to other objects that need to create counters and **Outmess** will be a link to some object that can handle the messages that **counter_class** cannot handle. These will include messages, other than the **display** message, that cannot be handled by **counter**. It can be the message stream link to some higher object in an object hierarchy, or just a link to a monitor process that ouputs error messages..

In the **new(Value,Counter)** message handled by the first clause **Value** will be the initial count value of the created counter and **Counter** will be a variable down which subsequent messages will be sent to the created counter. It becomes the first argument of the call

counter(Counter,Value,Back)

that sets up the counter. **Back** is a variable that will be used by the created counter to send messages back to **counter_class**. This message stream is therefore merged with the rest of the messages coming into **counter_class** to produce the new incoming message stream.

```
mode   counter_class(Messages?,Number?,Outmess^).
counter_class([new(Value,Counter)|Inmess],N,Out)  <-
        counter(Counter,Value,Back),  %create new counter Counter
        merge(Back,Inmess,Allmess),  %merge in its back comm. stream
        NewN is N+1,   % increment record of number of counters
        counter_class(Allmess,NewN,Out).
counter_class([how_many(Num)|More],N,Out)  <-
        Num = N, % retrieve or check
        counter_class(More,N,Out).
counter_class([kill|More],N,Out)  <- % a kill message passed up by
        NewN is N-1 &   % some killed counter object
        counter_class(More,NewN,Out);
counter_class([handle_for_me(display,Me)|More],N,Out)  <-
        Me = [retrieve(V)],  % ask Me for its value
        (data(V) &   % wait until value is returned then
            display_somehow(V)),  % display somehow
        counter_class(More,N,Out);
counter_class([Other|More],N,[Other|MoreOut])  <-
        counter_class(More,N,MoreOut).
```

Syntactic sugar

This style of representation of object classes and objects is a cliched form of PARLOG programming that can be surported by a front end that accepts syntactic sugar for the program. For Prolog, Definite Clause Grammars [Pereira & Warren 1980] is an example of the use of sugar. A possible syntactic sugar for the

counter_class and **counter** programs is:

> *class* counter.
> *class_arguments* Number?.
> *object_arguments* Value?.
> *class_messages*:
>> new(Value,Counter) -> *create_object* Counter *state* Value,
>>> Number *becomes* Number+1.
>> how_many(Num) -> Number=Num.
>> kill -> Number *becomes* Number-1.
>> handle_for_me(display,Me) -> *send* Me retrieve(V),
>>> (data(V) &
>>> display_somehow(V)).
>
> *object_messages*:
>> up -> Value *becomes* Value + 1.
>> down -> Value *becomes* Value - 1.
>> retrieve(Count) -> Count=Value.
>> kill -> *terminate_object, send_class* kill.

The sugar supresses the message stream aspects of the PARLOG representation and the explicit recursive calls. Ken Kahn and colleagues at Xerox Parc and Andrew Davison at Imperial College are producing front ends to accept such sugared input for the process representation of objects in parallel logic languages. Andrew Davison is building such an interface to PARLOG as one component of a PARLOG based knowledge representation system.

5. Other applications

[Broda & Gregory 1984] show how PARLOG can be used for discrete event simulation and in that paper present a graphical notation for PARLOG. As a high level language incorporating concurrency and communciation, PARLOG is a natural candidate for the specification of communicating systems. [Gregory et alia 1985] report on its use for the specification and simulation of communication protocols. An extension of PARLOG, incorporating the concept of a real time clock, has been used for specifyng the behaviour of a telecommunications switching system [Elshiewy 1987]. PARLOG has also been used to implement a subset of LOTUS, a specification language for communicating systems, enabling a LOTUS specification to be executed [Gilbert 1987a,b].

6. Current implementations

A sequential implementation, written in C running on Sun workstations, is the main system currently used by the PARLOG research group [Foster et alia 1986]. This has an interface to the Sun windows system and is based on an abstract PARLOG machine design [Gregory et alia 1987]. Licences for the implementation are available from the PARLOG Research Group, for Sun 3 or VAX under UNIX.

On the Sun 3 we have developed in PARLOG a programming environment, the PPS [Foster 1986], which uses windows and mouse to allow the user to interact with and control multiple evaluations. In the PPS a PARLOG program as a collection of data bases, or modules, with local name spaces. Programs in one data base can call relations defined in another data base. The linking is handled by the PPS. It also has an integrated editor which automatically archives old versions of progams. We are constructing other program development tools, such as debuggers [Huntbach 1987], to be integrated in the environment.

We have just started developing a parallel implementation on a six processor Sequent Balance, and we are investigating implementation on the sixteen agent prototype ALICE machine [Lam & Gregory 1987], [Darlington & Reeve 1981].

Acknowledgements

All the Imperial College work on PARLOG has been supported by the SERC, currently via three Alvey contracts. The author would also like to acknowledge the personal support of the SERC, through its Senior Fellowship Scheme.

I much appreciate the careful reading and helpful comments on a draft of this paper by Reem Baghat.

References

Broda, K. and Gregory, S. 1984. PARLOG for discrete event simulation. In *Proceedings of the 2nd International Conference on Logic Programming* (Uppsala, July), S.-A. Tarnlund (Ed.), Uppsala, pp.301-312.

Clark, K.L. and Foster, I.T. 1987. A declarative environment for concurrent logic programming, to appear in *Proceedings of Tapsoft 87 Conference* (Pisa, Italy).

Clark, K.L. and Gregory, S. 1981. A relational language for parallel programming. In *Proceedings of ACM Conference on Functional Languages and Computer Architecture* (Portsmouth, New Hampshire), Arvind and J. Dennis (Eds.), 171-178.

Clark, K.L. and Gregory, S. 1984a. PARLOG: parallel programming in logic. Research Report DOC 84/4, Dept. of Computing, Imperial College, London. Also in *ACM Transactions on Programming Languages and Systems*, 8(1), pp. 1-49.

Clark, K.L. and Gregory, S. 1984b. Notes on systems programming in PARLOG. In *Proceedings of International Conference on Fifth Generation Computer Systems* (Tokyo), H. Aiso (Ed.), Elsevier/North Holland, pp 299-306.

Clark, K.L. and Gregory, S. 1985. Notes on the implementation of PARLOG. *Journal of Logic Programming*, 2(1), pp 17-42.

Davison, A. 1987. Objects and Meta Objects in PARLOG, Research Report, PARLOG Research Group, Dept. of Computing, Imperial College, London.

Darlington, J. and Reeve, M. J. 1981. ALICE: a multiprocessor reduction machine. In *Proceedings of ACM Conference on Functional Languages and Computer Architecture* (Portsmouth, New Hampshire), Arvind and J. Dennis (Eds.),

Dijkstra, E. W. 1976. *A Discipline of Programming*. Prentice-Hall.

Elshiewy, N. A. 1987, Extended PARLOG: Logic Programming of Real Time Systems, Research Report, Computer Science Lab, Ericsson Telecom, Sweden.

Foster, I.T., 1986. *The PARLOG programming system: Reference Manual*, PARLOG Research Group, Dept. of Computing, Imperial College, London.

Foster, I.T., 1987. A meta interpreter in PARLOG for PARLOG with a meta call. Research Note, PARLOG Research Group, Dept. of Computing, Imperial College, London.

Foster, I.T., Gregory, S., Ringwood, G.A. and Satoh, K. 1986. A sequential implementation of PARLOG. In *Proceedings of 3rd International Logic Programming Conference* (London), Springer-Verlag, pp 149-156.

Gilbert, D., 1987a. Executable LOTOS: using PARLOG to implement an FDT, to appear in *Proceedings of Protocol Specification, Testing and verification VII*

(Zurich).

Gilbert, D., 1987b. Implementing LOTOS in PARLOG, Research Report, PARLOG Research Group, Dept. of Computing, Imperial College, London.

Gregory, S. 1987. *Parallel Logic Programming in PARLOG.* Addison-Wesley.

Gregory, S., Foster, I., Burt, A. D., Ringwood, G. A., 1987. An Abstract Machine for the Implementation of PARLOG on Uniprocessors. Research Report, PARLOG Research Group, Dept. of Computing, Imperial College, London.

Gregory, S., Neely, R. and Ringwood, G.A. 1985. PARLOG for specification, verification and simulation. In *Proceedings of the 7th International Symposium on Computer Hardware Description Languages and their Applications* (Tokyo, August), C.J. Koomen and T. Moto-oka (Eds.), Elsevier/North-Holland, pp. 139-148.

Hoare, C. A. R. 1978. Communicating sequential processes. CACM ,17(10), pp 666-677.

Huntbach, M. H. 1987. Algorithmic PARLOG Debugging. Research Report, PARLOG Research Group, Dept. of Computing, Imperial College, London.

Kahn, K., Tribble, E. D., Miller, M.S., Bobrow, D. G., 1986. Objects in Concurrent Logic Languages, in *Proceedings of OOPSLA '86* (Portland, Oregon), ACM.

Lam, M. and Gregory, G., 1987. PARLOG and ALICE: a Marriage of Convenience, to appear in *Proceedings of 4th International Logic programming Conference* (Melbourne), MIT Press.

Pereira, F. C. N. and Warren, D. H. D. 1980. Definite clause grammars for language analysis - a survey of the formalism and a comparison with augmented transition networks, *Artificial Intelligence* 13, pp 231-278.

Ringwood, G. A. 1987. PARLOG86 and the Dining Logicians, Research Report, PARLOG Research Group, Dept. of Computing, Imperial College, London. To appear in CACM.

Shapiro, E. Y. 1983. A subset of Concurrent Prolog and its interpreter. Tecnical Report TR-003, ICOT, Tokyo.

Shapiro, E. Y. and Mierowsky, C. 1984. Fair, biased, and self balancing merge operators. In *Proceedings of IEEE Symposium on Logic Programming* (Atlantic City, New Jersey), IEEE Computer Press, pp 83-90.

Shapiro, E. Y. and Takeuchi, A. 1983. Object oriented programming in Concurrent Prolog. In *New Generation Computing* 1, pp 25-48.

Takeuchi, A. and Furakawa, K. 1985. Bounded Buffer Communication in Concurrent Prolog. *New Generation Computing* 3(2), pp 145-155.

Ueda, K. 1985. Guarded Horn Clauses. ICOT Tecnical Report TR-103, ICOT, Tokyo.

FUNCTIONAL PROGRAMMING AND COMMUNICATING PROCESSES

(Some design considerations for a functional operating system)

David Turner
Computing Laboratory
University of Kent
Canterbury CT2 7NF
UNITED KINGDOM

Overview

This paper reports some of the initial results of a research project at the University of Kent for the construction of an operating system written entirely in a functional language. We are here primarily concerned with the internal structure of the operating system, seen as a network of communicating processes. The description in purely functional terms of such a network has until recently posed logical problems, a solution to which was proposed by W. Stoye in 1984. We have developed a refinement of Stoye's model which has stronger synchronisation properties, and permits each process to run in a separate address space, facilitating a distributed implementation. By introducing the concept of a wrapper-function, we enable message passing code to be statically type checked.

Background: The KAOS project

The aim of the KAOS (= Kent Applicative Operating System) project is to build a multi-user operating system written entirely in a purely applicative language.

We can see an operating system as being composed of three (essentially independent) components.

   (1) Kernel
   This is always running, it manages resources, and is the 'real' operating system.

(2) Tools
Editor(s), compiler(s), spelling-checkers, games, ...
Each of these is a separate program. The essential minimum is
an editor, and a compiler, but you can have as many other tools
as you want. In a well designed operating system most of the
code is here, and most of the functionality of the operating
system is provided at this level.

(3) Shell
This is the operating system as seen by the user when he logs
on. This provides the language in which the user 'talks to the
computer'.

There can be different shells for different users, presenting (perhaps very)
different interfaces to the operating system. We are interested in developing a
shell that provides a good programming environment for an applicative language, but
there could be another shell that implements BASIC. The structure of the operating
system as seen through a shell can be substantially different from the structure of
the operating system as seen by the person who wrote the kernel (and can differ from
one shell to another).

Note that one essential function of a general purpose shell (we leave aside special
purpose shells such as might run on a particular terminal and only permit the user
of that terminal to eg consult a timetable) is that it must provide the user with a
set of data structures that persist from session to session, and **some commands** for
updating them.

This implies that the language of the shell **must** be an imperative language, at least
in certain respects. Any attempt to pretend otherwise can only be an exercise in
self deception.

Does this mean that the project of producing a complete operating system written in
a functional language is somehow doomed to failure? Not at all. It is entirely
possible to write an interpreter for an imperative language (the shell in this case)
in an applicative one. The aim of the project is that all the code which **implements**
the operating system (at each of the three levels discussed above) be written in a
functional language.

As the language vehicle for this project we are using Miranda(*) - the advantages of

(*) 'Miranda' is a trademark of Research Software Ltd.

Miranda for our purpose are that it is purely functional, that it is statically typechecked (which we regard as essential for any large scale programming project) that it is a complete and well defined language, and that it is coming to be reasonably widely used (at the time of writing it is running at over 100 sites). We didn't use ML [Milner 84], although it has a somewhat stronger claim to be a standard vehicle, for the simple reason that it is not a functional language. Aside from the fact that ML permits assignment (already a sufficient disqualification for our purposes) ML does not support lazy evaluation, which is essential for what we are trying to do.

The notation of Miranda is based on higher order recursion equations and is similar to that of a number of other modern functional languages. We assume this style of notation is by now reasonably well known - for a more specific discussion of the features of Miranda the reader is referred to [Turner 85], [Turner 86].

The current status of the project, very briefly, is that we have some of the essential tools (level 2) written. There is a full screen editor 'medit', written in Miranda [Duncan 86] and (most of) a Miranda compiler in Miranda also exists. We have experimented with some simple shells written in Miranda.

The purpose of this paper is to report on the progress that has been made in designing a framework for the internal structure of the operating system, which involves communicating processes, traditionally a difficult area for functional programming.

It is an essential requirement of an operating system (even a single-user system) that it must pay attention to several tasks concurrently. For example we might expect it to run shells for several users, and perform background compilations, all at the same time. Even a very simple single-user one-job-at-a-time system must be ready to pay attention to interrupts at the same time as running the user's job.

The best model for this seems to be to structure the operating system as a number of independent processes. The processes run concurrently and send each other messages (and of course some processes receive messages from, or send messages to, the outside world). Some processes are always present and constitute the kernel, other processes go in and out of existence under the control of the kernel (for example user shells).

Each process has internal state (that is, it is not destined always to respond in the same way on receiving the same message) but there is no global state as such (i.e. the global behaviour is simply the product of the local behaviours). How may such a network of communicating processes be described in a functional language? We take this question in two parts, first the description of the individual process, then the way in which they are connected together.

Processes as functions over infinite lists

If we consider the behaviour of a process as the association of output events with individual input events, it is clearly not a function, since the output depends not only on the input event but also on the internal state. However, the internal state is itself a function of (some initial state and) the previous input history. It is therefore the case (at least for a deterministic process) that the output history, taken as a whole, is a function (determined by the initial state) of the input history, taken as a whole.

Such a process may be programmed in a functional language, in the following way. For simplicity we take the case of a process with a single input channel and a single output channel. Let the input messages be of type alpha, and the output messages of type beta. Let s0 be the initial state, let trans::alpha->state->state be the state transition function, and out::alpha->state->[beta] give the (perhaps empty) list of output messages in response to a particular input message.

```
process :: [alpha]->[beta]
process = p s0
    where
        p s (a:x) = out a s ++ p (trans a s) x
```

The notation used here (and in other examples in the paper) is that of Miranda.

That processes with internal state can be programmed in this way in a (lazy) functional language is now quite an old idea, current since at least the mid 70's, see e.g. [Kahn and McQueen 77], [Turner 76].

Networks of such processes can also be described. For example if we also have process' :: [beta]->[alpa], and it is connected in a loop with the above process, this can be programmed as

```
chanA :: [alpha]
chanB :: [beta]
chanA = process' chanB
chanB = process  chanA
```

If this is not to be deadlocked one of the processes must be a net producer (and allowing for this possibility requires a slight modification to our earlier schema for a process).

A typical example of programming in this style is shown by the Miranda program for the well known communicating-process solution to the Hamming numbers problem, see Figure 1.

To summarise the preceding paragraphs: Concurrent networks of communicating sequential processes can be programmed in a (lazy) functional language, elegantly and even efficiently, as recursions over infinite lists, and this fact has been known for about ten years. Does this then mean that the problem of how to describe the internal structure of an operating system in a functional language is essentially solved? Unfortunately not, for there is an important restriction on the behaviour of networks that can be described in this way - they must be **deterministic** (as must the individual processes).

That this must be so is immediately apparent from very basic properties of a functional notation. Given a network with a certain number of input lists, and a specified initial state, the list(s) of output messages must be uniquely determined by the given lists of input messages. Otherwise we shall be in the position of attempting to use a functional language to describe something that is not a function, an exercise which cannot succeed.

In particular this means that the output behaviour of the network cannot depend on the relative speed of arrival of input messages along different channels. We can only describe networks whose output is independent of the relative speeds of the processes of which it is composed (and likewise independent of the relative speeds of arrival of messages on different input ports of the whole network).

For an operating system this is quite unacceptable. We need to be able to deal with certain events, eg requests for resources, 'in the order in which they arise' (this concept need not be precise - if two events occur 'almost at the same time' we should be allowed to make an arbitrary decision as to which happened first). This means that the output behaviour of the network must be not independent of, but dependent on, the relative speeds of the processes of which it is composed. How can we modify the above method of describing networks of processes to permit us to program this?

The most straightforward approach is modify our representation of channels, as lists of messages, to add information representing the passage of time. We can pad out

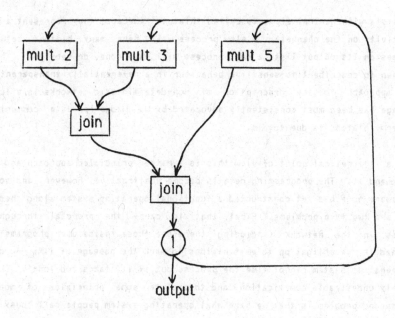

output = 1 : join (join (mult 2) (mult 3)) (mult 5)

where

mult n = map (n ×) output

join (a:x) (b:y) = a : join x (b:y), a < b

= b : join (a:x) y, a > b

= a : join x y,   a = b

FIGURE 1 The solution to the hamming numbers problem.

The problem is to print in ascending order all numbers of the form
$2^a 3^b 5^c$ where a, b, c can be any natural numbers.
There is nice solution to this problem in the form of a network of
communicating processes, sketched at the top of the figure. Below the
diagram we show the functional program, written in Miranda, which
describes this network.

the lists with neutral elements called 'hiatons' (because they represent a 'hiatus' in activity on the channel). A slow process will have many hiatons between the messages on its output list, a fast process will have none, or very few. The way is now open to describe time sensitive behaviour in a referentially transparent manner. This approach to the description of non-deterministic networks in a functional language has been most consistently advocated by W. Wadge [private communication], the term 'hiaton' is due to him.

From a theoretical point of view this is a rather principled approach and has much to commend it. The programming details become unattractive, however, and so far as I am aware none has yet constructed a functional operating system along these lines. There are two main problems. First that to carry the proposal through, every process in the network (including therefore those inside user programs) becomes enmeshed in the obligation to emit hiatons to mark the passage of time — otherwise the operating system cannot time the process out if it 'takes too long'. This seems a highly undesirable complication, and to violate some principles of modularity. The second problem is that we have what operating system people call 'busy waiting' — at any given time a significant proportion of the processes in the network will be 'counting hiatons' which seems a highly inefficient use of resources. In effect we have no real time interrupts, and are doing everything by polling.

We have therefore rejected the 'hiaton' approach for the KAOS project. An alternative approach is to add to our functional language some new primitives permitting the description of non-deterministic behaviour. For example we can add a non deterministic operation 'merge' that takes two (possibly infinite) lists and returns a list containing their elements 'in order of arrival'. Thus

        merge (a:x) y ==> a:merge x y
        merge x (b:y) ==> b:merge x y

The intention here is that the machine will use whichever of the above two reduction rules first becomes applicable. (Warning: this is not Miranda notation — the definition of 'merge' is not possible in Miranda, or in any other functional language. Read as a system of equations the above definition of 'merge' is just **inconsistent.**)

We also require that merge be 'fair' at least in the weak sense that every item on either input list is present 'eventually' in the result list. It turns out that all of the other non-deterministic primitives which have been proposed can be programmed in terms of fair merge. So adding merge to our functional language is in some sense enough to describe all non-deterministic networks. (Again we refer to results that have been known in the functional programming community for some years.)

The use of merge to create operating system like behaviour is described in [Henderson 82]. We give a sketch of how a two client/one server situation is programmed in Figure 2. The use of merge, or an equivalent primitive, to program substantial aspects of operating system behaviour in an otherwise functional language has been described by a number of authors, for example [Jones 83], [Abramsky and Sykes 85], [Friedman and Wise 78].

It seems to us that there are two basic objections to this approach, one practical, the other theoretical.

1) The communication paths within the network must be programmed in detail, by numerous uses of merge/unmerge, leading to what Backus has called "spaghetti programming" [private communication]. We lack the concept of an 'ether' permitting a process to send a message to any other process whose name is known.

2) 'merge' is not a function. It does not have side effects, but a call to merge can return different results on different occasions, even when the arguments are the same. (Recall that semantically, an argument is the 'same' if it computes the same value, regardless of by what method.) Referential transparency, that is the ability to employ equational reasoning in programs, has been destroyed. We may still be programming 'in a functional style', but this is no longer functional programming in any real sense.

A simple and ingenious scheme which overcomes both of these difficulties has recently been proposed by William Stoye of Cambridge University [Stoye 84], and it is upon this that our approach is based.

The sorting office - a global interconnection scheme

A sketch of Stoye's scheme is shown in Figure 3. The important change which has here taken place (and the step by which Stoye has advanced beyond the path opened up by Henderson et al) is that there is now only a single (infinitary) occurrence of 'merge' in the whole system, and it is **outside the language** (in Stoye's implementation it is part of the microcode which supports the abstract machine).

Each process has a single input list and a single output list. This is not a significant restriction since the input items can be labelled with information about their origin, and the output messages are always labelled with their intended

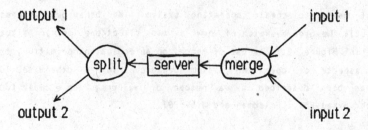

FIGURE 2 Using non-deterministic merge to schedule a resource between two clients.

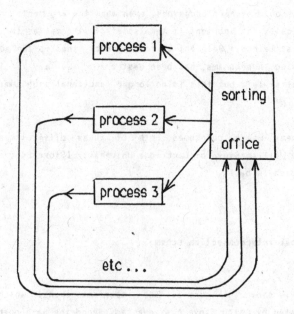

FIGURE 3 The structure of Stoye's functional operating system

destinations (so there would be no increase in power by allowing multiple output channels from each process). What is a significant restriction, of course, is that each process must be **sequential**, that is its output list must be uniqely determined by the sequence of arrival of messages on its input list — otherwise the process could not be described in a functional language, for the reasons discussed above.

[Note that this does not exclude the possibility of fine grain parallelism inside the implementation of each process — this would be `and-parallelism`, of the kind which arises from eg evaluating both sides of a plus operation in parallel, which is not a source of non-determinism. This consideration is orthogonal to the kind of parallelism we are discussing here.]

The output messages from each process are merged together and placed in the input lists of their addressees by a piece of apparatus called `the sorting office` — this is part of the abstract machine, and plays the role of the ether.

The output list of each process arises from the application of a certain list-to-list function (which we will call the `process body`) to the corresponding input list. In Stoye's scheme new processes are created by sending messages to a special process called the process-creation process. The contents of such a message is a function, namely the process body. On receiving it the process-creation process applies the body to a newly created input list (thus creating the desired process) and sends the address of the new input list back to the requesting process as a reply.

The process-creation process is also part of the abstract machine, and everyone knows its address (it is process number zero, say). Since new processes can arise dynamically, the number of processes in the system is unbounded in the general case, which is why we said earlier that the implied occurrence of `merge` inside the sorting office is in fact an infinitary merge.

Stoye implemented this scheme on SKIM 2 (a microcoded combinator reduction machine constructed at Cambridge) and used it to program a simple but quite useable operating system for this machine. The reduction machine was modified to timeslice itself among a set of reduction tasks (one for each process in existence) and to route messages to the correct destinations. The interested reader is referred to Stoye's thesis [Stoye 85] for details.

The important point for us about Stoye's scheme is that (given the rather simple modifications to the abstract machine) all of the code which describes the structure of the operating system can be now written in a purely functional language. We are therefore using this method (with certain modifications, see below) for our operating system, KAOS, now being written in Miranda. A fundamental design aim of the project was that we should carry the task through without compromising the functional nature of Miranda by adding referentially opaque features, such as `merge`, whence the decision to follow this route.

Each process in the operating system can be written in perfectly ordinary (deterministic) Miranda code. In fact to define the operating system we actually have to write code for the body of **just one process**, namely the boot process which creates all the other processes and thus calls the operating system into being!

[Aside: Some people have argued that Stoye's scheme is really a cheat, because merge is still `in there somewhere`, even if it is not visible in any of the functional code. Our response is that because there is now only a single invocation of merge in the whole life history of the system, it is possible to write down a purely declarative account of the behaviour of the whole network, and not merely of each individual process. We will not pursue this matter further here.]

Some refinements to the model

We now discuss some more detailed design decisions and their consequences. First how can we satisfy the requirements of static type-checking, a pervasive (and extremely valuable) feature of Miranda? In Stoye's thesis each message is a pair, consisting of the address to which it is being sent and some data item. Since there are no restrictions on the type of items which can be sent (so longer as sender and receiver are in agreement about the nature of the transaction) Stoye's compiler did not attempt to typecheck code which did message handling.

TYPE SECURITY

In our scheme the interfaces between processes are (statically) type secure. We sketch how this accomplished. We have it that all processes produce the **same** output type, namely

[message]

i.e. `list of message`. An object of type `message` is opaque (that is you cannot take it apart to find out what is in it) - the only thing a process can usefully do with a message is to put it in its output list. A data object is turned into a message by applying a `wrapper-function` (sometimes just `wrapper` for short). A wrapper function for objects of type alpha is called an alpha-wrapper, and is of type alpha->message.

Each process expects a specific kind of input item (not normally 'message', but some useful data item, say num, or tree or whatever). In the interests of static type checking we require that any given process has a single type of items in its input list (of course, this could be a union type, so there is no real loss of power). A process requiring its input list to be of type

[alpha]

is called an alpha-process. So we have many different kinds of process, e.g. num-process, tree-process and so on. Notice that in the interests of clarity we call the things which appear in input lists 'items', not messages (messages are the opaque objects in output lists). Note also that the body of an alpha-process is a function of type

[alpha]->[message]

Associated with each process is a wrapper function that can be used to send it messages. If it is an alpha-process the associated wrapper will be an alpha wrapper (and it is this discipline which enables us to ensure statically that processes receive only items of the right type in their input lists). The wrapper function carries then, two pieces of information - its type, saying what kind of object it is willing to wrap (this is for the use of the compiler only, since in a strongly typed language, such as Miranda, type information does not exist at run time) and the intended destination of the messages created by its use (this is for the use of the sorting office).

When a message passes through the sorting office, its wrapper function is stripped off, and the data item which it contained is placed in the input list of the destination process which was specified by the wrapper.

As the reader will by now be clear, 'message' is for us an abstract data type associated with wrapper functions. The underlying representation type (i.e. what a message 'really looks like' to the machine) is for us, as for Stoye, essentially just a '(destination,item)' pair. We will show later in this paper (after we have introduced the mechanism by which new processes are created) how the abstract data type message can be formally created from the concrete message apparatus by a Miranda **abstype** definition.

The underlying concrete message type we will call 'premessage', for clarity. The constructors of this type are not in scope for ordinary processes (e.g. we do not wish them to have access to process addresses directly). All normal communication takes place using wrappers.

SYNCHRONISATION

The next group of issues concern the nature of the buffering and the degree of inter process synchronisation in message passing. A closely related issue is, what kind of items should it be permitted to pass in a message (e.g. should we allow a message to contain an infinite object, such as the list of all prime numbers)?

We can take Stoye's decisions on these questions as a starting point. First, he allows arbitrary objects to be sent in messages, including both functions and infinite lists. This gets full marks for orthogonality, but has some not necessarily desirable implications for storage management. Both functions and lazy lists are `closure-objects', that is they can contain embedded references to any other item in the heap space of the process which created them. The implication is that in the general case the data structures of different processes will be inextricably intertwined, meaning that we are probably committed to a single monolithic heap space, shared by all processes. (Since Stoye was programming for a monoprocessor, with a single global address space, this was presumably not a disadvantage.)

On synchronisation and buffering, Stoye has the abstract machine simultaneously demanding output from all active processes, so there are no output queues, but each process can acummulate an unbounded queue of input items (implying that communication is completely asynchronous). Again these are not necessarily bad decisions (Stoye's system worked, and was even quite efficient) but for several reasons we have decided to do things differently.

We are concerned to avoid `dragging problems' in the communication between processes (meaning unbounded space requirements for as yet unevaluated expressions), and we also wish to support inter-process synchronisation. The latter, although still possible, is a somewhat unnatural activity in a system allowing unbounded input buffers. One is reminded of Keynes's remark about the difficulty of controlling something by `pushing on a piece of a string'. So, our decisions on these matters are:

1) Communication is synchronous

If process A attempts to send a message to process B (by placing a message created with B's wrapper on its output list), and process B has not yet demanded an input item, process A is **deactivated** until B is ready. This makes communication symmetrical between sender and receiver in its synchronisation properties – both must be ready to make the transaction. It also eliminates the need for any queues or buffers in the communication system – there will be no storage needs associated with the sorting office or with input or output lists.

An important consequence of this is that we can now program **data driven** concurrency (needed for example to program one producer/two consumer situations without introducing dragging problems). Trying to program data drive in a system with input buffers is the 'pushing on a piece of string' puzzle referred to earlier. Since it has been argued [Peyton Jones 87] that the occurrence of dragging problems is one of the most important obstacles standing in the way of a more general use of lazy functional languages, this seems an important advantage.

It is also worth pointing out that almost all recent theoretical work on communicating processes [Milner 80], [Hoare 85] assumes synchronous communication, and it may be useful to be able to draw on this body of knowledge.

2) Communication is hyperstrict

Some terminology. We say that function f is strict just when
    f BOTTOM = BOTTOM

where BOTTOM is the imaginary value deemed to be the result of expressions whose evaluation fails to terminate.

We say that f is **hyperstrict** if
    f x = BOTTOM

whenever x is not **totally defined**. Example, if the argument of f is a tree, f hyperstrict means that f fails if there is a BOTTOM anywhere in the tree.

We make wrapper functions hyperstrict. This means that items are **fully evaluated** before transmission to another process in a message. (Stoye does evaluation of messages to top-level only, so he has message passing strict but not hyperstrict). Our decision implies that only **discrete** (=finite, total) objects can be passed in messages. So not functions or e.g. infinite lists.

This decision further strenthens the synchronisation properties of the system. The major reason for the decision however is the following.

| Each process can have a separate heap space, which may be garbage collected independently of the heap space of every other process. Communication consists in copying a fully evaluated subgraph from one heap into another. |

This brings many benefits, including at least the following.

(i) The need for global garbage collection is eliminated.

(ii) Processes which run amock in their space requirements can be easily identified, observed, and dealt with. In view of the fact that we still lack a good understanding of the space behaviour of functional programs this is very desirable. By contrast, in a system with a monolithic heap 'containing intertwined data structures of all processes, the question, 'how much space is this process using' is not even meaningful.

(iii) Mapping the operating system onto a loosely coupled network of computers, each with its own local address space, becomes a relatively trivial exercise. (Actually the first implementation of KAOS is likely to be on a single large computer - however, knowing that it can be easily moved to a distributed implementation later is a definite plus.)

There is of course an associated disadvantage, namely the loss of orthogonality with respect to the types of items in messages. Certain values, specifically functions and infinite (lazy) objects can no longer be transmitted in messages. We remind the reader that the view of the operating system seen by the user through his shell need bear no simple relation to the internal structure of the operating system as supported by the kernel. So our decision DOES NOT IMPLY that e.g. functions will be in any way second class citizens as seen by the user. This means we may have to do some work in the intervening layers of the operating system, but operating systems already have to solve problems that are at least as hard as this one.

PROCESS CREATION

We do have however an immediate problem, namely how new processes can come into being. Stoye's method is to transmit a message containing a process body to a special address (that of the process-creation process). Since a process body is a function, this method is no longer open to us. We use instead an entirely different method (directly borrowed from UNIX).

In the situation where a process requires to initiate a new process, both the code for the continuation of the current process and the process body of the new process must both be present in the heap space of the current process. The process emits a special premessage, 'FORK', on its output list (this premessage should be considered as addressed to the abstract machine, rather than to another process).

The response of the machine to FORK is to duplicate the emitting process, by making a second copy of its heap image. The two processes distinguish themselves, each from the other, by reading the next item on their (now separated) input lists. Associated with each process is a small integer which is its process-id (hereafter 'pid' for short). In the case of one process (the 'parent') the next item on its input list is the pid of the child, while in the case of the child the next item on its input list is (say) 0, which is recognisable as not being a possible pid for a child.

All the processes in the system are descended, via invocations of FORK, from an initial 'boot' process (with pid=0, say). We are now ready to describe the nature of premessage passing as supported directly by the abstract machine. At this level we are working in terms of pid's, not wrapper functions, and don't yet have type security (this comes at the next stage, when we define the abstract type 'message' as supported by wrapper functions).

The data type of 'physical messages' as supported by the machine, is

```
premessage ::=   SEND pid item |
                 FORK |
                 WRITEDEV devid item |
                 READDEV devid |
                 KILL pid |
                 CLOSE pid
```

Here 'item' denotes a fully evaluated data object of arbitrary type, while 'pid' and 'devid' are just numbers. At any given time there are a number of processes in existence, each with its own heap space and an associated pid number. Each process can receive items on its input list and evaluates to a list of type

```
        [premessage]
```

Some processes will be **active** and others **suspended**. The active processes are subjected to simultaneous (in fact timesliced) demand for their output by the machine.

An active process becomes suspended
 - if it tries to read the next item in its input list when nothing has
   been transmitted.

- if it tries to SEND to a process which is not yet demanding input.
- if it issues a READDEV to a device with no ready data.
- it sends a WRITEDEV to a device which is not ready to write.

It becomes reactivated when the relevant data transfer is able to take place.

The action of the FORK premessage in creating new processes has already benn described above. A process ceases to exist, and its resources can be immediately reclaimed, if it receives the KILL premessage (clearly only certain very privileged processes should be allowed to send a KILL, but this security is a matter for higher levels of the system). The resources of a process can also be reclaimed if it terminates itself by returning [] (the empty list) as the remainder of its output list.

Sending CLOSE to a process causes the remainder of its input list to become []. This is somewhat more polite way of asking a process to leave than sending it a KILL. The process will discover, next time it tries to read its input list, that there are no more inputs, but it has the option of then doing some 'tidying up'.

The above is (in outline) a description of the lowest level of the system, as implemented in the abstract machine. In fact the type 'premessage' is not in scope for normal Miranda scripts, not even those which constitute the kernel of the operating system. Apart from a few processes that do lowest level communication with external devices, the sole use of 'premessage' in a Miranda script is in the definition of the abstract type 'message', shown in Figure 4.

The abstract type 'message' provides the type secure framework for interprocess communication in the rest of the system. It is implemented by a high level 'fork' which is applied to three continuations (functional arguments) for parent, child and failure respectively (the failure continuation is invoked if the fork cannot take place, eg because some resource is exhausted). Note that the parent continuation is supplied with the wrapper function for the child. Note also that the type of the high level 'fork' operation allows for the fact that parent and child will in general require input lists of two different types.

The function 'changetype' (definitely not permitted in normal Miranda scripts) is semantically equivalent to the identity function but has type '*-)**' so it can be used to smuggle things past the typechecker. Its purpose here is to permit the definition of (type secure) fork in terms of (not type secure) FORK to be accepted as legal by the compiler. Our current view is that there is only one other place in the operating system where the use of changetype will be necessary, namely in the loader (the program that converts compiled code to 'function').

```
%export message fork

%include <sys.private/changetype>

%include <sys.private/premessage>


|| process, wrapper are synonym types, defined for convenience only

process *  ==  [*] -> [message]

wrapper *  ==  * -> message


abstype message

with fork :: (wrapper ** -> process *) -> process ** -> process *

                -> process *

|| the implementation equations for the abstract type message follow

message == premessage

fork parent child fail (a : input)

= FORK : switch (changetype a)

    where

    switch (-1)  =  fail input

    switch 0     =  child (changetype input)

    switch n     =  parent (changetype (SEND n)) input
```

FIGURE 4

The Miranda script defining the abstract type message and the type
secure fork function in terms of the underlying FORK primitive

Readers unfamiliar with the Miranda **abstype** mechanism will find an account of it in [Turner 85]. The point to note here is that the distinction between abstract types and their representations exists only at compile time. At run time 'messages' and 'premessages' are indistinguishable. This means that the apparatus of wrapper functions, by which we have added type security to Stoye's scheme, has no associated run-time overhead. As far as the author is aware, Miranda's method of defining abstract data types is unique in having this property.

There are a number of points of detail which we haven't discussed here for lack of space. One issue is the apparently assymetrical nature of the communications established by 'fork', in that the parent is handed the child's wrapper but not vice versa. Seemingly, this would permit only 'downwards' communications, from ancestors to descendants. However, recall that the process body of the child is a function arising in the parent's namespace. The child may therefore inherit, as free variables, names for any and all wrapper functions known to the parent. This allows networks of arbitrary topology to be created.

Conclusions

Taking the requirements of the Kent operating system project as background, we have sketched a history of some of the methods by which people have sought to represent communicating processes in a functional programming language. It seems to us that the scheme of William Stoye is the first that permits the description of non deterministic behaviour without violating the requirements of referential transparency. We have described our own modifications to the Stoye scheme, permitting static type security in messages, synchronous communication, and separately garbage collected heap spaces.

Whether this scheme is sound as it stands or will require some further modifications in practice, we hope to find out by attempting to use it to build a real system.

From a theoretical point of view an important challenge is to show that equational reasoning can be applied to scripts involving 'fork' in a way that allows useful inferences about the behaviour of the processes.

Acknowledgements

Much of the above design emerged during a series of discussions with Robert Duncan (formerly of the University of Kent, now of the University of Sussex). I am extremely grateful to Robert for his inputs. In particular, the definition of fork in terms of FORK was first sketched by him. The KAOS project is supported by the Science and Engineering Research Council of Great Britain under grant number GR/D/26825. I am also grateful to ICL for their generous support in the form of a grant enabling me to concentrate on this and other research during the last two years.

[Note: 'UNIX' is a trademark of A T & T]

REFERENCES

S. Abramsky, R. Sykes "SECD-M: a Virtual Machine for Applicative Programming" in proceedings IFIP international conference on functional programming languages and computer architecture, Nancy, France, September 1985. (Springer LNCS vol 201.)

R. J. Duncan "Using the Miranda Screen Editor MEDIT" University of Kent Computing Laboratory, 1986.

D. P. Friedman, D. S. Wise "Applicative Multiprogramming", Indiana University Computer Science Department, Technical Report 72, January 1978.

P. Henderson "Purely Functional Operating Systems" in Functional Programming and its Applications, eds Darlington, Henderson and Turner, CUP 1982.

C. A. R. Hoare "Communicating Sequential Processes" Prentice Hall International 1985.

S. B. Jones "Abstract Machine Support for Purely Functional Operating Systems", Oxford University Programming Research Group Technical Monograph 34, August 1983.

G. Kahn, D. McQueen "Coroutines and Networks of Parallel Processes" in IFIP 77, North Holland.

R. Milner "A Calculus of Communicating Systems" LNCS 92, Springer-Verlag 1980.

R. Milner "The Standard ML Core Language", University of Edinburgh Department of Computer Science, October 1984.

S. Peyton-Jones "The Implementation of Functional Programming Languages", Prentice Hall International, March 1987.

W. Stoye "A New Scheme For Writing Functional Operating Systems", Cambridge University Compter Laboratory Technical Report 56, 1984.

W. Stoye "The Implementation of Functional Languages using Custom Harware" Ph D Thesis, Cambridge University Computer Laboratory, December 1985.

D. A. Turner "SASL Language Manual", St Andrews University Department of Computational Science, December 1976.

D. A. Turner "Miranda: A non-strict functional language with polymorphic types" in proceedings IFIP international conference on functional programming languages and computer architecture, Nancy, France, September 1985. (Springer LNCS vol 201)

D. A. Turner "An Overview of Miranda" SIGPLAN Notices, December 1986.

Garbage Collection in a Distributed Environment

Lex Augusteijn
Philips Research Laboratories Eindhoven
The Netherlands

Abstract

A garbage collector for a distributed system is described. This collector is of the mark and sweep type, each processor having its own garbage collector process, with access to local data only. In order to limit idle time for the processors in this system, the garbage collectors run on–the–fly, that is, concurrenly with the user program. The requirements put on the user program to achieve this are described. A new termination detection algorithm is imposed on the garbage collector, in order to detect a global state.

1 Introduction

In the frame of Esprit project 415, subproject A, a parallel object oriented language (POOL-T) has been designed (see e.g. [TA415,D0053,D0091,D0104]). In a POOL-T environment, objects (i.e. processes) are created and become obsolete during the execution of a program. In order to reclaim the memory occupied by obsolete objects, a *garbage collector* is needed. As a POOL-T program is supposed to be executed on a multiprocessor network, this garbage collector needs to be able to collect objects which are scattered over all processors in such a network. Each processor in the network is only able to access the objects located in its own memory. The garbage collector we present is a *distributed, on-the-fly* garbage collector, i.e. it is a set of garbage collector processes, one on each processor, which collect the obsolete objects in cooperation with each other and which run in parallel with the executing process. They can only access objects on their own processor. Therefore, in order to access other objects, they communicate to other garbage collectors. The algorithm used is a so called *mark and sweep* garbage collection algorithm.

The reason for needing an on-the-fly garbage collector is that the alternative, an interrupting one, would introduce a considerable amount of idle time in the system, since a garbage collector often has to wait in order to synchronize with other collectors.

The structure of this paper is as follows. In section 2 some details about POOL-T and the underlying architecture are presented. In section 3 we present some basic definitions and invariants which characterize a mark and sweep garbage collection process. In section 4 we describe how user-defined POOL-T objects should behave in order to allow this garbage collection process to be executed on-the-fly. In section 5 we describe how we obtain a distributed version of this on-the-fly garbage collector. We pay special attention to the problem of *termination detection*. A special object of class Synchronizer is used for the purpose of establishing global invariants, one of these being termination of a garbage collect cycle. This termination detection algorithm is treated in more detail in [D0183]. In section 6 we describe how the garbage collector is implemented in POOL-T. In section 7 the implementation of the synchronizer is described. In section 8 we give an abstraction of the executing process by means of a collection of POOL-T routines, which serve as an interface between the garbage collector and the executing process. In the appendix, a brief introduction in POOL-T is given.

2 Scope

The language POOL-T enables the programmer to describe a distributed program by a collection of cooperating processes, called *objects*. These objects are created dynamically (at run time) and have only access to their local variables, which are (references to) other objects. They communicate by sending each other *messages*. A message can contain *parameters* (references to objects again) and always delivers a *result* (also an object of course). An object sending a message is suspended until it receives the result. A message is only answered by a destination upon the execution of a so called *answer-statement* and if no message is available, it waits until one arrives (so we have a rendez-vous message passing mechanism). If a message it present, a *method* (which is a procedure) with the same name as the message is invoked, the parameters of the message become the parameters of the method. The result of the method is returned to the sender as the result of the message. Therefore the message passing mechanism behaves like a remote procedure call.

The machine on which POOL-T will be implemented, called DOOM (see e.g. [D0204,Odijk 87]), is a collection of von Neumann computers, connected by some message passing network. Each processor can handle several concurrent objects. While a message is travelling along the network, it is not acessible for any of the processors. Message travelling takes a limited, but unspecified time.

3 The mark and sweep algorithm

An object is *non-garbage* if it is either

1) Active, i.e. executable,
2) Sending, i.e. it has sent a message and is waiting for the result.
3) Accessible from a non-garbage object, i.e. some other non-garbage object holds a reference to it.

An object is *garbage* if it is not non-garbage.
We call non-garbage objects of type 1 and 2 *root* objects, since from their status it can be deduced immediately that they are non-garbage. Note that each non-garbage object is either a root object or accessible, directly or indirectly, from a root object.

Garbage collection is done in two phases, as usual, see e.g. [Dijk 78]. The first one is called the *marking* phase, the second one the *collection* phase. In the marking phase, all non-garbage objects are marked. The unmarked objects must then be garbage at the end of this phase. They are reclaimed in the collection phase.

Let G be the set of garbage objects at the beginning of the marking phase. We demand that all elements of G are collected at the end of the corresponding collection phase. (Note that we do not demand that there will be no garbage at all then: during the marking phase, new garbage may be created.)

The marking phase operates by means of *coloring of objects*. In this way, all non-garbage is marked (colored) by means of an iteration process, starting at the roots and proceeding with objects accessible from them until all non-garbage is marked.
We introduce the following coloring for objects :

Black, grey : non-garbage.
White : possibly garbage.

A black object is a non-garbage objects of which the direct *descendants* (i.e. objects to which it holds a reference) are non-white. Other non-garbage objects are white or grey. This is expressed by the following *invariants*:

SMOOTH	: There is no black to white reference.
G_WHITE	: $\forall x \in G.x$ is white.
R_NONWHITE	: All roots are non–white.
GC_INV	: **SMOOTH** $\wedge$ **G_WHITE** $\wedge$ **R_NONWHITE** .

Remark: in the sequel, we mean by 'greying' an object: make it grey if it was white, otherwise leave it unchanged.

The coloring process starts by establishing **GC_INV** by means of greying all objects and then whitening all non–roots. Note that an other order will do as well, but this one turns out be needed for the distributed version, see section 6.3. Then, grey objects are colored black, after greying their descendants. This continues, until the end of the marking phase where the following assertion is established:

NO_GREYS : There are no grey objects.

In order to guarantee the termination of this process, we have the following progress condition:

PROGRESS : The number of grey + white objects strictly decreases.

From **GC_INV** , **NO_GREYS** and the definition of garbage it follows that at the end of the marking phase, the following assertion holds :

WHITE_GARBAGE : $(\forall x \in G.x$ is white$) \wedge (x$ is white $\rightarrow x$ is garbage$)$
$\wedge$ there are no grey objects.

Therefore, once **NO_GREYS** is established, all we need to do to collect the elements of G, is to remove the white objects.

4 An on-the-fly version

In this section we informally show how a user program should behave in order not to violate the invariants and the progress condition of the collector, while running concurrently with it. It resembles the garbage collector in [Dijk 78] but it is of a much coarser grain size, since here the garbage collector is a concurrent process, rather then a concurrent processor. Since we have an on–the–fly garbage collector, the computation proper continues during garbage collection. We must however make sure that this does not violate **GC_INV** , **NO_GREYS** or **PROGRESS** . We consider an abstraction of the computation proper and call this the *mutator*, since it mutates the reference structure between objects.

- **G_WHITE**
  Since the mutator cannot access garbage objects (by the definition of garbage), it cannot violate **G_WHITE** .

- **SMOOTH**
  This assertion can be violated when some black object b is given a reference to a white object w. This can happen only when b is sent a message containing w as a parameter or by receiving w as a result. To avoid this, we need to color w grey as a part of this transmission. If w is local to the mutator, this is no problem at all. If it isn't, the coloring of w will cause a large overhead on the computation proper, since a remote message exchange will take place. Note however, that only b and the sender of the message are delayed by this, since other objects may now be scheduled instead.
  As we will see in section 5.2, this greying has to be performed by the sender of the message.

Remark 1: A solution to this problem is the following. Since the parameters of a message are a subset of the descendants of the sender, we might color all its descendants grey upon sending, rather than only the parameters. We can then color the sender itself black without violating **SMOOTH** . When this sender is going to send another time during the same marking phase, the parameters of this new message will be non–white, since they are descendants of a black object. Therefore, this new message may be sent without the coloring overhead. In this way, sending contributes to the marking phase of the garbage collection process and the overhead upon sending is reduced to once per sending object per marking phase. The same holds for the returning of a result. We do not treat this solution here because we want to concentrate on the bare algorithm rather than treating different optimizations.

Remark 2: Another optimization consists of administrating per processor whether or not a non–local object has been greyed allready during this marking phase. If this is the case, it not necessary to have it greyed again.

- **R_NONWHITE**
We can violate **R_NONWHITE** by turning a white object into a root. This only happens when a white object, waiting for a message to arrive, receives one. The mutator is obliged then to make it grey. We will treat this in the same way as the previous case, by coloring the parameters as well as the destination of a message. However, due to the latency of message transport, it may be the case that the destination is white again at the *arrival* of the message. This is the case when the message is sent in one cycle of the garbage collection, while it arrives in a next one. Then, although the destination was non–white upon sending, it may be whitened in the initialization of the subsequent cycle. If this happens to be case, it is colored grey at the arrival.

- **NO_GREYS**
Once **NO_GREYS** has been established, it cannot be violated by the mutator, since only white objects can be made grey, the only white objects are garbage objects and these are not accessible by the mutator.

- **PROGRESS**
New objects are created black during the marking phase. Since in POOL-T, they only hold references to NIL, GC_INV ∧ **PROGRESS** is not violated by creating a new object.
Furthermore, the mutator can only color white objects grey and this does not violate **PROGRESS** .

5 A distributed version

In this section, we explain how we can obtain a distributed version of the collection algorithm. The complete POOL text can be found in sections 6 and 7 below. It is annotated with assertions which we introduce here. The problem of establishing global assertion in a distributed environment is treated seperately in [DO183].

5.1 Introduction

We denote the garbage collectors by GC, possibly indexed by $i, j, \ldots$, to discriminate them. When $x\,(y, z)$ is an object, we denote its GC by $GC_{x(y,z)}$.

The on–the–fly solution sketched above can be transfered to a distributed system easily as far as termination is not concerned. The only adaption that has to be made is that a non–local descendant x which must be greyed, gives rise to a request message to GC_x. The main problem however, is the detection of the state NO_GREYS . This has become a global state, which can not be detected by local means: a *termination detection* algorithm must be used.

In a distributed environment, establishing of global assertions is a general problem. Several solutions to it have been published. Most of these solutions have a serious disadvantage for this algorithm. Since an object can hold a reference to another object anywhere in the system, each garbage collector must be able to communicate with any other garbage collector. In other words, the logical communication network between the processors is fully-connected, although the physical communication network does not need to be so. This feature makes most of the solutions in the literature very expensive in our case, since the states of all logical communication channels need to be recorded. Furthermore, an attempt to detect a global state may fail in many of these algorithms and they have to be restarted again. This is not the case in our solution, which follows a different approach. It is not fully distributed, in the sense that a special object, called a *synchronizer*, is introduced which serves in establishing global invariants. A fully distributed version however, can easily be derived from it and is sketched in [DO183]. The communication bandwith between this object and the garbage collectors will be very low, so it will not become a bottleneck. More algorithms for detection of global states in distributed systems can be found in the reference list of [Chan 86]. A very nice treatise on the combination of garbage collection and termination detection can be found in [Tel 86].

5.2 A general scheme

We now present a general scheme for the establishing of global assertions. We distinguish two cases:

- **A** Once some local assertion P has become true, concurrent collectors can not violate it. An example of this is the assertion "GC_INV ", which can only be affected by the collector on that processor during initialization, but not by others.

- **B** Once some local assertion P has become true, concurrent collectors, for which P does *not* hold may need to violate it again. In order to do so, they must sent a message to the appropriate collector. An example of this is the greying of descendants. A collector GC_i may have established NO_GREYS $_i$, while another collector GC_j may want to have a descendant x on GC_i be greyed, which would then violate NO_GREYS $_i$ again.

Note that in both cases, the state in which P holds globally, is a *stable* one, i.e. it is preserves until it is detected and new phase is initiated.

To case A, we present a simple solution. Once an assertion P has been established by a collector, it sents a done message to a special object of class Synchronizer. This synchronizer counts the number of done messages it has received and when all collectors have sent such a message, it concludes that P holds globally. It sents each collector a next_job message to inform it about that fact. After sending a done message, a collector does not need to wait. It can do local work which does preserve P, until it receives the next_job message.

The solution to case B is more complex. Suppose that we want to establish NO_GREYS globally and that NO_GREYS $_i$ is the local version of NO_GREYS for GC_i.

We define three states in which a collector can be:

- active, disquiet

- passive, disquiet

- passive, quiet

Note that an active collector is always disquiet. When a collector is quiet, NO_GREYS is guaranteed to hold there. A quiet collector can only become disquiet upon receiving a request message, being a request to grey an object, which would clearly violate NO_GREYS . This message can only be sent by another *disquiet* collector. This means that once all collectors are quiet, they remain so (a stable state).

Initially, all collectors are active. In finite time (by blackening local grey objects), a collector will turn from an active into a passive, quiet state. Once passive, it remains so, but it can change its state between quiescence and disquiescence (by receiving requests). Upon the transition from active to passive, each collector sends a so called done message to a synchronizer. As we will see, it is quaranteed that NO_GREYS holds globally, once all done messages have been sent. Note that each collector sends its done message exactly once since the transition from active to passive is made only once (per garbage collect cycle of course).

Each collector uses the method mark to color its grey objects to black. This method only terminates when NO_GREYS holds locally. Upon the start of the marking phase which must establish NO_GREYS globally, each collector calls its mark, which transforms its state from active into passive, quiet.

When marking, a collector GC_i that is greying the descendants of a local object may encounter a non-local descendant. This will give rise to the sending of a request message to another collector GC_j. When GC_j is quiet, it changes its state into disquiescence and calls mark to establish NO_GREYS again. In this case, we call GC_j a *child* of GC_i and GC_i the *father* of GC_j. Once GC_j is quiet again, the father-child relation is terminated and GC_j informs GC_i about this fact. When GC_j was already disquiet upon receiving a request message, we do not have to change its state and a father-child relation is not established.

We now introduce the following restrictions:

- A collector can be quiet only when it has no children.

- A collector can have at most one father.

Note that a passive collector is either quiet or a child of some other disquiet collector, which caused its disquiescence. We capture these characteristics in the following invariants.

I_1 : GC_i active $\rightarrow$ GC_i disquiet

I_2 : GC_i passive $\rightarrow$ GC_i has sent its done message

I_3 : GC_i father of GC_j $\leftrightarrow$ GC_j child of GC_i

I_4 : GC_i father of GC_j $\rightarrow$ GC_i, GC_j disquiet

I_5 : GC_i father of GC_k, GC_j father of GC_k, $\rightarrow$ $i = j$

I_6 : GC_i quiet $\leftrightarrow$ NO_GREYS $_i$ $\wedge$ GC_i.children $= 0$

I_7 : GC_i passive $\rightarrow$ GC_i quiet $\vee$ $\exists$ GC_j . GC_j father of GC_i

Moreover, we maintain:

I_8 : GC_i passive, disquiet $\rightarrow$
         $\exists$ $GC_o \cdots GC_m$. GC_0 father of GC_1 $\cdots$ father of GC_m father of GC_i,
         GC_0 active, $GC_1 \cdots GC_m$ passive, disquiet, $m \geq 0$

From these invariants we obtain:

I_9 : $(\forall i . GC_i \text{ passive}) \rightarrow (\forall i . \text{NO_GREYS }_i)$

Remark: It now becomes clear why the sender and not the receiver of a message has to color the parameters, as mentioned in section 4. Since the sender is a root, it is either grey or black by R_NONWHITE . When it is black, the parameters are non-white by SMOOTH and hence no greying needs to take place. When a sender s is grey, we may need to grey the parameters and the destination. If these are local to GC_s this is no problem at all, since GC_s is disquiet by the greyness of s and the greying will not disturb quiescence. If a parameter p or the destination d is non-local, a request must be sent to GC_p or GC_d, possibly disturbing quiescence. Then $GC_{d,p}$ become children of GC_s, which is no problem at all, since GC_s is disquiet. However, when the coloring is performed by GC_d instead of by GC_s, no guarantee exists that s is still grey at the arrival of a message, even when it was grey upon sending, due to the latency of message transport (it may be blackened in the mean time). Therefore, GC_d and GC_s may both be quiet and when GC_d or GC_p has to become disquiet by the greying of d or p, no disquiet father is available to let it become a child of.

We now construct a program which maintains these invariants and which establishes ($\forall$ i . GC_i passive).

6 Implementation of the collector

6.1 Avoiding deadlock

In order to avoid deadlock between collectors, which can occur when they send each other simultaneously a request message, we add to each collector a Marker process. The Collector keeps track of the administration of the collecting process, whereas the Marker takes grey objects to color them black. Before doing so, it first greys all descendants of such an object, in order not to violate **SMOOTH** . This leads to the communication scheme of figure 1.

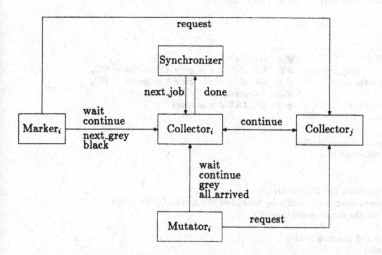

Figure 1: Communication diagram of the garbage collector.

The message wait adds children to a collector, whereas continue removes them. The marker can obtain a grey object by sending the message next_grey to its collector. The message all_arrived is used for synchronizing two subsequent cycles and is explained below. The other messages have been explained above or (in case of grey and black) are used for coloring objects.

6.2 The marker

A Marker process basically has the following (cyclic) behaviour.

- Take any grey object x.

- Color its descendants grey.

- Color x black.

A grey object x is obtained by sending the message next_grey to the Collector on the same processor as the Marker (i.e. to GC_x). Since x is grey for this Collector, it is disquiet. In order to maintain the invariants when a descendant y of x on another processor GC_y is greyed, GC_y potentially becomes a child of GC_x. Therefore, $GC_x.children$ is increased by means of the message wait. It will be decreased again by means of a message continue when the father-child relation terminates (wait and continue always come in pairs). This message continue is either sent by GC_y (when it is quiet again) or by the marker of GC_x (when GC_y was already disquiet, GC_y does not become a child then). This can be determined by the marker by means of the boolean result of the message request, by which GC_y is asked to grey y. It returns TRUE if GC_y was already disquiet, FALSE otherwise. We use this scheme for the mutator as well when it has to grey an object.

We now list the body and the most important methods of this class. Since some methods depend on the underlying implementation (e.g. the stack model of objects for retrieving the descendants), their implementation is not given here, but only their behaviour in terms of pre- and post-conditions.

```
CLASS Marker

VAR collector : Collector,        ##  The collector on this processor.
    collectors : Array(Collector),  ##  All collectors.
    x : Object

BODY
   ANSWER (init);
   DO TRUE THEN                   ##  GC_INV
      x ← collector ! next_grey ();  ##  GC_INV ∧ x is grey ∧ collector = GC_x
      grey_descendants (x);       ##  GC_INV ∧ x is grey ∧ collector = GC_x
                                  ##  ∧ descendants (x) are non-white
      collector ! black (x)       ##  GC_INV ∧ x is black
   OD


METHOD collector (x : Object) Collector :
##  Return the collector of x
END collector


METHOD grey_descendants (x : Object) Marker :
##  Grey the direct descendants of x by means of the method grey below.
##  It depends on the implementation of x.
   RETURN SELF
##  Descendants (x) are non-white.
END grey_descendants
```

```
METHOD grey (y : Object) Marker :
## INV : x is grey ∧ GC_INV ∧ collector = GCₓ
## I1 : INV ∧ gc_y = GCᵧ
LOCAL gc_y : Collector IN              ## INV
     gc_y ← collector (y);             ## I1
     IF Collector.id (gc_y, collector)
     THEN                              ## I1 ∧ GCₓ = GCᵧ
          collector ! grey (y)         ## INV ∧ y non–white
     ELSE                              ## I2 : I1 ∧ GCₓ ≠ GCᵧ
          collector ! wait (1);        ## I2 ∧ GCₓ.children ≥ 1
                                       ## (suppose GCᵧ to become a child of GCₓ)
          IF gc_y ! request (y, collector)
          THEN                         ## I2 ∧ y non–white ∧ GCₓ.children ≥ 1
                                       ## ∧ GCᵧ is not a child of GCₓ
               collector ! continue (1) ## I2 ∧ y non–white
          ## ELSE                      ## I2 ∧ y non–white
                                       ## (GCᵧ became a child of GCₓ)
          FI
     FI
     RETURN SELF
     ## INV ∧ y non–white
END grey

ROUTINE new (c : Collector, cols : Array(Collector)) Marker :
     RETURN NEW ! init (c, cols)
END new

METHOD init (c : Collector, cols : Array(Collector)) Marker :
     collector ← c;
     collectors ← cols ! copy ()                    ## Make a local copy
     RETURN SELF
END init

END Marker
```

6.3 The collector

We first introduce the following assertions. We use capitals for global assertions and lower case for their local versions.

quiet	No greys, no children here, the collector is quiet, the variable disquiet is FALSE.
all_grey	Only greys here.
QUIET	No greys, no children at all, all collectors are quiet.
NO_BLACKS	No blacks at all.
NO_WHITES	No whites at all.
GC_INV	As above.
gc_inv	Local version of GC_INV .
active	The done message has not been sent yet.
passive	The done message has been sent.
quiet	disquiet = FALSE.
s	At arrival of a message, sent from here, the destination and parameters are non–white. The same holds for the result of a message.
m	The mutator is in the marking mode, i.e. it preserves s.
S, M	Global versions of s, m.
father(GC_i, GC_j)	GC_i is the father of GC_j.

The marker above operates in close connection with the collector, e.g. either of them may send a *continue* message to a blocked collector as explained in section 6.2. In this section we present the implementation of the collector. It has the following (cyclic) behaviour:

- Initialy, all objects are black.

- Signal the mutator that new objects have to be created grey. Moreover, the mutator will enter the non–marking mode. This means that it does no longer maintain **s**. However, when a message arrives for a white destination, that destination is made grey. This is done to reduce the overhead for the mutator. Since there are only black objects, **SMOOTH** cannot be violated.

- All objects are greyed here. Since there are no white objects, **SMOOTH** cannot be violated.

- Wait until the other collectors have reached this state. Now, there are only grey objects in the entire system.

- All non–roots are made white here. Since there are no black objects, **SMOOTH** cannot be violated. By definition of G and root object, **G_WHITE** $\wedge$ **R_NONWHITE** holds now, hence **GC_INV** is established.

- Signal the mutator to enter the marking phase. The mutator now maintains **s** by greying the contents of messages at sending, hence **m** holds. Wait for old messages (sent before the start of this point) to arrive. They may contain white objects and their arrival at a black object will violate **SMOOTH** . However, since no black objects exists at this point, their arrival now is no problem.

- Wait until all collectors have reached this state. Now, all messages obey **S** and **M** holds.

- Signal the mutator that new objects have to be created black. This is necessary to guarantee the termination of the marking phase.

- Establish **quiet** by means of the method **mark**.

- Send a **done** message to the synchronizer.

- Now cyclicly wait for either a **request** or a **next_job** message. In the first case, the collector becomes disquiet and hence a child. Its father is stored in **father**. It then invokes **mark** again to restore **quiet** and stops being a child by sending a **continue** to the father. In the latter case, when a **next_job** message arrives (from the synchronizer), all collectors have send their **done** message, so no disquiet collector and hence no grey object remains (since I_8 holds). **QUIET** is now established.

CLASS Collector

```
VAR synchronizer : Synchronizer,
    marker : Marker,
    father : Collector,                    ##  Father of this collector
    children, greys : Integer,
    disquiet,
    ready : Boolean                        ##  ready → QUIET
```

```
BODY
    ANSWER (init);
    DO TRUE THEN                            ##   NO_WHITES ∧ all_black ∧ active ∧ m
        Mutator.grey_new_ones ();           ##   NO_WHITES ∧ active ∧ ¬ m
        color_all_grey ();                  ##   NO_WHITES ∧ all_grey ∧ active ∧ ¬ m
        sync1 ();                           ##   NO_BLACKS ∧ active ∧ ¬ m
        color_white ();                     ##   gc_inv ∧ NO_BLACKS ∧ active ∧ ¬ m
        await_arrivals ();                  ##   gc_inv ∧ NO_BLACKS ∧ s ∧ m ∧ active
        sync2 ();                           ##   gc_inv ∧ no_blacks ∧ S ∧ M ∧ active
        Mutator.black_new_ones ();          ##   gc_inv ∧ S ∧ M ∧ active
        mark ();
        synchronizer ! done ();             ##   gc_inv ∧ S ∧ M ∧ passive ∧ quiet

        ready ← FALSE;
        DO ¬ready THEN
        ## INV : gc_inv ∧ S ∧ M ∧ passive ∧ quiet
            SEL ANSWER (request) THEN       ##   gc_inv ∧ S ∧ M ∧ passive ∧ ¬ ready
                                            ##   ∧ ¬ quiet ∧ father (father,SELF)
                    mark ();                ##   INV ∧ father (father, SELF) ∧ ¬ ready
                    father ! continue (1)   ##   INV ∧ ¬ ready
            OR ANSWER (next_job) THEN       ##   INV ∧ QUIET
                    ready ← TRUE            ##   INV ∧ QUIET ∧ ready
            LES
        OD;                                 ##   INV ∧ QUIET ∧ ready
        collect ();                         ##   all_black ∧ S ∧ M ∧ NO_WHITES
        disquiet ← TRUE                     ##   all_black ∧ S ∧ M ∧ NO_WHITES ∧ active
    OD


METHOD request (x : Object, sender : Collector) Boolean :
##  INV : gc_inv ∧ S ∧ M ∧ sender.children > 0
    grey (x);                               ##   INV ∧ x non−white ∧ disq = disquiet
    RETURN disquiet
POST
    IF ¬disquiet
    THEN                                    ##   INV ∧ ¬ disquiet ∧ x non−white
                                            ##   ∧ father (sender,SELF)
            disquiet ← TRUE
            father ← sender                 ##   INV ∧ disquiet ∧ x non−white
                                            ##   ∧ father (father,SELF)
    FI
    ## INV ∧ x non−white ∧ disquiet ∧ (¬ disq → father(father,SELF)
END request


METHOD wait (n : Integer) Collector :
    ## children ≥ 0
    children ← children + n
    RETURN SELF
    ## children ≥ n
END wait


METHOD continue (n : Integer) Collector :
    ## children ≥ n
    children ← children − n
    RETURN SELF
    ## children ≥ 0
END continue


METHOD next_grey () Object :
## Return any grey object.
END next_grey
```

```
METHOD grey () Collector :
## Make x grey.
   RETURN SELF
END grey

METHOD black () Collector :
## Make x black.
   RETURN SELF
END black

METHOD mark () Collector :
## INV : GC_INV ∧ S ∧ M ∧ quiet = (children + greys = 0)
## I1 : INV ∧ disquiet = (children > 0 ∨ greys > 0)
## I2 : I1 ∧ ¬ quiet
   ## INV
   disquiet ← children > 0 | greys > 0;                    ## I1
   DO disquiet THEN                                        ## I2
      SEL ANSWER (grey)                                    ## I2
      OR greys > 0 ANSWER (next_grey)                      ## I2 ∧ greys > 0
      OR ANSWER (black)                                    ## INV
      OR ANSWER (wait)                                     ## I2 ∧ children > 0
      OR ANSWER (continue)                                 ## INV
      OR ANSWER (request)                                  ## I2
      LES;                                                 ## INV
      disquiet ← children > 0 | greys > 0                  ## I1
   OD                                                      ## I1 ∧ quiet
   RETURN SELF
   ## INV ∧ quiet
END mark

METHOD color_all_grey () Collector :
## Color all objects on this processor grey.
   RETURN SELF
END color_all_grey

METHOD color_white () Collector :
## Color all non-root objects on this processor white.
   RETURN SELF
END color_white

METHOD next_job () Collector :
   RETURN SELF
END next_job

METHOD sync1 () Collector :
## Send the done message and wait for all to establish all_grey
   ## NO_WHITES ∧ all_grey
   synchronizer ! done ();
   ANSWER (next_job)
   RETURN SELF
   ## NO_BLACKS
END sync1
```

METHOD await_arrivals () Collector :
Wait until the old messages from this processor have arrived. The mutator starts
preserving m by the call to the routine travelling.
Meanwhile, answer wait, grey, request and continue to allow message transport to go on.
LOCAL ready : Boolean IN
   ready ← Mutator.travelling () = 0;   ## **m**
   DO ˜ready THEN
       SEL ANSWER (all_arrived) THEN ready ← TRUE ## **m ∧ s**
      OR ANSWER (wait, grey, request, continue)   ## **m**
      LES
   OD
   RETURN SELF
   ## **m ∧ s**
END await_arrivals

METHOD all_arrived () Collector :
All old messages have arrived, new ones preserve s
RETURN SELF
s
END all_arrived

METHOD sync2 () Collector :
Send the done message and wait for all to establish m ∧ s
Meanwhile, answer wait, grey, request and continue to allow message transport to go on.
LOCAL ready : Boolean IN
   ## **m ∧ s**
   synchronizer ! done ();
   ready ← FALSE;
   DO ˜ready THEN
      SEL ANSWER (next_job) THEN ready ← TRUE ## **M ∧ S**
      OR ANSWER (wait, grey, request, continue)
      LES
   OD
   RETURN SELF
   ## **M ∧ S**
END sync2

ROUTINE new () Collector :
   RETURN NEW
END new

METHOD init (s : Synchronizer, cols : Array(Collector)) Collector :
   synchronizer ← s;
   marker ← Marker.new (SELF, cols);
   disquiet ← TRUE;
   ready ← FALSE;
   greys ← 0;
   children ← 0
   RETURN SELF
disquiet ∧ active ∧ NO_WHITES ∧ all_black ∧ children = 0 ∧ greys = 0
END init

END Collector

7   Implementation of the synchronizer

In this section we give the implementation of the synchronizer. As mentioned above, it counts the number of done messages sent by the different collectors. As soon as this number equals the number of processors in the system, it assumes that all collectors have sent their message and that some global assertion has been established. It then sends each collector in turn a next_job message in order to signal it about that fact.

As mentioned in section 5, it may be implemented as well as a tree of objects with the collectors in the leaves. These collectors send their done messages to their father in the tree, which on its turn sends its own message up in the tree once it has received the done messages from all of its sons. When the root has received all messages from its sons, all leaves are guaranteed to have send their done message and hence some global assertion is assumed to be established by this root. It informs his sons about that fact by sending them a next_job message, which is distributed through the tree down to the leaves. In this way, a global resource like one synchronizer can be avoided, thereby increasing the efficiency of this scheme. The tree can be allocated as a spanning tree of the processor network. We do not treat this second implementation any further here since we are not interested in the details of such optimizations.

We let the synchronizer create and initialize the different collectors. A collector is initialized after the creation of all other collectors, since each collector must know all the other ones in the system.

```
CLASS Synchronizer

VAR collectors : Array (Collector),
    number_of_processors : Integer

ROUTINE new (processors : Integer) Synchronizer :
    RETURN NEW ! init (processors)
END new

METHOD init (processors : Integer) Synchronizer :
LOCAL i : Integer IN
    number_of_processors ← processors;
    collectors ← Array (Collector).new (0, processors−1);
    i ← 0;
    DO i < processors THEN
        collectors ! put (i, Collector.new ()); i ← i + 1      ##  Create the collectors
    OD;
    i ← 0;
    DO i < processors THEN
        (collectors ● i) ! init (SELF, collectors); i ← i + 1  ##  Initialize the collectors
    OD
    RETURN SELF
END init

METHOD done () Synchronizer :
    RETURN SELF
END done

METHOD wait_for_all_done () Synchronizer :
LOCAL done_count : Integer IN
    done_count ← 0;
    DO done_count < number_of_processors THEN
        ANSWER (done); done_count ← done_count + 1
    OD
    RETURN SELF
END wait_for_all_done
```

```
METHOD give_all_next_job () Synchronizer :
LOCAL i : Integer IN
    i ← 0;
    DO i < number_of_processors THEN
        (collectors @ i) ! next_job (); i ← i + 1
    OD
RETURN SELF
END give_all_next_job

BODY
    ANSWER (init);
    DO TRUE THEN
        wait_for_all_done ();
        give_all_next_job ()
    OD

END Synchronizer
```

8 Implementation of the mutator

In this section, we model the mutator by a collection of routines of class Mutator. These routines can either be called by the garbage collector objects, or by the ordinary POOL-T objects which constitute the user program. The data of the mutator is modelled by the instance variables of this class. Although these are not visible inside the routines (according to the definition of POOL-T) we will not bother about that, since our aim is to give a formal model of the mutator process. By using routines and not methods, we avoid deadlock problems and we think to come closer to a realistic implementation, where the mutator will probably be implemented as a collection of run-time routines.

We need an indivisible operation in order to be able to preserve I_8: when greying the contents of a message sent by x, GC_x must be blocked (kept disquiet) by increasing its children when x is grey. The same holds for returning a result. The inspection of the color of x and the blocking must be indivisible since otherwise, x could be made black in the mean time and GC_x could become quiet. We indicate the indivisibility of such an operation by including it between $\ll$ and $\gg$.

Furthermore, we need direct access to the instance variables of an object. We use this for increasing children of the collector when blocking it during a send or return as an indivisible operation (a POOL-T send can never be indivisible).

Most routines will be clear from their text and their description in section 6.3. We assume the existence of a class Color with routines white, grey and black.

```
CLASS Mutator

VAR marking,                        ##   marking → m
    collector_waiting : Boolean,    ##   collector_waiting → collector is waiting for an
                                    ##   all_arrived message
    new_color : Color,              ##   The color of a new object
    number_of_cycles,               ##   The number of this GC-cycle
    travelling,                     ##   Number of messages sent but not delivered for this cycle
    old_travelling : Integer,       ##   Id. for the previous cycle
    collector : Collector           ##   The collector on this processor

## Routines to be called by the collector

ROUTINE grey_new_ones () Mutator :
    new_color ← Color.grey ();
    marking ← FALSE
    RETURN NIL
    ## ¬ m
END grey_new_ones
```

```
ROUTINE black_new_ones () Mutator :
    new_color ← Color.black ()
    RETURN NIL
END black_new_ones


ROUTINE travelling () Integer :
    number_of_cycles ← number_of_cycles + 1;    ##  Enter a new cycle
    old_travelling ← travelling;                ##  Adjust these counts
    travelling ← 0;                             ##
    marking ← TRUE                              ##  Establish m
    collector_waiting ← old_travelling > 0;     ##  The collector starts waiting for an all_arrived
                                                ##  message if the result is > 0

    RETURN old_travelling
    ## m
END travelling
```

Routines to be called by the user program

```
ROUTINE grey (x : Object) Integer :
## Color x grey.
## This is implemented as the method grey of class Marker.
## It returns the number of requests sent that did not create a child.
LOCAL gc_x : Collector,
      result : Integer IN
    gc_x ← collector (x);
    IF Collector.id (gc_x, collector)
    THEN collector ! grey (x)
    ELSE IF gc_x ! request (x, collector)
            THEN result ← 1                     ##  gc_x was disquiet
            ELSE result ← 0                     ##  gc_x was quiet
            FI
    FI
    RETURN result
END grey
```

```
ROUTINE send (s, d : Object, p : Pars, n : Integer, m : Method) Object :
## Send message m from s to d with n parameters in p.
LOCAL this_cycle,                                    ## The number of this cycle
      count,                                         ## Number of continues to send
      i : Integer
IN
    ≪ IF is_grey (s) & marking
    THEN ## GC, is disquiet
            collector.children ← collector.children + 1; ≫    ## GC, is blocked in disquiescence
            collector ! wait (n+1);                  ## For d and p
            count ← 1 + grey (d);                    ## Now grey d and p
            i ← 1;
            DO i ≤ n THEN
                count ← count + grey (p @ i); i ← i + 1
            OD;
            deliver_message (s,d,p,n, m);
            collector ! continue (count)
    ELSE ≫ ## Do not grey the contents of this message
         ## This message may become an old one, not obeying s
            this_cycle ← number_of_cycles;           ## Remember this cycle
            travelling ← travelling + 1;             ## The message starts travelling
            deliver_message (s,d,p,n,m);             ## May take some time
            IF this_cycle < number_of_cycle
            THEN ## It has become old while travelling
                    old_travelling ← old_travelling - 1;    ## The old message arrived
                    IF old_travelling = 0 & collector_waiting
                    THEN collector_waiting ← FALSE;  ## s
                            collector ! all_arrived ()    ## Release the collector
                    FI
            ELSE ## It did not become old
                    travelling ← travelling - 1      ## The message arrived
            FI
    FI
    RETURN wait_for_result ()                        ## Await the result of this message
END send


ROUTINE return (s, d, r : Object) Object :
## Return r from s to d, analogeous to send
LOCAL this_cycle,
      count : Integer
IN
    ≪ IF is_grey (s) & marking
    THEN collector.children ← collector.children + 1; ≫
            collector ! wait (1);                    ## For r
            count ← 1 + grey (r);
            deliver_result (s,d,r);
            collector ! continue (count)
    ELSE ≫ this_cycle ← number_of_cycles;
            travelling ← travelling + 1;
            deliver_result (s,d,r);
            IF this_cycle < number_of_cycle
            THEN old_travelling ← old_travelling - 1;
                    IF old_travelling = 0 & collector_waiting
                    THEN collector_waiting ← FALSE;  ## s
                            collector ! all_arrived ()
                    FI
            ELSE travelling ← travelling - 1
            FI
    FI;
    RETURN r
END return
```

9 Ackowledgements

I am greatly indebted to Frans Hopmans who supplied me with the first ideas concerning the termination detection in this algorithm. Furthermore, I would like to thank Wim Bronnenberg and Hans Oerlemans for reading this document and pointing out errors contained in it and the referees for their useful comments.

References

[TA415] *Parallel Architectures and Languages for A.I.P., a VLSI-directed Approach, A Technical Annex for project 415*, Oct. 1984. Philips Research Laboratories, EindHoven, The Netherlands.

[D0053] P. America, *Rationale for the design of POOL*. Doc.nr. 0053. Esprit project 415, subproject A. Philips Research Laboratories, EindHoven, The Netherlands.

[D0091] P.America, *Definition of the programming language POOL-T*. Doc.nr. 0091. Esprit project 415, subproject A. Philips Research Laboratories, EindHoven, The Netherlands.

[D0104] A. Augusteijn, *POOL-T User Manual*. Doc.nr. 0104. Esprit project 415, subproject A. Philips Research Laboratories, EindHoven, The Netherlands.

[D0183] Augusteijn, A. *Establishing global assertions in a distributed environment*. Doc. nr. 0183. Esprit project 415, subproject A Philips Research Laboratories, EindHoven, The Netherlands.

[D0204] Bronnenberg, W.J.H.J., Janssens, M.D., Odijk, E.A.M., van Twist, R.A.H. *The architecture of DOOM. Presentation at the Esprit-415 summerschool 1986*. Doc. nr. 0204. Esprit project 415, subproject A. Philips Research Laboratories, EindHoven, The Netherlands. To appear in Lecture Notes in Computer Science, Springer-Verlag.

[Chan 85] Chandy, K.M. and Lamport, L. *Distributed snapshots: Determining global states of distributed systems*. ACM Transactions on Computer Systems 3, 1 (February 1985), 63–75.

[Chan 86] Chandy, K.M. and Misra, J. *An Example of Stepwise Refinement of Distributed Programs: Quiescence Detection*. ACM Transactions on Programming Languages and Systems 8, 3 (July 1986), 326–343.

[Dijk 78] Dijkstra, E.W., Lamport, L., Martin, A.J. and Steffens, E.F.M. *On-the-Fly Garbage Collection: An Exercise in Cooperation*. Comm ACM 21, 11 (Nov. 1978), 966-975.

[Odijk 87] Odijk, E.A.M. *Presentation on Esprit project 415, subproject A (Philips Research)*. These proceedings.

[Tel 86] Tel, G., Tan, R.B. and van Leeuwen, J. *The Derivation of Graph Marking Algorithms from Distributed Termination Detection Protocols*. Techn. Rep. RUU-CS-86-11, Dept. of Computer Science, University of Utrecht, Utrecht, The Netherlands, 1986.

A Summary of POOL-T

In POOL-T, no distinction is made between data items and processes. Both are called *objects* and have a type, called their *class*. The behaviour of objects is specified by the programmer by means of the definition of the corresponding class, in which the attributes of the objects of that class (its *instances*) are listed. These attributes are:

- Local variables. In POOL-T, objects have access to their local variables only, not the variables of other objects. This gives rise to a powerful protection mechanism.

- Methods. These are local procedures of an object, acting on the local variables. A method always delivers a result.

- A body. In the body, the process behaviour of an object is specified. An object starts executing its body immediately after its creation.

- Routines. These are global procedures, with no global variables in scope. They are primarily used for the creation and initialisation of new objects.

Objects are created at run time by other objects. A program is started by creating one *root object* of some class specified by the programmer. This object usually creates the other objects which constitute the program.

Since no shared variables are present, objects communicate by sending each other *messages*. When some object a sends to object b a message m with parameters $p_1 \cdots p_n$, this is indicated by the expression $b \ ! \ m \ (p_1, \ldots, p_n)$ in the code of the class for object a. The object a waits until the result of the message is returned. The object b will answer m only upon the evaluation of the expression *ANSWER (m)*. When a message m is present, the method m will be invoked with the parameters of the message serving as actual parameters. When no message m is present, b waits until one arrives. Upon the evaluation *RETURN r* within the method m, the result of the method m, being the object r, is returned to a as a result of the message. As a consequence of this, a is woken up again. A result need not be returned at the end of a method invocation. It may be returned in the middle of it, resulting in the concurrent execution of the sender and of the last part of method of by receiver.

A message can be answered conditionally in a so called *select* statement, which reads *SEL* <*guarded-command*> {*OR* <*guarded-command*>} *LES*. Each guarded command consists of a boolean guard, an answer statement and a statement sequence. Its semantics is that exactly one guarded command is executed, its boolean guard must then be *TRUE* and a message named in the answer statement must be present. The correspoding method is then executed and afterwards the statement sequence. If more than one guard can be chosen, the one answering the first arrived message is executed. If necessary, the object waits until a guard can be chosen.

The expression *SELF* denotes the object executing that expression. It is most commonly used as the result of a method which should not return anything useful. This convention is made use of in the creation routines (often called *new*), where the expression $NEW \ ! \ init \ (p_1, \ldots, p_n)$ is returned. First a new object of the class in which the routine appears is created by the expression *NEW* and then a message *init* is sent to it. As the method *init* returns *SELF*, this new object is the result of the whole expresion, and hence of the routine.

When no body is present, the default body *DO TRUE THEN ANSWER ALL OD* is substituted. Most classes of this kind serve as abstract data types: their instances don't have any 'real' process behaviour, but they just offer some methods that operate on local data. Examples of these classes are the standard classes Integer, Boolean, Character, String and Array. Hence, integers and booleans etc., are objects as well.

Some syntactical sugar has been added for often occurring expression. E.g. $a + b$ abbreviates $a \ ! \ add \ (b)$, $a \ @ \ b$ abbreviates $a \ ! \ at \ (b)$ (e.g. array indexing), $\tilde{} a$ means $a \ ! \ not \ ()$ (e.g. boolean negation) and $\# a$ means $a \ ! \ size \ ()$.

Comments start with $\#\#$ and run to the end of the line.

DECIDABILITY OF BISIMULATION EQUIVALENCE
FOR PROCESSES GENERATING CONTEXT-FREE LANGUAGES

J.C.M. Baeten
Computer Science Department, University of Amsterdam

J.A. Bergstra *
Computer Science Department, University of Amsterdam;
Department of Philosophy, State University of Utrecht

J.W. Klop *
Centre for Mathematics and Computer Science, Amsterdam

(*): Authors partially supported by ESPRIT project 432, Meteor.

Abstract. A context-free grammar (CFG) in Greibach Normal Form coincides, in another notation, with a system of guarded recursion equations in Basic Process Algebra. Hence to each CFG a process can be assigned as solution, which has as its set of finite traces the context-free language (CFL) determined by that CFG. While the equality problem for CFL's is unsolvable, the equality problem for the processes determined by CFG's turns out to be solvable. Here equality on processes is given by a model of process graphs modulo bisimulation equivalence. The proof is given by displaying a periodic structure of the process graphs determined by CFG's. As a corollary of the periodicity a short proof of the solvability of the equivalence problem for simple context-free languages is given.

Introduction

The origin of the study of process semantics can be situated in the field of automata theory and formal languages. Typically, the abstract view that is taken in this field leaves from a process only its set of execution traces, the language determined by the process behaviour associated to some abstract machine. While this abstraction from all but the execution traces is the right one for a vast area of applications, Milner [Mi 1] observed in his seminal book that it precludes one from modeling in a satisfactory way certain features, such as deadlock behaviour, which arise when communication between abstract machines is considered. The same observation was made by Hoare, who initially provided his CSP with a trace semantics [Ho] but later preferred a less abstracting semantics - the so-called failure semantics [BHR]. In recent years much work has been done and is going on to study such process semantics which do not go all the way to the abstraction to trace sets or languages.

However, much less work has been done to explore the relationships between the 'classical' and well-established theory of automata and formal languages and the more recent views on processes. As one example of such an exploration we mention [BBKM], where the trace semantics is called linear time semantics (LT) and the less abstract process semantics is called branching time semantics (BT). For more work in the same direction, see [BMOZ] and [Me].

The present paper also addresses a question which arises from the comparison of LT and BT. The problem is as follows. As is well-known, the equality problem for context-free languages is unsolvable, meaning that it is undecidable whether two context free grammars have the same (finite) trace semantics. With the availability of more discriminating process semantics, such as Milner's bisimulation semantics or Hoare's failure semantics, it is natural to ask *whether the equality problem for context-free grammars is also unsolvable in such a finer semantics*. In this paper we only look at bisimulation semantics (the analogous question for failure semantics is very intriguing however, and to us wide open). For the question to make sense, we have to transpose the concept of a context-free grammar to the setting of 'process algebra' as we collectively call the algebraic approaches to process semantics which are exemplified by the work of Milner [Mi 1,2] and of Hoare [BHR]. This transposition is rather obvious: every context-free grammar can be converted (while retaining the same trace semantics) to a context-free grammar in Greibach Normal Form. And such a grammar in GNF is just another notation for what is known in process algebra as a process specification by means of a system of guarded recursion equations. (An alternative notation for a system of recursion equations can be obtained in 'μ-calculus', see [Mi 2] or [Me].)

So the question that we consider is:

Is the equality problem for context-free grammars in Greibach Normal Form, or, what is the same, for process specifications by means of systems of guarded recursion equations in the signature of Basic Process Algebra, solvable when 'equality' refers to bisimulation equivalence?

Here the word 'basic' in Basic Process Algebra (or BPA) indicates that only process operators + and · are present and no parallel or other operators. (Roughly, these operators can be compared with 'union' and 'concatenation', respectively, in trace semantics.)

Remarkably, the answer is affirmative, if we adopt the natural restriction to grammars without useless symbols and useless productions. In hindsight this is not too surprising, since processes under bisimulation semantics contain much more information than their abstractions, the corresponding finite trace sets (the context-free languages). The proof of the decidability is based upon the fact that the processes (under bisimulation semantics) which yield the context-free languages as their trace sets, display a very periodical structure which can be made explicit in the corresponding process graphs or transition diagrams. In Sections 7,8, we indicate how the method of this paper may be profitable when considering certain problems in the theory of formal languages: using the periodicity of the process graphs and the concept of bisimulation equivalence may help in obtaining decidability for the equivalence problem of subclasses of *deterministic* context-free languages.

The proof below employs in an essential way the supposition that the context-free grammar has no useless symbols and productions, useless as regards generating the context-free language. A more general question however would be the one without this assumption , that is the question: Is bisimulation equivalence decidable for all guarded recursive process specifications in BPA? This question is specific for process algebra and 'too general' to be of interest for the theory of formal languages when only sets of finite traces are considered, but would be of interest when also infinitary trace languages are considered.

Some of the easier proofs are omitted here; they can be found in the full version [BBK 2].

1. Context-free languages

For definitions and terminology concerning context-free grammars (CFG's) and context-free languages (CFL's) we refer to [HU]. In this preliminary section we recall some basic facts that will be used in the sequel. The following example fixes some notation:

1.1. EXAMPLE.(i) (This is Example 4.3 in [HU].)
$\{S \rightarrow aB, S \rightarrow bA, A \rightarrow a, A \rightarrow aS, A \rightarrow bAA, B \rightarrow b, B \rightarrow bS, B \rightarrow aBB\}$ is the CFG with variables S,A,B, terminals a,b and start symbol S. The corresponding CFL consists of all words $w \in \{a,b\}^*$ containing an equal non-zero number of a's and b's, as will be apparent from an inspection of the process graph determined by this CFG, in the sequel (Example 5.2.4).
(ii) Henceforth we will write CFG's using the bar notation, in which the CFG of (i) looks like

$$S \rightarrow aB \mid bA$$
$$A \rightarrow a \mid aS \mid bAA$$
$$B \rightarrow b \mid bS \mid aBB.$$

We will suppose that none of our CFL's contains the empty word ε; hence we may suppose that no CFG contains an ε-production, i.e. a production of the form A → ε. (As is well-known, this does not essentially restrict generality; cf. Theorem 4.3 in [HU].) A property of CFG's which is often used in the sequel is given by the following definition.

1.2. DEFINITION. (i) A CFG in which every production is of the form $A \rightarrow a \alpha$, where A is a variable, 'a' is a terminal, α is a possibly empty string of variables, is said to be in *Greibach Normal Form (GNF)*.
(ii) If moreover the length of α (in symbols) does not exceed 2, we will say that the CFG is in *restricted GNF*. (In [Ha] the format of restricted GNF is called "2-standard form".) E.g. the CFG in Example 1.1 is in restricted GNF.

It is well-known that every CFL (without ε) can be generated by a CFG in GNF. We even have:

1.3. THEOREM. *Every CFL without ε can be generated by a CFG in restricted GNF.* □

2. Basic Process Algebra.

The axiom system Basic Process Algebra or BPA consists of the following axioms:

Basic Process Algebra	Table 1
$x + y = y + x$	A1
$(x + y) + z = x + (y + z)$	A2
$x + x = x$	A3
$(x + y) \cdot z = x \cdot z + y \cdot z$	A4
$(x \cdot y) \cdot z = x \cdot (y \cdot z)$	A5

This axiom system is the core of a variety of more extensive process axiomatisations, including for instance axioms for parallel operators on processes as in ACP, Algebra of Communicating Processes (see [BK 1-3], [BBK 1], [BKO]). In this paper we will exclusively work in the setting of BPA. The signature of BPA consists of a set $A = \{a,b,c, ...\}$ of constants, called *atomic actions*, and the operators +, alternative composition, and ·, sequential composition. (The atomic actions will correspond with the terminal symbols from a CFG.) So, for instance, $a \cdot (b + c) \cdot d$ denotes the process whose first action is 'a' followed by a choice between b and c and concluding with action d. Often the dot · will be suppressed. In fact, the previous *process expression* denotes the same process as a(cd + bd), according to the axioms A1 and A4 of BPA. Note, however, that BPA does not enable us to prove that a(cd + bd) = acd + abd. By a *process* we mean an element of some algebra satisfying the axioms of BPA; the x,y,z in Table 1 vary over processes. Such an algebra is a *process algebra* (for BPA), e.g. the initial algebra of BPA is one.

In this paper we will be concerned with one process algebra only, namely the *graph model* of BPA consisting of *finitely branching process graphs modulo bisimulation*. All these concepts are treated in extenso in [BK 2, BBK 1]; for the sake of completeness of the present paper we will give a short exposition. Figure 1 (next page) contains two *process graphs*, g and h. Process graphs have a *root node* (indicated by the small arrow →) and have *edges* labelled with elements a,b,c,... from the action alphabet A. The two process graphs g,h displayed in Figure 1 are in fact *bisimilar*, that is: there exists a *bisimulation* between them. A bisimulation (from g to h) is a binary relation R with the set of nodes of g, NODES(g), as domain and NODES(h) as codomain, such that the roots of g,h are related and satisfying:

(i) if sRt and $s \rightarrow_a s'$ is an edge in g, then there is an edge $t \rightarrow_a t'$ in h such that s'Rt';
(ii) if sRt and $t \rightarrow_a t'$ is an edge in h, then there is an edge $s \rightarrow_a s'$ in g such that s'Rt'.

Indeed, a bisimulation between g,h in Figure 1 is obtained by relating the nodes which can be joined by a horizontal line. (Incidentally, this bisimulation is unique.) We indicate the fact that g,h are bisimilar thus: g ⇆ h. The notion of a bisimulation is originally due to Park [Pa].
Let $G = \{g,h,...\}$ be the set of all finitely branching process graphs ('finitely branching' means that a node has only finitely many outgoing edges). Operations + and · are defined on G as follows:

- if $g_1, g_2 \in G$ then the product $g_1 \cdot g_2$ results from appending (a copy of) g_2 at each terminal node (i.e. node without successors; this has nothing to do with the terminals in a CFG) of g_1, by identifying the root of g_2 with that terminal node;

- the sum $g_1 + g_2$ is the result of unwinding g_1, g_2 to g_1' resp. g_2' in order to make the roots acyclic (i.e. not lying on a cycle of steps) and, next, identifying the roots. (For a more detailed definition see [BK 2, BBK 1].)

Now it turns out that bisimilarity $\leftrightarrow$ is not only an equivalence on **G**, but even a congruence w.r.t. the operations just defined; and furthermore we have **G** / $\leftrightarrow$ ⊨ BPA, that is, the quotient structure **G** / $\leftrightarrow$ is a process algebra for BPA. We will refer to **G** / $\leftrightarrow$ as $\mathbb{G}$, the *graph model* of BPA.

Each process graph g ∈ **G** determines a set tr(g) of *completed traces*, starting at the root and continued as far as possible, that is: either terminating in an end node, or infinite. We will henceforth drop the word 'completed'. For instance, g as in Figure 1 has finite traces: a, bca,

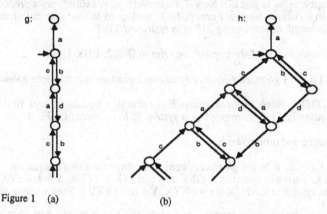

Figure 1   (a)   (b)

bcbdaca, and also infinite traces such as bdbdbd.... . We will refer to the set of *finite* traces of g as ftr(g). Now one can prove:

2.1. PROPOSITION. *Let* g,h ∈ **G** *be bisimilar. Then* tr(g) = tr(h), *and hence* ftr(g) = ftr(h). □

A proof will not be given here; see e.g. [BB, BBK 1]. The proposition entails that we can assign also to an element p of $\mathbb{G}$ (a 'process') a trace set tr(p) and a finite trace set ftr(p).

For use in the sequel, we need the following notion: if s is a node of process graph g ∈ **G**, then $(g)_s$ is the *subgraph* of g determined by s, that is the process graph with root s and having all nodes of g which are accessible from s. The edges of $(g)_s$ are inherited from g.

3. Recursive definitions

The model $\mathbb{G}$ of section 2 has the pleasant property that every system of guarded recursion equations has a unique solution in it. We will explain the syntax of such definitions (also called specifications) in this section, and also point out the relation with CFG's.

3.1. DEFINITION. (i) A *system of recursion equations* (over BPA) is a pair (X_0, E) where X_0 is a recursion variable and E is a finite set of recursion equations $\{X_i = s_i(X_0,...X_n) \mid i = 0,...,n\}$. We indicate the tuple $X_0,...,X_n$ by **X**. The $s_i(X)$ are process expressions in the signature of BPA, possibly containing occurrences of the recursion variables in **X**. The variable X_0 is the *root* variable. Usually we will omit mentioning the root variable when presenting a system of recursion equations, with the understanding that it is the first variable in the actual presentation.

(ii) Suppose that the right hand side of a recursion equation $X_i = s_i(X)$ is in normal form w.r.t. applications from left to right of axiom A4 in Table 1, i.e. $(x + y)z = xz + yz$. Such a recursion equation $X_i = s_i(X)$ is *guarded* if every occurrence of X_j $(j = 1,...,n)$ in $s_i(X)$ is preceded ('guarded') by an atom from the action alphabet; more precisely, every occurrence of X_j is in a subexpression of the form a·s' for some atom 'a' and expression s'. For instance, $X_0 = aX_1 + X_2 \cdot b \cdot X_2$ is not guarded, as the first occurrence of X_2 is unguarded; but the recursion equation $X_0 = c(aX_1 + X_2 \cdot b \cdot X_2)$ is guarded.

If the right hand side of $X_i = s_i(X)$ is not in normal form w.r.t. axiom A4, the recursion equation is said to be guarded if it is so after bringing the right hand side into A4-normal form.

A system of guarded recursion equations is also called a *guarded system*.

(iii) An expression *without visible brackets* is one in which all +-operators precede, in the term formation, the ·-operators. E.g. $aX_1 + X_2 \cdot b \cdot X_2$ is without visible brackets, but $c(aX_1 + X_2 \cdot b \cdot X_2)$ is not. A recursion equation is without visible brackets if its RHS is. Note that it is not possible to prove each expression in BPA equal to one without visible brackets.

(iv) If a system E of recursion equations is guarded and without visible brackets, each recursion equation is of the form $X_i = \Sigma_k \, a_k \cdot \alpha_k$ where α_k is a possibly empty product of atoms and variables (in case it is empty, $a_k \cdot \alpha_k$ is just a_k). Now if, moreover, α_k is exclusively a product of variables, E is said to be in *Greibach Normal Form (GNF)* , analogous to the same definition for CFG's. If each α_k in E has length not exceeding 2, E is in *restricted* GNF.

A well-known fact, for whose proof we refer to [BK 2, BBK 1], is:

3.2. PROPOSITION. *A guarded system of recursion equations has a unique solution in* $\mathbb{G}$. □

3.3. PROPOSITION. *Each guarded system* E *of recursion equations over* BPA *can, without altering the solution in* $\mathbb{G}$, *be converted to a system* E' *in restricted GNF.* □

The proof is routine and omitted here.

3.4. EXAMPLE.(i) Let E be the guarded system consisting of the single equation
$X = a(X + b)XX$. Then a conversion to GNF may yield $\{X = aYXX, Y = b + aYXX\}$.
(ii) Let E be the system in GNF $\{X = a + bXYX, Y = b + cYXY\}$. Then a conversion to restricted GNF may yield
$\{X = a + bUX, U = XY = aY + bUXY = aY + bUU, Y = b + cVY, V = YX = bX + cVV\}$.

Henceforth all our systems of recursion equations will be in restricted GNF. The reason to prefer the GNF format of systems of recursion equations or CFG's is that it implies in process algebra a well-understood theory of finding solutions. In principle it would also be possible to consider CFG's in say Chomsky Normal Form or even general CFG's; then the corresponding systems of recursion equations would in general be unguarded. Now, although such systems have always a solution in $\mathbb{G}$, these solutions are in general not unique for unguarded systems. Nevertheless one can associate to a system of recursion equations, possibly unguarded, a certain solution which has again the 'intended' CFL as finite trace set; but this is much less straightforward than for the guarded case.

3.5. NOTATION. If E is a system of recursion equations, E^t will denote the CFG obtained by replacing '+' by '|', and '=' by '→'. The start symbol of E^t is the root variable of E.

3.6. THEOREM. *Let* E *be in restricted GNF, with solution* $p \in \mathbb{G}$. *Then* ftr(p) *is just the CFL generated by* E^t. □

4. Normed processes

We will now describe a simplification algorithm to be applied to a system E of recursion equations in restricted GNF, yielding a system E' which does in general not have the same solution in the graph model $\mathbb{G}$, but which has the same finite trace set, i.e. determines the same CFL. The idea is to remove parts of E that do not contribute to the generation of the finite traces; cf. the similar procedure in [HU] to remove superfluous variables and productions from a CFG. The algorithm is essentially the same as the one in [HU], but the presentation below, using an underlining procedure, is more in line with our process algebra point of view.

4.1. DEFINITION. (i) A process graph g in **G** is *perpetual* if g has no finite (completed) traces. A process p in $\mathbb{G}$ is perpetual if p is represented by a perpetual process graph.

(ii) The *norm* of a process graph g, written |g|, is the least number of steps it takes from the root to reach a termination node, if g is not perpetual. (So |g| is the minimum length of a completed finite trace of g.) If g is perpetual, g has no norm.

(iii) The norm of a node s in process graph g, written |s|, is the norm of the subgraph determined by s (if this subgraph is not perpetual).

(iv) The norm of a process p is the norm of a representing process graph. A perpetual process has no norm. (It is an easy exercise to prove that bisimulations respect norms; hence the norm of a process is well-defined.)

(v) A process is *normed* if every subprocess has a norm.

4.2. PROPOSITION. *Every CFL is the finite trace set of a normed process* p, *recursively defined by means of a guarded system of recursion equations in restricted GNF.*

PROOF. Let E be a system of equations as in the proposition defining p. We will underline in an iterative procedure certain subexpressions in E, with the interpretation that an underlined subexpression stands for a non-perpetual process. The procedure is as follows:
(1) Underline all atoms in E.
(2) Extend underlinings $\underline{s}$ + t or s + $\underline{t}$, where s + t is a subexpression in E, to $\underline{s + t}$ resp. $\underline{s + t}$.

(3) If the RHS of a recursion equation in E is totally underlined, as in $X_i = \underline{s(X)}$, then the LHS is underlined: $\underline{X_i} = \underline{s(X)}$
(4) If a variable X_i is underlined, then every occurrence of X_i in E is underlined.
(5) Extend underlinings $\underline{s}.t$ to $\underline{s.t}$.

(6) Iterate these steps until no further underlining is generated.
(7) Erase all summands which are not totally underlined, and all equations whose left hand side consists of a variable which is not underlined.

Example: The system E = {X = aY + bXZ + cXX, Y = d + eYY, Z = aZ + bYZ} gets the underlining {$\underline{X} = \underline{a}\,\underline{Y}$ + b $\underline{X}$ Z + c $\underline{X}$ $\underline{X}$, $\underline{Y}$ = $\underline{d}$ + $\underline{e}\,\underline{Y}\,\underline{Y}$, Z = $\underline{a}$ Z + $\underline{b}$ $\underline{Y}$ Z}.

Hence the bold-face parts of E are discarded, yielding the system {x = aY + cXX, Y = d + eYY}.
    The remainder of the proof, to show that the resulting system indeed defines a normed process, is left to the reader. □

4.3. DEFINITION. Let E be a system of recursion equations which is invariant under the simplification procedure described in the proof of Proposition 4.2. Equivalently, E has a solution which is normed. Then E is called normed.

    We can now state the main problem of our paper. The *bisimulation equivalence problem* is the problem to decide whether two systems of recursion equations determine the same process (in G). The question is now: *Is the bisimulation equivalence problem for normed systems of recursion equations solvable?* In the remainder of this paper we show that this is indeed so, in remarkable contrast with the well-known fact that the 'finite trace equivalence problem' for such normed systems, or in other words, irredundant CFG's, is unsolvable. First we demonstrate in Section 5 a periodicity phenomenon of processes which are normed and recursively definable in BPA, the processes that can be said to be the underlying processes for the generation of CFL's.

5. Periodicity of normed processes

To each system E of recursion equations (henceforth always supposed to be normed and in restricted GNF) we will assign a process graph g(E) which represents the process defined by E and which displays the periodicity we are looking for. In order to describe g(E), we first define:

5.1. The universal tree t(E). This is the tree having as nodes all the words $w \in X^* = \{X_1,...X_n\}^*$, where $X_1,...X_n$ are the variables used by E. The top node is the empty word, and will be called the *termination node* . The first level of t(E) is as in Figure 2(a); the other levels of t(E) are inductively generated as follows: if w is a node of t(E), then its successors are as in Figure 2(b). It is important that the successors are $X_i w$ rather than $w X_i$.

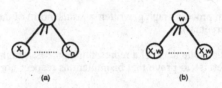

Figure 2

The tree t(E) will serve as the underlying node 'space' for the process graph g(E) determined by E, which will be defined below in subsection 5.3. A node from this space, i.e. a word $w \in X^*$, actually will denote the product of the (solutions for the) variables in w. E.g. if w = XYYXZ, then w denotes the process $\underline{X} \cdot \underline{Y} \cdot \underline{Y} \cdot \underline{X} \cdot \underline{Z}$ where $\underline{X}$ is the solution for the variable X, etc.

5.1.1. DEFINITION. (i) Let $w \in X^*$. The *translation* T_w is the mapping from X^* to X^* defined by: $T_w(v) = vw$, the concatenation of v followed by w. The *inverse translation* T_w^{-1} is the partial mapping from X^* to itself which removes the postfix w. A *shift* is an inverse translation followed by a translation: $T_w T_v^{-1}$. (So a shift replaces a postfix v by a postfix w.)

(ii) Let $w \in X^*$. The *length* of w, lth(w), is the number of symbols of w.

(iii) Let $v,w \in X^*$. The *(genealogical) distance* d(v,w) between v and w is the minimum number of steps (edges) necessary to go from v to w in the tree t(E), where E has variables **X**. Alternatively: let u be the maximal common postfix of v,w; let v = v'u and w = w'u; then d(v,w) = lth(v') + lth(w'). E.g. d(XYXZXXYZ, ZYYXXYZ) = lth(XYXZ) + lth(ZYY) = 7. (The reason for the term 'genealogical' will be clear in Section 5.2.)

(iv) Let $v,w \in X^*$. Then v,w are called *far apart* if d(v,w) > 3. (The number 3 is connected to the restriction in 'restricted GNF', as will be clear later.) Furthermore, let $X^* \supseteq V,W$. Then the sets V,W are far apart if all pairs $v \in V$, $w \in W$ are far apart.

(v) The *sphere with centre* w *and radius* r (a natural number), notation B(w,r), is the subset of X^* consisting of all v whose distance to w does not exceed r.

5.1.2. DEFINITION. (i) Let $V = \{V_i \mid i \in I\}$ be a collection of subsets of X^*. Suppose V contains a subcollection $W = \{W_j \mid j \in J\}$, $I \supseteq J$, such that every V_i ($i \in I$) can be obtained by translation of some W_j ($j \in J$), i.e. $V_i = T_w(W_j)$ for some w. Then **W** is called a *basis* (w.r.t. translations) for **V**.

(ii) Let $X^* \supseteq V,W$ and suppose for some U and v,w we have: $T_v(U) = V$, $T_w(U) = W$. Then we say that V,W are *equivalent modulo translation*, notation $V \equiv_T W$.

5.1.3. PROPOSITION. (i) $\equiv_T$ *is an equivalence relation.*
(ii) *If* $V \equiv_T W$ *then* V,W *differ by a shift.* □

5.1.4. PROPOSITION. (i) *Let* B_r *be the collection of all spheres with a fixed radius* r. *Then* B_r *has a finite basis.* (ii) B_r *is finitely partitioned by the translation equivalence.*

PROOF. (i) It is not hard to check that the spheres B(w,r) with lth(w) ≤ r form a basis.
(ii) Immediately from (i). □

5.1.5. EXAMPLE. See Figure 3, where X = X,Y and where B(YX,1) is indicated. A basis for the collection of all spheres with radius 1 is given by the three spheres B(ε,1) = {ε,X,Y}, B(X,1) = {ε,X,XX,YX} and B(Y,1) = {ε,Y,XY,YY}.

5.1.6. DEFINITION. (i) If a subset V of X^* is contained in some B(w,r), V is called r-*bounded*.
(ii) If $V = \{V_i \mid i \in I\}$ is a collection of subsets of X^*, and: $\exists r \forall i \exists w \; B(w,r) \supseteq V_i$, then the elements of **V** are *uniformly bounded*.

5.1.7. PROPOSITION. *Let* **V** *be a uniformly bounded collection of subsets of* X^*. *Then* **V** *is finitely partitioned by translation equivalence.*

PROOF. Clear from the preceding proposition, since the number of subsets of $B(w,r)$ is bounded by a constant depending only from r. $\square$

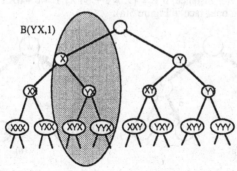

Figure 3

5.1.8. PROPOSITION. *Let* W *be a subset of* X^*, *where* X *is the list of variables used by* E, *such that :*
(i) $\exists c_1, c_2 \in \mathbb{N}$ $\forall w \in W$ $c_1 \le \text{lth}(w) \le c_2$,
(ii) W *cannot be partitioned into* W_1, W_2 *which are far apart.*
 Then W *is contained in a sphere* $B(w,r)$ *where* r *depends only from* c_1, c_2.

PROOF. It is not hard to check that for a pair of points in a set W as in the proposition, the distance is in fact bounded by $2(c_2 - c_1) + 2$. $\square$

 This proposition says that if horizontal slices of thickness $c_2 - c_1$ are taken from the tree $t(E)$, and the slices of the tree are further divided into 'parts' that are far apart, then the collection of these 'parts' is uniformly bounded. See Figure 4, where $X = X,Y$ and where the slices have thickness 1; the 'parts' are contained by the indicated rectangles.

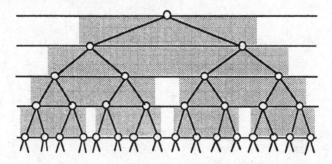

Figure 4

 Before defining the process graph $g(E)$, we make a simple observation about the relation of the length and the norm function. Our assumption is that E is normed, i.e. all perpetual parts have been pruned away as described in Proposition 4.2. That means that all subprocesses of the solution of E, which are of the form $w \in X^*$, have a norm $|w|$, the distance in steps to termination. It is easy to determine the relationship between $\text{lth}(w)$ and $|w|$:

5.1.9. PROPOSITION. *Let* E *be a normed system of recursion equations and* $|.|$ *the corresponding norm. Then:*
 (i) $|wv| = |w| + |v|$,
 (ii) $|w| = c_1.|X_1| + ... + c_n.|X_n|$ *where* c_i $(i = 1,...,n)$ *is the number of occurrences of* X_i *in* w,
 (iii) *the length function and the norm function are linearly equivalent in this sense: for some constants* n_1 *and* n_2 *we have for all* w: $|w| \le n_1.\text{lth}(w)$ *and* $\text{lth}(w) \le n_2.|w|$. $\square$

5.2. The process graph g(E). According to the equations in E, we now fill in, in the obvious manner, labeled edges in t(E). This will not give rise immediately to g(E), but first to an intermediate graph g'(E) from which g(E) originates by leaving out inaccessible parts (inaccessible from the root node, X_1). For instance, if E = {X = a + bYX, Y = c + dXY} then the upper part of t(E) gets the edges, drawn bold-face in Figure 5(a):

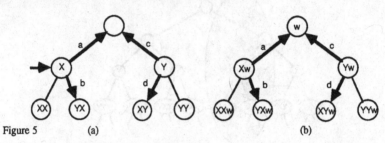

Figure 5   (a)   (b)

This basic figure (the bold-face part) corresponds just to the equations of E. But these equations give also rise to the following equations, for every w ∈ {X,Y}* (of course considered as a *product*):

$$Xw = (a + bYX)w = aw + bYXw$$
$$Yw = (c + dXY)w = cw + dXYw.$$

These equations yield the edges in t(E) as in Figure 5(b). So, the graph we want originates by reiterating the basic figure in Figure 5(a) wherever possible in t(E). The result is g'(E) as in Figure 6.

However, it is easily seen that large parts (the shaded rectangles in Figure 6) of the graph g'(E) are inaccessible from the root X. After leaving these out we have g(E), which has a 'linear' structure; it is the graph in Figure 1(a), Section 2.

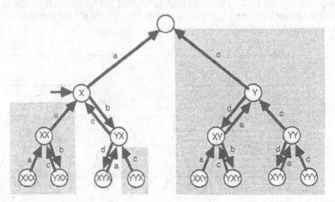

Figure 6

5.2.1. EXAMPLE. Let E be {X = a + bXY, Y = c + dYX}. Then g'(E) = g(E), i.e. g(E) uses all nodes of the tree t(E), as one easily verifies.

Note that by the restriction in 'restricted GNF' the only possible arrows (edges) in g(E) are:
(i)   from a node to itself,
(ii) from a node to its 'mother' (e.g. XX →$_a$ X in Figure 6),
(iii) from a node to a 'daughter' (e.g. XX →$_b$ YXX in Figure 6),
(iv) from a node to a 'sister',
(v) from a node to a 'niece'.
So, in all cases the nodes connected by an edge of g(E) have distance 0,1,2 or 3.

Henceforth we will present graphs g(E) *such that the norms are "respected graphically", i.e. a node with norm* n *will be positioned on level* n.

Example: if E = {X = a + bU, U = cX + dZX, Y = c + dZ, Z = aY + bUY}. Then g(E) is as in Figure 7.

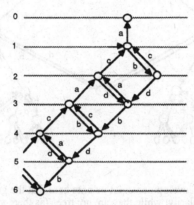

Figure 7

Note that the graphs of Figure 6 (the unshaded 'linear' graph also appearing in Figure 1(a), Section 2) and Figure 7 (also in Figure 1(b)) are bisimilar, as can be seen by relating all nodes on the same level. This example of two bisimilar process graphs shows that our bisimulation equivalence has nothing to do with the so-called "structural equivalence" or "strong equivalence" of CFG's (see [Sa 2], p.287), an equivalence notion which also happens to be decidable. (See also Problem 26 in Section 10.4 of [Ha].) Indeed, the "parenthesized versions" (see [Sa 2]) of both CFG's yield different languages (e.g. the word (b(c)(a)) is in the first CFL but not in the second, whereas (b(c(a))) is in the second but not in the first).

5.2.3. EXAMPLE. Let E be {X = a + bY + fXY, Y = cX + dZ, Z = gX + eXZ}. Then g(E) is (see Figure 8):

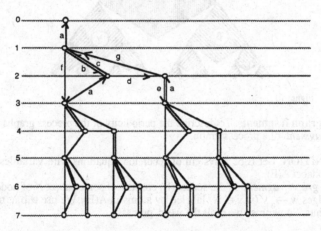

Figure 8

5.2.4. EXAMPLE. Let E be {X = dY + bZ, Y = b + bX + dYY, Z = d + dX + bZZ}. This example is the same as Example 1.1. The corresponding CFL consists of words with equal numbers of b's and d's.

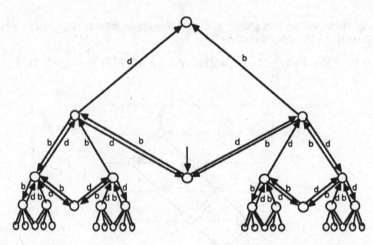

Figure 9

In advance to further developments, let us note here that the graphs g(E) as in the examples above exhibit a striking regularity; while they are not trees (as there are cycles present), the process graphs g(E) nevertheless have, from a more global point of view, a "tree-like" structure. For instance, in the last example there are three 'fragments' of the process graph which are strung together not only in tree-like fashion, but also in a regular way, as suggested in the following figure.

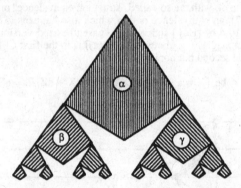

Figure 10

5.3. Process graph fragments. To describe the periodicity of the process graphs g(E), we need the notion of a *fragment* of a process graph.

5.3.1. DEFINITION. Let E be a system of recursion equations with variables $X = \{X_1,...,X_n\}$ and action alphabet A(E).
(i) A *process graph fragment* in the space t(E) consists of some subset N of nodes of X^* together with some edges $w \rightarrow_a v$ ($w,v \in N$) labeled by atoms in A(E). We use $\alpha,\beta,...$ to denote process graph fragments. Sometimes we omit the word 'process'.

(ii) Two graph fragments in t(E) are *disjoint* if they have no nodes in common.

(iii) A graph fragment is *connected* if it cannot be partitioned into two disjoint graph fragments.
Equivalently: a graph fragment is connected if each pair of points in it is connected by a path of consecutive edges, disregarding the direction of the edges.

(iv) If α,β are graph fragments, the *union* $\alpha \cup \beta$ is the graph fragment obtained by taking the union of the respective nodes and edges.

(v) *Translations* T_w of graph fragments and translation equivalence are defined as for node sets, with the extra understanding that a translation also respects labeled edges.

The following fact is obvious:

5.3.2. PROPOSITION. *If* α, α' *are graph fragments in* $g(E)$, *and* $\alpha \equiv_T \alpha'$, *then there are words* w, v *such that* $\alpha = T_v(T_w^{-1}(\alpha'))$. □

5.3.3. PROPOSITION. *Let* α *be a connected graph fragment of a process graph* $g(E)$. *Then the node set of* α *cannot be partitioned into two sets which are far apart.*

PROOF. Follows immediately from the fact, observed in subsection 5.2, that only nodes with distance 0,1,2 or 3 can be joined by an edge in the graph fragment. □

5.3.4. PROPOSITION. *Let* α *be a graph fragment of* $g(E)$ *such that*
(i) $\exists c_1, c_2 \in \mathbb{N} \; \forall w \in \alpha \; c_1 \leq |w| \leq c_2$, *and*
(ii) α *is connected.*
        Then α *is contained by a sphere* $B(w, r)$ *where* r *only depends (in a computable way) from* c_1, c_2 *and* E.

PROOF. By Propositions 5.3.3 and 5.1.8. □

5.3.5. PROPOSITION. *Let* $(\alpha_i)_{i \in I}$ *be a collection of fragments of* $g(E)$. *Let the* α_i *be uniformly bounded. (i) Then the collection is finitely partitioned by translation equivalence. (ii) Moreover, the number of elements of the partition can be computed from* E.

PROOF. (i): at once from Proposition 5.1.7. Part (ii) is routine. □

5.4. Regular decompositions. We are now arriving at the heart of the matter. First we will define what is meant by a 'regular decomposition' (also called 'periodical decomposition').

5.4.1. DEFINITION. A *regular* node-labeled tree T is a tree T with a labeling of the nodes, such that there are (modulo isomorphism of node-labeled trees) only finitely many subtrees.
        Note: the labels can be any mathematical objects - in our case they will be complicated objects, viz. translation equivalence classes of process graph fragments.

5.4.2. DEFINITION. A *regular decomposition* of the process graph $g(E)$ is a tree T where each node s is labelled with a process graph fragment α_s such that

- each α_s is a *finite* graph fragment in t(E),

- the union of all α_s is $g(E)$,

- for nodes s,t in T, α_s and α_t are disjoint iff s,t are not connected by a single edge in T,

- the collection of α_s (all nodes s in T) is finitely partitioned by translation equivalence,

- if $\underline{\alpha}_1, ..., \underline{\alpha}_k$ denote the finitely many equivalence classes in which the α_s are partitioned, and each label α_s is replaced by the label denoting its equivalence class, the resulting node-labeled tree T' is *regular*.

5.4.3. EXAMPLE. Let T' be the regular tree as in Figure 11. Then the actual tree T has the same tree structure and as node labels: fragments α_s which are translation equivalent in the way indicated by T'.

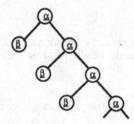

Figure 11

The following proposition is essential in the proof of the existence of a regular decomposition.

5.4.4. PROPOSITION. *Let* α *and* α' *be fragments of* g(E), *which are translation equivalent. Let* s *be a node in* α *which has a length not minimal in* α. *Suppose* s →$_a$ t *is an edge such that* α ∪ {s →$_a$ t} *is again a fragment of* g(E). *Let* s' *be the point in* α' *corresponding (after the same shift as from* α *to* α') *to* s.

Then there is a t' *and an edge* s' →$_a$ t' *such that* α' ∪ {s' →$_a$ t'} *is also a fragment of* g(E); *moreover, the two extended fragments are again translation equivalent by the same shift.*

PROOF. See Figure 12.

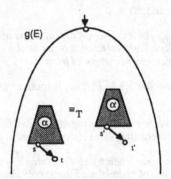

Figure 12

Since α ≡$_T$ α' there are w,v ∈ X* such that α' = T$_v$(T$_w^{-1}$(α)). So s = uw for some u ∈ X* and s' = uv. Since the length of s is not minimal in α, u is not empty. So s and s' start with the same variable; say s = X$_i$u'w and s' = X$_i$u'v. In particular, if s →$_a$ t is a step obtained from the recursion equation X$_i$ = ... + au" + ... (i.e. from the displayed summand, where u" ∈ X*) then t = u"u'w, and we have the step s' = X$_i$u'v →$_a$ u"u'v = t'. So the step s' →$_a$ t' is at least in g'(E) (the graph where also inaccessible parts are present, see Section 5.2). It is also in g(E), because t' is an accessible node. This is so as s' is accessible, being a node in α' which is in g(E). Therefore α' ∪ {s' →$_a$ t'} is indeed a fragment of g(E), and clearly it is equivalent to α ∪ {s →$_a$ t} by the same shift T$_v$T$_w^{-1}$. □

We will now define the decomposition which will be proved to be regular in Theorem 5.4.6.

5.4.5. DEFINITION. Let g(E) be the process graph corresponding to E.
(i) g(E) will be divided in fragments called *slices*, numbered 0,1,2,3,..... . Each slice has thickness d; we will also call d the *amplitude* of the decomposition.

(ii) The n-th slice (n = 0,1,2,3,...) contains the nodes s of g(E) with n.d ≤ |s| ≤ (n+1).d and moreover those nodes reachable by one step in g(E) from a node s with n.d < |s| < (n+1).d.
Example: in Figure 13 slice 1 of thickness 2 is displayed of the process graph in Figure 8.

(iii) The nodes s in the n-th slice with |s| ≤ n.d are called the *upper nodes* of the n-th slice; the nodes s with |s| ≥ (n+1).d are the *bottom nodes* of the n-th slice.

(iv) The n-th slice is now the fragment of g(E) obtained by taking the restriction of g(E) to the set of nodes of the n-th slice. (In the example of Figure 13: the bold-face part.)

(v) The n-th slice is divided in maximal connected fragments. These fragments, of all slices, together constitute the decomposition we want; we will say that the decomposition has amplitude d.

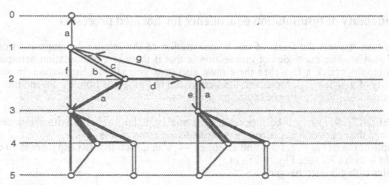

Figure 13

5.4.6. THEOREM. *Let* E *be a normed system of recursion equations in restricted GNF, in the signature of* BPA, *and let* g(E) *be the corresponding normed process graph. Then* g(E) *has a regular decomposition; moreover, the amplitude* d *of the decomposition can be chosen arbitrarily such that* $d \geq c(E)$ *for some constant* c(E) *computable from* E.

PROOF. Consider the decomposition with amplitude d as just defined.
(I). It is easy to see that the tree of fragments thus obtained is indeed a tree. To prove this, we must show that a situation (e.g.) as in Figure 14 cannot happen.

Figure 14

The reason that such a 'confluence' is impossible is that the bottom points of β and γ are too far apart, when d is sufficiently large. (It is trivial to give an estimation, depending on E, how large: it suffices to have the length of bottom points of a fragment at least 3 more than the length of top points.) Going downwards from such bottom points only increases the distance - hence there is no confluence possible.

(II) There are only finitely many labels (fragments) modulo translation equivalence. This follows from Propositions 5.3.4, 5.3.5.

(III) Next, we must prove the regularity of the decomposition. So consider two nodes s,t in T occupied by α_s, α_t with
$\alpha_s \equiv_T \alpha_t$. Let T_s, T_t be the subtrees of T determined by s resp. t. Further, let G_s, G_t be the graph fragments of g(E) obtained by taking the unions of all the labels in T_s resp. T_t.

CLAIM: $G_s \equiv_T G_t$. From the claim the regularity follows at once. The proof of the claim follows by repeated application of Proposition 5.4.4. □

In fact, the proof of Theorem 5.4.6 can also be applied on systems E which are not normed; an inspection of the definitions and arguments shows that everything carries over if instead of the norm |.|, the length lth is used (cf. Proposition 5.1.9). Thus we obtain

5.4.7. THEOREM. *Let* E *be a system of recursion equations in* BPA *in restricted GNF. Then the corresponding graph* g(E) *has a regular decomposition.* □

6. Decidability of bisimulation equivalence for normed processes

We can now harvest the fruits of our demonstration of the regular decomposition of normed process graphs. The main idea of this section is that if there is a bisimulation between normed process graphs $g(E_1)$, $g(E_2)$, then there must also be a 'periodical' bisimulation, in view of the periodicity of $g(E_1)$, $g(E_2)$. Moreover, the 'period' can be computed from E_1, E_2 and this yields the desired decidability. First we need some preparations.

6.1. DEFINITION. Let g,h be process graphs and let R be a relation with the nodes of g as domain and the nodes of h as codomain. A *bisimulation error* of R is
(i) a triple of nodes s,s' ∈ g, t ∈ h and an edge s →$_a$ s' in g such that sRt and there is no edge t →$_a$ t' in h with s'Rt' (see Figure 15), or
(ii) similar with g,h interchanged.

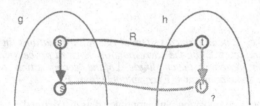

Figure 15

Clearly, R is a bisimulation iff R relates the roots of g,h and R contains no bisimulation errors.

6.2. DEFINITION. Let E_1, E_2 be normed systems of recursion equations in restricted GNF.
(i) Let R be a bisimulation between $g(E_1)$, $g(E_2)$. Then the *prefix up to* n, or n-*prefix*, is the restriction of R to the nodes of g,h whose level does not exceed n.

(ii) A *partial bisimulation* R between $g(E_1)$, $g(E_2)$ *up to level* n is a relation R with domain: the nodes of $g(E_1)$ with level ≤ n, and codomain: the nodes of $g(E_2)$ with level ≤ n, and such that R relates the roots of $g(E_1)$, $g(E_2)$ and contains no bisimulation errors.

(iii) Let $g(E_1)$, $g(E_2)$ be divided in slices of thickness d. Then a partial bisimulation between $g(E_1)$, $g(E_2)$ up to slice k is a partial bisimulation up to level d.k.

6.2.1. REMARK. Note that if graphs $g(E_1)$, $g(E_2)$ are drawn according to the convention that nodes with norm n are positioned on level n, all connections (i.e. related pairs of nodes) in a bisimulation between $g(E_1)$, $g(E_2)$ are 'horizontal'.

6.3. DEFINITION. Let $g(E_1)$, $g(E_2)$ be as in 6.2(iii), and suppose that regular decompositions of $g(E_1)$, $g(E_2)$ are given, with a common amplitude d. Let R be a partial bisimulation between $g(E_1)$, $g(E_2)$ up to slice k. We will define what it means for R to be d-*sufficient* (to extend R to a total bisimulation between $g(E_1)$, $g(E_2)$). (See Figure 16.)

Suppose, in the regular decomposition, that α is a fragment of slice k in $g(E_1)$, β one of slice k in $g(E_2)$. The successor fragments of α are $\alpha_1,...,\alpha_n$ and those of β are $\beta_1,...,\beta_m$ for some n,m. (Note that the top points of α_i (i = 1,...,n) are also in slice k, and likewise for β_j (j = 1,...,m)).

Suppose furthermore that fragments α,β are related by the partial bisimulation R, i.e. there is a pair of nodes $s \in \alpha$, $t \in \beta$ with sRt. Now suppose that at least one slice higher there are translation equivalent copies α',β' of α,β (which then must have successors $\alpha_1',...,\alpha_n'$ and $\beta_1',...,\beta_m'$, respectively, translation equivalent to their unprimed versions), such that the restriction of R to $\alpha \times \beta$ coincides, modulo translation equivalence $\equiv_T$, with the restriction of R to $\alpha' \times \beta'$. (Of course $\equiv_T$ extends to pairs of nodes (s,t) coordinate-wise.)

If for *each* pair α,β in the k-th slice such a copy α',β' exists, then the partial bisimulation R is called d-*sufficient*.

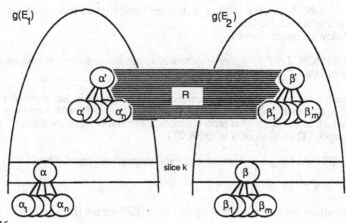

Figure 16

6.4. Let a partial bisimulation R as in 6.3 be given, which is sufficient. Then the *periodical continuation* of R is constructed as follows. Let α,β be as in 6.3. The partial bisimulation R is extended to $(\alpha_1 \cup ... \cup \alpha_n) \times (\beta_1 \cup ... \cup \beta_m)$ by copying the restriction of R to $(\alpha_1' \cup ... \cup \alpha_n') \times (\beta_1' \cup ... \cup \beta_m')$. This is done for all pairs α,β in slice k of $g(E_1)$, $g(E_2)$. It is now easily checked that the result is a partial bisimulation up to slice k+1, which again is sufficient; for, clearly the extended partial bisimulation does not contain a bisimulation error - if it did, the bisimulation error was copied from an earlier slice, quod non.

The *periodical continuation* of the sufficient, partial bisimulation R is obtained as the limit of this extension procedure. Clearly, it is a total bisimulation.

6.5. PROPOSITION. *Let* $g(E_1)$, $g(E_2)$ *be as before, and let* R *be a bisimulation between them. Then:*
(i) *each* n-*prefix of* R *is a partial bisimulation up to* n,
(ii) R *has a* d-*sufficient* M-*prefix for each* $M \geq N(E_1,E_2,d)$, *where* $N(E_1,E_2,d)$ *is some constant computable from* E_1,E_2 *and* d.

PROOF. (i) is obvious. (ii): the proof follows by elementary finiteness considerations; there are only finitely many possible relations $(\alpha \times \beta) \cap R$. $\square$

6.6. THEOREM. (i) *Let* E_1,E_2 *be normed systems of recursion equations (over BPA) in restricted GNF. Then the bisimilarity relation* $g(E_1) \pm g(E_2)$ *is decidable.*
(ii) *Equality of recursively defined normed processes in the graph model* $\mathbb{G}$ *of BPA is decidable.*

PROOF. (i) According to Theorem 5.4.6 the graphs $g(E_1),g(E_2)$ have a regular decomposition, with a common amplitude d. Now search through all (finitely many) relations between the nodes of $g(E_1),g(E_2)$ up to level $N = N(E_1,E_2,d)$. If there is no such relation which is a partial bisimulation up to N, there cannot be a bisimulation between $g(E_1),g(E_2)$, by Proposition 6.5(i). If there is such a bisimulation, this is revealed by finding a d-sufficient partial bisimulation up to N.
Part (ii) is a rephrasing of (i). $\square$

7. Simple context-free languages

In this section we derive, as an application of the method used in this paper, the well-known fact that *simple* CFL's have a decidable equivalence problem.

7.1. DEFINITION. (i) A *simple* CFG is a CFG in GNF such that there is no pair of different productions $A \to a\alpha$, $A \to a\beta$. Equivalently, in the notation of systems of guarded recursion equations in GNF: a system E is *simple* if it contains no recursion equation $X_i = \ldots + aw + av + \ldots$ for different $w,v \in X^*$. (ii) A CFL is simple if it can be obtained from a simple CFG.

7.2. DEFINITION. A process graph g is *deterministic* if there is no node $s \in g$ having two outgoing edges with the same label.
The following fact is obvious:

7.3. PROPOSITION. *Let E be a simple system of recursion equations in restricted GNF. Then* g(E) *is deterministic.* □

The reason for our interest in deterministic process graphs is that *if they are normed*, their bisimulation equivalence problem coincides with the equality problem for their finite trace sets. The proof of this fact, stated in the next proposition, is not trivial but also not difficult, and omitted in the present paper. (The full proof is in [BBK 2].)

7.4. PROPOSITION. *Let* g,h *be normed, deterministic process graphs. Then:*

$$g \leftrightarrow h \iff ftr(g) = ftr(h).$$ □

As a corollary we have the following fact from [KH] (or see [Ha], Section 11.10):

7.5. THEOREM (Korenjak - Hopcroft 1966)
The equivalence problem for simple CFL's is decidable.

PROOF. Immediate from Theorem 6.6(i), Proposition 7.3 and Proposition 7.4. □

8. Concluding remarks and questions

We have shown that equality of the processes generating CFL's is decidable, in remarkable contrast with the unsolvability of equality of CFL's. As equality of processes we mean here the equality obtained by dividing out the well-known bisimulation equivalence in the domain of process graphs. The proof of the decidability essentially uses the fact that the process graphs associated to CFG's in (restricted) Greibach Normal Form possess a tree-like periodical structure, which in itself is interesting. It should be noted that this periodicity holds for all process graphs g(E) with E a system of guarded recursion equations in Basic Process Algebra. However, in order to prove decidability of bisimulation equivalence for such graphs, we have adopted the restriction that they are normed; i.e. there are no redundant parts as regards the generation of the finite trace set, a CFL. From the point of view of CFG's and CFL's this is perfectly natural; but the general question for BPA remains: *Is bisimilarity of process graphs* g(E) *for all guarded recursive specifications* E *in BPA decidable?* Or, rephrased: *Is equality of all recursively defined processes in the graph model* $\mathbb{G}$ *of* BPA *decidable?* We conjecture that this is the case.
   It is conceivable that the method of this paper may be useful to approach some problems in the theory of formal languages. For instance, one can associate to push-down automata (PDA's) in a similar manner a process; and again one can prove that the process graph g(M) obtained by the description of the PDA M has a periodical decomposition as explained before. Now in the case of a deterministic PDA or DPDA, we find that g(M) is a deterministic process graph (cf. g(E) for a simple CFG, in Section 7). Just as for simple CFG's, the bisimilarity problem for such process graphs is equivalent to the equality problem for the corresponding finite trace sets, i.e. deterministic CFL's. Thus, in an attempt to settle the well-known equality problem for deterministic CFL's obtained by DPDA M, one can study the equivalent bisimilarity question for the process graphs g(M). The big problem here is the presence of final states and ε-steps. Without these, decidability can be proved by the method of this paper, and the result is that deterministic CFL's obtained via

acceptance by empty stack (rather than by final state) and such that the accepting DPDA has no ε-steps (or at least no stack-decreasing ε-cycles) have a decidable equality problem. (We do not know if this observation adds anything to the numerous partial decidability results regarding this question.)

Several other interesting questions remain. We conclude this paper with one of them:

8.1. QUESTION. The problem of this paper can also be considered in the setting of *readiness* or *failure semantics* instead of bisimulation semantics. (See [BKO] for an account of BPA with failure semantics or readiness semantics.) As these semantics are intermediate between bisimulation semantics and trace semantics, it is an interesting question whether decidability still holds. (We have no intuition for an answer.)

References

[BB]   J.C.M. Baeten, J.A. Bergstra, *Global renaming operators in concrete process algebra*, Report CS-R8521, Centre for Mathematics and Computer Science, Amsterdam 1985.

[BBK 1]   J.C.M. Baeten, J.A. Bergstra, J.W. Klop, *On the consistency of Koomen's Fair Abstraction Rule*, Report CS-R8511, Centre for Mathematics and Computer Science, Amsterdam 1985. To appear in Theoret. Comput. Sci.

[BBK 2]   J.C.M. Baeten, J.A. Bergstra, J.W. Klop, *Decidability of bisimulation equivalence for processes generating context-free languages*, Report CS-R8632, Centre for Mathematics and Computer Science, Amsterdam 1986.

[BBKM]   J.W. de Bakker, J.A. Bergstra, J.W. Klop, J.-J.Ch. Meyer, *Linear time and branching time semantics for recursion with merge*, in: Proc. 10th ICALP, Barcelona (J. Díaz, Ed.), Springer LNCS 154, 39-51, 1983; expanded version: Theoret. Comput. Sci. 34 (1984) 135-156.

[BHR]   S.D. Brookes, C.A.R. Hoare, W. Roscoe, *A Theory of Communicating Sequential Processes*, J. Assoc. Comput. Mach. 31, No.3, 560-599.

[BK 1]   J.A. Bergstra, J.W. Klop, *Process algebra for synchronous communication*, Inform. and Control 60 (1984) 109-137.

[BK 2]   J.A. Bergstra, J.W. Klop, *Algebra of communicating processes*, in: J.W. de Bakker, M. Hazewinkel, J.K. Lenstra, Eds., Proc. CWI Symp. Math. and Comp. Sci., North-Holland, Amsterdam 1986.

[BK 3]   J.A. Bergstra, J.W. Klop, *The algebra of recursively defined processes and the algebra of regular processes*, in: Proc. 11th ICALP, Antwerpen (J. Paredaens, Ed.), Springer LNCS 172, 82-94, 1984.

[BKO]   J.A. Bergstra, J.W. Klop, E.-R. Olderog, *Readies and failures in the algebra of communicating processes*, Report CS-R8523, Centre for Mathematics and Computer Science, Amsterdam 1985.

[BMOZ]   J.W. de Bakker, J.-J.Ch. Meyer, E.-R. Olderog, J.I. Zucker, *Transition systems, infinitary languages and the semantics of uniform concurrency*, in: Proc. 17th ACM STOC, Providence, R.I., 1985.

[Ha]   M.A. Harrison, *Introduction to Formal Language Theory*, Addison-Wesley 1978.

[Ho]   C.A.R. Hoare, *A model for communicating sequential processes*, in: "On the Construction of Programs" (R.M. McKeag and A.M. McNaughton, Eds.), 229-243, Cambridge Univ. Press, London/New York.

[HU]   J.E. Hopcroft, J.D. Ullman, *Introduction to Automata Theory, Languages, and Computation*, Addison-Wesley 1979.

[KH]   A.J. Korenjak, J.E. Hopcroft, *Simple deterministic languages*, Proc. of 7th Annual Symposium on Switching and Automata Theory, Berkeley, 36-46, 1966.

[Me]   J.-J.Ch. Meyer, *Programming calculi based on fixed point transformations: semantics and applications*, Ph.D. Thesis, Free University, Amsterdam 1985.

[Mi 1]   R. Milner, *A calculus of communicating systems*, Springer LNCS 92, 1980.

[Mi 2]   R. Milner, *A complete inference system for a class of regular behaviours*, J. Comput. and Syst. Sci. 28, 439-466, 1984.

[Pa]   D. Park, *Concurrency and automata on infinite sequences*, in: P. Deussen, Ed., Proc. 5th GI Conf. on Theor. Comp. Sci., Springer LNCS 104 (1981).

[Sa 1]   A. Salomaa, *Computation and automata*, Cambridge University Press 1985.

[Sa 2]   A. Salomaa, *Formal languages*, Academic Press, N.Y., 1973.

An Approach to Programming Process Interconnection Structures: Aggregate Rewriting Graph Grammars[*]

Duane A. Bailey
Janice E. Cuny
Computer and Information Sciences
University of Massachusetts
Amherst, Massachusetts 01003

Abstract

We describe a mechanism for generating families of process interconnection structures. Parallel programming environments that support individually programmed processor elements should allow the programmer to explicitly specify the necessary channels of communication at the level of logical abstraction of the algorithm. For highly parallel processors, the specification of this structure with traditional methods can be tedious and error-prone. *Aggregate rewriting graph grammars* provide a framework for describing families of regular graphs. Using this scheme, the difficulty of specifying an algorithm's communication structure is independent of its size. In addition, we note that *scripts* of derivation sequences generating different members of a family of structures can suggest an intra-family contracting map.

1. Introduction

When the processing elements of a parallel processor are individually programmed, explicit description of the necessary channels of communication often aids in the correct and efficient implementation of an algorithm. Knowledge of the underlying *communication structure* of an algorithm can provide redundancy needed for automatic error detection and correction, and it can provide structural information useful in mapping to a target architecture. Only a few parallel programming environments, however, support the explicit specification of communication structures[8,11].

Programmers are most effective when they work at the level of abstraction required by the algorithm. For programmers of parallel algorithms, this means communication structures should be logically depicted as graphs, as these representations usually accompany informal presentations of parallel algorithms. Graphical representations of communication structures serve as a basis for the display of mapping, control and debugging information. Programming environments that support graphical specification are currently very rudimentary: they rely on the programmer

[*]The Parallel Programming Environments Project at the University of Massachusetts is supported by the Office of Naval Research, contract N000014-84-K-0647. Duane Bailey was also supported by an American Electronics Association ComputerVision fellowship.

to draw each interconnection. This manual process is tedious, error prone and not feasible for large architectures. In addition, there is currently no support for the abstraction of *families* of communication structures. Description of graph families is necessary because most algorithms are designed in-the-small but are intended for arbitrarily large machines.

In this paper, we present a new form of graph grammar – called an aggregate rewriting graph grammar – and demonstrate its use in the specification of families of regular communication structures. This type of grammar facilitates description of regular structures at the programmer's level of abstraction. The resulting description is natural, compact and, in the case of recursively constructed graphs, a description that suggests contracting quotient maps[4].

In the next section, we informally describe aggregate rewriting graph grammars. The third section demonstrates the use of these grammars in describing a number of common network structures. The fourth section suggests mapping techniques naturally induced by recursive descriptions. Our final section discusses the use of aggregate rewriting grammars within a programming environment for highly parallel computation.

2. Aggregate Rewriting Graph Grammars

The use of graph grammars in Computer Science has been largely restricted to describing transformations on structures that are easily represented by graphs: databases, derivation trees

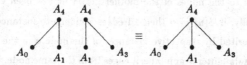

Figure 1: The two graphs shown above are equivalent; nodes generated with equivalent labels are identified.

of a compiler, operations on abstract data types, *etc.* These systems do not, in general, have the regularity that we would expect to find in process interconnection structures. For our domain, we have been able to define a restricted form of graph grammar that introduces and preserves regularity and thus forms a natural basis for our descriptions.

An aggregate rewriting graph grammar (subsequently, an AR grammar) is a sequential graph rewriting mechanism[3,10]. The subgraphs to be rewritten at each production step are *aggregates* of nodes – the union of occurrences of a production's left side – allowing massive, but regular, changes in the structure of the transformed graph.

---

[1]The set of strings, along with valid operations on those strings (such as the operations of concatenation and addition we use in this paper), is determined by the designer of the grammar.

Terminology

The labels on nodes of our graphs consist of a major label and a subscript. The subscript is an n-tuple of strings.[1] We assume that nodes are uniquely labeled: a graph containing two nodes with the same label is equivalent to the graph built by identifying those nodes as in Figure 1. For the purposes of this work, we also assume graphs have no duplicate arcs, and that each arc is undirected.

Each production identifies a *mother graph*, which is rewritten to a *daughter graph* similar to that of NCE grammars[6]; when the mother graph is restricted to a single node (node aggregate rewriting graph grammars, or NAR grammars) these grammars are similar to NLC grammars[7]. The application of a production rewrites an *aggregate* – the set of all occurrences of the mother graph in the host graph.[2] The aggregate is removed from the host graph, a distinct daughter graph is created for each instance of the mother graph, and the union of these new graphs is re-embedded into the remainder of the host graph. Unlike string grammars, however, there are often a number of possible re-embeddings; the arcs connecting the aggregate to the remainder of the host graph and the arcs connecting instances of the mother graph – called *interface arcs* – must be inherited by the image graph in some consistent manner. This is described by a *inheritance function* (or *connection function*[7]) which identifies the mapping of interface arcs between occurrences of mother and daughter graphs.

The inheritance function for AR grammars is a partial surjective function, ϕ, from the nodes of the daughter graph to the nodes of the mother graph; it has been described more formally elsewhere[1]. Informally, if $\phi(u) = v$ then all edges incident to instances of the node v of the mother graph are inherited by respective instances of the node u in the daughter graph. When two or more nodes of a daughter graph inherit edges from the same node, the inheritance function may be *partitioned* (written $\phi = \sum_i \phi_i$) to indicate that images of the two nodes will never share inherited edges. Copies of edges incident to two mother graph occurrences may never cross the partitioning of the inheritance function.

The effects of various inheritance functions are depicted in Figure 2. A host graph containing two occurrences of the node b is shown in (a). In (b), the inheritance function was not partitioned so all pairings of inheriting nodes from different daughter graphs inherited a copy of the host $b - b$ edge; in (c), the inheritance function was partitioned so only node instances from the same partition are incident to the same $b - b$ edge; and in (d), the inheritance function was not total, thus nodes labeled c did not inherit any edges.

A graph grammar generates graphs in the same way that a string grammar generates strings: a start-graph is iteratively rewritten by productions until each node of the graph is labeled with

---

[2]These occurrences may be constrained: for example, in this paper we assume a relation between the labels of a mother graph and its occurrence, and we extrapolate labels from the daughter graph that are consistent with each rewritten occurrence of the mother graph.

115

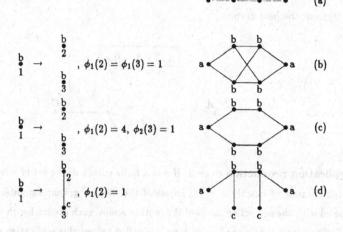

Figure 2: The various effects of inheritance functions on production application. The effect of rewriting the same host graph (a), using a total inheritance function without partitioning (b), a total inheritance function with partitioning (c), and a partial inheritance function (d).

terminal symbols. The *language* of a grammar is the set of all terminally labeled graphs that can be generated from a start-graph.

Production types

For the remainder of this paper, we assume the productions of AR grammars not allowed arbitrary connection functions, but rather are restricted to three production types that differ in the inheritance of interface arcs. These have the following semantics.

- **Relabeling productions.** The nodes of the mother graph are possibly relabeled and the injective mapping from mother to daughter nodes serves as the inheritance function. Thus, in the figure below, A is relabeled B and as a result, B inherits the arcs of A.

$$\boxed{A \quad C \xrightarrow{\text{rw}} B - C}$$

- **Extension productions.** The mother graph is rewritten to a larger daughter graph, as shown. An injective function from the mother graph to the daughter graph serves as the inheritance function. Excess nodes are not mentioned by the interface arcs and thus serve to 'extend' the host graph.

$$A \xrightarrow{\text{ext}} A - B - C$$

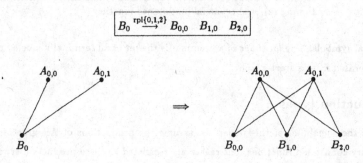

- **Replication production over S.** If S is a finite subset of the set of strings, the daughter graph consists of exactly $n = |S|$ copies of the mother graph; daughter graph nodes are labeled with the respective labels of the mother nodes, each prefixed with a distinct member of S. The power of this production type is detailed below: this replication production makes multiple copies of the node B_0 whose labels are prefixed with members of the string set $\{0, 1, 2\}$. Each receives a copy of the interface arcs mentioning B_0.

$$B_0 \xrightarrow{\text{rpl}\{0,1,2\}} B_{0,0} \quad B_{1,0} \quad B_{2,0}$$

Aggregates

The regularity of a communication network is often reflected by the labeling of its nodes. For example, the binary n-cube structure can be generated by labeling each of 2^n nodes with a binary number and connecting nodes whose labels differ in exactly one bit (see Figure 3). Aggregate rewriting graph grammars make use of the regularity of subscripts in labels by allowing productions to rewrite *aggregates* of nodes that are similarly labeled. A label specification may contain *variables* which potentially match labels that induce an *assignment*. For example, if string concatenation is written $S \cdot T$, then the label specification

$$S \cdot 0$$

matches strings ending in 0. A set of label specifications identifies an aggregate of nodes if a set of the nodes suggest a consistent assignment of variables in the specification. Thus, the specification

$$A_{0 \cdot S} - A_{1 \cdot S}$$

matches all pairs of A-labeled nodes differing in exactly the first digit, which also share an arc. This specification can be used, for example, to identify the diagonal arcs of Figure 3.

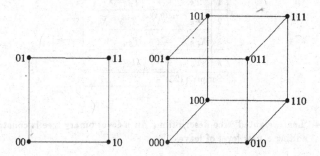

Figure 3: Two and three dimensional binary cubes. Each node is connected to all other nodes whose addresses differ in a bit. The 3-cube can easily be constructed by grafting two 2-cubes together.

Because mother and daughter graphs of productions specify aggregates, they become powerful rules for rewriting arbitrarily large structures simultaneously. Thus, while AR grammar productions are applied sequentially, they rewrite many subgraphs of a host graph in parallel. The result is the union of the daughter graphs, appropriately embedded.

In the next section, we present a number of examples of regular communication structures which are generated by AR grammars.

3. Examples

In this section we demonstrate the power of AR grammars for describing families of regular communication structures. The set of strings for generating labels is the set of digits in an appropriate base (usually binary). We shall assume nonterminal labels are upper-case roman letters (*e.g.* 'T'), while a single terminal label Ω is used. To aid in the interpretation of these grammars, we supplement these examples with *scripts* which indicate derivation sequences which generate the desired family of structures.[3]

Binary Trees

Several methods of generating binary trees are possible – we demonstrate two. The first is a 'leaf-weighted' construction (Figure 4), which appends a new layer of leaves on a n-level complete binary tree to generate an $(n + 1)$-level successor. The labeling of this tree is such that level n is labeled with n digit binary numbers. The children of a node are determined by appending either

---

[3]Scripts *do not* indicate all possible production sequences, however, they *do* generate all graphs in the language.

Leaf-weighted Tree		
Start-graph: T_λ		
1	$\dot{T}_S \xrightarrow{\text{ext}}$	$T_S - X_S$
2	$X_S \xrightarrow{\text{rpl}\{0,1\}}$	$X_{0,S} \quad X_{1,S}$
3	$X_{i,S} \xrightarrow{\text{rw}}$	$T_{S \cdot i}$
4	$T_S \xrightarrow{\text{rw}}$	Ω_S
Script: $(123)^n 4$		

Figure 4: 'Leaf-weighted' tree description. An n-level binary tree is constructed by adding a new level of leaves.

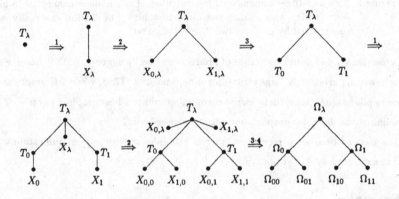

Figure 5: An example derivation of the grammar in Figure 4. Productions 1–3 add a new layer of leaves to the tree. Production 4 rewrites the labels to terminals. Note how $X_{0,\lambda}$ and $X_{1,\lambda}$ are identified with existing nodes T_0 and T_1 in the last steps.

a 0 or 1 on the node's label. The script for the leaf-weighted grammar indicates that the family can be derived by the derivation sequences $(123)^n 4$. Figure 5 shows a derivation for $n = 2$. The semantics of the production sequence $1 \cdot 2 \cdot 3$ is to generate a new layer of leaves, while production 4 terminates the derivation.

The second method (Figure 6) is 'root weighted': it generates a $(n + 1)$-level binary tree by generating two copies of an n-level binary tree, and then constructing a common root (Figure 7). From the script we note that $1 \cdot 2 \cdot 3$ is the sequence of production steps that increases the height by copying the tree (production 1) and generating a new root (production 2). While the labeling of this tree is identical to that of 'leaf-weighted' generation, we will see in the next section that the different generation of leaf- and root-weighted trees causes them to have distinct mapping characteristics.

Root-weighted Tree			
Start-graph: T_λ			
1	T_S	$\xrightarrow{\text{rpl}\{0,1\}}$	$T_{0,S}$ $T_{1,S}$
2	$T_{i,S}$	$\xrightarrow{\text{ext}}$	$T_{i.S} - X_S$
3	X_S	$\xrightarrow{\text{rw}}$	T_S
4	T_S	$\xrightarrow{\text{rw}}$	Ω_S
Script: $(123)^n 4$			

Figure 6: A 'root-weighted' tree grammar. A n-level binary tree is constructed by joining two copies of an $(n-1)$-level binary tree by mentioning a common root.

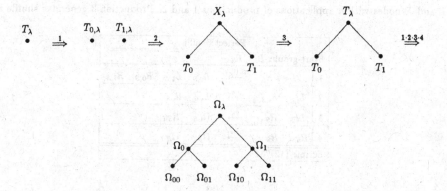

Figure 7: An example derivation of the 'root-weighted' tree grammar depicted in Figure 6. Productions 1–3 duplicate the tree and construct a common root.

m-Ary n-Cube			
Start-graph: C_λ			
1		C_S $\xrightarrow{\text{rpl}\{0,\ldots,m-1\}}$	$C_{0,S} \cdots C_{m-1,S}$
2	$C_{i,S}$ $C_{(j \neq i),S}$	$\xrightarrow{\text{rw}}$	$C_{S.i} - C_{S.j}$
3		C_S $\xrightarrow{\text{rw}}$	Ω_S
Script: $(12)^n 3$			

Figure 8: An m-ary n-cube grammar. The m copies of a m-ary, $(n-1)$-cube are joined together in productions 1 and 2.

Cubes

The binary (in general, m-ary) n-dimensional cube is constructed with the grammar depicted in Figure 8. The labels on the vertices of the n-dimensional binary cube structure are binary strings from 0 to $2^n - 1$. Each node is linked to vertices that differ in exactly one bit position. As the script shows, the productions 1 and 2 duplicate and connect smaller cubes to form larger cubes. Because each production matches an aggregate of nodes, the productions have the same semantics for arbitrarily sized host graphs.

Perfect shuffle

The perfect shuffle is described by the grammar found in Figure 9–a. This follows the original construction of Stone[12], which creates two copies of 2^n nodes (here, L_i and R_i) shuffles them, adds exchange arcs, and then reunites the relabeled copies. The script generates the 2^n copies of L and R nodes with n applications of productions 1 and 2. Production 3 generates shuffle arcs,

Perfect Shuffle							
Start-graph: L_λ	R_λ						
1	L_S	R_S	$\xrightarrow{\text{rpl}\{0,1\}}$	$L_{0,S}$	$L_{1,S}$	$R_{0,S}$	$R_{1,S}$
2	$L_{i,S}$	$R_{i,S}$	$\xrightarrow{\text{rw}}$	$L_{i \cdot S}$	$R_{i \cdot S}$		
3	$L_{i \cdot S}$	$R_{S \cdot i}$	$\xrightarrow{\text{rw}}$	$\Omega_{i \cdot S} - R_{S \cdot i}$			
4	$R_{S \cdot 0}$	$R_{S \cdot 1}$	$\xrightarrow{\text{rw}}$	$\Omega_{S \cdot 0} - \Omega_{S \cdot 1}$			
Script: $(12)^n 34$							

(a)

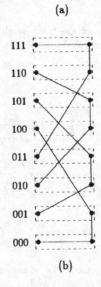

(b)

Figure 9: (a) Perfect shuffle grammar, and (b) node identification.

while production 4 generates exchange arcs. Identification of similarly labeled nodes causes the L_i and R_i to be thought of as the same logical node. Figure 9-b shows the identification of logical nodes.

We have seen in this section that AR grammars are capable of describing a variety of regular structures. Other structures, not presented here, such as SW-banyans[5] and cube connected cycles[9] have also been described with AR grammars in a similar fashion. We have found that manipulation of labels is an extremely powerful capability. In the next section we will show that the structure of the script can provide an aid to the mapping of large logical communication structures into small processor arrays.

4.   Mapping Techniques

One of the most important problems designers of parallel programming environment must address is the mapping of logical communication structures onto the physical communication network. It is often the case that the processor is too small to adequately handle the processes required by the algorithm.[4] Our description of *families* of communication structures does, however, allow us to identify special mappings that contract logical communication structures onto processors.

Fishburn and Finkel suggested a number of *quotient mappings* for common communication structures[4]. Essentially, if a n-process problem was to be mapped to a smaller m-processor array of the same family, a quotient map partitions the problem into m equivalence classes which are then mapped directly to the processor array.[5] Most of these mappings are identified by labeling the nodes of the graphs appropriately. For example, a square grid labeling each node with binary row and column binary indices from 0 to $2^n - 1$ can be reduced in size by dropping the least significant bit from both indices of each node.

Because AR grammars naturally suggest recursive descriptions of graph families the scripts provide a natural ordering of derivations. For example, a binary n-cube is generated by the derivation sequence $(1 \cdot 2)^n \cdot 3$. In the process of generating a $(n+1)$-cube, a smaller n-cube is first generated. Clearly, every node labeled S of an $(n+1)$-cube is attributable to exactly one node of an n-cube: the node labeled with n digit prefix of S. A natural mapping of a boolean $(n+1)$-cube into an n-cube is the one induced by this quotient map.

---

[4]Another problem occurs when the communication structure is not a member of the family of structures that may be easily mapped into the hardware. We will not discuss intra-family mappings induced by these descriptions in this paper.

[5]Ideally, this maps an identical number of processes to each processor, and maps the same number of logical channels to each physical channel. A counter-example can be found in complete binary trees, which fail to map evenly since $2^m - 1$ does not divide $2^n - 1$ for $1 < m < n$. However, augmenting trees with an extra node fixes this problem[2].

In general, recursively defined families have quotient maps suggested by their parameterized derivation sequences as described above. The implementor of the complete binary tree, for example, has the option of selecting either the leaf-weighted or root-weighted grammars which suggest the leaf-weighted and root-weighted quotient mappings defined by Fishburn and Finkel[4]. The ability to make this decision aids the user in fashioning a mapping of an arbitrarily large algorithm into the processor in a manner that is most efficient.

5. Conclusions

We have informally described AR grammars, which can be used to specify families of regularly structured graphs. In light of programming highly parallel processors, these grammars show promise in accurately describing a wide variety of structures. The power of aggregate rewriting productions allows the user to apply straightforward logical transformations on a structure in a manner that scales up. In addition, where computing resources are limited, the derivation scripts suggested by these grammars provide a useful basis for mapping large logical process structures onto smaller physical processor arrays.

As we expect highly parallel processors will soon be impossible to program by hand, graph construction tools must provide descriptive primitives that manipulate aggregates of nodes similarly. Furthermore, as the size of the problem increases we believe the user will find appropriate manipulation of labels a useful mechanism for generating node specific data. We believe aggregate rewriting graph grammars can provide support for future graphical interfaces to parallel programming environments.

References

[1] Duane A. Bailey and Janice E. Cuny. *Graph Grammar Based Specification of Interconnection Structures.* Technical Report 87-23, University of Massachusetts at Amherst, March 1987.

[2] Duane A. Bailey and Janice E. Cuny. *The Use of Shape Grammars in Processor Embeddings.* Technical Report A-86-23, University of Massachusetts at Amherst, July 1986.

[3] H. Ehrig, M. Pfender, and H. J. Schneider. Graph grammars: an algebraic approach. In *14th Conference on Switching and Automata Theory*, pages 167–179, 1973.

[4] John P. Fishburn and Raphael A. Finkel. Quotient networks. *IEEE Transactions on Computers*, C-31(4):288–295, April 1982.

[5] Rodney L. Goke. *Banyan Networks for Partitioning Multiprocessor Systems.* PhD thesis, University of Florida, 1976.

[6] D. Janssens and G. Rozenberg. Graph grammars with neighbourhood–controlled embedding. *Theoretical Computer Science*, 21:55–74, 1982.

[7] D. Janssens and G. Rozenberg. On the structure of node-label-controlled graph languages. *Information Sciences*, 20:191–216, 1980.

[8] Hungwen Li, Ching-Chy Wang, and Mark Lavin. Structured process: a new language attribute for better interaction of parallel architecture and algorithm. In *1985 International Conference on Parallel Processing*, pages 247–254, August 1985.

[9] Franco P. Preparata and Jean Vuillemin. The cube-connected cycles: a versatile network for parallel computation. *Communications of the ACM*, 300–309, May 1981.

10] H. J. Schneider. *Graph Grammars*, pages 314–331. *Lecture Notes in Computer Science*, Springer-Verlag, Berlin, September 1977.

11] Lawrence Snyder. Introduction to the configurable highly parallel computer. *Computer*, 15(1):47–56, January 1982.

12] Harold S. Stone. Parallel processing with the perfect shuffle. *IEEE Transactions on Computers*, C-20(2):153–161, February 1971.

Specifying Functional and Timing Behavior
for Real-Time Applications

Mario R. Barbacci[1,2] and Jeannette M. Wing[2]
Carnegie Mellon University
Pittsburgh, PA 15213, U.S.A.

Abstract

We present a notation and a methodology for specifying the functional and timing behavior of real-time applications for a heterogeneous machine. In our methodology we build upon well-defined, though isolated, pieces of previous work: Larch and Real Time Logic. In our notation, we strive to keep separate the functional specification from the timing specification so that a task's functionality can be understood independently of its timing behavior. We show that while there is a clean separation of concerns between these two specifications, the semantics of both pieces as well as their combination are simple.

1 Problem Context

Many computation-intensive, real-time applications require efficient concurrent execution of multiple *tasks* devoted to specific pieces of the application. Typical tasks include sensor data collection, obstacle recognition, and global path planning in applications such as robotics and vehicular control. Since the speed and throughput required of each task may vary, these applications can best exploit a computing environment consisting of multiple special and general purpose processors that are logically, though not necessarily physically, loosely connected. We call this environment a *heterogeneous machine*.

During execution time, *processes*, which are instances of tasks, run on possibly separate processors, and communicate with each other by sending messages of different types. Since the patterns of communication can vary over time, and the speed of the individual processors can vary over a wide range, additional hardware resources, in the form of switching networks and data buffers are required in the physical heterogeneous machine. Logically, *queues* are used to buffer data; processes dequeue data on queues attached to input ports and enqueue data from queues attached to output ports.

The application developer is responsible for prescribing a way to manage all of these

---

[1]Software Engineering Institute, [2]Department of Computer Science

This research is carried out jointly by the Software Engineering Institute, a Federally Funded Research and Development Center, sponsored by the Department of Defense, and by the Department of Computer Science, sponsored by the Defense Advanced Research Projects Agency (DOD), ARPA Order No. 4976, monitored by the Air Force Avionics Laboratory Under Contract F33615-84-K-1520. Additional support for J.M. Wing was provided in part by the National Science Foundation under grant DMC-8519254.

resources. We call this prescription a *task-level application description*. It describes the tasks to be executed, the assignment of processes to processors, the data paths between the processors, and the intermediate queues required to store the data as it moves from source to destination processes. A *task-level description language* is a notation in which to write these application descriptions.

We are using the term "description language" rather than "programming language" to emphasize that a task-level application description is not translated into object code in some kind of executable "machine language." Rather, it is to be understood as a description of the structure and behavior of a logical machine, that will be synthesized into resource allocation and scheduling directives. These directives are to be interpreted by a combination of software, firmware, and hardware in a heterogeneous machine.

```
task task-name
  ports                          -- Used for communication between a process and a queue
    port-declarations
  signals          -- Used for communication between a user process and the scheduler
    signal-declarations
  behavior          -- A description of the functional and timing behavior of the task
    requires predicate
    ensures predicate
    timing timing expression
  attributes                                        -- Additional properties of the task
    attribute-value-pairs
  structure      -- A process-queue graph describing the internal structure of a task
    process-declarations
    queue-declarations
    reconfiguration-statements
end task-name
```

Figure 1: A Template for Task Descriptions

We have an initial design of such a description language [3], a compiler for it, and a simulator that takes task descriptions as input. A task description (see Figure 1) contains information about four aspects of a task: (1) its interface to other tasks (**ports**) and to the scheduler (**signals**), (2) its functional and timing **behavior**, (3) its **attributes**, and (4) its internal **structure**, thereby allowing for hierarchical task descriptions. Reference [3] contains a more complete explanation of these and other features of the language. In this paper we focus on only one aspect: the information appearing in the **behavior** part of a task description.

2 Contributions
Formal specifications have been used successfully for specifying the functional behavior of software systems, e.g., individual program modules and abstract data types. These specifications have traditionally been used to verify a program's correctness ("is the right answer computed?"). Often, however, one is interested in not only the functional correctness of a system but also other properties, such as reliability, performance, security, and real-time behavior. Less work has focused on formally specifying these other properties of software systems, let alone their interactions with each other.

To our knowledge no work has addressed the formal integration of the formal specification of functional and timing behavior of software. The main contribution of this paper is exactly this integration of functional and timing specifications as embodied in our task description language.

We combine two separate formalisms: an axiomatic specification language, Larch [15, 16], used to specify functional behavior, and an event expression language used to specify timing behavior. Both are mapped to the same underlying logic, typed first-order predicate logic, so that their combination has a formal semantics.

Two significant aspects of our work are as follows:

- Since the formal semantics is relatively simple (first-order logic), not only can people easily understand our specifications but the specifications themselves can easily be subject to machine analysis.

- We build upon previous well defined and isolated pieces of research and combine them in a meaningful way. Their combination is applied in a context (heterogeneous machines) that itself is of growing interest to those involved in parallel architectures and languages.

3 Introduction to Larch

Before we describe the functional and timing specifications of a task, we give a brief introduction to Larch. We are keeping this introduction to Larch very short. The reader is encouraged to consult the appropriate references in the bibliography.

Larch uses a two-tiered approach to specifying program modules: a *trait* defines state-independent properties, and an *interface* specification defines state-dependent properties of a program. A trait is written in the Larch Shared Language (LSL), and it provides the assertion language used to express and define the meaning of the predicates of an interface specification.

```
QVals: trait
  introduces
    empty: → Q
    insert: Q, E → Q
    first: Q → E
    rest: Q → Q
    isEmpty: Q → Boolean
    isIn: Q, E → Boolean
  constrains Q so that
    Q generated by [ empty, insert ]
    for all q: Q, e, e1: E
        first(insert(empty), e)) = e
        first(insert(q, e)) = if isEmpty(q) then e else first(q)
        rest(insert(q, e)) = if isEmpty(q) then empty else insert(rest(q), e)
        isEmpty(empty) = true
        isEmpty(insert(q, e)) = false
        isIn(empty, e) = false
        isIn(insert(q, e), e1) = (e = e1) | isIn(q, e1)
```

a. A Trait for Queue Values

```
Enqueue = operation (q: queue, e: element)
    ensures q_post = insert(q, e)
Dequeue = operation (q: queue) returns (e: element)
    requires ~isEmpty(q)
    ensures q_post = rest(q) & e = first(q)
```

b. Interfaces for Queue Operations

Figure 2: A Larch Two-Tiered Specification for Queues

For a program module, such as a procedure, a Larch interface specification is written in a Larch Interface Language (LIL) and contains predicates about the states before and after the execution of the procedure. The Larch Interface Language to be used is specific to the programming language in which the procedure is written (e.g., C, Common Lisp, Ada, etc.). For this paper we will use a relatively simple interface language, such as would be defined for an Algol-like language.

Figure 2 depicts a Larch (two-tiered) specification of queues with Enqueue and Dequeue operations. The top part of the specification (Figure 2.a) is a trait written in LSL used to describe values of queues. A trait is akin to an algebraic specification (see Section 7 on Related Work). A set of operators and their signatures following **introduces** defines a vocabulary of terms to denote values of a type. For example, empty and insert(empty, 5) denote two different queue values. The set of equations following the **constrains** clause defines a meaning for the terms; more precisely, an equivalence relation on the terms, and hence on the values they denote. For example, from the above trait, one could prove that first(rest(insert(insert(empty, 5), 6))) = 6.

The bottom part of the specification (Figure 2.b) contains two interfaces written in our "generic" Larch interface language. They describe the functional behavior of two queue operations, Enqueue and Dequeue (queue operation names are used to write timing expressions, which are described later in this paper). A **requires** is a pre-condition on the state of an operation's input data that must be true upon operation invocation; an **ensures** is a post-condition on the state of an operation's input and output data that is guaranteed to be true upon operation termination. An omitted predicate is taken to be **true**. The specification for Dequeue states that Dequeue must be called with a non-empty queue and that it modifies the original queue by removing its first element and returning it.

4 Behavioral Information
The behavioral information in a task description is divided into two parts: a functional specification and a timing specification. In the next two subsections we describe informally the syntax and meaning of these two specifications. Section 5 gives the formal meaning, and in particular, the meaning of the combination of functional and timing specifications.

4.1 Functional Specifications
The functional information of a task description (see Figure 1) describes the behavior of the task in terms of predicates about the data in the queues, before and after each execution of the task. It consists of a **requires** clause and an **ensures** clause, together constituting a simple Larch interface specification. LSL is used as the assertion language in the predicates of these clauses.

A **requires** clause states what is required to be true of the data coming through the input ports; an **ensures** clause states what is guaranteed to be true of the data going out through the output ports. If one were to view each cycle of a task as one execution of a procedure, the **requires** and **ensures** are exactly the pre- and post-conditions on the functionality of that cycle.

A task implementation must satisfy the predicates, R and E, of the **requires** and **ensures** clauses. A task implementation is simply a program written in some programming language, e.g., C, Common Lisp, or Ada. Using Hoare-like notation, an implementation, Prog, *satisfies* the (functional) specification if:

$$\{R\} \ Prog \ \{E\}$$

It is up to the task implementor to show that a task implementation satisfies the functional specification as given by the **requires** and **ensures** clauses. This verification can be done formally — standard verification techniques can be used ([17, 18]) and some mechanical tools are available to aid this process ([13, 22, 24]). We defer to Section 5.2 for the definition of the meaning of the predicates in the presence of timing information.

```
task multiply
  ports
    in1, in2: in matrix;
    out1: out matrix;
  behavior
    requires  number_of_rows(first(in1)) = number_of_cols(first(in2));
    ensures   out1_post = insert(out1, first(in1) * first(in2));
end multiply;
```

Figure 3: The Functionality of a Matrix Multiplication Task

For example, consider a matrix multiplication task (Figure 3) that takes input matrices from two queues and outputs the result matrix on an output queue. The data traveling through these ports are of type matrix. Matrix values are specified using LSL just as for queue values, so "number_of_rows," "number_of_cols" and "*" would be defined in a trait about matrix values. The **requires** clause states that the task implementor may assume that the number of rows of the matrix entering through the port in1 equals the number of columns of the matrix entering through in2. The **ensures** clause states that the result of multiplying the two input matrices in one cycle is output to the queue attached to the output port.

4.2 Timing Specifications

The timing information describes the behavior of the task in terms of the operations that it performs on the queues attached to its input and output ports; this is the behavior of the task seen from the outside. A timing expression is a regular expression built from concurrent and sequential queue operations, with optional conditional expressions or guards that control when a subexpression is to be executed. Timing expressions are similar to a number of formalisms derived from Path Expressions [7].

The simplest timing expression is the name of a queue operation on the queue attached to a specific port, e.g., in1.Dequeue or OutPort.Enqueue. The duration of a queue operation or the delay between two operations is described by a time window, denoted by a pair of time values, $[T_{min}, T_{max}]$, defining the boundaries of the interval. The time window associated with a queue operation describes the minimum and maximum time needed to perform the operation (in1.Dequeue[15,25]) Intervals of time between queue operations are denoted by a Delay "operation" whose time window describes the minimum and maximum time consumed by the process in between queue operations.

A composite timing expression denotes the sequential and/or concurrent execution of operations on queues. Sequential composition is denoted by a space between operations; parallel composition is denoted by a "||" between operations. For example,

loop (in1.Dequeue[10,15] || in2.Dequeue) delay[*,30] out1.Enqueue

is a sequential timing expression that specifies two parallel Dequeue operations on the queues attached to the input ports in1 and in2, followed after some delay by an Enqueue on the queue attached to the output port out1. The Delay lasts some undetermined amount of time less than 30 seconds. The Dequeue operation on port in1 takes between 10 and 15 seconds to complete. The other two operations take some implementation dependent default time to complete. The keyword **loop** denotes a cyclic or repeating task.

---

1. The task is executed some integral number of times:

repeat *integer* => *expression*

2. The task is allowed to start during some time interval:

during *timewindow* => *expression*

3. The task is allowed to start no earlier than some time value:

after *timevalue* => *expression*

4. The is allowed to start no later than some time value:

before *timevalue* => *expression*

5. The task is allowed to start only if some predicate on the state of the input queues or the current time is true:

when *predicate* => *expression*

Table 1: Timing Expression Guards

An optional guard in a timing expression specifies a restriction on the execution of the associated timing expression, as shown in Table 1.

```
task multiply
  ports
    in1, in2: in matrix;
    out1: out matrix;
  behavior
    requires  number_of_rows(first(in1)) = number_of_cols(first(in2));
    ensures out1_post = insert(out1, first(in1) * first(in2));
    timing when (~isEmpty(in1) and ~isEmpty(in2)) =>
              ((in1.Dequeue || in2.Dequeue) delay[10,15] out1.Enqueue);
end multiply
```

Figure 4: The Timing of a Matrix Multiplication Task

For example, consider a revised matrix multiplication task (Figure 4). The **timing** clause states that the task does not start executing until both input queues contain data. Once that condition is satisfied, the task will remove its input data from both input queues concurrently (the Dequeue operations), will operate on the data for between 10 and 15 seconds (this "computation" time is lumped together under the delay operation), and finally will enqueue some output in the output queue. Notice another use of LSL in our specifications: the **when** condition places a constraint on the state of the queues (not on the state of the data in the queues). We use the trait from Section 3 to define the assertion language for predicates in a **when** guard.

5 Formal Meaning of Functional and Timing Specifications

We use Jahanian and Mok's Real-Time Logic (RTL) [19] to give meaning to our timing expressions. Furthermore, we use their logic to give meaning to the combination of our functional and timing specifications. We use four of their notational conventions:

Syntax	Meaning
$\uparrow$A	The start of an operation ("action" in RTL's terminology).
$\downarrow$A	The end of an operation.
@(E, i)	The time of the ith occurrence of event E, where events in our context are the start of an operation or the end of an operation. @ is an occurrence function that captures the notion of real-time.
P(t1, t2)	The interval of time during which the predicate P holds. P holds before or at t1, from t1 to t2, and at or after t2. If t1 and t2 are identical, then P holds at an interval around t1. For brevity, we will use P(t) when t1=t2 (i.e., "P holds around time t").

5.1 Assigning Meaning to Timing Specifications

In this section we describe the meaning of our timing specifications in terms of RTL logic. In the following discussion, we assume E, E1, and E2 are arbitrary timing expressions; A, A1, and A2 are operations; t1 and t2 are times (absolute or relative); a1 and a2 are absolute times; r1 and r2 are relative times; and W is a predicate of a **when** guard.

---

1. For any queue operation A, and for some implementation defined time window [T1,T2], the following axiom expresses the (default) duration of the operation:

$$\forall i \, [\, T1 \leq @(\downarrow A,i) - @(\uparrow A,i) \leq T2 \,]$$

2. For any queue operation A[t1,t2], with a duration defined by the time window [t1,t2], the following axiom expresses the duration of the operation:

$$\forall i \, [\, t1 \leq @(\downarrow A,i) - @(\uparrow A,i) \leq t2 \,]$$

3. For any sequence of queue operations, A = A1 ... An, the following axiom relates the start and end times of the composition to the start and end times of the individual operations:

$$\forall i \, [@(\uparrow A, i) = @(\uparrow A1, i) \wedge @(\downarrow A, i) = @(\downarrow An, i)]$$

4. For any parallel queue operations, A = A1 || ...|| An, the following axiom relates the start and end times of the composition to the start and end times of the individual operations:

$$\forall i \, [@(\uparrow A, i) = min(@(\uparrow A1, i), ..., @(\uparrow An, i)) \wedge @(\downarrow A, i) = max(@(\downarrow A1, i), ..., @(\downarrow An, i))]$$

5. Cycles in a repeating task do not overlap. The following two axioms express that an input operation cannot finish after the last output operation finishes, and that an output operation cannot start before the earliest input operation starts:

$$\forall i \, [\, max(@(\downarrow out_1,i),@(\downarrow out_2,i),....,@(\downarrow out_J,i)) > max(@(\downarrow in_1,i),@(\downarrow in_2,i),....,@(\downarrow in_K,i)) \,]$$

$$\forall i \, [\, min(@(\uparrow out_1,i),@(\uparrow out_2,i),....,@(\uparrow out_J,i)) > min(@(\uparrow in_1,i),@(\uparrow in_2,i),....,@(\uparrow in_K,i)) \,]$$

where J and K are the number of output and input queues, respectively.

Table 2: Axioms About Operation Start and End Times

To simplify the exposition, we introduce a simple rewrite rule: Any timing expression of the form "**repeat** n => E" can be rewritten as a sequence of n occurrences of the unguarded expression E ("E E E ... E"). Thus, the only guards we need to consider are **before**, **after**, **during**, and **when**. Table 2 gives the axioms that describe the start and end times of operations and composition of operations.

Timing Expression	M_{tb}(Timing Expression)
E =	M_{tb}(E) =
(E1)	M_{tb}(E1)
E1 ... En	M_{tb}((E1 E2) ...En)
E1 ||...|| En	$\wedge\, M_{tb}$(Ei || Ej) for all i ≠ j
E1 E2	M_{tb}(E1) $\wedge M_{tb}$(E2) $\wedge$
	$\forall\, i\, [\, @(\downarrow M_{to}(E1),\, i) \leq @(\uparrow M_{to}(E2),\, i)\,]$
E1 || E2	M_{tb}(E1) $\wedge M_{tb}$(E2) $\wedge$
	$\forall\, i\, [@(\uparrow M_{to}(E1),\, i) < @(\downarrow M_{to}(E2),\, i)\, \wedge$
	$@(\uparrow M_{to}(E2),\, i) < @(\downarrow M_{to}(E2),\, i)]$
when W => E1	M_{tb}(E1) $\wedge \forall\, i\, [\, W(@(\uparrow M_{to}(E1),\, i))\,]$
before a1 => E1	M_{tb}(E1) $\wedge \forall\, i\, [\, @(\uparrow M_{to}(E1),\, i) \leq a1\,]$
after a1 => E1	M_{tb}(E1) $\wedge \forall\, i\, [\, @(\uparrow M_{to}(E1),\, i) \geq a1\,]$
during [a1, a2] => E1	M_{tb}(E1) $\wedge \forall\, i\, [\, a1 \leq @(\uparrow M_{to}(E1),\, i) \leq a2\,]$
during [a1, r2] => E1	M_{tb}(E1) $\wedge \forall\, i\, [\, a1 \leq @(\uparrow M_{to}(E1),\, i) \leq a1 + r2\,]$
A[r1, r2]	$\forall\, i\, [\, @(\uparrow A,\, i) + r1 \leq @(\downarrow A,\, i) \leq @(\uparrow A,\, i) + r2\,]$
A[*, r1]	$\forall\, i\, [\, @(\downarrow A,\, i) \leq @(\uparrow A,\, i) + r1\,]$
A[r1, *]	$\forall\, i\, [\, @(\uparrow A,\, i) + r1 \leq @(\downarrow A,\, i)\,]$
A	true

a. M_{tb} -- Mapping from Timing Expressions to Booleans

Timing Expression	M_{to}(Timing Expression)
E =	M_{to}(E) =
loop E1	M_{to}(E1)
E1 ... En	M_{to}(E1) ... M_{to}(En)
E1 ||... || En	M_{to}(E1) || ... || M_{to}(En)
guard => E1	M_{to}(E1) for all guards, **when**, **before**, **during**, and **after**
A [t1, t2]	A
A	A

b. M_{to} -- Mapping From Timing Expressions to Operations

Table 3: Assigning Meaning to Timing Specifications

We assign a meaning to timing expressions by introducing a function, M_{tb} (Table 3.a), which maps timing expressions to Boolean values,

$$M_{tb} : \text{Timing Expression} \rightarrow \text{Boolean}.$$

In the definition of M_{tb} we use an auxiliary function, M_{to} (Table 3.b), which maps timing expressions to operations,

$$M_{to}: \text{Timing Expression} \rightarrow \text{Operation.}$$

M_{to} is needed because "start time" and "end time" are meaningful only for queue operations.

As an example of how to interpret the formalism intuitively, consider the entries for the **during** guard in Table 3.a. This guard specifies a time window during which the operation is allowed to start. The first time value of the window is the earliest start time allowed and must be an absolute time value. The second time value is the latest start time allowed and can be an absolute time value or a time value relative to the former. The meaning of the guarded expression is the conjunction of the meaning of the expression proper and a predicate stating the restriction on starting times.

5.2 Assigning Meaning to the Combined Specifications
Given a task description of the form:

> **task** *taskname*
> . . . . .
> **behavior**
>   **requires** Req ;
>   **ensures** Ens ;
>   **timing** E ;
> . . . . .
> **end** *taskname* ;

we give meaning to the predicates of the functional specification as related to time (i.e., at what times are these predicates to hold?) via a function M_f which maps from behavioral specifications to Boolean values:

$$M_f : \text{Predicate} \times \text{Timing Expression} \rightarrow \text{Boolean}$$

Pred.	Expr.	M_f(Predicate, Timing Expression)
Req	E	$M_f(\text{Req},E) = \forall i\ [\text{Req}(@(\uparrow M_{to}(E),i)) \wedge M_{tb}(E)]$
Ens	E	$M_f(\text{Ens},E) = \forall i\ [\text{Ens}(@(\downarrow M_{to}(E),i)) \wedge M_{tb}(E) \wedge \text{Consistent}(\text{Ens},E)]$

where Consistent(Ens, E) checks to see if the **ensures** Ens predicate is meaningful with respect to the timing expression E. Consistent is defined by using two auxiliary predicates, Uses and Depends:

For all input queues q_{in}, output queues q_{out}, elements in the output queues x:

Uses: element $\times$ input queue $\times$ output queue $\times$ Predicate $\rightarrow$ Boolean

Uses(x, q_{in}, q_{out}, Ens) =   true, if q_{in} *appearsIn* x $\wedge$ Ens => isIn(q_{out}, x);
                                  false, otherwise.
UsesSet(x, q_{out}, Ens) =   {q_{in} | Uses(x, q_{in}, q_{out}, Ens) } for all x such that isIn(q_{out}, x)

where "a *appearsIn* b" is a syntactic relation that checks if the text a occurs in the text b. Intuitively, Uses checks to see if the computation of x, the element enqueued on q_{out}, can be proven from the Ens to use any of the elements from q_{in}. In general, the element x is written in terms of a trait expression involving queue operators (e.g., first) as well as other type-specific operators (e.g,. *) as in the multiply example where x is taken to be first(in1) * first(in2).

For all input queues q_{in}, output queues q_{out}, elements in the output queues x, and for all $1 \leq i \leq$ length(q_{out}) where $i^{th}(q_{out})$ is first($rest^{i-1}(q_{out})$):

Depends: element × input queue × output queue × Timing Expression → Boolean

Depends($i^{th}(q_{out})$), q_{in}, q_{out}, E) =
  true, if E = E1 q_{out} E2 or E = E1 q_{out} || E2 or E = E1 || q_{out} E2, and
    q_{in} *appearsIn* E1 and q_{out} *appearsIn* E1 i-1 times;
  false, otherwise.
DependsSet(x, q_{out}, E) = {q_{in} | Depends(x, q_{in}, q_{out}, E) } for all x such that isIn(q_{out}, x)

Intuitively, Depends says that output elements can depend on only elements that were previously, or concurrently input.

We now define Consistent: Predicate × Timing Expression → Boolean as follows:

Consistent(Ens,E) = $\forall$ x, $\forall$ q_{out} [isIn(q_{out},x) => (Uses(x,q_{out},Ens) $\subseteq$ Depends(x,q_{out},E))]

Intuitively, we check to see that each element x in each output queue depends on only elements that have been dequeued from input queues strictly before or concurrently with the enqueueing of x.

5.3 Examples

In the absence of a timing expression, we can perform standard first-order reasoning on a functional specification. For example, if the multiply task's **ensures** predicate had the additional conjunct, first($out1_{post}$) = first(in1), then by equational reasoning (substitution of equals by equals), we see that the **ensures** predicate is satisfiable only if first(in1) * first(in2) = first(in1).

In the absence of a functional specification, we can use the axioms and rules of RTL plus our extensions listed in Section 5.1 to determine inconsistent timing expressions. For example, if the expression is in1 out1 in2, we can apply axiom 5 of Section 5.1 to show that, for each task cycle, the end of the last input operation (in2) cannot follow the end of the last output operation (out1), thus invalidating the timing expression.

```
task merge
    ports
        in1, in2: in item;
        out1: out item;
    behavior
        ensures out1_post = insert(insert(out1,first(in1)),first(in2));
        timing loop (in2 out1 in1 out1);
end merge;
```

Figure 5: Merge Task

More interestingly, however, is to show how a combined specification can be proven inconsistent, where in fact, each separately is consistent and meaningful. For example, consider a task that merges data coming from two input into one output queue, as shown in Figure 5.

The **ensures** clause specifies that the output queue's items be ordered such that the item from in1 is before that from in2, but the timing expression specifies that if the item from in1 is output on the queue out1, it must be the second, not first, item in the queue (here we assume that the output queue is initially empty.) This inconsistency can be formally proven:

UsesSet(first(out1), out1, Ens) = {in1}
DependsSet(first(out1), out1, E) = {in2}

Since the UsesSet is not a subset of the DependsSet for first(out1), Consistent(Ens, E) is false.

```
task divide
    ports
        a, b: in real;
        q, r: out real;
    behavior
        ensures first(q_post) * first(a) + first(r_post) = first(b)
        timing loop (a q b r);
end merge;
```

Figure 6: Divide Task

The example in Figure 6 illustrates why subsetting and not equality is used in the definition of Consistent. It also shows the use of the Ensures predicate and the need for equational reasoning about elements in a queue (see the second conjunct in the Uses predicate).

The **ensures** clause in the Divide task specifies that the quotient of b divided by a is in q and the remainder in r; however, the timing expression says that the computation of the quotient need depend on only what is in a, and not what is in b. This inconsistency can be formally proven since:

UsesSet(first(q), q, Ens) = {a, b}
DependsSet(first(q), q, E) = {a}

More specifically, to show UsesSet(first(q), q, Ens) = {a, b} we first note that:

Uses(*quotient*(first(a), first(b)), a, q, Ens) = true
Uses(*quotient*(first(a), first(b)), b, q, Ens) = true

since a and b both "appear in" the first argument (assume *quotient* is a trait operator for real numbers.)

Using equational reasoning on the Ens, we can show

first(q) = *quotient*(first(a), first(b))

By substitution, we get

Uses(first(q), a, q, Ens) ∧ Uses(first(q), b, q, Ens)

yielding:

UsesSet(first(q), q, Ens) = {a, b}

6 Examples

Figure 7 shows our multiply task with functional and timing information together. The figure shows two different multiply tasks, specified to have the same functionality but with different timing behavior. The **timing** expression in Figure 7.a states that the multiply task first checks that the input queues are non-empty, and if so perform two parallel Dequeue operations followed by an Enqueue operation. The **timing** expression in Figure 7.b states that the inputs come in sequentially instead of in parallel.

```
task multiply
  ports
    in1, in2: in matrix;
    out1: out matrix;
  behavior
      requires  number_of_rows(first(in1)) = number_of_cols(first(in2));
      ensures   out1_post = insert(out1, first(in1) * first(in2));
      timing when (~isEmpty(in1) and ~isEmpty(in2)) =>
                  ((in1.Dequeue || in2.Dequeue) delay[10,15] out1.Enqueue);
end multiply;
```

a. Parallel Input

```
task multiply
  ports
    in1, in2: in matrix;
    out1: out matrix;
  behavior
      requires  number_of_rows(first(in1)) = number_of_cols(first(in2));
      ensures   out1_post = insert(out1, first(in1) * first(in2));
      timing when (~isEmpty(in1) and ~isEmpty(in2)) =>
                  (in1.Dequeue in2.Dequeue delay[10,15] out1.Enqueue);
end multiply;
```

b. Serial Input

Figure 7: Matrix Multiplication Task

To further illustrate the richness of our specification language and to show the benefits of cleanly separating the functional from the timing information, we write three alternative descriptions for a task built into our library. This task, deal, has one input port and a number of output ports. Data dequeued from the input port is enqueued to one of the output ports, but this can be implemented in a number of ways, as illustrated in Figure 8.

In the examples, we will drop the name of the queue operation and use just the name of the port (i.e., in1 instead of in1.Dequeue). Since this paper introduces only two queue operations: Enqueue and Dequeue, and given that the former applies only to input queues and the other applies only to output queues, no confusion should occur as to which operation is implied.

The first example (Figure 8.a) states that we alternate the dequeuing of input and enqueueing of output and ensures that the first (second) output queue will see the first (second) element removed from the input queue. The second example (Figure 8.b) states that we dequeue all input before the output operations start, which themselves take place concurrently. It allows for the first dequeued element to be enqueued on either of the output queues, but ensures that the second dequeued element will not be enqueued to the same as the first. The third example (Figure 8.c) states that input data are dequeued and grouped in pairs before enqueueing them into the output ports. The first pair is enqueued to the first output queue; the second pair, to the second.

```
task deal
    ports
        in1: in matrix;
        out1, out2: out matrix;
    behavior
        ensures
            out1_post = insert(out1, first(in1)) &
            out2_post = insert(out2, second(in1));
        timing loop (in1 out1 in1 out2);
end deal;
```

a. Alternating Input and Output

```
task deal
    ports
        in1: in matrix;
        out1, out2: out matrix;
    behavior
        ensures
            (out1_post = insert(out1,first(in1)) &
             out2_post = insert(out2, second(in1))) |
            (out2_post = insert(out2, first(in1)) &
             out1_post = insert(out1, second(in1)))
        timing loop (in1 in1 (out1 || out2))
end deal;
```

b. Concurrent Output

```
task deal
    ports
        in1: in matrix;
        out1, out2: out matrix;
    behavior
        ensures
            out1_post = insert(insert(out1, first(in1)), second(in1)) &
            out2_post = insert(insert(out2, third(in1)), fourth(in1))
        timing loop (in1 in1 in1 in1 (out1 || out2) (out1 || out2))
end deal
```

c. Grouping Data

Assume that second(in1), third(in1), and fourth(in1) as abbreviations for first(rest(in1)), first(rest(rest(in1))), first(rest(rest(rest(in1)))), respectively, are defined in the trait for queues.

Figure 8: Deal Task

7 Related Work

The axiomatic approach to specifying a program's functional behavior has its origins in Hoare's early work on verification [17] and later work on proofs of correctness of implementations of abstract data types [18], where first-order predicate logic pre- and post-conditions are used for the specification of each operation of the type. The algebraic approach, which defines data types to be heterogeneous algebras [5], uses axioms to specify properties of programs and abstract data types, but the axioms are restricted to equations. Much work has been done on algebraic specifications for abstract data types [12, 11, 14, 6]; we use more recent work on Larch specifications [16] for program modules. None of this work addresses the formal specification of timing behavior of systems.

Operational approaches, such as those based on Timed Petri-net models [23, 26], are more commonly used for specifying behavior of real-time systems. Timed Petri-nets can be roughly characterized by whether "operation" time is assigned to the *transitions*, as in the original model by Ramchandani [23], or is assigned to the *places*, as in Sifakis' model [26]. In addition, both deterministic and stochastic timing are allowed, giving origin to a variety of models for specifying or evaluating performance requirements. This has been illustrated in recent work by Coolahan [9] (places, deterministic), Smith [27] (transitions, deterministic), Wong [28] (places, stochastic), and Zuberek [29] (transitions, stochastic). In contrast, our work takes a more axiomatic than operational approach to specifying timing behavior.

Specification and verification of timing requirements for real-time systems include recent work by Dasarthy [10], and by Lee, Gehlot, and Zwarico [20, 30]. This work as well as that by Jahanian and Mok, whose real-time logic we borrow, all focus on timing properties and not on functional behavior. Either states are left uninterpreted or predicates on states are simplistic, e.g., Boolean modes as in Jahanian and Mok's work. In contrast, since we have a formal means of specifying the functional behavior of tasks and the data on which they operate, we have a more expressive specification language with a richer semantics.

The programming model we have in mind for the developers of real time, concurrent applications is based on data flowing between computing elements. However, we do not impose a data driven computation model, a basic premise of most data flow languages [1]. Tasks in our applications are asynchronous and operate on their input and output queues according to a regime described by each task's timing expression. These requirements are difficult to satisfy in traditional data flow languages although a recent data flow language, LUSTRE, overcomes these limitations. LUSTRE [4, 8] supports the concept of timing in a stream language. LUSTRE is based on LUCID [2] with the addition of timing operators and user defined clocks associated with the variables (sequences of values). In the original version of the language [4] functions and operators required that all input variables be associated with the same clock (i.e., the input and output streams moved in lock-step). These restrictions have been relaxed in the latest version of the language [8]

8 Summary
Our approach to specifying the functional and timing behavior of real-time applications for a heterogeneous machine has the following characteristics:

- It takes advantage of two well defined, though isolated, pieces of previous work.
- There is a clean separation of concerns between the two specifications.
- The semantics of both specifications as well as their combination are simple.

In our language design, we strove to separate the functional specification from the timing specification so that a task's functionality could be understood independently of its timing behavior. This separation of concerns gives us the usual advantages of modularity. Different timing specifications can be attached to the same functional specification. Task implementors can focus on satisfying functionality first, timing second. Task validation can be performed separately. For example, one could use formal verification for functionality and simulation for timing. However, we are not completely satisfied with our definition of Consistent(Ens, E) (Section 5.2) since it depends on a syntactic relation, appearsIn, which is easy to check for but is probably too restrictive.

Since the semantics can be given in terms of first-order predicate logic, our specifications are amenable to machine manipulation and analysis. The algebraic style of Larch traits can be analyzed by rewrite-rule tools, e.g., Reve [21]; the two-state predicates of Larch interfaces and thus, task predicates, can be analyzed by verification systems that support first-order reasoning, e.g., Gypsy, HDM, and FDM [13, 24, 25]; formulae in real-time logic can be mechanically transformed into equivalent formulae in Presburger arithmetic [19]. However, though many of these tools are available, much work is needed to integrate them so our specifications could be fully machine-checked and analyzed.

Acknowledgements

We thank Al Mok for his assurance that we are using RTL properly and the anonymous referee for bringing to our attention the most recent development of LUSTRE.

References

[1]   W.B. Ackerman.
        Data Flow Languages.
        IEEE-CS Computer 15(2), February, 1982.

[2]   E.A. Ashcroft and W.W. Wadge.
        LUCID: The Data Flow Programming Language.
        Academic Press, 1985.

[3]   M.R. Barbacci and J.M. Wing.
        Durra: A Task-level Description Language.
        Technical Report CMU/SEI-86-TR-3, Software Engineering Institute, Carnegie Mellon
            University, 1986.

[4]   J-L. Bergerand, P. Caspi, N. Halbwachs, D. Pilaud, and E. Pilaud.
        Outline of a Real Time Data Flow Language.
        In *Proceedings of the IEEE-CS Real Time Systems Symposium*, pages 33-42. IEEE
            Computer Society Press, December, 1985.

[5]   G. Birkhoff and J.D. Lipson.
        Heterogeneous Algebras.
        Journal of Combinatorial Theory 8:115-133, 1970.

[6]   R.M. Burstall, and J.A. Goguen.
        Putting Theories Together to Make Specifications.
        In *Fifth International Joint Conference on Artificial Intelligence*, pages 1045-1058.
            August, 1977.
        Invited paper.

[7]   R.H. Campbell and A.N. Habermann.
        The Specification of Process Synchronization by Path Expressions.
        Lecture Notes in Computer Science.
        Springer-Verlag, 1974, pages 89-102.

[8]   P. Caspi, D. Pilaud, N. Halbwachs, and J.A. Plaice.
        LUSTRE: A Declarative Language for Programming Synchronous Systems.
        In *Procedings of the 14th Annual ACM Symposium on Principles of Programming
            Languages*, pages 178-188. ACM, January, 1987.

[9]   J.E. Coolahan and N. Roussopulos.
        A Timed Petri Net Methodology for Specifying Real-Time System Requirements.
        In *International Workshop on Timed Petri Nets*, pages 24-31. IEEE Computer Society
            Press, Torino, Italy, July, 1985.

[10]   Dasarthy.
        Timing Constraints of Real-Time Systems: Constructs for Expressing Them, Methods
            of Validating Them.
        IEEE Transactions on Software Engineering 11(1):80-86, January, 1985.

[11]   H. Ehrig and B. Mahr.
        Fundamentals of Algebraic Specification 1.
        Springer-Verlag, 1985.

[12]   J.A. Goguen, J.W. Thatcher, E.G. Wagner, and J.B. Wright.
        Abstract Data Types as Initial Algebras and Correctness of Data Representations.
        In *Proceedings from the Conference of Computer Graphics, Pattern Recognition and
            Data Structures*, pages 89-93. ACM, May, 1975.

[13]   D.I. Good, R.M. Cohen, C.G. Hoch, L.W. Hunter, and D.F. Hare.
        Report on the Language Gypsy, Version 2.0.
        Technical Report ICSCA-CMP-10, Certifiable Minicomputer Project, The University of
            Texas at Austin, September, 1978.

[14]   J.V. Guttag.
        The Specification and Application to Programming of Abstract Data Types.
        PhD thesis, University of Toronto, Toronto, Canada, September, 1975.

[15]   J.V. Guttag, J.J. Horning, and J.M. Wing.
        Larch in Five Easy Pieces.
        Technical Report 5, DEC Systems Research Center, July, 1985.

[16]   J.V. Guttag, J.J. Horning, and J.M. Wing.
        The Larch Family of Specification Languages.
        IEEE Software 2(5):24-36, September, 1985.

[17]   C.A.R. Hoare.
        An axiomatic basis for computer programming.
        Communications of the ACM 12(10):576-583, October, 1969.

[18]   C.A.R. Hoare.
        Proof of Correctness of Data Representations.
        Acta Informatica 1(1):271-281, 1972.

[19]   F. Jahanian and A.K. Mok.
        Safety Analysis of Timing Properties in Real-Time Systems.
        IEEE Transactions on Software Engineering 12(9):890-904, September, 1986.

[20]   I. Lee, and V. Gehlot.
        Language Constructs for Distributed Real-Time Programming.
        In *Proceedings of the Real-Time Systems Symposium*, pages 57-66. San Diego,
            December, 1985.

[21]   P. Lescanne.
        Computer Experiments with the REVE Term Rewriting System Generator.
        In *Proceedings of Tenth Symposium on Principles of Programming Languages*, pages
            99-108. ACM, Austin, Texas, January, 1983.

[22]   D.R. Musser.
       Abstract Data Type Specification in the Affirm System.
       IEEE Transactions on Software Engineering 6(1):24-32, January, 1980.

[23]   C. Ramchandani.
       Analysis of Asynchronous Concurrent Systems by Petri Nets.
       Technical Report TR-120, MIT Project MAC, 1974.

[24]   L. Robinson, and O. Roubine.
       SPECIAL - A Specification and Assertion Language.
       Technical Report CSL-46, Stanford Research Institute, Menlo Park, Ca., January,
           1977.

[25]   J. Scheid and S. Anderson.
       The Ina Jo Specification Language Reference Manual.
       Technical Report TM-(L)-6021/001/00, System Development Corporation, Santa
           Monica, CA, March, 1985.

[26]   J. Sifakis.
       Use of Petri Nets for Performance Evaluation.
       In *Proceedings of the IFIP Third International Workshop on Modeling and Performance
           Evaluation of Computer Systems*, pages 75-93. North-Holland Publishing Co.,
           Amsterdam, The Netherlands, 1977.

[27]   C.U. Smith.
       Robust Models for the Performance Evaluation of Hardware/Software Designs.
       In *International Workshop on Timed Petri Nets*, pages 172-180. IEEE Computer
           Society Press, Torino, Italy, July, 1985.

[28]   C.Y.Wong, T.S. Dillon, and K.E. Forward.
       Timed Places Petri Nets With Stochastic Representation of Place Time.
       In *International Workshop on Timed Petri Nets*, pages 96-103. IEEE Computer Society
           Press, Torino, Italy, July, 1985.

[29]   W.M. Zuberek.
       Performance Evaluation Using Extended Timed Petri-nets.
       In *International Workshop on Timed Petri Nets*, pages 272-278. IEEE Computer
           Society Press, Torino, Italy, July, 1985.

[30]   A. Zwarico and I. Lee.
       Proving a Network of Real-time Processes Correct.
       In *Proceedings of Real-Time Systems Symposium*, pages 169-177. San Diego,
           December, 1985.

Term Graph Rewriting

H.P. Barendregt[1], M.C.J.D. van Eekelen[1], J.R.W. Glauert[2],

J.R. Kennaway[2], M.J. Plasmeijer[1] and M.R.Sleep[2].

[1] University of Nijmegen, Nijmegen, The Netherlands. Partially supported by the Dutch Parallel Reduction Machine Project.
[2] School of Information Systems, University of East Anglia, Norwich, U.K. Partially supported by the U.K. ALVEY Project.

Abstract

Graph rewriting (also called reduction) as defined in Wadsworth [1971] was introduced in order to be able to give a more efficient implementation of functional programming languages in the form of lambda calculus or term rewrite systems: identical subterms are shared using pointers.

Several other authors, e.g. Ehrig [1979], Staples [1980a,b,c], Raoult [1984] and van den Broek et al. [1986] have given mathematical descriptions of graph rewriting, usually employing concepts from category theory. These papers prove among other things the correctness of graph rewriting in the form of the Church-Rosser property for "well-behaved" (i.e. regular) rewrite systems. However, only Staples has formally studied the soundness and completeness of graph rewriting with respect to term rewriting.

In this paper we give a direct operational description of graph rewriting that avoids the category theoretic notions. We show that if a term t is interpreted as a graph g(t) and is reduced in the graph world, then the result represents an actual reduct of the original term t (*soundness*). For weakly regular term rewrite systems, there is also a *completeness* result: every normal form of a term t can be obtained from the graphical implementation. We also show completeness for all term rewrite systems which possess a so called hypernormalising strategy, and in that case the strategy also gives a normalising strategy for the graphical implementation.

Besides having nice theoretical properties, weakly regular systems offer opportunities for parallelism, since redexes at different places can be executed independently or in parallel, without affecting the final result.

0. Introduction and background.

Graph rewriting is a well-known and standard technique for implementing functional languages based on term rewriting (e.g. Turner [1979a]), but the correctness of this method has received little attention, being simply accepted folklore. For both theory and practice, this makes a poor foundation, especially in the presence of parallelism. Staples [1980a,b,c] provides the only published results we are aware of. (A digested summary of these papers is in Kennaway [1984].) Wadsworth [1971] proves similar results for the related subject of pure lambda calculus.

Our principal result is that the notion of graph rewriting provides a sound and complete representation (in a sense precisely defined below) of *weakly regular* TRSs. A counterexample is given to show that for non-weakly regular TRSs completeness may fail: some term rewriting computations cannot be expressed in the corresponding graph rewrite system. A second result concerns the mapping of evaluation strategies between the term and the graph worlds. A counterexample is exhibited to show that an evaluation strategy which is normalising (i.e. computes normal forms) in the term world may fail to do so when it is transferred to the graph world. We prove that any strategy which satisfies a stronger condition of being *hypernormalising* in the term world is normalising (and indeed hypernormalising) in the graph world. We briefly consider the problem of defining a graph rewriting implementation of non-left linear term rewrite rules.

The general plan of the paper is as follows: Section 1 presents basic definitions, and introduces a linear syntax for terms represented as graphs. Section 2 introduces a category of term graphs. Section 3 defines the notion of graph rewriting, and section 4 introduces the notion of *tree rewriting* as a prelude to section 5, which develops our theory of how to relate the worlds of term and graph rewriting. Section 6 considers the problem of mapping strategies between the two worlds. Finally, section 7 gives a summary of the work.

1. Terms as trees and graphs.

1.1 DEFINITION.

(i) Let $\mathbf{F}$ be a (finite or infinite) set of objects called *function symbols*. A,B,... range over $\mathbf{F}$.

(ii) The set T of *terms* over $\mathbf{F}$ is defined inductively by:

$$A \in \mathbf{F}, \ t_1,...,t_n \in T \ \Rightarrow \ A(t_1,...,t_n) \in T \qquad\qquad (n \geq 0)$$

A() is written as just A. ∎

1.2 EXAMPLE.

Let $\mathbf{F}=\{0,S\}$. Then T $=\{0,S(0),0(S,S(0,0)), S(S,S,S)...\}$. Note that we do not assume that function symbols have fixed arities. This might appear inconvenient if one wished to represent, for example, the Peano integers, with a constant 0 and a successor operator S, since one also obtains extra "unintended" terms such as some of those listed above. When we define rewrite systems in section 3, we will see that this does not cause any problems. ∎

1.3 DEFINITION.

A *labelled graph* (*over* $\mathbf{F}$) is a triple (N,lab,succ) involving a (finite or infinite) set N of *nodes*, a function lab: N→$\mathbf{F}$, and a function succ:N→N*. In this case we say that the $n_1,...,n_k$ are the *successors* of n. The ith component of succ(n) is denoted by $succ(n)_i$. ∎

When we draw pictures of graphs, a directed edge will go from each node n to each node in succ(n), with the left-to-right ordering of the sources of the edges corresponding to the ordering of the components of succ(n). The identity of nodes is usually unimportant, and we may omit this information from pictures.

1.4 EXAMPLE.

Let $N=\{n_1,n_2,n_3\}$ and define lab and succ on N as follows.

$$lab(n_1)=G, \ lab(n_2)=A, \ lab(n_3)=B,$$
$$succ(n_1)=(n_2,n_3), \ succ(n_2)=(), \ succ(n_3)=().$$

This defines a labelled graph that can be drawn as:

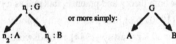

Using this notation, four more examples of graphs are the following.

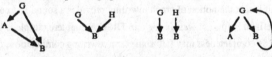

1.5 DEFINITION.

(i) A *path* in a labelled graph (N,lab,succ) is a list $(n_0,i_0,n_1,i_1,... ,n_{m-1},i_{m-1},n_m)$ where $m \geq 0$, $n_0,... ,n_m \in N$, $i_0,... ,i_{m-1} \in N$ (the natural numbers) and n_{k+1} is the i_k-th successor of n_k. This path is said to be *from* n_0 *to* n_m and m is the *length* of the path.

(ii) A *cycle* is a path of length greater than 0 from a node n to itself. n is called a *cyclic node*.

(iii) A graph is *cyclic* if it contains a cyclic node, otherwise it is *acyclic*. ∎

1.6 DEFINITION.

(i) A *term graph* (often, within this paper, simply a *graph*) is a quadruple (N,lab,succ,r) where (N,lab,succ) is a labelled graph and r is a member of N. The node r is called the *root* of the graph. (We do not require that every node of a term graph is reachable by a path from the root.) For a graph g, the components are often denoted by N_g, lab_g, $succ_g$, and r_g.

(ii) A path in a graph is *rooted* if it begins with the root of the graph. The graph is *root-cyclic* if there is a cycle containing the root.

When we draw pictures of term graphs, the topmost node is the root. ∎

Term graphs are exactly the graphs discussed in the paper Barendregt et al.[1987], which defines a language of generalised graph rewriting of which the rewriting treated in this paper is a special case.

1.7 DEFINITION. Let $g = (N,lab,succ)$ be a labelled graph and let $n \in N$. The *subgraph of* g *rooted at* n is the term graph $(N',lab',succ',n)$ where $N'=\{n' \in N \mid$ there is a path from n to $n'\}$ and lab' and $succ'$ are the restrictions of lab and $succ$ to N'. We denote this graph by $g|n$. The definition also applies when g is a term graph. ∎

1.8 EXAMPLES.

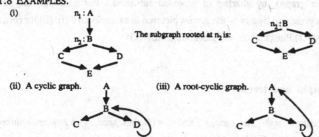

(i)

The subgraph rooted at n_2 is:

(ii) A cyclic graph.

(iii) A root-cyclic graph.

A formal description of a graph requires a complete specification of the quadruple $(N,lab,succ,r)$. When writing down examples of finite graphs, it is convenient to adopt a more concise notation, which abstracts away from details such as the precise choice of the elements of N. We will use a notation based on the definition of terms in definition 1.1, but with the addition of node-names, which can express the sharing of common subexpressions. The notation is defined by the following context-free grammar, with the restrictions following it.

1.9 DEFINITION (linear notation for graphs).

> graph   ::=   node | node + graph
> node   ::=   A(node,...,node) | x | x : A(node,...,node)

A ranges over **F**. x ranges over a set, disjoint from **F**, of *nodeids* ('node identifiers'). Any nodeid x which occurs in a graph must occur exactly once in the context x : A(node,...,node). Nodeids are represented by tokens beginning with a lower-case letter. Function symbols will be non-alphabetic, or begin with an upper-case letter. We again abbreviate A() to A. ∎

This syntax is, with minor differences, the same as the syntax for graphs in the language LEAN (Barendregt et al.[1987]). The five graphs of the examples 1.4 are in this notation: G(A,B), G(A(x:B),x), G(x:B) + H(x), G(B) + H(B) and x:G(A,B(x)). Note that multiple uses of the same nodeid express multiple references to the same node.

The definition of terms in 1.1 corresponds to a sublanguage of our shorthand notation, consisting of those graphs obtained by using only the first production for graph and the first production for node. *So terms have a natural representation as graphs.*

1.10 EXAMPLES.

(i) G(Plus(1,2), Plus(1,2))   (ii) G(Plus(n_1: 1, n_2: 2), Plus(n_1, n_2))

(iii) G(n:Plus(1,2), n)   (iv) n_1: Cons(3, n_1)

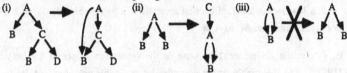

1.11 DEFINITION. A *tree* is a graph (N,lab,succ,r) such that there is exactly one path from r to each node in N. ■

Thus example (i) above is a tree, and (ii), (iii), and (iv) are not. Trees are always acyclic. Notice that a graph g is a finite tree iff g can be written by the grammar of 1.8 without using any nodeids.

The natural mapping of terms to graphs represents each term as a finite tree. However, some terms can also be represented as proper graphs, by sharing of repeated subterms. For example, the term G(Plus(1,2),Plus(1,2)) can be represented by any of the graphs pictured in example 1.10 (i), (ii), or (iii), as well as by the graphs G(Plus(x:1,2),Plus(x,2)) or G(Plus(1,x:2),Plus(1,x)).

2. Homomorphisms of graphs and trees.

2.1 DEFINITION. Given two graphs $g_1 = (N_1,\text{lab}_1,\text{succ}_1,r_1)$ and $g_2 = (N_2,\text{lab}_2,\text{succ}_2,r_2)$, a *homomorphism* from g_1 to g_2 is a map $f:N_1 \to N_2$ such that for all $n \in N_1$,

$$\text{lab}_2(f(n)) = \text{lab}_1(n)$$
$$\text{succ}_2(f(n)) = f(\text{succ}_1(n))$$

where f is defined by $f(n_1,...,n_k) = (f(n_1),...,f(n_k))$. That is, homomorphisms preserve labels, successors, and their order. ■

2.2 DEFINITION. Graph(F) is the category whose objects are graphs over F and whose morphisms are homomorphisms. Tree(F) is the full subcategory of Graph(F) whose objects are the trees over F. It is easy to verify that these are categories. ■

2.3 EXAMPLES. We shall write

$$g_1 \longrightarrow g_2$$

when there is a homomorphism from g_1 to g_2. We have the following pictures.

2.4 DEFINITION. (i) A homomorphism $f:g_1 \to g_2$ is *rooted* if $f(r_1)=r_2$.

(ii) An *isomorphism* is a homomorphism which has an inverse. We write g ~ g' when g and g' are isomorphic.

(iii) Two graphs are *equivalent* when they are isomorphic by a rooted isomorphism. We write g ≈ g' when g and g' are equivalent. ■

2.5 PROPOSITION. *(i) For any graphs g_1 and g_2 we have $g_1 \approx g_2 \implies g_1 \sim g_2$.*

(ii) Every rooted homomorphism from one tree to another is an isomorphism. ■

2.6 EXAMPLE. These two graphs are isomorphic but not equivalent (recall that in diagrammatic representations the root node is the topmost):

2.7 DEFINITION. Given any graph g=(N,lab,succ,r) we can define a tree U(g) which results from "unravelling" g from the root. We start with some examples.

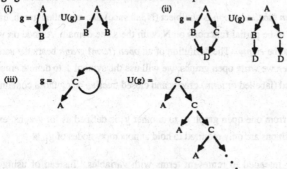

Now we give the formal definition. U(g) has as nodes the rooted paths of g. The root of U(g) is the path (r). For a path $p=(n_0,i_0,...,n_{m-1},i_{m-1},n_m)$, $lab_{U(g)}(p) = lab_g(n_m)$ and $succ_{U(g)}(p) = (p_1,...,p_k)$ where p_i is the result of appending $(i,succ_g(n_m)_i)$ to p. Clearly this is a tree. ■

2.8 PROPOSITION. *For every graph g there is a rooted homomorphism u_g: U(g)→g defined by:*

$$u_g(n_0,i_0,...,n_m) = n_m.$$ ■

2.9 PROPOSITION. *A graph g is a tree iff g ≈ U(g).* ■

2.10 DEFINITION. Two graphs g and g' are *tree-equivalent*, notation $g \approx_t g'$, if U(g) ≈ U(g'). ■

For example, the graphs of example 1.10 (i), (ii), and (iii) are all tree-equivalent. So are these two graphs:

3. Graph rewriting.

We now turn to rewriting. First we recall the familiar definitions of terms with free variables and term rewriting. We then explain informally how we represent terms with free variables as 'open' graphs, and define our notion of graph rewriting. Our definition is quite similar to the one in Staples [1980a].

3.1 DEFINITION (term rewriting). (i) Let **V** be a fixed set of function symbols, disjoint from **F**. The members of **V** are called *variables*, and are denoted by lower-case letters. An *open term* over a set of function symbols **F** is a term over **F**∪**V** in which every node labelled with a variable has no successors. An open term containing no variables (that is, what we have been calling simply a term) is a *closed* term.

(ii) A *term rewrite rule* is a pair of terms t_L and t_R (written $t_L \to t_R$) such that every variable occurring in t_R occurs in t_L. t_L and t_R are, respectively, the *left-* and *right-hand* sides of the *term rewrite rule* $t_L \to t_R$.

(iii) A term rewrite rule is *left-linear* if no variable occurs more than once in its left-hand side. ■

The usual definition of a term rewrite rule requires that t_L be not just a variable. However, our results are not affected by the presence of such rules, so we do not bother to exclude them.

In order to introduce graph rewriting, first we need some preparatory definitions.

3.2 DEFINITION. (i) An *open labelled graph* is an object (N,lab,succ) like a labelled graph, except that lab and succ are only required to be partial functions on N, with the same domain. A node on which lab and succ are undefined is said to be *empty*. The definition of an *open (term) graph* bears the same relation to that of a (term) graph. When we write open graphs, we will use the symbol ⊥ to denote empty nodes. As with terms, we talk of closed (labelled or term) graphs and closed trees as being those containing no empty nodes.

(ii) A *homomorphism* from one open graph g_1 to another g_2 is defined as for graphs, except that the "structure preserving" conditions are only required to hold at nonempty nodes of g_1. ■

Open term graphs are intended to represent terms with variables. Instead of using the set V of variables, we find it more convenient, for technical reasons, to follow Staples[1980a] by using empty nodes. The precise translation from open graphs to open terms is as follows. Given an open graph over F, we first replace each empty node in it by a different variable symbol from V, and then unravel the resulting closed graph over F∪V, obtaining an open term over F. Thus where a graph has multiple edges pointing to the same empty node, the term will have multiple occurrences of the same nodeid. For example, the graph Ap(Ap(⊥,w:⊥),Ap(⊥,w)) translates to the term Ap(Ap(x,z),Ap(y,z)):

We could obtain any term which only differs from this one by changes of variables. We shall treat such terms as the same.

We now turn to the graph representation of term rewrite rules. We only deal with left-linear rules in this paper. In 5.13 we discuss briefly the problems in graphically describing non-left-linear rules.

3.3 DEFINITION. (i) A *graph rewrite rule* is a triple (g,n,n'), where g is an open labelled graph and n and n' are nodes of g, called respectively the *left root* and the *right root* of the rule.

(ii) A *redex* in a graph g_0 is a pair $\Delta = (R,f)$, where R is a graph rewrite rule (g,n,n') and f is a homomorphism from g|n to g_0. The homomorphism f is called an *occurrence* of R. ■

Rather than introduce our formal definition of graph rewriting immediately, we begin with some examples. The formal definition is given in section 3.6.

3.4 TRANSLATION OF TERM RULES TO GRAPH RULES.

Let $t_L \to t_R$ be a left-linear term rewrite rule. We construct a corresponding graph rewrite rule (g,n,n'), where g is a labelled graph and n and n' are nodes of g. First take the graphs representing t_L and t_R. Form the union of these, sharing those empty nodes which represent the same variables in t_L and t_R. This graph is g. Take n and n' to be the respective roots of t_L and t_R. Here are two examples which should make the correspondence between term and graph rewrite rules clear.

(i) Term rule: Ap(Ap(Ap(S,x),y),z) → Ap(Ap(x,z),Ap(y,z))

   Graph rule: (n:Ap(Ap(Ap(S,x:⊥),y:⊥),z:⊥) + n':Ap(Ap(x,z),Ap(y,z)), n, n')

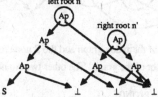

(ii) Term rule: head(cons(x,y)) → x

   Graph rule: (n:head(cons(x:⊥,⊥)), n, x)

3.5 INFORMAL DEFINITION OF GRAPH REWRITING.

A redex ((g,n,n'), f: g|n → g₀) in a graph g₀ is reduced in three steps. We shall use the following redex as an example: (g,n,n') is the S-rule above, g_0 = G(a,Ap(Ap(a:Ap(S,P),Q),R)) and f operates on n as indicated in the picture (which completely determines how f behaves on the rest of g|n).

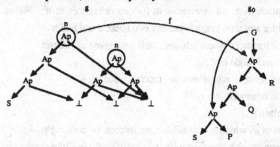

First (the *build* phase) an isomorphic copy of that part of g|n' not contained in g|n is added to g_0, with lab, succ, and root defined in the natural way. Call this graph g_1. Then (the *redirection* phase) all edges of g_1 pointing to f(n) are replaced by edges pointing to the copy of n', giving a graph g_2. The root of g_2 is the root of g_1, if that node is not equal to f(n). Otherwise, the root of g_2 is the copy of n'.

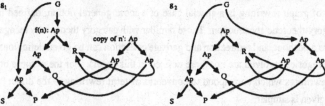

Lastly (the *garbage collection* phase), all nodes not accessible from the root of g_2 are removed, giving g_3, which is the result of the rewrite.

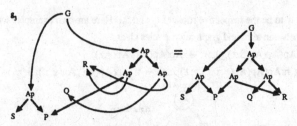

Note that the bottommost Ap node of the redex graph and the S node remain after garbage collection, since they are still accessible from the root of the graph. The other two Ap nodes of the redex vanish.

3.6 FORMAL DEFINITION OF GRAPH REWRITING.

We now give a formal definition of the general construction. Let $((g,n,n'), f: g|n \to g_0)$ be a redex in a graph g_0. The graphs g_1 (the build phase), g_2 (the redirection phase) and g_3 (the garbage collection phase) are defined as follows.

(i) The node-set N of g_1 is the disjoint union of N_{g0} and $N_{g|n'} - N_{g|n}$. The root is r_{g0}. The functions lab_{g1} and $succ_{g1}$ are given by:

$$lab_{g1}(m) = lab_{g0}(m) \qquad (m \in N_{g0})$$
$$= lab_g(m) \qquad (m \in N_{g|n'} - N_{g|n})$$
$$succ_{g1}(m)_i = succ_{g0}(m)_i \qquad (m \in N_{g0})$$
$$= succ_g(m)_i \qquad (m, succ_g(m)_i \in N_{g|n'} - N_{g|n})$$
$$= f(succ_g(m)_i) \qquad (m \in N_{g|n'} - N_{g|n}, succ_g(m)_i \in N_{g|n})$$

We write $g_1 = g_0 +_f (g,n,n')$.

(ii) The next step is to replace in g_1 all references to $f(n)$ by references to n'. We can define a substitution operation in general for any term graph h and any two nodes a and b of h.

$h[a:=b]$ is a term graph $(N_h, lab, succ, r)$, where lab, $succ$, and r are given as follows.

$lab(c) = lab_h(c)$ for each node c of N_h

if $succ_h(c)_i = a$ then $succ(c)_i = b$, otherwise $succ(c)_i = succ_h(c)_i$

if $r_h = a$ then $r = b$, otherwise $r = r_h$

With this definition, g_2 is $g_1[f(n):=n']$.

(iii) Finally, we take the part of g_2 which is accessible from its root, by defining $g_3 = g_2|r_{g2}$. We give this operation a name: for any term graph h, we denote $h|r_h$ by $GC(h)$ (*Garbage Collection*).

We denote the result of reducing a redex Δ in a graph g by $RED(\Delta,g)$. Collecting the notations we have introduced, we have

$$RED(((g,n,n'),f),g_0) = GC((g_0 +_f (g,n,n'))[f(n):=n']). \blacksquare$$

Our definition of graph rewriting is a special case of a more general notion, defined in Glauert et al.[1987] by a category-theoretic construction. Those familiar with category theory may recognise the build phase of a rewrite as a pushout, and redirection and garbage collection can be given definitions in the same style (though the categories involved are not those defined in this paper). For the purpose of this paper - describing graph rewritings which correspond to conventional term rewritings - the direct "operational" definition we have given is simpler.

3.7 DEFINITION. (i) If g reduces to g' by reduction of a redex Δ, we write $g \to^\Delta g'$, or $g \to g'$ if we do not wish to indicate the identity of the redex. The reflexive and transitive closure of the relation $\to$ is $\to^*$.

(ii) A *graph rewriting system* (GRS) over **F** consists of a pair (G,R) where **R** is a set of rewrite rules and G is a set of graphs over **F** closed under rewriting by the members of **R**.

(iii) We write $g \to_R g'$ if $g \to g'$ by reduction of a redex using one of the rules in **R**. The reflexive and transitive closure of $\to_R$ is $\to^*_R$. If clear from the context, we omit the subscript **R**.

(iv) A graph g such that for no g' does one have $g \to_R g'$ is said to be an R-normal form (or to be in R-normal form). If $g \to^*_R g'$ and g' is in R-normal form, we say that g' is an R-normal form of g, and that g has an R-normal form. Again, we often omit the R. ∎

Note that a GRS is not required to include all the graphs which can be formed from the given set of function symbols **F**. Any subset closed under rewriting will do. This allows our definition to automatically handle such things as, for example, sorted rewrite systems, where there are constraints over what function symbols can be applied to what arguments, or arities, where each function symbol may only be applied to a specified number of arguments. From our point of view, this amounts to simply restricting the set of graphs to those satisfying these constraints. So long as rewriting always yields allowed graphs from allowed graphs, we do not need to develop any special formalism for handling restricted rewrite systems, nor do we need to prove new versions of our results.

Our definition of a graph rewrite rule allows any conventional term rewrite rule to be interpreted as a graph rewrite rule, provided that the term rewrite rule is left-linear, that is, if no variable occurs twice or more on its left-hand side. As some of the following examples show, however, some new phenomena arise with graph rewrite rules.

3.8 EXAMPLES.

(i) Term rule: $A(x) \to B(x)$;   Graph rule: (n:A(x:⊥) + n':B(x), n, n')

   Graph: x:A(x);   Result of rewriting: x:B(x)

(ii) Term rule: $I(x) \to x$;   Graph rule:(n:I(n':⊥), n, n')

   Graph: I(3);   Result of rewriting: 3

(iii) The fixed point combinator Y has the term rewrite rule $Ap(Y,x) \to Ap(x,Ap(Y,x))$. This can be transformed into the graph rewrite rule $(n:Ap(Y,x:\perp) + n':Ap(x,Ap(Y,x)),n,n')$. However, it can also be given the graph rewrite rule: $(n:Ap(Y,x:\perp) + n':Ap(x,n'),n,n')$:

   (n:Ap(Y,x:⊥) + n':Ap(x,Ap(Y,x)),n,n')   (n:Ap(Y,x:⊥) + n':Ap(x,n'),n,n')

This captures the fact that the Böhm tree (Barendregt [1984]) of the term Ap(Y,x) is:

The graph rule can do all the 'unravelling' in one step, which in the term rewrite world requires an infinite sequence of rewritings.

(iv) Here is a more subtle example of the same phenomenon illustrated by (iii). Consider the term rewrite rule

$$F(Cons(x,y)) \rightarrow G(Cons(x,y))$$

Our standard representation of this as a graph rewrite rule is:

$$(\; n{:}F(Cons(x{:}\bot,y{:}\bot)) + n'{:}G(Cons(x,y)), \, n, \, n' \;)$$

Note that each application of this rule will create a new node of the form $Cons(...,...)$, which will have the same successors as an existing node $Cons\,(...,...)$. In a practical implementation, there is no need to do this. One might as well use that existing node, instead of making a copy of it. The following graph rewrite rule does this:

$$(\; n{:}F(z{:}Cons(\bot,\bot)) + n'{:}G(z), \, n, \, n' \;)$$

Both the languages Standard ML and Hope, which are languages of term rewriting, allow an enhanced form of term rewrite rules such as (using our syntax):

$$F(z{:}Cons(x,y)) \rightarrow G(z)$$

with precisely this effect. Of course, given referential transparency (which ML lacks) there is no reason for an implementation not to make this optimisation wherever there is an opportunity, even if the programmer does not. But providing this feature to the programmer may make his programs more readable.

(v) Term rule: $I(x) \rightarrow x$; Graph rule: $(\; n{:}I(n'{:}\bot), \, n, \, n' \;)$

   Graph: $x{:}I(x)$; Result of rewriting: $x{:}I(x)$

Example 3.8(v) is deliberately pathological. Consider the GRS for combinatory logic, whose rules are those for the S, K, and I combinators. The graph can be interpreted as "the least fixed point of I" (cf. the example of the Y combinator above), and in the usual denotational semantics in terms of reflexive domains should have the bottom, "undefined" value. As the graph reduces to itself (and to nothing else), it has no normal form. Thus our operational semantics of graph rewriting agrees with the denotational semantics. This is not true for some other attempts we have seen at formalising graphical term rewriting.

We now study some properties of graph rewrite systems. We establish a version of the theorem of finite developments for term rewriting, and the confluence of weakly regular systems. For reasons of space, the longer proofs are omitted from this paper. They appear in Barendregt et al. [1986].

3.9 PROPOSITION. *Garbage collection can be postponed. That is, given* $g \rightarrow^{\Delta 1} g_1 \rightarrow^{\Delta 2} g_2$, $\Delta_i = (R_i, f_i)$, $R_i = (g_i, n_i, n'_i)$ $(i = 1,2)$ *and* $g'_1 = (g +_{f1} R_1)[f(n) = n']$, *then* Δ_2 *is also a redex of* g'_1, *and* $g'_1 \rightarrow^{\Delta 2} g_2$. ∎

3.10 DEFINITION. Two redexes $\Delta_1 = ((g_1,n_1,n'_1),f_1)$ and $\Delta_2 = ((g_2,n_2,n'_2),f_2)$ of a graph g are *disjoint* if:

   (i) $f_2(n_2)$ is not equal to $f_1(n)$ for any nonempty node n of $g_1|n_1$, and

   (ii) $f_1(n_1)$ is not equal to $f_2(n)$ for any nonempty node n of $g_2|n_2$.

Δ_1 and Δ_2 are *weakly disjoint* if either they are disjoint, or the only violation of conditions (i) and (ii) is that $f_1(n_1) = f_2(n_2)$, and the results of reducing Δ_1 or Δ_2 are identical.

   A GRS is *regular* (resp. *weakly regular*) if for every graph g of the GRS, every two distinct redexes in g are disjoint (resp. weakly disjoint). ∎

3.11 PROPOSITION. *Let* $\Delta_1 = ((g_1,n_1,n'_1),f_1)$ *and* $\Delta_2 = ((g_2,n_2,n'_2),f_2)$ *be two disjoint redexes of a graph g. Let* $g \rightarrow^{\Delta 1} g'$. *Then either* $f_2(n_2)$ *is not a node of g', or there is a redex* $((g_2,n_2,n'_2),f)$ *of g' such that* $f(n_2) = f_2(n_2)$. ∎

3.12 DEFINITION. (i) With the notations of the preceding proposition, if $f_2(n_2)$ is not a node of g' then Δ_2/Δ_1 is the empty reduction sequence from g' to g'; otherwise, Δ_2/Δ_1 is the one-step reduction sequence consisting of the reduction of $((g_2,n_2,n'_2),f)$. This redex is the *residual* of Δ_2 by Δ_1 and is denoted by $\Delta_2//\Delta_1$. For weakly disjoint Δ_1 and Δ_2, Δ_2/Δ_1 is the empty reduction sequence from g' to g'. Δ_2/Δ_1 is not defined when Δ_1 and Δ_2 are not weakly disjoint, and $\Delta_2//\Delta_1$ is not defined when Δ_1 and Δ_2 are not disjoint.

(ii) Given a reduction sequence $g \to^{\Delta 1} \to^{\Delta 2} ... \to^{\Delta i} g'$ and a redex Δ of g, the *residual* of Δ by the sequence $\Delta_1...\Delta_i$, denoted $\Delta//(\Delta_1...\Delta_i)$ is $(\Delta//(\Delta_1...\Delta_{i-1}))//\Delta_i$ (provided that $(\Delta//(\Delta_1...\Delta_{i-1}))$ exists and is disjoint from Δ_i). ∎

3.13 PROPOSITION. *Let Δ_1 and Δ_2 be weakly disjoint redexes of g, and let $g \to^{\Delta i} g_i$ (i = 1,2). Then there is a graph h such that $g_1 \to^{\Delta 2/\Delta 1} h$ and $g_2 \to^{\Delta 1/\Delta 2} h$. That is, weakly disjoint redexes are subcommutative.* ∎

3.14 COROLLARY. *Every weakly regular GRS is confluent. That is, if $g \to^* g_i$ (i = 1,2), then there is an h such that $g_i \to^* h$ (i = 1,2).* ∎

3.15 DEFINITION. Let g be a graph and F be a set of disjoint redexes of g. A *development* of F is a reduction sequence in which the redex reduced at each step is a residual, by the preceding steps of the sequence, of a member of F. A *complete development* of F is a development of F, at the end of which there remain no residuals of members of F. ∎

3.16 PROPOSITION. *Every complete development of a finite set of pairwise disjoint redexes F is finite. In fact, its length is bounded by the number of redexes in F.* ∎

3.17 PROPOSITION. *Let F be a set of redexes of a graph g. Every finite complete development of F ends with the same graph (up to isomorphism). This graph is:*

$$GC((g +_{f1} R_1 +_{f2} ... +_{fi} R_i)[f_1(n_1) := n'_1]...[f_i(n_i):=n'_i])$$

where the redexes whose residuals are reduced in the complete development are $\Delta_1 = (f_1,R_1),...,\Delta_i = (f_i,R_i)$. ∎

Note that since we allow infinite graphs, a set of redexes F as in the last two propositions may be infinite. Nevertheless, it may have a finite complete development, if rewriting of some members of F causes all but finitely many members of F to be erased.

4. Tree rewriting.

In order to study the relationship between term rewriting and graph rewriting, we define the notion of *tree rewriting*. This is a formalisation of conventional term rewriting within the framework of our definitions of graph rewriting.

4.1 DEFINITION. (i) A *tree rewrite rule* is a graph rewrite rule (g,n,n') such that g|n is a tree.

For a set of tree rewrite rules R, the relation $\to_{tR}$ of *tree rewriting* with respect to R is defined by:

$$t_1 \to_{tR} t_2 \iff \text{ for some graph } g, t_1 \to_R g \text{ and } U(g) = t_2$$

(ii) A *tree rewrite system* (TreeRS) over F is a pair (T,R) where R is a set of tree rewrite rules and T is a set of trees over F closed under $\to_{tR}$. A *term rewrite system* (TRS) is a TreeRS, all of whose trees are finite.

When t_1 reduces to t_2 by tree rewriting of a redex Δ, we write $t_1 \to_t^\Delta t_2$, or $t_1 \to_t t_2$ when we do not wish to indicate the identity of the redex. ∎

Tree rewrite systems differ from conventional term rewrite systems in two ways. Firstly, infinite trees are allowed. We need to handle infinite trees, since they are produced by the unravelling of cyclic graphs. We need to handle cyclic graphs because some implementors of graph rewriting use them, and we do not want to limit the scope of this paper unnecessarily. Secondly, the set of trees of a TreeRS may be any set of trees over the given function symbols which is closed under tree rewriting. This is for the same reason as was explained above for GRSs.

If for each rule (g,n,n') in the rule-set, g is finite and acyclic, the set of all finite trees generated by the function symbols will be closed under tree rewriting. This is true for those rules resulting from term rewrite rules by our standard representation. Thus the conventional notion of a TRS is included in ours.

4.2 DEFINITION. Let $t, t_1,... t_i$ be trees, and $n_1,...,n_i$ be distinct nodes of t. We define $t[n_1:=t_1,...,n_i:=t_i]$ to be the tree whose nodes are

(i)   all paths of t which do not include any of $n_1,...,n_i$, and

(ii) every path obtained by taking a path p of t, which ends at n_j ($1 \leq j \leq i$) and contains no other occurrence of $n_1...n_i$, and replacing the last node of p by any path of t_j.

For any of these paths p, the label of p is the label of the last node in p, in whichever of $t, t_1,... t_i$ that came from. The successors function is defined similarly. ■

The results concerning disjointness, regularity, and confluence which we proved for graph rewriting all have versions for tree rewriting. Again we omit proofs. We also have the following:

4.3 PROPOSITION. *Unravelling can be postponed. That is, if $t_1 \rightarrow_t t_2 \rightarrow_t t_3$, then there are graphs g and g' such that*

(1) $t_2 = U(g)$ and $t_1 \rightarrow g$ (by graph rewriting)

(2) $g \rightarrow g'$ and $t_3 \rightarrow^*_t U(g')$. ■

5.   Relations between tree and graph rewriting.

In this section we prove our principal result: for weakly regular rule-systems, graph rewriting is a sound and complete implementation of term rewriting.

5.1 DEFINITION. Let (T,R) be a TreeRS.

(i) $L(T,R)$, the *lifting* of this system, is the GRS whose set of graphs is $L(T) = \{g \mid U(g) \in T\}$, and whose rule set is R (but now interpreted as graph rewrite rules). It is trivial to verify that $L(T)$ is closed under $\rightarrow_R$.

(ii) A *graphical term rewrite system* (GTRS) is a GRS of the form $L(T,R)$, where (T,R) is a term rewrite system.

(iii) A GRS (G,R) is *acyclic* if every member of G is acyclic. ■

When (T,R) is a term rewrite system, $L(T,R)$ represents its graphical implementation. There are two fundamental properties it must have to be a correct implementation, which we now define.

5.2 DEFINITION. (i) A TreeRS (T,R) is called *graph-reducible* if for every graph g in $L(T)$, if t is a normal form of $U(g)$ in (T,R), then there is a normal form g' of g in $L(T,R)$ such that $U(g') = t$, and if $U(g)$ has no normal form in (T,R), then g has no normal form in L(T,R).

    (ii) A GRS (G,R) is *tree-reducible* if there is a TreeRS (T,R) such that (G,R) = L(T,R), and such that if g' is a normal form of g in (G,R), then U(g') is a normal form of U(g) in (T,R), and if g has no normal form in (G,R), then U(g) has no normal form in (T,R). ∎

    L(T,R) is the graphical implementation of (T,R). Tree-reducibility of L(T,R) expresses soundness: every result which is obtainable by graph rewriting in L(T,R) is also obtainable by tree rewriting in (T,R). Graph-reducibility of (T,R) expresses completeness: every result which is obtainable by tree rewriting is also obtainable by graph rewriting. We shall see that every GTRS is tree-reducible, and every weakly regular TRS is graph-reducible. Not all GRSs, even those of the form L(T,R), are tree-reducible, nor is every TreeRS graph-reducible, as the following examples show.

5.3 EXAMPLE. Tree reducibility can fail when there are cyclic graphs. Consider the term rewrite rule $A(x)$ → $B(x)$, represented graphically by:

A cyclic graph may contain a single redex with respect to this rule, while its unravelling contains infinitely many:

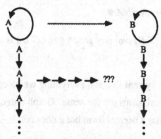

5.4 EXAMPLE. The following TreeRS is not graph-reducible:

    T: trees over {A,D,0,1,2}, with the following arities: A is binary, D is unary, and 0, 1, and 2 are nullary.

    R: $A(1,2)$ → 0; 1 → 2; 2 → 1; $D(x)$ → $A(x,x)$.

For a counterexample, consider the following tree rewriting sequence:

In the graph rewriting system we have:

In this example, the sharing of (tree) subterms in the graph world has excluded from the graph world certain rewrite sequences of the tree world. Distinct subterms of $A(1,1)$ correspond to the same subgraph of $A(x:1,x)$, forcing synchronized rewriting of siblings, which makes the normal form inaccessible.

5.5 DEFINITION.

    (i)   Redexes $\Delta = ((g,n,n'),f)$ and $\Delta' = ((g',m,m'),f')$ in a graph h are *siblings* if $hlf(n) \approx_t hlf(m)$.

    (ii)   For a redex $\Delta = ((U(g),n,n'),f)$ of a tree U(g) we define $u_g(\Delta)$ to be the redex $((g,n,n'),u_g \cdot f)$ of g.

(iii) For a redex Δ of a graph g, the set of redexes Δ' of $U(g)$ such that $u_g(\Delta') = \Delta$ is denoted by $u_g^{-1}(\Delta)$. For a set of redexes $\mathcal{F}$ of a graph g, $u_g^{-1}(\mathcal{F})$ denotes $\bigcup \{ u_g^{-1}(\Delta') \mid \Delta' \in \mathcal{F} \}$.

(iv) A redex Δ of a graph G is *acyclic* if $u_g^{-1}(\Delta)$ is finite. ∎

5.6 PROPOSITION. *Let $g \to g'$ by rewriting of an acyclic redex Δ. Then $U(g) \to^*_t U(g')$ by complete development of $u_g^{-1}(\Delta)$. For any redex Δ' of g, weakly disjoint from Δ, $u_g^{-1}(\Delta'//\Delta) = u_g^{-1}(\Delta')//u_g^{-1}(\Delta)$.* ∎

5.7 PROPOSITION. *Let $g \to^* g'$ by a complete development of a set $\mathcal{F}$ of disjoint acyclic redexes of g whose associated rewrite rules are acyclic. Then $U(g) \to^*_t U(g')$ by a complete development of $u_g^{-1}(\mathcal{F})$.* ∎

5.8 DEFINITION. (i) In a weakly regular GRS, the relation of *Gross-Knuth* reduction, notation $\to^{GK}$, is defined as follows

$g \to^{GK} g' \Leftrightarrow g \to^* g'$ by complete development of the set of all redexes of g.

(ii) In a weakly regular TreeRS we define *Gross-Knuth* reduction by

$t \to^{GK}_t t' \Leftrightarrow t \to^*_t t'$ by complete development of the set of all redexes of t. ∎

5.9 PROPOSITION. *Let (T,R) be a weakly regular TRS. Then $L(T,R)$ is weakly regular. Let g and g' be graphs in $L(T)$ such that $g \to^{GK} g'$. Then $U(g) \to^{GK}_t U(g')$.* ∎

5.10 PROPOSITION. *If every graph in $L(T)$ is acyclic, then $L(T,R)$ is tree-reducible. In particular, a graphical term rewrite system is tree-reducible.* ∎

5.11 PROPOSITION. *For any TreeRS (T,R) and any graph g in $L(T)$, g is a normal form of $L(T,R)$ iff $U(g)$ is a normal form of (T,R).* ∎

Thus in a graphical term rewrite system $L(T,R)$, everything which can happen can also happen in the term rewrite system, and all the normal forms are the same. Graph-reducibility may fail, however, since it may be that for some graph g, $U(g)$ has a normal form but g does not.

5.12 THEOREM. *Every weakly regular TRS is graph-reducible.*

PROOF. Let (T,R) be a weakly regular TRS. Let g be a graph of $L(T,R)$ such that $U(g)$ has a normal form. Proposition 5.7 relates the Gross-Knuth reduction sequences for g and $U(g)$ in the following way.

$$g \xrightarrow{GK} g_1 \xrightarrow{GK} g_2 \xrightarrow{GK} \cdots$$

$$U(g) \xrightarrow{GK}_t U(g_1) \xrightarrow{GK}_t U(g_2) \xrightarrow{GK}_t \cdots$$

It is a standard result that for regular TRSs, Gross-Knuth reduction is normalising (Klop [1980]), and the proof carries over immediately to weakly regular TreeRSs. Therefore the bottom line of the diagram terminates with some tree $U(g')$ in normal form such that g reduces to g' in $L(T,R)$. Therefore g' is a normal form of g, and (T,R) is graph-reducible. ∎

5.13 NON-LEFT-LINEARITY.

We shall now discuss non-left-linearity, and indicate why we excluded non-left-linear TRSs from consideration. In term rewriting theory, for a term to match a non-linear left-hand side, the subterms corresponding to all the occurrences of a repeated variable must be identical.

Our method of using empty nodes to represent the variables of term rewrite rules suggests a very different semantics for non-left-linear rules. Our representation of a term rule $A(x,x) \to B$ would be (n:A(x:⊥,x), n, x). This will only match a subgraph of the form a:A(b: ..., b). That is, the subgraphs matched by the repeated variable must be not merely textually equal, but identical - the very same nodes. If one is implementing graph rewriting as a computational mechanism in its own right, rather than considering it merely as an optimisation of term rewriting, then this form of non-left-linearity may be useful. However, it is not the same as non-left-linearity for term rules.

To introduce a concept more akin to the non-left-linearity of term rules, we could use variables in graphs, just as for terms, instead of empty nodes. A meaning must then be chosen for the matching of a graph A(Var1,Var1) where Var1 is a variable symbol, occurring at two different nodes. Two possibilities naturally suggest themselves. The subgraphs rooted at nodes matched by the same variable may be required to be equivalent, or they may only be required to be tree-equivalent. The latter definition is closer to the term rewriting concept.

When a variable occurs twice or more on the left-hand side of a rule, there is also a problem of deciding which of the subgraphs matched by it is referred to by its occurrences on the right-hand side. One method would be to cause those subgraphs to be first coalesced, replacing the equivalence or tree-equivalence which the matching detected by pointer equality. This technique may be useful in implementing logic programming languages, where non-linearity is much more commonly used than in functional term rewriting. Further investigation of the matter is outside the scope of the present paper.

Lastly, we note that although some term rewriting languages, such as SASL (Turner [1979b]) and Miranda (Turner [1986]), allow non-left-linear rules, they generally interpret the implied equality test neither as textual equality, nor as pointer equality, but as the equality operator of the language (although pointer equality may be used as an optimisation). In these languages, any program containing non-left-linear rules can be transformed to one which does not.

6. Normalising Strategies.

In this section we define the notion of an evaluation strategy in a general setting which includes term and graph rewrite systems. We then study the relationships between strategies for term rewrite systems and for the corresponding graph systems.

6.1 DEFINITION. (i) An *abstract reduction system* (*ARS*) is a pair $(O, \rightarrow)$, where O is a set of *objects* and $\rightarrow$ is a binary relation on O. This notion abstracts from term and graph rewrite systems. The transitive reflexive closure of $\rightarrow$ is denoted by $\rightarrow^*$.

(ii) An element x of an ARS is a *normal form* (nf) if for no y does one have $x \rightarrow y$.

(iii) An element x *has a normal form* if $x \rightarrow^* y$ and y is a normal form.

(iv) A *reduction sequence* of an ARS is a sequence $x_0 \rightarrow x_1 \rightarrow ... \rightarrow x_n$. The *length* of this sequence is n. A sequence of length 0 is *empty*. ■

6.2 DEFINITION. (i) Given an ARS $(O, \rightarrow)$, a *strategy* for this system is a function S which takes each $x \in O$ to a set $S(x)$ of nonempty finite reduction sequences, each beginning with x. Note that S can be empty.

(ii) S is *deterministic* if, for all x, $S(x)$ contains at most one element.

(iii) S is a *one-step strategy* (or *1-strategy*) if for every x in O, every member of $S(x)$ has length 1.

(iv) Write $x \rightarrow_S y$ if $S(x)$ contains a reduction sequence ending with y. By abuse of notation, we may write $x \rightarrow_S y$ to denote some particular but unspecified member of $S(x)$.

(v) An S-*sequence* is a reduction sequence of the form $x_0 \to_S x_1 \to_S x_2 \to_S \ldots$

(vi) S is *normalising* if for all x having a normal form any sequence

$$x_0 \to_S x_1 \to_S x_2 \to_S \ldots$$

must eventually terminate with a normal form. ■

6.3 DEFINITION. (i) Let S be a strategy of an ARS $(O, \to)$. *Quasi*-S is the strategy defined by:

quasi-S(x) = $\{x \to^* x' \to_S y \mid x' \text{ in } O\}$.

Thus a quasi-S path is an S-path diluted with arbitrary reduction steps.

(ii) A strategy S is *hypernormalising* if quasi-S is normalising. ■

A 1-strategy for a TreeRS or GRS can be specified as a function which takes the objects of the system to some subset of its redexes. This will be done from now on.

6.4 DEFINITION. Let S be a 1-strategy for a TreeRS (T,R). The strategy S_L for the lifted graph rewrite system L(T,R) is defined by $S_L(g) = u_g(S(U(g)))$. ■

For 1-strategies on TreeRSs, this is a natural definition of lifting. For multi-step strategies, it is less clear how to define a lifting, and we do not do so in this paper.

Although a 1-strategy for a TreeRS may be normalising, its lifting may not be. This may be because the lifting of the TreeRS does not preserve normal forms (e.g. as in example 5.4), or for more subtle reasons, such as in the following example.

6.5 EXAMPLE. Consider the following TreeRS:

Function symbols: A (binary), B, 1, 2 (nullary).

Rules: $1 \to 2$, $2 \to 1$, $A(x,y) \to B$.

By stipulating that A is binary and B, 1, and 2 are nullary, we mean, as discussed following definitions 3.7 and 4.1, that trees not conforming to these arities are not included in the system. Define a strategy S as follows (where the redexes chosen by S are boldfaced):

$$A(\mathbf{1},1) \to A(2,1) \qquad A(2,\mathbf{2}) \to A(2,1)$$

$$A(x,y) \to B, \text{ if neither of the preceding cases applies}$$

S takes the tree A(1,1) to normal form B in two steps. S_L takes the graph A(x:1,x) to A(x:2,x) and back again in an infinite loop.

The next theorem shows that if a 1-strategy S for a TreeRS is hypernormalising, then S_L is hypernormalising for the corresponding GRS.

6.6 THEOREM. *Let (T,R) be a TreeRS and let S be a 1-strategy for it. Let (G,R') be the lifting of (T,R). If S is hypernormalising then S_L is hypernormalising.*

PROOF. Assume S is hypernormalising. Let g be a graph in G having a normal form, and consider a quasi-S_L reduction sequence starting from g. By proposition 5.7 and the definition of S_L, we can construct the following diagram, where the top line is the quasi-S_L reduction sequence:

Since g has a normal form, so does U(g), so since quasi-S is normalising, the bottom line must stop at some point, with a normal form of U(g). Therefore the top line also stops, and must do so with a graph which unravels to the normal form in the bottom line. ■

6.7 EXAMPLE. The converse does not hold. If S_L is hypernormalising, S need not be. Consider the following TRS.

Function symbols: A (binary), B (nullary)

Rules: $A(x,y) \to B$ $\qquad$ $A(x,y) \to A(x,x)$

Every non-normal form of this system has the form $A(\alpha,\beta)$ for some terms α and β. Let S be the strategy:

$A(\alpha,\beta) \to_S A(\alpha,\alpha)$ $\qquad$ (if $\alpha \neq \beta$)

$A(\alpha,\alpha) \to_S B$

The first S_L-step in any quasi-S_L-sequence will produce either a graph of the form $A(x:\alpha,x)$ or the normal form B. In the former case, whatever extra steps are then inserted, the result can only be either another term of the same form or B. In the former case, the next S_L-step will reach B. Therefore S_L is hypernormalising. However, S is not hypernormalising. A counterexample is provided by the term $A(A(B,B),B)$. An infinite quasi-S sequence beginning with this term is:

$$A(A(B,B),B) \to_S A(A(B,B),A(B,B)) \to A(A(B,B),B) \to_S A(A(B,B),A(B,B)) \to ...$$

6.8 COROLLARY. *If a TreeRS (T,R) has a hypernormalising 1-strategy then it is graph reducible.*

PROOF. By theorem 6.5 the lifting (G,R) of the TreeRS has a normalising strategy. Now assume $U(g) = t$. Suppose g has no nf. Then the S_L path of g is infinite. This gives, by the construction of 6.6, an infinite quasi-S-path of t, hence t has no normal form. ■

An application of this result is that strongly sequential TRSs (in the sense of Huet and Lévy [1979]) are graph reducible. This follows from their theorem that the 1-strategy which chooses any needed redex is hypernormalising.

The condition that a strategy be hypernormalising is unnecessarily strong. Inspection of the proofs of the preceding theorem and corollary shows that the following weaker concept suffices.

6.9 DEFINITION. (i) Let S be a 1-strategy of a TreeRS (T,R). Then *sib-S* is the strategy defined by:

$$sib\text{-}S(x) = \{ x \to_S y \to^* z \mid \text{the sequence } y \to^* z \text{ consists of siblings of } S(x)\}.$$

That is, a sib-S path is an S-path diluted with arbitrary sib-steps from the reduction relation.

(ii) A strategy S is *sib-normalising* if sib-S is normalising. ■

6.10 THEOREM. *Let (T,R) be a TreeRS and let S be a 1-strategy for it. Let (G,R') be the lifting of (T,R). If S is sib-normalising then S_L is sib-normalising and (T,R) is graph-reducible.*

PROOF. Immediate from the proofs of theorem 6.6 and corollary 6.8. ■

7. Conclusion.

Graph rewriting is an efficient way to perform term rewriting. We have shown:

1. Soundness: for all TRSs, graph rewriting cannot give incorrect results.
2. Completeness: for weakly regular TRSs, graph rewriting gives all results.
3. Many normalising strategies (the hypernormalising, or even the sib-normalising ones) on terms can be lifted to graphs to yield normalising strategies there. In particular, for strongly sequential term rewrite systems, the strategy of contracting needed redexes can be lifted to graphs.

We have also given counterexamples illustrating incompleteness for non-weakly regular TRSs and for liftings of non-sib-normalising strategies.

References.

Barendregt, H.P.
    [1984]   *The Lambda Calculus: its Syntax and Semantics* (revised edition), North-Holland, Amsterdam.
Barendregt, H.P., M.C.J.D. van Eekelen, J.R.W. Glauert, J.R. Kennaway, M.J. Plasmeijer and M.R. Sleep
    [1986]   Term graph rewriting, Report 87, Department of Computer Science, University of Nijmegen, and also as Report SYS-C87-01, School of Information Systems, University of East Anglia.
    [1987]   Towards an intermediate language based on graph rewriting, these proceedings.
van den Broek, P.M. and G.F. van der Hoeven
    [1986]   Combinatorgraph reduction and the Church-Rosser theorem, preprint INF-86-15, Department of Informatics, Twente University of Technology.
Ehrig, H.
    [1979]   Introduction to the algebraic theory of graph grammars, in: *Graph grammars and their Applications in Computer Science and Biology*, ed. V. Claus, H. Ehrig, and G.Rozenberg. Lecture notes in Computer Science 73, Springer, Berlin, 1-69.
Glauert, J.R.W., J.R. Kennaway and M.R. Sleep
    [1987]   Category theoretic concepts of graph rewriting and garbage collection, in preparation, School of Information Systems, University of East Anglia.
Huet, G. and Lévy, J.J.
    [1979]   Call-by-need computations in non-ambiguous term rewriting systems, Report 359, IRIA-Laboria, B.P. 105, 78150 Le Chesney, France.
Kennaway, J.R.
    [1984]   An outline of some results of Staples on optimal reduction orders in replacement systems, Report CSA/19/1984, School of Information Systems, University of East Anglia, Norwich, England.
Klop, J.W.
    [1980]   *Combinatory Reduction Systems*, Mathematical Centre Tracts n.127, Mathematical Centre, Kruislaan 413, 1098 SJ Amsterdam.
Raoult, J.C.
    [1984]   On graph rewritings, *Theor. Comput. Sci.* 32, 1-24.
Peyton Jones, S.L.
    [1987]   *The Implementation of Functional Languages*, Prentice-Hall, London, to appear.
Staples, J.
    [1980a]   Computation on graph-like expressions, *Theor. Comput. Sci.* 10, 171-185.
    [1980b]   Optimal evaluations of graph-like expressions, *Theor. Comput. Sci.* 10, 297-316.
    [1980c]   Speeding up subtree replacement systems, *Theor. Comput. Sci.* 11, 39-47.
Turner, D.A.
    [1979a]   A new implementation technique for applicative languages, in: *Software: Practice and Experience* 9, 31-49.
    [1979b]   SASL Language Manual, "combinators" version, University of St. Andrews, U.K.
    [1986]   Miranda System Manual, Research Software Ltd., 1986.
Wadsworth, C.P.
    [1971]   Semantics and Pragmatics of the Lambda Calculus, D.Phil. thesis, Programming Research Group, Oxford University.

Towards
an Intermediate Language
based on
Graph Rewriting

H.P. Barendregt[2], M.C.J.D. van Eekelen[2], J.R.W. Glauert[1],
J.R. Kennaway[1], M.J. Plasmeijer[2] and M.R. Sleep[1].

[1]School of Information Systems, University of East Anglia, Norwich, Norfolk NR4 7TJ, U.K.,
partially supported by the U.K. ALVEY project,
[2]Computing Science Department, University of Nijmegen, Toernooiveld 1, 6525 ED Nijmegen, The Netherlands,
partially supported by the Dutch Parallel Reduction Machine Project.

Abstract.

Lean is an experimental language for specifying computations in terms of graph rewriting. It is based on an alternative to Term Rewriting Systems (TRS) in which the terms are replaced by graphs. Such a Graph Rewriting System (GRS) consists of a set of graph rewrite rules which specify how a graph may be rewritten. Besides supporting functional programming, Lean also describes imperative constructs and allows the manipulation of cyclic graphs. Programs may exhibit non-determinism as well as parallelism. In particular, Lean can serve as an intermediate language between declarative languages and machine architectures, both sequential and parallel.

1. Introduction.

Emerging technologies (VLSI, wafer-scale integration), new machine architectures, new language proposals and new implementation methods [VEG84] have inspired the computer science community to consider new models of computation. Several of these developments have little in common with the familiar Turing machine model. It is our belief that in order to be able to compare these developments, it is necessary to have a novel computational model that integrates graph manipulation, rewriting, and imperative overwriting. In this paper we present Lean, an experimental language based on such a model. In our approach we have extended Term Rewriting Systems [O'DO85, KLO85] to a model of general graph rewriting. With this model it should be possible to reason about programs, to prove correctness, and to port programs to different machines. The language as presented here does not yet meet all these goals, but we believe that it is a good step in the right direction.

A Lean computation is specified by an initial graph and a set of rules used to rewrite the graph to its final result. The rules contain graph patterns that may match some part of the graph. If the graph matches a rule it can be rewritten according to the specification in that rule. This specification makes it possible to first construct an additional graph structure and then link it into the existing graph by redirecting arcs.

Lean programs may be non-deterministic. The semantics also allows parallel evaluation where candidate rewrites do not interfere. There are few restrictions on Lean graphs (cycles are allowed and even disconnected graphs). Lean can easily describe functional graph rewriting in which only the root of the subgraph matching a pattern may be overwritten. Through non-root overwrites and use of global nodeids in disconnected patterns imperative features are also available.

In this paper we first introduce Lean informally. Then we show how a Lean program can be transformed to a program in canonical form with the same meaning. The semantics of Lean is explained using this canonical form. The semantics adopted generalises Staples' model of graph rewriting [STA80], allowing, for example, multiple redirections. A formal description of the graph rewriting model used in this paper can be found in [BAR87], as it applies to the special case of purely declarative term rewriting. After explaining the semantics we give some program examples to illustrate the power of Lean. The syntax of Lean and the canonical form is given in appendix A. Appendix B contains a summary of the predefined Lean rules.

2. General description of Lean.

2.1 Lean graphs.

The object that is manipulated in Lean is a directed graph called the *data graph*. When there is no confusion, the data graph is simply called *the graph*. Each node in the graph has an unique identifier associated with it (the *node identifier* or *nodeid*). Furthermore a node consists of a *symbol* and a possibly empty sequence of nodeids which define arcs to nodes in the graph. We do not assume that symbols have fixed arities. The data graph is a *closed* graph, that is, it contains no variables. It may be cyclic and may have disjoint components. This class of data graphs is, abstractly, identical to that discussed in [BAR87]. We refer to that paper for a formal discussion of the precise connection between graphs and terms.

Programming with pictures is rather inconvenient so we have chosen a linear notation for graphs. In this notation we use brackets to indicate tree structure and repeated nodeids to express sharing, as shown in the examples below. Nodeids are prefixed with the character '@'. Symbols begin with an upper-case character.

Lean notation: Graphical equivalent:

```
Hd (Cons 0 Nil);
```

```
@Cyclic: F @Cyclic;
```

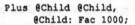

```
Plus @Child @Child,              @Child:Fac
     @Child: Fac 1000;
```

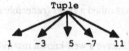

```
Tuple 1 -3 5 -7 11;
```

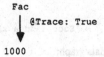

```
Fac 1000,                        @Trace: True
@Trace: TRUE;
```

2.2 Lean programs.

A *Lean program* consists of a set of *rewrite rules* including a *start rule*. A rewrite rule specifies a possible transformation of a given graph. The initial graph is not specified in a Lean program (see also section 4.2).

The left-hand-side of a rewrite rule consists of a Lean graph which is called a *redex pattern*. The right-hand-side consists of a (possibly empty) Lean graph called the *contractum pattern* and, optionally, a set of *redirections*. The patterns may be disconnected graphs and they are *open*, that is, they may contain *nodeid variables*. These are denoted by identifiers starting with a lower-case letter. Nodeids of the data graph may also occur in the rules. These are called *global nodeids*. When there can be no confusion with the nodeids in the data graph, we sometimes refer to the nodeid variables and the global nodeids in the rules just as nodeids. Here is an example program:

```
Hd (Cons a b)            → a                          ;

Fac 0                    → 1                          |
Fac n:INT                → *I n (Fac (-I n 1))        ;

F (F x)                  → x                          ;

Start                    → Fac (Hd (Cons 1000 Nil))   ;
```

The first symbol in a redex pattern is called the *function symbol*. Rules starting with the same function symbol are collected together forming a *rule-group*. The members of a rule-group are separated by a 'I'. Note that function symbols may also occur at other positions than the head of the pattern. A symbol which does not occur at the head of any pattern in the program is called a *constructor symbol*.

2.3 Rewriting the data graph.

The initial graph of a Lean program is rewritten to a final form by a sequence of applications of individual rewrite rules. A rule can only be applied if its redex pattern matches a subgraph of the data graph. A redex pattern in general consists of variables and symbols. An *instance* of a redex pattern is a subgraph of the data graph, such that there is a mapping from the pattern to that subgraph which preserves the node structure and is the identity on constants. This mapping is also called a *match*. The subgraph which matches a redex pattern is called a *redex* (*reducible expression*) for the rule concerned.

We will use the following rules which have a well-known meaning, as a running example to illustrate several concepts of Lean.

```
Add Zero z            → z                    | (1)
Add (Succ a) z        → Succ (Add a z)       ; (2)
```

Now assume that we have the following data graph:

```
Add (Succ Zero) (Add (Succ (Succ Zero)) Zero);
```

There are two redexes:

$\underline{\qquad}$ $\underline{\qquad}$ $\underline{\quad a \quad}$ $\underline{\qquad\qquad z \qquad\qquad}$	
Add (Succ Zero) (Add (Succ (Succ Zero)) Zero)	redex matching rule 2

$\underline{\qquad}$ $\underline{\qquad}$ $\underline{\qquad a \qquad}$ $\underline{\quad z \quad}$	
Add (Succ Zero) (Add (Succ (Succ Zero)) Zero)	redex matching rule 2

In graphical form this is:

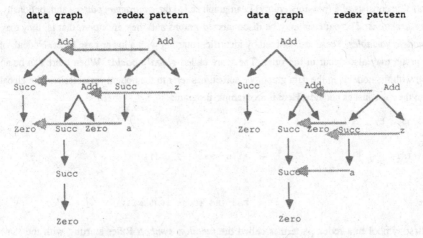

Note that there may be several rules for which there are redexes in the graph. A rule may match several redexes and a redex can match several rules. For instance, in the example above there is only one rule which matches any part of the data graph, but it matches two redexes. In general, therefore, there are many rewriting sequences for a given graph.

Evaluation of a Lean program is controlled by a *rewriting strategy*. In its most general form:

(1) It decides which rewritings to perform.

163

(2) It decides when to perform no further rewritings. The graph at this point is said to be in *strategy normal form*, or briefly, in *normal form*.

(3) It specifies what part of the resulting graph is the *outcome* of the computation.

For the purposes of graphical implementations of functional languages, strategies need only consider the subgraph of nodes accessible from the data root, for the purposes of identifying both redexes and terminal states. However, more general applications of Lean may not wish to be constrained in this way: for example, graphical rewrite rules may be used to represent non-terminating behaviours of practical interest such as operating systems.

The choices made by a rewriting strategy may affect the efficiency of rewriting, as well as its termination properties. In the future we aim to incorporate facilities into Lean to permit programmer control of strategy where necessary.

Once the strategy has chosen a particular redex and rule, rewriting is performed. The first step is to create an instantiation of the graph pattern specified on the right-hand-side of the chosen rule. This instantiation is called the *contractum*. In general this contractum has links to the original graph since references to nodeid variables from the left-hand-side are linked to the corresponding nodes identified during matching. A new data graph is finally constructed by redirecting some arcs from the original graph to the contractum. In most cases all arcs to the root node of the redex are redirected to the root node of the contractum as in Staples' model [STA80]. This has an effect similar to "overwriting" the root of the redex with the root of the contractum. This is what happens when no redirections are given explicitly in the rule. Explicit redirection of arbitrary nodes is also possible.

The process of performing one rewrite step is often called a *reduction*. The graph after one reduction is called the *result* of the reduction. Initially, the data graph contains a node with the symbol start. Hence, the rewriting process can begin with matching the start rule and hereafter rewriting is performed repeatedly until the strategy has transformed the graph to one which it deems to be in normal form.

[BAR87] gives a formal discussion of how graph rewrite rules with root-only redirection model term rewriting, and proves certain soundness and completeness results. The definition of rewriting given in that paper only covers rules of this form, but the extension of the formal description to the general cases of multiple and/or non-root redirection is straightforward.

The data graph of the previous example can be rewritten in the following way:

```
Add (Succ Zero) (Add (Succ (Succ Zero)) Zero)          → (2)
Succ (Add Zero (Add (Succ (Succ Zero)) Zero))          → (1)
Succ (Add (Succ (Succ Zero)) Zero)                     → (2)
Succ (Succ (Add (Succ Zero) Zero))                     → (2)
Succ (Succ (Succ (Add Zero Zero)))                     → (1)
Succ (Succ (Succ Zero))
```

Note that in this example the graph was actually a tree, and remained a tree throughout. There was no difference with a Term Rewriting System. In the following example there is a data graph in which parts are shared. Rewriting the shared part will reduce the number of rewriting steps compared to an equivalent Term Rewriting System.

```
Add @X @X,          @X: Add (Succ Zero) Zero                    → (2)
Add @X @X,          @X: Succ (Add Zero Zero)                    → (1)
Add @X @X,          @X: Succ Zero                               → (2)
Succ (Add @Z @X),   @X: Succ @Z,              @Z: Zero          → (1)
Succ (Succ Zero)
```

2.4 Predefined delta rules.

For practical reasons it is convenient that rules for performing arithmetic on primitive types (numbers, characters etc.) are predefined and efficiently implemented. In Lean a number of basic constructors for primitive types such as INT, REAL and CHAR are predefined. Representatives of these types can be denoted: for instance 5 (an integer), 5.0 (a real), '5' (a character). Basic functions, called *delta rules*, are predefined on these basic types.

The actual implementation of a representative of a basic type, is hidden for the Lean programmer. It is possible to denote a representative, pass a representative to a function or delta-rule and check whether or not an argument is of a certain type in the redex pattern.

```
Nfib 0              → 1                                                     |
Nfib 1              → 1                                                     |
Nfib n:INT          → ++I (+I (Nfib (-I n 1)) (Nfib (-I n 2)))             ;
```

In this example '0', '1' and '2' are denotations for some representation of the numbers 0, 1 and 2, '+I', '-I' and '++I' are function symbols for predefined delta rules defined on these representations. Hence, an integer consists of the unary constructor INT and an unknown representation. Note that in general one is allowed to specify just the constructor in the redex pattern of a rule. The value can be passed to a function by passing the corresponding nodeid (n in the example).

These predefined rules are however not strictly necessary. For instance, one could define numbers as: INT Zero to denote 0, INT (Succ Zero) to denote 1, INT (Succ (Succ Zero)) to denote 2 etc., and define a function for doing addition

```
PlusI (INT x) (INT y)           → INT (Add x y)                            ;
```

where Add is our running example. This kind of definition makes it possible to do arithmetic in a convenient way. However, for an efficient implementation one would probably not choose such a Peano-like representation of numbers, but prefer to use the integer and real representation and the arithmetic available on the computer.

3. Translating to canonical form.

Lean contains syntactic sugar intended to make programs easier to read and write. Explaining the semantics of Lean will be done with a form with all syntactic sugar removed known as *Canonical Lean*.

In this section we show how a Lean program can be transformed to its canonical form. Canonical Lean programs are valid Lean programs and are unaffected by this translation procedure. Every Lean program can be seen as a shorthand for its canonical form. Note that this section is all about syntax. The semantics of the canonical form are explained in section 4.

In the canonical form every node has a definition and definitions are not nested. Every redirection, including any redirection of the root, is done explicitly and in patterns all arguments of constructors are specified. In this canonical form a rewrite rule has the following syntax:

```
Graph                →            [ Graph , ] Redirections
```

The first Graph is the redex pattern. The second is the optional contractum pattern. Each pattern is represented as a list of node definitions of the form:

```
Nodeid:  Symbol { Nodeid }
```

Braces mean zero or more occurrences. The initial *Nodeid* identifies the node, *Symbol* is some function or constructor symbol and the sequence of nodeids identifies zero or more child nodes. Occurrences of nodeids before a colon are *defining* occurrences. Every nodeid must have at most one defining occurrence within a rule. Defining occurrences of global nodeids are allowed on the left-hand-side only. Within a rule a nodeid which appears on the right-hand-side must either have a definition on the right-hand-side or it must also appear on the left-hand-side.

3.1 Add explicit nodeids and flatten.

In the canonical form all nodes have explicit nodeids and there are no nested node definitions. Hence in each rule we have to introduce a new unique nodeid variable for every node that does not yet have one. Every nested node definition in the rule is then replaced by an application of the corresponding nodeid variable, and the definitions are moved to the outer level. Applying this transformation to our running example gives:

```
x: Add     y    z,
y: Zero                          → z                                          |
x: Add     y    z,
y: Succ    a                     → m: Succ n,
                                   n: Add   a z                               ;
```

All arguments of symbols (such as Add and Succ) have now become nodeids and brackets are no longer needed.

3.2 Specify the arguments of constructors.

In Lean one may write the following function which checks to see if a list is empty:

```
x: IsNil n,
n: Nil          →              t: TRUE                                        |
x: IsNil n,
n: Cons         →              t: FALSE                                       ;
```

Cons is a binary constructor symbol, but in Lean one may omit the specification of the arguments if they are not used elsewhere in the rule. This is not allowed in the canonical form hence the arguments are made explicit by introducing two new nodeid variables. Transformation of the example above will give:

```
x: IsNil n,
n: Nil          →          t: TRUE                            |
x: IsNil n,
n: Cons y z     →          t: FALSE                           ;
```

3.3 Make root redirections explicit.

The meaning of both rules in the running example is that the root of the pattern is redirected to the root of the contractum. Redirections are always made explicit in the canonical form. If no redirections are specified explicitly, a redirection is introduced to redirect the redex root to the contractum root. Note that if the right-hand-side of a rule consists only of a nodeid, the root of the redex is redirected to this nodeid. The running example with explicit redirections now becomes:

```
x: Add     y    z,
y: Zero              → x := z                             |
x: Add     y    z,
y: Succ    a         → m: Succ n,
                       n: Add  a z,
                       x := m                             ;
```

3.4 Define delta rules.

The predefined rules which are used in the program have to be explicitly added. We can assume that these rules are already in canonical form.

4. Semantics of Lean.

4.1 Graph terminology.

- Let F be a set of symbols and N be a set of nodes.
- Further, let C be a function (the *contents function*) from N to $F \times N^*$.
- Then C specifies a *Lean Graph* over F and N.
- If node n has contents $F\ n_1\ n_2\ ...\ n_k$ we say the node contains *symbol* F and *arguments* $n_1, n_2, ..., n_k$.
- There is a distinguished node in the graph which is the *root* of the graph.

In standard graph theory, a Lean graph is a form of directed graph in which each node is labelled with a symbol, and its set of out-arcs is given an ordering. In Lean nodes are denoted by their names, i.e. their nodeids. The canonical form defined in section 3 can be regarded as a tabulation of the contents function. We will explain the semantics of Lean using this canonical form.

4.2 The initial graph.

The initial graph is not specified in a program. It always takes the following form:

```
@DataRoot:    Graph @StartNode @GlobId₁ @GlobId₂ ... @GlobIdₘ,
@StartNode:   Start,
@GlobId₁:     Initial,
@GlobId₂:     Initial,
...
@GlobIdₘ:     Initial;
```

The root of the initial graph contains the nodeid of the start node which initially contains the symbol Start. The root node will always contain the root of the graph to be rewritten. Furthermore the root node contains all global nodeids addressed in the Lean rules. The corresponding nodes are initialised with the symbol Initial.

4.3 Operational semantics for rewriting.

Let G be a Lean graph, and R the set of rewrite rules. A reduction option, or *redop*, of G is a triple T which consists of a redex g, a rule r and a match μ. The match μ is a mapping from the nodes of the redex pattern p to the nodes of the graph G such that for every node x of p, if $C_p(x) = s\ x_1\ x_2 ... x_n$ then $C_g(\mu(x)) = s\ \mu(x_1)\ \mu(x_2) ... \mu(x_n)$. That is, μ preserves node structure. A redop introduces an available choice for rewriting the graph. A redop that is chosen is called a *rewrite* of the graph. The process of performing a rewrite is also called *rewriting*.

The contractum pattern may contain nodeid variables which are not present in the redex pattern. These correspond to the identifiers of new nodes to be introduced during rewriting. The mapping μ' is introduced taking as its domain the set of nodeid variables which only appear in the contractum pattern. Each of these is mapped to a distinct, new, nodeid which does not appear in G or R.

The domains of μ and μ' are distinct, but every nodeid variable in the contractum pattern is in the domain of one or the other. In order to compute the result of a rewrite one applies the mapping μ'' formed by combining μ and μ', to the contractum pattern resulting in the *contractum*.

Finally the new graph is constructed by taking the union of the old graph and the contractum, replacing nodeids in this union (and in the case that global nodeids are mentioned also in the rules) as specified by the redirections in the rewrite rule of the chosen redop.

Hence rewriting involves a number of steps:

1. A redop is chosen by the rewriting strategy. This gives us a redex in the graph G, a rule which specifies how to rewrite the redex and a mapping μ.

2. The contractum is constructed in the following way.
   - invent new nodeids (not present in G or R) for each variable found only in the contractum pattern.

This mapping is called μ'.

- apply μ", the combination of μ and μ', to the contractum pattern of the rule yielding the contractum graph C. Note that the contractum pattern, and hence C, may be empty.

3. The new graph G' is constructed by taking the union of G and C.

4. Each redirection in a rule takes the form O := N. In terms of the syntactic representation, this is performed by substituting N for every applied occurrence of O in the graph G' and in the rules R. The definition of O still remains. The nodeids O and N are determined by applying μ" to the left-hand-side and the right-hand-side of the redirection. All redirections specified in the rule are done in parallel. This results in the new graph G".

The strategy will start with a rewrite rule which matches the symbol start in the initial graph. When a computation terminates, its *outcome* is that part of the final graph which is accessible from the root. Thus a "garbage collection" is assumed to be performed at the end of the computation only. A real implementation may optimise this by collecting nodes earlier, if it can predict that so doing will not affect the final outcome. Which nodes can be collected earlier will in general depend on the the rule-set of the program and the computation strategy being used. Note that before the computation has terminated, nodes which are inaccessible from the root may yet have an effect on the final outcome, so they cannot necessarily be considered garbage. For certain strategies and rule-sets they will be, but inaccessibility is not in itself the definition of garbage.

Redirection of global nodeids has as a consequence that all references to the original global nodeid have to be changed. This includes the references to global nodeids made in the rewrite rules. Hence global nodeids can be viewed as *global* variables (they have a global scope), where nodeid variables are *local* variables (they have a meaning only within a single rule).

4.4 A small example.

We return to our running example with a small initial graph and see how rewriting proceeds. The rewriting strategy we choose will rewrite until the data graph contains no redexes only examining nodes accessible from the @DataRoot.

```
x: Add   y   z,
y: Zero                  →  x := z                              |  (1)
x: Add   y   z,
y: Succ a                →  m: Succ n,
                            n: Add  a z,
                            x := m                              ;  (2)
x: Start                 →  m: Add  n o,
                            n: Succ o,
                            o: Zero,
                            x := m                              ;  (3)
```

Initially we have the following graph:

```
@DataRoot : Graph @StartNode,
@StartNode: Start;
```

We now follow the rewrite steps.

1. The start node is the only redex matching rule (3). The mapping is trivial: $\mu(x) = $ @StartNode and the redex in the graph is:

```
@StartNode: Start;
```

2. Applying μ to the contractum scheme will leave this as it is while x does not appear in it. For all variables in the scheme we invent new nodeids and map the variables as follows: $\mu'(m) = $ @A, $\mu'(n) = $ @B, $\mu'(o) = $ @C, $\mu'(p) = $ @C. The contractum can now be constructed:

```
@A: Add  @B @C,
@B: Succ @C,
@C: Zero;
```

3. The union of C and G is G':

```
@DataRoot : Graph @StartNode,
@StartNode: Start,
@A: Add  @B @C,
@B: Succ @C,
@C: Zero;
```

4. We have to redirect $\mu''(x) = $ @StartNode to $\mu''(m) = $ @A. All applied occurrences of @StartNode will be replaced by occurrences to @A. The graph G" after rewriting is now:

```
@DataRoot : Graph @A,
@StartNode: Start,
@A: Add  @B @C,
@B: Succ @C,
@C: Zero;
```

This completes one rewrite. The start node will not be examined by the strategy anymore. Therefore it can be considered as garbage and it will be thrown away. The strategy will not stop yet because the graph still contains a redex accessible from the @DataRoot.

1. The strategy will choose the only redop. It matches rule 2: $\mu(x) = $ @A, $\mu(y) = $ @B, $\mu(z) = $ @C, $\mu(a) = $ @C;

2. Invent new nodeids and map the variables as follows: $\mu'(m) = $ @D, $\mu'(n) = $ @E. The contractum can now be constructed:

```
@D: Succ @E,
@E: Add  @C @C;
```

3. The union of C and G is G':

```
@DataRoot: Graph @A,
@A: Add  @B @C,
@B: Succ @C,
@C: Zero,
@D: Succ @E,
@E: Add  @C @C;
```

4. We have to redirect $\mu''(x) = $ @A to $\mu''(m) = $ @D. The graph G" after rewriting and removing garbage is:

```
@DataRoot: Graph @D,
@C: Zero,
@D: Succ @E,
@E: Add  @C @C;
```

It is now clear how this process may continue: @E is a redex and it matches rule 1: $\mu(x) = $ @E, $\mu(y) = $ @C, $\mu(z) = $ @C. The strategy chooses this redop, there is no new contractum graph but just a single redirection which takes $\mu''(x) = $ @E to $\mu''(z) = $ @C yielding the expected normal form:

```
@DataRoot: Graph @D,
@C: Zero,
@D: Succ @C;
```

5. Some Lean programs.

5.1 Merging lists.

The following Lean rules can merge two ordered lists of integers (without duplicated elements) into a single ordered list (without duplicated elements).

```
Merge    Nil      Nil        → Nil                        |
Merge    f:Cons   Nil        → f                          |
Merge    Nil      s:Cons     → s                          |
Merge    f:(Cons a b)
         s:(Cons c d)        → IF (<I a c)
                                 (Cons a (Merge b s))
                                 (IF (=I a c)
                                    (Merge f d)
                                    (Cons c (Merge f d)))  ;
```

<I, =I and IF are predefined delta rules (see appendix B) with the obvious semantics. Note that the right-hand-side of the last rule uses an application of the argument as a whole as well as its decomposition.

5.2 Higher order functions, currying.

In this example we show how higher-order functions are treated in Lean, by giving the familiar definition of the function Map.

```
Map        f         Nil        → Nil                           |  (1)
Map        f         (Cons a b) → Cons (Ap f a) (Map f b)       ;  (2)
Ap         (*I a)    b          → *I a b                        ;  (3)
Start                           → Map (*I 2) (Cons 3 (Cons 4 Nil)) ;  (4)
```

This can be rewritten, for example, in the following way:

```
Start                                                      → (4)
Map (*I 2) (Cons 3 (Cons 4 Nil))                          → (2)
Cons (Ap @L 3) (Map @L (Cons 4 Nil)),          @L:*I 2    → (3)
Cons (*I 2 3) (Map @L (Cons 4 Nil)),           @L:*I 2    → (*I)
Cons 6 (Map @L (Cons 4 Nil)),                  @L:*I 2    → (2)
```

```
Cons 6 (Cons (Ap @L 4) (Map @L Nil)),              @L:*I 2        → (3)
Cons 6 (Cons (*I 2 4) (Map @L Nil)),               @L:*I 2        → (*I)
Cons 6 (Cons 8 (Map @L Nil)),                      @L:*I 2        → (1)
Cons 6 (Cons 8 Nil)
```

Rule (3) of this example will rewrite (Ap (*I 2) 3) to its uncurried form (*I 2 3) which makes multiplication possible. One will need such an "uncurry" rule for every function which is used in a curried manner. Note that during rewriting the node @L:(*I 2) is shared. In this case sharing only saves space, but not computation.

5.3 Graphs with cycles.

The following example is is a solution for the Hamming problem: it computes an ordered list of all numbers of the form $2^n 3^m$, with n,m ≥ 0. We use the map and merge functions of the previous examples.

```
Ham       → Cons 1 (Merge (Map (*I 2) Ham) (Map (*I 3) Ham))              ;
```

A more efficient solution to this problem can be obtained by means of creating cyclic sharing in the contractum making heavy use of computation already done. The new definition is:

```
x: Ham     → Cons 1 (Merge (Map (*I 2) x) (Map (*I 3) x))                ;
```

5.4 Copying a tree structure.

This example is very straightforward if the structure of tree nodes is known. Here is a program which copies a binary tree structure.

```
Copy       (Bin left right)    → Bin (Copy left) (Copy right)     |
Copy       (Leaf x)            → x                                ;
```

In the present version of Lean it is not possible to copy an arbitrary unknown data structure. We hope to support more general solutions in a future version of Lean.

5.5 Counting specific rewrites via global assignment.

```
r: Hd (Cons a b),
@HdCount: Total n:INT          → newvalue: Total (++I n),
                                 r := a,
                                 @HdCount := newvalue            ;

r: Start                       → nr: Hd (Cons 1 (Cons 2 Nil)),
                                 initvalue: Total 0,
                                 r := nr,
                                 @HdCount := initvalue           ;
```

We are dealing with disconnected graphs and patterns in this example. The global nodeid @HdCount in the graph is addressed in a rewrite rule. The integer value in @HdCount will be increased each time a head of a list is taken. Global nodeids and arbitrary redirections in rewrite rules make other styles of programming possible involving globals and side effects. Here, the retention of the canonical notation forces the user to make his text inelegant. Perhaps a useful danger signal, both to reader and writer?

5.6 Unification using redirection.

This program implements a simple unification algorithm. It operates on representations of two types, returning "cannot unify" in case of failure. The types are contructed from three basic types I, B and Var and a composing constructor Com. Different type variables are represented by distinct nodes. Repeated type variables are represented by shared nodes. References to such a shared node are taken to be references to the same variable.

```
root: Start                              → Unify t1 t2 root,
                                           t1: Com i t1,
                                           t2: Com i (Com i t2),
                                           i: I                       ;

   Unify x                x          r → x
o: Unify t1:(Com x y)     t2:(Com p q) r → n: Com (Unify x p r) (Unify y q r),
                                           o := n, t1 := n, t2 := n   |
o: Unify t1:Var           t2         r → o := t2, t1 := t2           |
o: Unify t1               t2:Var     r → o := t1, t2 := t1           |
   Unify t1:Com           t2:I       r → n: "cannot unify", r := n   |
   Unify t1:Com           t2:B       r → n: "cannot unify", r := n   |
   Unify t1:I             t2:Com     r → n: "cannot unify", r := n   |
   Unify t1:B             t2:Com     r → n: "cannot unify", r := n   |
   Unify t1:I             t2:B       r → n: "cannot unify", r := n   |
   Unify t1:B             t2:I       r → n: "cannot unify", r := n   ;
```

5.7 Combinatory logic.

Here we show the Lean equivalent of a well-known TRS using explicit application: combinatory logic.

```
Ap (Ap (Ap S a) b) c)     → Ap (Ap a c) (Ap b c)                      |
Ap (Ap K a) b)            → a                                         ;

Start         → Ap (Ap (Ap S (Ap K K)) (Ap S K)) (Ap (Ap K K) K))  ;
```

6. Future work.

Lean is the result of collaboration between two research groups: the Dutch Parallel Reduction Machine (DPRM) group at Nijmegen and the Declarative Alvey Compiler Target Language (DACTL) group at UEA. Recognising the current instability of emerging languages and architectures, both groups wish to identify a computational model appropriate to a new generation rewriting model of computing. The DPRM group has developed a subset of Lean, called Clean [BRU87], for the support of purely functional languages. Dactl0 [GLA87] predates Lean, and includes some concepts not present in Lean. In the future, our groups plan to continue to collaborate on further developing and refining the computational model and the Lean language based on it. It is intended that later versions of Lean and Dactl will converge.

Because rewriting strategies have a critical influence on efficiency and outcome, future versions of

Lean aim to offer the programmer explicit control. Strategies should be based mainly on local information so that concurrent evaluation is not constrained. One approach is to employ fine grain control annotations so that a rule may nominate which of the nodes it creates should be considered as roots for future redexes. Dactl0 adopts this approach. Its main advantage is that a simple execution model is obtained. Another approach is to have a high level specification of strategies and a formalism for combining strategies during evaluation. This approach holds out promise for global reasoning [EEK86]. We believe that the way forward should involve a careful combination of these approaches. At the high level formally specified strategy information should be used, allowing analysis and transformation of programs using abstract interpretation techniques. Correctness preserving translation tools would then convert such a program into a form using a small set of well-designed control primitives suitable for efficient parallel implementation.

Besides strategies, there are several other concepts that may be incorporated in Lean in the near future. These include: more general typing; annotations to allow compiler optimisations; interfacing with the outside world; modules and separate compilation facilities; support for unification.

7. Conclusions.

Lean is an experimental language for specifying computations in terms of graph rewriting. It is very powerful since there are few restrictions on the graph that is transformed and the transformations that can be performed.

The graph rewriting model underlying Lean is of independent interest as a general model of computation for parallel architectures. It includes as special cases, more restricted systems, such as Graph Rewriting Systems which model Term Rewriting Systems. For these GRSs certain soundness and completeness results are shown in [BAR87].

Lean is designed to be a useful intermediate language for those language implementations which rely on graph rewriting. Compilers targetted to Lean are being implemented for functional languages. Interpreters for Lean are under development [JAN87]. A first version of a compiler for a restricted subset of Lean (Clean) is now running on a Vax750 (Unix) [BRU87]. The performance is encouraging.

8. Acknowledgements.

We would like to thank Jan-Willem Klop of the Centre for Mathematics and Computer Science in Amsterdam for his explanations, Tom Brus and Maarten van Leer of the University of Nijmegen and Nic Holt of ICL for their valuable comments.

9. References.

[BAR87] Barendregt, H.P., Eekelen, M.C.J.D. van, Glauert, J.R.W., Kennaway, J.R., Plasmeijer, M.J., Sleep, M.R., "Term Graph Reduction", these proceedings, 1987.

[BRU87] Brus, T., Eekelen, M.C.J.D. van, Leer, M. van, Plasmeijer, M.J., "Clean - A Language for Functional Graph Rewriting", University of Nijmegen, Internal Report nr. 95, February 1987.

[EEK86] Eekelen, M.C.J.D. van, Plasmeijer, M.J., "Specification of rewriting strategies in Term Rewriting Systems", University of Nijmegen, Workshop on Graph Reduction, Santa Fe, 1986.

[GLA87] Glauert, J.R.W., Kennaway, J.R., Sleep, M.R., "DACTL: A Computational Model and Compiler Target Language Based on Graph Reduction", University of East Anglia 1987, Internal Report SYS-C87-03.

[JAN87] Jansen, T, "Interpreting Lean", Masters thesis, University of Nijmegen, may 1987.

[KLO85] Klop, J.W., "Term rewriting systems", Notes for the Seminar on Reduction Machines, Ustica 1985, to appear.

[O'DO85] O'Donnell, M.J., "Equational Logic as a Programming Language", Foundations of Computing Series, MIT Press, 1985.

[STA80] Staples, J., "Computation on Graph-like Expressions", Theor. Comp. Sc. 10, North-Holland, 1980, pp. 171-185.

[VEG84] Vegdahl, Steven R., "A Survey of Proposed Architectures for the Execution of Functional Languages", IEEE Transactions on Computers, vol. c-33, no. 12, december 1984.

Appendix A : Syntax

LeanProgram	=	{ RuleGroup }.
RuleGroup	=	Rule { '|' Rule } ';'.
Rule	=	Graph '->' Graph [',' Redirections]	Graph '->' Redirections.
Graph	=	[Nodeid ':'] Node { ',' NodeDefinition }.
NodeDefinition	=	Nodeid ':' Node .
Node	=	Symbol { Term }.
Term	=	Nodeid	[Nodeid ':'] Symbol	[Nodeid ':'] '(' Node ')'.
Redirections	=	Redirection { ',' Redirection }	Nodeid { ',' Redirection }.
Redirection	=	Nodeid ':=' Nodeid.

For the canonical form of Lean replace the following rules in the syntax above;

Rule	=	Graph '->' [Graph ','] Redirections.
Graph	=	NodeDefinition { ',' NodeDefinition }.
Term	=	Nodeid.
Redirections	=	Redirection { ',' Redirection }.

Appendix B : Predefined Delta Rules.

Name	Type		Description
EXP	REAL	-> REAL	exponent
LOG	REAL	-> REAL	logarithm base e
LOG10	REAL	-> REAL	logarithm base 10
SQRT	REAL	-> REAL	square root
POW	(REAL,REAL)	-> REAL	x^y
NOT	BOOL	-> BOOL	invert
AND	(BOOL,BOOL)	-> BOOL	and
OR	(BOOL,BOOL)	-> BOOL	or
XOR	(BOOL,BOOL)	-> BOOL	exclusive or
=B	(BOOL,BOOL)	-> BOOL	equal
<>B	(BOOL,BOOL)	-> BOOL	not equal
+C	(CHAR,CHAR)	-> CHAR	plus
-C	(CHAR,CHAR)	-> CHAR	minus
++C	CHAR	-> CHAR	increment
--C	CHAR	-> CHAR	decrement
=C	(CHAR,CHAR)	-> BOOL	equal
<>C	(CHAR,CHAR)	-> BOOL	not equal
<C	(CHAR,CHAR)	-> BOOL	lower than
>C	(CHAR,CHAR)	-> BOOL	higher than
<=C	(CHAR,CHAR)	-> BOOL	lower or equal
>=C	(CHAR,CHAR)	-> BOOL	higher or equal
+S	(STRING,STRING)	-> STRING	concatenate strings
SLICE	(STRING,INT,INT)	-> STRING	slice string
INDEX	(STRING,INT)	-> CHAR	index string
UPDATE	(STRING,INT,CHAR)	-> STRING	replace char
LENGTH	STRING	-> INT	length of string
=S	(STRING,STRING)	-> BOOL	equal
<>S	(STRING,STRING)	-> BOOL	not equal
<S	(STRING,STRING)	-> BOOL	lower than
>S	(STRING,STRING)	-> BOOL	higher than
<=S	(STRING,STRING)	-> BOOL	lower or equal
>=S	(STRING,STRING)	-> BOOL	higher or equal
RTOI	REAL	-> INT	convert REAL to INT
ITOR	INT	-> REAL	convert INT to REAL
CTOI	CHAR	-> INT	convert CHAR to INT
ITOC	INT	-> CHAR	convert INT to CHAR
ITOS	INT	-> STRING	transform to string
RTOS	REAL	-> STRING	transform to string
BTOS	BOOL	-> STRING	transform to string
CTOS	CHAR	-> STRING	transform to string
ABORT	STRING	-> halt	write string, stop.

Name	Type		Description
IF	(BOOL,*,*)	-> *	normal IF
READLINES	STRING	-> [STRING]	read file
READCHARS	STRING	-> [CHAR]	read file
+I	(INT,INT)	-> INT	plus
-I	(INT,INT)	-> INT	minus
*I	(INT,INT)	-> INT	times
/I	(INT,INT)	-> INT	divide
DIV	(INT,INT)	-> INT	divide
MOD	(INT,INT)	-> INT	modulo
NOT%	INT	-> INT	bit NOT
AND%	(INT,INT)	-> INT	bit AND
OR%	(INT,INT)	-> INT	bit OR
XOR%	(INT,INT)	-> INT	bit XOR
ROTL%	(INT,INT)	-> INT	bit rotate left
++I	INT	-> INT	increment
--I	INT	-> INT	decrement
=I	(INT,INT)	-> BOOL	equal
<>I	(INT,INT)	-> BOOL	not equal
<I	(INT,INT)	-> BOO	lower than
>I	(INT,INT)	-> BOOL	higher than
<=I	(INT,INT)	-> BOOL	lower or equal
>=I	(INT,INT)	-> BOOL	higher or equal
RANDOM		-> INT	random number
+R	(REAL,REAL)	-> REAL	plus
-R	(REAL,REAL)	-> REAL	minus
*R	(REAL,REAL)	-> REAL	times
/R	(REAL,REAL)	-> REAL	divide
++R	REAL->REAL		increment
--R	REAL->REAL		decrement
=R	(REAL,REAL)	-> BOOL	equal
<>R	(REAL,REAL)	-> BOOL	not equal
<R	(REAL,REAL)	-> BOOL	lower than
>R	(REAL,REAL)	-> BOOL	higher than
<=R	(REAL,REAL)	-> BOOL	lower or equal
>=R	(REAL,REAL)	-> BOOL	higher or equal
SIN	REAL	-> REAL	sinus
COS	REAL	-> REAL	cosinus
ASIN	REAL	-> REAL	arcsinus
ACOS	REAL	-> REAL	arccosinus
ATAN	REAL	-> REAL	arctangens
ATAN2	(REAL,REAL)	-> REAL	arctangens x/y

DISTRIBUTED GARBAGE COLLECTION

USING REFERENCE COUNTING

D I Bevan*

GEC Research Ltd
Hirst Research Centre
East Lane
Wembley
Middlesex
HA9 7PP

ABSTRACT

We describe here an elegant algorithm for the real-time
garbage collection of distributed memory. This algorithm
makes use of reference counting and is simpler than
distributed mark-scan algorithms. It is also truly real-time
unlike distributed mark-scan algorithms. It requires no
synchronisation between messages and only sends a message
between nodes when a reference is deleted. It is also
relatively space efficient using at most five bits per
reference.

INTRODUCTION

One of the common objections to the widespread use of functional
programming languages has been that their implementations have
traditionally been considerably more inefficient than those of
imperative languages. This has led to a large amount of research into
ways of implementing functional languages on multiprocessor systems
[4,7,8,9]. In order to do this, algorithms are necessary for garbage
collecting distributed memory which minimise the amount of
communication. This paper describes a simple and efficient solution to
this problem making use of reference counting.

Previous Work

Most previous work on parallel garbage collection has made use of
the mark-scan technique. The first parallel garbage collection algorithm
was described in [17], where Steele considered a dual processor system;
one processor, known as the mutator, running the user program and the
other being a special purpose garbage collection processor. Several
other algorithms of this sort were also produced (see for example [5].

---

*Research partially funded by ESPRIT project 415: Parallel
Architectures and Languages for AIP - A VLSI Directed Approach.

and [13]).

Hudak and Keller in [10] were the first to describe an algorithm suitable for multiprocessor systems. Their algorithm is also a modification of the sequential mark-scan algorithm. All the processors cooperate in both phases of the collection but marking can proceed in parallel with execution of the user program. Hughes [12] describes another mark-scan algorithm for use on a distributed system. Each processor is able to garbage collect its local memory independently of the rest of the system, and each local garbage collection contributes a little to global garbage collection. It is similar to an algorithm described by Mohamed-Ali in [16] but, as Hughes admits, neither his nor Mohamed-Ali's algorithm is truly real-time since any particular computation may be delayed for a long time while its processor does a garbage collection.

Reference Counting

The reference counting method of garbage collection has a number of advantages over the mark-scan method. Firstly, mark-scan algorithms have to visit every accessible object in order to mark it at each collection. Reference counting algorithms, however, visit objects only as they are being processed. Secondly, mark-scan algorithms, especially distributed ones, may not delete objects until long after they become inaccessible. Reference counting algorithms delete objects as soon as they become inaccessible. Thirdly, distributed mark-scan algorithms are complicated and difficult to prove correct (see [5]) and much synchronisation is necessary between the collector and mutator.

However, reference counting also suffers from a serious drawback. Objects accessible from themselves, and thus part of a circular structure, are not deleted at all. Hughes, basing his work on previous work by Bobrow [2], describes in [11] a solution to this problem in the uniprocessor case by keeping a separate reference count for each maximally strongly connected component of the program graph. Aertes describes an equivalent method in [1]. Other solutions to this problem are to be found in [3] and [6]. The algorithm described here will not collect circular data structures but can probably be adapted to do so by making use of the ideas in these papers.

Distributed Reference Counting

There has been very little work on algorithms for distributed reference counting. The only known algorithm other than that described in this paper is described by Lermen and Maurer in [14] and [15]. However, this algorithm has a number of severe shortcomings which the one described below does not have. Firstly, for the algorithm to work correctly, the communications medium between two nodes must deliver messages in the order they are sent. Secondly, for the deletion of a reference there has to be synchronisation of communication between the node with the object containing the reference and the node with the referenced object. Thirdly, a reference can only be moved from one node to another by duplicating it and then deleting the original reference. Lermen and Maurer's algorithm is also inefficient. Each object on a node has to keep two separate reference counts for each other node. Finally, the communications overhead is at least three times the number of references copied between different nodes.

The algorithm described here was discovered independently by the author but the basic idea is mentioned briefly in [19] where it is attributed to Arvind. In contrast to Lermen and Maurer's algorithm, it makes no requirements of the communications medium and no synchronisation is necessary. It is also possible to move a reference from one node to another with no overhead. It needs only one reference count of at most three bits per object and at most two extra bits per reference. Its communications overhead is restricted to one message when a reference is deleted.

THE BASIC ALGORITHM

We assume that our machine consists of a number of nodes and that on each node there are a number of objects. These objects may contain references to other objects (or indeed themselves), possibly on other nodes. At any time a reference may be deleted or a new object may be created and a reference to it created from an object already in existence. Similarly, at any time, a reference may be copied from one object to another. We require that no object be deleted if it is referenced and that objects be deleted when they are no longer referenced.

Weighted References

In order to achieve this, we associate with each reference a positive weight and with each object a reference count. The algorithm attempts to maintain the following invariant.

The reference count of an object is equal to the sum of the weights of the references to it.

This ensures that the reference count of an object is zero if and only if it is not referenced by another object. An object can thus be deleted if its reference count is zero. We consider the different possible operations on references separately.

When a new object is created with a reference from some object already in existence, the new object may be given an arbitrary reference count and the reference to it a weight equal to that reference count (see figure 1(i)). This maintains the invariant.

When a reference is duplicated, its weight is split between the two resulting references in such a way that the sum of the weights of the resulting references is equal to the original weight of the initial reference (see figure 1(ii)). This maintains the invariant without needing to communicate with the object referenced or to change its reference count.

When a reference to an object is deleted, the reference count of

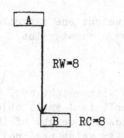

(i) A new object B is created
with a reference from A.

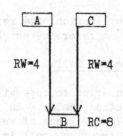

(ii) The reference from A
to B is duplicated.

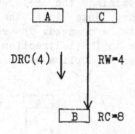

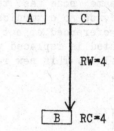

(iii) The reference from A to B is deleted.

Figure 1.

the object needs to be reduced by the weight of the reference. To achieve this, a message, known as a decrement reference count (DRC) message, is sent to the object. This message contains the weight of the deleted reference. When an object receives a DRC message, it decrements its reference count by the weight contained in the message (see figure 1(iii)). Thus the invariant is maintained.

When the reference count of an object reaches zero, the object may be deleted. In order to do this all its references to other objects must first be deleted by sending DRC messages to each object referenced.

The invariant given above now holds if there are no DRC messages in transit. The following invariant holds all the time.

The reference count of an object is equal to the sum of the weights of the references to it added to the sum of the weights contained in DRC messages in transit to it.

IMPLEMENTATION

The algorithm, as described above, is not implementable because it requires reference weights to take arbitrarily decreasing positive values and reference counts to take arbitrary sums of these. For implementation we restrict reference weights to be positive integers, (in fact we restrict them further to be powers of two), and deal with the duplication of a reference with weight one separately. We also have a maximum reference weight and reference count value.

Indirection Cells

In order to cope with references with weight one, we make use of indirection cells. An indirection cell is a small object consisting of a single reference of weight one. Since the weight of the reference in an indirection cell is always one, its value need not be stored. When we wish to duplicate a reference with weight one we create an indirection cell containing a copy of the reference to be duplicated and having a maximum reference count. This indirection cell can be created on the same node as the object containing the reference to be duplicated, so no communication is necessary. Note that the reference count of referenced object does not need to be changed. The reference to be duplicated is replaced with a reference to the indirection cell with maximum weight. This new reference can then be duplicated as normal (see figure 2).

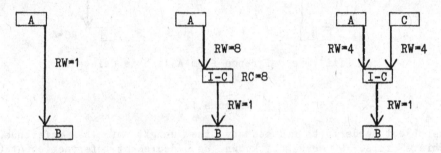

Duplication of a reference with weight one
using an indirection cell (I-C).

Figure 2.

Powers Of Two

To implement the above algorithm we attach to each reference field in an object a reference weight field (RWF), and to each object a reference count field (RCF). We note that we can restrict reference weights to being powers of two since we only need to halve their values when duplicating references. This being the case we can save space by storing in the RWF the binary (base two) logarithm of the reference weight rather than the reference weight itself. Similarly, when a DRC message is sent, the contents of the RWF of the reference being deleted can be put in the message.

If we use b bits for the RWFs, then RWFs can contain values from 0 to 2^b-1, representing reference weights of powers of two from 1 to $2^{(2^b-1)}$. Reference counts can then vary from 0 to $2^{(2^b-1)}$. However we need never store a reference count of zero since an object with zero reference count can be deleted. So if we store in a RCF one less than the reference count of the object, we only need 2^b-1 bits for RCFs (see figure 3).

One bit reference weight field				Two bit reference weight field			
RWF	RW	RCF	RC	RWF	RW	RCF	RC
0	1	0	1	00	1	000	1
1	2	1	2	01	2	001	2
				10	4	010	3
				11	8	011	4
						100	5
						101	6
						110	7
						111	8

Relationship of the contents of a reference weight field (RWF)
to the reference weight (RW) and the contents of a reference
count field (RCF) to the reference count (RC).

Figure 3.

The Complete Algorithm

We can now rewrite our algorithm in terms of the contents of the
RWFs and RCFs. Let $RWF(r)$ be the contents of the RWF of a reference r,
$RCF(x)$ be the contents of the RCF of an object x, and $con(m)$ be the
contents of a DRC message m. The invariant can now be written as
follows.

For any object x, $RCF(x)$ equals the sum of $2^{RWF(r)}$ for each
reference r, to x, plus the sum of $2^{con(m)}$ for each DRC
message m, in transit to x, minus one.

When a new object x, is created with a reference r, to it from some
object already in existence, then $RCF(x)$ is set to its maximum value
(all ones). $RWF(r)$ is also set to its maximum value (all ones).

When a reference r, is duplicated (the new reference being s) and
$RWF(r)$ is not zero, then both $RWF(r)$ and $RWF(s)$ are set to the original
value of $RWF(r)-1$.

When a reference r, with $RWF(r)$ equal to zero is duplicated, an
indirection cell, i, is created containing this reference. The original
reference is replaced by a reference s, to the indirection cell. $RCF(i)$
and $RWF(s)$ are set to their maximum values (all ones). The reference s,
to the indirection cell is now duplicated.

When a reference r, to an object is deleted, a DRC message m, is
sent to the object with $con(m)$ set to $RWF(r)$.

When an object x, receives a DRC message m, with 2^con(m) less than or equal to RCF(x), RCF(x) is decremented by 2^con(m).

When an object x, receives a DRC message m, with 2^con(m) equal to RCF(x)+1, it deletes all its references to other objects and x is deleted itself.

PERFORMANCE

We performed a number of simulation runs to investigate the space and time efficiency of the algorithm. The space efficiency, measured as the number of bits for reference counting per reference, depends on a trade-off between the size of the RWFs and RCFs, and the number of indirection cells that need to be created. If we have small RWFs and RCFs, we need to create indirection cells more often.

The number of indirection cells created depends on how many times, on average, references are duplicated, or equivalently on the mean number of references to an object. This, in functional programming systems, is dependent on the amount of program graph in an object. In general, large objects contain subgraphs which are essentially trees, which, if distributed amongst smaller objects such as binary apply nodes and cons cells, would lead to many objects which were referenced only once.

This is born out in practice. Most of the architectures for functional languages have used small cells and have reported 70-80% of all objects being only referenced once. (This is equivalent to an average of between 1.45 and 1.25 references to an object.) This has led people to suggest the use of small RCFs. For example Wise and Friedman [20] and Stoye et al [18] suggest the use of a single bit in the reference count field. At the same time, our simulations with larger object size have given figures of 35-60% of objects being referenced once, with the average number of references to an object between 2.3 and 1.6.

Space Overhead

If we are given the sizes, |RCF| and |RWF|, of the RCF and RWF respectively, and the size of an address field, |AF|, then we can calculate the number of bits used by the reference counting per reference. If #refs is the number of references to an object and #ics the number of indirection cells used by these references, then the number of bits used in the reference counting of these references is given by the following formula.

$$(\#ics + 1).|RCF| + \#refs.|RWF| + \#ics.|AF|$$

Each indirection cell and the object referenced has a RCF. Each reference uses one RWF (the reference from an indirection cell does not need a RWF because its reference weight is always 1). Each indirection cell contains a reference which means an extra address field is necessary. By making use of this formula and the fact that |RCF| = 2^|RWF|-1, we were able to get information on the average number of bits needed for each reference by the algorithm. We used our simulation data to give us the distribution of values of #refs and to calculate the mean value of #ics for a given value of #refs. The results obtained are plotted in figure 4.

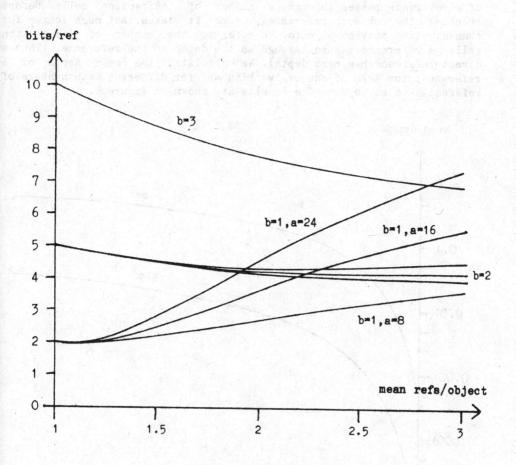

bits/ref

mean refs/object

Number of bits needed per reference.
(b = |RWF|, a = |AF|)

Figure 4.

As can be seen from the diagram, from the point of view of minimising the number of bits used by the algorithm, it is best to use only one bit in the RWF (and one in the RCF) with 24 bit addresses unless the mean number of references to an object exceeds 1.9 (or even more if smaller address fields are used). Not until the mean number of references approaches 3 is it worth using more than two bits in the RWF (and three in the RCF).

Reference Depth

The disadvantage with using small RWFs and RCFs is the proliferation of indirection cells. The main problem this causes is that if a reference passes through a number of indirection cells before reaching the object referenced, then it takes that much longer for communication between objects. We refer to the number of indirection cells a reference passes through as the depth of the reference. (Thus a direct reference has zero depth). We calculated the mean depth of a reference for RWFs of one or two bits and for different mean numbers of references to an object. The results are shown in figure 5.

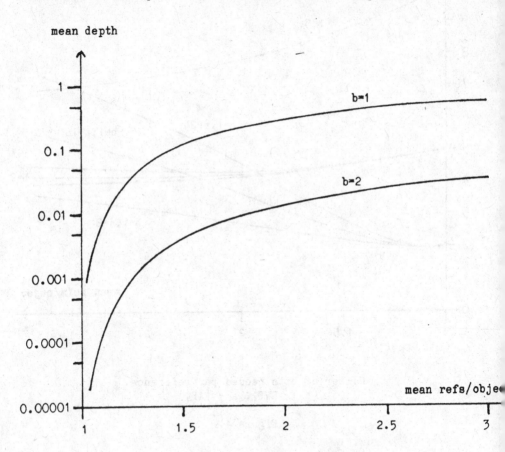

Mean depth of a reference.
$(b = |RWF|)$

Figure 5.

We see from the diagram that with a one bit RWF (and a one bit RCF), the mean depth of a reference is over 0.1 if the mean number of references to an object is above 1.5. This rises to 0.5 if the mean number of references is 2.5. This means that a large proportion of references pass through at least one indirection cell (i.e. have positive depth). Using a two bit RWF (and consequently a 3 bit RCF) provides about a sixteen fold improvement. The mean depth of a reference is only 0.005 when the mean number of references to an object is 1.5. This means that less than one in two hundred references have positive depth. If the mean number of references to an object increases to 2.5 the mean depth is still only 0.02.

SUMMARY

We have described an elegant distributed reference counting algorithm and an efficient implementation of it. Its major advantages are (i) it is considerably simpler than any similar algorithm, (ii) it is truly real-time, (iii) it does not require any synchronisation of messages, (iv) it requires a message to be sent only when a reference is deleted, (v) it is relatively space efficient, using at most five bits per reference. Its main disadvantage is that, in its present form, it will not collect circular structures.

ACKNOWLEDGEMENTS

The author is grateful to Simon Peyton Jones for suggesting the use of indirection cells, and to Geoffrey Burn, Chris Hankin and Penny Bevan for reading earlier drafts of this paper.

REFERENCES

[1] Aertes J.P.H., "Implementing SASL Without Garbage Collection", EUT-Report 81-WSK-05, Eindhoven University of Technology, 1981.

[2] Bobrow D.G., "Managing Reentrant Structures Using Reference Counts", ACM Transactions on Programming Languages and Systems 2(3), 1980, pp 269-273.

[3] Brownbridge D.R., "Cyclic Reference Counting for Combinator Machines", in [7], pp 273-288.

[4] Darlington J., Reeve M., "ALICE - A Multiprocessor Reduction Machine for the Parallel Evaluation of Applicative Languages", Proc. ACM Conference on Functional Programming Languages and Computer Architecture, New Hampshire 1981.

[5] Dijkstra E.W., Lamport L., Martin A.J., Scholten C.S., Steffens E.F.M., "On-the-Fly Garbage Collection: An Exercise in Cooperation", Comm. ACM 21(11), 1978, pp 966-975.

[6] Friedman D.P., Wise D.S., "Reference Counting Can Manage the Circular Environments of Mutual Recursion", Information Processing Letters 8 1.

[7] Goos G., Hartmanis J., "Functional Programming Languages and Computer Architecture", Proc. ACM Conference on Functional Programming Languages and Computer Architecture, Nancy, 1985, Springer-Verlag Lecture Notes in Computer Science 201.

[8] Hankin C.L., Osmon,P.E., Shute M.J., "COBWEB: A Combinator Reduction Architecture", in [7], pp 99-112.

[9] Hudak P., Goldberg G., "Experiments in Diffused Combinator Reduction", Proc. ACM Conference on Lisp and Functional Programming, Austin, 1984, pp 167-176.

[10] Hudak P., Keller R.M., "Garbage Collection and Task Deletion in Distributed Applicative Processing Systems", Proc. ACM Conference on Lisp and Functional Programming, 1982, pp 168-178.

[11] Hughes J., "The Design and Implementation of Programming Languages", Technical Monograph PRG-40, Oxford University Computing Laboratory Programming Research Group, 1984, pp 99-115.

[12] Hughes J., "A Distributed Garbage Collection Algorithm", in [7], pp 256-272.

[13] Kung H., Song S., "An Efficient Parallel Garbage Collection System and its Correctness Proof", Technical Note, Department of Computer Science, Carnegie-Mellon University, Pittsburgh, 1977.

[14] Lermen C-W., Maurer D., "A Protocol For Distributed Reference Counting", Proc. ACM Conference on Lisp and Functional Programming, Cambridge, Mass., 1986, pp 343-350.

[15] Lermen C-W., Maurer D., "A Protocol For Distributed Reference Counting and its Correctness Proof", to appear as report SFB 124, Universität des Saarlandes, West Germany, 1986.

[16] Mohamed-Ali K.A., "Object-Oriented Storage Management and Garbage Collection in Distributed Processing Systems", PhD Thesis, Report TRITA-CS-8406, Royal Institute of Technology, Stockholm, 1984.

[17] Steele G.L., "Multiprocessing Compactifying Garbage Collection", Comm. ACM 18(9), 1975, pp 495-508.

[18] Stoye W.R., Clarke T.J.W., Norman A.C., "Some Practical Methods for Rapid Combinator Reduction", Proc. ACM Conference on Lisp and Functional Programming, Austin, 1984, pp 159-166.

[19] Thomas R.E., "A Dataflow Architecture with Improved Asymptotic Performance", Report MIT/LCS/TR-265, Massachusetts Institute Of Technology, 1981.

[20] Wise D.S., Friedman D.P., "The One-Bit Reference Count", BIT 17, 1977, pp 351-359.

Rigorous Development of a Distributed Calendar System

Ulla Gamwell Dawids and Hans Henrik Løvengreen

Department of Computer Science
Building 344, Technical University of Denmark
DK–2800 Lyngby, Denmark

Abstract

Many formal languages and notations for specification of concurrent and distributed systems have been presented, but few of these have been applied in larger scale. In this paper we try to apply some of these within a method for rigorous development of distributed systems. The development method is illustrated on a simplified version of a realistic application: a distributed calendar system.

1 Introduction

Today, data-processing systems consisting of work-stations connected by local-area networks have become standard technology. For such inherently concurrent and distributed systems a number of "distributed" software products, e.g. file servers and mail systems, are now becoming commercially available.

Also from a theoretical viewpoint, concurrency and distribution have received much attention. This has resulted in a number of models and specification languages for concurrency, e.g. temporal logic, CCS, TCSP, and Petri Nets. Although most of the formal notions have nice compositional properties, there is still a large gap between the toy examples handled by the theories (e.g. concatenation of buffers) and the distributed systems being implemented.

In order to "bridge the gap" between theory and practice, we believe that *rigorous development methods* for distributed systems are needed. By a rigorous development method we understand a construction procedure supported by formal specification and implementation languages making it possible to state the system requirements precisely throughout the development. Also, the formal basis of such a method should make it possible to verify each development step formally although we question whether this is feasible in practice. This sense of *rigorous* follows that advocated in [Jones 80] for software development in general.

In the master's thesis of the first author [Dawids 86] such rigorous development has been tried out on different problems of somewhat larger size. In the present paper, we illustrate the approach on a simplified example.

The paper is organized as follows: The emphasis is on the example in section 4 showing the development of a simple distributed calendar system. Before that we briefly introduce the development method and the languages used in this paper, viz. fairly standard versions of temporal logic and CSP [Hoare 85]. Following the development example, we shortly describe how the development steps may be be verified. A verification example from the calendar system is given in the appendix. Finally, we summarize our experience from the work and list a number of outstanding problems.

2   The Development Method

The development method is based on:

- A *model* of what a distributed system is and how it behaves.

- A *specification language* in which to express properties of system behaviour.

- An *implementation language* in which to express behaviour in a direct, operational way.

For distributed systems, we use the following general model:

> A *distributed system* consists of a collection of processes which interact with each other and with the environment by means of message passing over directed channels.

The channels connecting processes of the system are called *internal channels*. The channels leading to and from the environment are called *external channels*. At this point, we need not make further assumptions about the communication, e.g. whether it is synchronous or asynchronous.

Different *views* may be applied to distributed systems as illustrated in figure 1. As usual, we see that if we consider a process to be itself a (sub-)system, the process view coincides with the external view of this sub-system. This allows for *hierarchical decomposition* of distributed systems.

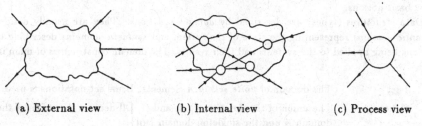

(a) External view   (b) Internal view   (c) Process view

Figure 1: System views

The *model of behaviour* for distributed systems may then be defined in terms of the communications taking place over the channels. Corresponding to the different system views, we may talk about *external behaviour*, *internal behaviour*, and *process behaviour*.

Development Steps

The development method in general consists of a number of system descriptions moving from abstract and external views of the system towards the process implementation. The principal kinds of descriptions are:

- **Central Specification:** A definition of the functions to be provided by the system when seen as a central, sequential system. The purpose of this description is to get a good idea of which task the system is to perform before considering the problems concerned with concurrency. The specification may be given in an algebraic, pre/post-condition, or explicit functional style. An explicit functional specification may later be used as a starting point for the internal protocol as described in e.g. [Lamport 82].

- **External System Specification:** A definition of the required properties of the external behaviour of the system when seen as a reactive one.

- **Internal System Specification**: A description of the process and communication structure of the system and a definition of the properties of its internal behaviour. Hereby we determine the *protocol* that must be followed in order to satisfy the external specification. The internal specification is based on a *system-wide* viewpoint describing how the processes are intended to co-operate.

- **Process Specification**: A description of the properties of the behaviour of an individual constituent process. In this description, the actual nature of the communication mechanism becomes important.

- **Process Implementation**: A "program" defining a concrete behaviour for an individual constituent processes.

In section 5, we address the question of how to verify one kind of specification against another.

3 Notation

3.1 The Functional Language

For the central specification, we use the functional meta-language *Meta-IV* of the so-called VDM-method. The language and its use is extensively described in [Bjørner 82] — here, we only introduce a few basic notions.

Data structures (types) are described by *domain equations*. They are usually divided into *semantic domains* representing the state of the system and *syntactic domains* describing the operations being applied to the systems and their results. The domain constructors of main interest are:

A-set	The domain of *finite sets* of A-elements. Usual set-notations is used.
$A\|B\|C$	The *union* of the domains A, B, and C. $[A]$ denotes the union of the domain A and the singleton domain $\{\underline{nil}\}$.
$A \overrightarrow{m} B$	The domain of *finite maps* from a subset of A to B. $m + [a \mapsto b]$ denotes a map which is like m except that the element a is mapped to b.
$A :: B \times C \times D$	The domain A of *named trees*, i.e. tuples of B, C, and D elements marked with the symbol A. An object in this domain is constructed by $\underline{mk}\text{-}A(b,c,d)$. Components of a tree-object may be selected by *selector functions* of the form $\underline{s}\text{-}X$ where X is a domain name or an explicitly given field-name.

Constraints imposed on semantic domains are specified by *invariance predicates*. Syntactic domains are constrained relatively to the current state by *well-formedness predicates*. The *semantic functions* which describe the effect of the operations may be specified either imlicitly by *pre- and post-conditions* or explicitly by *function expressions*.

3.2 A Behaviour Model

We here briefly outline the behaviour model used in this paper which is based on the one in [Chaochen 86]. The model is rather similar to that of [Nguyen 86].

We consider a distributed system to be a *network* consisting of a number of processes connected by directed, named communication channels as in figure 1(b). Each channel c has an *input end* and an *output end*. The *alphabet* of a network N is denoted by $\alpha(N)$ and consists of the set of channel-ends connected to processes of the network. The the *internal channels* of N have both ends in $\alpha(N)$, the *external channels* only one. A process may be seen as a network without internal channels.

We consider channels to be *typed*, i.e. each channel c has an associated set of possible message values M_c. In the present paper, we furthermore assume that communication is *synchronous*, that is, channels have no buffer capacity.

Observation

Our notion of network behaviour is based on *discrete time*; at each instant of the discrete time, the state of the system is observed.

We assume that only the channels of the system are observable: at each channel-end we can observe how the process connected to this end affects the channel. We may either observe *communication events*, i.e. the passing of messages over the channels, or the capability of the processes to engage in a communication. To record the state of a channel c we associate two *basic variables* to c — one for the input end $\mathcal{I}_c$ and one for the output end $\mathcal{O}_c$. The variables may take the following values:

$m \in M_c$ The process is receiving/sending a message m over c.

req   The process is requesting a communication over c.

rej   The process is rejecting communication over c.

clo   The process has closed the channel end.

A consequence of this model is that we assume that the system is observed at least as often as communications may take place or the capabilities may change, but the exact interval is of no importance when real-time aspects are not considered. Also, the model allows us to represent *true concurrency* to some extent since we may observe several communications on different channels at the same moment of time.

Now, we may start the system and our discrete clock and record the observations s_i made at each discrete point of time: $s_0, s_1, s_2, \ldots$. Such a recording will be called a *course* of the system. The *behaviour* of a system consists of all conceivable courses of the system. Since the communication is synchronous, these are all courses which can possibly be observed when the network is put in different environments being more or less willing to communicate. By the *external behaviour* of a system we understand the possible courses when the observation is restricted to the external channels.

3.3   Temporal Logic

We specify the behaviour of a network by specifying properties which must be satisfied for each course in the behaviour. For expressing properties of courses (infinite sequences of observations) we use a linear time temporal logic. Assertions are constructed from *atomic predicates* whose truth can be determined from an observation (and an assignment to quantified variables), *logical connectives* ($\land, \lor, \neg, \Rightarrow$) and quantifiers ($\forall, \exists$) having their usual meaning, plus the following temporal operators:

$\Box P$ P is true from now on.

$\Diamond P$ P will eventually become true (or is true now).

$\triangledown P$ P has been true (or is true now).

P until Q P is true until Q becomes true (if ever). Trivially true if Q is true now. Note that Q is not required to become true (weak until).

$\bigcirc P$ P will be true in the next moment of time. When applied to a term, $\bigcirc t$, it denotes the value of t in the next state.

A formal definition of these operators along the lines in e.g. [Koymans 83] is straightforward.

A temporal formula is satisfied for a course iff it is true at the beginning of that that course. A temporal formula is satisfied for a behaviour iff it is satisfied for any course in the behaviour. A temporal formula must mention only variables within the alphabet of the network specified.

Notational Abbreviations

Liveness properties are specified using the usual *leads-to* operator which is defined by:

$$P \rightsquigarrow Q \quad \triangleq \quad \Box (P \Rightarrow \Diamond Q)$$

In order to shorten our specifications (and to make them less model-dependent), we introduce a number of *channel predicates* defined in terms of the basic channel variables:

$$
\begin{aligned}
pass(c,m) &\triangleq \mathcal{I}_c = m \wedge \mathcal{O}_c = m \\
isreq(c) &\triangleq \mathcal{I}_c = \mathbf{req} \ \underline{\text{until}} \ (\exists\, m)(pass(c,m)) \\
osreq(c,m) &\triangleq \mathcal{O}_c = \mathbf{req} \ \underline{\text{until}} \ pass(c,m) \\
iwreq(c) &\triangleq (\Box \Diamond \mathcal{I}_c = \mathbf{req}) \ \underline{\text{until}} \ (\exists\, m)(pass(c,m)) \\
owreq(c,m) &\triangleq (\Box \Diamond \mathcal{O}_c = \mathbf{req}) \ \underline{\text{until}} \ pass(c,m)
\end{aligned}
$$

$pass(c,m)$ denotes that the message m is passing on the channel c. By definition, $pass(c,m)$ will be true only in one step of time. The moment before, both ends must have been requesting, and the next moment the input and output ends either request or reject further input/output or they have been closed down.

The *strong requests*, $osreq(c,m)$ and $isreq(c)$, denote that the controlling process will do nothing but communicate (m) on c. The *weak requests*, $iwreq(c)$ and $owreq(c)$, denote that the process from time to time will attempt to communicate on c until a communication (of m) takes place.

Auxiliary Variables

Even though most safety-properties can be specified using the before-operator, such properties are often more conveniently specified in terms of the *state* of the system. We here think of the state as a summary of the communication history of system. This state may be used in specifications through a number of *auxiliary state variables*. The value of these variables must be uniquely determined from the past values of the basic (channel) variables $\mathcal{I}$ and $\mathcal{O}$. For each auxiliary variable, this is done by specifying its initial value and how the various communications of the system change the value. This may be expressed by a temporal assertion of the form:

$$
\begin{aligned}
S = s_0 & \\
\wedge \quad \Box\, (\quad & (pass(c_1,m_1) \wedge \bigcirc S = F(S,c_1,m_1)) \\
\vee \quad & (pass(c_2,m_2) \wedge \bigcirc S = F(S,c_2,m_2)) \\
& \vdots \\
\vee \quad & \underline{\text{unchanged}})
\end{aligned}
$$

The initial value of the state variable S is defined to be s_0. Each time a message is passed on one of the channels of the system, the second part of the definition states how the state variable is changed by specifying that the value in the next step (the $\bigcirc$-operator) must be a function F

of previous value and the communication. Communications not explicitly mentioned should not change the variable as indicated by the unchanged-symbol.[1]

The notion of auxiliary variables resembles that of *abstract state functions* in [Lamport 83a], [Lamport 83b] and the *conceptual state* notion in [Stark 86]. The temporal notation used here is from [Chaochen 86].

3.4 A Version of CSP

As our implementation language, we here use a version of (Theoretical) CSP close to that presented in [Hoare 85], but restricted to the following operators:

$SKIP$	Successful termination.
$c \, ! \, v \to P$	Outputs v on c and then behaves like P.
$c \, ? \, m : M \to P$	Binds input on c to m and then behaves like P.
$P \, [] \, Q$	External choice between P and Q.
$P \sqcap Q$	Internal choice between P or Q.
$P \parallel Q$	Parallel composition of P and Q with internal communication synchronized. External channels must be used by at most one of P and Q at a time.

In [Chaochen 86] it has been shown how such a subset of CSP can be given a *temporal semantics* by considering these expressions to represent temporal formulas.

To shorten our CSP specification we abbreviations like:

$$\forall_{j \in 1..n} \; C_{ij} \, ! \, v \to P \quad \triangleq \quad C_{i,1} \, ! \, v \to C_{i,2} \, ! \, v \to \ldots \to C_{i,n} \, ! \, v \to P$$

$$[]_{j \in 1..n} \; C_{ij} \, ! \, v \to P_{(j)} \quad \triangleq \quad (C_{i,1} \, ! \, v \to P_{(1)} \, [] \, C_{i,2} \, ! \, v \to P_{(2)} \ldots [] \, C_{i,n} \, ! \, v \to P_{(n)})$$

4 Example: A Distributed Calendar System

4.1 Introduction

The problem concerns a situation occuring frequently in our everyday life. In connection with jobs and other activities we all have to participate in a number of different meetings and arrangements with a number of different persons. To keep track of these appointments we use a calendar but sometimes it can be hard to survey the situation when the telephone rings continuously about new meetings while one is trying to arrange a meeting oneself.

The Problem

We have a fixed number of persons each having a calendar. A person is making appointments about meetings involving a number of other persons and in the calendar a note is made of every appointment.

A person can propose a meeting by asking the persons involved if they want to participate. They may in return approve or reject a meeting depending on whether they have a meeting already. Each person must carefully update the calendar according to the appointments agreed upon.

Our objective is now to develop a system which can be consulted by persons who want to arrange meetings. The system keeps in order the calendars of the individual persons and carries out the arrangements concerning the meetings.

---

[1] We here require the changes to the auxiliary variables to be deterministic. Thereby, a specification can always be seen as a specification of properties of the basic variables. Complications due to simultaneous changes are not relevant for this paper.

A Distributed Calendar System

We suppose that a fixed number of persons are associated to the system. These persons are called the *clients* of the system. A client may consult the system to propose a meeting and the system then later on reports back the result of the arrangements.

To keep the problem simple, we make the following assumptions: Meetings cover whole days. A proposal for a meeting only includes the participants of the meeting — no preferred dates. If two clients, independently of each other, propose meetings concerning the same group of participants, these meetings are considered to be different. A person is not asked whether he/she wants to participate in a meeting proposed by somebody else; if the calendar allows it, a meeting is arranged.

The calendar system must be *consistent*, i.e. it must never arrange conflictning meetings and clients should have the same view of which meetings have been arranged. Furthermore, the system should be *effective*, i.e. it should try to arrange as many meetings as possible.

It may happen, however, that conflicting meetings are proposed concurrently and thus we are forced to make a decision upon which meeting shall actually take place. Many strategies can be proposed to solve that problem, but usually one strives for solutions which give a *fair* treatment of every person. In this simple calendar system, however, we do not want to treat the aspect of fairness. If conflicting meetings are proposed, they may all be rejected or one of them may succeed. We do not decide upon which meeting should be favoured and thus a person can be prevented from ever arranging a meeting. (In [Dawids 86] it is illustrated how the treatment of fairness increases the complexity of the system significantly.)

4.2 A Central Specification

In order to increase our understanding of the system, we start by giving a central, sequential model of the system using the notation described in section 3.1.

Semantic Domains

We here consider the system as a central agent managing all the calendars. So the system state consists of a collection of uniquely identified calendars, one for each associated person. Each calendar consists of a number of dates on which at most one meeting can be arranged. A meeting is identified by the set of identifiers (Id) constituting the participants including the person initiating the meeting. By convention, a date of the calendar is free if the set of identifiers associated to it is empty. This leads to the following semantic domains:

$$Calendar\_System = Id \vec{m} Calendar$$
$$Calendar = Date \vec{m} Id\text{-}\underline{set}$$

As the invariance constraint we require that meetings can only involve persons associated to the calendar system and that if a person has a note in the calendar about a meeting then every participant must have a note of that meeting, too.

$$\underline{inv}\text{-}Calendar\_System(CS) \triangleq$$
$$(\forall\ i \in \underline{dom}\,CS)$$
$$(\forall\ d \in \underline{dom}\,CS[i],\ m \in Id\text{-}\underline{set})\ (CS[i][d] = m \Rightarrow (\forall\ j \in m)(j \in \underline{dom}\,CS \land CS[j][d] = m))$$

Syntactic Domains

Each person connected to the system can consult the system to propose a meeting. A proposal (*Input*) is made by identifying oneself and listing the (other) persons who should attend the meeting. The system will in return (*Output*) either give a negative answer to the proposer or give a positive answer to every participant of the meeting. A negative result just includes the name of the person to which the result is sent. A positive result contains the name of the person to which the result is sent, the date on which the meeting is to be held, and the set of persons participating in the meeting.

$$
\begin{aligned}
Operations &= Input \mid Output \\
Input &:: Id \times Id\text{-}\underline{set} \\
Output &:: Result\text{-}\underline{set} \\
Result &= Pos\_Result \mid Neg\_Result \\
Pos\_Result &:: Id \times Date \times Id\text{-}\underline{set} \\
Neg\_Result &:: Id
\end{aligned}
$$

Since a proposal for a meeting can include only persons associated to the calendar system we impose the well-formedness constraint:

$$is\text{-}wf\text{-}Input(\underline{mk}\text{-}Input(id,ids),CS) \triangleq id \in \underline{dom}\,CS \wedge (\forall\, i \in ids)(i \in \underline{dom}\,CS \wedge i \neq id)$$

Semantic Functions

We specify the system by a function *Evolve*. This function takes as arguments an *Input* and a *Calendar System*. These must both fulfil the constraints presented above. As a result the function returns a (new) calendar system and a set of *Results*. The function can be specified by a pair of *pre- and postconditions*, but we here choose to present an *explicit functional description* since it will give a hint about the protocol to be used later.

To evaluate the result of a proposal, the system must examine the calendars to find a common free date. If such a date does not exist, a negative answer is returned to the proposer and the calendars are left unchanged. If such a date does exist, every participant receives a positive result about the meeting and the calendar of each participant is updated.

$$
\begin{aligned}
&Evolve(\underline{mk}\text{-}Input(id,ids),CS) \triangleq \\
&\quad \underline{let}\ part = \{id\} \cup ids\ \underline{in} \\
&\qquad \underline{let}\ dset = Free\_Dates(part,CS)\ \underline{in} \\
&\qquad \underline{if}\ dset = \{\} \\
&\qquad\qquad \underline{then}\ (\{\underline{mk}\text{-}Neg\_Result(id)\},CS) \\
&\qquad\qquad \underline{else}\ \underline{let}\ d \in dset\ \underline{in} \\
&\qquad\qquad\qquad \underline{let}\ CS' = Update\,CS(CS,d,part)\ \underline{in} \\
&\qquad\qquad\qquad (\{\underline{mk}\text{-}Pos\_Result(id,d,part) \mid id \in part\ \},CS') \\
&\underline{type}\ Evolve:\ Input \times Calendar\_System \overset{\sim}{\to} Output \times Calendar\_System
\end{aligned}
$$

where

$$
\begin{aligned}
&Free\_Dates(idset,CS) \quad \triangleq \{\ d \in Dates \mid (\forall\, id \in idset)(CS[i]/d] = \{\})\} \\
&Update\_CS(CS,d,idset) \quad \triangleq \\
&\quad \underline{let}\ Update\_Cal(CS,d,meeting,idset) = \\
&\qquad \underline{if}\ idset = \{\} \\
&\qquad\qquad \underline{then}\ CS \\
&\qquad\qquad \underline{else}\ \underline{let}\ id \in idset\ \underline{in} \\
&\qquad\qquad\qquad Update\_Cal(CS + [id \mapsto (CS[id] + [d \mapsto m])],d,meeting,\ idset\backslash\{id\}) \\
&\quad \underline{in}\ Update\_Cal(CS,d,idset,idset)
\end{aligned}
$$

4.3   External System Specification

In this and the following sections, we again consider the system to be a reactive one interacting with the clients through communication channels.

External system interface

The system is supposed to maintain a calendar for each client. A *Calendar* here consists of a finite number of dates to which meetings may be associated. A *Meeting* is identified by the initiator, the (other) participants and a number. The number is used to identify a meeting uniquely since a client is capable of arranging several meetings concerning the same participants.[2] In the distributed version, a *Result* from the system indicates a date and the meeting which has been arranged on this date. By convention, the value *nil* is returned if the meeting could not be arranged. The basic domains of the distributed solution are thus:

$$
\begin{array}{ll}
Calendar & = Date \; \vec{m} \; [Meeting] \\
Meeting & :: \; Init : Id \times Part : Id\text{-}\underline{set} \times No : INTG \\
Result & :: \; [Date] \times Meeting
\end{array}
$$

Each client i is connected to the system via two external channels. I_i is used for proposals and O_i is used for results:

$$
\begin{array}{lll}
I_i & : \quad Meeting & \text{— Input channel from Client}_i. \\
O_i & : \quad Result & \text{— Output channel to Client}_i.
\end{array}
$$

Specification conventions

In an atomic formula, an argument may be replaced by "-". This means that the value of the argument is irrelevant and the notation is equivalent to existential quantification over the appropiate domain just outside the atomic formula.

Thoughout the specifications we assume that *Clients* denotes a fixed, finite set of names of the persons associated with the system. These names will be used to identify the various channels and processes in the system, e.g. Agent$_i$ is the agent-process associated with client i. Furthermore, the free variables of each formula are implicitly assumed to be universally quantified over the following domains:

$$
\begin{array}{ll}
i, j, k & \text{ranges over } Clients. \\
m & \text{ranges over } Meeting. \\
d & \text{ranges over } Date. \\
x & \text{ranges over } Date \cup \{\underline{nil}\}.
\end{array}
$$

Preconditions

As already mentioned, we require meetings to be uniquely identified. This requirement to the system environment may be expressed by:

(PRE) $\Box \; (pass(I_i,m) \Rightarrow i = \underline{s}\text{-}Init(m) \wedge i \notin \underline{s}\text{-}Part(m) \subseteq Clients \wedge \bigcirc\Box \; \neg \; pass(I_i,m))$

This property will be a precondition for all of the following formulas. The environment may implement this property by letting each client assign a unique number to each of its proposed meetings. The precondition ensures that all communication events can be ascribed to a unique proposal.

---

[2]The requirement of uniqueness is not crucial, but simplifies the specification a great deal. Instead, we could have specified the properties in terms of the number of occurrences of the various events.

External safety properties

We here state what the system is allowed to do. First of all, results are sent only to participants of a meeting. If a result is sent to the initiator, this client must have proposed the meeting. If sent to another participant, the result must be positive.

(ES1) $\Box$ $(pass(O_i, \underline{mk}\text{-}Result(x,m))$
$$\Rightarrow (i = \underline{s}\text{-}Init(m) \land \triangledown\, pass(I_i,m)) \lor (i \in \underline{s}\text{-}Part(m) \land x \neq \underline{nil}))$$

ES1 also ensures that the system does not arrange meetings by itself. This follows from the fact that the initator must have proposed a meeting and the liveness property EL3 below that ensures that if one participant receives a positive result then every other participant, including the initiator, must receive the result, too.

We also require any results about the same meeting to be identical and that conflicting meetings are not arranged, i.e. for a given client, no two positive results about different meetings may indicate the same date.

(ES2) $\Box$ $(\triangledown\, pass(O_i, \underline{mk}\text{-}Result(x_1,m)) \land pass(O_j, \underline{mk}\text{-}Result(x_2,m)) \Rightarrow x_1 = x_2)$

(ES3) $\Box$ $(\triangledown\, pass(O_i, \underline{mk}\text{-}Result(d_1,m_1)) \land pass(O_i, \underline{mk}\text{-}Result(d_2,m_2)) \land m_1 \neq m_2 \Rightarrow d_1 \neq d_2)$

(ES4) $\Box$ $(pass(O_i, \underline{mk}\text{-}Result(\text{-},m)) \Rightarrow \bigcirc\Box\, \neg\, pass(O_i, \underline{mk}\text{-}Result(\text{-},m)))$

Since ES3 does not by itself prevent a result from being repeated, we have added this (less important) requirement as ES4.

External liveness properties

To have a useful system we must require that the system accepts the proposals of the clients. However, in order to allow implementations with limited buffer capacity, we require the clients to be "attentive" if they are to be served. By attentive, we mean willing to accept any output from the system:

$$attentive(i) \triangleq osreq(O_i,\text{-}) \rightsquigarrow pass(O_i,\text{-})$$

The system must accept input from any attentive client and when input is accepted, an output is guaranteed to be offered:

(EL1) $attentive(i) \Rightarrow \Box\Diamond\, iwreq(I_i)$

(EL2) $pass(I_i,m) \rightsquigarrow osreq(O_i, \underline{mk}\text{-}Result(\text{-},m))$

These two properties together express that deadlock cannot occur.

In order to maintain consistency we require that if the system passes a positive result to a client then every (attentive) participant of the meeting must at some time be offered a (positive) result about that meeting, too. We cannot require that the results are actually passed to the clients as we do not know whether they are willing to communicate.

(EL3) $\Box$ $((attentive(i) \land i = \underline{s}\text{-}Part(m)) \lor i = \underline{s}\text{-}Init(m)$
$$\Rightarrow (pass(O_j, \underline{mk}\text{-}Result(d,m)) \rightsquigarrow \triangledown\, osreq(O_i, \underline{mk}\text{-}Result(\text{-},m)))$$

This formula is characterized by the combination of the $\rightsquigarrow$ operator and the $\triangledown$ operator which is needed because we do not know in which order the outputs are being offered at the different agents.

Comments on the External Specification

The above properties have been selected so as to express the required properties with a clear distinction between safety and liveness aspects and trying to avoid redundancy. Users of the system, however, are probably more interested in properties such as: "if a client receives a positive result about a meeting, then the meeting must have been requested by somebody and the other (attentive) participants plus the initiator will receive the same result too":

$$pass(O_i,\ \underline{mk}\text{-}Result(d,m))\ \wedge\ j = \underline{s}\text{-}Init(m)$$
$$\Rightarrow\ (\ \bigtriangledown\ pass(I_j,m)\ \wedge$$
$$\Diamond\ (\forall\ k \in \underline{s}\text{-}Part(m)\cup\{j\})$$
$$(attentive(k)\ \vee\ k = j \Rightarrow\ \bigtriangledown\ osreq(O_k,\ \underline{mk}\text{-}Result(d,m)))$$

Fortunately, this property can be proved from ES1, ES2, and EL3 by temporal reasoning.

4.4   Internal System Specification

We now consider the system as a collection of independent *agents* each managing the calendar of a single client. When a client consults its agent to propose a meeting, the agent carries out the necessary arrangements with the other agents, updates the calendar if necessary and reports the result to the client. Each agent has admittance only to its own calendar, and the only way to get information about the calendars of the other clients is to communicate with their agents.

In this step of the development, the *protocol* is determined. The explicit functional version of the central specification was based on the idea of collecting the free dates of every participant indicating whether a meeting was possible. We transfer this idea to the distributed system by letting the agent of the client who proposed the meeting arrange the meeting. This agent relays the proposal to every agent of a participant of the meeting, and they in return answer with a set of free dates of the client's calendar or with an empty set of dates if they reject the meeting. The agent of the initiator must then inform the other agents about the result of its investigations and send output to its client.

Network structure

The protocol is based on a broadcast structure. Every agent is connected to every other agent and one agent disseminates the information about a meeting to every participant. Between any pair of agents we thus need two channels along which proposals are relayed, two channels along which answers are passed, and two channels to report the results. Two channels are needed for each kind of communication since the channels are unidirected. The network and protocol structure of the system is illustrated in figure 2.

Let $i, j \in$ Clients, $i \neq j$. Then the complete set of channels and their associated message types is given by:

I_i :	*Meeting*	— Input channel from Client$_i$
P_{ij} :	*Meeting*	— Proposal channel from Agent$_i$ to Agent$_j$.
A_{ij} :	*Answer*	— Answering channel from Agent$_i$ to Agent$_j$.
R_{ij} :	*Result*	— Result channel from Agent$_i$ to Agent$_j$.
O_i :	*Result*	— Output channel to Client$_i$.

The only new message type is Answer defined by:

Answer	::	*Date-set* × *Meeting*

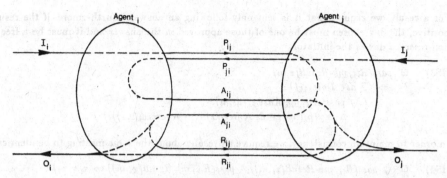

Figure 2: Network structure of the calendar system

In order to express the internal safety properties, we introduce an auxiliary variable for each client i, $Calendar_i$, holding the calendar of this client. The relation between the communication events and the auxiliary variable $Calendar_i$ is defined by:

$$Calendar_i \triangleq [d \mapsto \underline{nil} \mid d \in dataset_0]$$
$$\wedge \; \Box \; (\; (pass(O_i, \underline{mk}\text{-}Result(d,m)) \wedge \bigcirc Calendar_i = Calendar_i + [d \mapsto m])$$
$$\vee \; \text{unchanged})$$

The calendar always contains a fixed set of days, $dataset_0$, e.g. covering a whole year. Initially, every date of the calendar is free, and upon the sending of a positive output to the client the calendar is updated.

In order to simplify the specification of safety properties, we use the following abbreviations:

$$free_i(d) \triangleq Calendar_i[d] = \underline{nil}$$

$$reserved_i(d,m) \triangleq (\exists \; ds \in Date\text{-}set)(\exists \; j \in Clients)$$
$$(\; \triangledown \; pass(A_{ij}, \underline{mk}\text{-}Answer(ds,m)) \wedge d \in ds \; \wedge$$
$$\neg \; (\; (\exists \; x \in [Date])(\triangledown \; pass(R_{ji}, \underline{mk}\text{-}Result(x,m)) \wedge x \neq d)$$
$$\vee \; Calendar_i[d] = m))$$

That a date d at a client i is *free* simply means that no meeting has yet been arranged on this day. A date may, however, be *reserved* for a meeting which means that it has been passed as (part of) an answer to a proposal from another agent and it is not yet known whether the meeting will be arranged on this day or not. As soon as a result telling that the day was not chosen for the meeting is received, the day will no longer be reserved. Also, if the day is actually chosen for the meeting, it will remain reserved until the result is passed to the client and the day thereby recorded as occupied in the calendar.

Internal safety properties

An agent relays only proposals received from its client and only to participants of the meeting.

(IS1) $\quad \Box \; (pass(P_{ij}, m) \Rightarrow \triangledown \; pass(I_i, m) \wedge j \in \underline{s}\text{-}Part(m))$

An agent only sends answers about meetings for which is has received a proposal and every date approved must be free and not reserved for another meeting:

(IS2) $\quad \Box \; (pass(A_{ij}, \underline{mk}\text{-}Answer(ds,m)) \wedge m \neq m'$
$$\Rightarrow \triangledown \; pass(P_{ji}, m) \wedge (\forall \; d \in ds) \; (\; free_i(d) \wedge \neg \; reserved_i(d,m')))$$

For a result, we require that it is sent only following an answer. Furthermore, if the result is positive, the day chosen must be one of those approved in the answer and it must be a free and non-reserved day of the initiator.

(IS3) $\Box$ $(pass(R_{ij}, \underline{mk}\text{-}Result(x,m))$
            $\Rightarrow$ $(\exists\ ds \in Date\text{-}\underline{set})$
                $(\ \bigtriangledown\ pass(A_{ji}, \underline{mk}\text{-}Answer(ds,m))$
                $\wedge\ (x \neq \underline{nil} \Rightarrow x \in ds\ \wedge\ free_i(x)\ \wedge\ \neg\ reserved_i(x,\cdot))))$

In order to maintain consistency, we require all results about the same meeting to be identical:

(IS4) $\Box$ $(\bigtriangledown\ pass(R_{ij}, \underline{mk}\text{-}Result(x_1,m))\ \wedge\ pass(R_{ik}, \underline{mk}\text{-}Result(x_2,m)) \Rightarrow x_1 = x_2)$

The last safety properties concern the sending of output from an agent to its client. An agent only passes a result about a meeting to its client if either the client is the initiator of the meeting or it is a positive result received from another agent. For the initiator, the result is not given until the (same) result has been sent to every participant, and we still require the day to be free and non-reserved.

(IS5) $\Box$ $(pass(O_i, \underline{mk}\text{-}Result(x,m))\ \wedge\ k = \underline{s}\text{-}Init(m)$
            $\Rightarrow$ $(i = k\ \wedge\ (\forall\ j \in \underline{s}\text{-}Part(m))(\bigtriangledown\ pass(R_{ij}, \underline{mk}\text{-}Result(x,m)))\ \wedge\ \bigtriangledown\ pass(I_i,m)\ \wedge$
                $(x \neq \underline{nil} \Rightarrow free_i(x)\ \wedge\ \neg\ reserved_i(x,\cdot)))$
            $\vee\ (\bigtriangledown\ pass(R_{ki}, \underline{mk}\text{-}Result(x,m))\ \wedge\ x \neq \underline{nil})$

As the last safety property we still require that at most one result is output about each meeting

(IS6) $\Box$ $(pass(O_i, \underline{mk}\text{-}Result(\cdot,m)) \Rightarrow \bigcirc\Box\ \neg\ pass(O_i, \underline{mk}\text{-}Result(\cdot,m)))$

It should be noted that the safety properties are somewhat redundant in order to allow for meetings with no participants except for the initiator.

Internal liveness properties

The internal liveness properties express the overall structure of the protocol.

As in the external specification we require that agents are obliging to attentive clients:

(IL1) $attentive(i) \Rightarrow \Box\Diamond\ iwreq(I_i)$

When an agent has received a proposal for a meeting from its client, it must relay the proposal to the other participants and an agent must send an answer to every proposal.

(IL2) $(\forall\ j \in \underline{s}\text{-}Part(m))(pass(I_i,m) \rightsquigarrow pass(P_{ij},m)))$

(IL3) $pass(P_{ij},m) \rightsquigarrow pass(A_{ji}, \underline{mk}\text{-}Answer(\cdot,m)))$

A proposal is relayed to every agent of a participant and they in return send an answer. When the agent who initiated the proposals knows whether the meeting is arranged or not, it must send back the result.

(IL4) $pass(A_{ji}, \underline{mk}\text{-}Answer(\cdot,m)) \rightsquigarrow pass(R_{ij}, \underline{mk}\text{-}Result(\cdot,m))$

Finally, we present the properties ensuring that the results are output to the clients. When an agent has received a proposal from its client, has found out the result, and sent it to all other participants, it is certain that the result will be offered to the client at some time.

(IL5) $\bigtriangledown\ pass(I_i,m) \wedge (\forall\ j \in \underline{s}\text{-}Part(m))\ (\bigtriangledown\ pass(R_{ij}, \underline{mk}\text{-}Result(\text{-},m)))$
    $\leadsto \bigtriangledown\ osreq(O_i, \underline{mk}\text{-}Result(\text{-},m))$

When an agent receives a positive result from another agent, it must relay it to the client provided the client is attentive. A negative result should not be relayed as the client did not initiate the meeting him/herself.

(IL6) $attentive(i) \Rightarrow (pass(R_{ji}, \underline{mk}\text{-}Result(d,m)) \leadsto osreq(O_i, \underline{mk}\text{-}Result(\text{-},m)))$

4.5 Process Specification

In the process specification we narrow our point of view and specify the behaviour of a single agent, $Agent_i$. The safety properties of a process directly correspond to those of the internal specification, the only difference being that we consider these to be specifications of which communications $Agent_i$ is allowed to do.

Also the process liveness properties follow those of the internal specification. E.g. the property that a proposal is followed by an answer is converted into two properties saing that after a proposal, a process will be ready to input an answer and after receiving a proposal, a process will try to output an answer. However, great care must be taken in order to ensure that messages are passed at the right moments and that the properties can actually be implemented.

Being so similar to the internal specification, we here omit the process specification and pass directly to the process implementation.

4.6 Process Implementation

We conclude our development by presenting a CSP specification of the behaviour of an agent.

The overall protocol has already been settled, but a few details have to be considered. An agent is either *active* or *passive*. Initially, an agent is passive; when it receives input from its client it becomes active and remains so while arranging the meeting. The active agent relays the proposal to every participant of the meeting, awaits their answers, and sends back the result. When this is done the agent returns to the passive state.

When a passive agent receives a proposal from another agent, it returns the free dates of the calendar and awaits the result. When the result is received, the calendar is updated and if the result is positive, this is relayed to the client.

To avoid deadlock, an agent must always willing to accept new proposals from other agents. For simplicity, we here decide that whenever an agent is waiting either for a result or an answer it rejects new proposals by answering with an empty set of dates. This is done by a "background" process, $Refuse\_Proposals_i$.

In the CSP specification we use a number of parameters to record the state of an agent. When an agent is passive its state consists of the calendar, cal. An active agent needs, besides the calendar, three state components: The meeting it is arranging, m, the set of agents from which it awaits an answer, ids, and the set of dates which has been approved until now, $dates$.

$Agent_i(cal) \triangleq Passive\_Agent_i(cal)$

$Refuse\_Proposal_i \triangleq (\ [\,]_{j \in Clients}\ P_{ji}\ ?\ m : Meeting \rightarrow A_{ij}\ !\ \underline{mk}\text{-}Answer(\{\},m) \rightarrow$
$(\ R_{ji}\ ?\ r : Result \rightarrow SKIP$
$\|\ Refuse\_Proposal_i\ )$
$\|\ Refuse\_Channel_i\ ?\ s : Stop \rightarrow SKIP)$

$Passive\_Agent_i(cal) \triangleq$
$\quad (I_i \ ? \ m : Meeting \rightarrow (\forall_{j \in s\text{-}Part(m)} \ P_{ij} \ ! \ m \rightarrow$
$\qquad\qquad\qquad (Active\_Agent_i(cal,m,\underline{s}\text{-}Part(m),\{d \mid cal/d] = \underline{nil}\}))$
$\qquad\qquad\qquad) \parallel Refuse\_Proposal_i$
$\quad [] \, []_{j \in Clients} \ P_{ji} \ ? \ m : Meeting \rightarrow$
$\qquad\qquad\qquad (A_{ij} \ ! \ \underline{mk}\text{-}Answer(\{d \mid cal/d] = \underline{nil}\},m) \rightarrow$
$\qquad\qquad\qquad\qquad (\ R_{ji} \ ? \ \underline{mk}\text{-}Result(d,m) : Result \rightarrow$
$\qquad\qquad\qquad\qquad\qquad O_i \ ! \ \underline{mk}\text{-}Pos\_Result(d,m) \rightarrow$
$\qquad\qquad\qquad\qquad\qquad Refuse\_Channel_i \ ! \ stop() \rightarrow$
$\qquad\qquad\qquad\qquad\qquad Passive\_Agent_i(cal + [d \mapsto m])$
$\qquad\qquad\qquad\qquad [] \ R_{ji} \ ? \ \underline{mk}\text{-}Result(\underline{nil},m) : Result \rightarrow$
$\qquad\qquad\qquad\qquad\qquad Refuse\_Channel_i \ ! \ stop() \rightarrow$
$\qquad\qquad\qquad\qquad\qquad Passive\_Agent_i(cal))$
$\qquad\qquad\qquad) \parallel Refuse\_Proposal_i)$

$Active\_Agent_i(cal,m,ids,dates) \triangleq$
$\quad \underline{if} \ ids = \{\} \ \underline{then} \ \underline{if} \ dates = \{\} \ \underline{then} \ \forall_{j \in s\text{-}Part(m)} \ R_{ij} \ ! \ \underline{mk}\text{-}Result(\underline{nil},m) \rightarrow$
$\qquad\qquad\qquad\qquad\qquad O_i \ ! \ \underline{mk}\text{-}Result(\underline{nil},m) \rightarrow$
$\qquad\qquad\qquad\qquad\qquad Refuse\_Channel_i \ ! \ stop() \rightarrow$
$\qquad\qquad\qquad\qquad\qquad Passive\_Agent_i(cal)$
$\qquad\qquad\qquad \underline{else} \ \sqcap_{d \in dates} \ \forall_{j \in s\text{-}Part(m)} \ R_{ij} \ ! \ \underline{mk}\text{-}Result(d,m) \rightarrow$
$\qquad\qquad\qquad\qquad\qquad O_i \ ! \ \underline{mk}\text{-}Result(d,m) \rightarrow$
$\qquad\qquad\qquad\qquad\qquad Refuse\_Channel_i \ ! \ stop() \rightarrow$
$\qquad\qquad\qquad\qquad\qquad Passive\_Agent_i(cal + [d \mapsto m])$
$\quad \underline{else} \ []_{j \in ids} \ A_{ji} \ ? \ \underline{mk}\text{-}Answer(ds,m) : Answer \rightarrow$
$\qquad\qquad Active\_Agent_i(cal,m,ids \backslash \{j\},dates \cap ds)$

This program is, of course, not a perfect solution to the problem, but could be a reasonable one if implemented on a broadcast network.

5 Verification Principles

In this section, we briefly describe how the development steps may be verified. We do not present a formal proof system, but the rules are similar to those of [Nguyen 86] where the justification can be found. Some experience from the verification of the calendar system is mentioned and a single proof example is given in the appendix.

Central vs. External Specification

Regarding this relationship, we have not yet any clear ideas on how to formalize it. The problem is that two different abstract view of the system are to be compared: a sequential, functional one with reactive and concurrent one. We would, however, like to express that when the concurrent system is *quiescent* (at rest), its state should correspond to one in the central case and that a single proposal should result in a quiescent state corresponding to the one obtained by applying the corresponding operation to the central system. It is likely that the *transaction* concept from database theory is applicable here.

External vs. Internal Specification

In this case, we are dealing with two specifications based on the same behaviour model and expressed in the same language. If S_I is the internal specification and S_E an external specification, we therefore just have to show that $S_I \Rightarrow S_E$.

In principle, this can be done within the temporal logic. However, since the specifications also contain some rather indirect parts, viz. the auxiliary variables, the arguments become more operational and must be carried out at a meta-level (see appendix). Alternatively, specific proof rules may be established to handle auxliary variables as in [Lamport 83b] and [Stark 86].

Internal vs. Process Specification

The problem is here how to *compose* specifications. Suppose a network N consists of processes $P_1 \ldots P_n$ satisfying specifications $S_1 \ldots S_n$. To show a network property S_I is satisfied we have to show that it follows from the conjunction of the S_i's plus the following *communication medium properties* expressing that the communication is synchronous and strongly fair:

$$\text{Sync}_N \triangleq \Box \ (\forall \ c \in Internal\_channels(N)) \ (\mathcal{I}_c \in M_c \ \lor \ \mathcal{O}_c \in \ M_c \Rightarrow \mathcal{I}_c = \mathcal{O}_c)$$

$$\text{Fair}_N \triangleq \ (\forall \ c \in Internal\_channels(N)) \ (iwreq(c) \land osreq(c) \rightsquigarrow pass(c,m))$$

Although this is a simple verification principle, also here the presence of auxiliary variables makes it necessary to use meta-level arguments.

Process Specification vs. Process Implementation

Here we are dealing with a relationship between two different languages. In both [Chaochen 86] and [Barringer 85] is has been tried to give a temporal semantics to CSP in order to obliterate this distinction. The semantics, however becomes rather operational (of course) and seems difficult to apply directly. We feel that operational, meta-level reasoning is still the only practical way to approach this verification step.

6 Discussion

We have presented a method for rigorous development of distributed systems and illustrated it by a reasonably practical example. Of the steps within the method we emphasize the central and the internal specification. The central specification gives us a good understanding of the functionality of the system and establishes most of the data-structures to be used. The internal specification gives us a system-wide view of the protocol idea, but still allowing for different protocol-implementations.

Our framework is to be given a formal basis consisting of a system model plus specification and implementation languages. In this paper we have been using a model based on synchronous communication and presented our specifications in temporal logic and CSP. Alternatively, we could have used the similar model of [Nguyen 86]. Furthermore, in [Dawids 86] it has been shown that the asynchronous, quiescent-trace based model of Misra and Chandy [Johnsson 85] is also applicable. Many other models, e.g. based on partial order semantics, are potential candidates.

Since we aim at developing methods which can be used for real *software engineering*, we have chosen to present an example of somewhat larger size than usual in papers on specification. The example shows that it is possible to express the various specification steps in a formal way and that is possible to verify the development using rigorous arguments based on the formal behaviour model. Truly formal proofs, however, seem to be feasible only in a few cases.

We find the temporal specifications to be quite readable due to the ability to talk about communication events in contrast to methods based on trace-predicates. Concerning the external and internal specifications, however, we think they suffer from the usual problem of axiomatic methods in that it can be difficult find the right set of axioms corresponding to the intended system-model. For example, the present specification allows for the following implementation of the agents:

$$Agent_i \ \triangleq \ I_i \ ? \ m{:}Meeting \ \rightarrow \ O_i \ ! \ \underline{mk}\text{-}Result(\underline{nil},m) \ \rightarrow \ Agent_i \qquad\qquad (!)$$

One way to improve on this situation could be to make the specification more state-oriented as described in e.g. [Lamport 83a] and [Chandy 86]. Another possibility could be to link the central and the external specification more closely together.

Of course, the idea of a development method is not to apply proofs afterwards, but rather let them direct the development. Here, especially the step from the external to the internal specification seems to lack a methodological basis. The idea of stepwise protocol refinement, as described in [Chandy 86], may be a proper solution, but it should probably be supported by a number of "standard solutions" to handle e.g. deadlock and fairness issues.

From the present and other examples, we conclude that rigorous development of distributed systems is possible, but in order to handle the number of systems which are to be constructed, the emphasis should, perhaps, rather be put on developing a simple conceptual framework for distributed computing within which a number of (formally verified) "building blocks" can be put together in a coherent manner.

Acknowledgements

The authors would like to thank Zhou Chaochen for providing the ideas for the behaviour model used in this paper, Dines Bjørner for pointing out the calendar problem to be of interest, plus Ni Haichu, Anders P. Ravn, and the referees for many helpful comments.

References

[Barringer 85]   H. Barringer, R. Kuiper, and A. Pnueli: *A Compositional Temporal Approach to a CSP-like Language.* In proceedings of IFIP Conference: The Rôle of Abstract Models in Information Processing, Vienna 1985.

[Bjørner 82]   Dines Bjørner and Cliff B. Jones: *Formal Specification and Software Development.* Prentice-Hall International 1982.

[Chandy 86]   Mani Chandy and Jayadev Misra: *An Example of Stepwise Refinement of Distributed Programs: Quiescence Detection.* ACM Transactions on Programming Languages and Systems, Vol. 8, No. 3, pp. 326–346, July 1986.

[Chaochen 86]   Zhou Chaochen and Ni Haichu: *A Temporal Semantics of CSP and its Soundness.* In proceedings of ICCC'86, Beijing, October 1986.

[Dawids 86]   Ulla Gamwell Dawids: *On Principles for Rigorous Development of Distributed Systems.* M.Sc. thesis, Department of Computer Science, Technical University of Denmark, August 1986.

[Hoare 85]   C.A.R. Hoare: *Communicating Sequential Processes.* Prentice-Hall International 1985.

[Johnsson 85]   Bengt Johnsson: *A Model and Proof System for Asynchronous Networks.* In proceedings of 4nd Annual ACM Symposium on Principles of Distributed Computing, August 1985.

[Jones 80]   Cliff B. Jones: *Software Development: A Rigorous Approach.* Prentice-Hall International 1980.

[Koymans 83]   R. Koymans, J. Vytopil, and W.P. de Roever: *Real-time Programming and Asynchronous Message Passing.* In proceedings of 2nd Annual ACM Symposium on Principles of Distributed Computing, Montreal, August 1983.

[Lamport 82]   Leslie Lamport: *An Assertional Correctness Proof of a Distributed Algorithm.* Science of Computer Programming, Vol. 2, pp. 175-206, 1982.

[Lamport 83a]   Leslie Lamport: *Specifying Concurrent Program Modules*. ACM Transactions on Programming Languages and Systems, Vol. 2, No. 2, April 1983.

[Lamport 83b]   Leslie Lamport: *What Good is Temporal Logic*. In proceedings of IFIP'83, pp. 657–668, North-Holland 1983.

[Nguyen 86]   Van Nguyen, Alan Demers, David Gries, and Susan Owicki: *A Model and Temporal Proof System for Networks of Processes*. Distributed Computing, Vol. 1, No. 1, pp. 7–25, 1986.

[Stark 86]   Eugene W. Stark: *Proving Entailment Between Conceptual State Specifications*. In proceedings of ESOP'86, Lecture Notes in Computer Science Vol. 213, pp. 197–209, Springer-Verlag 1986.

Appendix: Verification Example

Proof of ES3

Proposition: For any $i \in Clients$:

$$\Box \ (pass(O_i, \underline{mk}\text{-}Result(\cdot, m)) \Rightarrow i = \underline{s}\text{-}Init(m) \lor i \in \underline{s}\text{-}Part(m)).$$

Proof: Follows from PRE, IS1, IS2 and IS3 by tracing back i.

Let $Pass_1 \triangleq pass(O_i, \underline{mk}\text{-}Result(d_1, m_1))$ and $Pass_2 \triangleq pass(O_i, \underline{mk}\text{-}Result(d_2, m_2))$.

Assume $m_1 \neq m_2$ and that "now", the following holds: $\bigtriangledown Pass_1 \land Pass_2$. To prove ES3 we then have to show that $d_1 \neq d_2$ follows from the internal properties.

From the proposition we have two cases:

Case 1: $i = \underline{s}\text{-}Init(m_2)$. Since two outputs over the same channel cannot take place at the same time, $Pass_1$ must have taken place strictly before $Pass_2$ and we therefore now have $\neg free_i(d_1)$. But according to IS5, d_2 must be free now in order let $Pass_2$ occur and therefore $d_1 \neq d_2$.

Case 2: $i \in \underline{s}\text{-}Part(m_2)$. Let $k = \underline{s}\text{-}Init(m_2)$. From IS5 it follows that

$$\bigtriangledown \ pass(R_{ki}, \underline{mk}\text{-}Result(d_2, m_2))$$

and therefore from IS2 and IS3 there exists a set of dates ds such that

$$\bigtriangledown \ (pass(A_{ik}, \underline{mk}\text{-}Answer(ds, m)) \land d_2 \in ds \land free_i(d_2))$$

Let t_{A2} be the point of time where this answer was (first) passed.

As a positive result is received about the meeting m_2 now, IS4, IS5, and IS6 ensure that no negative, nor positive result about this meeting has previously been received, i.e.

$$\neg \ (\bigtriangledown \ pass(R_{ki}, \underline{mk}\text{-}Result(x, m_2)) \land x \neq d_2 \ ) \land \neg \ \bigtriangledown \ pass(O_i, \underline{mk}\text{-}Result(d_2, m_2))$$

According to the definition of *reserved* it follows that since t_{A2}, d_2 must have been reserved.

If $Pass_1$ has taken place before t_{A2}, d_1 must have been non-free at t_{A2} and therefore $d_2 \neq d_1$.

If $Pass_1$ has taken place at t_{A2} or later, we have two cases:

Case 2.1: $i = \underline{s}\text{-}Init(m_1)$. From IS5 it then follows that d_1 must have been unreserved when $Pass_1$ took place and therefore $d_1 \neq d_2$.

Case 2.2: $i \in \underline{s}\text{-}Part(m_1)$. As above, we conclude that at some time t_{A1}, Agent$_i$ must have given an answer containing d_1 and from this time on, d_1 has been reserved or non-free. Whatever t_{A1} comes before or after t_{A2} we are therefore led to conclude that $d_1 \neq d_2$.

Since in any case $\bigtriangledown Pass_1 \land Pass_2 \Rightarrow d_1 \neq d_2$, ES3 holds.

A Reduction Semantics for Imperative Higher-Order Languages

Matthias Felleisen, Daniel P. Friedman

Computer Science Department, Indiana University, Bloomington, IN 47405, USA

Abstract

Imperative higher-order languages are a highly expressive programming medium. Compared to functional programming languages, they permit the construction of safe and modular programs. However, functional languages have a simple reduction semantics, which makes it easy to evaluate program pieces in parallel. In order to overcome this dilemma, we construct a conservative extension of the λ-calculus that can deal with control and assignment facilities. This calculus simultaneously provides an algebraic reasoning system and an elegant reduction semantics of higher-order imperative languages. We show that the evaluation of applications can still take advantage of parallelism and that the major cost of these evaluations stems from the necessary communication for substitutions. Since this is also true for functional languages, we conjecture that if a successful parallel evaluation scheme for functional languages is possible, then the same strategy will also solve the problem of parallel evaluations for imperative programming languages.

1. *Pro* Imperative Higher-Order Languages

A programming language is a medium for expressing thoughts about problems and their solutions. This statement is folk wisdom, yet, it has been ignored since programming became an activity performed on real machines. In the beginning, programming languages were considered as command languages for computers. This view grew out of the popular imperative programming languages for the early computing machines and the necessity for maximal utilization of scarce resources.

Another phase in programming language research was determined by the advent of non-von-Neumann computer architectures. The realization was that the traditional way of processing programs had a bottleneck and that this bottleneck should be eliminated in favor of as much parallel processing as possible. But, instead of implementing redesigned traditional languages on these modern machines, new languages were invented. The prevailing opinion was [4, 17] that "increasing performance by exploiting parallelism must go hand in hand with making the programming of *these* machines easier."[1] This argument, together with a trend for more mathematical languages, ignited interest in applicative languages [1].

Applicative languages are easy to implement on non-traditional reduction architectures. They have a simple operational model based on reduction semantics. However, these languages lack abstractions for expressing evaluation control and state change because these facilities invalidate ordinary reduction semantics and thus complicate parallelization of program evaluations. Programmers must simulate these imperative effects in applicative languages by using and optimizing tricks of denotational semantics, *e.g.*, accumulators, auxiliary functions, or the clumsy passing around of state variables. Again, the burden is borne by the programmer.

Our basic premise is that the language user should not feel any restrictions caused by the underlying implementation machine. We agree that a language must have a clean, mathematical reasoning system, but, we also insist that a language must include control and assignment facilities as fundamental abstractions for expressing evaluation control and state change. They are necessary ingredients for secure, modular, and compositional programming.

The starting point of our development is the λ-calculus [2], more precisely, the λ-value-calculus [20], which is simultaneously a language and a reasoning system. Its advantage is that all objects, including functions, are first-class, *i.e.*, there is no restriction on their use. The programming language contains two additional facilities which preserve this property. One gives full access and control over

---

[1] [17, p.350], emphasis ours.

the current continuation of an expression; the other abstracts the right to reassign a value to a variable. Programming paradigms such as logic, functional, or object-oriented programming are easily emulated in this language by implementing the respective constructs as syntactic abstractions [3, 13].

Recently [6, 7] we presented two extensions of the λ_v-calculus which independently model control and assignment facilities. Here we demonstrate that the two extensions can be unified. The new calculus automatically yields a reduction semantics for imperative higher-order languages. The standard reduction strategy of the calculus reveals considerable potential for parallelism in the evaluation of programs. A minor result is the introduction of a new control construct. While simplifying the reductions of the control calculus [6], it syntactically subsumes all traditional control constructs and permits the design of an entirely new class of programs [5].

The emphasis here is on the development of the reduction semantics since it is crucial for the parallel implementation of programs. The reader who is more interested in the proof system is referred to the earlier reports,[2] but the relevant material is repeated here for completeness. In the next section we formalize the syntax and semantics of the programming language and demonstrate with a few examples how some commonly found facilities of other languages are simple syntactic abstractions. The third section contains the transformation of our abstract machine semantics into a program rewriting system. The derivation method is new; some of the intermediate stages are remotely related to Plotkin-style operational semantics [19]. In Section 4 we reformulate the rewriting system as a set of freely applicable notions of reduction. Section 5 addresses implementation issues. An alternative definition of standard evaluation reveals that the reduction system for the programming language offers ample opportunity for evaluating programs in parallel.

2. The Programming Language

The programming language is an idealized version of such imperative higher-order programming languages as ISWIM [14], GEDANKEN [22], and Scheme [23]. Its term set $\Lambda_{\mathcal{F}\sigma}$ is an extension of the term set Λ of the λ-calculus. The two new kinds of expressions are $\mathcal{F}$-applications and σ-abstractions. An $\mathcal{F}$-application is of the form $(\mathcal{F}M)$ where M is an arbitrary expression; when evaluated, it applies M to a functional abstraction of its current continuation, i.e., a functional representation of the rest of the computation. These abstractions have the same status and behavior as functions created by λ-abstractions. The syntax of a σ-abstraction is $(\sigma x.M)$ for a variable x and a term M. The abstraction does not bind the variable, but abstracts the right to reassign a value to the variable. When invoked on a value, a σ-abstraction performs the reassignment and then continues to evaluate its body, which yields a result for the entire application. The meaning of the remaining constructs should be adapted accordingly: variables are assignable placeholders for values, abstractions correspond to call-by-value procedures, and applications invoke the result of the function part on the value of the argument part. The syntax is summarized in Definition 2.1.

The sets of free and bound variables of a term M, $FV(M)$ and $BV(M)$, are defined as usual; the only binding construct in the language is the λ-abstraction. The set of assignable variables in M, $AV(M)$, contains all variables that occur in the variable position of a σ-abstraction. Terms with no free variables are called *closed terms* or *programs*. To avoid syntactic issues, we adopt Barendregt's *α-congruence convention* of identifying ($\equiv_\alpha$ or just $\equiv$) terms that are equal modulo some renaming of bound variables and his *hygiene convention* which says that in a discussion, free variables are assumed to be distinct from bound ones. Substitution is extended in the natural way and we use the notation $M[x := N]$ to

---

[2] C. Talcott [24] and I. Mason [18] also have designed reasoning systems for control and [first-order] assignment abstractions, respectively. However, their systems are not extensions of λ-calculi, but are equational theories based on rewriting machines similar to the ones we present in Section 3. Neither addresses the issue of reduction systems; work on a unification of the two systems is in progress [personal communication].

Definition 2.1: The programming language $\Lambda_{\mathcal{F}\sigma}$

The improper symbols are λ, $($, $)$, $.$, $\mathcal{F}$, and σ. *Vars* is a countable set of variables. The symbols $x, y, \ldots$ range over *Vars* as meta-variables but are also used as if they were elements of *Vars*. The *term set* $\Lambda_{\mathcal{F}\sigma}$ contains

— *variables:* x if $x \in$ *Vars*;

— *abstractions:* $(\lambda x.M)$ if $M \in \Lambda_{\mathcal{F}\sigma}$ and $x \in$ *Vars*;

— *applications:* (MN) if $M, N \in \Lambda_{\mathcal{F}\sigma}$;

— $\mathcal{F}$-*applications:* $(\mathcal{F}M)$ if $M \in \Lambda_{\mathcal{F}\sigma}$;

— σ-*abstractions:* $(\sigma x.M)$ if $x \in$ *Vars* and $M \in \Lambda_{\mathcal{F}\sigma}$.

The union of variables, abstractions, and σ-abstractions is referred to as the set of *(syntactic) values.*

Definition 2.2: The CESK-transition function

$$\langle x, \rho, \theta, \kappa \rangle \overset{CESK}{\longmapsto} \langle \ddagger, \emptyset, \theta, (\kappa \, \mathrm{ret} \, \theta(\rho(x))) \rangle \tag{1}$$

$$\langle \lambda x.M, \rho, \theta, \kappa \rangle \overset{CESK}{\longmapsto} \langle \ddagger, \emptyset, \theta, (\kappa \, \mathrm{ret} \, \langle \lambda x.M, \rho \rangle) \rangle \tag{2}$$

$$\langle MN, \rho, \theta, \kappa \rangle \overset{CESK}{\longmapsto} \langle M, \rho, \theta, (\kappa \, \mathrm{arg} \, N \, \rho) \rangle \tag{3}$$

$$\langle \ddagger, \emptyset, \theta, ((\kappa \, \mathrm{arg} \, N \, \rho) \, \mathrm{ret} \, F) \rangle \overset{CESK}{\longmapsto} \langle N, \rho, \theta, (\kappa \, \mathrm{fun} \, F) \rangle \tag{4}$$

$$\langle \ddagger, \emptyset, \theta, ((\kappa \, \mathrm{fun} \, \langle \lambda x.M, \rho \rangle) \, \mathrm{ret} \, V) \rangle \overset{CESK}{\longmapsto} \langle M, \rho[x := n], \theta[n := V], \kappa \rangle \tag{5}$$

$$\text{where } n \notin Dom(\theta)$$

$$\langle \mathcal{F}M, \rho, \theta, \kappa \rangle \overset{CESK}{\longmapsto} \langle M\gamma, \rho[\gamma := \langle \mathrm{p}, \kappa \rangle], \theta, (\mathrm{stop}) \rangle \tag{6}$$

$$\langle \ddagger, \emptyset, \theta, ((\kappa \, \mathrm{fun} \, \langle \mathrm{p}, \kappa_0 \rangle) \, \mathrm{ret} \, V) \rangle \overset{CESK}{\longmapsto} \langle \ddagger, \emptyset, \theta, (\kappa \otimes \kappa_0 \, \mathrm{ret} \, V) \rangle \tag{7}$$

$$\langle \sigma x.M, \rho, \theta, \kappa \rangle \overset{CESK}{\longmapsto} \langle \ddagger, \emptyset, \theta, (\kappa \, \mathrm{ret} \, \langle \sigma x.M, \rho \rangle) \rangle \tag{8}$$

$$\langle \ddagger, \emptyset, \theta, ((\kappa \, \mathrm{fun} \, \langle \sigma x.M, \rho \rangle) \, \mathrm{ret} \, V) \rangle \overset{CESK}{\longmapsto} \langle M, \rho, \theta[\rho(x) := V], \kappa \rangle. \tag{9}$$

---

denote the result of substituting all free variables x in M by N.

The semantics of $\Lambda_{\mathcal{F}\sigma}$-programs is defined via an abstract state-transition machine. The machine manipulates quadruples of control strings, environments, stores, and continuations. A *control string* is either the symbol $\ddagger$ or a $\Lambda_{\mathcal{F}\sigma}$-expression. A variable γ is reserved for exclusive use in machine transitions. *Environments*, denoted by ρ, are finite maps from variables to semantic values and locations. *Stores*, denoted by θ, are finite maps from locations and semantic values to semantic values; stores are the identity map on values. We use the set of natural numbers as locations. If f is an environment or store, then $f[x := y]$ is like f except at the place x where it is y. The set of *semantic values* is the union of closures and program points. A *closure* is an ordered pair $\langle M, \rho \rangle$ composed of an abstraction M and an environment ρ whose domain covers the free variables of the abstraction. Depending on the kind of abstraction, a closure is called λ- or σ-closure. A *program point* is a p-tagged continuation code.

A *continuation code* remembers the remainder of the computation during the evaluation of the current control string. The domain of continuations consists of two subdomains: p- and ret-continuations. A ret-continuation $(\kappa \, \mathrm{ret} \, V)$ consists of a p-continuation code κ and a semantic value V. The value is supplied to the p-continuation so that it can finish whatever is left to do. p-Continuations are defined inductively and have the following intuitive function with respect to an evaluation:

— **(stop)** stands for the initial continuation, specifying that nothing is left to do;

— $(\kappa \arg N \rho)$ indicates that N is the argument part of an application, that ρ is the environment of the application, and that κ is its continuation;

— $(\kappa \operatorname{fun} V)$ represents the case where the evaluation of a function part yielded V as a value, and κ is the continuation of the application.

Machine states of the form $\langle M, \emptyset, \emptyset, (\operatorname{stop}) \rangle$ are *initial*; if V is a closure and θ is defined on all locations which are used by V then $\langle \ddagger, \emptyset, \theta, ((\operatorname{stop}) \operatorname{ret} V) \rangle$ is a *terminal* state.

The CESK-transition function is displayed in Definition 2.2. The first five rules evaluate the functional subset of $\Lambda_{\mathcal{F}\sigma}$. They correspond to the transition rules of the SECD-machine [16]. The store component is superfluous with respect to this subset and could be merged with the environment. (CESK6) and (CESK7) describe the evaluation of an $\mathcal{F}$-application and the application of a continuation to a value; (CESK8) and (CESK9) define the effect of an assignment application.

The evaluation of an $\mathcal{F}$-application directly corresponds to the informal description of $\mathcal{F}$. The $\mathcal{F}$-argument is applied to γ, which stands for the current continuation. The current continuation is transferred out of the register into a p-closure and this gives the program total control over its use. In particular, the decision about when to use the continuation is left to the program.

The application of a continuation in a $\Lambda_{\mathcal{F}\sigma}$-program results in the concatenation of the applied continuation to the current one with the auxiliary function $\otimes$:

$$\kappa \otimes (\operatorname{stop}) = \kappa$$
$$\kappa \otimes (\kappa' \arg N \rho) = (\kappa \otimes \kappa' \arg N \rho)$$
$$\kappa \otimes (\kappa' \operatorname{fun} V) = (\kappa \otimes \kappa' \operatorname{fun} V)$$

This causes the machine to evaluate the applied continuation as if it were a function. If the applied continuation does not affect its continuation during the evaluation, the result is returned to the point of application.

The effect of an assignment application depends on three different factors. First, occurrences of variables are disambiguated via the environment, but the store contains the associated current value. Second, the store component of a CESK-evaluation is always present. The only operations on the store are updates and extensions. Unlike the environment, it never shrinks nor is it removed from its register. Third, the rules (CESK8) and (CESK9) jointly manipulate the location-value association in the store according to an intuitive understanding of assignment. (CESK8) produces a σ-closure from a σ-abstraction and the current environment. Thus the transition rule (CESK9) changes the value of the variable that was lexically visible at definition time. Because of the constant presence of the store, every subsequent occurrence of this variable refers to the new value.

In order to abstract from the machine details, we define an evaluation function that maps programs to value-store pairs:

$$eval_{CESK}(M) = \langle V, \theta \rangle \text{ iff } \langle M, \emptyset, \emptyset, (\operatorname{stop}) \rangle \overset{CESK^+}{\longmapsto} \langle \ddagger, \emptyset, \theta, ((\operatorname{stop}) \operatorname{ret} V) \rangle.$$

When we refer to the extensional semantics of $\Lambda_{\mathcal{F}\sigma}$, we mean this $eval_{CESK}$-function. The intension behind this function with respect to the CESK-machine is the CESK-transition function. In other words, $eval_{CESK}$ defines *which* value-store pair is the result of a program, and the transition function says *how* this result is computed.

The distinction between extensional and intensional semantics is extremely important for our development. From the extensional point of view, which is that of a programmer, the programming language is—exactly like the λ-calculus—an entirely sequential language. To an outside observer this means that events in an evaluation are totally ordered. No function in our language nor in the λ-calculus can thus compute the mathematical (symmetric) or-function. However, the sequentiality of our intensional semantics depends on the granularity of the event representation. We shall see a number of different machine architectures, each of which is extensionally equivalent to, but intensionally rather different from the CESK-machine.

At this point, we clarify the formal semantics with a few programming examples. Beyond providing insight into the semantics, these examples also illustrate some of the expressiveness of imperative higher-order languages. Lack of space prohibits broader treatment of this issue. The interested reader is referred to the literature.

$\mathcal{F}$-applications are closely related to the call/cc-function in Scheme [3]. There are two essential differences. First, when call/cc is applied to a function, it provides this function access to the current continuation, but it also leaves the continuation in its register. This effect can be achieved by an $\mathcal{F}$-application if the $\mathcal{F}$-argument immediately invokes the continuation. Second and more important, call/cc applies its argument to a continuation object, which, when applied in turn, discards the current continuation; an $\mathcal{F}$-application, however, simply provides its argument with a function that upon invocation performs the same action as the current continuation. Hence, a simulation of call/cc must pass a function to the call/cc argument which ignores its current continuation, or, in terms of $\mathcal{F}$-applications, the object must grab the continuation without using it. Putting all this together produces the following equivalence:

$$\text{call/cc} \equiv \lambda f.\mathcal{F}(\lambda k.k(f(\lambda v.\mathcal{F}(\lambda d.kv)))).$$

Landin's J-operator [15] and Reynolds's **escape**-construct [21] are also closely related language facilities. Both are syntactic variations on call/cc [8] and hence, we omit detailed treatment. None of these facilities can implement an $\mathcal{F}$-application as a syntactic abstraction because of the abortive effect of their continuation objects.

The assignment abstraction is more conventional. In traditional expression-oriented languages, statements usually come together with a block like **begin** $\langle stmt \rangle$ **result** $\langle exp \rangle$. This is a block that first performs the statement-part and then evaluates the expression-part to return a result. Together with ordinary assignment this block can express an assignment abstraction as a function:

$$\sigma x.M \equiv (\lambda v.(\textbf{begin } x := v \textbf{ result } M))$$
where v is a fresh variable.

The inverse relationship is expressed by

$$\textbf{begin } x := N \textbf{ result } M \equiv (\sigma x.M)N.$$

The choice of σ-abstractions over assignment statements is for syntactic and proof-technical reasons only.

The implementation of call/cc and ordinary assignment as syntactic abstraction makes clear that all programs that were written with these facilities can also be written in $\Lambda_{\mathcal{F}\sigma}$. However, there are control constructs that are more easily defined with $\mathcal{F}$. For example, the operation halt, which is implicitly used in the definition of call/cc, is realized by grabbing and ignoring the current continuation:

$$\text{halt} \stackrel{df}{=} \lambda x.\mathcal{F}(\lambda d.x).$$

An exit-facility in a function-body is an equally simple use of $\mathcal{F}$. Suppose we want an abstraction

$$(\textbf{function } x \text{ } Body)$$

which is like an ordinary function, except that its function body may contain exit-expressions of the form

$$(\text{exit } Exp).$$

The effect of an exit-expression is an immediate return to the function caller with the value of Exp. When cast into continuation terminology, this description leads to the obvious implementation of function- and exit-expressions: an exit-expression resumes the continuation of the function-application. With call/cc we get:

$$(\text{function } x \ Body) \overset{df}{=} \lambda x.\text{call/cc}(\lambda \epsilon.Body_\epsilon),$$

$$(\text{exit } Exp) \overset{df}{=} (\epsilon \ Exp).$$

We hereby assume that exit's ϵ and the ϵ in the call/cc-expression are the same. Although all of these programming constructs look functional, the reader should be aware that the presence of $\mathcal{F}$ makes them imperative.

Assignment abstractions are also imperative in nature, but they give rise to a different class of programs. In conjunction with higher-order functions it is easy to program reference cells with σ-abstractions. The three operations on a cell are: mk-cell, which creates a new cell with given contents; deref, which looks up the current contents of a cell; and set-cell, which changes the contents of a cell to a new value and returns this value upon completion. An implementation of this set of functions is:

$$\text{mk-cell} \overset{df}{=} \lambda x.\lambda m.mx(\sigma x.x),$$

$$\text{deref} \overset{df}{=} \lambda c.c(\lambda xs.x),$$

$$\text{set-cell} \overset{df}{=} \lambda c.c(\lambda xs.s).$$

The definition of set-cell clarifies why we call σ-abstraction "an abstraction of the right to reassign a value to x." When set-cell is applied to a cell, it returns a σ-abstraction, which upon application changes the content of the cell.

The implementation strategy for single-value cells generalizes to full Lisp-cons cells and Smalltalk-objects in a straightforward manner. Furthermore, with mutable cells a program can create circular structures to model self-referential dependencies in the real-world. A use of state variables for remembering the current control state of a computation leads to simple implementations of such facilities as coroutines [10], backtrack points [9], and relations [11].

In summary, we have demonstrated that the programming language (together with an appropriate syntax preprocessor [13]) is interesting and expressive. Its semantics is defined via an abstract machine that is derived from a denotational specification via a well-explored technique [12, 21, 25]. An implementation of the machine on stock hardware is straightforward and reasonably efficient. Given its character as a rewriting system, a reduction or a rewriting machine could also serve as an implementation vehicle, but, such an implementation could not utilize the inherent parallelism in these machines. The intensional specification of the semantics is sequential in nature and any attempt to exploit parallelism on the basis of these specifications remains *ad hoc*. The underlying reason is that the structure of the machine states and the state representations are too closely tied to conventional architectures. However, we doubt that any of the state components besides the control string is *natural* in the sense that it is unavoidable for the specification of the language semantics. An elimination of these extra components can clearly improve the comprehensibility of the machine activities and should give more insight into the intensional aspects of the language semantics.

3. From the CESK-Machine to a Control String-Rewriting System

An evaluation of a program on the CESK-machine is a sophisticated interplay between the control string and the other three auxiliary components. In the course of program evaluation, parts of the control string are mapped to values in the environment-store system, others become a part of the continuation code. At other points control strings are shuffled back from the auxiliary components into the control string register. Our objective in this section is to integrate the extra state components into the control string by extending the programming language.

3.1. Eliminating Environments

Environments map free variables of a control string to their meaning. They directly correspond to stacks on traditional machines. For machines which only simulate stacks, quasi-substitution generally improves the performance. Instead of storing away the meaning of free variables, quasi-substitution replaces all free variables in a control string by their meaning. For the CESK-machine this means that applications of λ-closures to values now place values and locations in the control string. The Λf_σ-language is modified accordingly. Otherwise, the system remains the same.

3.2. Eliminating Continuations

An inspection of some sample evaluations on the CESK-machine reveals that the continuation code is like a control string memory. Those pieces of the control string that are of no interest to the current computation phase are shifted to the continuation stack. This is equally true for (syntactic) values in the control string register. Such a step causes the machine to look in the continuation code for what to do next. In case the two parts of an application have been identified as proper values, the appropriate action, i.e., a function, continuation, or assigner invocation, is performed; otherwise, the search is continued.

From the perspective of the program as a whole, the machine searches through the term until it finds a value in the left part of an application. Then it backs up and continues the search in the right part of the application. Once an application with two values—a *redex*—has been found, a computation step changes the corresponding subterm. During the search phase the *context* of the redex is moved to the continuation. In other words, the p-continuation encodes the textual context of a redex, and it is therefore quite natural to represent p-continuation codes as contexts. Informally, an applicative context—or sometimes context for short—is a term with a hole in it such that the path from the root to the hole goes through applications only. Let $C[\ ]$ stand for a context, then the inductive definition is:[3]

— $[\ ]$ is the empty context or hole,

— $VC[\ ]$ is a context where V is a value, and

— $C[\ ]M$ is a context where M is arbitrary.

If $C[\ ]$ is a context, then $C[M]$ is the term where the hole is filled with the term M.

The definition of applicative contexts captures the dynamic character of the search phase in the correct way. The context hole corresponds to the current search area. If a value is in the left part of an application, the search moves to the right; otherwise, the search space is narrowed down to the left part.

Once the continuation representation uses contexts, the control string and the continuation component can be merged. First, the holes of the contexts are filled with the respective term, $\updownarrow$'s are simply dropped. Then all the search rules are eliminated. These two steps together yield a control string-store machine whose transition function is displayed in Definition 3.1. All other concepts are modified appropriately.

3.3. The Control String-Rewriting System

After the elimination of environments and continuations we are left with a system that is solely based on control strings and stores. The role of the store is characterized by the three transition rules (CS1), (CS2), and (CS5): they use, extend, and modify the store. The crucial rule is (CS2). It replaces bound variables of a λ-abstraction by a new, distinct location and thus gradually builds the store. Future

---

[3] Generally, contexts are defined in a broader sense, i.e., as a term with at least one hole and no restriction on the location of the hole. Since we only use applicative contexts in this paper, the terminology should not cause any confusion.

Definition 3.1: The CS-machine

$$\langle C[n], \theta \rangle \xrightarrow{CS} \langle C[\theta(n)], \theta \rangle \tag{1}$$

$$\langle C[(\lambda x.M)V], \theta \rangle \xrightarrow{CS} \langle C[M[x := n]], \theta[n := V] \rangle \quad \text{where } n \notin Dom(\theta) \tag{2}$$

$$\langle C[\mathcal{F}M], \theta \rangle \xrightarrow{CS} \langle M\langle \mathbf{p}, C[\ ]\rangle, \theta \rangle \tag{3}$$

$$\langle C[\langle \mathbf{p}, C_0[\ ]\rangle V], \theta \rangle \xrightarrow{CS} \langle C[C_0[V]], \theta \rangle \tag{4}$$

$$\langle C[(\sigma n.M)V], \theta \rangle \xrightarrow{CS} \langle C[M], \theta[n := V] \rangle \tag{5}$$

---

references to a bound variable are resolved via the always-present store. A request for the current value of a variable causes a store lookup; an instruction to change the current value results in a modified store. It is therefore important to understand the nature of bound variables.

At this point we must recall the α-congruence convention about bound variables in terms. According to this convention, the name of a bound variable is irrelevant (up to uniqueness). Abstractions like $\lambda x.x$ and $\lambda y.y$ are considered to be the same. This actually means that the programming language is the quotient of Λ over $\equiv_\alpha$. From this perspective, a λ-abstraction is an expression together with a relation that determines which parts of the expression are equivalent. The relationship is manifested by occurrences of the bound variable.

A unification of our ideas on the role of the CS-store and the nature of bound variables directly leads to an abstracted view of the store. The intention behind the replacement of bound variables by unique locations in the bodies of λ-abstractions is to retain the *static* α-equivalence for the rest of the computation, i.e., as a *dynamic* relation, even after the $\lambda x.$-part has disappeared. Hence, if we want to integrate the store into the control string language, we must find a way to express this dynamic relationship.

The most natural possibility is a labeling scheme. Instead of placing a location into the program text and the value into the store, the value could be labeled with the location and placed into the text as a *labeled value*.[4] With respect to the transition relation, we replace

$$\langle C[(\lambda x.M)V], \theta \rangle \xrightarrow{CS} \langle C[M[x := n]], \theta[n := V] \rangle \quad \text{where } n \notin Dom(\theta)$$

by

$$C[(\lambda x.M)V] \longmapsto C[M[x := V^n]] \text{ where } n \text{ is not used in the rest of the program.}$$

V^n is the labeled version of the value V. With this labeling technique it is indeed possible to re-interpret lookups and assignments as term manipulations.

The effect of an assignment relies on the introduction of a new substitution operation. In the extended term language, a σ-application looks like

$$(\sigma U^n.M)V$$

when it is about to be evaluated. The assignable variable has been replaced by a labeled value; all other related variable positions carry the same label. When it is time to perform the above σ-application, all these occurrences of an n-labeled value must be replaced by n-labeled values V. To implement this, we introduce the labeled value substitution $M[n := V]$. The result of $M[n := V]$ is a term like M except

---

[4] Labeled terms have also been used for the investigation of the regular λ-calculus [2, p.353]. Although our problem is unrelated to these investigations we have adopted the notation in order to avoid the introduction of an entirely new concept.

Definition 3.2: The C-rewriting system

$$C[V^n] \overset{C}{\longmapsto} C[V[n := V]] \tag{1}$$

$$C[(\lambda x.M)V] \overset{C}{\longmapsto} C[M[x := V^n]] \quad \text{where } n \text{ is fresh} \tag{2}$$

$$C[\mathcal{F}M] \overset{C}{\longmapsto} M\langle \mathbf{p}, C[\ ]\rangle \tag{3}$$

$$C[\langle \mathbf{p}, C_0[\ ]\rangle V] \overset{C}{\longmapsto} C[C_0[V]] \tag{4}$$

$$C[(\sigma U^n.M)V] \overset{C}{\longmapsto} C[M][n := V] \tag{5}$$

The labeled term substitution $L[n := V]$ is defined by:

$x[n := V] = x,\ U^n[n := V] = V^n,\ U^m[n := V] = U[n := V]^m$ if $n \neq m$,

$(\lambda x.M)[n := V] = \lambda x.M[n := V]$,

$(MN)[n := V] = (M[n := V]N[n := V])$,

$(\mathcal{F}M)[n := V] = (\mathcal{F}M[n := V])$,

$(\sigma X.M)[n := V] = (\sigma X[n := V].M[n := V])$,

$\langle \mathbf{p}, C[\ ]\rangle[n := V] = \langle \mathbf{p}, C[\ ][n := V]\rangle,\ [\ ][n := V] = [\ ]$.

---

that all subterms labeled n are replaced by V^n. With this new operation, the assignment transition is definable as

$$C[(\sigma U^n.M)V] \longmapsto C[M][n := V].$$

At first glance, a variable lookup merely strips off the label from the labeled value which is now already sitting in the right position. Yet, a closer look reveals that this strategy has a minor flaw: it cannot deal with circular or self-referential assignments. When the label n appears not only in $C[M]$ but also in V, the equivalence-positions in V are not affected by the labeled value substitution. There are two obvious ways out of this dilemma. First, we can blame the assignment statement and require that self-referential assignment builds a circular or infinite term. Second, we can find a more intelligent lookup transition that is knowledgeable about circularities. In other words, the assignment transition only updates the equivalence classes within the program and leaves the equivalence positions within the new value alone. The complimentary lookup transition is then something like a by-need continuation of the latest assignment transition or their equivalence class:

$$C[V^n] \longmapsto C[V[n := V]].$$

This version of the lookup transition simultaneously strips off a label and updates all equivalence positions within the value.

Definition 3.2 contains the formalization of the transition function. With respect to changes in the language $\Lambda_{\mathcal{F}\sigma}$, we leave it at the above informal description. The *eval*-function for the rewriting semantics maps programs directly to values:

$$eval_C(M) = V \text{ iff } M \overset{C}{\longmapsto}{}^* V.$$

The correspondence between the CESK- and the C-rewriting semantics is captured in the following

Theorem 1 (C-Simulation). *There is a morphism* Unload *such that for all programs* $M \in \Lambda_{\mathcal{F}\sigma}$

$$eval_C(M) = \text{Unload}(eval_{CESK}(M)).$$

Proof. The proof has four parts, each establishing the correctness of one of the transformations in this section. For each part, we define a principal morphism that models the crucial idea of the corresponding transformation step. Based on this morphism, an induction on the number of evaluation steps shows that two corresponding states in two evaluation sequences are related by this morphism. The four morphisms are:

$$R(\langle M, \rho \rangle) = M[x_1 := \rho(x_1)] \dots [x_n := \rho(x_n)] \quad \text{where } FV(M) = \{x_1, \dots, x_n\}$$

for eliminating environments;

$$\left. \begin{array}{l} S((\text{stop})) = [\ ] \\ S((\kappa\,\text{arg}\,N)) = C[[\ \ ]S(N)] \\ S((\kappa\,\text{fun}\,F)) = C[S(F)[\ \ ]] \end{array} \right\} \quad \text{where } S(\kappa) = C[\ \ ]$$

for representing p-continuations as contexts;

$$T(\ddagger, (C[\ \ ]\,\text{ret}\,V)) = C[V]$$
$$T(M, C[\ \ ]) = C[M]$$

for merging continuations and control strings; and

$$U(x, \theta) = x,$$
$$U(n, \theta) = U(\theta(n), \theta[n := (\lambda x.x)])^n,$$
$$U(\lambda x.M, \theta) = \lambda x.U(M, \theta),$$
$$U(MN, \theta) = U(M, \theta)U(N, \theta),$$
$$U(\mathcal{F}M, \theta) = \mathcal{F}U(M, \theta),$$
$$U(\langle p, C[\ \ ] \rangle, \theta) = \langle p, U(C[\ \ ], \theta) \rangle,$$
$$U([\ \ ], \theta) = [\ \ ],$$
$$U(\sigma X.M, \theta) = (\sigma U(X, \theta).U(M, \theta))$$

for folding the store into the control string. The rest of the proof is tedious, but routine. The required morphism Unload is the composition of U, S, and R. □

Theorem 1 stipulates a redefinition of $eval_{CESK}$:

$$eval_{CESK}(M) = \text{Unload}(V, \theta) \text{ iff } \langle M, \emptyset, \emptyset, (\text{stop}) \rangle \stackrel{CESK^+}{\longmapsto} \langle \ddagger, \emptyset, \theta, ((\text{stop})\,\text{ret}\,V) \rangle$$

since the user is only interested in the final values and their relationship to the rest of the store. Given this, the claim of the theorem is that $eval_C$ and $eval_{CESK}$ extensionally define the same semantics.

The advantages of the C-rewriting system are obvious. The domain of the transition function is a minor variant of $\Lambda_{\mathcal{F}\sigma}$; the function itself only consists of five rules. Continuations have become something more intuitive, namely, the textual context of an evaluation redex. Labeled values, though complex at first glance, also have a number of advantages. For example, a vacuously abstracted variable causes the CESK-machine to enlarge the domain of the store; in the C-rewriting system the labeled value simply disappears and with it the useless label. Unfortunately, the transition rules are context dependent. It is therefore impossible to freely apply these rewriting rules to subterms. In the next section, we derive a reduction calculus that is equivalent to the C-rewriting system with the desired properties.

4. The λ_v-CS-Calculus

The context dependency of the C-rewriting transition rules has two entirely different aspects. First, the requirement that $C[\ \ ]$ is an applicative context enforces the correct timing of rewriting steps. Since there is exactly one partitioning of a program into a redex and a context, only one action is possible at any given time. Second, the context of such a pair represents the current continuation and can thus become a part of the program in the form of a program point. The latter dependency can apparently be eliminated by encoding a context as a term, but the former is inherent: by their very nature, imperative actions must happen in a certain order.

Because of the dichotomy between timing and context dependency there is no hope of finding a set of entirely context-free reduction relations. The closest we can get is a system where the dependency is confined to a particular point. The root of the term offers itself for this purpose. If there is no context to a redex, the entire extent of the reduction step is known. Therefore, the obvious solution is to distribute the transition work to two sets of relations: ordinary reductions, whose task it is to move a C-redex-like term to the root, and special relations, which perform the imperative action at the root of a program. We refer to these special steps as computation rules or steps and mark them with $\triangleright$ instead of the customary $\rightarrow$ for notions of reduction.

The computation rule for a λ-application $(\lambda x.M)V$ has the same form as the C-transition rule (C2) without context:

$$(\lambda x.M)V \triangleright_{\beta_\sigma} M[x := V^n]$$

where n neither occurs in M nor in V. Given that this rule is applicable when the redex is at the root of the term or, put differently, in the empty context, the inductive definition of applicative contexts requires us to consider two more cases: the embedding of a λ-application to the left of an arbitrary term N and to the right of a value U. In the first case, the C-rewriting semantics says that after the completion of the β-step the modified λ-body $M[x := V^n]$ and N form an application $M[x := V^n]N$. Since the second case is symmetric to the first, we suggest the two λ-reductions:

$$((\lambda x.M)V)N \longrightarrow (\lambda x.MN)V,$$
$$U((\lambda x.M)V) \longrightarrow (\lambda x.UM)V.$$

Like the β-rule itself, these reductions rely on the hygiene convention and assume that the set of free variables in N and U, respectively, is disjoint from the set of bound variables in M.

Although the proposed λ-reductions and computations obviously simulate (C2) in the right way, it is disappointing to realize that the ordinary β_v-reduction

$$(\lambda x.M)V \longrightarrow M[x := V] \qquad (\beta_v)$$

is lost. One would expect that an extension of the Λ-language as a programming language would be orthogonal with respect to the original constructs and that therefore the new calculus would be an extension of the λ_v-calculus. The flaw in our development is the convention that *assignable* and *non-assignable* variables are the same kind of objects. The solution is to split the variable set into two disjoint subsets, one for each category. Accordingly, the β-rewriting rule is split into two different transitions and the set of reductions is extended with the β_v-relation. This decision simultaneously makes our calculus-extension conservative and clarifies why a λ-application for an assignable variable must *bubble up* to the top of a term. While an ordinary β-reduction discards the sharing relation of the λ-abstraction, a $\triangleright_{\beta_\sigma}$-computation retains it for the rest of the computation and hence, if these transitions are in accord with the original semantics, they establish these dynamic sharing relations at the appropriate time.

The simulation of assignment with reductions and computation rules is now straightforward. A σ-application can work its way to the top of a term with rules similar to those for a λ-application. The computation rule becomes

$$(\sigma U^n.M)V \triangleright_\sigma M[n := V].$$

For the delabeling step (C1) this technique does not work since a labeled value V^n does not contain a natural continuation part. Our solution is to replace all assignable variables by a delabel-application of the form $(\mathcal{D}\,x\,M)$ where M is expected to consume the proper value of x after the delabeling transition. A $\mathcal{D}$-application at the top simply delabels the labeled value and applies M to the value:

$$(\mathcal{D}\,V^n M) \rhd_{\mathcal{D}} MV[n := V].$$

If $(\mathcal{D}\,V^n M)$ is to the left of some expression N, the $\mathcal{D}$-application must somehow incorporate the argument N into the consumer expression in order to move closer to the top. According to the intuitive semantics of $\mathcal{D}$-applications, the entire application would first delabel V^n, then apply M to the resulting value, and finally, the result of this application would consume N. Abstracting from the value, this informal description is captured in the λ-abstraction $\lambda v.MvN$ and hence, the two necessary reductions for $\mathcal{D}$-applications are:

$$(\mathcal{D}\,V^n M)N \to (\mathcal{D}\,V^n(\lambda x.MxN)),$$
$$U(\mathcal{D}\,V^n M) \to (\mathcal{D}\,V^n(\lambda x.U(Mx))).$$

Finally, we turn to the simulation of $\mathcal{F}$-applications. The crucial idea is that a context $C[\;]$ can be perceived as a function of its hole. Based on this observation, the C-transition rules (C3) and (C4) could be replaced by

$$C[\mathcal{F}M] \longrightarrow M(\lambda x.C[x])$$

without changing the extensional semantics of the C-rewriting system. For a reduction simulation of this rule this means that $\mathcal{F}$-applications must encode their context and apply this to their argument. For the top-level computation rule this is rather simple:

$$\mathcal{F}M \rhd_{\mathcal{F}} M(\lambda x.x)$$

is the required relation. For the other cases, we must again consider the two inductive cases of a context definition. Consider the expression $(\mathcal{F}M)N$ and suppose it is embedded in a context $C[\;]$. Clearly, the function $\lambda f.fN$ is a correct encoding of the immediate context of the $\mathcal{F}$-application. The rest of the context, i.e., $C[\;]$, can be encoded by another $\mathcal{F}$-application and by building this part of the continuation into the expression $\lambda f.fN$. Putting these ideas together, the reductions for $\mathcal{F}$-applications should be

$$(\mathcal{F}M)N \longrightarrow_{\mathcal{F}} \lambda\kappa.M(\lambda f.\kappa(fN)),$$
$$U(\mathcal{F}M) \longrightarrow_{\mathcal{F}} \lambda\kappa.M(\lambda v.\kappa(Uv)).$$

The new language and its reduction and computation relations are summarized in Definition 4.1.[5] Constructing the rest of the calculus is almost standard [2, 6, 7] and we omit it. With respect to the capabilities of the λ_v-CS-calculus as a reasoning system the first important question is whether the calculus is consistent. The answer is expressed in the form of a (generalized) Church-Rosser Theorem:

Theorem 2 (Church-Rosser). *The computation relation, that is, the union of the computation relations and the transitive-reflexive and compatible closure of the reduction relations, satisfies the diamond property.*

Proof. The proof is a generalization of the Martin-Löf proof for the Church-Rosser Theorem for the traditional λ-calculus [2]. □

Equally important, but more relevant for our investigation of evaluation functions is the question whether the system defines an evaluation function that is extensionally equivalent to $eval_{CESK}$. For

---

[5] The original description of the assignment facet [7] contains the erroneous β_σ-reduction: $(\lambda x.M)V \longrightarrow M[x := V^n]$. As pointed out above, a reduction like this could establish the dynamic sharing relationships at the wrong time. However, in the standard computation function this rule is valid and hence, can be used as a shortcut: see also Section 5 below.

Definition 4.1: The λ_v-CS-calculus

The improper symbols are λ, $($, $)$, $.$, $\mathcal{F}$, σ, and $\mathcal{D}$. $Vars = Var_\lambda \cup Var_\sigma$ is a countable set of variables. The set of labels is an arbitrary, infinite set. The set of values contains variables and abstractions. U and V range over values, n over labels, and X over Var_σ and labeled values. Λ_{CS} contains

- *variables:* x if $x \in Var_\lambda$;
- *λ-abstractions:* $(\lambda x.M)$ if $M \in \Lambda_{CS}$ and $x \in Vars$;
- *applications:* (MN) if $M, N \in \Lambda_{CS}$;
- *$\mathcal{F}$-applications:* $(\mathcal{F}M)$ if $M \in \Lambda_{CS}$;
- *σ-abstractions:* $(\sigma x.M)$ and $(\sigma V^n.M)$ if $M, N \in \Lambda_{CS}$ and $x \in Var_\sigma$;
- *$\mathcal{D}$-applications:* $(\mathcal{D}\,x\,M)$ and $(\mathcal{D}\,V^n\,M)$ if $M \in \Lambda_{CS}$ and $x \in Var_\sigma$.

All variables in the following notions of reductions are in Var_λ unless explicitly stated otherwise:

$$(\lambda x.M)V \xrightarrow{\beta_v} M[x := V] \text{ where } V \text{ is a value,} \qquad (\beta_v)$$

$$U((\lambda x.M)V) \xrightarrow{\beta_R} (\lambda x.(UM))V \text{ where } x \in Var_\sigma, \; U \text{ and } V \text{ are values} \qquad (\beta_R)$$

$$((\lambda x.M)V)N \xrightarrow{\beta_L} (\lambda x.(MN))V \text{ where } x \in Var_\sigma, \; V \text{ is a value} \qquad (\beta_L)$$

$$U(\mathcal{F}M) \xrightarrow{\mathcal{F}_R} \mathcal{F}\lambda\kappa.M(\lambda v.\kappa(Uv)) \text{ where } U \text{ is a value} \qquad (\mathcal{F}_R)$$

$$(\mathcal{F}M)N \xrightarrow{\mathcal{F}_L} \mathcal{F}\lambda\kappa.M(\lambda f.\kappa(fN)) \qquad (\mathcal{F}_L)$$

$$U((\sigma X.M)V) \xrightarrow{\sigma_R} (\sigma X.(UM))V \text{ where } U \text{ and } V \text{ are values} \qquad (\sigma_R)$$

$$((\sigma X.M)V)N \xrightarrow{\sigma_L} (\sigma X.(MN))V \text{ where } V \text{ is a value} \qquad (\sigma_L)$$

$$U(\mathcal{D}\,X\,M) \xrightarrow{\mathcal{D}_R} (\mathcal{D}\,X\,(\lambda v.U(Mv))) \text{ where } U \text{ is a value} \qquad (\mathcal{D}_R)$$

$$(\mathcal{D}\,X\,M)N \xrightarrow{\mathcal{D}_L} (\mathcal{D}\,X\,(\lambda v.MvN)) \qquad (\mathcal{D}_L)$$

The top-level computation rules are

$$(\lambda x.M)V \rhd_{\beta_\sigma} M[x := V^n] \text{ where } x \in Var_\sigma, \; V \text{ is a value, and } n \text{ is fresh} \quad (\beta_\sigma)$$

$$(\mathcal{F}M) \rhd_{\mathcal{F}} M(\lambda x.x) \qquad (\mathcal{F}_T)$$

$$(\sigma U^n.M)V \rhd_\sigma M[n := V] \text{ where } V \text{ is a value} \qquad (\sigma_T)$$

$$(\mathcal{D}\,V^n\,M) \rhd_\mathcal{D} MV[n := V] \qquad (\mathcal{D}_T)$$

---

the traditional λ-calculus, this is the standard reduction function which always reduces the leftmost-outermost redex first. With the notion of an applicative context, the definition of a standard reduction function becomes

$$M \longmapsto_{scsv} N \text{ iff there are } P, Q, \text{ and } C[\;] \text{ such that}$$
$$P \text{ reduces to } Q, M \equiv C[P], \text{ and } N \equiv C[Q].$$

Since we have generalized the notion of a calculus to a system that may contain computation relations, we must also provide for these rules in the evaluation function. We call the resulting function standard computation function, denote it by $\overset{\rhd}{\longmapsto}_{scsv}$, and define it as:

$$\overset{\rhd}{\longmapsto}_{scsv} = \longmapsto_{scsv} \cup \rhd_{\beta_\sigma} \cup \rhd_{\mathcal{F}} \cup \rhd_\sigma \cup \rhd_\mathcal{D}.$$

The evaluation function for programs is simply the transitive-reflexive closure of this standard computation function:

$$eval_{csv}(M) = V \text{ iff } M \overset{\triangleright \;\;\bullet}{\longmapsto}_{scsv} V.$$

Its correctness is captured in

Theorem 3 (Standard Simulation). *There is a (n injective) morphism* D *such that for all programs* $M \in \Lambda_{\mathcal{F}\sigma}$,

$$eval_{CESK}(M) = V \text{ iff } eval_{csv}(\mathsf{D}(M)) = \mathsf{D}(V).$$

Proof. The morphism D is a transformation that replaces all assignable variables and labeled values by $(\mathcal{D} \; X \; \lambda x.x)$. Now, it is easy to show by induction on the structure of the context $C[\;\;]$ that

$$C[(\mathcal{D} \; V^n \; M)] \overset{\triangleright \;\;\bullet}{\longmapsto}_{scsv} C[MV[n := V]], \text{ and}$$
$$C[\sigma U^n.M)V] \overset{\triangleright \;\;\bullet}{\longmapsto}_{scsv} C[M][n := V].$$

A similar result for $C[\mathcal{F}M]$ can also be obtained, but the details are rather technical because the standard computation relation actually produces an encoding of $\lambda x.C[x]$ and not the function itself. We refer the interested reader to our earlier report [6]. Given Theorem 1, these equivalences are sufficient to prove the theorem. $\square$

The crucial consequence of this simulation theorem is that the $eval_{csv}$-function is yet another semantics for $\Lambda_{\mathcal{F}\sigma}$, but unlike the previous evaluation function the standard computation function is *not sequential* in nature. In the next section we compare the two semantic frameworks in more depth and discuss the relevance of this result with respect to implementation.

5. Parallelism for Imperative Languages

The potential for parallel evaluation of $\Lambda_{\mathcal{F}\sigma}$ programs can best be seen from the definition of the function *Eval* in Definition 5.1, which is an (extensionally) equivalent reformulation of the $eval_{csv}$-function. Because of the two-level definition of the calculus, the *Eval*-function needs an auxiliary function *seval*, which returns the value or semi-value of an expression. A semi-value is a top-level redex and causes another cycle of the *Eval*-function; a value is the final result. On one hand, the auxiliary function is actually superfluous. An obvious way to merge *seval* with *Eval* is by introducing a top-level symbol (by a loader/compiler) that *syntactically* marks the root of the term. On the other hand, factoring out this definition facilitates a discussion about a realization of this semantics, because *seval* performs nearly all of the work.

The first interesting point about *seval* is that a functional program is evaluated with almost no loss of efficiency compared to an evaluator for the functional subset of our language. Second and more important, the two parts of an application can still be evaluated in parallel. The intuitive reason behind this parallelism is that imperative effects do not take place immediately, but cause the bubbling-up of the respective semi-value. Thus, if an assignment is to happen, this is indicated by a σ-application in the corresponding branch of the application. Although this may cause a momentary suspension of other evaluations, the coordination is natural and built into the system so that there is no real need for artificial communication.

Unfortunately, this scheme has two major problems. First, the *seval*-function apparently does not require the (semi-) value of the argument part of an application when the function part yields a semi-value. Second, even though the bubbling-up of imperative redexes is a natural means of coordinating imperative effects, it implies that one step of the sequential rewriting machine is replaced by a possibly long sequence of reduction steps. Indeed, the bubbling-up movement may be considered as the counterpart of the von-Neumann bottleneck. The speed of the evaluation function greatly depends on its optimal implementation.

Definition 5.1: The *Eval*-function

Let U and V range over values; S over semi-values, that is, $\mathcal{F}$-, $\mathcal{D}$-, σ-, and λ-applications (whose variables are in Var_σ); M, N, P, and Q over arbitrary terms; and X over labeled values. Then the *Eval*-function is defined as:

$$Eval(M) \equiv \begin{cases} Eval(N[x := V^n]) & \text{if } seval(M) \equiv (\lambda x.N)V \quad (*) \\ Eval(N(\lambda x.x)) & \text{if } seval(M) \equiv (\mathcal{F}N) \\ Eval(N[n := V]) & \text{if } seval(M) \equiv (\sigma U^n.N)V \\ Eval(NV[n := V]) & \text{if } seval(M) \equiv (\mathcal{D} V^n N) \\ seval(M) & \text{otherwise.} \end{cases}$$

where *seval* is defined in four inductive clauses:

$$seval(V) \equiv V \text{ and } seval(S) \equiv S;$$

and, if $seval(M) \equiv U$ and $seval(N) \equiv V$, then

$$seval(MN) \equiv \begin{cases} seval(P[x := V]) & \text{if } U \equiv \lambda x.P, \, x \in Var_\lambda \\ UV & \text{otherwise;} \end{cases}$$

and, if $seval(M) \equiv U$ and $seval(N) \equiv S$ then

$$seval(MN) \equiv \begin{cases} (\lambda x.UP)V & \text{if } S \equiv (\lambda x.P)V \quad (*) \\ \mathcal{F}\lambda\kappa.P(\lambda v.\kappa(Uv)) & \text{if } S \equiv \mathcal{F}P \\ (\sigma X.UP)V & \text{if } S \equiv (\sigma X.P)V \\ \mathcal{D} X(\lambda v.U(Pv)) & \text{if } S \equiv \mathcal{D} XP; \end{cases}$$

and, finally, if $seval(M) \equiv S$, then

$$seval(MN) \equiv \begin{cases} (\lambda x.PN)V & \text{if } S \equiv (\lambda x.P)V \quad (*) \\ \mathcal{F}\lambda\kappa.P(\lambda f.\kappa(fN)) & \text{if } S \equiv \mathcal{F}P \\ (\sigma X.PN)V & \text{if } S \equiv (\sigma X.P)V \\ \mathcal{D} X(\lambda v.PvN) & \text{if } S \equiv \mathcal{D} XP. \end{cases}$$

At this point, Theorem 3 plays an important role. According to this theorem, the reduction system and the rewriting system are equivalent and hence, some of the insight gained from the rewriting system can be added to the realization of the *seval*-function. With respect to the first point, Theorem 3 clarifies that in most cases the (semi-) value of an argument part is needed independently of the value of the corresponding function part. For example, one consequence of Theorem 3 and the preceding discussion is that the evaluation function need not bubble-up a λ-application with an assignable variable to the root of a program. Once *seval* encounters such an application, it is the correct time to perform a substitution with a labeled value. The only condition is that the label be unique. This condition can be guaranteed in various ways and therefore, the three clauses (*) for bubbling-up a λ-application in Definition 5.1 are superfluous:

$$seval(MN) = seval(P[x := V^n]) \text{ if } seval(M) = \lambda x.P, x \in Var_\sigma ,$$
$$\text{and } seval(N) = V.$$

Furthermore, after bubbling up a σ- or $\mathcal{D}$-application the *seval* resumes the evaluation of the applications all the way down to the place where the imperative redex started. Based on these arguments, *seval* may as well evaluate both pieces of an application when encountering it the first time. Only grabbing a continuation in the function part will ever require suspension of evaluation of an argument part. But even then, the stopping point is clearly marked by the arrival of an $\mathcal{F}$-application and, since continuations are rarely thrown away, the early evaluation may still be useful later. In other words, this special case represents the only instance of speculative parallelism in our system.

Finally, Theorem 3 also points to some major shortcuts with respect to the bubbling-up movement. Since σ-applications must resume evaluation of the σ-body after the top-level step and since $\mathcal{D}$- and $\mathcal{F}$-applications build up new β-redexes, the respective reduction sequences can benefit from an immediate evaluation of the internal redexes of their right-hand sides. For example, the ordinary evaluation of $(M(N(\mathcal{D}\ (\lambda x.x)^n\ L)))$ proceeds as follows:

$$
\begin{aligned}
(M(N(\mathcal{D}\ (\lambda x.x)^n\ L))) &\longrightarrow (M(\mathcal{D}\ (\lambda x.x)^n\ (\lambda x.N(Lx)))\\
&\longrightarrow (\mathcal{D}\ (\lambda x.x)^n\ (\lambda x.M((\lambda x.N(Lx))x))\\
&\longrightarrow (\lambda x.M((\lambda x.N(Lx))x)(\lambda x.x)\\
&\longrightarrow M((\lambda x.N(Lx))(\lambda x.x))\\
&\longrightarrow M(N(L(\lambda x.x)))
\end{aligned}
$$

but, a parallel reduction of the internal β-redexes shortens this evaluation:

$$
\begin{aligned}
(M(N(\mathcal{D}\ (\lambda x.x)^n\ L))) &\longrightarrow (M(\mathcal{D}\ (\lambda x.x)^n\ (\lambda x.N(Lx)))\\
&\longrightarrow (\mathcal{D}\ (\lambda x.x)^n\ (\lambda x.M(N(Lx))))\\
&\longrightarrow (\lambda x.M(N(Lx)))(\lambda x.x)\\
&\longrightarrow M(N(L(\lambda x.x))).
\end{aligned}
$$

The internal reductions must be aware of free variables, yet, since these variables stand for values, they can be treated as such until their "contents" is needed for the function position of a proper application. This has the advantage that the end-consumer of the value can immediately absorb the variable x and the value for x arrives sooner at its final destination, $e.g.$, $seval$ can immediately begin with the evaluation of Lx in the above example.

Given the acceptance of $Eval$ as a parallel evaluator and the preceding arguments about possible improvements, it seems that the really expensive part of our schema is the substitution algorithm. It imposes a necessary communication among the processors. Put differently, this argument means that the cost of evaluating imperative programs should be comparable to the cost of evaluating applicative programs since for the latter communication costs also constitute the central obstacle to parallel evaluations. In applicative languages this cost may be avoided by compiling programs into combinator form where variables do not exist and substitution is unnecessary. Based on on-going research, we conjecture that a similar compilation scheme can be developed for $\Lambda_{\mathcal{F}\sigma}$ and the λ_v-CS-calculus.

6. Summary

In the preceding sections we demonstrated how an intensionally sequential semantics for an imperative higher-order language can be transformed into an extensionally equivalent, yet intensionally parallel semantics. In Section 5 we discussed a series of improvements to this semantics. Based on this discussion, we believe that if a successful parallelization for functional languages is possible, then the same strategy will also lead to a successful parallelization for imperative programming languages.

Many of the issues raised in Section 5 call for a thorough analysis. In particular, the demand for a combinator-based target system for imperative higher-order languages is a challenging problem. Despite a lack of obvious answers to many questions, we hope that our analysis stimulates research in programming languages for programmers.

Acknowledgement. Matthias Felleisen is supported by an IBM Graduate Research Fellowship. The work is also supported in part by the NSF grants DCR 85 01277 and DCR 83 03325.

References

1. BACKUS, J. Can programming be liberated from the von Neumann style? A functional style and its algebra of programs, *Comm. ACM* **21**(8), 613–641.

2. BARENDREGT, H.P. *The Lambda Calculus: Its Syntax and Semantics*, North-Holland, Amsterdam, 1981.

3. CLINGER, W.D., D.P. FRIEDMAN, M. WAND. A scheme for a higher-level semantic algebra, in *Algebraic Methods in Semantics*, J. Reynolds, M. Nivat (Eds.), 1985, 237–250.

4. DENNIS, J.B. Programming generality, parallelism and computer architectures, *Information Processing* **68**, 1969, 484–492.

5. FELLEISEN, M., D.P. FRIEDMAN, B. DUBA, J. MERRILL. Beyond continuations, Technical Report No 216, Indiana University Computer Science Department, 1987.

6. FELLEISEN, M., D.P. FRIEDMAN. Control operators, the SECD-machine, and the λ-calculus, *Formal Description of Programming Concepts III*, North-Holland, Amsterdam, 1986, to appear.

7. FELLEISEN, M., D.P. FRIEDMAN. A calculus for assignments in higher-order languages, *Proc. 14th ACM Symp. Principles of Programming Languages*, 1987, 314-325.

8. FELLEISEN, M. Reflections on Landin's J-operator: a partly historical note, *Computer Languages*, 1987, to appear.

9. FRIEDMAN, D.P., C.T. HAYNES, E. KOHLBECKER. Programming with continuations, in *Program Transformations and Programming Environments*, P. Pepper (Ed.), Springer-Verlag, 1985, 263–274.

10. HAYNES, C.T., D.P. FRIEDMAN, M. WAND. Obtaining coroutines from continuations, *Computer Languages* **11**(3/4), 1986, 143–153.

11. HAYNES, C. T. Logic continuations, *Proc. Third International Conf. Logic Programming*, London, Springer-Verlag, 1986, 671–685; also to appear in *Journal of Logic Programming*, 1987.

12. HENSON, M.C., R. TURNER. Completion semantics and interpreter generation, *Proc. 9th ACM Symp. Principles of Programming Languages*, 1982, 242–254.

13. KOHLBECKER, E, M. WAND. Macro-by-example: deriving syntactic transformations from their specifications, *Proc. 14th ACM Symp. Principles of Programming Languages*, 1987, 77–85.

14. LANDIN, P.J. The next 700 programming languages, *Comm. ACM* **9**(3), 1966, 157–166.

15. LANDIN, P.J. An abstract machine for designers of computing languages, *Proc. IFIP Congress*, 1965, 438–439.

16. LANDIN, P.J. The mechanical evaluation of expressions, *Computer Journal* **6**(4), 1964, 308–320.

17. MAGÓ, G.A. A network of microprocessors to execute reduction languages, *Int. Journal of Computer and Information Sciences* **8**, 1979, 349–385; 435–471.

18. MASON, I. A. *The Semantics of Destructive Lisp*, Ph.D. dissertation, Stanford University, 1986.

19. PLOTKIN, G.D. A structural approach to operational semantics, Technical Report DAIMI FN-19, Aarhus University, Computer Science Department, 1981.

20. PLOTKIN, G.D. Call-by-name, call-by-value, and the λ-calculus, *Theoretical Computer Science* **1**, 1975, 125–159.

21. REYNOLDS, J.C. Definitional interpreters for higher-order programming languages, *Proc. ACM Annual Conference*, 1972, 717–740.

22. REYNOLDS, J.C. GEDANKEN—A simple typeless language based on the principle of completeness and the reference concept, *Comm. ACM* **13**(5), 1970, 308–319.

23. SUSSMAN G.J., G. STEELE. Scheme: An interpreter for extended lambda calculus, Memo 349, MIT AI-Lab, 1975.

24. TALCOTT, C. *The Essence of Rum—A Theory of the Intensional and Extensional Aspects of Lisp-type Computation*, Ph.D. dissertation, Stanford University, 1985.

25. WAND, M., D.P. FRIEDMAN. Compiling lambda-expressions using continuations and factorizations, *Computer Languages* **3**, 1978, 241–263.

Petri Net Models for

Algebraic Theories of Concurrency

(extended abstract)

Rob van Glabbeek and Frits Vaandrager

Centre for Mathematics and Computer Science
P.O. Box 4079, 1009 AB Amsterdam, The Netherlands

In this paper we discuss the issue of interleaving semantics versus True concurrency in an algebraic setting. We present various equivalence notions on Petri nets which can be used in the construction of algebraic models:
(a) the occurrence net equivalence of Nielsen, Plotkin & Winskel;
(b) bisimulation equivalence, which leads to a model which is isomorphic to the graph model of Baeten, Bergstra & Klop;
(c) the concurrent bisimulation equivalence, which is also described by Nielsen & Thiagarajan, and Goltz;
(d) partial order equivalences which are inspired by work of Pratt, and Boudol & Castellani.
A central role in the paper will be played by the notion of real-time consistency. We show that, besides occurrence net equivalence, none of the equivalences mentioned above (including the partial order equivalences!) is real-time consistent. Therefore we introduce the notion of ST-bisimulation equivalence, which is real-time consistent. Moreover a complete proof system will be presented for those finite ST-bisimulation processes in which no action can occur concurrently with itself.
Note: Partial support received from the European Communities under ESPRIT project no. 432, An Integrated Formal Approach to Industrial Software Development (METEOR).

Introduction

One of the most controversial issues in the theory of concurrency is the issue of interleaving semantics versus True concurrency. People advocating interleaving semantics model the parallel composition of two processes by interleaving the atomic actions performed by these processes. A typical equation valid in interleaving semantics is: $a \| b = a \cdot b + b \cdot a$. The intended meaning of this equation is that when you observe the parallel composition of atomic actions a and b, either you see first the a and then the b, or you see first the b and then the a. The interleaving fans are aware of the fact that for some applications their approach is not realistic (for example in those places where real-time or fairness aspects are important). But since reality is extremely complicated one needs some simplifying assumptions, and they argue that the interleaving assumption is a good one: it allows for the construction of very elegant mathematical models of concurrency in which specification and verification of large concurrent systems is feasible.

The True concurrency adherents on the contrary think that interleaving models are very unrealistic. With an enormous enthusiasm they present all kinds of examples, formulated in terms of Petri nets, event structures or Mazurkiewicz traces, which show that the interleaving approach is bizarre.

Another controversy in the theory of concurrency which we would like to mention here is the issue of linear time versus branching time. It has to do with the equation: $a \cdot (b + c) = a \cdot b + a \cdot c$. Here the intended meaning is that when you observe first a *and then* b or c, this is just the same as when you observe a and then b or a and then c. Most True concurrency theories use this equation because the people who developed these theories thought there was nothing against it. The major part of the interleaving adherents however, reject the equation because they think that the timing of the choices in a process is often essential. They argue that for the proper description of features like deadlock behaviour, divergence, fair abstraction and interrupt mechanisms, information concerning the timing of choices is crucially important. Because we also think that very often the timing of choices is relevant, we are interested in branching time models.

The discussion in this paper takes place in the setting of ACP, the Algebra of Communicating Processes, as described in [BK1-3]. Until now all models studied in the ACP framework were based on the interleaving assumption and it was very difficult to deal with real-time aspects of concurrent systems. However, real-time aspects are often important (or even vital) in the design of concurrent systems. The major reason which motivated our excursion into the domain of True concurrency, was that doing this might help us answer the following question:

Can the language of ACP be used to specify real-time concurrent systems?

When True concurrency adherents argue that the interleaving approach is not realistic, the 'interleavers' answer that their approach at least makes algebraic system verification possible. This leads to our second question:

Is it possible to perform algebraic system verifications in a non-interleaved semantics?

Petri nets, introduced in 1962 by Petri in his now famous thesis ([Pe]), is the best known framework in which both True concurrency and branching time can be modelled. For this reason we have decided to define our models in terms of Petri nets. Furthermore there are a lot of interesting theoretical results concerning Petri nets, which we might use. Last but not least we have chosen Petri nets because they have nice graphical representations. Pictures are important, not only from a didactical point of view, but also to make the analysis of the models easier.

A lot of people have been trying to combine ideas from CCS and ACP-like theories with True concurrency. NIELSEN, PLOTKIN & WINSKEL [NPW] were (as far as we know) the first ones who looked for a branching time non-interleaved model of concurrency. In [W1] an event structure semantics is presented for CCS and related languages. In [GM] a semantics for CCS is presented based on the notion of occurrence nets. [Po] presents non-interleaved versions of various equivalences like observation equivalence and failure equivalence, in the setting of Petri nets.

However, in none of these papers much attention is paid to *algebraic laws* valid in the various models. Only in a recent paper by BOUDOL & CASTELLANI [BC] this issue is studied. But their paper only deals with the case in which there is no communication possible between the components of a system (communication will be dealt with in a paper by them which is now in preparation).

In the first section of this paper we present a short review of part of the theory of ACP. Section 2 contains the basic definitions about Petri nets which we need in the rest of the paper. Moreover the fundamental notion of *occurrence net equivalence* is defined. In section 3 we define the ACP-operators on Petri nets. Some of the definitions are adopted from other authors, whereas some others (notably the sequential composition) are new here.

In section 4 we present our first algebraic model, which is based on the occurrence net equivalence. We will argue that in this model there are not enough laws valid to make practical system verifications possible. Still the occurrence net equivalence is important theoretically: it gives the identifications which, from an observational point of view, should be made in any case. In section 4 we also give the semantical notion of *bisimulation equivalence*, which leads to an interleaved Petri net model of the axiom system ACP, which is isomorphic to the graph model of BAETEN, BERGSTRA & KLOP [BBK1]. Finally section 4 contains a non-interleaved model for a subset of ACP, based on the notion of *concurrent bisimulation equivalence*. This equivalence, which can be situated between occurrence net and bisimulation equivalence, is also described by NIELSEN & THIAGARAJAN [NT] and GOLTZ [G]. All the equivalences in section 4 respect branching time.

In section 5 we add the concept of causality. Causality is not respected by the concurrent (or ordinary) bisimulation equivalence. We present the *pomset equivalence,* which is derived from PRATT [Pr1-2], and closely related to the trace theory of MAZURKIEWICZ [M1-2], see also [AR]. The pomset equivalence does respect causality but violates branching time. This brings us to the *pomset bisimulation equivalence,* which is inspired by BOUDOL & CASTELLANI [BC]. The pomset bisimulation equivalence respects both causality and branching time. However, we will argue that it does not fully respect the combination of both concepts. We propose a refinement of this notion which is more satisfactory in this sense.

Section 6 is a digression into the domain of real-time semantics. We give a real-time interpretation of process algebra, using the notion of timed Petri nets as presented in, for example, CARLIER, CHRETIENNE & GIRAULT [CCG]. New in our approach is the notion of *real-time consistency.* An equivalence relation on Petri nets is real-time consistent if it does not identify nets with a different real-time behaviour. A model based on a real-time consistent equivalence makes it possible to reason about concurrent systems in a real-time consistent manner without having to deal with the full complexity of real-time. A major result of this paper is that, except for the occurrence net equivalence, all previously described equivalences (including the partial order equivalences!) are *not* real-time consistent.

Therefore we present in section 7 a new equivalence, which *is* real-time consistent: the *ST-bisimulation equivalence.* This equivalence leads to a model for the ACP operators. We give a complete axiomatisation for finite processes in which no action can occur concurrently with itself. The structure of the complete axiomatisation is remarkable: if one wants to prove that two terms represent the same process in ST-bisimulation semantics, one first has to translate these terms into other ACP-terms. Thereafter one has to prove the equivalence of the new terms using the axioms of ACP (including the interleaving axiom CM1!!). If and only if this succeeds, the original terms are equivalent in the non-interleaved ST-bisimulation semantics. In our view the results of section 7 show that in principle the language of ACP can be used to specify real-time concurrent systems and to perform algebraic system verifications.

Due to lack of space almost all the proofs have been omitted. Also the topic of solving recursion equations is skipped here. For these issues we refer to the full paper [GV].

§1 A LANGUAGE FOR COMMUNICATING PROCESSES

In this section we present a language for reasoning about processes in an algebraical way - that is without referring to particular models - which is based on the axiom system ACP of BERGSTRA & KLOP [BK 1-3]. ACP starts from a collection A of given atomic actions. These actions are taken to be indivisible, and form a parameter of the axiom system. For each atomic action $a \in A$ there is a constant a in the language, representing the process, starting with an a-step and terminating after some time. Furthermore we have a special constant δ, denoting deadlock, the acknowledgement of a process that it cannot do anything any more, the absence of an alternative. We will write $A_\delta = A \cup \{\delta\}$. In ACP a process can end in two ways: by terminating successfully or by reaching a state of deadlock. Now processes can be built up from smaller ones by means of sequential, alternative and parallel composition operators. If x and y are two processes, then $x \cdot y$ is the process that starts the execution of y after completion of x (x must have terminated successfully), and $x + y$ is the process that can do either x or y. We do not specify whether the choice between the alternatives is made by the process itself, or by the environment, but it should be made at the beginning of $x + y$. The merge of two processes, $x\|y$, executes the processes x and y simultaneously and independently, except for communication actions. In ACP, communication between parallel processes is modelled by means of a binary communication function $\gamma:A_\delta\times A_\delta\to A_\delta$, which is commutative, associative and has δ as zero element. γ forms a second (and last) parameter of the system. If $\gamma(a,b)=c\neq\delta$ this means that if a occurs in a process x and b occurs in y then in the merge $x\|y$ the processes x and y can communicate by synchronising the actions a and b. The synchronous performance of a and b is then regarded as a performance of the communication action c. In a merge, communication is never forced: the process $x\|y$ can either execute the actions a and b independently or perform the communication action c instead. This leaves open the possibility that x finds a communication partner in the environment, outside y, for instance in a context $(x\|y)\|z$. However, synchronisation can be forced by means of the encapsulation operator ∂_H. Here H is a set of atomic actions. Operator ∂_H blocks actions from H by means of a renaming into δ. It is used to *encapsulate* a process, i.e. to make communications with the environment impossible. In ACP there are also two auxiliary operators $\|\_$ and $|$, which are used for reducing concurrency to nondeterminism. Here we will skip them for the moment. Below we give the formal signature of our language, as well as some basic axioms.

1.1. Signature.

S (Sort):	P	(the set of processes)
F (Functions):	$+:P\times P\to P$	(alternative composition or sum)
	$\cdot:P\times P\to P$	(sequential composition or product)
	$\|:P\times P\to P$	(parallel composition or merge)
	$\partial_H:P\to P$	(encapsulation; $H\subseteq A$)
C (Constants):	$\delta\in P$	(deadlock)
	$a\in P$	(atomic actions; $a\in A$)

1.2. Note.
In a product $x\cdot y$ we will often omit the $\cdot$. About leaving out parentheses: we take $\cdot$ to be more binding than other operations and $+$ to be less binding than other operations. In case of an associative operator, we also leave out parentheses.

1.3. Axioms.
These are presented in table 1. Here $a\in A_\delta;x,y,z\in P;H\subseteq A$.

$x+y = y+x$	A1	$\partial_H(a) = a$ if $a\notin H$	D1	
$x+(y+z) = (x+y)+z$	A2	$\partial_H(a) = \delta$ if $a\in H$	D2	
$x+x = x$	A3	$\partial_H(x+y) = \partial_H(x)+\partial_H(y)$	D3	
$(x+y)z = xz+yz$	A4	$\partial_H(xy) = \partial_H(x)\cdot\partial_H(y)$	D4	
$(xy)z = x(yz)$	A5			
$x+\delta = x$	A6	$x\|y = y\|x$	C1	
$\delta x = \delta$	A7	$(x\|y)\|z = x\|(y\|z)$	C2	

TABLE 1

1.4. Recursion.
A *Recursive specification* E is a set of equations $\{x=t_x\,|\,x\in V_E\}$ with V_E a set of variables and t_x a process expression for $x\in V_E$. Only the variables of V_E may appear in t_x. A solution of E is an interpretation of the variables of V_E as processes (in a certain domain), such that the equations of E are satisfied.

The Recursive Definition Principle (RDP) tells us that every recursive specification has a solution. We conjecture that all models presented here satisfy RDP. For a substantiation of this conjecture we refer to [GV].

Recursive specifications are used to define (or specify) processes. Our language can be made recursive, by adding the syntactic constructs $<x|E>$ (with $x\in V_E$), denoting the x-component of one of the solutions of E. This limits the class of models of the language to the ones satisfying RDP. However, in this extended abstract recursive constructs will not be used.

§2 PETRI NETS
In this section we will define the elements of the models that will be constructed in this paper. This is not the place to give an extensive introduction into the theory of Petri Nets. For this we refer to [R] or [RT].

2.1. DEFINITION: Let A be a given alphabet.
i) A *labelled marked net* (over A) is a 5-tuple $N = (S,T,F,M_{in},l)$ where:
- S is a set of *places* or *S-elements;*
- T is a set of *transitions* or *T-elements*, $S\cap T=\varnothing$;
- $F\subseteq S\times T\cup T\times S$, F is called the *flow relation*, $T\subseteq ran(F)$;
- $M_{in}:S\to\mathbf{N}$, M_{in} is called the *initial marking;*
- $l:T\to A$, l is called the *labelling function.*

ii) For $x\in S\cup T$ ${}^\bullet x = \{y\,|\,yFx\}$ is called the *preset* of x; $x^\bullet = \{y\,|\,xFy\}$ is called the *postset* of x.

2.2. The well known graphical representation of nets is as follows. Places and transitions are represented as circles and boxes, respectively. The flow relation is indicated by arcs between the corresponding circles and boxes. Transitions are inscribed by their labels. The initial marking is represented by placing dots (*tokens*) in the corresponding circles.

2.3. DEFINITION: Let $N = (S, T, F, M_{in}, l)$ be a labelled marked net.
i)   A function $M : S \rightarrow \mathbb{N}$ is called a *marking* of N;
ii) Let M be a marking. We say that $t \in T$ is *M-enabled* (*enabled*, to *occur* or to *fire*), notation $M[t>$, if
     $\forall s \in {}^{\bullet}t : M(s) \geqslant 1$;
iii) Let M, M' be markings and let $t \in T$. We say that M' *t-follows* M, and *results from firing t*, notation $M[t>M'$, if:
     a. $M[t>$
     b. $\forall s \in S$:

$$M'(s) = \begin{cases} M(s)-1 & \text{if } s \in {}^{\bullet}t - t^{\bullet} \\ M(s)+1 & \text{if } s \in t^{\bullet} - {}^{\bullet}t \\ M(s) & \text{otherwise} \end{cases}$$

iv) Let M be a marking. A sequence $\alpha = t_1 * \cdots * t_n \in T^*$ is *M-enabled*, notation $M[\alpha>$, if there exist $M_0, \ldots, M_n$ such that $M_0 = M$ and for $1 \leqslant i \leqslant n$: $M_{i-1}[t_i > M_i$. We say that M_n is *obtained from M by firing* α, notation $M[\alpha > M_n$. We also say that M_n is *reachable* from M;
v)   Let M, M' be markings, let $\alpha = t_1 * \cdots * t_n \in T^*$, and let $M[\alpha > M'$. In this case we say that the sequence $\sigma = l(t_1) * \cdots * l(t_n) \in A^*$ is *M-enabled*, notation $M[\sigma>$. We also say that M' *is obtained from M by firing* σ, notation $M[\sigma > M'$;
vi) For each marking M, $[M>$ is the set of markings reachable from M;
vii) N is called *safe* if for each $M \in [M_{in}>$ and for each $s \in S$: $M(s) \leqslant 1$. In this case each marking reachable from M_{in} can be considered as a subset of S.

2.4. DEFINITION: Let $N = (S, T, F, M_{in}, l)$ be a safe labelled marked net.
i)   Let M be a reachable marking of N and let U be a subset of T. We say that U is *M-enabled*, notation $M[U>$, if:

     a. $\forall t \in U \; \forall s \in {}^{\bullet}t : M(s) = 1$

     b. $\forall t, t' \in U : t \neq t' \Rightarrow {}^{\bullet}t \cap {}^{\bullet}t' = \emptyset$ (Because N is safe, this implies ${}^{\bullet}t \cap (t')^{\bullet} = \emptyset$.)
ii) N has *bounded parallelism* if for every $M \in [M_{in}>$, and $U \subseteq T$ such that $M[U>$, we have that U is finite.

2.5. *Note.* In this paper we will only consider safe labelled marked nets, which have bounded parallelism and a non-empty initial marking. We will use the word *net* to denote such a structure. For $i = 0, 1, \ldots$, and nets N_i, we will denote the components of N_i by resp. S_i, T_i, F_i, $(M_{in})_i$ and l_i. Let λ be some infinite cardinal, and let A be a given set of atomic actions. $\mathbb{N}_\lambda(A)$ is the set of nets over alphabet A such that the cardinality of the sets of places and transitions is less than λ.

2.6. *Occurrence nets.* Above we have introduced the notion of a Petri net. Furthermore we have defined the dynamic behaviour of a net in terms of its markings and the firing rule. Most Petri nets have the property that the state (marking) which results after a number of transitions has been fired, gives us almost no information about this firing sequence. Consider for example the net in figure 1:

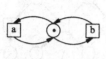

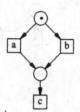

FIGURE 1   FIGURE 2

There is only one state, so we have absolutely no information about the firing sequence of a's and b's leading to it. Figure 2 presents another example. The state which results from firing the a-transition, could have been caused also by the firing of the b-transition.

Below we will define the fundamental notion of occurrence nets - a subclass of acyclic nets with places which can only be forwardly branched. Occurrence nets have the property that each transition can fire only once. Furthermore we can deduce from the state of the net which were the transitions leading to it. Occurrence nets were introduced in NIELSEN, PLOTKIN & WINSKEL [NPW]. Our definition is taken from WINSKEL [W2].

2.6.1. DEFINITION: An *occurrence net* is a net (S,T,F,M_{in},l) for which the following restrictions are satisfied:

1) $\forall s \in S : |{}^{\bullet}s| \leqslant 1$;

2) $s \in M_{in} \Leftrightarrow {}^{\bullet}s = \varnothing$;

3) F^+ (the transitive closure of F) is irreflexive and $\forall t \in T : \{t' \in T \mid t'F^*t\}$ is finite;

4) The *conflict relation* $\sharp$ is irreflexive, where for $x,y \in S \cup T$: $x \sharp y \Leftrightarrow \exists t,t' \in T : t \neq t', {}^{\bullet}t \cap {}^{\bullet}t' \neq \varnothing, tF^*x$ and $t'F^*y$.

2.6.2. PROPOSITION: *Let* $N = (S,T,F,M_{in},l)$ *be an occurrence net. Then:* $\forall t \in T \, \exists M \in [M_{in}> : M[t>$ *and* $\forall s \in S \, \exists M \in [M_{in}> : s \in M$. *In words: N does not contain superfluous transitions or places.*

2.7. Unfolding. By means of the notion of *unfolding* we will now relate to each net an occurrence net. As pointed out by [NPW] and [W2], the behaviour of the unfolding of a net is exactly the same as the behaviour of the net itself; the only difference is that the unfolding has a "memory" in which the dynamic history is stored. Definition 2.7.1 is rather technical, but the reader can learn the essential properties of the unfolding operator from examples 2.7.2 and theorem 2.8.

2.7.1. DEFINITION: Let N_0 be a net. The *unfolding* of N_0, notation $\mathcal{U}(N_0)$, is the net N_1 defined inductively as follows. $S_1, T_1, F_1, (M_{in})_1$ and $\mathfrak{M}$ are the least sets satisfying:

1. $(M_{in})_1 \subseteq S_1 \subseteq \{(t,s) \mid t \in T_1 \cup \{*\}, s \in S_0\}$;
2. $T_1 \subseteq \{(M,t) \mid M \subseteq S_1, t \in T_0\}$;
3. $F_1 \subseteq S_1 \times T_1 \cup T_1 \times S_1$;
4. $\mathfrak{M} \subseteq Pow(S_1)$;
5. $(M_{in})_1 = \{(*,s) \mid s \in (M_{in})_0\} \in \mathfrak{M}$;
6. If, for some index set I, $\{(t_i,s_i) \mid i \in I\} \in \mathfrak{M}$ and $\{s_i \mid i \in I\}[t>$ then:

$$t' = (\{(t_i,s_i) \mid i \in I \text{ and } s_i \in {}^{\bullet}t\}, t) \in T_1$$

$$\{(t',s) \mid s \in t^{\bullet}\} \subseteq S_1$$

$$\{(t_i,s_i) \mid i \in I \text{ and } s_i \notin {}^{\bullet}t\} \cup \{(t',s) \mid s \in t^{\bullet}\} \in \mathfrak{M}$$

$$\{((t_i,s_i),t') \mid i \in I \text{ and } s_i \in {}^{\bullet}t\} \cup \{(t',(t',s)) \mid s \in t^{\bullet}\} \subseteq F_1$$

l_1 is the function from T_1 into A defined by: $(m,t) \in T_1 \Rightarrow l_1((m,t)) = l_0(t)$.

2.7.2. EXAMPLES:

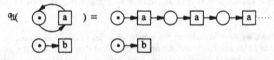

FIGURE 3

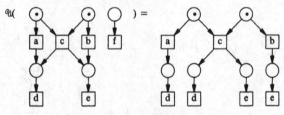

FIGURE 4

2.8. THEOREM: *Let* N_0 *be a net, let* $N_1 = \mathcal{U}(N_0)$, *and let* $\mathfrak{M}$ *be as defined in section 2.7.1. Then:*

i) $\mathfrak{M} = [(M_{in})_1>$;

ii) N_1 *is an occurrence net;*

iii) *If* N_0 *is an occurrence net, then* N_1 *is isomorphic to* N_0 *(two nets are considered isomorphic if they only differ in the names of places and transitions).*

2.8.1. REMARK: For $\lambda > \aleph_0$ we have that $\mathcal{U} : \mathbf{N}_\lambda(A) \to \mathbf{N}_\lambda(A)$.

2.9. DEFINITION: Two nets N_0 and N_1 are *occurrence net equivalent*, notation $N_0 \equiv_{occ} N_1$, iff $\mathfrak{U}(N_0)$ is isomorphic to $\mathfrak{U}(N_1)$.

Clearly, $\equiv_{occ}$ is an equivalence relation. Note that theorem 2.8 implies that in each equivalence class of $\equiv_{occ}$ there is, up to isomorphism, exactly one occurrence net.

2.10. Root-unwinding. For the proper definition of some of the process operators we need to work with nets which have acyclic roots, i.e. the places of the initial marking have no incoming arrows. What we could do in order to reach this situation is a restriction of the domain to a subset of nets which have acyclic roots, for example to occurrence nets. Or we could start the definitions of the operations with the unfolding of the nets involved. We do not like the first solution because we think that in a lot of applications it is very natural to work with nets with cyclic roots. The second solution is also not favoured by us since the operation of unfolding a net is very complicated. This means that, in order to add two nets one has to perform an awful amount of work. Moreover, the operation of unfolding refers heavily to the token-game and is therefore very operational. We are interested in a *general* non-operational construction that relates, with a minimum amount of work, to every net an occurrent equivalent net with acyclic roots. The simplest solution we could find is the *root-unwinding* operation presented below. The construction resembles one in GOLTZ [G], but, due to the fact that our nets can be infinite and we want to stay in axiomatic set theory, our construction is a bit more complicated. But as explained above, if someone does not like the operation he or she can just skip the definition and work with unfoldings instead.

2.10.1. DEFINITION: We define the *root-unwinding* map $\mathfrak{R}: \mathbf{N}_\lambda(A) \to \mathbf{N}_\lambda(A)$ as follows. Let $N_0 \in \mathbf{N}_\lambda(A)$. Let $M_{cyc} = \{s \in (M_{in})_0 \mid {}^\bullet s \neq \varnothing\}$ be the set of cyclic root elements, and let $M_{cyc}^c = \{s^c \mid s \in M_{cyc}\}$ be a copy of this set. Then $\mathfrak{R}(N_0)$ is the net N_1 obtained by adding the places in M_{cyc}^c, and put them in the initial marking instead of the elements of M_{cyc}:

$$S_1 = S_0 \cup M_{cyc}^c \quad \text{and} \quad (M_{in})_1 = ((M_{in})_0 - M_{cyc}) \cup M_{cyc}^c$$

We define a set $\mathbf{U}$ by:

$$\mathbf{U} = \{M_{cyc} - (\bigcup_{t \in X} {}^\bullet t) \mid X \text{ a finite subset of } T_0\}$$

Note that the cardinality of $\mathbf{U}$ is less than λ. For each $U \in \mathbf{U}$ and $t \in T_0$ such that ${}^\bullet t \cap U$ is non-empty, we introduce a new transition $<U,t>$ such that:

$${}^\bullet <U,t> = ({}^\bullet t - U) \cup \{s^c \mid s \in {}^\bullet t \cap U\} \quad \text{and} \quad <U,t>^\bullet = t^\bullet$$

The label of $<U,t>$ is the label of t. Because the cardinality of $\mathbf{U}$ is less than λ, the number of new transitions in the root-unwinding N_1 is also less than λ. Thus we avoid the cardinality problem that arises if we introduce a new transition $<U,t>$ for every subset U of M_{cyc}.

2.10.2. EXAMPLE:

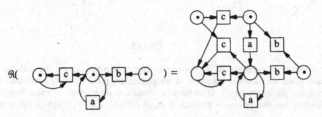

FIGURE 5

2.10.3. LEMMA: *Let $N_0 \in \mathbf{N}_\lambda(A)$ and let $N_1 = \mathfrak{R}(N_0)$. Then:*

i) $N_0 \equiv_{occ} N_1$;

ii) $\forall s \in (M_{in})_1 : {}^\bullet s = \varnothing$;

iii) *If $\forall s \in (M_{in})_0 : {}^\bullet s = \varnothing$, then N_1 is identical to N_0.*

§3 Definition of ACP operators on Nets

In this section we will define the operators of section 1 on the set $N_\lambda(A)$ of nets. All the models which are presented in this paper are constructed by dividing out an equivalence relation on nets, which is a congruence with respect to the operators as defined here.

3.1. An atomic action $a \in A$ is interpreted as:

3.2. δ is represented by the net:

Execution of the process associated with a net terminates when, after firing a number of transitions, no token is left. So the process a terminates after the firing of its transition. The process δ however cannot terminate because there is no transition that can remove the token of the initial marking.

3.3.1. $+$: The definition of the $+$ is from GOLTZ & MYCROFT [GM]. By means of a cartesian product construction, conflicts are introduced between all pairs of initial transitions of the two nets involved. Let $N_0, N_1 \in N_\lambda(A)$, $N_2 = \Re(N_0)$ and $N_3 = \Re(N_1)$. $N_4 = N_0 + N_1$ is defined by:

$$S_4 = (S_2 - (M_{in})_2) \cup (S_3 - (M_{in})_3) \cup (M_{in})_2 \times (M_{in})_3$$

$$T_4 = T_2 \cup T_3$$

$$F_4 = ((F_2 \cup F_3) \cap (S_4 \times T_4 \cup T_4 \times S_4)) \cup \{((s_0, s_1), t) \mid (s_0, t) \in F_2 \text{ or } (s_1, t) \in F_3\}$$

$$(M_{in})_4 = (M_{in})_2 \times (M_{in})_3$$

$$l_4 = l_2 \cup l_3$$

3.3.2. EXAMPLE:

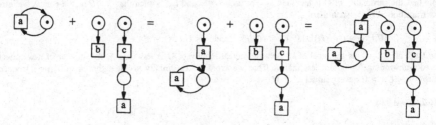

FIGURE 6

3.4.1. $\cdot$: Below we present a definition of the $\cdot$-operator. In the definition we use the well-known construction of *complements*: for each place we introduce a number of complementary places in such a way that a place contains a token iff the complementary places are empty. If all the new places contain a token we know that the old places are empty, and thus execution of the first process is finished. If $N_0, N_1 \in N_\lambda(A)$ and $N_2 = \Re(N_1)$, define $N_3 = N_0 \cdot N_1$ by:

$$S_3 = S_0 \cup (S_2 - (M_{in})_2) \cup (S_0 \times (M_{in})_2)$$

$$T_3 = T_0 \cup T_2$$

$$(M_{in})_3 = (M_{in})_0 \cup (S_0 - (M_{in})_0) \times (M_{in})_2$$

Besides the arrows of F_0 and $F_2 \cap (S_3 \times T_3 \cup T_3 \times S_3)$, F_3 contains arrows defined by:

$$[(s, t) \in F_0 \wedge (t, s) \notin F_0 \wedge s' \in (M_{in})_2] \Rightarrow (t, (s, s')) \in F_3$$

$$[(t, s) \in F_0 \wedge (s, t) \notin F_0 \wedge s' \in (M_{in})_2] \Rightarrow ((s, s'), t) \in F_3$$

$$[(s_0, s_1) \in S_0 \times (M_{in})_2 \wedge (s_1, t) \in T_2] \Rightarrow ((s_0, s_1), t) \in F_3$$

The labelling function is given by: $l_3 = l_0 \cup l_2$.

3.4.2. EXAMPLE:

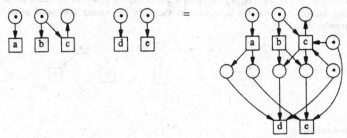

FIGURE 7

3.5. ‖: If $N_0, N_1 \in \mathbb{N}_\lambda(A)$, obtain $N_2 = N_0 \| N_1$ by taking the disjoint union of N_0 and N_1, adding transitions:

$$\{(t,u) \mid t \in T_0, \ u \in T_1, \ \gamma(l_0(t), l_1(u)) \neq \delta\}$$

and taking: $l_2((t,u)) = \gamma(l_0(t), l_1(u))$, ${}^\bullet(t,u) = {}^\bullet t \cup {}^\bullet u$ and $(t,u)^\bullet = t^\bullet \cup u^\bullet$.

3.6.1. ∂_H: Let $N \in \mathbb{N}_\lambda(A)$. $\partial_H(N)$ is obtained from N by omitting the transitions with labels in H and the flow pairs they occur in.

3.6.2. EXAMPLE: Let $\gamma(a,b) = c$, and let $H = \{a,b\}$. Then:

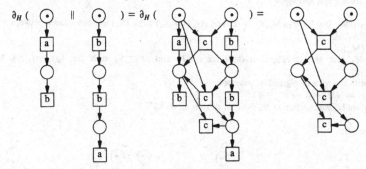

FIGURE 8

§4 OCCURRENCE NET, BISIMULATION AND CONCURRENT BISIMULATION SEMANTICS

In section 3 we defined the operators of section 1 on the Petri net domains of section 2. Thus we are able to associate nets to process expressions in a compositional way. Now a Petri net model can be obtained by dividing out a congruence relation on a domain $\mathbb{N}_\lambda(A)$. In such a model several processes - which are regarded to have the same behaviour - are identified. In fact the suitability of a congruence is determined by those aspects of the behaviour of concurrent systems we are interested in. Since we want to build proof systems for verifying that two processes have the same behaviour, and since we will use the constructed models as a criterion for establishing the validity of the proof systems, it is no good solution not to identify any processes at all (to select the identity as congruence). On the contrary, our purpose is to identify any two processes for which we can find no interesting property that discriminates between them. Of course it is application dependent which properties should be considered as interesting. Therefore we will describe a variety of possibilities. Each of the equivalences mentioned in this paper gives rise to another process semantics.

4.1. Occurrence net semantics.

The least identifying semantics of this paper is based upon occurrence net equivalence, as defined in section 2.9. Occurrence net semantics was already employed by NIELSEN, PLOTKIN & WINSKEL [NPW], WINSKEL [W2] and GOLTZ & MYCROFT [GM]. It carefully respects the local structure of nets, but the identity of places and transitions is not preserved. However, in an algebraic approach in which we have operators like + and ·, this loss of identity is unavoidable, because the definition of these operators only makes sense if we identify a net N with $\mathfrak{R}(N)$.

4.1.1. PROPOSITION: $\equiv_{occ}$ is a congruence w.r.t. the operators of section 1.
4.1.2. PROPOSITION: $\mathbb{N}_\lambda(A) / \equiv_{occ}$ satisfies the axioms of table 1, except for axioms A3, A4 and A5.

As illustrated in figure 9, the model $N_\lambda(A)/\equiv_{occ}$ does not even identify processes like a and $a+a$, which behave very much the same. Hence we argue that in this model there are not enough laws valid to make practical system verifications possible.

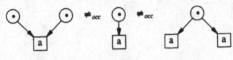

FIGURE 9

4.2. Bisimulation semantics.

In the occurrence net semantics of the previous section the structure of processes is carefully respected, but, due to the low degree of identification, there are not enough laws for algebraic system verification. Now we will look at an opposite point in our spectrum. *Bisimulation semantics* is firmly based upon the interleaving assumption. Consequently, some features of concurrency, like causal dependencies, cannot be modeled any more. However, for this semantics rich algebraic theories are available which can be - and have been - used for verification of several kinds of systems.

As far as this paper is concerned, the virtue of bisimulation semantics is twofold. Firstly, it gives rise to powerful algebraic tools which can be used for all applications in which properties like causality and real-time behaviour are unimportant and the interleaving assumption is harmless. And secondly, it will turn out to be a valuable expedient for axiomatising non-interleaved semantics.

We start by defining *bisimulation equivalence* or *bisimilarity*. The original notion, although defined on graphs instead of nets, is due to PARK [Pa]. It can be regarded as a refinement of MILNER'S *observational equivalence* [Mi]. Clause 4 below represent an idea from the ACP framework: the distinction between deadlock and successful termination (cf. section 1.0, section 3.2, and figure 12).

4.2.1. DEFINITION: Let $N_0, N_1 \in N_\lambda(A)$. A relation $R \subseteq Pow(S_0) \times Pow(S_1)$ is a *bisimulation* between N_0 and N_1, notation $R: N_0 \leftrightarrow N_1$, if:
1. $(M_{in})_0 \ R \ (M_{in})_1$;
2. if $M_0 \ R \ M_1$ and $M_0[t_0 > M'_0$, then there are $t_1 \in T_1$ and $M'_1 \subseteq S_1$ such that $l_0(t_0) = l_1(t_1)$, $M_1[t_1 > M'_1$ and $M'_0 \ R \ M'_1$;
3. as 2 but with the roles of N_0 and N_1 reversed;
4. $M_0 \ R \ M_1 \ \Rightarrow \ (M_0 = \emptyset \Leftrightarrow M_1 = \emptyset)$.
N_0 and N_1 are *bisimilar*, notation $N_0 \leftrightarrow N_1$, iff there is an $R: N_0 \leftrightarrow N_1$.

4.2.2. EXAMPLES:

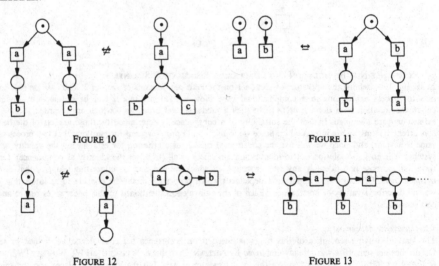

FIGURE 10

FIGURE 11

FIGURE 12

FIGURE 13

4.2.3. PROPOSITION: $\leftrightarrow$ is an equivalence relation on $N_\lambda(A)$, which is a congruence w.r.t. the operators of section 1.
4.2.4. PROPOSITION: $N_\lambda(A)/\leftrightarrow$ satisfies the axioms of table 1.
4.2.5. PROPOSITION: Let $N \in N_\lambda(A)$. Then $N \leftrightarrow \mathcal{U}(N)$. So $\equiv_{occ} \Rightarrow \leftrightarrow$.

4.3. Petri nets and process graphs.

Since bisimulation semantics is based on the interleaving assumption, the model presented above does not really use the expressive power of Petri nets. In fact we claim that for $\lambda > \aleph_0$, the model $N_\lambda(A) / \leftrightarrow$ is isomorphic to the graph model $G_\lambda(A) / \leftrightarrow$ of [BBK1] (if we omit all τ's from this model). The usefulness of an interleaved Petri net model is (in our view) establishing a connection between the 'classical' graph models and the non-interleaved Petri net models in this paper. Furthermore, we think that the definition of the parallel composition operator is more natural in the Petri net model than it is in the graph model. Below, we try to make the relation between the two models more explicit.

4.3.1. DEFINITION: Let $N_0 \in N_\lambda(A)$. The *sequentialisation* of N_0, notation $\mathcal{S}(N_0)$, is the net N_1 defined by:

$$S_1 = [(M_{in})_0 > - \{\varnothing\}$$

$$T_1 = \{(M,t) \mid M \in S_1, \, t \in T_0 \text{ and } M[t>\}$$

$$F_1 = \{(M,(M,t)) \mid (M,t) \in T_1\} \cup \{((M,t),M') \mid (M,t) \in T_1, \, M[t>M' \text{ and } M' \neq \varnothing\}$$

$$(M_{in})_1 = \{(M_{in})_0\}$$

$$l_1((M,t)) = l_0(t) \text{ for } (M,t) \in T_1$$

Because each reachable marking M of net N_0 can be characterized by a sequence $\sigma \in T^*$ with $(M_{in})_0[\sigma > M$, we have that the cardinality of S_1 is less than λ. Thus $\mathcal{S}$ is a function from $N_\lambda(A)$ into $N_\lambda(A)$.

4.3.2. EXAMPLE:

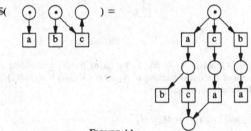

FIGURE 14

4.3.3. LEMMA: *Let $N_0 \in N_\lambda(A)$ and let $N_1 = \mathcal{S}(N_0)$. Then:*

i) $N_0 \leftrightarrow N_1$;

ii) $|(M_{in})_1| = 1$;

iii) $\forall t \in T_1 : |{}^\bullet t| = 1$ and $|t^\bullet| \leqslant 1$;

iv) $\mathcal{S}(N_1)$ *is isomorphic to* N_1.

4.3.4. REMARK: Lemma 4.3.3 says that each element of $N_\lambda(A) / \leftrightarrow$ contains a process-graph-like Petri net. In fact there is a 1-1 correspondence between sequentialisations of nets and τ-less process graphs. This is illustrated below.

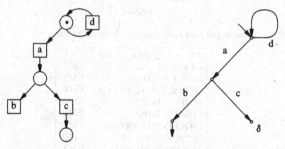

FIGURE 15

4.4. A complete proof system.

Now we will present a sound and complete proof system for bisimulation semantics; that is, a set of rules and axioms such that an equation $t = t'$ holds in the model $N_\lambda(A) / \leftrightarrow$ if and only if it can be proved from the rules and axioms in this set. The proof system consists of the equational theory ACP of BERGSTRA & KLOP [BK1-3] (which deals with closed terms) plus a limit rule for open terms. In ACP we use two auxiliary operators $\underline{\parallel}$ (left-merge) and $|$ (communication merge). The process $x \underline{\parallel} y$ is the process $x \| y$, but with the restriction that the first step comes from x, and $x | y$

is $x\|y$ with a communication step as the first step. These operators are used in the reduction of concurrency to non-determinism, which is the basic simplification introduced by the interleaving approach.

4.4.1.1. $\mathbb{L}$: If $N_0, N_1 \in \mathbb{N}_\lambda(A)$, obtain $N_2 = N_0 \mathbb{L} N_1$ by taking $N_0 \| N_1$ and adding a new S-element $ROOT$, which will become the only element of the initial marking of N_2. For each $t \in T_0$ and $M \subseteq S_0$ for which $(M_{in})_0[t > M$, we add a new T-element t^0 and put:
$-l_2(t^0) = l_0(t)$

$-{}^\bullet(t^0) = \{ROOT\}$ and $(t^0)^\bullet = M \cup (M_{in})_1$

4.4.1.2. EXAMPLE: Let $\gamma(a,b)=c$. Then:

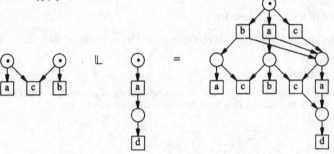

FIGURE 16

4.4.2.1. $|$: If $N_0, N_1 \in \mathbb{N}_\lambda(A)$, obtain $N_2 = N_0 | N_1$ by taking $N_0 \| N_1$ and adding a new S-element $ROOT$, which will become the only element of the initial marking of N_2. Let $(M_{in})_0[t_0 > M_0$, $(M_{in})_1[t_1 > M_1$ and $\gamma(l_0(t_0), l_1(t_1)) = c \neq \delta$. Then we add a new T-element (t_0, t_1) and put:
$-l_2((t_0,t_1)) = c$

$-{}^\bullet(t_0,t_1) = \{ROOT\}$ and $(t_0,t_1)^\bullet = M_0 \cup M_1$

4.4.2.2. EXAMPLE: Let $\gamma(a,b)=c$. Then:

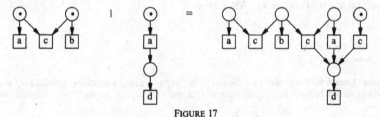

FIGURE 17

4.4.3. ACP consists of the axioms A and D of table 1 and the axioms CM below.

$x\|y = x\mathbb{L}y + y\mathbb{L}x + x\|y$	CM1
$a\mathbb{L}x = ax$	CM2
$(ax)\mathbb{L}y = a(x\|y)$	CM3
$(x+y)\mathbb{L}z = x\mathbb{L}z + y\mathbb{L}z$	CM4
$(ax)\|b = (a\|b)x$	CM5
$a\|(bx) = (a\|b)x$	CM6
$(ax)\|(by) = (a\|b)(x\|y)$	CM7
$(x+y)\|z = x\|z + y\|z$	CM8
$x\|(y+z) = x\|y + x\|z$	CM9
$a\|b = \gamma(a,b)$	CM10

TABLE 2

Furthermore, we have the *limit rule* (LR) of BAETEN & BERGSTRA [BB]. It states that if an equation holds for all finite processes (i.e. if it holds after any substitution of closed terms for the variables in this equation) then it holds for all processes. Now the axioms C of table 1 are derivable from ACP+LR.

4.4.4. PROPOSITION: $\underline{\leftrightarrow}$ *is also a congruence w.r.t. the operators* $\|$ *and* $|$.

4.4.5. PROPOSITION: $\mathbf{N}_\lambda(A)\,/\,\underline{\leftrightarrow}\,\vDash\,$ACP+LR, *i.e.* $\mathbf{N}_\lambda(A)\,/\,\underline{\leftrightarrow}$ *is a model of* ACP+LR.

4.4.6. THEOREM: $\mathbf{N}_\lambda(A)\,/\,\underline{\leftrightarrow}\,\vDash\,t=t'\;\Leftrightarrow\;$ACP+LR $\vdash t=t'$, *i.e.* ACP+LR *is a sound and complete proof system.*

4.5. Concurrent bisimulation semantics.

In this section we present a non interleaved variant of bisimulation semantics. This *concurrent bisimulation semantics* takes explicitly into account the possibility that in a process like $a\|b$ the actions a and b occur concurrently (besides the possibilities that they occur one after the other, or synchronise into a communication action $\gamma(a,b)$). Definition 4.5.2 of the concurrent bisimulation, but without our termination clause 4, also appeared in [NT] and [G].

4.5.1. DEFINITION: Let $N = (S,T,F,M_{in},l)$ be a net, let M,M' be markings of N and let U be a subset of T. We say that M' *U-follows* M, and *results from firing the transitions in* U *concurrently*, notation $M[U>M'$, if:

a. $M[U>$ (see definition 2.4)

b. $\forall s \in S$:

$$M'(s) = \begin{cases} M(s)-1 & \text{if } \exists t \in U : s \in {}^\bullet t - t^{\bullet} \\ M(s)+1 & \text{if } \exists t \in U : s \in t^{\bullet} - {}^\bullet t \\ M(s) & \text{otherwise} \end{cases}$$

Note that if M is reachable and $M[U>M'$ then U must be finite (since N displays only bounded parallelism, see 2.5) so M' is reachable again.

4.5.2. DEFINITION: Let $N_0, N_1 \in \mathbf{N}_\lambda(A)$. A relation $R \subseteq Pow(S_0) \times Pow(S_1)$ is a *concurrent bisimulation* between N_0 and N_1, notation $R : N_0 \underline{\leftrightarrow}_c N_1$, if:

1. $(M_{in})_0\ R\ (M_{in})_1$;
2.   if $M_0\ R\ M_1$ and $M_0[U_0>M'_0$, then there are $U_1 \subseteq T_1$ and $M'_1 \subseteq S_1$ such that $l_0(U_0)=l_1(U_1)$, $M_1[U_1>M'_1$ and $M'_0\ R\ M'_1$ (here $l_i(U_i)$ denotes the multiset of labels of the transitions in U_i);
3.   as 2 but with the roles of N_0 and N_1 reversed;
4. $M_0\ R\ M_1\;\Rightarrow\;(M_0=\varnothing\,\Leftrightarrow\,M_1=\varnothing)$.

N_0 and N_1 are *concurrently bisimilar*, notation $N_0\underline{\leftrightarrow}_c N_1$, iff there is an $R : N_0\underline{\leftrightarrow}_c N_1$.

4.5.3. PROPOSITION: $\underline{\leftrightarrow}_c$ *is an equivalence relation on* $\mathbf{N}_\lambda(A)$, *which is a congruence w.r.t. the operators of section 1.*

4.5.4. PROPOSITION: $\mathbf{N}_\lambda(A)\,/\,\underline{\leftrightarrow}_c$ *satisfies the axioms of table 1.*

4.5.5. PROPOSITION: $\equiv_{occ}\;\Rightarrow\;\underline{\leftrightarrow}_c\;\Rightarrow\;\underline{\leftrightarrow}$.

4.5.6. EXAMPLE:

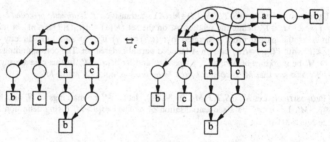

FIGURE 18

4.5.7. REMARK: The algebraic equivalent of figure 18 is the identity:

$$a(b\|c)+(a\|c)b = a(b\|c)+(a\|c)b+ab\|c$$

Here we see that the algebraic approach allows us to represent a rather complex Petri net by means of a relatively simple formula.

§5 PARTIAL ORDER SEMANTICS

The equation

$$a\|b=ab+ba,\tag{i}$$

which holds in the interleaved bisimulation semantics of section 4.2, is rejected in the concurrent bisimulation semantics of section 4.5. The reason for rejecting this equation is that the left hand side leaves open the possibility that a and b occur simultaneously, whereas this option is not present at the right hand side. The True concurrency adherents also reject this equation, but for a more fundamental reason: in $a\|b$ the actions a and b occur *independently*, while in $ab+ba$ there is a *causal* link between them: a occurs before b or b occurs before a. In order to point out the difference more sharply the following notation will be used.

All models of concurrency investigated in this paper (except the one based on occurrence equivalence) satisfy the axioms A1-3 from table 1, expressing that the alternatives in a choice can be regarded to form a set. Now write $x \subseteq y$ for $x+y=y$. From A1, A2 and A3 respectively it follows that $\subseteq$ is antisymmetrical, transitive and reflexive, and hence a partial order. Now the formula

$$ab\|c \subseteq (a\|c)b + a(b\|c) \qquad \text{(ii)}$$

(cf. section 4.5.7) does hold in concurrent bisimulation semantics: in $ab\|c$ there are five possibilities: c occurs before a, simultaneous with a, between a and b, simultaneous with b, or after b. Each of these possibilities is already present at the right hand side, so the summand $ab\|c$ says nothing new and can be deleted. However, (ii) is incompatible with True concurrency: in $ab\|c$ the action c occurs independently of both a and b, while in $(a\|c)b + a(b\|c)$ the c action occurs either causally before b or causally behind a.

Hence the True concurrency approach depends in a subtle way on a philosophically complicated issue like causality (for a philosophical discussion of the concept of causality see HOSPERS [Ho]). However, it is also possible to reject formulas like (ii) on more earthly grounds, as for example real-time behaviour. If we suppose that the execution of an atomic action takes a fixed amount of time (or that a fixed amount of time elapses between the instantaneous occurrence of an atomic action and the following action), and if we furthermore assume that c takes as much time as a and b together, then $ab\|c$ can be executed much faster than $(a\|c)b + a(b\|c)$.

This section is devoted to the causal approach to True concurrency. In the next section the real-time approach will be examined. There we will see to what extent these approaches coincide. After some preliminaries we start with the definition of the pomset equivalence, a partial order approach stemming from PRATT [Pr1-2], which is a variant of trace theory as originated by MAZURKIEWICZ (see [M1-2] and [AR]).

5.1. Causality.

5.1.1. DEFINITION: An *A-labelled partial ordered set* is a triple $(X, <, l)$ with X a set, $<$ a partial order on X, and $l : X \to A$ a labelling function. Two such sets $(X_0, <_0, l_0)$ and $(X_1, <_1, l_1)$ are *isomorphic* if there exists a bijective mapping $f : X_0 \to X_1$ such that $f(x) < f(y) \Leftrightarrow x < y$ and $l_1(f(x)) = l_0(x)$.

A *partial ordered multiset (pomset)* over A is an isomorphy class of A-labelled partial ordered sets. As usual, pomsets can be made setlike by requiring that the elements of the sets X should be chosen from a given set.

A *totally ordered multiset (tomset)* over A can be defined similarly. There exists a 1-1 correspondence between sequences $\sigma \in A^*$ and finite tomsets. Let $\hat{\sigma}$ denote the tomset corresponding with σ. A sequence $\sigma \in A^*$ is a *sequentialisation* of a pomset ρ, if $\hat{\sigma}$ can be obtained by expanding the partial order of ρ into a total one.

5.1.2. DEFINITION: Let $N = (S, T, F, M_{in}, l) \in \mathbb{N}_\lambda(A)$. A transition t' is *directly preceded* by a transition t if $t' \cap {}^\bullet t' \neq \varnothing$. For $\alpha = t_1 * \cdots * t_m \in T^*$ define the relation $<$ on the set $Oc(\alpha) = \{(t_i, i) \mid 1 \leq i \leq m\}$ of numbered occurrences of transitions in α as the partial order generated by: $(t_i, i) < (t_j, j)$ if $i < j$ and t_j is directly preceded by t_i. This makes $(Oc(\alpha), <, l')$ with $l'(t_i, i) = l(t_i)$ into an A-labelled partial ordered set. The corresponding pomset is denoted by $pom(\alpha)$.

Let M, M' be markings of N, $\alpha \in T^*$, $\rho = pom(\alpha)$ and let $M[\alpha > M']$. In this case we say that ρ is *M-enabled*, notation $M[\rho >$. We also say that M' *is obtained from M by firing* ρ, notation $M[\rho > M']$.

5.1.3. PROPOSITION: Let $N = (S, T, F, M_{in}, l) \in \mathbb{N}_\lambda(A)$, let M, M' be markings of N, and let ρ be a pomset over A such that $M[\rho > M']$. Let $\sigma \in A^*$ be a sequentialisation of ρ. Then $M[\sigma > M']$ (using definition 2.3.(v)). Note that we cannot conclude $M[\hat{\sigma} > M']$.

5.2. Pomset semantics.

5.2.1. DEFINITION: The set $pom(N)$ of pomsets (with termination information) of a net $N \in \mathbb{N}_\lambda(A)$ is given by $pom(N) = \{pom(\alpha) \mid M_{in}[\alpha >\} \cup \{(pom(\alpha), \sqrt{}) \mid M_{in}[\alpha > \varnothing\}$. Two nets $N_1, N_2 \in \mathbb{N}_\lambda(A)$ are *pomset equivalent*, notation $N_1 \equiv_{pom} N_2$, if $pom(N_1) = pom(N_2)$.

5.2.2. EXAMPLES: (Note that the first two nets *are* identified in concurrent bisimulation semantics.)

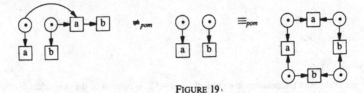

FIGURE 19

5.2.3. PROPOSITION: $\equiv_{pom}$ is an equivalence relation on $\mathbf{N}_\lambda(A)$, which is a congruence w.r.t. the operators of section 1.

5.2.4. PROPOSITION: $\mathbf{N}_\lambda(A)\,/_{\equiv_{pom}}$ satisfies the axioms of table 1.

5.2.5. PROPOSITION: $\equiv_{occ}\;\Rightarrow\;\equiv_{pom}$.

5.3. Pomset bisimulation semantics.

Although the partial order approach sketched above preserves causality, other features of concurrency get lost. The equation

$$a(b+c) = ab+ac \tag{iii}$$

is not valid in (concurrent) bisimulation semantics, since the timing of the choice between b and c is different on the left and right hand side. However, (iii) is satisfied in $\mathbf{N}_\lambda(A)\,/_{\equiv_{pom}}$, so in this model all information about the timing of choices is lost. As argued by (for instance) MILNER [Mi], this implies that deadlock behaviour cannot be described in the model. Thus we encountered bisimulation equivalences, respecting branching time but violating causality, and pomset equivalence which respects causality but violates branching time. Now the natural question arises whether the virtues of both approaches can be combined or not, i.e. if a model of concurrency exists respecting both causality and branching time. Such a model was presented by BOUDOL & CASTELLANI [BC]. A variant of this model, adapted to the setting of the present paper will be treated below (Boudol and Castellani used a different language, and event structures instead of Petri nets).

5.3.1. DEFINITION: Let $N_0,N_1\in\mathbf{N}_\lambda(A)$. A relation $R\subseteq Pow(S_0)\times Pow(S_1)$ is a pomset bisimulation between N_0 and N_1, notation $R:N_0\overset{\leftrightarrow}{{}_{pom}}N_1$, if:
1. $(M_{in})_0\ R\ (M_{in})_1$;
2. if $M_0\ R\ M_1$ and for $\alpha_0\in T_0^*$ $M_0[\alpha_0>M'_0$, then there are $\alpha_1\in T_1^*$ and $M'_1\subseteq S_1$ such that $pom(\alpha_0)=pom(\alpha_1)$, $M_1[\alpha_1>M'_1$ and $M'_0\ R\ M'_1$;
3. as 2 but with the roles of N_0 and N_1 reversed;
4. $M_0\ R\ M_1\ \Rightarrow\ (M_0=\varnothing\Leftrightarrow M_1=\varnothing)$.

N_0 and N_1 are pomset bisimilar, notation $N_0\overset{\leftrightarrow}{{}_{pom}}N_1$, iff there is an $R:N_0\overset{\leftrightarrow}{{}_{pom}}N_1$.

5.3.2. EXAMPLES:

$$a(b\|c)+(a\|c)b\ \overset{\leftrightarrow}{\not{}}_{pom}\ a(b\|c)+(a\|c)b+ab\|c\quad\text{(as for }\equiv_{pom}\text{, in contrast with }\overset{\leftrightarrow}{{}_c}\text{, see (ii) in §5.0)}\tag{a}$$

$$a\|b+ab\ \overset{\leftrightarrow}{\not{}}_{pom}\ a\|b\ \overset{\leftrightarrow}{{}_{pom}}\ a\|b+a\|b\quad\text{(as for }\equiv_{pom}\text{, see figure 19)}\tag{b}$$

$$a\|(b+c)+a\|b+(a+c)\|b\ \overset{\leftrightarrow}{{}_{pom}}\ a\|(b+c)+(a+c)\|b\quad\text{(taken from [BC])}\tag{c}$$

5.3.3. PROPOSITION: $\overset{\leftrightarrow}{{}_{pom}}$ is an equivalence relation on $\mathbf{N}_\lambda(A)$, which is a congruence w.r.t. the operators of section 1.

5.3.4. PROPOSITION: $\mathbf{N}_\lambda(A)\,/_{\overset{\leftrightarrow}{{}_{pom}}}$ satisfies the axioms of table 1.

5.3.5. PROPOSITION: $\equiv_{occ}\;\Rightarrow\;\overset{\leftrightarrow}{{}_{pom}}\;\Rightarrow\;\overset{\leftrightarrow}{{}_c}$, $\overset{\leftrightarrow}{}$ and $\equiv_{pom}$.

5.4. Combining causality and branching time.

The formula (ii) respects branching time, but violates causality. It holds in concurrent bisimulation semantics, but does not hold in pomset or pomset bisimulation semantics. On the other hand the formula

$$ab\|c\subseteq a(b+d)\|c \tag{iv}$$

respects causality but violates branching time. It holds in pomset semantics, but not in (concurrent) bisimulation or pomset bisimulation semantics. The combination of (ii) and (iv):

$$ab\|c\subseteq a(b+d)\|c+(a\|c)b+a(b\|c) \tag{v}$$

respects both causality and branching time. However, it violates the idea behind the combination of these two concepts. The right hand side will perform an a and a c action, and either a b or a d. The action c can occur causally before b or causally behind a. It is also possible that c occurs independent of both a and b, but in that case c occurs also independent of the choice between b and d. The summand $ab\|c$ adds the possibility that c occurs independent of both a and b, but causally behind the choice in favour of b. Hence (v) violates the real combination of causality and branching time. Nevertheless it is satisfied in pomset bisimulation semantics. The model based on the following generalised pomset bisimulation equivalence does not have this disadvantage. However, in [BC], BOUDOL & CASTELLANI presented a proof system for a language without communication, that is sound and complete for closed terms with respect to pomset bisimulation semantics. Such a result is not available for the generalised version.

5.4.1. DEFINITION: Let $N_0,N_1\in\mathbf{N}_\lambda(A)$. A relation $R\subseteq Pow(S_0)\times Pow(S_1)$ is a generalised pomset bisimulation between N_0 and N_1, notation $R:N_0\overset{\leftrightarrow}{{}_{gpom}}N_1$, if:
1. $(M_{in})_0\ R\ (M_{in})_1$;
2. if $M_0\ R\ M_1$ and for $\alpha_0=t_{01}*t_{02}*\cdots*t_{0n}\in T_0^*$, $M_0\ [t_{01}>M_{01}\ [t_{02}>M_{02}\cdots\ [t_{0n}>M_{0n}$, then there are $\alpha_1=$

$t_{11} * t_{12} * \cdots * t_{1n} \in T_1^-$ such that $pom(\alpha_0) = pom(\alpha_1)$, $M_1 [t_{11} > M_{11} [t_{12} > M_{12} \cdots [t_{1n} > M_{1n}$, and $M_{0i} R M_{1i}$ for $1 \leq i \leq n$;

3. as 2 but with the roles of N_0 and N_1 reversed;

4. $M_0 R M_1 \Rightarrow (M_0 = \emptyset \Leftrightarrow M_1 = \emptyset)$.

N_0 and N_1 are *generalised pomset bisimilar*, notation $N_0 \underline{\leftrightarrow}_{gpom} N_1$, iff there is an $R : N_0 \underline{\leftrightarrow}_{gpom} N_1$.

5.4.2. EXAMPLES:

$$ab \| c + a(b+d) \| c + (a \| c)b + a(b \| c) \quad \not\underline{\leftrightarrow}_{gpom} \quad a(b+d) \| c + (a \| c)b + a(b \| c) \quad \text{(unlike } \underline{\leftrightarrow}_{pom}, \text{ see (v))} \qquad \text{(a)}$$

$$a \| (b+c) + a \| b + (a+c) \| b \quad \underline{\leftrightarrow}_{gpom} \quad a \| (b+c) + (a+c) \| b \quad \text{(as for } \underline{\leftrightarrow}_{pom}, \text{ see 5.3.2(c))} \qquad \text{(b)}$$

5.4.3. PROPOSITION: $\underline{\leftrightarrow}_{gpom}$ *is an equivalence relation on* $\mathbf{N}_\lambda(A)$, *which is a congruence w.r.t. the operators of section 1.*

5.4.4. PROPOSITION: $\mathbf{N}_\lambda(A) / \underline{\leftrightarrow}$ *satisfies the axioms of table 1.*

5.4.5. PROPOSITION: $\equiv_{occ} \Rightarrow \underline{\leftrightarrow}_{gpom} \Rightarrow \underline{\leftrightarrow}_{pom}$.

§6 REAL-TIME SEMANTICS

In this section we will describe a possible real-time interpretation of process algebra. First we show how real-time behaviour can be attached to Petri nets. This gives the timed Petri net model as presented in, for example, CARLIER, CHRETIENNE & GIRAULT [CCG]. In BAETEN, BERGSTRA & KLOP [BBK2] it is shown how operational rewrite systems can be used to give real-time semantics for the ACP language. The intuition behind this semantics is comparable with the intuition behind the timed Petri nets. New in our approach is the notion of *real-time consistency*. An equivalence relation on Petri nets is real-time consistent if it does not identify nets with a different real-time behaviour. A model based on a real-time consistent equivalence makes it possible to reason about concurrent systems in a real-time consistent manner without having to deal with the full complexity of real-time. We show that the concurrent and pomset bisimulation equivalences are not real-time consistent. However, in the next section we will present an equivalence relation on nets which *is* real-time consistent.

6.1. Timed Petri nets. Let $N = (S, T, F, M_{in}, l)$ be a safe labelled marked net. Time is introduced in the following manner. We assume the presence of a function $\tau : A \to \mathbf{R}^+$. The τ-function associates a (fixed) processing time with each atomic action. Here we have chosen the range of τ to be the set $\mathbf{R}^+$, but this could also have been $\mathbf{Q}^+$ or $\mathbf{N}^+$. We assume that τ has a positive lower bound in order to avoid Zeno's paradox. Further we restrict ourselves to nets in $\mathbf{N}_\lambda(A)$ (so we have bounded parallelism). As a consequence of these assumptions the set of points in time at which some transition starts or ends firing, will be discrete. In case a transition u fires at time t, it removes the tokens from the input places. $\tau(l(u))$ time units later tokens are placed in the output places of u. We assume that it takes no time to resolve conflicts: when a transition can fire, it will fire immediately, or it will be disabled immediately. This means that we have maximal parallelism. We make these intuitions formal in the following definitions:

6.2. DEFINITION: Let $N = (S, T, F, M_{in}, l) \in \mathbf{N}_\lambda(A)$ and let $\tau : A \to \mathbf{R}^+$. An *instantaneous description* is a 4-tuple (M, U, ρ, t) where:

- $M \subseteq S$ is the set of places with a token;
- $U \subseteq T$ is the set of transitions which are firing. If a transition is firing, its input places are already empty
 $(\forall u \in U : {}^\bullet u \cap M = \emptyset)$, whereas its output places are still empty;
- $\rho : T \to [0, \infty)$ is a function which gives for each transition the residual processing time. $\rho(u) = 0$ for those transitions which are not firing;
- $t \in [0, \infty)$ is the time.

We will now define a transition relation $\to$, which tells how one instantaneous description can evolve into another.

6.3. DEFINITION: Let $N = (S, T, F, M_{in}, l) \in \mathbf{N}_\lambda(A)$, $\tau : A \to \mathbf{R}^+$ and let (M, U, ρ, l) be an instantaneous description of N. The binary relation $\to$ is defined by:

1. if $M[u>$, $\rho'(u) = \tau(l(u))$ and $\rho'(\overline{u}) = \rho(\overline{u})$ if $\overline{u} \neq u$, then: $(M, U, \rho, t) \to (M - {}^\bullet u, U \cup \{u\}, \rho', t)$;

2. if $u \in U$ and $\rho(u) = 0$, then: $(M, U, \rho, t) \to (M \cup u^\bullet, U - \{u\}, \rho, t)$;

3. if $\forall u \in T : \neg M[u>$, $U \neq \emptyset$, $0 < \Delta t = \min\{\rho(u) | u \in U\}$, $\rho'(u) = \rho(u) - \Delta t$ if $u \in U$, and $\rho'(u) = 0$ otherwise, then: $(M, U, \rho, t) \to (M, U, \rho', t + \Delta t)$.

6.4. DEFINITION: Let $N \in \mathbf{N}_\lambda(A)$. A *real-time execution* of N is a sequence $< I_i >_{i < n}$ of instantaneous descriptions of N such that $I_0 = (M_{in}, \emptyset, \lambda x. 0, 0)$ and $I_i \to I_{i+1}$ for $i < n$.

The following definition is derived from REED & ROSCOE [RR].

6.5. DEFINITION: A *timed action* is an ordered pair (t,a), where a is an atomic action and $t \in [0, \infty)$ is the time at which it occurs. The set $[0, \infty) \times A$ of all timed actions is denoted TA. The set of *timed traces* is:

$$(TA)'_{\leq} = \{\sigma \in TA^* \mid \text{if } (t,a) \text{ precedes } (t',a') \text{ in } \sigma, \text{ then } t \leq t'\}$$

6.6. In a trivial way we can associate a timed trace with each real-time execution of a net $N \in \mathbb{N}_\lambda(A)$: we take the sequence of actions executed by the system, together with their starting times. Let $tt_\tau : \mathbb{N}_\lambda(A) \to (TA)'_{\leq}$ be the function which, for given $\tau : A \to \mathbb{R}^+$, associates with each net the set of its timed traces.

6.7. DEFINITION: An equivalence relation $\equiv$ on $\mathbb{N}_\lambda(A)$ is called *real-time consistent*, if for all $\tau : A \to \mathbb{R}^+$ with the property $\exists \epsilon > 0 \ \forall a \in A: \tau(a) > \epsilon$, and for all $N_0, N_1 \in \mathbb{N}_\lambda(A)$: $N_0 \equiv N_1 \Rightarrow tt_\tau(N_0) = tt_\tau(N_1)$.

6.8. PROPOSITION: *The equivalence relation $\underleftrightarrow{}_{gpom}$ is not real-time consistent.*
PROOF: Below we give two nets which are generalised pomset bisimilar, but have different timed traces.

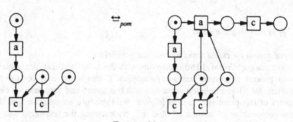

FIGURE 20

If we define communication by $\gamma(r,s) = c$ and if $H = \{r,s\}$, then we can express the identity algebraically as follows:

$$\partial_H(ar \| r \| s) = \partial_H(ar \| r \| s) + ac\delta$$

Assume $\tau(a) = \tau(c) = 1$. Now any real-time execution of the net on the left will start with an a and a c action. The net on the right however, has also the possibility to start with an a action only, followed by a c action after 1 time unit.

6.9. COROLLARY: *The equivalence relations $\underleftrightarrow{}_{pom}$, $\underleftrightarrow{}_c$, $\underleftrightarrow{}$ and $\equiv_{pom}$ are not real-time consistent.*

6.10. QUESTION: Is $\underleftrightarrow{}_{gpom}$ real-time consistent for fully observable process expressions, as defined in section 7.5.2?

§7 ST-BISIMULATION SEMANTICS

In this section we present a non-interleaved Petri net model for the theory of section 1, together with a complete proof system for closed process expressions without autoparallelism (cf. section 7.3). The model is based on a real-time consistent equivalence on nets, called *ST-bisimulation equivalence*. The idea behind ST-bisimulation equivalence is rather simple: A bisimulation can be viewed as a relation between the states of two systems. In the graph model of [BBK1], the states are the nodes in the graphs. In the bisimulation equivalence on Petri nets which we presented in the previous sections, the states of the system are distributed entities: namely the set of places containing a token. In the philosophy leading to the ST-bisimulation the state of a system is the set of places containing a token, together with the sequence of transitions which are firing, in the order they started firing. This is just what one obtains when leaving out the real-time information from the instantaneous descriptions as defined in section 6.2 (the order of the transitions can be derived from the function ρ in 6.2).

7.1.1. DEFINITION: Let $N_0, N_1 \in \mathbb{N}_\lambda(A)$. A relation $R \subseteq (Pow(S_0) \times T_0^*) \times (Pow(S_1) \times T_1^*)$ is an *ST-bisimulation* between N_0 and N_1, notation $R: N_0 \underleftrightarrow{}_{ST} N_1$, if:
1. $((M_{in})_0, \epsilon) \ R \ ((M_{in})_1, \epsilon)$;
2. if $(M_0, \sigma_0) \ R \ (M_1, \sigma_1)$ and $M_0[t_0\rangle$, then there is a $t_1 \in T_1$ such that $l_0(t_0) = l_1(t_1)$, $M_1[t_1\rangle$ and $(M_0 - {}^\bullet t_0, \sigma_0 * t_0) \ R \ (M_1 - {}^\bullet t_1, \sigma_1 * t_1)$;
3. as 2 but with the roles of N_0 and N_1 reversed;
4. if $(M_0, \sigma_0 * t_0 * \rho_0) \ R \ (M_1, \sigma_1 * t_1 * \rho_1)$ and $|\sigma_0| = |\sigma_1|$, then $(M_0 \cup t_0{}^\bullet, \sigma_0 * \rho_0) \ R \ (M_1 \cup t_1{}^\bullet, \sigma_1 * \rho_1)$;
5. as 4 but with the roles of N_0 and N_1 reversed;
6. $(M_0, \sigma_0) \ R \ (M_1, \sigma_1) \Rightarrow ((M_0, \sigma_0) = (\varnothing, \epsilon) \Leftrightarrow (M_1, \sigma_1) = (\varnothing, \epsilon))$.
N_0 and N_1 are *ST-bisimilar*, notation $N_0 \underleftrightarrow{}_{ST} N_1$, iff there is an $R: N_0 \underleftrightarrow{}_{ST} N_1$.

7.1.2. EXAMPLES: Define communication by $\gamma(r,s) = c$ and let $H = \{r,s\}$. Then:

$$\partial_H(ar\|r\|s) + ac\delta \ \not\leftrightarrow_{ST} \ \partial_H(ar\|r\|s) \ \leftrightarrow_{ST} \ (a\|c)\delta \quad \text{(both parts unlike } \leftrightarrow_{pom} \text{ and } \leftrightarrow_{gpom}, \text{ see §6.8)} \quad \text{(a)}$$

$$ab\|c + a(b+d)\|c + (a\|c)b + a(b\|c) \ \not\leftrightarrow_{ST} \ a(b+d)\|c + (a\|c)b + a(b\|c) \quad \text{(unlike } \leftrightarrow_{pom} \text{ see §5.4)} \quad \text{(b)}$$

$$a\|(b+c) + a\|b + (a+c)\|b \ \leftrightarrow_{ST} \ a\|(b+c) + (a+c)\|b \quad \text{(as for } \leftrightarrow_{pom} \text{ and } \leftrightarrow_{gpom} \text{ see example 5.3.2(c))} \quad \text{(c)}$$

The second part of example (a) shows that ST-bisimulation does not respect causality. Both parts together show that pomset bisimulation and ST-bisimulation are incomparable.

7.1.3. PROPOSITION: $\leftrightarrow_{ST}$ *is an equivalence relation on* $N_\lambda(A)$, *which is a congruence w.r.t. the operators of section 1.*

7.1.4. PROPOSITION: $N_\lambda(A) / \leftrightarrow_{sr}$ *satisfies the axioms of table 1.*

7.1.5. PROPOSITION: *All implications between the equivalences of this paper are displayed below:*

7.2. THEOREM: $\leftrightarrow_{ST}$ *is real-time consistent.*

7.3. A complete proof system for closed terms without autoparallelism.

A net is said to have *autoparallelism* if two transitions with the same label can fire concurrently (from some reachable marking). A closed process expression has autoparallelism if this is the case for the associated net. Next we will present a proof system for ST-bisimulation semantics which is sound and complete for closed terms without autoparallelism. The structure of this proof system is as follows: We introduce an operator *split* that splits any atomic action a into the sequential composition of actions a^+ and a^-, representing the beginning and the end of a. Then we prove that $N_0 \leftrightarrow_{ST} N_1$ iff $split(N_0) \leftrightarrow split(N_1)$. Now we already have a proof system for $\leftrightarrow$, which is sound and complete for closed terms, namely ACP. Thus, a proof system for $\leftrightarrow_{ST}$ can be obtained from ACP, by adding a sound set of axioms for the *split* operator that allows any closed term $split(t)$ to be rewritten into a closed ACP-term (without occurrences of the *split* operator). In this way the interleaving based axiom system ACP can be used to prove identities in the non-interleaved ST-bisimulation semantics.

7.3.1. Syntax. Formally, this idea will be implemented by a two-sorted algebra. We have a sort P of processes (the processes in a domain with ST-bisimulation semantics) and an auxiliary sort SP of split processes, in a domain with interleaving. On P we have the constants and operators of section 1; on SP we have constants δ, a^+, a^- (for $a \in A$), the operators $+$, $\cdot$, $\|$ and δ_H of section 1, and the auxiliary operators $\mathbin{\|\mkern-9mu\_}$ and $\mathbin{|}$ of section 4.4. Furthermore there is a unary operator $split : P \to SP$.

7.3.2. Semantics. Let A be a set of atomic actions and $\gamma : A_\delta \times A_\delta \to A_\delta$ a communication function. We define the set of split actions $A^\pm$ and the communication function $\gamma : A_\delta^\pm \times A_\delta^\pm \to A_\delta^\pm$ by:

$$A^\pm = \{a^+, a^- \mid a \in A\} \qquad \gamma(a^+, b^+) = \gamma(a,b)^+ \qquad \gamma(a^-, b^-) = \gamma(a,b)^- \qquad \gamma(a^+, b^-) = \delta$$

Now we give a model for this two-sorted signature. The set $N_\lambda(A) / \leftrightarrow_{sr}$ will be the domain of processes and $N_\lambda(A^\pm) / \leftrightarrow$ will be the domain of split processes. In order to define the operator $split : N_\lambda(A) / \leftrightarrow_{sr} \to N_\lambda(A^\pm) / \leftrightarrow$ we first define $split : N_\lambda(A) \to N_\lambda(A^\pm)$ and then check that the pair $(\leftrightarrow_{ST}, \leftrightarrow)$ is a congruence for this operator. The remaining constants and operators are defined as before.

7.3.2.1. split: Let $N_0 \in N_\lambda(A)$. $N_1 = split(N_0) \in N_\lambda(A^\pm)$ is defined by:

$$S_1 = S_0 \cup T_0$$

$$T_1 = \{t^+, t^- \mid t \in T_0\}$$

$$F_1 = \{(s,t^+) \mid (s,t) \in F_0\} \cup \{(t^+, t) \mid t \in T_0\} \cup \{(t, t^-) \mid t \in T_0\} \cup \{(t^-, s) \mid (t,s) \in F_0\}$$

$$(M_{in})_1 = (M_{in})_0$$

$$l_1(t^+) = (l_2(t))^+ \quad \text{and} \quad l_1(t^-) = (l_2(t))^-$$

So $split(N)$ is obtained from N, by replacing any net segment

That $(\leftrightarrow_{ST}, \leftrightarrow)$ is a congruence for *split*, follows from the following proposition.

7.3.3. PROPOSITION: *For any* $N_0, N_1 \in N_\lambda(A)$: $N_0 \leftrightarrow_{ST} N_1 \Rightarrow split(N_0) \leftrightarrow split(N_1)$.

7.3.4. PROPOSITION: *For any* $N_0, N_1 \in \mathbf{N}_\lambda(A)$ *without autoparallelism:* $split(N_0) \rightleftharpoons split(N_1) \Rightarrow N_0 \rightleftharpoons_{ST} N_1$.

7.3.5. *The split rule.* Let SPR be the rule $split(x) = split(y) \Rightarrow x = y$. Proposition 7.3.4 states its soundness for processes without autoparallelism. Furthermore proposition 4.4.6 states the soundness of ACP on sort SP. Now let SPLIT be a sound set of axioms, such that for any closed process expression p of sort P there is a closed ACP-expression q such that SPLIT $\vdash split(p) = q$. Then it follows trivially that SPLIT + ACP + SPR is a sound and complete proof system for closed terms without autoparallelism. So it suffices to find a suitable version of SPLIT. This we will do in three stages.

7.4. *The case without communication.* Suppose that $\gamma(a,b) = \delta$ for $a,b \in A$. Let SP^* be the theory presented in the left upper block of table 3, but with SP3 replaced by SP3*: $split(x\|y) = split(x)\|split(y)$. Then SP^* is sound with respect to the model of section 7.3.2 and for any closed process expression p of sort P there is a closed ACP-expression q of sort SP such that $SP^* \vdash split(p) = q$.

7.5. *The case with fully observable processes.* If we just expand the approach of section 7.4. with communication as defined in 7.3.2, then a serious problem arises: SP3* is not sound any more. Counterexample (if $\gamma(a,b) = c$):

$$split(a\|b) = a^+(a^-b^+b^- + b^+(a^-b^- + b^-a^-)) + b^+(b^-a^+a^- + a^+(b^-a^- + a^-b^-)) + c^+c^-$$

$$split(a)\|split(b) = a^+(a^-b^+b^- + b^+(a^-b^- + b^-a^- + c^-)) +$$
$$+ b^+(b^-a^+a^- + a^+(b^-a^- + a^-b^- + c^-)) + c^+(b^-a^- + a^-b^- + c^-)$$

Note that $split(a)\|split(b)$ is a very unrealistic process since certain actions can end before they begin. It turns out that sometimes a^+ communicates with b^+, while a^- and b^- occur independently. In order to disable this suspicious behaviour we will introduce a state operator $\lambda_\emptyset$, that renames actions a^- into δ if they are not preceded by an action a^+. Then we can replace axiom SP3* by SP3 (see table 3).

For the general theory of state operators see BAETEN & BERGSTRA [BB]. Our state operator remembers which actions are currently firing. This memory is located in a subscript S, with S ranging over $Pow(A)$. So we add operators $\lambda_S : SP \rightarrow SP$ to our signature for $S \subseteq A$. The axioms for λ_S are presented in the right-hand half of table 3.

$split(x + y) = split(x) + split(y)$	SP1		$\lambda_S(\delta) = \delta$		L1
$split(xy) = split(x) \cdot split(y)$	SP2		$\lambda_S(a^+) = a^+$		L2
$split(x\|y) = \lambda_\emptyset(split(x)\|split(y))$	SP3		$\lambda_S(a^-) = a^-$ if $a \in S$		L3
$split(\partial_H(x)) = \partial_{H^\pm}(split(y))$	SP4		$\lambda_S(a^-) = \delta$ if $a \notin S$		L4
$split(\delta) = \delta$	SP5		$\lambda_S(a^+x) = a^+ \cdot \lambda_{S \cup \{a\}}(x)$		L5
$split(a) = a^+ \cdot a^-$	SP6		$\lambda_S(a^-x) = a^- \cdot \lambda_{S - \{a\}}(x)$ if $a \in S$		L6
			$\lambda_S(a^-x) = \delta$ if $a \notin S$		L7
$split(x) = split(y) \Rightarrow x = y$	SPR		$\lambda_S(x + y) = \lambda_S(x) + \lambda_S(y)$		L8

TABLE 3

Now SP + L allows any closed process expression $split(p)$ with p of sort P to be rewritten in a closed ACP-term. However, the axiom SP3 is still not sound for all processes. Therefore we will first limit ourselves to a restricted domain of processes, for which its soundness can be proved.

7.5.1. DEFINITION: The alphabet $\alpha(N)$ of a net N is the set of labels of transitions which are M-enabled from a marking $M \in [M_{in}>$. Remark that if $N_0 \rightleftharpoons N_1$ then $\alpha(N_0) = \alpha(N_1)$. Now the alphabet $\alpha(p)$ of a closed process expression p is the alphabet of the associated net.

7.5.2. DEFINITION: A closed process expression p is *fully observable* if for any subexpression $x\|y$ of p we have $\alpha(x) \cap \alpha(y) = \emptyset$, and for any $a,c \in \alpha(x)$, $b,d \in \alpha(y)$ we have:

$$a \neq \gamma(a,b) \neq b$$
$$\gamma(a,b) = \gamma(c,d) \neq \delta \Rightarrow a = c \wedge b = d$$

In this case any action can be traced back to the components in a merge it originated from. Obviously a fully observable process expression has no autoparallelism.

7.5.3. PROPOSITION: *The axiom SP3 holds for fully observable closed process expressions* $u\|v$. *Hence* $SP + ACP + L + SPR$ *is sound and complete for fully observable closed process expressions.*

7.6. The general case, but still without autoparallelism. This case can be derived from the previous one by first doing some 'preprocessing' to make closed terms fully observable. For details see our full paper [GV].

7.7. CONJECTURE: We can make the proof system sound and complete for processes in which at most n transitions with the same label can occur concurrently by splitting atomic actions into the sequential composition of $n + 1$ parts.

REFERENCES

[AR]   AALBERSBERG, I.J.J. & G. ROZENBERG, *Theory of traces,* Technical Report No. 86-16, Institute of Applied Mathematics and Computer Science, University of Leiden, 1986.

[BB]   BAETEN, J.C.M. & J.A. BERGSTRA, *Global renaming operators in concrete process algebra,* CWI Report CS-R8521, Amsterdam, 1985.

[BBK1] BAETEN, J.C.M., J.A. BERGSTRA & J.W. KLOP, *On the consistency of Koomen's fair abstraction rule,* CWI Report CS-R8511, Amsterdam, 1985, to appear in Theor. Comp. Sci.

[BBK2] BAETEN, J.C.M., J.A. BERGSTRA & J.W. KLOP, *An operational semantics for process algebra,* CWI Report CS-R8522, Amsterdam, 1985, to appear in: Proc. Banach semester, Warschau 1985, North-Holland.

[BK1]   BERGSTRA, J.A. & J.W. KLOP, *Process algebra for synchronous communication,* Information & Control 60 (1/3), 1984, pp. 109-137.

[BK2]   BERGSTRA, J.A. & J.W. KLOP, *Process Algebra: Specification and Verification in Bisimulation Semantics,* In: Proc. CWI Symposium Math. & Comp. Sci. (M. Hazewinkel, J.K. Lenstra & L.G.L.T. Meertens, eds.), North Holland, 1986, pp. 61-94.

[BK3]   BERGSTRA, J.A. & J.W. KLOP, *Algebra of Communicating processes with abstraction,* Theor. Comp. Sci. 37(1), 1985, pp. 77-121.

[BC]   BOUDOL, G. & I. CASTELLANI, *On the semantics of concurrency: partial orders and transition systems,* Rapports de Recherche No 550, INRIA, Centre Sophia Antipolis, 1986.

[CCG]   CARLIER, J., CHRETIENNE & C. GIRAULT, *Modelling scheduling problems with timed Petri nets,* In: Advances in Petri Nets 1984 (G. Rozenberg, ed.), Springer LNCS 188, 1985, pp. 62-82.

[GV]   VAN GLABBEEK, R.J. & F.W. VAANDRAGER, *Petri net models for algebraic theories of concurrency,* to appear as: CWI Report CS-R87.., Amsterdam, 1987.

[G]   GOLTZ, U., *Building Structured Petri Nets,* Arbeitspapiere der GMD 223, Sankt Augustin, 1986.

[GM]   GOLTZ, U. & A. MYCROFT, *On the relationship of CCS and Petri nets,* In: Proc. ICALP 84 (J. Paredaens, ed.), Springer LNCS 172, 1984, pp. 196-208.

[Ho]   HOSPERS, J., *An Introduction to Philosophical Analysis,* second edition, Prentice-Hall, Inc., Englewood Cliffs, N.J., 1967.

[M1]   MAZURKIEWICZ, A., *Concurrent program schemes and their interpretations,* Report DAIMI PB-78, Computer Science Department, Aarhus University, Aarhus, 1978.

[M2]   MAZURKIEWICZ, A., *Semantics of concurrent systems: a modular fixed-point trace approach,* In: Advances in Petri Nets 1984 (G. Rozenberg, ed.), Springer LNCS 188, 1985, pp. 353-375.

[Mi]   MILNER, R., *A calculus for Communicating Systems,* Springer LNCS 92, 1980.

[NPW]   NIELSEN, M., G.D. PLOTKIN & G. WINSKEL, *Petri nets, event structures and domains, part I.* Theor. Comp. Sci., 13(1), 1981, pp. 85-108.

[NT]   NIELSEN, M. & P.S. THIAGARAJAN, *Degrees of Non-Determinism and Concurrency: A Petri Net View,* In: Proc. of the 5th Conf. on Found. of Softw. Techn. and Theor. Comp. Sci. (M. Joseph & R. Shyamasundar, eds.), Springer LNCS 181, 1984, pp. 89-118.

[Pa]   PARK, D.M.R., *Concurrency and automata on infinite sequences,* Proc. 5th GI Conference (P. Deussen, ed.), Springer LNCS 104, 1981, pp. 167-183.

[Pe]   PETRI, C.A., *Kommunikation mit Automaten,* Schriften des Institutes für Instrumentelle Mathematik, Bonn, 1962.

[Po]   POMELLO, L., *Some equivalence notions for concurrent systems. An overview.* In: Advances in Petri Nets 1985 (G. Rozenberg, ed.), Springer LNCS 222, 1986, pp. 381-400.

[Pr1]   PRATT, V.R., *On the Composition of Processes,* Proc. of the 9th POPL, 1982, pp. 213-223.

[Pr2]   PRATT, V.R., *Modelling Concurrency with Partial Orders,* International Journal of Parallel Programming, Vol. 15, No. 1, 1986, pp. 33-71.

[RR]   REED, G.M. & A.W. ROSCOE, *A Timed Model for Communicating Sequential Processes,* In: Proc. ICALP 86 (L. Kott, ed.), Springer LNCS 226, 1986, pp. 314-323.

[R]   REISIG, W., *Petri Nets, An Introduction,* EATCS Monographs on Theoretical Computer Science, Springer-Verlag, 1985.

[RT]   ROZENBERG, G. & P.S. THIAGARAJAN, *Petri nets: basic notions, structure, behaviour.* In: Current Trends in Concurrency, Overviews and Tutorials (J.W. de Bakker, W.P. de Roever, G. Rozenberg, eds.), Springer LNCS 224, 1986, pp. 585-668.

[W1]   WINSKEL, G., *Event structure semantics for CCS and related languages,* In: Proc. 9th ICALP (M. Nielsen & E.M. Schmidt, eds.), Springer LNCS 140, 1982, pp. 561-576.

[W2]   WINSKEL, G., *A new definition of morphism on Petri net,* In: Proc. STACS 84 (M. Fontet, K. Mehlhorn, eds.), Springer LNCS 166, 1984, pp. 140-150.

A Computational Model for Distributed Systems Using Operator Nets

Janice I. Glasgow and Glenn H. MacEwen
Department of Computing and Information Science
Queen's University
Kingston, Canada, K7L 3N6

1. Introduction

A distributed system consists of a finite set of processes and channels. It can be represented as a labeled, directed graph in which the nodes denote processes and the arcs denote communication channels. *Operator nets* [Ashcroft 1985] is a graphical language which provides a method for describing interprocess communication and parallelism in a distributed computing environment. The purpose of this paper is to define a denotational semantics for operator nets that computationally models distributed systems. Such a model specifies a system's behavior by defining abstract and operational interpretations of communication.

An operator net consists of a set of nodes and a set of directed arcs. A program in the language is a set of equations that relates the output arc of a node to a function or operator applied to the input arcs of the node. These equations can themselves be considered a language: the functional programming language Lucid [Wadge 1985]. Although Lucid was originally developed for program verification, it has more recently been considered as a special-purpose language for implementing operator nets.

Properties of a distributed system can be expressed in the operator net model in terms of the *histories* of an operator net and *events* that occur in such a net. A history is similar to the notion of a global state [Chandy 1985]. Each arc of an operator net is associated with a possibly infinite history sequence of values. For any particular time, a history is a record (or snapshot) of these history sequences. An event of an operator net describes the result of a function application that maps a history onto a more defined history. Section 2 of the paper presents a general framework for operator nets as well as a behavioral semantics for the language that can be used to model computations in a distributed system.

Specification and verification of systems that run concurrently are viewed very differently from proving correctness in sequential programs. Rather than concentrating on what a program computes at termination, the primary concern is with system behavior. Reasoning about distributed systems involves properties that describe the system whenever it is operating: this implies that it is necessary to specify and to prove properties related to the interaction of processes computing in parallel. To simplify this we introduce *relations* in the model, which include a relation between events and messages *(causality)*, a relation between events *(precedes)*, and a relation between messages *(depends on)*. In Section 3 of the paper we define these relations and show how they can be used to express abstract constraints on distributed systems.

The operator net approach to specification allows us to express properties of a distributed system on two levels. At the abstract level, we use the relations of the computational model combined with predicate logic to express constraints on a system. This level of specification leaves out operational details and allows us to express nondeterminism. By defining process nodes as operator net functions and providing equations that express the communication between processes as applications of these functions, we can provide an executable specification of the system that is very close to a practical implementation. Verifying that this operational specification adheres to the corresponding abstract constraints is straightforward; it uses a proof system based on Lucid transformation and verification rules. A discussion of this topic is also included in Section 3.

2. Operator Nets

An operator net is a graph consisting of nodes and directed arcs. Each arc of a net has an associated infinite sequence of values (history sequence); each node corresponds to a function that accepts input history sequences from incoming arcs and produces an output sequence along its outgoing arc.

While operator nets are syntactically similar to dataflow nets [Arvind 1977, Dennis 1975], they completely separate the operational semantics from the mathematical semantics. With this approach there are several computational methods for achieving the same mathematical meaning. Operator nets intuitively reflect the concept of data flowing through a network. Since there is no notion of explicit sequencing or flow of control in the language, computations are naturally distributed.

The variables of an operator net program have as values infinite sequences that can be thought of as objects that change with time. Modal operators (*first, next, fby, whenever,* etc) are used to express both recursive and iterative computations in a purely functional way.

In this section, we shall describe the syntax and a denotational semantics of the language of operator nets. We extend this semantics to a behavioral semantics for operator nets that describes how the fixpoint solution to a set of equations can be derived by computing a sequence of successively better approximations to the solution.

In the computational model described by the behavioral semantics, each arc can be considered as a communication channel that carries message values from one process to another. To model message passing correctly, we define the behavioral semantics as follows:

- History sequences are nonintermittent, i.e. an undefined value cannot precede a defined value;
- For any history sequence, at most one new defined value can be added to the sequence at any step in a computation; and
- New values can be added to any subset of the set of history sequences at any step of a computation.

Operationally, these restrictions on the behavioral semantics imply that: a process can produce ordered messages along its outgoing channel; at any step in a computation, at most one new message can be produced for a particular process; messages can be produced concurrently at several distinct processes at any step in a computation.

2.1 The Operator Net Model

A general framework for the language of operator nets has been previously described [Ashcroft 1985]. In this section we present a syntax and semantics for this model.

2.1.1 Syntax

An operator net consists of a directed graph and a set of related function definitions. There are several types of nodes that can be used in an operator net. These include:

- *Operator nodes,* that are associated with particular operator symbols;
- *Function nodes,* that are associated with the names of function definitions;
- *Fork nodes,* that are used for replicating data; and
- *Input and output nodes,* that are used to interface with the external environment.

A function or an operator node has the same number of input arcs as the arity of its associated function definition or operator. These input arcs are assumed to be ordered. A fork node has one input and an arbitrary number of identical output arcs. We consider two classes of arcs for an operator net. An arc is an *input* arc to the net if it is the output of an input node. All other arcs are considered *computed* arcs.

There is a one-to-one mapping between the set of function definitions and the nodes of an operator net. Recursive function definitions and nested operator nets are both allowed in the model. Figure 1 illustrates the directed graph for an operator net that solves a modified version of Hamming's problem [Dijkstra 1976]. This operator net defines the ordered infinite sequence of integer values of the form $2^i 3^j$.

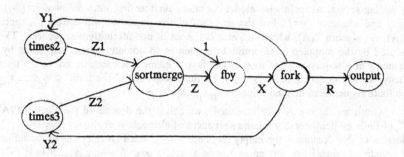

Figure 1 Modified Hamming's Problem

This operator net contains node *fby*, where fby is a modal operator defined for sequences $X = \langle x_0, x_1, ... \rangle$ and $Y = \langle y_0, y_1, ... \rangle$ as:

$$X \text{ fby } Y = \langle x_0, y_0, y_1, ... \rangle.$$

Thus the sequence resulting from X fby Y consists of the first value of X followed by the entire sequence Y. The operator net also contains output node *output* and function nodes: *times2*, *times3* and *sortmerge*. The corresponding function definitions for these nodes are given below.

$$times2(x) = 2 * x$$

$$times3(x) = 3 * x$$

```
sortmerge(x,y) = if first y >  first x
                    then first x fby sortmerge(next x,y)
                 elseif first x >  first y
                    then first y fby sortmerge(x,next y)
                    else first y fby sortmerge (next x, next y)
                 fi;
```

The modal operators *first* and *next* used in the preceding definition are defined for any sequence $X = \langle x_0, x_1, ... \rangle$ of an operator net as:

$$first X = \langle x_0, x_0, ... \rangle \text{ and next } X = \langle x_1, x_2, ... \rangle.$$

2.1.2 Semantics

Each operator net is associated with a continuous algebra A consisting of elementary data objects D. The domain D is a set with a flat complete partial ordering $\leq_A$ on D and a least element $\perp$ (bottom or undefined), which is less than all other elements. The operators of algebra A must be continuous, but need not be strict.

Algebra A is extended to a continuous sequence algebra I(A), which has as its universe the set of all infinite sequences of elements of the universe of A. Ordering on the algebra I(A) is pointwise and the infinite sequence consisting of bottoms is the least element. Operators on the objects of I(A) are pointwise extensions of the operators of algebra A. I(A) is enlarged to E(A) by adding several nonpointwise modal operators such as *first, next, followed-by (fby), as-soon-as (asa)* and *whenever (wvr)*. For the purposes of this paper we will consider a specialization of E(A), the algebra P(A), whose universe is the set of nonintermittent sequences. This algebra is induced by the mapping of intermittent sequences to nonintermittent sequences by making all elements of a sequence $\perp$ as soon as the first $\perp$ element is encountered. In the interest of simplicity, we will denote a partially defined infinite sequence of the form $< x_0,x_1,...,x_i,\perp,\perp,...>$ as the finite sequence of defined values $< x_0,x_1,...,x_i>$.

Given an algebra A with domain D, we define the domain of the algebra P(A) as the set P^ω of finite or denumerably infinite sequences of elements over the set $P = D - \{\perp\}$. The least element of this domain is the empty sequence $< >$, which corresponds to the infinite sequence of undefined values. For sequences $X = < x_0,x_1,...>$ and $Y = < y_0,y_1,...>$ in P^ω, the relation $\leq_P$ is defined for X and Y as:

$$X \leq_P Y \text{ if and only if } length(X) \leq length(Y) \text{ and } x_i \leq_A y_i, \text{ for all } i,$$

where length is a function that returns the number of defined values in a sequence. Any increasing chain $X0 \leq_P X1 \leq_P ...$ in P^ω has a *least upper bound* (lub) which we will call the *limit* of the chain. If X is the limit of such a chain, denoted $\cup \{X0,X1,...\}$, then for all Xi, $Xi \leq_P X$. Since there exists a least element in P^ω, and since there is a limit to any chain in the domain, P^ω is a complete partial order (cpo). Operations of the algebra P(A) are continuous functions. Thus for any operation f in P(A) and chain

$$X1 \leq_P X2 \leq_P X3 \leq_P ...$$

in P^ω, there is also a chain

$$f(X1) \leq_P f(X2) \leq_P f(X3) \leq_P ... \text{ (monotonicity), such that}$$

$$f(\cup \{X1, X2, X3,...\}) = \cup \{f(X1),f(X2),f(X3),...\}.$$

If we label all the arcs in an operator net with a distinct variable name, then for each function or operator node of the net we express the relationship between the input arcs and the output arc as an application of the function or operator. For example, the corresponding equation for the node:

is $c = foo(a,b)$, where *foo* is defined by the function definition associated with node foo. A fork node with input a and outputs b1, b2,... and bn has associated equations $b1 = a$, $b2 = a$,... $bn = a$.

The set of equations and function definitions for an operator net are used to specify the meaning for the net as the unique minimal solution for the set of equations. Since these equations are over cpo's, where operators are continuous, such a solution can be determined using conventional fixpoint theory [Manna 1974]. This technique is similar to that used in Kahn's "simple language for parallel processing" [Kahn 1974, 1977]. Consider Hamming's problem as described by the operator net graph in Figure 1. The equations for this net are:

$$Y1 = X$$
$$Y2 = X$$
$$R = X$$
$$Z1 = times2(Y1)$$
$$Z2 = times3(Y2)$$
$$Z = sortmerge(Z1,Z2)$$
$$X = 1 \text{ fby } Z$$

A solution to this set of equations is:

$$R = X = Y1 = Y2 = \ <1,2,3,4,6,8,...> \ = 2^i 3^j$$
$$Z1 = \ <2,4,6,8,12,16,...>$$
$$Z2 = \ <3,6,9,12,18,24,...>$$
$$Z = \ <2,3,4,6,8,9,...>$$

There are several computational methods that can be used to determine such a solution. In the next section we will define a behavioral semantics that describes one such method.

2.2 A Behavioral Semantics for Operator Nets

The semantics for operator nets defined in the previous section were concerned only with a solution to the set of equations for the net, not with a method by which the solution could be determined. In this section we describe a model for operator nets that corresponds to communication in a distributed system. We do this by computing the history sequences for a net in a stepwise fashion, where each step of the computation corresponds to a finite approximation to the solution of the set of equations for the net. The solution can be defined as the limit to such a chain of approximations. This continuous mathematics approach [Stoy 1977] allows for a description of operator nets that is intermediate between the mathematical model presented in Section 2.1 and an actual system implementation.

A *history* of an operator net is a tuple of history sequences wherein each sequence corresponds to an arc in the net. The domain of histories can be constructed from the sequence domains described in the previous section. If a net has n arcs, then the domain of histories H for the net is defined as the domain product:

$P_1 \times P_2 \times \dots \times P_n$, where $P_i = P^\omega$ for all i, $1 \leq i \leq n$.

The minimal element of H is the tuple consisting of totally undefined sequences $(< \ >)$. The relation $\leq_H$ is a partial order for histories defined for any two histories h1 and h2 of an operator net O as:

$$h1 \leq_H h2 \text{ if and only if } b_{h1} \leq_P b_{h2} \text{ for all arcs b of O,}$$

where b_h denotes the value of the history sequence for arc b in history h. Any chain of histories has a limit that is also in the domain H, therefore H is a cpo.

Since we wish to interpret arcs of an operator net as communication channels that are normally considered as queues, computation in the model corresponds to *piped evaluation* [Conway 1963]. In a pipeline operator net, values occur on the arcs in exactly the order in which they are produced. That is, a value b_i of history sequence b cannot be defined if a preceding value b_j (j < i) is undefined.

In our behavioral semantics for operator nets, we wish to consider a node of a net as a process that consumes input history sequences and produces an output sequence. The functions that transform these streams of messages are assumed to be monotonic and continuous. In terms of stream processing this implies the following desirable properties [MacQueen 1979]:

If a process consumes input, it can only produce more output. It cannot modify previous output *(monotonicity)*.

A process cannot produce output only after an infinite amount of computation *(continuity)*.

An *event* of an operator net corresponds to concurrent processing at one or more nodes of the net. The result of this processing is a history determined by applying a function, *newhistory,* to a history and a set of arcs (output arcs of the processing nodes). The new history may vary from the previous history only in the values of the history sequences of the specified arcs. Thus the result of an event is that the new history is a better approximation than was the previous history to a solution for the equations of the operator net.

We define the behavioral semantics for operator nets in terms of computations of a net. A *computation* is a sequence of events, where each event occurs in the history that was a result of the previous event in the sequence. We are particularly interested in computations that result in a history chain whose limit defines a fixpoint to the function newhistory. Such a computation determines a solution to the set of equations for an operator net.

We have now presented an intuitive discussion of a behavioral semantics for operator nets. In the remainder of this section, we shall formally define the concepts of history, event and computation and show how they can be used to find the solution to the set of equations for an operator net.

Definition 2.1 History

A *history* h for an operator net O is a tuple of sequences $(a1_h, a2_h, \dots, an_h)$, where for each arc ai $(1 \leq i \leq n)$ in O, ai_h is a sequence of values for arc ai. ai_h is called a history sequence.

An event of an operator net O is a triple (h,B,h'), where h and h' are histories of the net and B is a set of computed arcs of O. Such an event is said to occur in history h and result in history h'. The new history h' can differ from h only in the values for history sequences for arcs in set B. At most one new value is added to any such sequences. Thus, history h' is equal or more defined than was the previous history h (h $\leq_H$ h'). Events are defined in terms of a function *newhistory* that maps a history and a set of computed arcs for an operator net onto a new history.

Definition 2.2 Event

For any operator net O with set of arcs {a1,...,an}, an event of O is a triple (h,B,newhistory(h,B)) such that:

B is some set of computed arcs of O and newhistory is defined:

newhistory(h1,B) = $(a1_{h2},...,an_{h2})$ where for all ai ($1 \leq i \leq n$),

if ai $\in$ B such that ai_{h1} is the finite sequence $< ai_0,...,ai_{k-1} >$ and ai is defined by equation:

$$ai = foo(b1,...,bj) \text{ for operator or function foo and}$$
$$ai_k = (foo(b1_{h1},...,bj_{h1}))_k \neq \perp$$

then $ai_{h2} = < ai_0,...,ai_{k-1},ai_k >$

otherwise $ai_{h2} = ai_{h1}$.

The function *newhistory* described in the preceding definition is continuous in the first variable since:

If h and h' are any two histories for some operator net O such that h $\leq_H$ h' and B is some set of computed arcs of O then
newhistory(h,B) $\leq_H$ newhistory(h',B)   (monotonicity).

If h is the least upper bound (limit) of a chain of histories {$h_1,h_2,...$} and B is some set of computed arcs of O then
newhistory(h,B) = $\cup$ {newhistory(h_1,B), newhistory(h_2,B),...}.

The result of an event (h,B,h') is that the new history h' is equal or more defined than the previous history h. This relation is stated and proved formally in the following theorem.

Theorem 2.1

For any event (h,B,h') of an operator net O, h $\leq_H$ h'.

Proof:

Assume that (h,B,h') is an event of operator net O. By Definition 2.2, h' = newhistory(h,B), for some set B of computed arcs of O. For any arc a of operator net O,

a) If a $\in$ B such that $a_h = < a_0,a_1,...,a_{k-1} >$
then $a_{h'} = < a_0,a_1,...,a_k >$ or $a_{h'} = a_h$.

Since $(a_h)_i \leq_A (a_{h'})_i$ for all i $\geq$ 0, by the definition of the relation $\leq_P$, $a_h \leq_P a_{h'}$.

b) Otherwise $a_h = a_{h'}$, thus $a_h \leq_p a_{h'}$.

Therefore for all arcs a in O, $a_h \leq_p a_{h'}$, which implies $h \leq_H h'$, by the definition of the relation $\leq_H$.

$\square$

An event is a single step in a computation of a solution (or partial solution) of an operator net. The preceding theorem guarantees that for any single event (h,B,h'), $h \leq_H h'$. If we define a sequence of events such that the first event occurs in some initial history and each subsequent event occurs in the history resulting from the previous event then the histories resulting from the events form a chain. An initial history for an operator net is the history that consists of the undefined sequence for all computed arcs of the net.

Definition 2.3 Computation

A sequence of events $e_1,e_2,...$ is a *computation* of an operator net O with initial history h_0 and resulting in history h if and only if

- for all events e_i in the sequence, e_i is (h_{i-1},B_i,h_i) for some set B_i of computed arcs of O, and

-h is the limit of the possibly infinite chain of histories, $\{h_0,h_1,...\}$.

We say that a history h is a *valid history* for an operator net O if and only if it is the result of some computation of O. Similarly e is a *valid event* of an operator net if h is a valid history and e = (h,B,h') for some set B of computed arcs of O. For the remainder of the paper, we will use the terms event and history of an operator net to mean valid event and valid history of the net.

Recall the operator net for the modified Hamming's problem of Figure 1. The initial history h_0 for this operator net is defined as the n tuple consisting of the undefined sequence < > for all computed arcs of the net and <1,1,1,...> for the input arc. Suppose now we have a computation resulting in history h, where h partially defines the history sequences as follows:

$Z1_h = <2,4,6,8>$
$Z2_h = <3,6>$
$Z_h = <2,3,4,6,8>$
$R = Y1_h = Y2_h = <1,2,3,4>$
$X_h = <1,2,3,4>$

We can now define an event e = $(h,\{X,Z,Z2\},h')$ such that h' is the history defined by an application of function newhistory:

$h' = newhistory(h,\{X,Z,Z2\})$

Using Definition 2.2, history h' is defined:

$Z1_{h'} = Z1_h$
$Y1_{h'} = Y1_h$
$Y2_{h'} = Y2_h$

$$R_{h'} = R_h$$
$$Z2_{h'} = <3,6,9>$$
$$Z_{h'} = <2,3,4,6,8>$$
$$X_{h'} = < 1,2,3,4,6>$$

The result of event e is that one new value is added simultaneously to the history sequences for arcs Z2 and X. A new value was not added to the sequence for arc Z since it was already as defined as it could be, given the current values of the history sequences for the arcs Z1 and Z2 which define Z.

To prove that the behavioral semantics can be used to determine the solution of an operator net, we define the concept of a *complete computation*. A computation is complete for an operator net O if it results in a history h such that for any set B of computed arcs of O, newhistory(h,B) = h. Any computation which terminates, either naturally or by deadlock, is complete, since no additional processing (applications of function newhistory) will result in a new history.

An infinite computation may also result in a fixpoint for newhistory and thus be complete. In fact the result of the infinite computation $e_0, e_1, ...$, where $e_i = (h_{i-1}, B, h_i)$ for B the set of <u>all</u> computed arcs of B, is a fixpoint of the function newhistory.

Theorem 2.2

Given an operator net O, the history that results from a complete computation in O is a solution to the set of equations for the operator net.

Proof:

Assume that history h is the result of a complete computation for some operator net O such that h is not a solution to the equations of O. Then there must exist an equation

$$b = f(a1, a2, ..., an) \text{ in O such that } b_h \neq f(a1_h, a2_h, ..., an_h)$$

Let b_k be the first element in the sequence such that

$$(b_h)_k \neq (f(a1_h, a2_h, ..., an_h))_k.$$

It must be the case that length(b) = k, since by Definitions 2.2 and the continuity of f, if $(b_h)_k$ is defined then it must have the value $(f(a1_h, a2_h, ..., an_h))_k$. Thus b_h is a sequence containing k defined values: $< b_0, b_2, ..., b_{k-1} >$.

Let h' = newhistory(h,{b}). By Definition 2.2, $(b_{h'})_k = (f(a1_h, a1_h, ..., an_h))_k \neq (b_h)_k$.

Thus $b_h \neq b_{h'}$. But by the definition of complete computation, h = newhistory(B,h) = h'. Since we have a contradiction, our initial assumption that h is not a solution to the set of equations for O is false.

$\square$

3. Reasoning in Operator Nets

In this section we introduce relations in operator nets and show how they can be used to specify and to verify properties of distributed systems.

3.1 Relations in Operator Nets

The concept of the temporal ordering of events is necessary for expressing certain properties of distributed systems. To do this, we discuss some fundamental relationships between objects in the operator net model. Formal definitions of these properties is currently under investigation.

In the previous section, we saw that an event describes the action that results from an application of the function newhistory. There is a direct relationship between an event and the new values that are added to the history sequences of the arcs for the event. In such a case, we say that the new values were *caused* by the event. Thus a value is caused an event (h,B,h') if the value was undefined in the history in which the event occurs (h), and defined in the history that is the result of the event (h').

We are also concerned whether the computation of a value in a sequence *depends on* values in other sequences. To determine such a relation we must consider the definition for the history sequence that contains the value. For instance, if we have a node of the form:

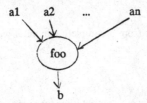

where foo is a pointwise function such that b = foo(a1,a2,...an), then for any history h such that b_i is a value on sequence b in history h, we say that value b_i depends on values $a1_i$, $a2_i$,... and an_i (where aj_i is the ith value of sequence aj in history h for all j). This relation is transitive. That is, if a value u depends on a value v and v depends on w, then u also depends on w. Thus we can trace dependence through several nodes of an operator net.

Properties that correspond to the relative order of events are also important. Thus, we define the relation *precedes* that denotes whether an event occurs before another event. This can easily be determined by examining the histories that the event occurs and results in. For example, if event e1 results in history h1 and e2 occurs in history h2 such that $h1 \leq_H h2$ then e1 precedes e2.

3.2 Specification of Distributed Systems Using Operater Nets

Distributed systems consist of processes and communication channels. In the operator net model, processes are represented as nodes defined by operator net (or Lucid) functions. Channels of the system correspond to directed arcs in the operator nets. We can consider the state of a channel in terms of the history sequence for the channel. Although consumed and unconsumed values are not distinguished on these sequences, this information can be determined by looking at the global state (history) of the net.

Using the behavioral model for operator nets we can specify properties of distributed systems. This is illustrated by two examples. The first example presents an abstract specification for the Hamming's problem operator net defined in Section 2. The second example illustrates how operator nets can be used to specify the asynchronous networks of Brock and Ackerman.

Example 3.1 Hamming's Problem

Section 2 presented an operational specification for the modified version of Hamming's problem. Using the behavioral model for operator nets, we can also express high-level constraints that must be satisfied for an operational interpretation of the net to be correct. If O is the operator net for the Hamming's problem, then the constraints on O are:

If h is any history of O such that $R_h = <r_0, r_1,...>$ then it must be the case that:

- For all values r_n in R_h, $r_n = 2^i * 3^j$ for some integers i and j,

- For all values r_m and r_n in R_h, m < n if and only if $r_m < r_n$, and

- For all values r_n and r_{n+1} in R_h, there does not exist a value v such that:

$$r_n < v < r_{n+1} \text{ and } v = 2^i * 3^j \text{ for some integers i and j.}$$

If history h is the result of a complete computation of O then length(R_h) is infinite.

This abstract specification for Hamming's problem ensures that any history sequence for arc R is ordered, contains only values of the form $2^i * 3^j$, and does not omit any such values from the sequence. It also states that a complete computation must result in the infinite sequence that contains all such values. It is possible to verify that the operational specification for operator nets described in Section 2 satisfies these constraints.

Example 3.2 Brock Ackerman Net

Brock and Ackerman [Brock 1981] have described an example which demonstrates that processes specified using history sequences give rise to an inconsistency in the sense that two nets that behave differently cannot be specified uniquely. We overcome this inconsistency in the operator net model by the use of relations. The example consists of two networks, O1 and O2, as illustrated in Figure 2.

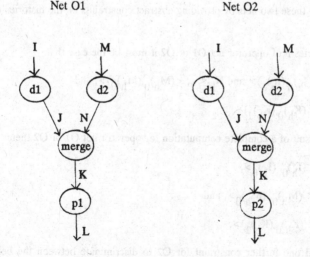

Net O1   Net O2

Figure 2 Brock Ackerman Nets

The processes *d1* and *d2* each consume one value from their input sequence and write it twice on their output sequence, i.e.

d1(x) = d2(x) = first x fby (first x fby ⊥)

where ⊥ denotes the undefined sequence.

Process *p1* sequentially transfers two values from its input to its output sequence.

p1(x) = first x fby (next x fby ⊥)

p2 is similar to p1 in the sense that it copies the first two values of its input sequences, but it behaves differently. The first value is not written until the second value is read. Thus process p2 must have some sort of memory. One way to specify this as an operator net function would be:

p2(x) = hd(y) fby (hd(tl(y)) fby ⊥)
      where y = [first x, first next x]

The operations *hd* and *tl* are list operations which select the first and remainder of a list. By constructing a list of the first two elements of x and then decomposing it, we guarantee that the first value of the output sequence for p2 cannot be produced until the second input value has been consumed.

    The above function definitions for the nodes d1, d2, p1 and p2 specify an actual implementation or executable specification for processes of the Brock Ackerman networks. Communication between the channels of the network can be expressed by operator net equations:

J = d1(I)
N = d2(M)
K = merge(J,N)
L = p1(K)   (or L = p2(K))

We can also specify these two nets by providing abstract constraints on the histories of the operator net.

    For all histories h of operator net O1 or O2 it must be the case that:

$$J_h \leq_P\ <(I_h)_0,(I_h)_0)> \text{ and } N_h \leq_P\ <(M_h)_0,(M_h)_0)>, \text{ and}$$

$$L_h \leq_P\ <(K_h)_0,(K_h)_1)>$$

If h is the result of a complete computation for operator net O1 or O2 then:

$$J_h = <(I_h)_0,\ (I_h)_0>,$$

$$N_h = <(M_h)_0,\ (M_h)_0>, \text{ and}$$

$$L_h = <(K_h)_0,(K_h)_1)>.$$

We now add one further constraint for O2 to discriminate between the behavior of the two nets:

If event (h,B,h') of net O2 causes value $(L_{h'})_0$ then length(K_h) $\geq$ 2.

This final constraint guarantees that p2 can only produce an output value once it has received at least two input values.

In this example we did not define the node *merge*. In the current model, it is impossible to provide operator net equations that express a nondeterministic merge. We can express such behavior though at the abstract level. In our previous work on modelling a multilevel secure network, we expressed abstract constraints on a merge node which ensured that the output sequence of such a node was in fact a proper merge of the input sequences [Glasgow 1986]. In the future, we hope to extend the denotational semantics for operator nets to allow for nondeterminate operators. Keller has discussed techniques for representing such operators [Keller 1977].

The general framework for operator nets described by the semantics in Section 2 would not allow for a specification of the Brock Ackerman nets that would distinguish between the behaviors of processes p1 and p2. To do so it is necessary to consider the relations on an operator net.

An alternative method for specifying the properties of distributed systems based on *behaviors* and *temporal logic* has also been used to specify the Brock Ackerman nets [Nguyen 1986]. The most significant difference between the two approaches to specification is that the temporal logic model only considers finite sequences of events. The limitations implied by this restriction are discussed in the final section of the paper.

The combination of Lucid and operator nets has been used extensively as a specification method in the development of the multi-level secure system SNet [MacEwen 1984, 1987; Glasgow 1984, 1985a, 1985b, 1986]. The concept of message passing through a network was intuitively represented as an operator net. Operator nodes were used to represent the active elements (hosts and computers) and message processing functions of a network. Security constraints of the network were expressed as Lucid functions that defined the process nodes. This approach allowed us to express high-level constraints, and by successive refinements also express operational constraints on the SNet model.

3.3 Verification of Distributed Systems Using Operator Nets

An important motivation for using operator nets to specify distributed systems is their correspondence to the Lucid programming language. Since Lucid was initially designed for the purpose of verification, it is associated with a set of inference/transformation rules that allow formal reasoning about programs [Ashcroft 1976].

An operator net consists of unordered equations expressing equalities among the history sequences for the arcs. These equations can be used to mathematically derive desired properties about the system that the operator net is describing. In particular, one can reason about properties that change with time without introducing explicit time parameters. This is possible because Lucid, or the equations of operator nets, can be thought of as a modal or tense logic. Within a particular sequence for an operator net, we interpret time asynchronously. That is, successive positions in a sequence represent the advancement of a local clock. Global time is expressed in terms of relations on the histories of an operator net. Events and values can be compared using the *precedes, causes* and *depends on* relations.

Reasoning about time in an operator net can be done using an *induction rule* for histories. If property P holds in the initial history h_0, and if assuming that P holds in history h implies that P holds in history h' = newhistory(h,B) for any set B of the arcs of the operator net, then P holds for all possible histories of the net.

Lucid also provides a large number of *transformation rules* that allow changes to be made in a program while preserving its meaning. These rules, combined with the interpretation of operator nets described in this paper, could form the basis of a general proof technique for distributed systems.

4. Discussion

This paper describes an interpretation of operator nets that corresponds to a computational model of message passing in a distributed system. We consider such a system to be a net consisting of process nodes that communicate via directed arcs. Abstract properties of a system are expressed using relations on events and messages of an operator net. Corresponding operational specifications can be written using Lucid equations that define a node as a mathematical function, and the history sequence associated with the output arc of the node as the function applied to the input arc sequences. Nodes of an operator net can be refined to allow for several levels of abstraction in the development of a system specification. Operational specifications are executable and can be easily transformed into a practical implementation. The multi-level secure system SNet has been developed and implemented on a distributed architecture using this approach [Glasgow 1986]. At the time of this development though, a formal model for computationally modelling distributed systems using operator nets did not exist. Thus we had no formal basis for the particular model we were using for performing proofs in the SNet system.

The behavioral semantics described in this paper relate, in a non-shared memory environment, to the parallel programming schemata developed by Karp and Miller [Karp 1969]. Both models are concerned with the problem of specifying properties of concurrent computation. They also share the approach of first, defining a level of abstraction that leaves certain details unspecified and second, emphasizing properties that hold no matter how the details are specified. The earlier work of Karp and Miller promises to be useful in providing a basis for the future development of decision procedures for properties such as determinacy, boundedness and termination in the operator net model.

The operational approach to system development using an executable specification language is not new. PAISley [Zave 1982], which is an example of such a language, is composed of asynchronous parallel processes where each process goes through a sequence of states. A functional syntax is used to map a process state to its successor.

Zave has discussed the potential of applicative languages for operational specifications. She concludes that [Zave 1983]:

> The main problem with the use of purely applicative languages as operational specification languages concern comprehensibility and modifiability. With no concept of state (memory) to capture the results of computations, complex applicative programs can prove hard to understand.

The Lucid/Operator net family of applicative languages contradicts this statement. The concept of state is easily captured in the infinite history sequences of an operator net. Complex programs and parallel processing can be described using the behavioral semantics for operator nets. Specifications at this level can be easily modified and refined, as was discovered in the design and development of SNet. As well, the mathematical semantics of Lucid provide transformation and verification rules to aid in reasoning about systems.

Another controversial statement made by Zave is:

> PAISley is more complete than any other operational specification language because it alone includes timing properties.

Relative timing properties can be captured abstractly by operator net relations and operationally by modal operators in the language. Also, two approaches to real time specification using Lucid and operator nets have been developed [Faustini 1986; Skillicorn 1986]. The latter approach is based on the behavioral model of operator nets described in this paper.

A popular approach for modelling networks is the use of *traces* [Misra 1981; Pratt 1982]. A trace is similar to a history in that it represents the state of a network after some computation. It has been pointed out though, that liveness properties, such as progress and termination, are difficult to specify using traces [Nguyen 1986]. This is because such properties deal with complete, possibly infinite history sequences. Traces specify only finite computations. Since histories of operator nets are continuous, properties concerning the limit of a chain of histories can be specified. It should be pointed out, that preserving continuity prohibits the equations of operator nets from expressing nondeterminism. To reason about nondeterminism, we currently consider non-deterministic processes as input nodes of the net whose properties are expressed using abstract operator net constraints.

Several other languages for modeling distributed systems have previously been developed. One technique is *temporal logic* [Manna 1984], which provides a means of expressing properties of time sequences and ordering of events. An extension to the trace model that uses temporal logic assertions on the behavior of a system has also been proposed [Nguyen 1984]. Although this model is effective for both synchronous and asynchronous networks, it is still limited in both expressibility and the ability to refine specifications. The modal operators of Lucid are similar to temporal operators in their ability to express properties of time sequences. A sound and complete proof system, which has been developed for the temporal logic approach, is a topic for future research in operator nets.

Another approach to describing time dependencies is the *event model* [Chen 1983]. This model specifies two relationships among events or messages in a distributed system. These are the *precedes* relation which represents time order, and the *enables* relation which represents causality. This approach, unlike operator nets, does not include an interpretation of either of these relations.

A graphical model for studying parallel computations is the *Petri net* [Peterson 1981]. A Petri net consists of two types of nodes, called transitions and places, directed arcs, and fixed simulation rules. Similar to Petri nets, operator nets provide a simple graphical structure as a visual aid to a system and are able to model properties at many levels of abstraction. Both models are also able to deal with causality and dependence between events. Unlike Petri nets though, operator nets are capable of describing "high-level" properties of flow of data as well as "low-level" control aspects of computation.

The behavioral semantics of operator nets provide a formal model for a distributed system that is an intermediate point between the actual system and a mathematical model. They allow for a separation of the operational considerations from the mathematical semantics in a way that makes a distributed system's description comprehensive. They allow properties of safety and liveness to be expressed as well. Properties related to concurrency can also be expressed in an operator net by considering events that correspond to a set of processes computing in parallel.

Acknowledgements: The authors would like to thank Ed Ashcroft, Bob Tennent, Prakash Panangaden, Selim Akl and David Skillicorn for valuable discussions and useful comments on earlier drafts of this paper.

References

[Arvind 1977]
"Some Relationships Between Asynchronous Interpreters of Dataflow", in *Formal Description of Programming Language,* IFIP Working Group 2.2, 1977.

[Ashcroft 1976]
E.A. Ashcroft and W.W. Wadge, Lucid, "A Formal Theory for Writing and Proving Programs", *SIAM J. Comput.,* 5, No. 3, pp. 336-354, 1976.

[Ashcroft 1985]
E.A. Ashcroft and R. Jagannathan, "Operator Nets", in *Proceedings of IFIP TC-10 Working Conference on Fifth-Generation Computer Architectures,* North Holland, 1985.

[Brock 1981]
J.D. Brock and W.B. Ackerman, "Scenarios: A Model of Nondeterminate Computation", *International Colloquium on Formalization of Programming Concepts,* 1981.

[Chandy 1985]
K.M. Chandy and L. Lamport, "Distributed Snapshots: Determining Global States of Distributed Systems", *ACM Transactions on Computer Systems,* Vol. 3, No. 1, pp. 63-75, 1985.

[Chen 1983]
B. Chen and R.T. Yeh, "Formal Specification and Verification of Distributed Systems", *IEEE Transactions on Software Engineering,* Vol. SE-9, No. 6, pp. 710-721, 1983.

[Conway 1963]
M.E. Conway, "Design of a Separable Transition-diagram Compiler", *Communication of the ACM 6,* pp. 396-408, 1963.

[Dijkstra 1976]
E.W. Dijkstra, *A Discipline of Programming,* Prentice-Hall, Englewood Cliffs, New Jersey, 1976.

[Faustini 1986]
A.A. Faustini and E.B. Lewis, "Toward a Real-Time Dataflow Language", *IEEE Software,* pp. 29-35, January 1986.

[Faustini 1983]
A.A. Faustini, S.G. Mathews and A.A. Yaghi, "The pLucid Programming Manual", Department of Computer Science, University of Arizona, Tempe, Arizona, 1983.

[Glasgow 1984]
J.I. Glasgow, F. Ouabdesselam, G.H. MacEwen, T. Mercouris, "Specifying Multi-level Security in a Distributed System", *NBS/DOD Computer Security Conference,* Gaithersburg, MD, September, 1984.

[Glasgow 1985a]
J.I. Glasgow, G.H. MacEwen, "Lucid: A Specification Language for Distributed Systems", *Verification Workshop III,* Watsonville, California, Feb. 1985, also appears in *ACM Software Engineering Notes,* August 1985.

[Glasgow 1985b]
J.I. Glasgow, G.H. MacEwen, "A Two-level Security Model for a Secure Network", *Proceedings of the Eighth National Computer Security Conference,* Gaithersburg, MD. September 1985.

[Glasgow 1986]
J.I. Glasgow, G.H. MacEwen, "The Development and Proof of a Formal Specification for a Multi-level Secure System," *ACM Transactions on Computer Systems,* Vol. 5, No. 2, May 1987.

[Kahn 1974]
G. Kahn, "The Semantics of a Simple Language for Parallel Processing", *Proceedings of IFIP Congress 74,* pp. 471-475, 1974.

[Kahn 1977]
G. Kahn and D. McQueen, "Coroutines and Networks of Parallel Processes," *Proceedings of IFIP Congress 77,* pp. 993-998, 1977.

[Karp 1969]
R.M. Karp and R.E. Miller, "Parallel Program Schemata", *Journal of Computer and System Sciences:* 3, pp. 147-195, 1969.

[Keller 1977]
R.M. Keller, "Denotational Models for Parallel Programs With Indeterminate Operators," *Formal Descriptions of Programming Languages,* North-Holland, Amsterdam, 1977.

[MacEwen 1984]
G.H. MacEwen, Z. Lu and B. Burwell, "Multi-Level Security Based on Physical Distribution", *Proceedings of IEEE Symposium on Security and Privacy,* Oakland, pp. 167-177, April, 1984. Also presented at NBS/DOD Computer Security Conference, Gaithersburg, MD, September 1984.

[MacEwen 1987]
G.H. MacEwen, V. Poon and J. Glasgow, "A Model for Multilevel Security Based on Operator Nets", *Proceedings of the IEEE Symposium on Security and Privacy,* Oakland, April 1987.

[MacQueen 1979]
D.B. MacQueen, "Models for Distributed Computing", *INRIA Report #351,* April 1979.

[Manna 1974]
Z. Manna, *Mathematical Theory of Computation*, McGraw Hill, 1974.

[Manna 1984]
Z. Manna, A. Pnueli, "Adequate Proof Principles for Invariance and Liveness Properties of Concurrent Programs", *Science of Computer Programming 4,* pp. 257-289, 1984.

[Misra 1981]
J. Misra and K.M. Chandy, "Proofs of Networks of Processes," *IEEE Trans. Software Eng.* SE -7, pp. 417-526, July 1981.

[Nguyen 1984]

V. Nguyen, D. Gries and S. Owicki, "A Model and Temporal Proof System for Networks of Processes," *11th Annual Princ. of Prog. Lang.,* pp. 121-131, 1984.

[Nguyen 1986]
V. Nguyen, A. Demers, D. Gries and S. Owicki, "A Model and Temporal Proof System for Networks of Processes," *Distributed Computing,* Vol 1, No. 1, 1986.

[Peterson 1981]
J.L. Peterson, "Petri Net Theory and the Modeling of Systems", *Prentice-Hall,* Englewood Cliffs, NJ, 1981.

[Pratt 1982]
V. Pratt, "On the Composition of Processes," *9th Annual ACM Symp. Princ. of Prog. Lang.,* pp. 213-223, 1982.

[Skillicorn 1986]
D. Skillicorn, J.I. Glasgow, "Real-Time Specification Using Lucid", Department of Computing and Information Science, Queen's University, Technical Report, 1986.

[Stoy 1977]
J.E. Stoy, *Denotational Semantics: The Scott-Strachey Approach to Programming Language Theory,* MIT Press, Cambridge, Mass., 1977.

[Wadge 1985]
W.W. Wadge, E.A. Ashcroft, *Lucid, the Dataflow Programming Language*, Academic Press, 303 pages, 1985.

[Zave 1983]
P. Zave, "Operational Specification Language", *ACM Annual Conference,* pp. 214-222, October, 1983.

[Zave 1982]
P. Zave, "An Operational Approach to Requirements Specification for Embedded Systems", *IEEE Transactions on Software Engineering SE-8,* pp. 250-269, May 1982.

Design and Proof of Communicating Sequential Processes

E. Pascal GRIBOMONT

Philips Research Laboratory, Brussels

Abstract. An old principle connecting concurrent processes with sequential non-deterministic ones is revisited. Associated with a transformation technique, it leads to a methodology for an incremental design and verification of CSP networks. The starting point is a non-deterministic program. This program and its invariant are transformed step by step into a CSP network, without introducing new variables. The methodology is illustrated by the synthesis of a simple solution to the mutual exclusion problem.

1. Introduction

The experience shows that the design and the verification of a program turns to be tricky when parallel execution is involved. Nevertheless, there exists for a long time a technique which allows to reduce parallel composition into sequential composition (see [Ash70]). More precisely, a set S of concurrent processes can be replaced by a single non-deterministic sequential program S' such that an invariance property P holds for S if and only if it holds for S'. Some liveness properties like termination can also be studied by this transformation. This reduction technique is recalled with more details in the next section.

The usefulness of this transformation technique is limited by two drawbacks. First, this technique is valid only when the statements of the concurrent processes are executed one at a time; this "interleaving" semantics does not allow true concurrent execution. Second, the size of the sequential non-deterministic program obtained by the reduction technique is proportional to the product of the sizes of the concurrent processes.

In the third section we show that these drawbacks strongly reduce when the concurrent processes do not share variables but communicate synchronously. This is the case for many parallel algorithms, written in programming languages like Ada, CSP and OCCAM (see [Hoa78], [Mis81], [May83], [Ger84]). In this framework, the reduction technique gives rise to a non-deterministic program of moderate size. The invariance and liveness properties of this program are then proved rather easily.

In addition, the equivalent non-deterministic program can be seen as the last element of a sequence of programs; in this sequence, the first elements would correspond to coarse-grained parallel programs, while the last ones would correspond to fine-grained parallel programs. This refinement technique allows an incremental design of the program and the proof. It is illustrated in section four by the design of an algorithm which ensures access in mutual exclusion to a resource shared by distributed stations.

Comments about the synthesis of concurrent programs, and comparison with related works, appear in the last section.

2. The reduction technique

It is convenient to represent a process P by a set of transitions. A transition is a triple (L, S, M), where S is a statement and L, M are control points; L and M are respectively the origin and the extremity of the transition.

Let us consider a very simple example. The classical program

$$y := 1;$$
$$while \ x > 0 \ do$$
$$y := y * x;$$
$$x := x - 1.$$

for computing the factorial of x, can be translated into the following set of transitions:

$$(L_1, \ y := 1 \ , \ L_2)$$
$$(L_2, \ x > 0 \ \longrightarrow \ y := y * x \ , \ L_3)$$
$$(L_3, \ x := x - 1 \ , \ L_2)$$

An execution is a finite or infinite sequence of transitions. The origin of the first executed transition is a distinguished control point named the initial control point. The origin of a transition occurring further in the sequence is the extremity of the previous transition. A transition modelling a conditional statement can be executed only when the condition is true.

Let us consider again the example depicted above. If the execution is started with the initial condition $x = n$ (n is a natural number), the first transition is executed once, and then the second and the third ones are executed n times, strictly alternating. Since the value of x has decreased to 0, the execution halts.

An invariant is a set of formulas, true at the beginning of the execution and respected by each transition. Here is an invariant for the example:

$$at \ L_1 \ \Rightarrow \ (x = n \land n \geq 0)$$
$$at \ L_2 \ \Rightarrow \ (0 \leq x \leq n \land y * x! = n!)$$
$$at \ L_3 \ \Rightarrow \ (0 < x \leq n \land y * (x - 1)! = n!)$$

The location predicate $at\ L$ is true when the execution lies at the control point L. An immediate consequence of the invariant is the following formula:

$$(at\ L_2 \land x = 0) \implies y = n!$$

This formula expresses the partial correctness of the program.

Let us now consider the concurrent execution of two processes P and Q. $P \parallel Q$ can be defined as follows:

An execution of $P \parallel Q$ is obtained by interleaving in an arbitrary way an execution of P with an execution of Q.

This simple operational definition suggests that $P \parallel Q$ can still be represented by a set of transitions, which is designed as follows:

- The set of control points of $P \parallel Q$ is the Cartesian product of the sets of control points of P and Q.
- For each transition (L_1, S, L_2) in P and for each control point M in Q, create the transition $(L_1 M, S, L_2 M)$ in $P \parallel Q$.
- For each transition (M_1, T, M_2) in Q and for each control point L in P, create the transition (LM_1, T, LM_2) in $P \parallel Q$.

The set of transitions obtained by this transformation is the sequential non-deterministic representation of $P \parallel Q$. "Non-deterministic" means that several executable transitions can issue from the same control point.

It is not necessary to list all the transitions of the sequential equivalent program explicitly; listing all the transitions of the components is sufficient. More precisely, the non-deterministic program equivalent to $P \parallel Q$ can be seen as a transition system defined as follows:

- The transistions simply are the transitions of P and the transitions of Q.
- A transition (N_1, U, N_2) can be executed only when $at\ N_1$ is true; after the execution, $at\ N_2$ is true.
- At every time, exactly one location predicate for each process is true.
- If L_0 and M_0 are the initial control points of P and Q respectively, $at\ L_0$ and $at\ M_0$ are true at the beginning of the execution.

This way of reducing parallel programs to sequential ones is valid only when two underlying conditions are fulfilled.

First, the statements of P and Q are not executed concurrently, but one after another. This hypothesis is true when the concurrent processes are executed on a single shared processor.

Second, we suppose that the statements are "atomic", that is, non-interruptible statements, executed as a whole. Indeed, the "granularity" of the statements, which does not matter in sequential programming, has a critical importance in parallel programming. In addition, if P and Q contain respectively p and q control points, then $P\|Q$ contains pq control points.

The canonical form of an invariant of $P\|Q$ is as follows:

$$\bigwedge_{L \in P_{cp}, M \in Q_{cp}} (at\ L \wedge at\ M) \Rightarrow I(L, M)$$

where P_{cp}, Q_{cp} are the set of control points of the processes; $I(L, M)$ is a relation between the variables of P and Q which holds every time the executions of P and Q respectively lie at L and at M.

The generalization to the parallel composition of three or more processes is straightforward.

The canonical form can be used for short programs only. For medium-sized or large programs, more economical forms are needed. See e.g [Owi76] and [Gri77] for examples. Whatever the form may be, the design of an invariant is usually difficult when concurrency is involved, since many transitions between many states must be taken into account.

3. Concurrency with synchronous communication

When the concurrent processes interfere only by synchronous communication, important simplifications occur. Before presenting them, we describe the concept of synchronous communication.

A process P can send a message to a process Q only if there exists a channel from P to Q. Let C be such a channel. It is one-way and can be used by processes P and Q only. If e is an expression in P and x a variable of Q, the distributed assignment $x := e$ is performed when P executes the output statement $C!e$ and Q executes the input statement $C?x$. Such communication statements can be executed only in "matching pair", that is, one of them is an input statement, the other is an output statement and both refer to the same channel. Each time a communication statement is encountered in the execution of a process, the execution of this process is suspended until the partner is prepared to execute a matching statement. At that time, the distributed assignment is performed and the execution of both processes can go on.

3.1. Reduction of CSP networks.

We can know compare general parallelism and parallelism restricted to synchronous communication.

Let (L_1, S, L_2) and (M_1, T, M_2) be transitions of P and Q respectively.

In the general case, this pair of transitions will give rise to four transitions in $P\|Q$:

$$(L_1M_1, S, L_2M_1)$$
$$(L_1M_2, S, L_2M_2)$$
$$(L_1M_1, T, L_1M_2)$$
$$(L_2M_1, T, L_2M_2)$$

Now, if P and Q are processes communicating only as described above, without shared memory, various possibilities can occur.

First, if S and T are matching communication statements, only the transition

$$(L_1M_1, S\|T, L_2M_2)$$

will be added to $P\|Q$, where $S\|T$ stands for the adequate distributed assignment.

Second, if S and T are internal statements, that is, if they do not involve any communication, a similar simplification occurs; only the transition

$$(L_1M_1, S\|T, L_2M_2)$$

will be introduced. $S\|T$ stands now for the concurrent execution of S and T; since the concurrent processes do not share any variable, no distinction exist between $S\|T$, $S;T$ and $T;S$.[1]

Third, if S is a communication statement with process Q, while T is not a matching statement, the pair (S, T) will not give rise to any transition of $P\|Q$ at all.

Let us now introduce a last, but important, simplification. We consider again the example of the factorial program. The pair of transitions

$$(L_2, x > 0 \longrightarrow y := y * x, L_3)$$
$$(L_3, x := x - 1, L_2)$$

could be replaced by the single transition

$$(L_2, x > 0 \longrightarrow y := y * x; x := x - 1, L_2)$$

which can also be written

$$(L_2, x > 0 \longrightarrow (y, x) := (y * x, x - 1), L_2)$$

Such a simplification, which allows to decrease the number of control points, is not valid when general concurrency is involved; this is the reason why the concept of

---

[1] provided that both S and T terminate; non-terminating internal statements are not considered here.

"atomic" statement is introduced in parallel programming. However, the replacement of (L_1, S, L_2) and (L_2, T, L_3) by $(L_1, S; T, L_3)$ is valid when parallelism is restricted to synchronous communication, except when both S and T contain communication statements.

3.2. From non-deterministic programs to CSP networks.

The reduction procedure can be used in the reverse way, and a transition like

$$(L_1M_1, R, L_2M_2)$$

can be split into

$$(L_1, S, L_2), \quad (M_1, T, M_2)$$

provided that the converse transformation is valid. When it is not, the statement R has to be split sequentially first, in order to obtain the following:

$$(L_1M_1, A, L_3M_3)$$

$$(L_3M_3, B, L_2M_2)$$

where L_3, M_3 may be new labels and $A; B$ is equivalent to R. Afterwards, the parallel splitting of A and B can be attempted. However, the sequential splitting could falsify some required invariance property; in any case, the invariant must be adapted. If this adaptation is not possible, the intended splitting is not valid.

For simple programs, the adaptation of the invariant is easy, as demonstrated in the following section. A more formal approach is needed for complex programs; it is presented and illustrated in [Grb85].

When transforming a non-deterministic program into a CSP network, only two kinds of transformations will be allowed. A transition may be split into two subtransitions, to be executed sequentially, or concurrently if they involve a communication between processes. These transformations will give rise to the introduction of new labels, but new variables are never introduced. This technique will not succeed if the starting point is not well chosen.

Comment. When no sequential splitting is performed, no adaptation of the invariant is needed. The partial correctness rule presented in [Apt 86] corresponds to this case.

4. An example

The principle of correspondence between concurrent systems and non-deterministic programs was primarily introduced to reduce concurrent programs into sequential ones (see [Ash70]). However, the reverse transformation is useful too. This is demonstrated in the following example.

4.1. Description of the problem.

We consider a resource shared by n distributed computing stations. The resource is directed by a controller which must provide access in mutual exclusion. A station p is initially in a non-critical section (state p_0). It performs internal computation until access to the shared resource becomes necessary, that is, until an internal condition, denoted crs_p, becomes true. At this moment, a request is sent to the controller. The access can be delayed (waiting state p_1). When the permission has been granted by the controller, the station may use the resource (state p_2), until the internal condition crs_p becomes false; at this time, the station releases the resource and returns to its non-critical section (state p_0). At every time, the station p is in one and only one of its three possible states.

The controller deals with a variable $INCS$ and a waiting queue E. $INCS$ is intended to record the number of the station currently lying in its critical section; its value will be 0 when no station performs its critical section. E is intended to record the numbers of the waiting stations.

4.2. A very simple solution.

The mutual exclusion problem is solved by the following transition system, which simply translates the informal description given in the previous paragraph.

1. $(p_0, \neg crs_p \longrightarrow [\ ], p_0)$, $\forall p$
2. $(p_0, < crs_p \wedge INCS = 0 \longrightarrow INCS := p >, p_2)$, $\forall p$
3. $(p_0, < crs_p \wedge INCS \neq 0 \longrightarrow E := E \cup \{p\} >, p_1)$, $\forall p$
4. $(p_2, crs_p \longrightarrow [\ ], p_2)$, $\forall p$
5. $(p_2 q_1, < \neg crs_p \wedge q \in E \longrightarrow (INCS, E) := (q, E \setminus \{q\}) >, p_0 q_2)$, $\forall p, q$
6. $(p_2, < \neg crs_p \wedge E = \emptyset \longrightarrow INCS := 0 >, p_0)$, $\forall p$

Only relevant control points have been mentioned in the transitions. For instance, the transition

$$(p_2 q_1, < \neg crs_p \wedge q \in E \longrightarrow (INCS, E) := (q, E \setminus \{q\}) >, p_0 q_2)$$

can be executed only when $(at\ p_2 \wedge at\ q_1)$ is true; after the execution, $(at\ p_0 \wedge at\ q_2)$ is true. The truth values of the other location predicates are not changed. Initially, $at\ p_0$ is true for each station p.

The notation $[\ ]$ stands for an arbitrary internal computation which is not described here; we only suppose that $[\ ]$ always terminates.

The value of the predicate crs_p is modified by the internal computation only. We suppose that crs_p is false infinitely often; this means that station p cannot remain in its critical section forever.

The notation $<B \longrightarrow S>$ means that, when B is true, S is executed without interference with other transitions (this is noted *await B do S* in [Owi76]).

The first transition and the fourth one are models for the computation performed by the station p in its non-critical section and in its critical section respectively. The second and the third transitions correspond to the requesting procedure: station p requests the access and this access is granted at once (transition 2) or delayed (transition 3). Lastly, transitions 5 and 6 concern the releasing procedure: when the station p releases the resource, this resource is attributed to a waiting station r (transition 5) or becomes idle (transition 6).

The system is intended to provide a fair service; the requirements are:

Mutual exclusion. At every time, the resource is assigned to at most one station.

No idleness. The resource remains idle only when the waiting queue is empty.

No deadlock. The system can always proceed.

No starvation. A waiting station is never delayed forever.

No unwanted access. Only the numbers of the waiting stations are put on the queue.

The initial conditions are:

$$\forall p \, (at \, p_0) \, \land \, INCS = 0 \, \land \, E = \emptyset$$

The fairness principle is assumed: if a transition can be executed infinitely often, it will be executed infinitely often. In addition, the convention introduced before about crs_q ensures that the stations behave fairly: none of them can remain in its critical section forever.

4.3. The proof.

A classical distinction is made between invariance properties and liveness properties. We consider first invariance properties, which assert that some relation between program variables and control points is always true.

The classical way to prove an invariance property is to design an invariant which implies it. This is independent from the fairness principle.

An interesting invariance property is the following:

$$
\begin{aligned}
& \forall p : (at \, p_2 \, \Rightarrow \, INCS = p) \\
\land \quad & (INCS = 0 \, \Rightarrow \, E = \emptyset) \\
\land \quad & \forall p : (p \in E \, \Rightarrow \, at \, p_1)
\end{aligned}
$$

This property formalizes **Mutual exclusion, No idleness** and **No unwanted access** described in the previous paragraph. It can be rewritten as follows:

$$\forall\, p: [\,at\; p_0 \;\Rightarrow\; p \notin E\,]$$
$$\wedge \quad \forall\, p: [\,at\; p_2 \;\Rightarrow\; (INCS = p \,\wedge\, p \notin E)\,] \qquad (I_1)$$
$$\wedge \quad (INCS = 0 \;\Rightarrow\; E = \emptyset)$$

The design of an adequate invariant is immediate: I_1 is respected by each transition.

In the framework of transition systems, **no deadlock** is also an invariance property, asserting that, at every moment, at least one transition is executable. Let us investigate deadlock possibilities in our example. It is first observed that station p will be locked in its waiting state if its number does not belong to the queue; this situation will be avoided if the following invariance property holds:

$$\forall\, p: [\,at\; p_1 \;\Rightarrow\; p \in E\,]$$

Let I_2 be the conjunction of this formula with I_1. It is easily checked that I_2 remains an invariant of the system. Especially, the transition $(p_0 \to p_1)$ puts the number p on the queue while the transition $(p_1 \to p_2)$ removes p from the queue. It is now possible to check that no deadlock can occur; this is not done here since a stronger property will be proved later.

4.4. An implementation in CSP.

The solution presented above can be implemented as such if each station knows the state of the other stations and of the variables $INCS$ and E. In this framework, a specific resource controller is not needed: all the stations cooperate to ensure an adequate utilization of the shared resource.

However, we are interested in the case where the stations and the shared resource are distant and can exchange information by synchronous communication only. The algorithm described above can still be used in this framework, but some transformations are needed first. The resource is associated with a controller, which can receive messages from the stations and send answers. The variables $INCS$ and E are the property of this controller; they cannot be accessed directly by the stations.

Most transitions of the system involve cooperation between a station and the controller or between two stations. In order to obtain a CSP implementation, we have to restrict this cooperation to synchronous communication.

Let us consider first transitions 2 and 3:

$$(p_0, < crs_p \,\wedge\, INCS = 0 \;\longrightarrow\; INCS := p >, p_2), \; \forall\, p$$
$$(p_0, < crs_p \,\wedge\, INCS \neq 0 \;\longrightarrow\; E := E \cup \{p\} >, p_1), \; \forall\, p$$

First, a request is transmitted from the station p to the controller; second, the controller grants the access if $INCS = 0$, or puts p on the queue if not. These transitions are split in such a way that the new transitions involve at most one communication. As the controller becomes an explicit process, it receives labels. The location predicate $at\ C$ is true when the controller is idle; in this state, it is able to receive messages from the stations. The controller is in the location C_p when a request from the station p has been received, but not processed yet. The transitions 2 and 3 are thus replaced by:

$$(p_0C, < crs_p \longrightarrow skip >, p_1C_p), \ \forall p$$
$$(p_1C_p, < INCS = 0 \longrightarrow INCS := p >, p_2C), \ \forall p$$
$$(p_1C_p, < INCS \neq 0 \longrightarrow E := E \cup \{p\} >, p_1C), \ \forall p$$

The formula I_2 is no longer an invariant. The transition $(p_0C \to p_1C_p)$ can falsify the assertion $[at\ p_1 \Rightarrow p \in E]$.

This assertion is thus replaced by $[at\ p_1 \Rightarrow (\neg at\ C_p \Leftrightarrow p \in E)]$.

The transition $(p_1C_p \to p_1C)$, which involves two processes, is acceptable only if a synchronization statement is performed between the processes. As we do not want to introduce more communication statements than necessary, we will try to replace this transition by

$$(C_p, < INCS \neq 0 \longrightarrow E := E \cup \{p\} >, C), \ \forall p$$

from which the label p_1 has been removed. This becomes evident if the assertion $[at\ C_p \Rightarrow at\ p_1]$ could be added to the invariant. The intended invariant is thus:

$$\begin{aligned}
&\forall p: [at\ p_0 \Rightarrow p \notin E] \\
\wedge \ &\forall p: [at\ p_1 \Rightarrow (\neg at\ C_p \Leftrightarrow p \in E)] \\
\wedge \ &\forall p: [at\ p_2 \Rightarrow (INCS = p \wedge p \notin E)] \quad\quad (I_3) \\
\wedge \ &\forall p: [at\ C_p \Rightarrow (at\ p_1 \wedge p \notin E)] \\
\wedge \ &(INCS = 0 \Rightarrow E = \emptyset)
\end{aligned}$$

It is easy to check that I_3 is respected by each transition.

We consider now transition 5 and 6:

$$(p_2q_1, < \neg crs_p \wedge q \in E \longrightarrow (INCS, E) := (q, E \setminus \{q\}) >, p_0q_2), \ \forall p, q$$
$$(p_2, < \neg crs_p \wedge E = \emptyset \longrightarrow INCS := 0 >, p_0), \ \forall p$$

First, a release message is transmitted from the station p to the controller; second, the resource is attributed to a waiting station, if the queue is not empty, or becomes idle, if the queue is empty.

The transitions are split as follows:

$$(p_2q_1C, \; < \neg crs_p \; \longrightarrow \; skip >, \; p_0q_1C'_p) , \;\; \forall \, p, q$$
$$(p_0q_1C'_p, \; < q \in E \; \longrightarrow \; (INCS, E) := (q, E \setminus \{q\}) >, \; p_0q_2C) , \;\; \forall \, p, q$$
$$(p_2C, \; < \neg crs_p \; \longrightarrow \; skip >, \; p_0C'_p) , \;\; \forall \, p$$
$$(p_0C'_p, \; < E = \emptyset \; \longrightarrow \; INCS := 0 >, \; p_0C) , \;\; \forall \, p$$

The controller is in the state C'_p when a release message has been transmitted from the station p to the controller, but has not been processed yet; in this state, the value of $INCS$ is p.

The invariant is adapted easily, by adding the assertion $[\,at \; C'_p \; \Rightarrow \; INCS = p\,]$.

Let us note that the first new transition is an instance of the third one and can be removed.

The second new transition could not be implemented in CSP since it involves three processes. However, the station p does not seem to play any effective role in this transition; the label p_0 is thus removed, and the transition is generalized into:

$$(q_1C'_p, \; < q \in E \; \longrightarrow \; (INCS, E) := (q, E \setminus \{q\}) >, \; q_2C) , \;\; \forall \, p, q$$

However, this transition should not be executed when a station is in its critical section. When this transition can be executed, the value of $INCS$ is p; no station other than p could be in its critical section.

In order to avoid this case, the assertion $[\,at \; C'_p \; \Rightarrow \; \neg at \; p_2\,]$ is tentatively added to the invariant.

Similarly, the station p does not play any active role in the transition $(p_0C'_p \to p_0C)$, which tentatively is generalized into

$$(C'_p, \; < E = \emptyset \; \Rightarrow \; INCS := 0 >, \; C)$$

The system we have obtained is:

1. $(p_0, \; \neg crs_p \; \longrightarrow \; [\,], \; p_0) , \;\; \forall \, p$
2. $(p_0C, \; < crs_p \; \longrightarrow \; skip >, \; p_1C_p) , \;\; \forall \, p$
3. $(p_1C_p, \; < INCS' = 0 \; \longrightarrow \; INCS := p >, \; p_2C) , \;\; \forall \, p$
4. $(C_p, \; < INCS \neq 0 \; \longrightarrow \; E := E \cup \{p\} >, \; C) , \;\; \forall \, p$
5. $(p_2, \; crs_p \; \longrightarrow \; [\,], \; p_2) , \;\; \forall \, p$
6. $(p_2C, \; < \neg crs_p \; \longrightarrow \; skip >, \; p_0C'_p) , \;\; \forall \, p$
7. $(q_1C'_p, \; < q \in E \; \longrightarrow \; (INCS, E) := (q, E \setminus \{q\}) >, \; q_2C) , \;\; \forall \, p, q$
8. $(C'_p, \; < E = \emptyset \; \longrightarrow \; INCS := 0 >, \; C) , \;\; \forall \, p$

The intended invariant is now:

$$\forall p: [at\ p_0 \Rightarrow p \notin E]$$
$$\wedge \quad \forall p: [at\ p_1 \Rightarrow (\neg at\ C_p \Leftrightarrow p \in E)]$$
$$\wedge \quad \forall p: [at\ p_2 \Rightarrow (INCS = p \wedge p \notin E)]$$
$$\wedge \quad \forall p: [at\ C_p \Rightarrow (at\ p_1 \wedge p \notin E)] \qquad (I_4)$$
$$\wedge \quad \forall p: [at\ C'_p \Rightarrow (\neg at\ p_2 \wedge INCS = p)]$$
$$\wedge \quad (INCS = 0 \Rightarrow E = \emptyset)$$

It is checked easily that I_4 is respected by all the transitions.

The current version of the transition system is nothing but the non-deterministic program equivalent to the following CSP network:

Station $p\ (p = 1, \ldots, n)$:

$$(p_0, \neg crs_p \longrightarrow [\ ], p_0)$$
$$(p_0, crs_p \longrightarrow REQ_p!, p_1)$$
$$(p_1, OK_p?, p_2)$$
$$(p_2, crs_p \longrightarrow [\ ], p_2)$$
$$(p_2, \neg crs_p \longrightarrow END_p!, p_0)$$

Controller:

$$(C, REQ_q?, C_q), \quad q = 1, \ldots, n$$
$$(C_q, < INCS = 0 \longrightarrow INCS := q >, C), \quad q = 1, \ldots, n$$
$$(C_q, < INCS \neq 0 \longrightarrow E := E \cup \{q\} >, C), \quad q = 1, \ldots, n$$
$$(C, END_q?, C'_q), \quad q = 1, \ldots, n$$
$$(C'_q, < E = \emptyset \longrightarrow INCS := 0 >, C), \quad q = 1, \ldots, n$$
$$(C_q, < E = \{r\} \cup E' \longrightarrow (INCS, E := r, E'); OK_r! >, C), \quad q = 1, \ldots, n$$

The communication statements do not implement any actual communication, but only synchronization; that is the reason why no argument has been mentioned.

This result is rather satisfactory but can be improved. In its present state, the controller cannot receive a message before having processed the previous one. This is not a drawback for requests: since stations may access the shared resource only in turn, it is convenient to process the requests strictly in sequence. On the contrary, it could be more efficient to allow the concurrent processing of a request and a release. The natural way to achieve that is by splitting the controller into two separate processes. However, these processes, being not distant, would communicate by sharing the variables E and $INCS$. The current structure of the controller and the target structure are depicted on fig. 1. The intended modification, which implies the introduction of a new label C', is easily modelled: it is sufficient to replace the label C by the label C' in the last three transitions of the controller. The equivalent transition system is modified accordingly. The formula I_4 is still an invariant of the system.

4.5. Liveness properties.

We will now outline the proof of **no starvation**. This property expresses that when a station p tries to access the resource, it gains the access and then returns into its non-critical state within a finite delay. Let us recall first a now classical notation: the formula

$$A \rightsquigarrow B$$

is true if each time A is true, then B will be true within a finite delay.

Comments. This delay may be zero. B does not necessarily remain true forever. The relation $\rightsquigarrow$ is reflexive and transitive.

We have to prove the following formula:

$$(at\ p_0 \wedge crs_p) \rightsquigarrow (at\ p_0 \wedge \neg crs_p)$$

This will be achieved by establishing the following sequence of formulas:

$$a)\quad (at\ C_p) \rightsquigarrow (at\ C)$$
$$b)\quad (at\ C'_p) \rightsquigarrow (at\ C')$$
$$c)\quad (at\ p_0 \wedge crs_p) \rightsquigarrow (at\ p_1)$$
$$d)\quad (at\ p_1) \rightsquigarrow (p \in E \vee at\ p_2)$$
$$e)\quad (p \in E) \rightsquigarrow (at\ p_2)$$
$$f)\quad (at\ p_2) \rightsquigarrow (at\ p_2 \wedge \neg crs_p)$$
$$g)\quad (at\ p_2 \wedge \neg crs_p) \rightsquigarrow (at\ p_0 \wedge \neg crs_p)$$

All these formulas are rather immediate consequences of the fairness principle: if a transition can be executed infinitely often, it will be executed infinitely often. Let us consider the first formula. When $at\ C_p$ is true, then $at\ p_1$ is true. Either the transition 3 or the transition 4 remains executable until one of them is effectively executed, which will occur within a finite delay. After this execution, $at\ C$ is true. Other formulas are proved in the same way. Formal technique for proving liveness properties are presented in [MaP84].

Let us observe that these formulas also imply that deadlock is not possible.

5. Conclusion

A method was introduced to design and prove CSP networks, starting from a non-deterministic program. It is interesting to compare this method with others recently proposed. Afterwards, the ideas which have led to the method proposed in this paper are summarized.

A design method for CSP is described in [Moi85]. Starting from a sequential non-deterministic program, and a partition of its variables into n sets, this method provides an equivalent CSP networks of n processes. This method always succeeds; this is an advantage, but the resulting network contains new variables and can be very inefficient if the initial program and the partition of the variables are not well chosen.

The method proposed here will not succeed if the starting point is not well chosen: the designer will discover that the splitting of a transition would destroy the invariant. Such failures are helpful and can lead to a better starting point.

The technique of stepwise refinement, which is used in this paper to obtain a CSP implementation of an abstract algorithm, has been used in a more general way in [Cha86], to design various solutions to a non-trivial problem. The method of this author is more powerful than ours, since it starts from scratch (and not from a coarse-grained solution) and, by successive steps, can lead to a detailed solution. However, each step may involve some kind of creativity; there is no distinct separation between a first, creative phase, and a second one, during which only technical refinements are tried. We feel that allowing only a restricted kind of refinement makes the designer's task easier. Let us mention that the principle of stepwise refinement appeared already in [Dij78], where a coarse-grained and a fine-grained versions of the same algorithm were presented. In [Grb85], this principle is developed into a methodology for parallel programming.

Ideally, the starting point for the design of a concurrent system is a formal specification of its intended behaviour. This approach is explored in [MaW84]: the specification is formalized in propositional temporal logic. If the formula is consistent, a model is produced; this model can be transformed in a concurrent system. This technique is restricted to finite-states systems, but this includes the synchronization part of non-finite-states systems. However, the complexity of the procedure producing the model prevents this technique to be used for large finite-states systems.

Many authors have presented methods in which processes are considered in isolation (see e.g. [Owi76], [Apt80]). This is not our case, since we adopted the position explained in [Lam83]: the design of a distributed algorithm requires reasoning about all the processes together, and it is this global reasoning that is reflected in assertions about the global state. Some recent works, as [Apt86] and [Cha86], show that global reasoning leads to simpler proofs.

The method presented here is based on two ideas.

On the one hand, in the general area of problem solving, the separation of concerns is often helpful. This is especially true for concurrent programs. The task of the designer will be easier if a clear distinction is made between the algorithmic phase and the implementation phase.

On the other hand, an efficient way to understand a complex concurrent system is as follows. First, the system is reduced to an as simple transition system as possible. This abstract form emphasizes the algorithmic subtleties of the program. Afterwards, this form is refined step by step, until the original form is obtained. This allows to check the correctness of the algorithm and its implementation.

The starting point of the method is thus an abstract algorithm. It is usually a rather short piece of code; the formalism of transition systems seems well suited to write it. The size of the corresponding invariant remains moderate. During the implementation phase of the design, the basic algorithm is refined step by step until an implementable version is obtained. The size of the program and its invariant does not usually remain low; that is the reason why we suggest that only simple, restricted forms of stepwise refinements would be used. Especially, the introduction of new variables is not recommended during the implementation phase.

When writing a concurrent system, the designer has to deal with the inherent difficulty of programming and the inherent complexity of parallelism, but has not to deal with both of them at the same time.

The example developed here is rather simple and the last version is not much bigger than the first one. However, for more substantial applications, the difference between the abstract algorithm and an actual implementation can be more impressive. See [Grb85] for examples, and also for a more formal presentation of the refinement technique.

Bibliography

[Apt80] K.R. APT, N. FRANCEZ and W.P. DE ROEVER, "A Proof System for Communicating Sequential Processes", ACM Toplas, vol. 2, pp. 359-385, 1980

[Apt86] K.R. APT, "Correctness Proofs of Distributed Termination Algorithms", ACM Toplas, vol. 8, pp. 388-405, 1986

[Ash70] E.A. ASHCROFT and Z. MANNA, "Formalization of Properties of Parallel Programs", Machine Intelligence, vol. 6, pp. 17-41, 1970

[Cha86] M. CHANDY and J. MISRA, "An Example of Stepwise Refinement of Distributed Programs: Quiescence Detection", ACM Toplas, vol. 8, pp. 326-343, 1986

[Dij78] E.W. DIJKSTRA and al., "On-the-Fly Garbage Collection: An Exercise in Cooperation", CACM, vol. 21, pp. 966-975, 1978

[Ger84] R. GERTH and W.P. DE ROEVER, "A proof system for concurrent ADA programs", SCP, vol. 4, pp. 159-204, 1984

[Grb85] P. GRIBOMONT, "Méthode progressive de synthèse et de vérification de programmes parallèles", thèse de doctorat, université de Liège, 1985

[Gri77] D. GRIES, "An exercise in Proving Parallel Programs Correct", CACM, vol. 20, pp. 921-930, 1977

[Hoa78] C.A.R. HOARE, "Communicating Sequential Processes", CACM, vol. 21, pp. 666-677, 1978

[Lam83] L. LAMPORT, "An Assertional Correctness Proof of a Distributed Algorithm", SCP, vol. 2, pp. 175-206, 1983

[MaP84] Z. MANNA and A. PNUELI, "Adequate proof principles for invariance and liveness properties of concurrent programs", SCP, vol. 4, pp. 257-289, 1984

[MaW84] Z. MANNA and P.L. WOLPER, "Synthesis of Communicating Processes from Temporal Logic Specifications", ACM Toplas, vol. 6, pp. 68-93, 1984

[May83] D. MAY, "OCCAM", ACM Sigplan Notices, vol. 18, pp. 69-79, 1983

[Mis81] J. MISRA and K.M. CHANDY, "Proofs of Networks of Processes", IEEE Trans. on Software Engineering, vol. SE-7, pp. 417-426, 1981

[Moi85] A. MOITRA, "Automatic construction of CSP programs from sequential non-deterministic programs", SCP, vol. 5, pp. 277-307, 1985

[Owi76] S. OWICKI and D. GRIES, "An Axiomatic Proof Technique for Parallel programs", Acta Informatica, vol. 6, pp 319-340, 1976

Parallel Programming in Temporal Logic

Roger Hale and Ben Moszkowski
Computer Laboratory, University of Cambridge,
Corn Exchange Street, Cambridge CB2 3QG, England

1 Background

For some time now temporal logic has been an accepted tool for reasoning about concurrent programs. More recently, we have shown that temporal logic specifications may be executed directly [Mos86,Hal87], and have tested our methods on a number of concurrent systems, ranging from hardware devices to high-level algorithms. Out of this work has come the programming language, *Tempura*, which is a subset of Moszkowski's *Interval Temporal Logic* [Mos83].

Having had some experience in using Tempura, we believe that there is a need to compare it with other parallel programming paradigms. For this purpose we have chosen four algorithms from the literature. The first one is a simple scheduling algorithm, the second is for the evaluation of parsed expressions, the third is a graph traversal algorithm, and the final one performs a mergesort on an array of processors. These algorithms take up the central section of this paper, but first there is a description of Interval Temporal Logic (ITL) and a short account of Tempura. Our review of ITL is not intended to be a tutorial, but is sufficient for an understanding of the paper. The paper concludes with a discussion of where ITL stands in relation to some other parallel programming paradigms.

2 Interval Temporal Logic

Like all temporal logics, ITL extends classical first-order logic with operators for relating behaviour at different times. This means that the familiar logical operators, such as "and" and "not", all appear in ITL, but there are in addition some special temporal operators which stand for notions involving time, like "... and then ...", "always", and "next".

2.1 The Computational Model

A computation, in our view, is a sequence of one or more discrete steps, each step being characterised by the values of some collection of variables. In principle, if it is known what all the variables are and what values they can take, then the (usually infinite) set of all possible computations, Σ, is determined. A particular computation, $\sigma \in \Sigma$, is a sequence of steps,

$$\sigma = \langle \sigma_0, \ldots, \sigma_n \rangle,$$

the length of the computation, n, being the number of *transitions* between states.

The formulae which describe the properties of computations are composed as follows. Syntactically, any formula of classical predicate logic with quantification is also a formula of ITL. Furthermore, any formula p may be prefixed by one of the temporal operators $\Box$ ("always"), $\Diamond$ ("sometimes") or $\bigcirc$ ("next") to form a new property, and any two formulae, p_1 and p_2, may be combined using the so-called *chop* operator to give a new property $p_1 ; p_2$ ("p_1 and then p_2"). The semantics of these operators are described informally below and summarised in figure 1.

2.2 First Order Logic and Parallel Composition

First order logic is contained within ITL, and therefore all the classical operators appear in ITL too. For example, if the formulae p_1 and p_2 describe the behaviours of two processes, then their logical conjunction $p_1 \wedge p_2$ describes the computation that results when p_1 and p_2 are run in parallel. If p_1 holds the value of X constant, and p_2 gives it an initial value of 7, then their conjunction constrains X to have the value 7 on every step.

In a similar way, the disjunction of two process descriptions $p_1 \vee p_2$ describes a computation on which one or the other may occur, and the negation $\neg p$ is true of any process which doesn't behave like p.

2.3 Variables and Quantifiers

To make life easier for ourselves, we distinguish three kinds of variables:

- *Interval variables*, whose values depend on entire computations (they are functions of intervals).

- *State variables*, which depend only on state. To make them into functions of computations, we adopt the convention that the value of a state variable on a sequence of states is its value on the first of those states.

- *Static variables*, which do not change in value during a computation.

Interval variables do not seem very useful for describing deterministic computations. Consequently only state and static variables are used in the following, and these we differentiate by a simple naming convention. Names beginning with a capital letter (like I and *Temp*) belong to state variables, whereas those starting with a lower case letter (such as i and *temp*) are static.

Predicate symbols in ITL are analogous to computational procedures; they allow us to parameterise specifications. For example, an array of n identical processors operating in parallel could be specified as follows:

$$p(0) \wedge \ldots \wedge p(n-1).$$

An equivalent, but more concise specification uses *universal quantification*:

$$\forall i < n : p(i)$$

(read "for all i less than n ..."). The dual construction, *existential quantification*, asserts that there is at least one value of each quantified variable for which the associated statement is true. For example, the assertion

$$\exists I : (p_1(I) \wedge \exists I : p_2(I))$$

can be satisfied if we can find one computation on which variable I behaves according to $p_1(I)$, and another on which I's behaviour is given by $p_2(I)$, provided that both computations agree on the behaviour of every variable except I. This is like declaring new variables with local scope.

So far we have only shown how to refer to a computation as a whole. Let us now look at some temporal operators which focus on parts of a computation.

2.4 Chop and Sequential Behaviour

The basic sequencing operator of ITL is *chop* (;). The construction $p_1 ; p_2$ is satisfied by a computation which can be split into two parts such that p_1 is true on the first, and p_2 on the second. Note, however, that the two subcomputations have a state in common: the initial step of the second is also the final step of the first.

Many other temporal operators can be defined in terms of chop. Amongst these are the "always" and "sometimes" operators which characterise temporal logics. The property $\Diamond p$ holds if p holds sometimes, *i.e.* if the computation can be split apart so that p is true on the second part, and a property always holds, $\Box p$, if its negation is not sometimes true.

$$\Diamond p \equiv_{\text{def}} true \, ; p \quad \text{and} \quad \Box p \equiv_{\text{def}} \neg \Diamond \neg p.$$

Both of these operators refer to tail computations. Variants which refer to other parts of a computation may also be defined.

2.5 Next and Timing

So far we have shown how to describe parallel and sequential behaviour, but not how to refer to a specific point in a computation. It is the "next" operator, $\bigcirc$, which makes this possible. A computation satisfies the property $\bigcirc p$ if p holds on the tail subcomputation comprising the second and all subsequent steps. There must be a second step or else $\bigcirc p$ cannot be true for any p. Thus, for example, the property $\neg \bigcirc true$ holds on any computation which has exactly one state, and so computation length can be made explicit.

To introduce the next operator it is necessary to suppose that computation proceeds according to the tick of some global clock, so that there always will be a well-defined next state. Where this is not a reasonable assumption one might avoid using next, but an alternative is to describe a computation relative to several different clocks by means of *temporal projection*. Some simple examples of projection are given in [Mos86] and [Hal87].

2.6 Correctness

We denote that a computation σ has property p by writing

$$\sigma \models p$$

("σ satisfies p"). A property which is true of all computations is said to be valid. This is written

$$\models p.$$

If *spec* is a general behaviour that some program ought to have (such as sorting a list of integers), and *imp* is a more restricted property satisfied by the computations of some program (a merge-sort, for instance), then our program may be said to meet the specification if those computations which satisfy *imp* also satisfy *spec*. This will be true if

$$\models pgm \supset spec,$$

provided, of course, that there is a computation satisfying *pgm*.

To prove such an assertion of correctness one can reason directly in terms of the semantics, but this is generally unsatisfactory being tedious and error-prone. It is much better to have a systematic, preferably automated proof theory. A completely automatic proof system for ITL does not seem to be viable as any decision procedure must have at least exponential complexity. However, the problem can be made tractable by focussing on useful parts of the logic, such as Tempura, and by relying on manually guided verification systems, such as Gordon's verification system for higher-order logic [Gor87]. Some progress has been made with this approach, and will be reported in future work.

$$\langle \sigma_0, \ldots, \sigma_n \rangle \models p_1 \wedge p_2 \quad \text{iff} \quad \langle \sigma_0, \ldots, \sigma_n \rangle \models p_1 \quad \text{and} \quad \langle \sigma_0, \ldots, \sigma_n \rangle \models p_2$$

$$\langle \sigma_0, \ldots, \sigma_n \rangle \models \neg p \quad \text{iff} \quad \text{it is not the case that} \quad \langle \sigma_0, \ldots, \sigma_n \rangle \models p$$

$$\langle \sigma_0, \ldots, \sigma_n \rangle \models p_1 \, ; p_2 \quad \text{iff} \quad \langle \sigma_0, \ldots, \sigma_i \rangle \models p_1 \quad \text{and} \quad \langle \sigma_i, \ldots, \sigma_n \rangle \models p_2 \quad \text{for some } i \leq n$$

$$\langle \sigma_0, \ldots, \sigma_n \rangle \models \Box p \quad \text{iff} \quad \langle \sigma_i, \ldots, \sigma_n \rangle \models p \quad \text{for all } i \leq n$$

$$\langle \sigma_0, \ldots, \sigma_n \rangle \models \bigcirc p \quad \text{iff} \quad n > 0 \quad \text{and} \quad \langle \sigma_1, \ldots, \sigma_n \rangle \models p$$

Figure 1: Semantics of the operators.

3 Tempura

Tempura is an executable subset of ITL. It is loosely similar to other logic-based languages in that execution of a program p produces a computation which satisfies p, but is completely unlike them in being a parallel language which supports an algorithmic style of programming.

3.1 Program Semantics

A formula, p, of ITL is a Tempura program if, after eliminating quantifiers and expanding predicates, it can be transformed into the canonical form:

$$p \equiv \bigwedge_{i=0}^{n} \bigcirc^i p_i,$$

where the notation $\bigcirc^i$ denotes i applications of the next operator and each p_i is a conjunction of equations which assign values to program variables. The transformation of program p into canonical form is carried out iteratively. On the first iteration $p \ (= q_0)$ is transformed into an equivalent form $p_0 \wedge \bigcirc q_1$, where p_0 is a conjunction of equations. On the second iteration the reduction is repeated, transforming q_1 into $p_1 \wedge \bigcirc q_2$, and so forth until finally the process terminates on the nth iteration, when the term q_n cannot be reduced ($q_n = p_n \wedge \neg \bigcirc true$). The result is to define a class of computations of length n which agree on the variable assignments made by the p_i.

As a simple illustration, the program $\Box(X = 0) \wedge \bigcirc(\neg \bigcirc true)$ has the canonical form

$$\Box(X = 0) \wedge \bigcirc(\neg \bigcirc true) \quad \equiv \quad (X = 0) \wedge \bigcirc(X = 0).$$

Here, $p_0 \equiv p_1 \equiv (X = 0)$ and $q_1 \equiv (X = 0) \wedge (\neg \bigcirc true)$.

The reduction technique does not work for arbitrary formulae, because not every formula can be reduced to a conjunction of the above form. To admit disjunction into programs (other than in Boolean expressions) would increase considerably the complexity of the execution algorithm, since in general one must use back-tracking to satisfy the property $p_1 \vee p_2$. To handle the negation, $\neg p$, one must in addition assume a "closed world". Furthermore, an exhaustive search of the solution space is much more costly than the equivalent for a first-order language because of the additional temporal dimension. Although these constructs could be incorporated into a language based on temporal logic, Tempura is restricted to a part of ITL for which satisfiability can be determined efficiently and deterministically.

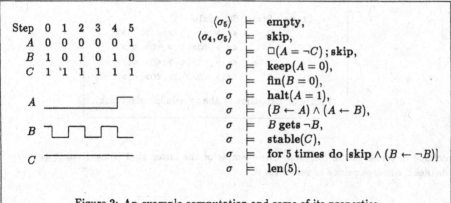

Figure 2: An example computation and some of its properties.

3.2 Derived Operators

There is a natural correspondence between certain logical operators and certain aspects of programming. For example, the conjunction and chop operators model parallel and sequential composition, and existential quantification corresponds to the introduction of local variables. Other concepts, such as unit delay and assignment, have no direct analogue, but may easily be defined within ITL. Consequently, a body of new operators has arisen to simplify the expression of such ideas. Some of the most useful of these are defined below.

In the following definitions p denotes an arbitrary property and n stands for a natural number. Variable x is static (unchanging), and A, B and C depend on state. More generally, A, B and C might be replaced by expressions.

empty	$\equiv_{\text{def}}$	$\neg \bigcirc true$	(the zero-length interval)
skip	$\equiv_{\text{def}}$	$\bigcirc$ empty	(the unit-length interval)
keep(p)	$\equiv_{\text{def}}$	$\Box(\neg\text{empty} \supset p)$	(on all but the last state)
fin(p)	$\equiv_{\text{def}}$	$\Box(\text{empty} \supset p)$	(on the last state)
halt(C)	$\equiv_{\text{def}}$	$\Box(\text{empty} \equiv C)$	(interval termination)
$A \leftarrow B$	$\equiv_{\text{def}}$	$\exists x : [x = B \wedge \text{fin}(A = x)]$	(assignment)
A gets B	$\equiv_{\text{def}}$	keep $\exists x : [x = B \wedge \bigcirc(A = x)]$	(unit delay)
stable(A)	$\equiv_{\text{def}}$	A gets A	(constant value)
if C then p_1 else p_2	$\equiv_{\text{def}}$	$(C \supset p_1) \wedge (\neg C \supset p_2)$	(conditional)
for n times do p	$\equiv_{\text{def}}$	if $n = 0$ then empty	
		else $[p\,;\text{for } n-1 \text{ times do } p]$	(repetition)
len(n)	$\equiv_{\text{def}}$	for n times do skip	(interval length)

Figure 3.2 gives an example to make these definitions more concrete. It sets out a number of properties which are true of a system of three variables, A, B and C, during a computation σ. The system oscillates between two states a few times before entering a third. It is apparent from this example that Tempura embodies ideas from conventional imperative programming as well as some which are more akin to dataflow. Examples of the former kind are the destructive assignment, $A \leftarrow B$ and the various repetitive constructs, such as **while** loops, which can be

```
    State   Step   Schedule
    0       0      << >,< >,< >,< >,< >>
    1       1      << >,<0>,< >,<0>,< >>
    2       2      <<1>,<0>,< >,<0>,<1>>
    3       3      <<1>,<0>,<2>,<0>,<1>>
```

Figure 3: Execution of the scheduling algorithm.

defined in terms of the **for** loop. An example of the latter kind is the term A **gets** B which defines a whole sequence of values for A.

4 Some Parallel Algorithms

In this section we describe four parallel algorithms, all taken from the literature. The first one is a simple scheduling algorithm, the second is for the evaluation of parsed expressions, the third is a graph traversal algorithm, and the final one performs the so-called odd-even mergesort using an array of processors. We describe each one in a general manner, using a model of computation based on discrete time and shared variables, and then give the corresponding Tempura program and show a sample behaviour.

4.1 A Scheduling Algorithm

Suppose there are a number of interdependent activities that are to be performed concurrently, subject to certain scheduling constraints. These activities might, for example, be lecture courses, some of which require others to have been given previously, or they might be phases in a large software development project. For ease of exposition, let us consider only five activities, $a_0 \ldots a_4$, with the following constraints: a_4 must be done after a_3, a_2 must be done after both a_0 and a_3, and a_0 must be done after a_1. These constraints form a partial ordering which is represented as follows:

$$a_3 \prec a_4, \quad a_0 \prec a_2, \quad a_3 \prec a_2, \quad a_1 \prec a_0,$$

$make\_schedule(n, constraints, Schedule, Step) \quad \equiv_{def}$
$\quad \wedge \mathbf{halt}(\forall i < n : Schedule_i \neq \langle \rangle)$
$\quad Step = 0 \wedge Step \mathbf{\ gets\ } Step + 1$
$\quad \wedge \forall i < n :$
$\qquad [\mathbf{halt}(\forall j \in constraints_i : Schedule_j \neq \langle \rangle) \wedge \mathbf{keep}(Schedule_i = \langle \rangle)] ;$
$\qquad [\mathbf{skip} \wedge Schedule_i \leftarrow \langle Step \rangle \wedge \mathbf{keep}(Schedule_i = \langle \rangle)] ;$
$\qquad [\mathbf{stable}(Schedule_i)]$

Figure 4: The scheduling algorithm.

$$make\_timed\_schedule(n, constraints, costs, Start, Stop, Step) \quad \equiv_{def}$$
$$\wedge \, halt(\forall i < n : Stop_i \neq \langle \, \rangle)$$
$$Step = 0 \wedge Step \text{ gets } Step + 1$$
$$\wedge \forall i < n :$$
$$[\mathbf{halt}(\forall j \in constraints_i : Stop_j \neq \langle \, \rangle)$$
$$\wedge \, \mathbf{keep}(Start_i = \langle \, \rangle) \wedge \mathbf{keep}(Stop_i = \langle \, \rangle)] \, ;$$
$$[\mathbf{len}(costs_i) \wedge \mathbf{fin}(Stop_i = \langle Step \rangle) \wedge Start_i \leftarrow \langle Step \rangle$$
$$\wedge \, \mathbf{keep}(Start_i = \langle \, \rangle) \wedge \mathbf{keep}(Stop_i = \langle \, \rangle)] \, ;$$
$$[\mathbf{stable}(Start_i) \wedge \mathbf{stable}(Stop_i)]$$

Figure 5: The revised scheduling algorithm.

and here is a suitable schedule:

$$\text{Step } 0 : \quad a_1, a_3$$
$$\text{Step } 1 : \quad a_0, a_4$$
$$\text{Step } 2 : \quad a_2$$

Er [Er83] proposes a parallel algorithm for generating a schedule from a partial order. Each abstract task a_i has its own associated process which waits until the scheduling of all tasks that must be done during earlier phases. Immediately afterwards, the process i records the current phase and indicates that a_i can be performed.

Let us look at how to implement this algorithm in Tempura. The overall form of the associated predicate is as follows:

$$make\_schedule(n, constraints, Schedule, Step).$$

There are four parameters. The first one, n, is the number of tasks. The variable *constraints* contains an n-element list of the scheduling restrictions imposed by the partial order. Each element $constraints_i$ is itself a list of those tasks that a_i must wait for. Thus, in our example, *constraints* has the following value:

$$\langle \langle 1 \rangle, \langle \, \rangle, \langle 0, 3 \rangle, \langle \, \rangle, \langle 3 \rangle \rangle.$$

For instance, $constraints_2$ has the value $\langle 0, 3 \rangle$ since task a_2 must wait for both a_0 and a_3.

The variable *Schedule* is a list which shows when each task must be started. When the scheduling algorithm starts, each entry is initialised to the empty list, $\langle \, \rangle$. This indicates that the time at which to start the task is not yet determined. Upon a task being scheduled, the entry in *Schedule* is altered to $\langle Step \rangle$, where *Step* is the computation step at which the task is to be begun. As the algorithm proceeds, the variable *Step* is incremented to equal the computation step currently under investigation. Figure 3 shows the values of the variables *Step* and *Schedule* throughout the algorithm's execution, and the algorithm itself is given in figure 4.

The lifetime of each abstract task is divided into three phases. In the first it waits for the other tasks on which it depends to complete, in the second it is activated for one step and its start time recorded, and in the third phase the task is finished. The algorithm terminates when all the tasks have finished.

We assert that our algorithm produces a correct schedule, *i.e.* if $a_i \prec a_j$ then a_i will be scheduled before a_j:

$$\models before(i, j) \wedge make\_schedule(n, constraints, Schedule, Step) \supset \mathbf{fin}(Schedule_{i,0} < Schedule_{j,0}),$$

```
State  Step  Start                           Stop
0      0     << >,< >,< >,< >,< >,< >>       << >,< >,< >,< >,< >,< >>
1      1     << >,<0>,< >,< >,< >,< >>       << >,<1>,< >,< >,< >,< >>
2      2     <<1>,<0>,< >,< >,< >,< >>       <<2>,<1>,< >,< >,< >,< >>
3      3     <<1>,<0>,< >,<0>,< >>           <<2>,<1>,< >,<3>,< >>
4      4     <<1>,<0>,< >,<0>,< >>           <<2>,<1>,< >,<3>,< >>
5      5     <<1>,<0>,<3>,<0>,<3>>           <<2>,<1>,<5>,<3>,<5>>
```

Figure 6: Execution of the revised scheduling algorithm.

where the predicate *before* is true if $a_i \prec a_j$.

$$before(i,j) \quad \equiv_{def} \quad (i \in constraints_j) \lor (\exists k \in constraints_j : before(i,k)).$$

The recursion is well-founded because the constraints form a partial order.

Unfortunately, the algorithm just described does not necessarily produce the schedule which requires the least time to execute, because it does not take account of the time that may be required to perform a task. In effect, it has been assumed that each task is completed in a single step. However, if it takes more time to carry out a_3 than a_1 and a_0 put together, then it is better to schedule a_4 after a_0, not at the same time.

An improved algorithm is specified by the predicate

$$make\_timed\_schedule(n, constraints, costs, Start, Stop, Step)$$

in figure 5. The new variable *costs* is a list of the execution times of each task. In our example, *costs* has the value

$$\langle 1, 1, 2, 3, 2 \rangle.$$

Task a_3, for example, takes three units of time. Two other new variables, *Start* and *Stop*, take the place of *Schedule*. They both have the same structure as *Schedule*, but *Start* is a list which shows when to start each task, and *Stop* shows when each task finishes. The structure of the algorithm is the same as before, but now the phase during which task a_i is active has duration $costs_i$. Figure 6 shows the values of *Start* and *Stop* during the execution of this algorithm.

4.2 Evaluating an Expression Tree

Now let us consider a problem with a strict hierarchy. Suppose that our goal is to evaluate simple arithmetic expressions in-place. We assume that the expressions have been parsed into a tree representation. For example, the parsed form of the expression

$$((1+2) \times 3) + ((4 \times 5) + (6+7))$$

would be the binary tree shown in figure 7. During evaluation this tree is to be transformed into the integer 42. In order to calculate this value as quickly as possible, the subexpressions represented by the children of each node may be evaluated in parallel. A sample parallel evaluation is given in figure 8.

The evaluation algorithm is given by the predicate *eval_tree* in figure 9. It is is a straightforward use of recursion. If the tree is already an integer, then we are done. Otherwise, the arguments are evaluated, and the corresponding operator applied to calculate the result. The

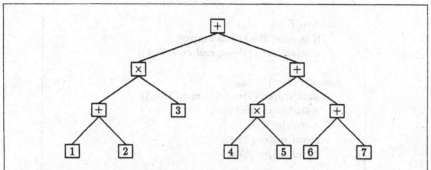

Figure 7: Tree representation of the expression $((1 + 2) \times 3) + ((4 \times 5) + (6 + 7))$

arguments are evaluated by applying *eval_tree* recursively to each in parallel, but one must be careful because these parallel evaluations do not necessarily take the same time to complete. Thus, one of the arguments may need to be kept stable while waiting for the other evaluation to complete. This can be seen in the predicate *eval_args*. Another detail to watch is that the structure of the node must be maintained while its arguments are evaluated. Thus, if the node starts out as a "+"-node, it must remain a "+"-node until its arguments are ready.

Suppose that addition and multiplication are both instantaneous, and that their results can be assigned to a memory location in one step. The predicates *add* and *multiply* have this behaviour.

$$add(A, B, C) \quad \equiv_{\text{def}} \quad \textbf{skip} \wedge (C \leftarrow A + B),$$
$$multiply(A, B, C) \quad \equiv_{\text{def}} \quad \textbf{skip} \wedge (C \leftarrow A \times B).$$

These specifications can be executed in Tempura, and the result of executing the whole program for our example expression is shown in figure 8. Notice that the number of steps required to evaluate the expression is equal to the depth of the tree.

$$\models \quad eval\_tree(Tree) \quad \supset \quad \textbf{len}(depth(Tree)) \wedge Tree \leftarrow tree\_val(Tree),$$

where *depth* and *tree_val* are recursively defined functions. The function *depth* returns the depth of a binary tree, and *tree_val* returns its value.

Figure 10 shows what happens if the multiplication instruction is slower, taking a time dependent on its arguments. In this case it satisfies the specification:

$$multiply(A, B, C) \quad \supset \quad \textbf{len}(\text{if } A = 0 \text{ then } 1 \text{ else } A) \wedge (C \leftarrow A \times B).$$

Any suitable adder or multiplier can be used in this program.

```
Step   Tree
0      <"+",<"*",<"+",1,2>,3>,<"+",<"*",4,5>,<"+",6,7>>>
1      <"+",<"*",3,3>,<"+",20,13>>
2      <"+",9,33>
3      42
```

Figure 8: Evaluation of the expression $((1 + 2) \times 3) + ((4 \times 5) + (6 + 7))$.

$eval\_tree(Tree)$ $\equiv_{def}$
    if $is\_num(Tree)$ then empty
    else$[eval\_args(Tree) ; eval\_expr(Tree)]$

$eval\_args(Tree)$ $\equiv_{def}$
    $halt(is\_num(Tree_l) \wedge is\_num(Tree_r))$
    $\wedge stable(struct(Tree))$
    $\wedge stable(Tree_{op})$
    $\wedge eval\_subtree(Tree_l)$
    $\wedge eval\_subtree(Tree_r)$

$eval\_subtree(Tree)$ $\equiv_{def}$
    $eval\_tree(Tree) ; stable(Tree)$

$eval\_expr(Tree)$ $\equiv_{def}$
    if $Tree_{op} = $ "+" then $add(Tree_l, Tree_r, Tree)$
    else if $Tree_{op} = $ "×" then $multiply(Tree_l, Tree_r, Tree)$
    else...

Figure 9: An algorithm to evaluate parsed expressions.

4.3   Traversing a Graph

Now imagine a network of processors which can communicate by sending and receiving messages along bidirectional channels. Each processor is represented as a node of a connected graph, and each communication channel as an edge joining two nodes. A processor is aware of its immediate neighbours, but beyond that has no knowledge of the topology of the network. In this section we look at a distributed algorithm for traversing such a graph. The algorithm we describe is due to Chang [Cha82]. It provides a basis for many useful control functions in a distributed system. It can, for example, be used to decide upon an identity for a new processor which is added to the network.

The method works as follows. To begin with one particular node (the "initiator") sends out a message to each of its neighbours. These messages, called "explorers", are then propagated outwards, step-by-step, to every other node in the network. When a node receives its first explorer from a neighbouring vertex, v_a, it sends out new explorers in parallel to each of its other neighbours. Subsequently, it may also receive explorers from its other neighbours, and to these it sends acknowledgement messages, called "echoes". Each node records the arrival of echoes, and when it has received all that it expects (one echo from every neighbour except v_a), it acknowledges its first explorer by sending an echo to neighbour v_a. The traversal is complete when the initiator has received an echo from each of its neighbours. A few steps of this algorithm are illustrated for an example network in figure 11.

If the echo messages carry information about those parts of the network which they have traversed, then we can gradually build up a picture of the topology of the network as echoes return towards the source. Finally, when all echoes have returned, the source node has a complete list of the processors on the network. To give an identity to a newly connected processor, it merely

```
Step   Tree
0      <"+",<"*",<"+",1,2>,3>,<"+",<"*",4,5>,<"+",6,7>>>
1      <"+",<"*",3,3>,<"+",<"*",4,5>,13>>
2      <"+",<"*",3,3>,<"+",<"*",4,5>,13>>
3      <"+",<"*",3,3>,<"+",<"*",4,5>,13>>
4      <"+",9,<"+",20,13>>
5      <"+",9,33>
6      42
```

Figure 10: Expression evaluation with slow multiplication.

has to choose an unused one.

In the following ITL description of the algorithm we shall confine our attention to the control aspects of the algorithm. Thus, we need only regard messages as Boolean values (either present or not). Processors communicate through shared variables. Thus, assuming that there may be at most one explorer or echo in transit between each pair of processors at any one time, we may model the communication network as a pair of Boolean arrays, one called *Explorer* to represent explorers, the other called *Echo* representing echoes. Both *Explorer* and *Echo* are in fact *partial arrays*, being defined only for those pairs (i, j) for which there is a connection from processor i to processor j.

Each node has an active phase when it is dispatching explorers; and the predicate *explore*, which describes this part of the algorithm, has the following general form

$$explore(i, explore\_list, echo\_list),$$

where the variable i is the identity of the node, *explore_list* is a list of neighbouring nodes to be explored, and *echo_list* identifies those nodes to which echoes should be returned. The echo algorithm is given in figure 12 where it can be seen that the body of *explore* is a parallel composition of five other predicates. Four of these describe the communications between node i and its neighbours; the other one counts echoes as they arrive, and halts the exploration when all the expected ones have been received. The four communication predicates are:

- *send(M, i, nbrs)*, which specifies just one initial transmission of message M from node i to each of the neighbouring nodes held in *nbrs*.

- *reply(M, i, nbrs)*, which is like *send* but the transmission occurs at the end of the computation.

- *copy(M, M', i, nbrs)*, which always acknowledges a message M from one of its neighbours by returning M'.

- *no(M, i, nbrs)*, which ensures that no M is transferred from node i to any of the specified neighbours. It is necessary to assert this because there is no frame assumption.

The initiator is always in the exploratory phase, since it is responsible both for sending out the initial explorers and for determining when the algorithm is complete. Each of the other nodes must wait passively until it receives an explorer from neighbour v_a whereupon it also enters the active phase. After receiving its quota of echoes, it returns its own echo to v_a and reverts to the

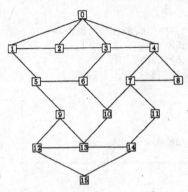

(a) The graph to be traversed.

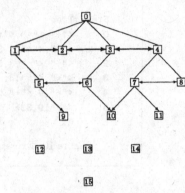

(d) Step 3: Echoes return.

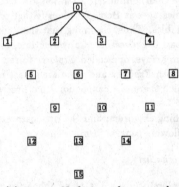

(b) Step 1: Node 0 sends out explorers.

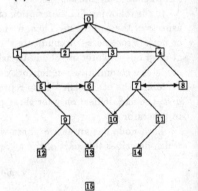

(e) Step 4: Traversal continues.

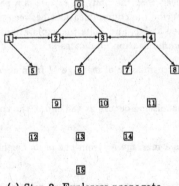

(c) Step 2: Explorers propagate.

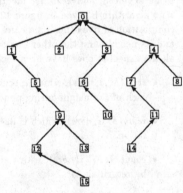

(f) Paths of the final echoes.

Figure 11: Traversal of a graph (Explorers are thin arrows, Echoes are bold).

$$node(i, nbrs) \quad \equiv_{def}$$
$$\exists a : [\textbf{halt}(\exists j \in nbrs : Explorer_{j,i})$$
$$\wedge no(Explorer, i, nbrs) \wedge no(Echo, i, nbrs)] ;$$
$$[a = \min(j \in nbrs : Explorer_{j,i}) \wedge explore(i, nbrs \setminus \langle a \rangle, \langle a \rangle)] ;$$
$$[no(Explorer, i, nbrs) \wedge no(Echo, i, nbrs)]$$

$$explore(i, explore\_list, echo\_list) \quad \equiv_{def}$$
$$monitor\_echoes(i, explore\_list)$$
$$\wedge send(Explorer, i, explore\_list)$$
$$\wedge copy(Explorer, Echo, i, explore\_list)$$
$$\wedge reply(Echo, i, echo\_list)$$
$$\wedge no(Explorer, i, echo\_list)$$

$$send(M, i, nbrs) \quad \equiv_{def} \quad \forall j \in nbrs : [\textbf{skip} \wedge (M_{i,j} \leftarrow true)] ; [M_{i,j} \text{ gets } false]$$

$$reply(M, i, nbrs) \quad \equiv_{def} \quad \forall j \in nbrs : \Box[M_{i,j} = \textbf{empty}]$$

$$copy(M, M', i, nbrs) \quad \equiv_{def} \quad \forall j \in nbrs : [M'_{i,j} \text{ gets } M_{j,i}]$$

$$no(M, i, nbrs) \quad \equiv_{def} \quad \forall j \in nbrs : [M_{i,j} \text{ gets } false]$$

$$monitor\_echoes(i, nbrs) \quad \equiv_{def}$$
$$\exists EchoCount :$$
$$EchoCount = |nbrs|$$
$$\wedge EchoCount \text{ gets } [EchoCount - (\sum_{j \in n} \text{ if } Echo_{j,i} \text{ then } 1 \text{ else } 0)]$$
$$\wedge \textbf{halt}(EchoCount = 0)$$

Figure 12: The graph traversal algorithm.

passive state. The predicate $node(i, nbrs)$ captures this behaviour. Finally, the whole network is simply the parallel composition of all the node specifications:

$$\forall i < |net| : \textbf{if } i = initiator \textbf{ then } explore(i, net_i, \langle \rangle) \textbf{ else } node(i, net_i),$$

where net is a connectivity list such that net_i is a list of the neighbours of node i. The behaviour of this algorithm is illustrated in figure 11.

4.4 The Perfect Shuffle

A "perfect shuffle" of a deck of cards is achieved when the deck is divided equally into two halves, which are then shuffled in such a way that cards from each of the two halves alternate in the shuffled deck. The corresponding operation on an array of n data elements permutes the elements of an array according to the permutation s, where

$$s(i, n) = \begin{cases} 2i & 0 \leq i < n/2 \\ 2i + 1 - n & n/2 \leq i < n \end{cases}$$

$$shuffle\_net(n, Inst, Data) \quad \equiv_{def}$$
$$\forall i < n:$$
$$Data_i \text{ gets}$$
$$\text{if } Inst_i = \text{``shuffle''} \text{ then } Data_{s(i,n)}$$
$$\text{else if } Inst_i = \text{``unshuffle''} \text{ then } Data_{s^{-1}(i,n)}$$
$$\text{else } Data_i$$

Figure 13: A perfect shuffle network (s is the shuffle permutation).

and we assume that n is a power of 2. Surprisingly, this operation is used in a number of important parallel algorithms, from the Fast Fourier Transform to matrix transposition. An example of its use in a sorting algorithm is given in the next section.

The perfect shuffle can be performed directly in hardware by an array of n processing cells in which cell i is connected to cell $s(i, n)$. Each cell in the shuffle network holds a single element of data, $Data_i$, and has a control input, $Inst_i$, to define what operation is to be performed at each computation step. We may suppose that only three operations are possible: shuffle, unshuffle, and no-operation. The first two of these cause data elements to flow around the network in the appropriate direction, the last leaves data elements unchanged. A shuffle network of n cells may therefore be described by the predicate $shuffle\_net$ as shown in figure 13.

It is interesting to note that both the shuffle and unshuffle operations can also be performed in $n/2 - 1$ computation steps on a linearly connected array of processing cells with operations for shifting data to the left or right. Such an array of cells is defined in figure 14. The shuffle is performed by means of the triangular sequence of exchanges defined by the predicate $shuffle\_cntl$ in figure 15, and may be simulated by executing the parallel composition of the controller and cell array:

$$shuffle\_cntl(n, Inst) \wedge linear\_net(n, Inst, Data).$$

An example is shown in figure 16, where the instructions "shiftleft", "shiftright" and "noop" are represented as "<--", "-->". and " - ", respectively. Combining the shuffle controller in parallel with the linear network causes the data elements to be shuffled in $n/2 - 1$ steps (if we take a

$$linear\_net(n, Inst, Data) \quad \equiv_{def}$$
$$\forall i < n:$$
$$Data_i \text{ gets}$$
$$\text{if } Inst_i = \text{``shiftright''} \text{ then } Data_{i-1}$$
$$\text{else if } Inst_i = \text{``shiftleft''} \text{ then } Data_{i+1}$$
$$\text{else if } Inst_i = \text{``compareright''} \text{ then } min(Data_i, Data_{i+1})$$
$$\text{else if } Inst_i = \text{``compareleft''} \text{ then } max(Data_i, Data_{i-1})$$
$$\text{else } Data_i$$

Figure 14: A linear network of comparator cells.

$shuffle\_cntl(n, Inst) \quad \equiv_{def}$
$\quad$ **for** $i < n/2 - 1$ **do** [skip
$\quad\quad \wedge\forall\, 0 \leq j < n/2 - i - 1:$
$\quad\quad\quad Inst_j = $ "noop"
$\quad\quad \wedge\forall\, n/2 - i - 1 \leq j < n/2 + i:$
$\quad\quad\quad Inst_j = $ **if** $odd(i + j)$ **then** "shiftleft" **else** "shiftright"
$\quad\quad \wedge\forall\, n/2 + i \leq j < n:$
$\quad\quad\quad Inst_j = $ "noop"]

Figure 15: The shuffle controller for a linear network.

data exchange to be our basic computation step).

$\models shuffle\_cntl(n, Inst) \wedge linear\_net(n, Inst, Data) \supset len(n/2 - 1) \wedge \forall i < n : Data_i \leftarrow Data_{s(i,n)}$

In the next section we discuss a sorting algorithm which uses the perfect shuffle.

4.5 Parallel Merging

There are a variety of sorting and merging algorithms that do multiple comparisons in parallel [BDHM84]. Let us consider the so-called odd-even mergesort. This merges two sorted lists to form a longer sorted list. The merger is performed on a linearly connected row of comparator cells. Each comparator can only communicate with its two immediate neighbours (the boundary cells have only one neighbour, of course) and receives instructions from a central controller about what to do. Initially the left half of the row contains one sorted list and the right half contains another. After the merge the entire row is sorted.

The row is the linear network of comparator cells defined in figure 14. A cell can perform five operations: a shift either to the right or to the left, a comparison and possible exchange with either the right or left neighbour, and a no-operation which leaves the data unchanged. The controller for the merger is recursively defined. The base case is for merging two cells and only requires a single comparison. The left cell is instructed to "compareright", and the right cell to "compareleft". In a larger row we first "unshuffle" the row, then recursively merge each half in parallel, then "shuffle" the row, and finally compare each cell having an odd numbered index with its even-indexed neighbour (*e.g.* 1 and 2).

Step	Data	Inst
0	<0,1,2,3,4,5,6,7>	< - , - , - ,<--,-->, - , - , - >
1	<0,1,2,4,3,5,6,7>	< - , - ,<--,-->,<--,-->, - , - >
2	<0,1,4,2,5,3,6,7>	< - ,<--,-->,<--,-->,<--,-->, - >
3	<0,4,1,5,2,6,3,7>	

Figure 16: An example of the shuffle on a linear network.

$$
\begin{aligned}
&merge\_cntl(n, Inst) \quad \equiv_{\text{def}} \\
&\quad unshuffle\_cntl(n, Inst) \,; \\
&\quad [merge\_cntl(n/2, Inst_{0..n/2}) \wedge merge\_cntl(n/2, Inst_{n/2..n})] \,; \\
&\quad shuffle\_cntl(n, Inst) \,; \\
&\quad oddeven\_compare\_cntl(n, Inst)
\end{aligned}
$$

Figure 17: The controller for the parallel merge.

Figure 17 shows the main predicate for the controller. The shuffle is achieved by the sequence of exchanges discussed in the previous section, and the unshuffle by applying the same sequence of operations in reverse, though both operations could equally well be done in a single step on the perfect shuffle network.

Once we have the controller and comparators specified, the overall system can be constructed by combining them in parallel.

$$
merge(n, Data) \quad \equiv_{\text{def}} \quad \exists Inst : [merge\_cntl(n, Inst) \wedge linear\_net(n, Inst, Data)].
$$

Here is a statement of the correctness of the merger:

$$
\models \quad sorted(Data_{0..n/2}) \wedge sorted(Data_{n/2..n}) \wedge merge(n, Data) \quad \supset \quad \text{fin}(sorted(Data))
$$

where the predicate *sorted* tests whether its list argument is sorted, and the notation $Data_{i..j}$ denotes the sublist of *Data* from element i up to $j - 1$. Figure 18 shows the values of *Inst* and *Data* during a sample execution of the predicate *merge*. For brevity, operations "shiftleft", "shiftright", "compareleft", "compareright", and "noop" are represented as "<--", "-->", "<-?", "?->" and " - ", respectively.

5 Discussion

Now we come to examine some of the issues relating ITL to other models of concurrent computation, and discuss some of the advantages and drawbacks of each approach.

5.1 Discrete Computation Sequences

The view of computation as a sequence of discrete steps is well established, and provides a natural way to express dynamic behaviour. With good reason it is common to many languages and formalisms besides ITL, including conventional imperative languages like *Pascal*.

Functional programming [Hen80] offers an alternative in which certain types of functions are interpreted as executable descriptions of computations. The functions themselves have no built-in notion of state, and therefore dynamic behaviour must be modelled indirectly by means of recursion. One can also represent time-dependent variables as lists of values, or explicitly as functions of time.

Perhaps the strongest argument in support of functional languages has been their mathematical elegance and simplicity relative to conventional imperative languages. However, this argument does not seem to hold up against ITL.

```
Step  Data               Inst
0     <1,3,4,6,0,2,5,7>  < - ,<--,-->,<--,-->,<--,-->, - >
1     <1,4,3,0,6,5,2,7>  < - , - ,<--,-->,<--,-->, - , - >
2     <1,4,0,3,5,6,2,7>  < - , - , - ,<--,-->, - , - , - >
3     <1,4,0,5,3,6,2,7>  < - ,<--,-->, - , - ,<--,-->, - >
4     <1,0,4,5,3,2,6,7>  <?->,<-?,?->,<-?,?->,<-?,?->,<-?>
5     <0,1,4,5,2,3,6,7>  < - ,<--,-->, - , - ,<--,-->, - >
6     <0,4,1,5,2,6,3,7>  < - ,?->,<-?, - , - ,?->,<-?, - >
7     <0,1,4,5,2,3,6,7>  < - , - , - ,<--,-->, - , - , - >
8     <0,1,4,2,5,3,6,7>  < - , - ,<--,-->,<--,-->, - , - >
9     <0,1,2,4,3,5,6,7>  < - ,<--,-->,<--,-->,<--,-->, - >
10    <0,2,1,3,4,6,5,7>  < - ,?->,<-?,?->,<-?,?->,<-?, - >
11    <0,1,2,3,4,5,6,7>
```

Figure 18: A sample execution of the merge program.

Let us return to our tree evalutaion example. This algorithm is naturally recursive, and in its basic form has a simple dynamic behaviour in which each step depends in a straightforward way on its predecessor. One would therefore expect a functional form to be easy to construct, and so it is. Indeed, the naive Tempura function presented in figure 19 is more concise than the temporal algorithm of figure 9. Our function uses a list to hold the values of the expression tree. However, to accommodate a multiplier with different timing characteristics is no longer a straightforward substitution of one predicate for another, but now requires more state information to be somehow introduced. What was trivial in the temporal version has now become awkward because of the lack of state memory.

5.2 First Order Logic

The programming language Prolog [CM81] uses Horn clauses in first order logic as a means of specifying computations. In subsequent work Clark and Gregory [CG86], Shapiro [Sha84] and others have generalised this framework to model concurrent systems, but in so doing have sacrificed the formal purity of the original.

Just as in the functional case, first order logic does not admit the idea of change, but the same techniques may be used to represent dynamic behaviour indirectly, with similar advantages and drawbacks. The use of history lists seems to be most popular with the advocates of Prolog-based concurrent languages, but it is not clear that this is a practical way to represent the changes over time of large data structures.

5.3 The Need for Intervals

The use of classical temporal logic for reasoning about parallel programs is widespread [Pnu81], and it has also been proposed as a basis for programming [Tan83]. The principal advantage of sticking to classical temporal logic is that it has a well-understood proof theory. However, there are also definite gains to be made by adopting the interval-based approach, the most important of these being clarity of expression, particularly in the study of timing and sequencing issues. Furthermore, Moszkowski [Mos83] has given a general method for translating an ITL formula

---

$$eval\_tree\_fn(\,Tree\,) \quad \equiv_{def}$$
$$\textbf{if } is\_num(\,Tree\,) \textbf{ then } Tree$$
$$\textbf{else } eval\_tree\_fn(\,append(\langle eval\_args\_fn(\,Tree_0)\rangle,\ Tree))$$

$$eval\_args\_fn(\,T\,) \quad \equiv_{def}$$
$$\textbf{if } is\_num(T_l) \wedge is\_num(T_r) \textbf{ then } eval\_expr\_fn(T)$$
$$\textbf{else } \langle T_{op},\ eval\_subtree\_fn(T_l),\ eval\_subtree\_fn(T_r)\rangle$$

$$eval\_subtree\_fn(\,T\,) \quad \equiv_{def}$$
$$\textbf{if } is\_num(T) \textbf{ then } T \textbf{ else } eval\_args\_fn(T)$$

$$eval\_expr\_fn(\,T\,) \quad \equiv_{def}$$
$$\textbf{if } T_{op} = \text{``+''} \textbf{ then } T_l + T_r$$
$$\textbf{else if } T_{op} = \text{``}\times\text{''} \textbf{ then } T_l \times T_r$$
$$\textbf{else} \ldots$$

Figure 19: A functional program to evaluate an expression tree.

---

involving chop into an equivalent formula without chop. Using this translation, one can move between the two branches of temporal logic.

The essential idea of the translation is to existentially introduce boolean variables to mark the end-points of subcomputations. A marker is false during the subcomputation and becomes true at the end, and therefore takes the place of empty in ITL. Here, by way of illustration, is a translation of the predicate $eval\_tree$ of figure 9:

$$eval\_tree'(\,Tree, Done\,) \quad \equiv_{def}$$
$$\textbf{if } is\_num(\,Tree\,) \textbf{ then } Done$$
$$\textbf{else } \exists Done' : [eval\_args'(\,Tree, Done')] \wedge [(\neg Done)\ \text{U}\ (Done' \wedge eval\_expr'(\,Tree, Done))],$$

where U is the strong until operator. It is apparent that for all but the simplest programs, the translated form is considerably more opaque than the original version using chop, and since the translation can be automated, it is difficult to see any justification at all for not using chop.

5.4 Concurrency and Communication

ITL has a simple model based on true (synchronous) parallelism, and communication by means of shared variables. Languages such as CSP [Hoa85] have taken a wholly different approach, modelling concurrency as arbitrary interleavings of sequential events, and assuming a particular style of channel communication from the outset. Which is the better approach depends to a great extent on the application, but some general points can be made.

CSP is not derived from a logic, and so needs to be augmented before any kind of formal proof can be done. It is also much more sophisticated semantically than ITL, a difference which is especially striking when one considers concurrent composition. Both of these facts make it easier to reason about Tempura programs. On the other hand, the built-in communication primitives make it easier to model asynchronous communicating processes in CSP. Our graph traversal example showed that, when applied in a naive way, the use of shared variables for communication, coupled with the lack of a frame assumption, can lead to some awkwardness in the specification.

Finally, we should note that it is not hard to describe asynchronous parallelism in ITL using the projection operator [Mos86]. It is also possible to define message passing disciplines within ITL, but how to achieve this in a general way is the subject of research.

5.5 Determinism

Tempura programs are deterministic, and as a result have a relatively straightforward and efficient execution mechanism. In contrast, the execution of a program written in Prolog or one of its derivatives will, in general, require resolution and backtracking. It is possible to conceive an executable subset of ITL which would permit nondeterminism. Indeed, the programming language *Tokio* [FKTM86] is just such a subset.

The advantage of a nondeterministic model is that a wider class of formulae are executable. Apart from a more complex execution algorithm, the disadvantages are firstly that one loses the equivalence between a program (together with its input data) and its computation sequence, and secondly that one can no longer guarantee that the execution of a given program will be the same on different runs or on different interpreters.

It remains to be seen whether nondeterministic execution is of sufficient value to outweigh the drawbacks, or whether one really only needs nondeterminism in the specification language (which is the same for both cases).

References

[BDHM84] D. Bitton, D. J. DeWitt, D. K. Hsiao, and J. Menon. A taxonomy of parallel sorting. *ACM Computing Surveys*, 16(3):287–318, September 1984.

[CG86] K. L. Clark and S. Gregory. Parlog: parallel programming in logic. *ACM Transactions on Programming Languages and Systems*, 8(1):1–49, January 1986.

[Cha82] E. J. H. Chang. Echo algorithms: depth-first parallel operations on general graphs. *IEEE Transactions on Software Engineering*, 8(4):391–401, July 1982.

[CM81] W. F. Clocksin and C. S. Mellish. *Programming in Prolog*. Springer-Verlag, Berlin, 1981.

[Er83] M. C. Er. A parallel computation approach to topological sorting. *Computer Journal*, 26(4):293–295, April 1983.

[FKTM86] M. Fujita, S. Kono, H. Tanaka, and T. Moto-oka. Tokio: logic programming language based on temporal logic and its compilation to prolog. In *Proceedings of the Third International Conference on Logic Programming*, London, July 1986.

[Gor87] M. J. C. Gordon. *HOL: A Proof Generating System for Higher Order Logic*. Technical Report 103, Computer Laboratory, University of Cambridge, England, 1987.

[Hal87] R. W. S. Hale. Temporal logic programming. In A. Galton, editor, *Temporal Logic and Its Applications*, Academic Press, London, 1987. (In preparation).

[Hen80] P. Henderson. *Functional Programming: Application and Implementation*. Prentice-Hall International, London, 1980.

[Hoa85]   C. A. R. Hoare. *Communicating Sequential Processes*. Prentice Hall, London, 1985.

[Mos83]   B. C. Moszkowski. *Reasoning about Digital Circuits*. PhD thesis, Department of Computer Science, Stanford University, 1983.

[Mos86]   B. C. Moszkowski. *Exceuting Temporal Logic Programs*. Cambridge University Press, Cambridge, England, 1986.

[Pnu81]   A. Pnueli. The temporal semantics of concurrent programs. *Theoretical Computer Science*, 13:45–60, 1981.

[Sha84]   E. Y. Shapiro. Sysytems programming in concurrent prolog. In *Proceedings of the Eleventh Annual ACM Symposium on Principles of Programming Languages*, Salt Lake City, USA, January 1984.

[Tan83]   C. Tang. Toward a unified logic basis for programming languages. In *Proceedings of the IFIP Congress 1983*, North-Holland, Amsterdam, 1983.

"RUTH : A Functional Language for Real-Time Programming"

Dave Harrison

Department of Computing Science

University of Stirling

Stirling FK9 4LA

Scotland, United Kingdom

Abstract

This paper introduces the real-time programming language RUTH which is a functional language based on the lazy language LispKit LISP [8]. RUTH is a semantically pure functional language in which the concept of a Process is encapsulated by the more general concept of a function. Communication between Processes is modelled by streams of timestamped values. RUTH programs take as input a tree of integers which is lazily evaluated as the program executes to produce node values representing the current time. Taking real-time information as an input data structure allows RUTH programs to define and react to real-time events without loosing referential transparency and allows us to define a formal semantics without the complication of including timing information.

1. INTRODUCTION

A real-time system can be categorised as one whose correctness depends not only upon the values of its inputs and outputs and their relative ordering but also upon their absolute ordering in time. In other words not only upon what happens but also upon when it happens. In [13] it is argued that real-time systems are qualitatively different from conventional data processing systems because of this. Whereas we prefer a conventional system to produce some result even if it takes longer than expected, a real-time system must produce its outputs within a particular period of time or not at all. For example any delay in sending a new value for engine speed to an engine controller could result in the engine becoming unstable. Once that has occurred sending the delayed value will only make matters worse. Conversely if a conventional system produces a result earlier than expected this is a benefit; in a real-time system it may well be a disaster. The production of a result before the external system is ready to receive it may well cause the result to be lost. Even worse, if a result is produced early it is probable that new input data will also be read early and that data is likely to be invalid (for example due to sensor settling times). This will invalidate all subsequent computation.

So in a real-time system the major part of the correctness of the system is whether it interacts with its environment within specified periods of time or Time Windows. (cf. [7]). Real-time systems vary from "soft" systems in which the Time Windows are large compared to the speed of a software implementation (eg. electronic timetabling systems) to "hard" systems in which the Time Windows are small (eg. signal processing). At the "soft" end of this range real-time systems merge into conventional systems as we reach the stage where the requirement is simply that a result must be produced eventually (ie. the Window stretches to infinity). Such systems can be handled without any explicit notion of time and thus by conventional programming languages. At the "hard" end of the range real-time systems merge into hard wired electronics as we reach the stage at which software is simply not fast enough (ie. the Window is of the order of micro-seconds wide). Between the two extremes lie a large class of problems such as Machine Control, Animation and Operating Systems. It is problems in this domain that RUTH is designed to address.

Imperative programming languages deal with real-time in terms of execution time (e.g. explicitly programmed wait loops) and non-determinance (e.g. real-time Clock interrupts). Functional programming languages, on the other hand, have no concept of execution time and are totally determinate, being simply a definition of an expression mapping their input data structures to their output data structures. Functional programming languages also exhibit the property of referential transparency. In [14] this is defined as follows.

> "The only thing that matters about an expression is its value, and any expression can be replaced by any other equal in value. Moreover, the value of an expression is, within certain limits, the same whenever it occurs."

The limits mentioned are simply the scope of declaration of all of the identifiers used in the expression. For example the expression $x + f(x)$ is always equal to $f(x) + x$ in a programming language with referential transparency. Imperative languages violate referential transparency by their use of the assignment statement. If within the body of $f(x)$ the identifier x is changed by assignment then the two expressions will not be equal. This makes it impossible to consider the behaviour of f in isolation. We must always be aware that it may have "side effects" on other values in our programs. Worse, if $f(x)$ changes the value of x then we cannot predict the value of the expression $x + f(x)$ unless we know whether x or $f(x)$ is evaluated first. In a functional language, on the other hand, there is no way we can change the value of a declared identifier and so we preserve referential transparency.

Both determinance and referential transparency greatly simplify the formal semantics of a language and this has several advantages. Without a formal semantics there is no way we can reason about programs. Yet real-time systems are those we would most like to be able to reason about and prove correct, since as pointed out in [13], incorrect behaviour is usually not transparently recoverable in a real-time system. That is, incorrect actions by software cannot simply be "rolled-back" and forgotten about. They will have produced a (possibly disastrous) reaction from the external world such as causing an aeroplane to crash. Secondly, trying to satisfy the timing requirements of a real-time system can result in very complex algorithms. The ability to write simple clear algorithms which do not satisfy the timing requirements and then automatically transform them into more efficient versions can help solve this problem [6] but without a formal semantics the definition of transformation rules is impossible. Finally, the simpler the semantics of a language the more confidence a user is likely to have that programs written using it are correct. For these reasons the language RUTH is purely functional. The very properties that give functional programming languages their clarity and formal tractability (determinance and referential transparency) make it impossible for them to handle real-time in the same way as imperative languages. Therefore an alternative technique must be found.

Several methods for solving this problem have been proposed. In [11] and [12] a non-determinate choice primitive is introduced into LispKit LISP, the chosen alternate being that which is available first in real-time. PFL [9] also includes a non-determinate choice primitive of this type and reference to the current value of system time is given by a non-referentially transparent primitive. ART [2] is a purely functional language which associates with each data value its time of creation (a timestamp) and uses streams of such objects to model real-time input/output so allowing timing information to be handled by the program. The "discrete" approach used by ART, in which all data has a time associated with it, contrasts sharply with the "continuous" approach taken by the LUCID family of languages [1], [7] and the ARCTIC language [5]. Instead of every value being associated with a time of creation, values are treated as functions of time. Thus each time has a value associated with it.

This paper describes (and outlines the Denotational Semantics of) the language RUTH which is purely a functional language using timestamps and real-time Clocks to deal with real-time events. Abstracting all timing information into an input data structure allows us to ignore real-time considerations in the formal semantics without loosing the ability to talk about real-time in our programs. The paper is divided into three parts. Firstly Channels are introduced. Channels are infinite streams of timestamped messages in which the timestamps correspond to the time at which the messages were placed in the Channel. Then a method is given for allowing functional programs to reference real-time by supplying a real-time Clock as an input to the program. Finally the method by which RUTH functions are used to define real-time Processes is shown.

2. TIMESTAMPS AND CHANNELS

Consider a RUTH function F

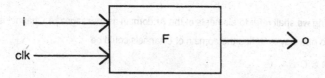

F takes as inputs a Channel i and a Clock clk and produces the Channel o as output. All the messages in i and o have timestamps defining the real-time at which they were placed in the Channels. This relationship between timestamps and real-time is the most important feature of the RUTH programming language as i allows us to specify timing requirements and to react to real-time events explicitly in RUTH programs Unfortunately enforcing such a relationship is non-trivial as we shall see later. In RUTH timestamps are represented by the domain of natural numbers (**N**). This seems natural in digital computers which can only represent discrete values accurately. We assume that our timestamps represent values in real-time with a error of 1/2 a "tick". Provided the duration of a "tick" in discrete time is small enough we can treat ou timestamps as accurate representations of the continuous values. We shall assume that this is the case. Th domain of values allowed on Channels is that of Atoms (**A**). Each Channel is an infinite sequence of pairs o numbers and Atoms where such pairs are drawn from the domain of Time Stamped Atoms (**At**) defined

$$At = N \otimes A$$

Where "$\otimes$" denotes the coalesced product of two domains [4]. That is, for any two domains D_1, D_2

$$D_1 \otimes D_2 = \{<d_1, d_2> \mid d_1 \in D_1, d_2 \in D_2, d_1 \neq \perp, d_2 \neq \perp\} \cup \{\perp\}$$

So the elements of **At** are all possible pairs of Natural Numbers and Atoms plus the undefined element $\perp$ (rea bottom). (cf. The domain T(**A**) in [2]). In order to construct elements of **At** we use

$$\{\_,\_\} : N \times A \rightarrow At$$

Throughout this paper "_" is used to denote the position of arguments in domain element constructors. Fo example { t, a } denotes the Atom a stamped with the time t. A consequence of using the "$\otimes$"domai constructor is that if either the Natural Number or the Atom are undefined then the element of **At** constructe from them is also undefined. That is

$$\{\perp, a\} = \{t, \perp\} = \{\perp, \perp\} = \perp$$

This means it is impossible to put partially evaluated messages on Channels since we cannot be sure whethe a value is defined or not until it has been completely evaluated. Two selectors are used on elements of **At**

obj	: At $\rightarrow$ A	*obj*	({ t, a }) = a
stamp	: At $\rightarrow$ N	*stamp*	({ t, a }) = t

In the following we shall refer to elements of the **At** domain as messages. A Channel is simply an infinite list messages so one way to define the domain of Channels could be

$$Ch = At \otimes Ch$$

A Channel is a coalesced pair comprising the first message on the Channel (its "Head") and the list messages following the first on the Channel (its "Tail"). Since a Channel is just a list of messages the Tail o

Channel is itself a Channel. This doesn't quite define the behaviour we need however. The "⊗" operator demands that both the Head and the Tail of the Channel are fully evaluated so that it can be sure that they are fully defined. This causes us two problems. Firstly, Channels are infinite data structures so evaluating the Tail will take infinite time. Secondly, if the Tail turns out to be undefined then the Channel we are trying to construct will be undefined. Although we may have had a perfectly well defined message at the Head we cannot send this message because of an error in producing the Tail. (These problems in producing elements of our Channel domain are modelled in the mathematics by the fact that it has only one element - the undefined element $\perp$.) This is clearly undesirable, the property we wish for our Channels is that whilst the message we wish to send must be fully defined we do not care about any subsequent messages. This property is usually called *Head Strictness* because we strictly insist that the Head message is defined but do not care about the messages in the Tail. We denote this "don't care" situation by a technique known as Domain Lifting [4]. For any domain D the lifted domain $D_\perp$ is defined

$$D_\perp = \{ <true, d> \mid d \in D \} \cup \{ \perp \}$$

The elements of the domain $D_\perp$ are produced by taking each element (including the undefined element $\perp$) from the domain D and pairing it with "true". We then add a new undefined element to $D_\perp$. The consequence of this is that the undefined element in D ($\perp$) becomes a defined element in $D_\perp$ ($<true, \perp>$). There is no way that we can construct the undefined element of $D_\perp$ from elements of the domain D. The operator *lift* is used to construct elements of $D_\perp$ from a domain D by pairing elements of D with true as above. The operator *drop* takes elements of the domain $D_\perp$ and returns the second part of the pair thus producing an element of D. So for any domain D with member d

lift $: D \rightarrow D_\perp$	*lift* (d) = <true, d>
drop $: D_\perp \rightarrow D$	*drop* (<true, d>) = d

Replacing the domain which is the second argument of "⊗" in the definition of the Channel domain by its lifted counterpart we obtain

$$Ch = At \otimes Ch_\perp$$

Now there is no need to try to evaluate the Tail of the Channel since it will always be defined in $Ch_\perp$ (We must still evaluate the Head since our Channel will still be undefined if the Head is undefined.) This definition of Channels is recursive and we rely on the underlying theory of domains (see [14]) to guarantee that the solution of the defining equation is the domain which we require. To construct elements of Ch we use the infix operator ":"

$$\_ : \_ \qquad : At \times Ch_\perp \rightarrow Ch$$

If at $\in$ **At** and $ch_\perp \in$ **Ch**$_\perp$ then at : $ch_\perp \in$ **Ch**. Two selectors are defined to return the first element of a Channel and to return the Channel with that element removed.

front	: $Ch \rightarrow At$	*front* $(at: ch_\perp)$ = at	
rest	: $Ch \rightarrow Ch_\perp$	*rest* $(at : ch_\perp)$ = $ch_\perp$	

We define RUTH functions in terms of our semantic functions in the usual way by defining the semantic function "$\mathcal{E}_v$" (Evaluate). $\mathcal{E}_v$ takes a syntactic RUTH expression and a mapping from syntactic identifiers to semantic values (an environment) and returns a semantic value.

$$\mathcal{E}_v : EXP \rightarrow (ID \rightarrow Val) \rightarrow Val$$

Here EXP denotes the set of syntactic expressions, ID the set of syntactic identifiers (which is contained within EXP) and **Val** is the domain of semantic values (that is, possible results of a RUTH expression). We denote the environment in which the identifier I maps to the value v as

$$[I \rightarrow v]$$

We shall use I to denote syntactic identifiers throughout this paper. Environments can be constructed from other environments by using the "$\oplus$" operator.

$$\rho \oplus [I \rightarrow v] = \lambda x. \underline{If} x = I \ \underline{Then} v \ \underline{Else} \rho[x]$$

Where $\rho \in$ (ID $\rightarrow$ **Val**). This says that the environment $\rho \oplus [I \rightarrow v]$ is the same as the environment ρ save that the variable I is mapped to the value v. In the following ρ will be used to denote environments. The Atom part of the Head message in a Channel is referenced by the RUTH function HeadCh ("Head-Channel") and the function Time returns the timestamp of the Head message. The Tail of the Channel is returned by the function TailCh ("Tail-Channel"). We give first the RUTH type signatures of these functions and then their semantics in terms of the semantic functions given above. For simplicity we shall follow the practice of ignoring domain injections and projections assuming that the reader can infer them from the context.

HeadCh : chan $\rightarrow$ atom	$\mathcal{E}_v$ [HeadCh (E)] ρ = *obj* (*front* ($\mathcal{E}_v$ [E] ρ))
Time : chan $\rightarrow$ num	$\mathcal{E}_v$ [Time (E)] ρ = *stamp* (*front* ($\mathcal{E}_v$ [E] ρ))
TailCh : chan $\rightarrow$ chan	$\mathcal{E}_v$ [TailCh (E)] ρ = *drop* (*rest* ($\mathcal{E}_v$ [E] ρ))

Here chan is the RUTH type corresponding to elements of the domain **Ch**, atom is the type corresponding to the domain **A**. num corresponds to the domain **N** (which is a sub-domain of **A** just as num is a sub-type of atom). Here (and in the following) E denotes a syntactic expression. The RUTH Channel constructor is called ConsCh (Cons-Channel). It is defined

ConsCh : atom x num x chan → chan

$$\mathcal{E}_v [\, ConsCh\,(\,E_1,\,at(\,E_2\,),\,E_3\,)]\,\rho \;=\; \{\,\mathcal{E}_v[\,E_2\,]\,\rho,\,\mathcal{E}_v[\,E_1\,]\,\rho\,\} : \textit{lift}\,(Tail)$$

where

$$Tail = \textit{If } stamp\,(front\,(\mathcal{E}_v[\,E_3\,]\,\rho\,)) > \mathcal{E}_v[\,E_2\,]\,\rho \;\underline{\textit{Then}}\;\mathcal{E}_v[\,E_3\,]\,\rho \;\underline{\textit{Else}}\;\bot$$

The first argument to ConsCh evaluates to an atom. The syntactic expression at(E_2) denotes that the atom is to be timestamped with the number which is the result of evaluating E_2. The result of evaluating E_3 (the Tail of the Channel) is lifted to denote that it is not required to construct the Channel and may be delayed. However when we do finally evaluate the Tail we check that the timestamp of its Head message is greater than that we have just calculated for E_1. If it is not then the Tail is undefined. This ensures that the timestamps in our Channels are strictly increasing.

Using these functions we can write RUTH programs that can respond to when inputs occur in a deterministic way. For example a function to merge two Channels into one based on the time of production of the inputs (a timewise merge) would be

merge : chan x chan x num → chan
merge   = <u>lambda</u> (ch1, ch2, d).

       <u>If</u> Time (ch1) ≤ Time (ch2)

       <u>Then</u> ConsCh (HeadCh (ch1), at(Time (ch1) + d), merge (TailCh (ch1), ch2, d))
       <u>Else</u> ConsCh (HeadCh (ch2), at(Time (ch2) + d), merge (ch1, TailCh (ch2), d))

This function simply compares the times of availability of the messages at the Head of the two Channels and constructs a Channel containing the earlier of the two messages and the timewise merging of the remainders. Each time a message is output from the merge its timestamp is increased by d. This specifies that messages must be output from merge d time units after they arrive. The question is will this definition of merge evaluate fast enough to meet this requirement? The functions Time, HeadCh and TailCh are strict in their argument; that is they insist that at least the first message in the Channel is fully evaluated. Whilst this gives RUTH the synchronisation between Processes that is required in a real-time language it is a little restrictive in use. The expression

Time (ch1) ≤ Time (ch2)

cannot be evaluated unless the first message in both ch1 and ch2 is fully evaluated. However all we are trying to determine is which of the two Channels produces a message first. If ch1 has produced a message and ch2 has not then the above expression is obviously true and we need not wait for ch2. In many situations we certainly would not want to wait for ch2 to produce a message. For example if ch1 carried messages from a smoke detector while ch2 carried messages from a keyboard. It highly likely that if a smoke detector has sensed the presence of smoke it will be a considerable time before another key is pressed on the keyboard. We would wish to pass on the smoke detector signal immediately and not have to wait for a keyboard input. In terms of our timing requirement keeping a message in one Channel waiting until a message arrives in the other means we will almost certainly keep messages waiting for longer than d time units. What we would like to be able to test is whether or not a message is available in a single Channel. Such a test is real-time dependent a message may not be available at one instant but may be placed in the Channel at the next. Any test of availability must take account of this. Since RUTH timestamps denote the actual time at which a message is placed in a Channel we can easily define such a test - the Ready function

Ready : chan x num $\rightarrow$ boolean

$$\mathcal{E}_v [\text{Ready} (E_1, E_2)] \rho = stamp\,(front\,(\mathcal{E}_v [E_1] \rho)) \leq \mathcal{E}_v [E_2] \rho$$

Where boolean is the type corresponding to the domain of Boolean values {true, false, $\perp$} and is a sub-type of atom. This is semantically identical to (ie. produces the same result as) the expression Time (E_1) $\leq E_2$ since

$$\mathcal{E}_v [\text{Time} (E_1) \leq E_2] \rho = stamp\,(front\,(\mathcal{E}_v [E_1] \rho)) \leq \mathcal{E}_v [E_2] \rho$$

but the advantage of using Ready over using the Time function is that we can rely on the timestamps being the actual real-time at which the messages are placed in the Channel. If we are evaluating the expression Ready (ch, n) and the Channel ch has a fully evaluated message then Ready can be evaluated instantly; if not we need only wait until the time n has passed at which point we can safely return false. After the real-time denoted by n has passed any message subsequently placed in the Channel will have a timestamp greater than n. So Ready will not be blocked waiting for input in ch whereas if Time were used we would be blocked waiting for a message so that we could return the value of its timestamp. This ability to "short circuit" the evaluation of Ready depends on all messages in a Channel being given timestamps equal to the real time at which they are placed in the Channel. The problems associated with ensuring that this condition is met will be considered below in Section 3. Now we can write a merge function as follows

merge : chan x chan x num x num $\rightarrow$ chan
merge   = lambda (ch1, ch2, d, n).
       If Ready (ch1, n)
     Then If Ready (ch2, n)
           Then If Time(ch1) $\leq$ Time(ch2) Then ans1 Else ans2
           Else ans1
       Else If Ready (ch2, n) Then ans2 Else merge (ch1, ch2, d, n + k)

<u>where</u>

ans1 = ConsCh (HeadCh (ch1), at(Time (ch1) + d), merge (TailCh (ch1), ch2, d, n + k))

ans2 = ConsCh (HeadCh (ch2), at(Time (ch2) + d), merge (ch1, TailCh (ch2), d, n + k))

k = {a constant number}

This function looks slightly more complex than the merge function given above but that is because it explicitly considers the cases in which either or both of the Channels has not yet produced a value. Both Channels are tested using Ready to determine if they have a message available at time n. If neither has a message then the merge function is called recursively with n increased by k. If only one Channel has a message then that message will be taken. If both Channels have a message with a timestamp less than n then the one with the lower timestamp (ie. that arrived first) is taken.

Here k is a constant determining the "sampling rate" of the merge, that is how often merge checks for messages. If the sampling rate is too slow (ie. k > d) then we will certainly violate the timing requirement by keeping a message waiting for longer than d time units. However we don't want the sampling rate to be faster than merge can cope with. If each evaluation of merge takes i units and i > k then our value for n is going to fall further and further behind the current time. Thus we must eventually violate the timing requirement. So the correct value for k is in the range i < k < d. (Obviously in the case where d < i there is no way we can satisfy the timing requirement.) We know the value of d but determining that of i is more problematical. In [2] the semantics of the language ART are parameterised with the time each expression takes to evaluate. Techniques like this will give us some notion of the value of i but in general will not be strictly accurate due to operational considerations, for example DMA on I/O slowing down memory access. The more low level detail we include in our semantics the more accurate our "timing" will become. However a simple formal semantics was one of the major reasons for using a functional language in the first place and such detatil will only complicate matters. The use of a range of values (Time Windows) to define how long an expression should take to evaluate will save us from including too much low-level operational detail in our semantics, but we will still need to know general facts such as evaluation order. Using a range of values for time introduces non-determinancy into any language with an explicit notion of time and so is not suitable for RUTH. Much more work needs to be done in this area and as we shall see in the next Section the approach taken in RUTH is to abstract all information about the passage of time into input real-time Clocks.

Notice that this new version of merge computes exactly the same ordering of messages from ch1 and ch2 as that given earlier and the merged messages are given exactly the same timestamps. In the first version the value of i depended on the arrival of the next messages from ch1 and ch2 and we could be almost certain it would eventually exceed d. In the new version we are using the Ready test and will not waste time waiting for unavailable messages. Consequentially our new version of merge has a much better chance of satisfying the timing requirements since its value for i will be lower. In Section 3 we shall return to this point in our discussion of "Time Partial Correctness".

In general a Process will produce not one but a number of Channels as its result. Before going any further we shall introduce the way this is expressed in RUTH. We define the domain of Tuples **Tp**

$$Tp = Ch \otimes ... \otimes Ch$$

That is a tuple is a collection of Channels. The constructor and selector for the domain of Tuples are

Constructor $<\_, ..., \_>$: **Ch x ... x Ch → Tp**

Selector *select* : **Tp x N → Ch**

$$select \, (<ch_0, ..., ch_m, ..., ch_n>, m) = ch_m$$

In RUTH tuples are constructed using the RUTH primitive Tuple and elements are selected from tuples using Select. These functions are defined

Tuple : chan x ... x chan → tuple $\qquad \mathcal{E}_v \, [Tuple \, (E_0, ..., E_n)] \, \rho = < \mathcal{E}_v \, [E_0] \, \rho, ..., \mathcal{E}_v \, [E_n] \, \rho >$

Select : tuple x num → chan $\qquad \mathcal{E}_v \, [Select \, (\, E_1, E_2 \,)] \, \rho = select \, (\, \mathcal{E}_v \, [E_1] \, \rho, \mathcal{E}_v \, [E_2] \, \rho \,)$

Here tuple is the RUTH type corresponding to the domain **Tp**. We shall ignore tuples for most of the rest of this paper. They will become important only in Section 4 when we discuss configuring RUTH functions into Process Networks. In the next section we go on to consider the Clock trees which are supplied as input to RUTH programs and show how they can be used both to provide timestamps for the messages placed in Channels and to provide reference to the real-time.

3. CLOCKS AND "REAL" REAL-TIME

In [3] Burton introduces a method by which a tree of *decisions* may be input to a functional program allowing non-determinate choices to be made whilst preserving referential transparency. Once a *decision* is referenced from the tree it becomes fixed in the usual lazy evaluation manner. However the value to which particular *decision* is bound depends only on the external system. Burton suggests that if the tree contains values for the current time instead of *decisions* this method can be used to allow real-time information to be input to a functional program. In RUTH each program is supplied with a tree of time values (or Clock) as Burton suggests. Each RUTH Process is given a different sub-tree of the Clock so that each Process has a unique notion of the current time. The reason for using a tree in preference to a linear list for our Clocks is so that we can extract different sub-trees. The way this is done will be explained in Section 4. The Processes themselves treat their Clocks as simple lists of time values. A Clock tree is composed of a node holding an integer value denoting the current time and two sub-trees denoting the times of future events. As the tree is (lazily) evaluated each of the nodes is instantiated with the value of system time at the time *at which the node is evaluated*. The effect is as if each time the program demands the value of an unevaluated node in the Clock tree a message is printed at a console asking the user to input the current value of time from his watch. The input value is then assigned to the node. Taking real-time information as an input data structure to our programs allows us to ignore real-time aspects in our formal semantics. Thus we avoid the problems involved in correctly "timing" a semantics whilst retaining the ability to handle real-time explicitly in our programs. Since Clocks are input data structures we can write time dependent RUTH programs in a purely functional way. The domain of Clocks is defined

$$\text{Clk} = \text{N} \otimes \text{Clk}_\perp \otimes \text{Clk}_\perp$$

A Clock is thus an integer and two lifted Clocks. The sub-Clocks are lifted to denote that they need not be evaluated before the integer value is used. This is as we'd expect since they contain the times of events that have not yet occurred. For the same reason the values contained in the nodes of the sub-trees must be strictly greater than the value contained in the node of the parent tree. Once again we define semantic functions to allow us to construct and select from Clocks

Constructor $\{\_,\_,\_\} : \text{N} \times \text{Clk}_\perp \times \text{Clk}_\perp \to \text{Clk}$

Selectors $time$: $\text{Clk} \to \text{N}$ $time\,(\{t, lc, rc\}) = t$

       $left$: $\text{Clk} \to \text{Clk}_\perp$ $left\,(\{t, lc, rc\}) = lc$

       $right$: $\text{Clk} \to \text{Clk}_\perp$ $right\,(\{t, lc, rc\}) = rc$

The simplest RUTH primitives using Clock trees are the functions HeadClk and TailClk. (The names were chosen to emphasise the point that to a RUTH function a Clock is just a list of time values).

HeadClk : clock → num $\mathcal{E}_v [\, \text{HeadClk}\,(E)] \,\rho = time\,(\,\mathcal{E}_v\,[E]\,\rho\,)$

TailClk   : clock → clock $\mathcal{E}_v [\, \text{TailClk}\,(E)]\,\rho = drop\,(left\,(\,\mathcal{E}_v\,[E]\,\rho\,))$

clock is the RUTH type corresponding to the domain **Clk**. HeadClk takes a Clock as an argument and returns the integer at the node. When HeadClk is evaluated the node will be instantiated with the current value of real-time (provided the node has not already been evaluated) thus allowing RUTH programs easy access to timing information. Obviously the programmer should be careful that HeadClk is not supplied with a Clock which has already had its node instantiated. Otherwise the value returned by HeadClk will not represent the current real-time. TailClk simply returns the left sub-tree of the Clock so that as far as a RUTH programmer is concerned the Clock is simply a list. With HeadClk and TailClk we can write functions which respond to the passage of time without recourse to non-determinance. For example the following function waits until after a given time and then returns the first message in its input Channel, effectively delaying receipt of the message.

Input_After : chan x clock x num → atom

Input_After = lambda (ch, clk, when).

      If HeadClk (clk) < when

    <u>Then</u> Input_After (ch, TailClk (clk), when)

    <u>Else</u> HeadCh (ch)

Even in real-time systems we still need to handle non real-time outputs. For example the logging of errors in an engine control system. The only timing restriction is that all errors should be logged "eventually". This is well towards the "soft" end of the real-time spectrum as the correct functioning of the engine controller doesn't depend on how fast it can log mistakes. The way we specify non real-time outputs in RUTH is via an additional form of ConsCh in which we provide a Clock rather than an explicit time as the second argument. When the message is finally placed in the output Channel the node value of the Clock is instantiated to the current time as before and the current time is used as the timestamp of the message.

ConsCh : atom x clock x chan → chan

$$\mathcal{E}_v [\text{ConsCh} (E_1, E_2, E_3)] \rho = \{ time (\mathcal{E}_v [E_2] \rho), \mathcal{E}_v [E_1] \rho \} : lift (\text{Tail})$$

<u>where</u>

Tail = <u>If</u> stamp (front ($\mathcal{E}_v [E_3] \rho$)) > time ($\mathcal{E}_v [E_2] \rho$) <u>Then</u> $\mathcal{E}_v [E_3] \rho$ <u>Else</u> ⊥

Provided the Clock has not already been instantiated the message will automatically receive a timestamp equal to the real time at which it is placed in the output Channel. This style of "don't care" timestamping is used by all conventional programs which have no knowledge of real-time. It simply defines the output to occur as soon as operationally possible. The merge we defined earlier had a timing restriction on its outputs. If there were no such restriction then we could write merge as below.

merge : chan x chan x clock → chan

merge   = <u>lambda</u> (ch1, ch2, clk).

      <u>If</u> Ready (ch1, n)

      <u>Then</u> <u>If</u> Ready (ch2, n)

            <u>Then</u> <u>If</u> Time (ch1) ≤ Time (ch2) <u>Then</u> ans1 <u>Else</u> ans2

            <u>Else</u> ans1

      <u>Else</u> <u>If</u> Ready (ch2, n) <u>Then</u> ans2 <u>Else</u> merge (ch1, ch2, tc)

      <u>where</u>

      n   = HeadClk (clk)

      tc   = TailClk (clk)

      ttc = TailClk (TailClk (clk))

      ans1 = ConsCh (HeadCh (ch1), tc, merge (TailCh (ch1), ch2, ttc))

      ans2 = ConsCh (HeadCh (ch2), tc, merge (ch1, TailCh (ch2), ttc))

Once again this merge produces exactly the same ordering of messages as the merges given previously. The difference here is that we give no fixed values for the timestamps, relying on them to be calculated as each message is sent.

Earlier we noted that a non-blocking implementation of the Ready test relies on the fact that all messages in Channels have a timestamp equal to the real time at which they were placed in the Channel. By imposing certain syntactic constraints upon RUTH programs it is possible to ensure that Clock values are not re-used. If we then insist that only "don't care" timestamping is used we can be sure that output messages will always have valid timestamps. Defining these syntactic restrictions is non-trivial and enforcing them will cause us two major problems. Firstly we would no longer have the ability to give explicit timestamps to messages and so to define outputs to occur at particular times. Slightly less seriously the syntactic restrictions required will severly cramp a functional program's style.

To avoid these problems we impose the run-time restriction that a message may only be placed in an output Channel from a RUTH Process if its timestamp is equal to the current real-time. If it is not then the Process producing the message is in error and the message cannot be sent. This is easy to check at run-time and allows us to implement the non- blocking Ready test. (Operationally we also allow messages with timestamps greater than the current time to be placed in output Channels. The receiving Process will just not be able to access them until the times denoted by their timestamps have arrived. Allowing a Channel to carry messages to be received in the future causes no problems for implementation of the Ready test; it is messages that are to be received *in the past* that cannot be allowed.) This gives us the notion of "Time Partial Correctness" mentioned in Section 2. A RUTH Process may contain a correct statement of its timing requirements but under certain evaluation strategies may fail to produce any result because it does not execute quickly enough to satisfy them. RUTH Processes are guaranteed to produce only correct results but whether they produce any results at all is at the mercy of the way in which they are evaluated. This is similar to the standard notion of Partial Correctness [6] in which it is possible to transform a program from one form to another without changing its meaning. There is no guarantee that the new version of the program will terminate in all the cases in which the original did. Likewise the new version may well terminate in cases where the original did not. The only guarantee is that if the programs do terminate they produce the correct result. Similarly by transforming a correct RUTH Process it may be possible to produce a version which will satisfy the timing requirements. It is equally possible to transform a Process into one that will definitely not satisfy them. The two versions of merge given in Section 2 are examples of this. Although they both specify exactly the same Channel we would expect the second version to produce output in cases where the first would not. HeadCh and Input_After are also semantically equivalent and one can be transformed into the other. We would expect a program using HeadCh to produce output in cases where one using Input_After did not due to the delay introduced by Input_After.

At the start of this section we commented on the need for input Clocks to be tree structured so that different sub-trees could be extracted to supply independent timing information to different Processes. In the next section we define what a RUTH Process is, how its Clock tree is extracted from the input Clock and how it is used.

4. PROCESSES AND SUB-PROCESSES

Most real-time systems are composed of a set of independent communicating Processes. In RUTH a Process is simply an expression mapping a set of input Channels and a Clock to a set of output Channels. To emphasise that a Process is totally independent of the rest of the system we wrap the expression in an enclosing Process definition. For example the "don't care" merge Process given above would be defined

Process Merge_Process

Input ch1, ch2

Clock clk

Is   (merge (ch1, ch2, clk)

       where

       merge = ...) ;

This says that the Process Merge_Process takes two input Channels which it calls ch1 and ch2 and an input Clock which it calls clk. The output from Merge_Process is defined by the expression following "Is" (the Process Expression). The Process Expression may involve only the identifiers ch1, ch2 and clk (along with any identifiers it defines itself) so that a Process has no knowledge of the rest of the system beyond that supplied via its input Channels and Clock. A Process definition is interpreted as the definition of a function from its input Channels and Clock to a set of output Channels. We use the semantic function $\mathcal{E}_p$ (Evaluate Process) to define this

$$\mathcal{E}_p : \text{PROC} \rightarrow (\text{ID} \rightarrow \textbf{Val})$$

$$\mathcal{E}_p \, [\text{Process} \, I \, \underline{\text{Input}} \, I_0, ... , I_n \, \underline{\text{Clock}} \, I_c \, \underline{\text{Is}} \, E:] = [\, I \rightarrow \mathcal{E}_v \, [\, \underline{\text{lambda}} \, (I_0, ... , I_n, I_c).E] \, \rho \,]$$

where

$$\rho = [\,]$$

The result of evaluating a Process definition is an environment mapping the Process Name I to the function which results from evaluating the Process Expression E as if it were a function of $I_0, ... , I_n$ (its input Channels) and I_c (its Clock). This function is called the Process Function. Notice that the environment with which we evaluate the Process Function is empty, only its arguments may be used within the Process Expression. Process Function is supplied with its arguments via a Process Application which is similar to function application. For the merge Process above a Process Application could be

out = Merge_Process inp1, inp2

This defines the Channel out to be the result of applying the Merge_Process to the Channels inp1 and inp2. Although Merge_Process produces only one output Channel in general a Process will produce a tuple of output Channels. Using the semantic function $\mathcal{E}_a$ (Evaluate Process Application) we define the meaning of a Process Application. We need two definitions of $\mathcal{E}_a$ to cope with the fact that the Process Application may define a single Channel or a tuple of Channels.

$$\mathcal{E}_a : \text{PROC\_APP} \rightarrow \text{Clk} \rightarrow (\text{ID} \rightarrow \text{Val}) \rightarrow (\text{ID} \rightarrow \text{Val})$$

$$\mathcal{E}_a \, [O = I \, I_0, \ldots, I_m](\text{clk})(\rho) \qquad = [\, O \rightarrow \rho \, [I] \, (\, \rho \, [I_0], \ldots, \rho \, [I_m], \text{clk}) \,] \tag{1}$$

$$\mathcal{E}_a \, [O_0, \ldots, O_n = I \, I_0, \ldots, I_m](\text{clk})(\rho) = [\, O_0 \rightarrow ch_0 \,] \oplus \ldots \oplus [\, O_n \rightarrow ch_n \,] \tag{2}$$

where

$$ch_0 = select \, (\, \rho \, [I] \, (\, \rho \, [I_0], \ldots, \rho \, [I_m], \text{clk}), 0)$$

...

$$ch_n = select \, (\, \rho \, [I] \, (\, \rho \, [I_0], \ldots, \rho \, [I_m], \text{clk}), n)$$

The result of a Process Application is an environment mapping the output Channel names $O_0, \ldots, O_n$ to the tuple of Channels which results from applying the Process Function called I (in the given environment ρ) to the Channels called $I_0, \ldots, I_m$ (in ρ) and the Clock tree supplied to $\mathcal{E}_a$. This Clock is extracted from the input Clock to the whole system via the semantic function *extract*.

$$extract : \text{Clk} \times \text{N} \rightarrow \text{Clk}$$

$$extract = \lambda \, (\text{clk}, n). \; \underline{\textit{If}} \; n = 0 \; \underline{\textit{Then}} \; drop \, (left \, (\text{clk})) \; \underline{\textit{Else}} \; extract \, (drop \, (right \, (\text{clk})), n)$$

Thus for any $n \geq 0$ *extract* returns a unique sub-tree of the given Clock. We connect Process Applications together using the Configuration construct. For example a four way "don't care" merge could be defined

Configuration merge4
Output out
Input inp1, inp2, inp3, inp4
Is int1 = Merge_Process inp1, inp2 ;
  int2 = Merge_Process inp3, inp4 ;
  out = Merge_Process int1, int2 ;

Here we have a network of three Process Applications taking four Channels as input which the Configuration calls inp1, inp2, inp3 and inp4, and producing the Channel called out as output. Two internal Channels named int1 and int2 are used to carry the results of the merging inp1 with inp2 and inp3 with inp4 respectively. Each Channel is used as input to exactly one Process and is output from exactly one Process. Channel names which appear only on the left hand side of a Process Application denote output Channels from the Configuration and must also appear in the list of Channels following Output. Likewise Channel names which only appear on the right hand side of a Process Application denote input Channels to the Configuration and must appear in the list of names following Input. Conceptually the Configuration's input (resp. output) Channels are the output (resp. input) Channels of the external world. We use the semantic function $\mathcal{E}_c$ (Evaluate Configuration) to define the meaning of a Configuration.

$\mathcal{E}_c : \text{CONF} \rightarrow \text{Clk} \rightarrow (\text{Ch x. ..x Ch}) \rightarrow \text{Tp}$

$\mathcal{E}_c$ [Configuration I Output $O_0, \dots , O_m$ Input $I_0, \dots , I_n$ Is $PA_0; \dots ; PA_k;$] (clk)($ch_0, \dots , ch_n$)

$= < \rho [O_0], \dots , \rho [O_m] >$

where

$\rho = fix (\lambda \rho". \rho' \oplus \mathcal{E}_a [PA_0](\text{extract}(clk, 0))(\rho") \oplus \dots \oplus \mathcal{E}_a [PA_k](\text{extract}(clk, k))(\rho"))$

$\rho' = [I_0 \rightarrow ch_0] \oplus \dots \oplus [I_n \rightarrow ch_n]$

$fix = \lambda f. ((\lambda x. f (x (x))) (\lambda x. f (x (x))))$

We supply the Configuration with a Clock, clk and a set of input Channels $ch_0, \dots , ch_n$. The Channels are bound to the input identifiers $I_0, \dots , I_n$ in the initial environment ρ'. The result of the Configuration is the tuple of Channels mapped to by the output Channel names $O_0, \dots , O_m$ in the final environment ρ, which contains definitions for all the Channels named in the Configuration. To calculate ρ we start with ρ' which has definitions for all the input Channels. We can get definitions for all the other Channels by evaluating the Process Applications which define them. Each Process Application is supplied with a unique Clock taken from the input Clock by *extract*. The Process Applications also require an environment mapping in which all their input Channels are defined. Since the definitions of Channels used in the Process Applications may be mutually recursive (ie. the contents of Channel x may depend on Channel y which may itself depend on Channel x) the only environment containing this information is ρ. We use the function *fix* to return the environment which the fixed point of the function defining ρ. Effectively using *fix* allows us to say that ρ is the environment we would get from evaluating each of the Process Applications if we already knew the value of ρ. (For the theoretical background supporting *fix* see [14].) By using Configurations it is possible to define any network communicating Processes as a set of RUTH Process Applications connected via Channels.

5. CONCLUSIONS AND FURTHER WORK

Functional programming languages define a mapping between input data structures and output data structures with no consideration given to the particular method of execution being used to evaluate them. Unfortunately when considering real-time systems the method of execution (and many other operational details) become important because they effect the times at which particular calculations are carried out and thus the way in which the program will react to real- time events. The functional language RUTH handles such problems by taking real-time information as an input data structure, allowing programs written in RUTH to react to real-time events in a programmer defined way whilst still maintaining the property of referential transparency. Because of this programs written in RUTH may be reasoned about and transformed in much the same way as other functional languages.

A full denotational definition of RUTH exists as does an implementation of a subset of the language based on the LispKit SECD machine [8]. This implementation only allows single input Channel to single output Channel programs to be written and uses mark-sweep garbage collection instead of an incremental method more suited to real-time programming but is otherwise complete. At present I am engaged in defining a formal SECD machine based model to be used as a basis for the implementation of RUTH in OCCAM [10]. The combination of OCCAM and the Transputer is well suited to the implementation of both parallel computers and real-time systems and is thus ideal for the implementation of RUTH. It is hoped to configure a RUTH system across several Transputers and so examine the use of RUTH in the design and implementation of Distributed Operating Systems along the lines of the work done in [12]; a problem for which the functional style of programming seems very appropriate.

ACKNOWLEDGEMENTS

I would like to thank the referees for their helpful comments. I would also like to thank Simon Jones for making me write (and re-write) this paper and Simon Finn and Paul Williamson for many interesting discussions, some of which concerned this work.

REFERENCES

[1] "Automatic Control Systems Programming using a Real Time Declarative Language"
J.L. Bergarand, P. Caspi, N. Halhwachs and J.A. Plaice
From : IFAC / IFIP Symposium on Software for Computer Control {SOCOCO 86}
Graz (Austria) May 1986

[2] "Applicative Real-Time Programming"
M. Broy
Proceedings IFIP 1983.
North-Holland Information Processing 83.

[3] "Nondeterminism with referential transparency in Functional Programming Languages."
F.W. Burton
Department of Electrical Engineering and Computer Science - University of Colorado at Denver.

[4] "The Semantics of Lazy {and Industrious} Evaluation"
R. Cartwright and J. Donahue

Proceedings 1982 Symposium on Lisp and Functional Programming, Pittsburg USA

[5] "Arctic : A Functional Language for Real-Time Control"
R.B. Dannenberg
Proceedings 1984 Symposium on Lisp and Functional Programming, Austin, Texas USA.

[6] "Program Transformation"
J. Darlington
In :   Functional Programming and its Applications
        Eds. J. Darlington, P. Henderson and D.A. Turner
        Cambridge University Press 1982

[7] "Toward a Real-Time Dataflow Language"
A.A. Faustini and E.B. Lewis
IEEE Software. January 1986

[8] "The LispKit Manual"
P. Henderson, G.A. Jones and S.B. Jones
Oxford University Computing Laboratory, Programming Research Group Monograph 32

[9] "PFL : A Functional Language for Parallel Programming"
S. Holmstrom
Proceedings Declarative Programming Workshop
University College London 11-13th April 1983

[10] "OCCAM Programming Manual"
Inmos Ltd.
Prentice-Hall International Series in Computer Science 1984

[11] "Abstract Machine Support for Purely Functional Operating Systems"
S.B. Jones
University of Stirling Department of Computing Science, T.R.15

[12] "A Range of Operating Systems Written In A Purely Functional Style"
S.B. Jones
University of Stirling Department of Computing Science, T.R.16

[13] "On Real-Time Distributed Computing"
G. Le Lann
Proceedings IFIP 1983.
North-Holland Information Processing 83.

[14] "Denotational Semantics : The Scott-Strachey Approach to Programming Language Theory"
J. Stoy
MIT Press 1977

A COMPOSITIONAL PROOF THEORY FOR REAL-TIME DISTRIBUTED MESSAGE PASSING.

Jozef Hooman *

Department of Mathematics & Computing Science
Eindhoven University of Technology
P.O. box 513
5600 MB Eindhoven
The Netherlands

ABSTRACT

A compositional proof system is given for an OCCAM-like real-time programming language for distributed computing with communication via synchronous message passing. This proof system is based on specifications of processes which are independent of the program text of these processes. These specifications state (1) the assumptions of a process about the behaviour of its environment, and (2) the commitments of that process towards that environment provided these assumptions are met. The proof system is sound w.r.t a denotational semantics which incorporates assumptions regarding actions of the environment, thereby closely approximating the assumption/commitment style of reasoning on which the proof system is based. Concurrency is modelled as "maximal parallelism"; that is, if a process can proceed it will do so immediately. A process only waits when no local action is possible and no partner is available for communication. This maximality property is imposed on the domain of interpretation of assertions by postulating it as separate axiom. The timing behaviour of a system is expressed from the viewpoint of a global external observer, so there is a global notion of time. Time is not necessarily discrete.

1. INTRODUCTION

Recently attention has been drawn to the discrepancy between the growing number of real-time applications - industrial process control, telecommunication, life support systems in hospitals, avionics systems used for guidance and control, to mention but a few - and the existing theoretical background for such systems. For concurrency and hard time limits make the design and development of real-time embedded systems very complex, and certainly testing is not sufficient to validate a program. Also, in many real-time applications failure is very expensive and can have disastrous consequences. So, especially in this area of real-time systems, there is a growing need for formal specification and verification techniques in order to provide assistance in the "lost world" of real-time software development (see [Glass]).

The Esprit project DESCARTES provides a context for investigating these problems. A simple language is considered for capturing the essential features of real-time in the context of distributed message passing. It is based on CSP (Communicating Sequential Processes [Hoare]), a language for concurrent programs with communication via synchronous message-passing. Contrary to CSP, where communicating partners explicitly name each other, here communication occurs along unidirectional channels between pairs of processes. Added is the real-time statement *DELAY d*, which suspends the execution for the specified number of time units. Such a DELAY-statement may occur in the guard of an alternative command. Together with the underlying execution model this gives the opportunity to program a time-out. The execution model is that of *"maximal parallelism"*. That is, if a process can proceed it will do so immediately. A process only waits when no local action is possible and no partner is available for communication. As soon as an action becomes possible execution must proceed.

---

* supported by Esprit Project 937: Debugging and Specification of Ada Real-Time Embedded Systems (DESCARTES).
Electronic-mail address: mcvax!eutrc3!wsinjh.UUCP or wsdcjh@heithe5.BITNET .

New in this paper is a compositional Hoare-style proof system for safety properties of real-time distributed processes. The maximal parallelism constraint is modeled as an axiom for the domain of interpretation of assertions which may be used throughout the proof system. To obtain specifications of processes which are independent of their program text, Hoare triples are extended with invariants which should hold throughout program execution. This is needed in particular when specifying the communication and timing behaviour of nonterminating processes - the usual kind of processes when considering real-time - independent of their text. The invariants do not refer to any internal state of the process during execution.
What should be the form of such an invariant?

In general, the behaviour of a process depends on its environment; for instance on the values sent by the environment. Incorporating real-time makes this dependency even greater. The timing behaviour of a process will now also depend on the time at which the environment is ready to communicate, on how long a communication is enabled by the environment, etc. Consequently, knowledge about the environment is an important factor in the design of a real-time process. Therefore, we aim at *specifying processes within their environment*, and in the resulting specifications *the knowledge about that environment should be reflected by imposing suitable assumptions*.

To allow process behaviour to be specified relative to such assumptions, we adopt the assumption/commitment-style of reasoning as described in [ZBR,ZRE84]. Using this formalism, the invariant of a process in our specifications consists of two parts:
an *assumption* describing the expected behaviour of the environment, and
a *commitment* which is guaranteed by the process itself, as long as the environment does not violate the assumption.
When two processes are composed in parallel, we then have to verify that the assumptions of one process about joint communications correspond to the commitments of the other process for these joint communications.

How can we adapt this assumption/commitment based formalism to deal with real-time? In the formalism of [ZBR] an assumption describes the communication behaviour of a process. Note that the communication behaviour of environment and process is identical when restricting to joint communications, since a channel connects exactly two processes and communication is synchronous. This simple picture changes when dealing with real-time. In our proof system we must be able to make assumptions concerning "wait actions" of the environment, that is;
- when is the environment ready to start a communication, when does it start waiting,
- how long will the environment wait for a particular communication,
- when does the environment stop waiting for a communication.
Next observe that such wait actions concerning joint communications are different for environment and process. Consequently, we distinguish between wait actions of the process and wait actions of the environment. This distinction is reflected in the proof system as follows. The assumption of a process refers to the wait actions of the environment, whereas the commitment refers to the wait actions of that process itself.

In our semantics wait actions are represented by so called *wait records*, which denote the waiting period of a process for a communication. Because the assertions in the specification will refer to wait actions of the environment, *environment* wait records are included in the semantics too. By means of these environment records the maximal parallelism constraint is imposed on *every* element of the semantic domain by requiring that, for a particular channel, the waiting period denoted by a wait record does not overlap with the waiting period denoted by an environment wait record. Consequently, when processes are composed in parallel no explicit check on maximality is needed. At parallel composition we only have to check additionally that the assumptions made by one process concerning the wait records of the environment must be fulfilled by the other process as far as it concerns their joint channels.

The aim is a *compositional* proof system, that is, the specification of a composite construct should be verifiable in terms of the specifications of its syntactic constituents, without knowing the structure of these constituents. For the parallel composition of two processes the goal is, in principle, a simple conjunction of the commitments of their specifications. By incorporating environment wait records and imposing maximal parallelism as a separate axiom, we avoid a separate clause for checking maximal parallelism in the parallel composition rule.

The introduction of wait records raises the question whether it is possible to characterise real-time distributed message passing in a compositional fashion *without* such records. If termination, communication along channels, and the time communication takes place are the observables of a process, the answer to this question is no. Specifically, the full abstraction result of [HGR] implies that if wait records - or something equivalent - are not included in the denotational semantics, then it is possible to give two programs with the same semantics, but observably different behaviour. So, given our specific observables, without wait records the semantics would be unsound.

The semantics given in [KSRGA] served as starting point for our semantics, and it has been changed to come as close as possible to that of [ZRE]. The global notion of time used in [KSRGA] is maintained in our semantics. This is justified because we want to express the timing behaviour of a system from the viewpoint of a global external observer with his own clock. So, at the level of reasoning there is a conceptual global clock. New is that, in deviation of [KSRGA], time is not necessarily discrete.

This paper is structured as follows. Chapter 2 contains the syntax of the language considered and its intuitive semantics. In chapter 3 a denotational semantics is defined. The correctness formula and the assertion language are described in chapter 4. The main chapter is chapter 5, where a compositional proof system is given for our real-time programming language for distributed computing with communication via synchronous message passing. The conclusion can be found in chapter 6, together with a discussion of future work.

ACKNOWLEDGEMENTS

The author thanks the members of the EUT-team involved in Esprit project DESCARTES and Amir Pnueli for clarifying discussions. Especially Willem-Paul de Roever and Rob Gerth provided many useful comments and valuable advice; in fact they rewrote the paper after having been presented with my draft. All this, however, would have been of no use hadn't it been for the work of Job Zwiers on compositionality of proof systems for concurrent networks, and the insight in their intricacies which he shared with the author.

2. SYNTAX

In this chapter we give the syntax of a real-time programming language for distributed synchronous message-passing. Communication takes place through unidirectional channels which connect exactly two processes. There is a delay-statement, which may appear in the guard of an alternative statement, too. Such a delay-branch causes a time-out if no communications were offered during the delay period. We separate the concepts of parallel composition and hiding of internal communications by introducing an explicit hiding operator [..].

In the syntax below D will stand for a channel name, d and e for expressions, b for a boolean expression, and x for a program variable.

Language construction $L ::= S \mid N$

Statement $S ::= SKIP \mid x := e \mid IO \mid DELAY\ d \mid S_1; S_2 \mid [N] \mid A \mid *A$

Alternative $A ::= [\overset{n_1}{\underset{i=1}{\square}} b_i \rightarrow S_i \; \overset{n_2}{\underset{i=1}{\square}} b_i'; IO_i \rightarrow S_i' \; \overset{n_3}{\underset{i=1}{\square}} b_i''; DELAY\ d_i \rightarrow S_i'']$

Input/Output $IO ::= D!e \mid D?x$

Network $N ::= S_1 \parallel S_2$

A boolean expression b_i' or b_i'' is omitted if it is *TRUE*.

2.1 Informal semantics

- **SKIP**   skip: only affects the execution time.
- **x := e**   assignment: the value of expression e is assigned to the variable x.
- **D !e**   output: send the value of expression e through channel D; this action synchronizes with a corresponding input command.
- **D?x**   input: receive via channel D a value and assign this value to the variable x; this action synchronizes with a corresponding output command.
- **DELAY d**   delay: suspends the execution for (the value of) d time units. A delay statement with a negative value is equivalent to a delay statement with a zero value.
- **$S_1; S_2$**   sequential composition: execute S_2 after having executed S_1.
- **[N]**   hiding: the internal channels of network N are no longer visible.
- **A**   alternative: A guard is open if the boolean part evaluates to true. Following [KSRGA] we give priority to purely boolean guards. So if at least one of the b_i is true then select non-deterministically one of the open purely boolean guards and execute the corresponding branch. If none of the purely boolean guards is open and none of the other guards is open execution aborts. Otherwise, let *mindelay* be the minimum of the delay-values of the open delay-guards (infinite if there are no open delay-guards). If within *mindelay* time units at least one IO-command of the open IO-guards can be executed, select non-deterministically one of them and execute the guard and the corresponding branch. Otherwise, if no IO-guard can be taken within *mindelay* time units, one of the open delay-guards with delay value equal to *mindelay* is selected.
- ***A**   iteration: repeated execution of alternative A as long as at least one of the guards is open. When none of the guards is open execution terminates.
- **$S_1 \parallel S_2$** network: parallel execution of S_1 and S_2, based on the maximal parallelism model; no process ever waits unnecessarily, if execution can proceed it will do so immediately.

2.2 Syntactic restrictions

First some definitions:
var (L) denotes the program variables occurring in language construction L,
chan (L) denotes the set of visible channel names in language construction L, and
type (IO) denotes the channel of the IO-command.

ex. $chan(E!5; D?x \parallel D!2; F!3) = \{D, E, F\}$, and $chan([E!5; D?x \parallel D!2; F!3]) = \{E, F\}$. □

In a network $S_1 \parallel S_2$ the concurrent processes S_1 and S_2 are not allowed to have shared variables. Thus $var(S_1) \cap var(S_2) = \emptyset$. Furthermore it is required that S_1 and S_2 do not have joint input channels or joint output channels. So the joint channels of $S_1 \parallel S_2$, i.e. $chan(S_1) \cap chan(S_2)$, are exactly those channels through which S_1 and S_2 may communicate with each other.

Throughout this paper we use $\equiv$ to denote syntactic equality.

3. SEMANTICS

In [KSRGA] a denotational semantics has been given for CSP-R, a language similar to that of the previous chapter but with communication by means of process naming instead of channels. That semantics is based on the linear history semantics for CSP of [FLP]. The basic domain consists of non-empty prefix-closed sets of pairs of states and (finite) histories. To characterise maximal parallelism, such a history contains besides "communication records", which denote actual communications, also "no-match records" to denote that a process is waiting for a communication. Furthermore, the length of a trace represents the time. In view of the desired proof system, which should be based on the assumption/commitment type of correctness formula from [ZBR,ZRE84], we reformulate this semantics. The new semantics should be as close as possible to the semantics described in [ZRE], which is formulated in terms of trace-state pairs, where a *trace* is defined as a sequence of communication records only.

We extend a trace-state pair to a 5-tuple, consisting of components for the communication trace, the set of wait records of the process, the set of wait records of the environment, the state and the time. *Wait records* denote the waiting of a process for a communication. In our proof system we want to express assumptions concerning wait actions of the environment, so the semantics contains also a set of *environment* wait records. These environment wait records are used to model maximal parallelism, by requiring that for every tuple in the semantic domain the set of wait records and the set of environment wait records satisfy this maximality constraint. That is, for a particular channel there is no overlap of the waiting periods denoted by a wait record and an environment wait record.
We take the same global notion of time as in [KSRGA]; however, we do not assume discreteness of time.

In the next section we describe 5-tuples, which form the basis of our semantic domain of denotations. In section 3.2 an ordering on these tuples is defined, which is used for a formal definition of correctness formulae in chapter 4, and which is needed to obtain, in section 3.3, a complete partial order as domain of denotations. Finally, the particular function defining the semantics is given in section 3.4.

3.1 Our basic 5-tuples

In this section we define our basic 5-tuples, which form the basis of the semantic domain.
Assume a given time domain $TIME$, and a domain VAL for values of identifiers. To avoid an elaborate distinction between the types $TIME$ and VAL, e.g. the distinction between $TIME$-expressions and VAL-expressions, we choose VAL such that $VAL = TIME$. Furthermore we assume that VAL contains the nonnegative integers, and $v+w$, $v<w$, $v=w$ are defined in VAL.
The basic domain of denotations for the semantics of a process consists of sets of tuples $(\tau,W,W^e,\sigma,\alpha)$, where:

- τ is a communication trace; a sequence of <u>communication records</u> (t,D,v), with $t \in TIME$, D a channel name and $v \in VAL$. Informal meaning: at time t a communication via channel D starts and v is the communicated value.

- W is a set of <u>wait records</u> of that process; a wait record has the form (l,u,D), with $l,u \in TIME$ and D a channel name. Informal meaning: wait from time l up to time u for a communication via channel D.

- W^e is a set of wait records of the *environment*.

- σ is a state; a mapping from identifiers to values ($\sigma \in STATE$) or $\perp$, indicating an unfinished computation.

- $\alpha \in TIME \cup \{\perp\}$.

Such a 5-tuple indicates a "point" in a computation, i.e., it reflects the state of affairs in a computation at a certain point of time.
A tuple $(\tau,W,W^e,\sigma,\alpha)$ with $\sigma \neq \perp$, $\alpha \neq \perp$ models a finished computation, which terminates at time α in state σ, with trace τ and set of wait records W produced during the computation. W^e represents the assumption about the wait actions performed by the environment up to and including termination time α.
Tuples $(\tau,W,W^e,\sigma,\alpha)$ with $\sigma = \perp$ and $\alpha = \perp$, modeling unfinished computations, are needed to obtain prefix closed sets of 5-tuples, and to model infinite computations through an infinite chain of approximations.

3.2 Ordering on tuples

In this section we extend the usual prefix ordering for sequences to our 5-tuples.
In the sequel s will stand for the tuple $(\tau, W, W^e, \sigma, \alpha)$, and similar $s' = (\tau', W', W^{e'}, \sigma', \alpha')$, $\hat{s} = (\hat{\tau}, \hat{W}, \hat{W}^e, \hat{\sigma}, \hat{\alpha})$, etc.

The ordering $\leqslant$ on tuples is defined as follows: $s' \leqslant s$ denotes that either $s' = s$, or s' precedes s in a computation. In the latter case, s' represents an unfinished computation at a certain point of time, say $\hat{\alpha}$. Then $\sigma' = \perp$, $\alpha' = \perp$ and τ', W' and $W^{e'}$ are the *restriction* of τ, W and W^e, resp., to $\hat{\alpha}$, or s' denotes the initial tuple of a computation $(<>, \varnothing, \varnothing, \perp, \perp)$
($<>$ denotes the empty trace).

To formalise this, define the restriction, $\tau \downarrow \alpha$, of a trace τ to a time α as the initial prefix of τ for which the following holds: $(t, D, v) \in \tau \downarrow \alpha \ \rightleftarrows \ (t; D, v) \in \tau \ \wedge \ t \leqslant \alpha$.
The restriction, $W \downarrow \alpha$, of a set of wait records W to time α is defined as follows:
$W \downarrow \alpha = \{ (l, u, D) \in W \mid u \leqslant \alpha \}$.
Then the ordering on tuples, $s' \leqslant s$, is defined by
$s' = s \ \vee \ (\alpha' = \perp \ \wedge \ \sigma' = \perp \ \wedge \ \exists \hat{\alpha} (\ \tau' = \tau \downarrow \hat{\alpha} \ \wedge \ W' = W \downarrow \hat{\alpha} \ \wedge \ W^{e'} = W^e \downarrow \hat{\alpha} \ )) \ \vee$
$s' = (<>, \varnothing, \varnothing, \perp, \perp)$.

3.3 Domain of denotations

In this section the tuples and their ordering are used to define the semantic domain of denotations. (We assume the reader to be familiar with complete partial orderings, see [deB].)
This semantic domain $I\!D$ is restricted to those tuples that satisfy the **maximal parallelism constraint**, that is, never two processes both wait for the same communication. For the wait records in a tuple s this means that W and W^e never contain wait records for the same communication that overlap in time. Let $[..,..>$ denote a left closed, right open interval, and let W and W' be sets of wait records. Then we formulate this constraint as follows:

$MP(W, W') \ \rightleftarrows \ \forall (l, u, D) \in W \ \forall (l', u', D) \in W' : [l, u> \ \cap \ [l', u'> \ = \ \varnothing$.

Furthermore, traces occurring in tuples of the semantic domain will always be *time-ordered* :
for a trace τ, predicate *time$-$ordered* (τ) is true iff the sequence of time stamps in the records of τ is non decreasing. So in the sequel we restrict us to the following set of tuples:

$I\!B = \{(\tau, W, W^e, \sigma, \alpha) \mid MP(W, W^e) \wedge time-ordered(\tau)\}$.

Let U be a set of tuples. The prefix closure of U is defined as $\mathbf{PFC}(U) = \{ s' \mid s' \leqslant s , s \in U \}$. U is called prefix closed iff $PFC(U) = U$.

The basic domain of denotations is the set of all nonempty, prefix closed subsets of $I\!B$
$I\!D = \{D \mid D \subseteq I\!B \ \wedge \ D \neq \varnothing \ \wedge \ PFC(D) = D\}$. Then $(I\!D, \subseteq)$ is a complete partial order, with the singleton set $\{(<>, \varnothing, \varnothing, \perp, \perp)\}$ as least element.

3.4 The function defining the semantics

Finally the particular function defining the semantics is given.
Assume a function T has been given, which assigns to every *atomic* statement S (i.e. skip, assignment, io, delay) and state σ an interval $T_\sigma(S)$, such that the execution time of this statement in this state is an element of the given interval. For the alternative statement A $T_\sigma(A)$ denotes the overhead needed to execute this statement (e.g. evaluation of boolean guards, selection of an open guard, etc.). We assume that there is no overhead for the other composite constructs.
Assume the existence of semantic functions $[\![..]\!]$ for VAL expressions e and boolean expressions b : $[\![e]\!]\sigma$, $[\![b]\!]\sigma$.

Let $WAIT = \{(l, u, D) \mid l, u \in TIME, l \leqslant u\}$ and
$WAIT_t = \{(l, u, D) \in WAIT \mid u \leqslant t\}$, for $t \in TIME$.

The variant of a state $\sigma \neq \perp$, $\sigma[^v\!/\!_x]$, is defined as $\begin{cases} \sigma[^v\!/\!_x](x) = v \\ \sigma[^v\!/\!_x](y) = \sigma(y) , \text{ if } y \not\equiv x. \end{cases}$

The semantics is now defined as a function M which maps a language construction L, given an initial state ($\neq \perp$) and starting time, to an element of D: $M : L \rightarrow (STATE \times TIME \rightarrow D)$.

skip

The semantics of the *skip* statement shows that the time component is updated with the execution time of this statement; all possible execution times between the bounds given by the T-function are included. Furthermore the environment may add a set of wait records E. Again all possibilities are included with the restriction that the upper bound of these records should be less then or equal to the termination time, i.e. $\alpha+t$. When processes are composed in parallel it is checked that for joint communications the set of environment wait records of one process equals the actual wait records of the other process.

$$M(SKIP)(\sigma, \alpha) = PFC(\{(<>, \varnothing, E, \sigma, \alpha+t) \mid E \subseteq WAIT_{\alpha+t} \wedge t \in T_\sigma(SKIP)\})$$

assignment

The *assignment* statement has a similar semantics, now also the state is updated.

$$M(x := e)(\sigma, \alpha) = PFC(\{(<>, \varnothing, E, \sigma[\llbracket e \rrbracket \sigma /_x], \alpha+t) \mid E \subseteq WAIT_{\alpha+t} \wedge t \in T_\sigma(x := e)\})$$

delay

The *delay* statement updates the time component α with the specified time given by the T-function. This T-function should be such that $t \in T_\sigma(DELAY\ d)$ implies $t \geqslant \llbracket d \rrbracket \sigma$. Since a negative delay value yields a zero delay, the function *nonneg*, defined below, is applied to the delay value;

$$nonneg(v) = \begin{cases} 0 & \text{if } v < 0, \\ v & \text{if } v \geqslant 0. \end{cases}$$

$$M(DELAY\ d)(\sigma, \alpha) = PFC(\{(<>, \varnothing, E, \sigma, \alpha+nonneg(t)) \mid$$
$$E \subseteq WAIT_{\alpha+nonneg(t)} \wedge t \in T_\sigma(DELAY\ d)\})$$

output

For the *output* command we include a communication record in the semantics. Assume the process has to wait w time units, then the actual communication starts at point of time $\alpha+w$.
Waiting for w time units is denoted by wait record $(\alpha, \alpha+w, D)$. Since waiting time w depends on the other process, we take all possible values for w.
The maximal parallelism constraint imposes a restriction on the wait records of the environment. These environment wait records must not overlap with the just added wait record of the process itself, so these overlapping records are excluded.

$$M(D!e)(\sigma, \alpha) = PFC(\{(<(\alpha+w, D, \llbracket e \rrbracket \sigma)>, \{(\alpha, \alpha+w, D)\}, E, \sigma, \alpha+w+t) \mid$$
$$w \in TIME \wedge w \geqslant 0 \wedge t \in T_\sigma(D!e) \wedge$$
$$E \subseteq WAIT_{\alpha+w+t} \wedge MP(E, \{(\alpha, \alpha+w, D)\})\})$$

input

The semantics of the *input* statement is similar to the output command, now the value received is not known, and we include all possible values. Again environment wait records which overlap with the waiting time are excluded.

$$M(D?x)(\sigma, \alpha) = PFC(\{(<(\alpha+w, D, v)>, \{(\alpha, \alpha+w, D)\}, E, \sigma[v/_x], \alpha+w+t) \mid$$
$$w \in TIME \wedge w \geqslant 0 \wedge v \in VAL \wedge t \in T_\sigma(D?x) \wedge$$
$$E \subseteq WAIT_{\alpha+w+t} \wedge MP(E, \{(\alpha, \alpha+w, D)\})\})$$

sequential composition

In order to define the semantics of sequential composition, the semantic function is extended to initial tuples by defining $\overline{M(L)} : \{s \in B \mid \sigma \neq \perp\} \rightarrow D$.
First the *concatenation* of two tuples s_1 and s_2 is defined by
$$s_1 s_2 = (\tau_1 \tau_2, W_1 \cup W_2, W_1^e \cup W_2^e, \sigma_2, \alpha_2).$$
Then $\overline{M(L)}\hat{s} = \{\hat{s}s \mid s \in M(L)(\hat{\sigma}, \hat{\alpha}) \wedge MP(W^e, \hat{W}) \wedge MP(\hat{W}^e, W)\}$. Note that there is an explicit check to guarantee that the concatenation satisfies the maximal parallelism constraint.

Define the extension of a function $X : STATE \times TIME \to I\!D$ to a set $U \in I\!D$, $X^* : I\!D \to I\!D$:
$X^*(U) = \{ s \mid \exists s_u : s_u \in U \wedge \sigma_u \neq \bot \wedge s \in \overline{X} s_u \} \cup \{ s_u \mid s_u \in U \wedge \sigma_u = \bot \}$. Then

$$M(S_1 ; S_2)(\hat{\sigma}, \hat{\alpha}) = M(S_2)^*(M(S_1)(\hat{\sigma}, \hat{\alpha}))$$

hiding

Hiding of internal communications just means the projection on external channels:

$$M([N])(\sigma, \alpha) = [M(N)(\sigma, \alpha)]_{chan([N])}$$

with for $U \in I\!D$ projection on a set *cset* is defined as follows:

$$[U]_{cset} = \{ ([\tau]_{cset}, [W]_{cset}, [W^e]_{cset}, \sigma, \alpha) \mid (\tau, W, W^e, \sigma, \alpha) \in U \} \text{ where}$$

$[\tau]_{cset}$ denotes the restriction of τ to records with channel name in *cset*, and

$$[A]_{cset} = \{ (l, u, D) \mid (l, u, D) \in A \wedge D \in cset \}, \text{ for } A \subseteq WAIT.$$

alternative

For the semantics of the *alternative* construction consider two cases:

- at least one of the purely boolean guards is true; then, because of priority for these branches, take the union of the semantics of all branches with a true purely boolean guard.
- none of the purely boolean guards is true:
  - if a communication is possible before the minimal delay period has elapsed, include the usual communication record and wait records for all open i/o-guards.
  - take one of the open delay branches with minimal delay if there was no communication available for the open communication guards within this delay period. This last restriction is denoted by wait records for the channels of open i/o-guards, with interval length equal to the minimal delay period.

Again the wait records of the environment are restricted in order to satisfy the maximal parallelism constraint.

Let $A \equiv [\overset{n_1}{\underset{i=1}{\Box}} b_i \to S_i \ \overset{n_2}{\underset{i=1}{\Box}} b_i' ; IO_i \to S_i' \overset{n_3}{\underset{i=1}{\Box}} b_i'' ; DELAY \ d_i \to S_i'']$, define

$mindelay = min\{ nonneg([d_i]\sigma) \mid [b_i'']\sigma \} \quad (min(\varnothing) = \infty)$

$ioset = \{ type(IO_i) \mid [b_i']\sigma \}$ and abbreviate $\{(l, u, cset)\} = \{ (l, u, D) \mid D \in cset \}$.

$M(A)(\sigma, \alpha) =$

$\overset{n_1}{\underset{i=1}{\bigcup}} \{ M(S_i)(\sigma, \alpha + t) \mid [b_i]\sigma \wedge t \in T_\sigma(A) \}$, if $\overset{n_1}{\underset{i=1}{\bigvee}} [b_i]\sigma$, and otherwise

$\overset{n_2}{\underset{i=1}{\bigcup}} M(S_i')^*(PFC\{(<(\alpha + t + w, D, v)>, \{(\alpha + t, \alpha + t + w, ioset)\}, E, \overline{\sigma}, \alpha + t + w + t') \mid$

$\qquad [b_i']\sigma \wedge t \in T_\sigma(A) \wedge t' \in T_\sigma(D!e) \wedge w \in TIME \wedge 0 \leqslant w < mindelay \wedge$

$\qquad E \subseteq WAIT_{\alpha + t + w + t'} \wedge MP(E, \{(\alpha + t, \alpha + t + w, ioset)\}) \wedge$

$\qquad \begin{cases} IO_i \equiv D!e \to v = [e]\sigma \wedge \overline{\sigma} = \sigma \\ IO_i \equiv D?x \to v \in VAL \wedge \overline{\sigma} = \sigma[^v/_x] \end{cases} \})$

$\cup \overset{n_3}{\underset{i=1}{\bigcup}} M(S_i'')^*(PFC\{(<>, \{(\alpha + t, \alpha + t + mindelay, ioset)\}, E, \sigma, \alpha + t + nonneg(t')) \mid [b_i'']\sigma \wedge$

$\qquad nonneg([d_i]\sigma) = mindelay \wedge t \in T_\sigma(A) \wedge t' \in T_\sigma(DELAY \ d_i) \wedge$

$\qquad E \subseteq WAIT_{\alpha + t + nonneg(t')} \wedge MP(E, \{(\alpha + t, \alpha + t + mindelay, ioset)\}) \})$

iteration

The semantics of the *iteration* statement is defined by the following fixed point equation:

$$M(*A) = \mu(\lambda_X \cdot \lambda_{\sigma,\alpha}. \text{ if } \bigvee_{i=1}^{n_1} [\![b_i]\!]\sigma \ \vee \ \bigvee_{i=1}^{n_2} [\![b_i{}']\!]\sigma \ \vee \ \bigvee_{i=1}^{n_3} [\![b_i{}'']\!]\sigma \quad \text{then } X^*(M(A)(\sigma,\alpha))$$

$$\text{else} \quad PFC\{(<>,\varnothing,E,\sigma,\alpha+t) \mid E \subseteq WAIT_{\alpha+t} \ \wedge \ t \in T_\sigma(A)\}),$$

with μ the least fixed point operator.

parallel composition

In the semantics of the *parallel composition* $S_1 \| S_2$ it is checked that assumptions made by one process concerning the wait records of the environment must be fulfilled by the other process as far as it concerns joint communications.

A trace of $S_1 \| S_2$ is a merge of traces from S_1 and S_2, that is, projected on the channels of S_i it should yield a trace of S_i (for $i = 1,2$), and it should not contain other channels than those of S_1 and S_2.

Let $jchan = chan(S_1) \cap chan(S_2)$ and define $max(\alpha_1,\alpha_2) = \bot$ if $\alpha_1 = \bot \ \vee \ \alpha_2 = \bot$.

$$M(S_1 \| S_2)(\hat{\sigma},\hat{\alpha}) = \{(\tau, W_1 \cup W_2, W_1^e \cup W_2^e - [W_1^e \cup W_2^e]_{jchan}, \sigma, max(\alpha_1,\alpha_2)) \mid$$

$$(\tau_i, W_i, W_i^e, \sigma_i, \alpha_i) \in M(S_i)(\hat{\sigma},\hat{\alpha}) \wedge i \in \{1,2\} \wedge [\tau]_{chan(S_i)} = \tau_i \ \wedge$$

$$(D \notin chan(S_1,S_2) \rightarrow [\tau]_D = <>) \wedge time-ordered(\tau) \wedge$$

$$[W_1]_{jchan} = [W_2^e]_{jchan} \wedge [W_2]_{jchan} = [W_1^e]_{jchan} \wedge$$

$$(\sigma_1 \neq \bot \ \wedge \ \sigma_2 \neq \bot \ \rightarrow \ \sigma(x) = \begin{cases} \sigma_i(x) & , x \in var(S_i) \\ \hat{\sigma}(x) & , x \notin var(S_1,S_2) \end{cases}) \wedge$$

$$(\sigma_1 = \bot \ \vee \ \sigma_2 = \bot \ \rightarrow \ \sigma = \bot)\}$$

4. SPECIFICATION LANGUAGE

In this chapter our specification language is defined. First we give an informal introduction to correctness formulae in section 4.1. Section 4.2 lists a number of expressions from the assertion language. The examples of section 4.3 should give an impression of the type of specifications intended. Restrictions on assertions are formulated in section 4.4. Section 4.5 concerns the validity of assertions and correctness formulae.

4.1 Correctness formulae

In this section the correctness formulae used in the proof system are introduced. Our aim is a compositional proof theory for safety properties, in which it is possible to specify the behaviour of a process relative to assumptions about the behaviour of its environment. Therefore we extend Hoare triples with two parts, an

- **assumption** specifying the expected communication behaviour of the environment (the waiting for a communication included), and a
- **commitment**, which is guaranteed to hold by the process itself, as long as the assumption concerning earlier behaviour has not been violated by the environment.

Important is that assumption and commitment reflect, respectively, the externally visible behaviours of environment and process. That is, they refer to a communication trace of externally visible channels and to wait records concerning these channels. Consequently, assumption and commitment must not contain program variables or internal channels. Clearly the assumption refers to *environment* wait records, whereas the commitment refers to wait records of the process itself. In addition we require that assumption and commitment do not refer to the time component.

We use the following notation: $(A,C) : \{p\} \, L \, \{q\}$, meaning informally:

assume that p holds for the initial tuple (in $I\!B$) in which L starts executing, then:

(1) C holds for the initial tuple of L,

(2) C holds after every communication and wait action of L, provided A held after all communications and wait actions of L before this particular one,

(3) q holds for the final tuple if and when L terminates, provided A held after all communications and wait actions of L, up to and including the moment of termination.

Observe that the coupling between A and C is checked whenever the set of wait records or the trace of L changes. This is justified, since A and C do not refer to the program variables or to the time component. Furthermore, assertions are restricted (see section 4.4) such that their validity is not changed by adding *environment* wait records.

4.2 Assertion language

In this section we list a number of expressions from the assertion language. A complete syntax is given in [H].

In our assertions it is possible to refer to the components of a tuple; to the

- trace of communication records by π,
- set of wait records by W,
- set of environment wait records by W^e,
- program variables,
- time component by means of the special variable *time*.

$[\pi]_{cset}$ denotes the **projection** of the trace π on a set of channel names *cset*, and is defined as the maximal subtrace of π with channel names in *cset* (in the sequel denoted as π_{cset}).

$[W]_{cset}$ denotes the maximal subset of W with channel names in *cset* (denoted as W_{cset}). Similar for $[W^e]_{cset}$. We often omit brackets and commas in *cset*, e.g. W_D, π_{BD}.

Similar $[te]_{cset}$ denotes the projection of a trace expression *te* (i.e. an expression denoting a trace) on a set of channel names *cset*.

In the sequel assertions are restricted to those where π, W and W^e occur only *projected*, that is, within the scope of a projection $[...]_{cset}$. The precise restrictions on the assertion language are formulated in section 4.4.

Because a trace is a sequence of records, we use an index to refer to a particular record, e.g. $\pi_B[i]$ refers to the i-th communication record in trace projection π_B.

Furthermore, we can select the fields of a communication record:

- *tim* selects the time stamp,
- *comm* selects the channel name, and
- *val* selects the communicated value.

$|te|$ denotes the length of a trace expression *te*.

In assertions we use <u>logical variables</u> to relate assumption, commitment, precondition and postcondition. These variables do not occur in the program text, so the value they denote is not affected by program execution. Quantification is only allowed over logical variables.

In order to apply correct substitutions distinguish between three types of logical variables:

- logical trace variables : t,
- logical wait variables : w, and
- logical *VAL* variables : v.

Let $var(p)$ be the set of <u>program</u> variables occurring in assertion p,

and $chan(p)$ is defined as the set of channel names occurring in projections. Remember that we restrict us to assertions in which π, W and W^e only occur projected.

To denote that a trace expression te_1 is an <u>initial prefix</u> of trace expression te_2, we use the abbreviation $te_1 \leqslant te_2$, defined as follows: $\exists t : te_1 \hat{\ } t = te_2$.

4.3 Examples of specifications

The examples below should give an impression of the type of specifications intended.

ex. 1 Take the following T-function: $T(x := x + 1) = [3,4]$, $T(IO) = [1.5, 3.5]$. Then

$$(TRUE, TRUE): \{time = v\} \, B?x \, ; \, x := x+1 \, ; \, D!x \, \{time - v \in [6,11]\} \qquad \square$$

Assume for the following examples: $T(DELAY \ d) = [d, d]$, $T(IO) = [1,1]$, and $T(A) = [1,1]$.

ex. 2 Consider the following informal specification:

$(environment \ waits \ for \ the \ first \ comm. \ via \ D \ from \ time \ 2 \ up \ to \ the \ actual \ comm. , TRUE):$
$\{execution \ starts \ at \ time \ 0 \ and \ the \ trace \ of \ channel \ D \ is \ initially \ empty\}$
DELAY 5 ; D!3
$\{termination \ at \ time \ 6\}.$

This can be expressed formally as follows:

$$(\pi_D \neq <> \ \rightarrow \ (2, tim(\pi_D[1]), D) \in W_D^e, TRUE):$$
$$\{time = 0 \ \wedge \ \pi_D = <>\} \ \textbf{DELAY 5 ; D!3} \ \{time = 6\}. \qquad \square$$

ex. 3 The correctness formula below contains an informal assumption:

$(the \ environment \ does \ not \ communicate \ via \ channel \ D \ in \ time \ interval \ [1,6], TRUE):$
$\{\pi_D = <> \ \wedge \ time = 0\} \ [\textbf{DELAY 5} \rightarrow x := 5 \ \square \ \textbf{D!3} \rightarrow x := 6] \{x = 5\}.$

This assumption can be formalised as follows: $|\pi_D| \geqslant 1 \ \rightarrow \ tim(\pi_D[1]) \notin [1,6].$ $\qquad \square$

ex. 4 This example demonstrates how two concurrent processes mutually make assumptions about the waiting period for a communication of the other. Consider assumption

$A_1 \equiv (|\pi_D| \geqslant 1 \ \rightarrow \ (2, tim(\pi_D[1]), D) \in W_D^e) \ \wedge \ (|\pi_D| \geqslant 2 \ \rightarrow \ (13, tim(\pi_D[2]), D) \in W_D^e)$

and commitment

$C_1 \equiv (|\pi_D| \geqslant 1 \ \rightarrow \ (5, tim(\pi_D[1]), D) \in W_D) \ \wedge \ (|\pi_D| \geqslant 2 \ \rightarrow \ (8, tim(\pi_D[2]), D) \in W_D)$

then

$$(A_1, C_1): \{\pi_D = <> \ \wedge \ time = 0\} \ S_1 \equiv \textbf{DELAY 5 ; D!3 ; DELAY 2 ; D!6} \ \{time = 14\}.$$

Note that the commitment C_1 of this process expresses that the waiting period for the second D-communication starts at time 8, which depends on the assumption in A_1 about when the first D-communication of the environment is enabled.

The second concurrent process has an "inverted" assumption/commitment pair,

let $A_2 \equiv C_1[^{W^e}/w]$ and $C_2 \equiv A_1[^W/w^e]$ then

$$(A_2, C_2): \{\pi_D = <> \ \wedge \ time = 0\} \ S_2 \equiv \textbf{DELAY 2 ; D?x ; DELAY 7 ; D?x} \ \{time = 14\}.$$

Note that the assumption of one process is justified by the commitment of the other. Then the parallel composition rule will allow us to derive:

$$(TRUE, TRUE): \{\pi_D = <> \ \wedge \ time = 0\} \ S_1 \| S_2 \ \{time = 14\}. \qquad \square$$

4.4 Restrictions on the assertion language

For a correctness formula $(A, C): \{p\} \ L \ \{q\}$ the following restrictions are imposed upon the assertions A, C, p and q:

- $var(A, C) = \emptyset$; program variables must not occur in A and C, since A and C should express the communication interface only.
- W does not occur in A; an assumption must only mention the wait records of the environment and the trace.
- W^e does not occur in C; a commitment must only mention the wait records of the process itself and the trace.
- the special variable *time* does not occur in A and C.

By imposing this constraint (and the first restriction), the validity of A and C depends on the trace and the wait records only, and not on the time component. Consequently, we have to check preservation of the validity of A and C, and their coupling, only after an occurrence of a communication or wait action, and not when merely time passes. Future research will investigate the consequences of allowing the special variable *time* to occur in A and C.

- π, W and W^e must occur *projected*, that is within the scope of a projection $[..]_{cset}$.
- W^e is allowed in p and q, but all assertions must be <u>monotone</u> in W^e:
  an assertion p is called *monotone in* W^e iff $p \rightarrow \forall E \subseteq WAIT : p^{[W^e \cup E/_{W^e}]}$.
  That is, the validity of p is not changed by adding environment wait records.
  Also assumption A must be monotone in W^e.
  <u>example</u> The following assertions are not monotone:
  $W_D^e = \varnothing$, $\quad (5,7,B) \notin W_B^e$, $\quad W_D^e \subseteq \{(0,5,D),(9,10,D)\}$.
  Examples of monotone assertions:
  $W_D^e \neq \varnothing$, $\quad (5,7,B) \in W_B^e$, $\quad W_D^e \supseteq \{(0,5,D),(9,10,D)\}$.
  □

4.5 *Validity of assertions and correctness formulae*

This section concerns the interpretation of the assertion language and a formal definition of correctness formulae. An assertion p is interpreted in a logical variable environment γ, which assigns values to logical variables, and a tuple $s = (\tau, W, W^e, \sigma, \alpha) \in I\!B$, notation: $[\![p]\!]\gamma s$.
If p contains free program variables $(var(p) \neq \varnothing)$ or the special variable *time*, then p is only interpreted in tuples s with $\sigma \neq \bot$ and $\alpha \neq \bot$.

An assertion p is called <u>valid,</u> denoted by $\models p$, iff $\forall \gamma \forall s \in I\!B : \sigma \neq \bot \wedge \alpha \neq \bot \rightarrow [\![p]\!]\gamma s$.

For the formal interpretation of a correctness formula we need the $<$ relation on tuples, defined as: $s' < s \rightleftharpoons s' \leqslant s \wedge (\tau' \neq \tau \vee W' \neq W)$.

<u>Notation:</u> $\hat{s}_\bot = (\hat{\tau}, \hat{W}, \hat{W}^e, \bot, \bot)$.

Now a correctness formula is called <u>valid,</u> denoted by $\models (A,C) : \{p\} L \{q\}$, iff

$$\forall \gamma \forall \hat{s} \in I\!B, \hat{\sigma} \neq \bot, \hat{\alpha} \neq \bot : [\![p]\!]\gamma \hat{s} \rightarrow \forall s \in \overline{M(L)}\hat{s} : (\forall s'(\hat{s}_\bot \leqslant s' < s \rightarrow [\![A]\!]\gamma s') \rightarrow [\![C]\!]\gamma s) \wedge$$

$$(\sigma \neq \bot \rightarrow (\forall s'(\hat{s}_\bot \leqslant s' \leqslant s \rightarrow [\![A]\!]\gamma s') \rightarrow [\![q]\!]\gamma s)).$$

5. PROOF SYSTEM

Important in the proof system, which will be formulated in this chapter, is how we deal with maximal parallelism. In the assertion language the **maximal parallelism constraint** is formulated as follows:

(MP) $\qquad \forall v_1 v_2 v_3 v_4 : (v_1,v_2,D) \in W_D \wedge (v_3,v_4,D) \in W_D^e \rightarrow [v_1,v_2 > \cap [v_3,v_4 > = \varnothing$,

where D is a channel name, and v_1,v_2,v_3,v_4 are logical VAL variables.
Observe that it is allowed to use axiom scheme MP for every implication in the assertion language, since assertions are only interpreted in tuples from $I\!B$ (remember that every tuple in $I\!B$ satisfies the maximal parallelism constraint w.r.t. W and W^e (see chapter 3)).
<u>Conclusion:</u> Maximal parallelism is modeled as the axiom MP which is imposed on the domain of interpretation of assertions in our system. That is, this axiom can be used to prove implications between assertions, for instance, when applying the consequence rule.

The rules and axioms of our proof system are given in three groups. In section 5.1 the rules and axioms related to atomic statements of our language are presented, and in section 5.2, those related to composite constructs. In section 5.3 general axioms and rules related to all language constructions are given, and soundness of the system is stated (which is proved in the appendix of [H]). Section 5.5 contains an example demonstrating the use of assumptions and commitments in combination with parallel composition and hiding.

5.1 Rules and axioms for atomic statements

First we give rules and axioms for skip, assignment, delay and i/o-commands. These rules and axioms have in common that in order to prove $(A, C): \{p\} S \{q\}$ the implication $p \rightarrow C$ has to hold (C should hold initially). Following [ZRE84] these implications are avoided by proving $(A, C): \{p \wedge C\} S \{q \wedge C\}$.

For an arbitrary T-function the skip axiom would have the following form (note that *time* does not occur in C):

$$(A, C): \{\forall t \in T(SKIP): q [^{time + t}/_{time}] \wedge C\} \, SKIP \, \{q \wedge C\}$$

In order to avoid explicit mentioning of the T-function in every rule of the proof system we take one specific T-function. It represents assumptions about the execution time which are similar to those in [KSRGA], where atomic actions take one time unit, except for the *DELAY d* statement which takes exactly d time units. To be precise: in the sequel we adopt the following T-function:

$T(SKIP) = T(x := e) = T(D!e) = T(D?x) = T(A) = [1,1]$ (closed interval), and
$T(DELAY \, d) = [d, d]$.

skip

(skip) $(A, C): \{q [^{time + 1}/_{time}] \wedge C\} \, SKIP \, \{q \wedge C\}$

assignment

(assignment) $(A, C): \{q [^{time + 1}/_{time}, {}^e/_x] \wedge C\} \, x := e \, \{q \wedge C\}$

delay

Remember that a negative delay value yields a zero delay, so the function *nonneg* is applied, which is defined as follows: $nonneg(v) = \begin{cases} 0 & \text{if } v < 0, \\ v & \text{if } v \geq 0. \end{cases}$

(delay) $(A, C): \{q [^{time + nonneg(d)}/_{time}] \wedge C\} \, DELAY \, d \, \{q \wedge C\}$

output

For the output command we have to prove that given the precondition:
- commitment C holds for the final state (which is represented by the substitution), and
- the postcondition holds in the final state (also the time is updated), provided assumption A holds in the final state.

Note that in general we do not know the length of the waiting period for this communication, thus we have to prove commitment and postcondition for all possible wait values w.

Let $subst \equiv {}^{W \cup \{(time, time + w, D)\}}/_W, {}^{\pi^{\cdot}(time + w, D, e)}/_{\pi}$.

(output) $\dfrac{p \wedge C \rightarrow \forall w \in TIME, w \geq 0: C[subst] \wedge (A[subst] \rightarrow q[subst, {}^{time + w + 1}/_{time}])}{(A, C): \{p \wedge C\} D!e \{q \wedge C\}}$

As observed above, it is allowed to use axiom MP for every implication between assertions. This will be used in the following example, where assumption A is strong enough to determine the waiting period.

example We want to prove the following formula:

$$(A \equiv \pi_D \neq <> \rightarrow (7, tim(\pi_D[1]), D) \in W_D^e, C \equiv TRUE):$$

$$\{p \equiv \pi_D = <> \wedge time = 4\} \, D!3 \, \{time = 8\}.$$

First take the following auxiliary postcondition: $q \equiv (7, time - 1, D) \in W_D^e \wedge (4, time - 1, D) \in W_D$.

By using the output rule we can prove $(A, C): \{p\} D!e \{q\}$,

since $p \wedge C \wedge A[subst] \rightarrow (7, time + w, D) \in W_D^e \wedge time = 4$, and

$q[subst, {}^{time + w + 1}/_{time}] \rightleftharpoons (7, time + w, D) \in W_D^e \wedge (4, time + w, D) \in W_D \cup \{(time, time + w, D)\}$,

thus $p \wedge C \wedge A[subst] \rightarrow q[subst, {}^{time + w + 1}/_{time}]$, for all $w \in TIME, w \geq 0$.

By using the maximal parallelism axiom MP for channel D we can derive from the post condition q: $[7, time - 1 > \cap [4, time - 1 > = \emptyset$.

Since $l \leqslant u$ for a wait record $(l,u,...)$ we can derive: $time - 1 = 7$, and thus: $time = 8$.
Then the consequence rule, which will be formulated later, leads to the desired result.
□

input
The input rule has the same structure as the output rule. Since the received value is not known in general, we have to prove commitment and postcondition for all possible input values.
Let $subst \equiv {}^{W \cup \{(time, time+w, D)\}}/_W, {}^{\pi'(time+w, D, v)}/_{\pi}$.

(input)

$$\frac{p \wedge C \rightarrow \forall w \in TIME, w \geqslant 0 \; \forall v \in VAL : C[subst] \wedge (A[subst] \rightarrow q[subst, {}^{time+w+1}/_{time}, {}^{v}/_{x}])}{(A,C):\{p \wedge C\} D?x \{q \wedge C\}}$$

As we saw above, A may contain enough information to be more specific about the waiting period for the communication. In addition, A can specify the value that will be received by an input.

<u>example</u> Using the input rule, we can prove $(\pi_D \leqslant <(..,D,5)>, TRUE): \{\pi_D = <>\} D?x \{x = 5\}$.
□

5.2 Rules for composite constructs

Next we give rules for sequential composition, hiding, alternative, iteration and parallel composition. Since we give a *compositional* proof system, to each composite construct corresponds a rule in which a specification of the construct can be derived from its constituents without any further knowledge of the structure of these components (see [HdeR] for more details).

sequential composition

(sequential composition)
$$\frac{(A,C):\{p\}S_1\{r\}, \; (A,C):\{r\}S_2\{q\}}{(A,C):\{p\}S_1;S_2\{q\}}$$

hiding
The hiding rule allows us to encapsulate internal communications.

(hiding)
$$\frac{(A,C):\{p \wedge \pi_{jchan} = <> \wedge W_{jchan} = \varnothing\} S_1 \parallel S_2 \{q\}}{(A,C):\{p\}[S_1 \parallel S_2]\{q\}}$$

where $jchan = chan(S_1) \cap chan(S_2)$, and provided $chan(A,C,p,q) \cap jchan = \varnothing$.

alternative
For the alternative construct we have two rules; a consequence of purely boolean guards having priority.
Let $A \equiv [\; \overset{n_1}{\underset{i=1}{\square}} b_i \rightarrow S_i \; \overset{n_2}{\underset{i=1}{\square}} b_i';IO_i \rightarrow S_i' \; \overset{n_3}{\underset{i=1}{\square}} b_i'';DELAY \; d_i \rightarrow S_i'' \;]$.
The first rule is applied if one of the purely boolean guards evaluates to true.
Assertion $\bar{p}$ holds after the overhead required by the alternative statement (one time unit) and before execution of a S_i-branch.

(alt1)
$$\frac{p \rightarrow \bar{p}[{}^{time+1}/_{time}], \; (A,C):\{\bar{p} \wedge b_i\}S_i\{q\}, \; i=1,..,n_1}{(A,C):\{p \wedge \overset{n_1}{\underset{i=1}{\bigvee}} b_i\} A \{q\}}$$

In the second rule none of the purely boolean guards is true. In order to define the minimal delay period and the set of "open" IO-guards, we have to know which booleans are true. So we have to guess the set of true boolean guards:
S is the set of indices i such that b_i' is true, and T is the set of indices i such that b_i'' is true.
Define for sets $S \subseteq \{1,...,n_2\}$ and $T \subseteq \{1,...,n_3\}$:
$mindelay = min\{ nonneg(d_i) \mid i \in T\}$, $(min(\varnothing) = \infty)$
$ioset = \{ type(IO_i) \mid i \in S\}$, and abbreviate $\{(l,u,cset)\} = \{ (l,u,D) \mid D \in cset \}$.
Expression $B_{S,T}$ checks the guess, represented by S and T, for booleans:
let $S^c = \{i \mid i \notin S \wedge 1 \leqslant i \leqslant n_2\}$ and $T^c = \{i \mid i \notin T \wedge 1 \leqslant i \leqslant n_3\}$ then

$$B_{S,T} \equiv \bigwedge_{k \in S} b_k{}' \wedge \bigwedge_{k \in S^c} \neg b_k{}' \wedge \bigwedge_{k \in T} b_k{}'' \wedge \bigwedge_{k \in T^c} \neg b_k{}''.$$

For a wrong guess $B_{S,T}$ yields FALSE in the premiss of an implication in the rule, thus satisfying this implication trivially.

Assertion $\bar{p}$ holds after a *DELAY*-guard and before a $S_i{}''$-branch, and assertion p_i holds after the IO_i-guard and before the $S_i{}'$-branch.

Let

$$subst_1 \equiv {}^{W \cup \{(time+1,time+1+w,ioset)\}}\!/_W, \, {}^{\pi^{\smallfrown}(time+1+w,D,e)}\!/_\pi$$

$$subst_2 \equiv {}^{W \cup \{(time+1,time+1+w,ioset)\}}\!/_W, \, {}^{\pi^{\smallfrown}(time+1+w,D,v)}\!/_\pi$$

$$subst_3 \equiv {}^{W \cup \{(time+1,time+1+mindelay,ioset)\}}\!/_W.$$

(alt2)   for all $S \subseteq \{1,..,n_2\}$, $T \subseteq \{1,..,n_3\}$:

$$p \wedge C \rightarrow \neg \bigvee_{i=1}^{n_1} b_i$$

$B_{S,T} \wedge p \wedge C \rightarrow \forall w \in TIME : 0 \leqslant w < mindelay \rightarrow C[subst_1] \wedge$

$\qquad\qquad (A[subst_1] \rightarrow p_i[subst_1, {}^{time+mindelay+2}\!/_{time}])$ if $IO_i = D\,!e$, $i = 1,..,n_2$

$B_{S,T} \wedge p \wedge C \rightarrow \forall w \in TIME \; \forall v \in VAL : 0 \leqslant w < mindelay \rightarrow C[subst_2] \wedge$

$\qquad\qquad (A[subst_2] \rightarrow p_i[subst_2, {}^{time+mindelay+2}\!/_{time}], {}^v\!/_x])$ if $IO_i = D?x$, $i = 1,..,n_2$

$(A,C):\{p_i \wedge b_i{}'\} S_i{}' \{q\}$, $i = 1,..,n_2$

$B_{S,T} \wedge p \wedge C \rightarrow C[subst_3] \wedge (A \rightarrow \bar{p}[subst_3, {}^{time+mindelay+1}\!/_{time}])$

$(A,C):\{\bar{p} \wedge nonneg(d_i) = mindelay \wedge b_i{}''\} S_i{}'' \{q\}$, $i = 1,..,n_3$

$$\overline{\qquad\qquad\qquad\qquad (A,C):\{p \wedge C\} A \{q \wedge C\} \qquad\qquad\qquad\qquad}$$

iteration

Define $b \equiv \bigvee_{i=1}^{n_1} b_i \vee \bigvee_{i=1}^{n_2} b_i{}' \vee \bigvee_{i=1}^{n_3} b_i{}''$, then

(iteration) $$\frac{(A,C):\{p \wedge b\} A \{p\} \, , \, p \wedge \neg b \rightarrow q[{}^{time+1}\!/_{time}]}{(A,C):\{p\} *A \{q\}}$$

parallel composition

In [ZBR,ZRE84] the rule for parallel composition has the following form:
given specifications $(A_i, C_i):\{p_i\} S_i \{q_i\}$ for both components,
choose a network assumption A for $S_1 \parallel S_2$, and check $A \wedge C_i \rightarrow A_j$, for $(i,j) \in \{(1,2),(2,1)\}$.
This results in a specification $(A, C_1 \wedge C_2):\{p_1 \wedge p_2\} S_1 \parallel S_2 \{q_1 \wedge q_2\}$,
provided certain restrictions on the assertions are met.

Typically, in $A \wedge C_i \rightarrow A_j$ assumptions concerning joint channels are verified; the remaining assumptions about external communications are maintained in A. A straightforward adaptation of this rule is not possible; suppose we try a rule of the following form:

$$(A_i, C_i):\{p_i\} S_i \{q_i\}, \; i = 1,2$$

$$\cdots$$

$$\frac{A \wedge C_1[{}^{w^e}\!/_w] \rightarrow A_2 \, , \, A \wedge C_2[{}^{w^e}\!/_w] \rightarrow A_1}{(A, \cdots):\{\cdots\} S_1 \parallel S_2 \{\cdots\}}$$

Then consider the valid formula:

$$(A_1 \equiv (7,tim(\pi_D[1]),D) \in W_D^e, C_1 \equiv (7,tim(\pi_D[1]),D) \notin W_D):$$

$$\{\pi_D = <> \wedge W_D = \emptyset \wedge time = 0\} \, \mathbf{S_1} \equiv D!3 \, \{time = 8\}.$$

If we take the parallel composition of S_1 and an other process S_2 with $D \notin chan(S_2)$, the new assumption of $S_1 \parallel S_2$ should be $A \equiv A_1$, since D is an external channel of this network. But then $A \wedge C_1[{}^{w^e}\!/_w] \rightarrow FALSE$ and we can prove every arbitrary assumption A_2 for S_2.

These problems can be avoided by taking care that the sets of channel names occurring in projections of W^e in both components of the conjunction $A \wedge C_i[^{W^e}/w]$ are disjoint.

Let $wchan(p)$ denote the set of channel names occurring in projections enclosing W or W^e in assertion p, and let $jchan = chan(S_1) \cap chan(S_2)$.

For the network assumption A we require that W^e does <u>not</u> occur projected on joint channels: $wchan(A) \cap jchan = \varnothing$. Furthermore <u>project</u> the commitments C_1 and C_2 such that W occurs only inside projections on joint channels in C_1 and C_2.

The <u>W-projection</u> of an assertion p on a set of channel names $cset$ is defined as follows:

$p|^W cset \equiv \exists w : p[^{[W]_{cset} \cup [w]_{comp}}/w]$, where $comp = chan(p) - cset$, (convention: $[w]_\varnothing = \varnothing$)

and w a logical wait variable not occurring in p.

<u>example</u> Compare the W-projection of $(7,8,D) \in W_{BD}$ on channel D:

$(7,8,D) \in W_{BD} \; |^W \; \{D\} \;\rightleftarrows\; (7,8,D) \in [W]_{BD} \; |^W \; \{D\} \;\rightleftarrows\; \exists w : (7,8,D) \in [[W]_D \cup [w]_B]_{BD} \;\rightleftarrows\;$
$\exists w : (7,8,D) \in [W]_D \cup [w]_B \;\rightleftarrows\; (7,8,D) \in W_D$,

with the W-projection of $(7,8,B) \in W_{BD}$ on D:
$(7,8,B) \in W_{BD} \; |^W \; \{D\} \;\rightleftarrows\; \exists w : (7,8,B) \in [W]_D \cup [w]_B \;\rightleftarrows\; \exists w : (7,8,B) \in [w]_B \;\rightleftarrows\; TRUE$.
□

(parallel composition) $\quad (A_i, C_i) : \{p_i \wedge W_{jchan} = \varnothing\} \, S_i \, \{q_i\}, \; i = 1,2$

$q_1[^{v_1 v_1}/_{time}, ^{w_1}/_w, ^{w_3}/_{w^e}] \wedge q_2[^{v_2}/_{time}, ^{w_2}/_w, ^{w_4}/_{w^e}] \wedge time = max(v_1, v_2) \wedge$

$\qquad W = w_1 \cup w_2 \wedge W^e = w_3 \cup w_4 - [w_3 \cup w_4]_{jchan} \;\rightarrow\; q$

$C_1[^{w_1}/_w] \wedge C_2[^{w_2}/_w] \wedge W = w_1 \cup w_2 \;\rightarrow\; C$

$$\frac{(C_1|^W jchan)[^{w^e}/_w] \wedge A \;\rightarrow\; A_2 \;, \quad (C_2|^W jchan)[^{w^e}/_w] \wedge A \;\rightarrow\; A_1}{(A,C) : \{p_1 \wedge p_2 \wedge W_{jchan} = \varnothing\} \, S_1 \parallel S_2 \, \{q\}}$$

with v_1, v_2, w_1, w_2, w_3 and w_4 logical VAL variables not occurring free in C or q, and provided $wchan(A) \cap jchan = \varnothing$,
$chan(p_i, q_i, A_i, C_i) \cap chan(S_j) \subseteq chan(S_i)$, and $var(p_i, q_i) \cap var(S_j) = \varnothing$, for $(i,j) \in \{(1,2),(2,1)\}$.

The last two restrictions denote that assertions of one process are not allowed to refer to program variables or external channels of the other process.

5.3 General rules and axioms

The following rules and axioms are applicable to every language construction.
The **consequence** rule is a straightforward extension of the usual rule in Hoare logic: one can strengthen the assumption and weaken the commitment.

(consequence) $\qquad \dfrac{A \rightarrow A'\,, p \rightarrow p'\,, \; (A', C') : \{p'\} \, L \, \{q'\} \,, q' \rightarrow q \,, C' \rightarrow C}{(A,C) : \{p\} \, L \, \{q\}}$

substitution

(substitution) $\qquad \dfrac{(A,C) : \{p\} \, L \, \{q\}}{(A,C) : \{p[^e/_v, ^f/_t, ^g/_w]\} \, L \, \{q\}}$

where v, t and w are a logical VAL variable, a logical trace variable and a logical wait variable, resp., and where e, f and g are an arbitrary VAL expression, a trace expression and a wait expression, resp., and provided v, t and w do not occur free in A, C or q.

In order to achieve a relative complete proof system a few more rules are necessary, e.g. invariance, conjunction and extension (see [ZRE84],[H]).
<u>Theorem:</u>
All rules and axioms of the above given proof system are sound w.r.t. the given semantics.
See the appendix of [H] for a proof of this theorem.

5.4 Example

The following example demonstrates the use of assumptions and commitments in combination with parallel composition and hiding. Consider the following processes:

$S_{11} \equiv D_1?x \; ; x := x+1 ; B!x$

$S_{12} \equiv D_2?y_1 ; y_1 := y_1+1 ; B?y_2 ; y_2 := y_2+y_1 ; F!y_2$

$S_2 \equiv [D_1!0 \parallel D_2!0] ; [F?z \rightarrow SKIP \,\square\, DELAY \; 5 \rightarrow error := 1]$.

Suppose we want to prove $(TRUE, TRUE) : \{error = 0\} [[S_{11} \parallel S_{12}] \parallel S_2] \{error = 0 \wedge z = 2\}$.

For an easy formulation we define the following predicates:

"*env waits for D from v* " denotes the assumption that the environment waits for the first communication via channel D starting at point of time v.

"*env waits for D from v and sends $\bar{v}$*" expresses the waiting for the first communication along channel D starting at point of time v, until the communication takes place with communicated value $\bar{v}$. "*wait for D from v* " and "*wait for D from v and send $\bar{v}$*" express similar commitments for the process itself. Formal definitions:

$env \; waits \; for \; D \; from \; v \; and \; sends \; \bar{v} \equiv \pi_D \neq <> \rightarrow (v, tim(\pi_D[1]), D) \in W_D^e \wedge val(\pi_D[1]) = \bar{v}$

$env \; waits \; for \; D \; from \; v \qquad\qquad\;\; \equiv \pi_D \neq <> \rightarrow (v, tim(\pi_D[1]), D) \in W_D^e$

$wait \; for \; D \; from \; v \; and \; send \; \bar{v} \quad\; \equiv \pi_D \neq <> \rightarrow (v, tim(\pi_D[1]), D) \in W_D \wedge val(\pi_D[1]) = \bar{v}$

$wait \; for \; D \; from \; v \qquad\qquad\qquad \equiv \pi_D \neq <> \rightarrow (v, tim(\pi_D[1]), D) \in W_D$.

Note: *wait for D from v and send $\bar{v}$* $\equiv$ (*wait for D from v and receive $\bar{v}$*)$[^W/_{w^e}]$.

"*wait for D_1, D_2 from v* " abbreviates "*wait for D_1 from v $\wedge$ wait for D_2 from v* ".

For S_{11} and S_{12} we can prove:

$(env \; waits \; for \; D_1 \; from \; v \; and \; sends \; 0, \; wait \; for \; D_1 \; from \; v \; \wedge \; wait \; for \; B \; from \; v+2 \; and \; send \; 1):$
$$\{time = v \; \wedge \; \pi_B = <> \; \wedge \; \pi_{D_1} = <>\} \, S_{11} \, \{TRUE\}$$

and

$(env \; waits \; for \; D_2 \; from \; v \; and \; sends \; 0 \wedge env \; waits \; for \; B \; from \; v+2 \; and \; sends \; 1,$
$$wait \; for \; D_2 \; from \; v \; \wedge \; wait \; for \; F \; from \; v+4 \; and \; send \; 2):$$
$$\{time = v \; \wedge \; \pi_B = <> \; \wedge \; \pi_{FD_2} = <>\} \, S_{12} \, \{TRUE\}.$$

With the parallel composition rule (and the consequence rule for the precondition) this leads to (observe that the commitment of S_{11} about channel B justifies the assumption of S_{12} about this channel):

$(env \; waits \; for \; D_1, D_2 \; from \; v \; and \; sends \; 0,$
$$wait \; for \; D_1, D_2 \; from \; v \; \wedge \; wait \; for \; F \; from \; v+4 \; and \; send \; 2):$$
$$\{time = v \; \wedge \; \pi_{D_1 D_2 F} = <> \; \wedge \; \pi_B = <>\} \, S_{11} \parallel S_{12} \, \{TRUE\}.$$

Hiding of joint channel B gives

$(env \; waits \; for \; D_1, D_2 \; from \; v \; and \; sends \; 0,$
$$wait \; for \; D_1, D_2 \; from \; v \; \wedge \; wait \; for \; F \; from \; v+4 \; and \; send \; 2):$$
$$\{time = v \; \wedge \; \pi_{D_1 D_2 F} = <>\} \, [S_{11} \parallel S_{12}] \, \{TRUE\}.$$

For S_2 we can prove:

$(env \; waits \; for \; D_1, D_2 \; from \; v \; \wedge env \; waits \; for \; F \; from \; v+2+\bar{v} \; and \; sends \; 2 \wedge \bar{v} < 5,$
$$wait \; for \; D_1, D_2 \; from \; v \; and \; send \; 0):$$
$$\{time = v \; \wedge \; \pi_{D_1 D_2 F} = <> \; \wedge \; error = 0\} \, S_2 \, \{error = 0 \wedge z = 2\}.$$

Using the parallel composition rule we obtain

$$(TRUE, TRUE) : \{time = v \; \wedge \; error = 0 \wedge \pi_{D_1 D_2 F} = <>\} \, [S_{11} \parallel S_{12}] \parallel S_2 \, \{error = 0 \wedge z = 2\}.$$

Applying the hiding rule leads to

$$(TRUE, TRUE) : \{time = v \; \wedge \; error = 0\} [[S_{11} \parallel S_{12}] \parallel S_2] \{error = 0 \wedge z = 2\}.$$

Using the substitution rule, with substitution $[^{time}/_v]$ in the precondition, we obtain the desired result:
$$(TRUE, TRUE) : \{error = 0\} [[S_{11} \parallel S_{12}] \parallel S_2] \{error = 0 \wedge z = 2\}. \qquad \square$$

6. CONCLUSION AND FUTURE WORK

A compositional proof system has been formulated for a real-time programming language for distributed computing with communication via synchronous message passing. In this proof system it is possible to specify assumptions about the expected behaviour of the environment of a process, and to formulate a commitment concerning the behaviour of the process itself, relative to these assumptions. Assumption and commitment are expressed as invariants, thus allowing the specification of nonterminating processes. Maximal parallelism is modeled by imposing a separate axiom on the domain of interpretation of assertions.

An essential restriction on the assertion language is that the special variable *time* must not occur in assumption or commitment. The next step in our research is to drop this restriction. Thereafter we hope to investigate the relation with liveness properties, in view of Lamport's statement ([La]) that real-time properties can be expressed as safety properties.

Another interesting topic concerns changing the computation model: instead of maximal parallelism, where every process has its own processor, we plan to study the real-time behaviour resulting from the implementation of all processes on one processor together with some scheduling policy. For this seems to be what current practice in real-time programming is about - at least within our Esprit project. Also other communication primitives, such as asynchronous communication and broadcast, will be studied.

We expect the extension of the proof system with recursion in the style of [ZRE] to be straightforward. Finally relative completeness of the proof system is expected to proceed along the same lines as the relative completeness proof of the [ZRE]-system; it will be considered as soon as [Z] becomes available.

A. REFERENCES

[deB]   de Bakker, J.W., Mathematical Theory of Program Correctness, Prentice Hall, (1980).

[FLP]   Francez, N., Lehman, D., Pnueli, A., A Linear History Semantics for Distributed Programming, TCS 32, (1984), 25-46.

[Glass]   Glass, R.L., The "Lost world" of Software Debugging and Testing, CACM 23, (1980), 264-271.

[Hoare]   Hoare, C.A.R., Communicating Sequential Processes, CACM 21, (1978), 666-677.

[H]   Hooman, J., A Compositional Proof Theory for Real-Time Distributed Message Passing, Tech. Report CSN86/10 , Eindhoven University of Technology, (1987).

[HdeR]   Hooman, J., de Roever, W.P., The quest goes on: a survey of proof systems for partial correctness of CSP, Current Trends in Concurrency, LNCS 224, (1986), 343-395.

[HGR]   Huizing, C., Gerth, R., de Roever, W.P., Full Abstraction of a Real-Time Denotational Semantics for an OCCAM-like Language, POPL 87, (1987), 223-237.

[KSRGA]   Koymans, R., Shyamasundar, R.K., de Roever, W.P., Gerth, R., Arun-Kumar, S., Compositional Semantics for Real-Time Distributed Computing, Report no. 68, University of Nijmegen, to appear in Information and Control, (1986).

[La]   Lamport, L., What Good Is Temporal Logic?, Information Processing 83, R.E. Manson (ed.), North Holland, (1983), 190-222.

[Z]   Zwiers, J., Ph.D. Thesis, to appear, Eindhoven University of Technology, (June 1987).

[ZBR]   Zwiers, J., de Bruin, A., de Roever, W.P., A proof system for partial correctness of dynamic networks, Logics of Programs 83, LNCS 164, (1983).

[ZRE84]   Zwiers, J., de Roever, W.P., van Emde Boas, P., Compositionality and concurrent networks: soundness and completeness of a proofsystem, Report no. 57, University of Nijmegen, (1984).

[ZRE]   Zwiers, J., de Roever, W.P., van Emde Boas, P., Compositionality and concurrent networks: soundness and completeness of a proofsystem, ICALP 85, LNCS 194, (1985).

STREAM:
A SCHEME LANGUAGE FOR FORMALLY DESCRIBING DIGITAL CIRCUITS

Carlos Delgado Kloos

Departamento de Informática y Teoría de Sistemas

E.T.S. Ing. Telecomunicación, Univ. Politécnica de Madrid

Ciudad Universitaria - 28040 Madrid - Spain

EUNet: cdk@goya.uucp - EAN: cdk@etsitm.iris

Abstract

For formally reasoning about, transforming, and verifying hardware designs
it is necessary to have a formal framework with a sound semantical basis. We
present a language, called STREAM, with these purposes. With it, one can describe stream processing agents for modelling all kinds of concurrent systems. Two styles of composition of agents are defined: an applicative style,
in which streams are named, and a functional style, with which also a topology can be defined.

The language is used for the description of digital circuits at different
levels of detail. First a non-hardware-specific system level is studied.
Then the register-transfer and gate level are characterized and modelled
with STREAM. It is shown that apart from being able to describe loosely
coupled systems in general, also synchronous and even asynchronous systems
can easily be modelled.

1. INTRODUCTION

Among the outcomes of the "software crisis" (the problem of getting correct and
efficient computer programs) was on the one hand the treatment of programs as formal
objects, of which one could prove theorems (as e.g. show equivalence in behaviour of
two programs or verify a program correct w.r.t. a specification), and on the other
hand the formalization of the process of program construction. To be able to do the
latter, one can include in one wide spectrum language all the constructs that are
needed in the program development. In the case of software this would be some high
level constructs for expressing specifications, as could be e.g. predicate logic,
some constructs for high level programming, as are found in applicative, functional,

or procedural programs, and some assembler language features. The inclusion of all constructs in one language has the advantage that one can perform the program design without changing the language, only the style (cf. [3]).

If we want to repeat this idea in the hardware area, we encounter some difficulties. To master the often very high complexity of digital systems, some description levels have become usual: system level, register-transfer level, gate level, switch level, etc. Unfortunately, the description languages at these levels differ very much from one another. Moreover, they don't always cover all aspects involved. Some additional features are sometimes assumed or explained in natural language. Therefore, it is a non-trivial task to include all the different expression mechanisms within one single framework.

In contrast to usual sequential programming, we deal here with concurrent systems. Thus we have to consider issues of parallelism and synchronization, which makes the treatment more difficult. Apart from the behavioural description, topological and geometrical considerations come into the scene and become of more importance the lower we go in the hierarchy of levels.

For being able to apply formal techniques for the description of digital circuits one needs to have a formally defined language. It should be possible to describe it intended behaviour by means of some of the techniques of semantic definition, be this in an algebraic, denotational, operational, or some other way. This opens the door to a number of different methods for the high-level design and development of hardware systems. Methods for verification w.r.t. an initial specification or of stepwise transformation of a specification into a final version become then applicable (cf [11]).

Especially at the final stages of a hardware design, graphical representations are usual and useful. Therefore a graphical variant to the textual form should be very convenient.

In the sequel we define a language which covers all the aspects mentioned above. I is a concurrent language in which behaviour and connectivity or topology can be described. Moreover, it is possible to instantiate it to use it to describe software and hardware in all the different levels mentioned. In this paper we will only give intuitively the syntax and semantics of the language. A formal definition of the semantics does not pose difficulties. A denotational semantics can be seen in [9]. An algebraic definition of a related language is presented in [10]. The definition i form of a continuous abstract data type lays the basis for getting correctness-preserving transformation rules out of the axioms of the type.

2. THE STREAM LANGUAGE

2.1. Streams

A digital circuit is a concurrent system. At different points of the circuit, several values succeed in time. Independently of the type of the data, we model this succession of values using "streams" (cf. [8]). Streams constitute a very basic concept for the description of concurrent communicating systems (see e.g. [4]). A stream is a finite or infinite sequence of values. We use the following notation for streams:

    <<   (or >>) represents the empty stream
    <1<   (or >1>) represents a stream with only one value: 1
    <1,2< (or >2,1>) here 1 is the first and 2 the second element
    <1,2,3,...< (or >...,3,2,1>)   represents the infinite stream of all natural num-
                       bers in ascending order.

We denote by STR(D) the set of all streams over a given set D of data values and define over it functions for getting the first element and the rest of a stream and for appending a value to a stream:

    first: STR(D) → D⊥
    rest: STR(D) → STR(D)
    append: D x STR(D) → STR(D)

D⊥ is the flat domain whose elements are that of D and the bottom element ⊥. With these functions together with the nullary function that yields the empty stream and a definedness predicate, a continuous abstract data type can be defined (see [15]). It resembles the type for stacks, but for the streams also infinite objects are allowed. STR(D) forms an algebraic domain w.r.t. the prefix ordering for streams, which is defined as

$$s_1 \le s_2 \iff \text{there exists stream s: } s_2 = conc(s_1,s)$$

where conc is the concatenation operation for streams. All finite streams are partial elements. Only the infinite ones are total. This corresponds to the intuition, where we would have to wait till the end of times to have all the information of a point under observation. As we cannot wait so long, we content ourselves with the incomplete information contained in the partial streams.

Streams have been used to model the semantics of loosely ([4]) and tightly ([5]) coupled systems, and of concurrent languages based on the concept of shared memory ([6]). We want to use them now to describe hardware.

2.2. The language

STREAM is a scheme language. For illustration purposes we are going to present it instantiated with the set of natural numbers, i.e. for D=N. The name **STREAM** refers to the underlying basic concept, but also can be understood as an acronym for STandard REpresentation of Algorithms for Microelectronics. The programs written in **STREAM** are called agents. The semantics of an agent is a stream processing function.

We could have based the primitive agents of the language on the functions defined for the streams (first, rest, append). This has been done for example in the data flow language LUCID (see e.g. [16]). We prefer to go a step further and define the primitive agents more in accordance with the further applications. Our language resembles more the data flow language of Dennis in [12].

2.2.1. Primitive agents

In this section we present the primitive agents, showing a textual and a graphical representation together with an intuitive semantics.

For each element d∈D, we define an append agent d& with one input and one output:

d&

The stream at the output equals the stream at the input with d appended to the beginning. With agents like this connected in series we can construct any finite stream. We can also build infinite streams using feedback. Later on we will see these composition functions.

For each n-ary function f over D, we define the lifted agent f* with n inputs and one output:

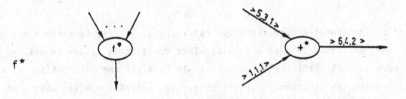

f*

The first element of the output stream is obtained by applying the function f to the first elements of the input streams. The same is true for the rest of the input and output streams. Thus f* performs the function f repeatedly on all tuples of input values. Note that the streams are defined over the set D rather than over the flat domain D⊥. This means that if an input stream is empty, there is no first element, and therefore we cannot apply f to get an output value. In other words, f* is strict in STR(D). If f is nullary (n=0), then there are no input streams and the output stream is an infinite constant stream.

The two classes of agents we have seen are parameterized on the underlying set D. We will now see two further agents used for conditionally routing data values. The first of their inputs requires a stream of boolean values. The other streams are all of type STR(D) for some D.

The distribution agent distributes data values according to a stream of boolean values:

The first boolean value is inspected, if it exists. If it is **true**, then the first data value, if existent, is taken to the left output (to the first output in the textual representation); if it is **false** to the right (resp. second) one. The two input values are consumed and the procedure is repeated for the successive values.

Dually, a selection agent is defined. It selects data values from two input streams and takes them to the output, according to an input stream of boolean values.

It is possible to lift these agents from functions over the basic values. Then D has to be extended by a further value indicating the absence of a proper value ([10]).

2.2.2. Composition of agents

To build **STREAM** nets we have to compose the primitive agents. Two alternative composition styles will be presented.

The applicative style names the objects that are processed, as is done e.g. in the lambda calculus. Therefore in our case the streams are named. Each stream in the net gets a different name. Graphically, the streams can be associated to the input and output lines of the agents. Connecting two agents means then joining lines, i.e. stating that the stream on the output line of an agent coincides with the stream on the input line of another (or the same!) agent. One output line can be joined to several input lines, but not the other way around. Imposing that two output streams be equal violates the cause-effect relationship. This restriction corresponds to the prohibition that two identifiers be equal at the left-hand side of multiple declarations in (applicative) programming languages.

As an example we will consider a net for the continuous computation of the mean value. The n-th element of the output stream equals the mean value of the n first elements of the input stream. This net would be described applicatively as follows:

a := 0& d
b := 0& e
c := 1& c
d := a +° g
e := b +° c
f := d +° e

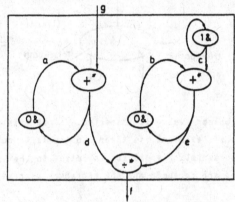

A second composition style, the functional style, is considered. This is inspired on the notation of combinators and on the functional programming style (cf. [2]). Here streams are not named explicitly. Instead, we take advantage of a linear ordering which is supposed for the input streams and for the output streams of an agent.

We define several composition functions. The function for parallel composition produces from two agents the agent that results from the juxtaposition of inputs and the juxtaposition of outputs. In the textual form we use the operator ‖ and in the graphical form we just draw one agent beside the other. The function for serial composition produces from two agents the agent that results by joining the outputs from the first agent to the inputs of the second. For doing so, the number of streams joined must coincide. In the textual form we have the operator ⟹. It can be shown that these two functions are associative. Therefore, they can be extended to compose more agents. They are not commutative. A third interesting function is the feedback function, which connects the first output of an agent to its first input. This function introduces recursion at the level of streams. For expressing this textually, we use the operator C.

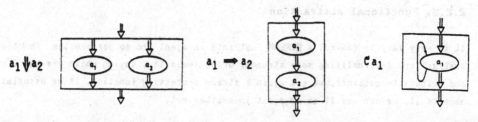

$a_1 \Downarrow a_2$ $a_1 \Rightarrow a_2$ $\mathcal{C} a_1$

For getting the same possibilities of connection allowed by the naming mechanism of the applicative style, some more primitive agents have to be introduced. The forking agent creates a second copy of a stream. It corresponds to using an identifier twice. This is a basic building block for creating multiple copies. The permuting agent permutes two neighbouring streams. It allows to change the linear ordering defined on inputs and outputs. This is a basic building block for constructing agents that permute more streams. The sink agent allows to forget a stream. It corresponds to the situation in which a stream created at an output is not used further.

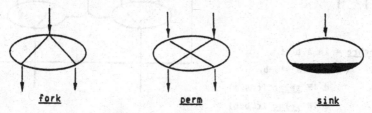

fork   perm   sink

The STREAM net for computing the mean value could be described in the functional style as follows (we suppose the parallel composition function of greater priority than the serial composition function):

$$[\mathcal{C} \ (0\& \Downarrow \underline{id}^* \Rightarrow +^* \Rightarrow \underline{fork})] \ \Downarrow \ [\mathcal{C} \ (0\& \Downarrow \mathcal{C} \ (1\& \Rightarrow \underline{fork}) \Rightarrow +^* \Rightarrow \underline{fork})] \Rightarrow +^*$$

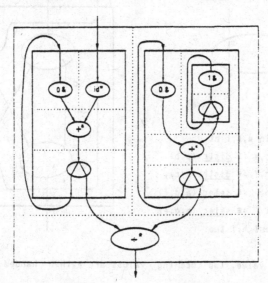

2.2.3. Functional abstraction

It is very easy to convert a **STREAM** net into an agent and so perform the functional abstraction. Internalising some streams, or equivalently, saying which are the inputs and outputs to consider, we get again a stream processing function. If we associate a name to it, we can use it as an agent in another net.

We now present two useful nets that will be used afterwards as agents.

 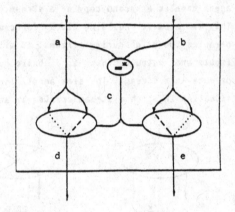

agent <u>synchro</u> = in a,b ni

    c := a =° b,

    d := <u>selec</u> (c,a,a),

    e := <u>selec</u> (c,b,b)

out d,e tuo

The synchronizing agent <u>synchro</u> shortens the longer of the two streams to the length of the shorter by taking its prefix.

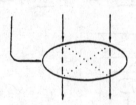 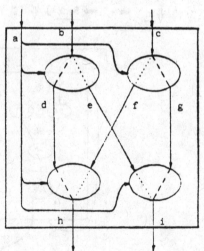

agent <u>comm</u> = in a,b,c ni

    d,e := <u>distr</u> (a,b),

    g,f := <u>distr</u> (a,c),

    h := <u>selec</u> (a,d,f),

    i := <u>selec</u> (a,g,e)

out h,i tuo

For each boolean value, two incoming values are either handed through straight or permuted.

3. THE SYSTEM LEVEL

At this level we specify systems independently of their further implementation as
software or hardware. With **STREAM** it is straightforward to specify loosely coupled
systems. We assume buffers at the connecting lines for the streams.

The concept of stream is an underlying notion of the data flow approach. In fact a
data flow graph can be directly interpreted as a **STREAM** net. Other frameworks can
also be translated into **STREAM**, as for instance a system of recursively defined coroutines as in [1]. A stream can be assigned to each of the routines. Imperative
programs can also be modelled with the **STREAM** language. The strictness of the program
constructs is modelled by using synchronization agents. For more details see [9].

As a simple example of a **STREAM** net, we consider the factorial function. The net
could look graphically as follows:

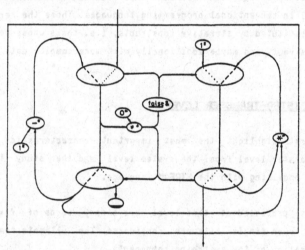

A textual form can be easily deduced. Note that there are many different execution
sequences. On the left loop we could first build a stream with decreasing values down
to zero, and then consume these values to form the product in the right loop. Another
possibility is that both loops proceed in lockstep, the right loop consuming a value
as soon as it is produced by the left one.

It is out of the scope of this paper to show how this net for the factorial function
relates to classical programs in recursive or iterative form. A mapping for automatic
translation of procedural programs into **STREAM** has been defined in [9].

Note that a loop has to be controlled always by an append agent d& to guarantee
correct working conditions. In the example above, both loops were controlled by
true&, that provided the starting condition. Another example is:

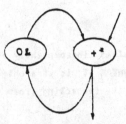

This net computes the accumulative sum of all input elements. O& (now in the loop itself) provides the first element on the left input, so that an addition can be carried out when an element arrives at the right input. Without O& the net would be in a deadlock condition.

It could be interesting to use recursively defined agents at the beginning. If we are heading for software, this would yield recursive functions. But if we want to design hardware, the recursion on agents has to be eliminated and replaced by recursion on streams, i.e. by agents with feedback. This recursion conversion is similar to recursion removal in conventional programming languages. There the recursion of the functions is substituted by iterative constructs, i.e. those whose semantics is intrinsically recursive (, and maybe additionally with more complex data structures).

4. THE REGISTER-TRANSFER LEVEL

Let us first highlight the most important characteristics that distinguish the register-transfer level from the system level and then study the implications they have on the modelling with the STREAM language.

The elements processed at this level are binary words of fixed length. Sometimes subwords or even single bits are considered. The ultimate reason for this is the digital operation of the switching components.

Another characteristic of register-transfer systems is the synchronous mode operation. All activities are controlled by a global clock. The clocking scheme is introduced in order to eliminate transitory values from the circuitry. In one clock period sufficient time is left for all signals to adapt to the new values and eventually stabilize.

We also have to keep in mind that this level is just over the gate level and has been created as an abstract view of it. Therefore, all processing functions that we consider here should be implementable with gates.

The fact that we only have available the data type of bit words means that we have to code everything into it: characters, boolean values, (a finite subset) of integers or reals, etc. It also means that we have to design agents for operating with this type. For example: formation of a subword, selection of a bit, or shifting, shuffling and reflecting of the bits of a word. For doing this, we have to convert a stream of bit words into a tuple of streams of bits. For the reflection of 4-bit-words we have:

$$\text{agent } \underline{\text{4-refl}} = (\underline{\text{perm}} \Downarrow \underline{\text{id}}^* \Downarrow \underline{\text{id}}^*) \Longrightarrow$$
$$(\underline{\text{id}}^* \Downarrow \underline{\text{perm}} \Downarrow \underline{\text{id}}^*) \Longrightarrow$$
$$(\underline{\text{perm}} \Downarrow \underline{\text{perm}}) \Longrightarrow$$
$$(\underline{\text{id}}^* \Downarrow \underline{\text{perm}} \Downarrow \underline{\text{id}}^*) \Longrightarrow$$
$$(\underline{\text{perm}} \Downarrow \underline{\text{id}}^* \Downarrow \underline{\text{id}}^*)$$

The assumption of synchronicity imposes a severe restriction on the agents we can use. With the **STREAM** language we can immediately describe loosely coupled systems. A very illustrative example for this kind of systems is the post system. If an addressee is not at home, all the arriving letters will wait in queue until (s)he comes back and takes them in the same order to read (process) them. The queues are modelled by our streams (and the buffers we suppose on every connection line). Synchronicity means now that there is no queuing up: after the sender has sent a letter, this has to be read by the addressee before the next is sent. But it means more: if an agent has two input lines and a value arrives on the first one, then a value has to arrive also at the second line before the next value can be sent on the first line. Therefore, to keep the whole system going, on each time unit values have to be produced and consumed on each line. Everybody has to send a letter, even if (s)he has nothing to say! (S)he would then send an empty letter.

An agent is called <u>synchronizable</u>, iff we get a value on <u>every</u> output line in response to a value consumed on <u>every</u> input line. We have seen agents that don't fulfil this condition. For instance, the <u>selec</u> and <u>distr</u> agents are not synchronizable, because <u>selec</u> consumes one value from the boolean line and one value from only one of the other input lines; <u>distr</u> produces one value on only one of the output lines.

To model the absence of a value carrying information, we introduce a new value: the absence value ∧ (it models "the empty letter") and define new selection and distribution agents:

agent <u>rt-sel</u> = <u>comm</u> ⟹ (<u>id</u>°∥ <u>sink</u>)
agent <u>rt-dis</u> = (<u>id</u>°∥ <u>id</u>°∥ ∧°) ⟹ <u>comm</u>

<u>id</u> is the identity function.

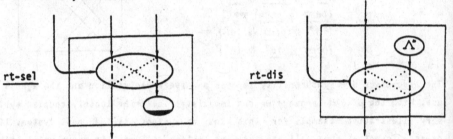

Note that <u>rt-sel</u> is a simple multiplexor and <u>rt-dis</u> a simple demultiplexor.

But we now have three basic values: 0, 1, and ∧. What we can do is identify ∧ with one of the other two. For the following we will make ∧ = 0, which is the option more often taken.

How do we model the synchronizing clock? A clock periodically repeats the same values. We abstract in our model from real time and only consider a sequence of events. Therefore, the simplest way to model a clock would be by an infinite stream of 1's, for example. We synchronize all activities to this clock using the <u>synchr</u> agent we have seen before. In this way, the stream of 1's becomes the sequencing reference for the other agents.

All the components at this level have to be eventually implemented by gates. For gate networks with no feedback loops, i.e. combinational circuits, the modelling is very easy, or the other way around: a specified behaviour is easy to implement with gate components. The synchronous mode operation allows us to forget the transitory values and just concentrate on the stationary ones, which are given by the laws of boolean algebra. For instance, the **STREAM** net

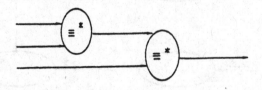

directly corresponds to the gate network

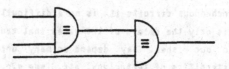

In the previous section, we have said that for the proper functioning of a net with a feedback loop an append agent must be present. The implementation of the append agent O& is a D-flip-flop with value O stored initially. Other kinds of flip-flops, as the RS- or the JK-flip-flop, can also be modelled in **STREAM** (cf. [9]). As an example, we show the **STREAM** agent and the register-transfer network of a Johnson counter with three-bit-words. An n bit Johnson counter is a sequential circuit that outputs a sequence of bit words, such that the n-1 last bits of a word equal the n-1 first bits of the previous word and the first bit is equal to the negation of the last bit of the previous word.

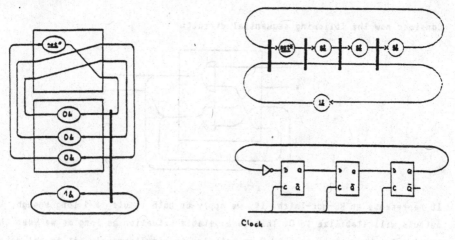

Of course in this case instead of inverting the Q output of the last flip-flop, one would take advantage of the available inverted output $\overline{Q}$. The flip-flops to be used for the implementation should be either master-slave or edge-triggered, in order to guarantee that input and output will never have a direct connection through the flip-flops.

5. THE GATE LEVEL

In the preceding section we have seen that in a synchronous system the behaviour of a gate network can be understood very easily and modelled straightforwardly with a **STREAM** net. This is so because the delays are known. They are imposed by a clock. The period is chosen long enough to let the network stabilize.

In the case of asynchronous circuits it is more difficult to predict the real behaviour, because it is only the delays of the gates that count and these cannot be adjusted precisely to our wishes. They depend on many uncontrollable things such as temperature, charactersitics of technology, etc. (see e.g. [13]). For instance, consider an equivalence gate and suppose that a transition occurs at both inputs. Let's also assume that this transition should in principle take place at the same time because both signals are driven by the same source. Therefore, in theory the output should not change. Nevertheless, in practice it could be the case that the transition on one input takes place a little later than on the other. The cause for this could be a delay due to a longer path or to slower gates. In this case, between the two transitions the output would try to change and give a little pulse. This is an undesired pulse, because it can affect temporarily or permanently subsequent stages. This effect, called hazard, cannot be modelled with the domain STR({0,1}).

Consider now the following sequential circuit:

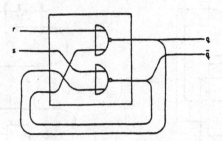

It represents an RS-nor-latch. If we apply on both inputs a 1 long enough, the two outputs will stabilize to 0. This is a stable situation as long as we keep the 1 on the inputs. When we go back to 0 on both inputs simultaneously, it is not possible to predict the outputs without knowing the delays of the gates. Ideally, if the delays are equal, the outputs would oscillate between [0,0] and [1,1]. In practice they stabilize either to [0,1] or to [1,0] depending on which gate is faster. This effect is called a race. In this case it is a critical race, because the final values will depend on the delays. This is also an undesired effect. Therefore, [1,1] is prohibited as an input pair, although it would suffice to prohibit the transition from [1,1] to [0,0].

How can we model hazards, oscillations, and races within our framework? Eichelberger gave in 1965 the ideas for the detection of hazards in combinational and sequential circuits, that led to the ternary simulation algorithm ([14]). Here three values are considered: 0, 1, and a third one for indicating the uncertainty of having one of these two. It is possible to adapt these ideas to our framework and, even more, one can apply the techniques of fixpoint semantics to them and get a much simpler, clearer, and more systematic theory.

We will instantiate the streams now with a superset of B, the set T with three elements: 0, 1, and ?. On this set we define an ordering $\subseteq$ in the following way:

$$? \subseteq 0 \qquad ? \subseteq 1$$

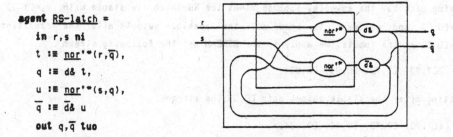

Therefore, $(T, \subseteq)$ is a flat domain. This ordering $\subseteq$ has nothing to do with the ordering $\leq$ in the generic domain of streams, nor with the flat ordering in $D^{\perp}$. We extend every n-ary boolean function $f: B^n \rightarrow B$ to $f': T^n \rightarrow T$ as follows:

$$f'(t_1,\ldots,t_n) = \underset{t_1 \subseteq b_1}{\cap} \ldots \underset{t_n \subseteq b_n}{\cap} \{f(b_1,\ldots,b_n)\}$$

$\cap$ is is the greatest lower bound. It can be seen that f' is monotonic and continuous. Eichelberger gave only a verbal explanation for getting f' for a given f.

Consider now a circuit with n+m inputs and m outputs. The outputs are the outputs of the m gates contained in the circuit. Let

$$f: B^{n+m} \rightarrow B^m \quad \text{or} \quad f: B^n \rightarrow (B^m \rightarrow B^m)$$

be the binary function, assuming the gates were ideal devices without delay. We now feedback the m outputs of the circuit to the last m inputs. We say that the circuit is <u>stable</u> with an input tuple $v \in B^n$, if $f(v)$ is the identity function, or stated in other terms, if there exists a tuple $w \in B^m$ that is a fixpoint of $f(v)$. For a given $f(v)$ there might be none, one, or several tuples w fulfilling this condition. The RS-latch, for instance, is only stable with the output pair $[0,0]$ for the input pair $[1,1]$. But for the input pair $[0,0]$, there are two possible stable situations: $[0,1]$ and $[1,0]$. We also extend this definition of stability straightforwardly to f'. We represent the RS-latch by the following **STREAM** net:

agent <u>RS-latch</u> =
    in r,s **ni**
    t := <u>nor</u>'*(r,$\overline{q}$),
    q := d& t,
    u := <u>nor</u>'*(s,q),
    $\overline{q}$:= $\overline{d}$& u
    out q,$\overline{q}$ **tuo**

The append agents represent the delays of the gates and hold the internal state.

We want to model the asynchronous behaviour in response to an input transition from $v_i \in B^n$ to $v_r \in B^n$ with the only information about the delays that they are finite. Assuming the circuit initially stable with output tuple $w_i \in B^m$, we want to know all possible output tuples that could occur for all possible delay situations.

First we apply the stream $\langle p_m, ..^m.., p_m \langle$ to the net, where $p_m = v_i \cap v_r \in T^n$. p_m has a ? on each line that presents a transition. As a result, we get at the output:

$$\langle w_i, f'(p_m)(w_i), f'(p_m)^2(w_i), ..., f'(p_m)^m(w_i)\langle$$

The superscript indicates repeated application of a function. Due to the monotonicity of f', we see that w_i is a postfixpoint of $f'(p_m)$ and that the sequence of values is decreasing. As the domain is finite, the sequence is stationary. The stationary value is always reached in at most m steps. A value of the output tuple may change to ? or not change at all. The worst case is that it changes due to a ? on one input line that has to propagate through all the m gates. Let's call $q_m \in T^n$ the stationary tuple. It is therefore a fixpoint of $f'(p_m)$, i.e. f' is stable with p_m and q_m.

We now turn to the final input tuple and see whether it can bring the output into a tuple which is more defined than q_m. We apply the stream $\langle v_r, ..^m.., v_r \langle$ and get at the output:

$$\langle q_m, f'(v_r)(q_m), f'(v_r)^2(q_m), ..., f'(v_r)^m(q_m)\langle$$

q_m is a prefixpoint of $f'(v_r)$. Again due to monotonocity, the sequence is increasing and stationary in at most m steps. Let's call the stationary value $q_r \in T^m$. It is a fixpoint of $f'(v_r)$, i.e. we have reached again a stable situation, now with input tuple v_r and output tuple q_r. q_r represents all possible stationary values that could appear in the circuit due to different delay configurations. If it is purely boolean, the circuit will always enter into this tuple. A position in this tuple with ? means that this position could be 0 or 1 in a real circuit or that it could be oscillating between them. ? indicates therefore the possibility of an oscillation or the presence of a race or hazard in general.

Coming back to the example, suppose that the RS-latch is stable with $v_i = [1,1]$ and $w_i = [0,0]$ and we want to know all the possible outputs after the transition to $v_r = [0,0]$ at the inputs. We apply in the STREAM net the following stream

$$\langle [?,?], [?,?], [0,0], [0,0]\langle$$

getting after the stable output pair [0,0] the stream

$$\langle [?,?], [?,?], [?,?], [?,?]\langle.$$

We see that [?,?] at the input sets the output to [?,?], from which it doesn't recover after applying [0,0]. No purely boolean output can be predicted with the information we have. If we apply the above method to a non-prohibited initial state we would get the corresponding purely boolean result.

With this simple well-known example we have shown that even asynchronous behaviour can be appropriately described in our framework.

6. CONCLUSION

In our approach, the language was designed thinking first on the semantics and then looking to the different domains of application. In this way we get a small number of simple primitives with a clean behaviour and can see better the difference in the communication mechanisms of the different kinds of systems. In other approaches often an existing language is taken (e.g. Pascal, Ada) with was designed for other purposes than hardware description and is forced to model some of the hardware features.

It is useful to describe related kinds of systems, that usually have been defined with different notations, in one and the same framework in order to really discern where the differences are. This is especially useful if one aspires to design VLSI systems from the functional specification to the final implementation using one development system to support it and to have a common semantics underlying this development. That is what we have done defining STREAM. The agents written in this language are intuitively easy to understand. Nevertheless, a formal semantics has been defined, for allowing the possibility of formal manipulation. Two forms of representation have been defined: a textual one, suitable for computer processing, and a graphical one, which is easier to understand intuitively and relates to the classical schematics. For composing agents into STREAM nets we have shown two styles: a first one, which we call applicative, to define connectivities and a second one, the functional style, to define topologies.

Some aspects have not been tackled here, partly for lack of space, partly for still being in a research phase. The switch level (cf. [7]) can also be modelled within our approach (see [9]). In this way a very wide spectrum of the VLSI design activity can be covered. Future extensions will be the introduction of geometrical aspects in order to reach the symbolic and geometrical layout levels. A timing abstraction mechanism, which fits well with the idea of streams, has to be defined precisely. Many things remain to be done. What we have presented is the fundamentals of an approach that looks very promising.

Acknowledgements

Some of the ideas in this paper are essentially a product of my Ph. D. Thesis ([9]), which was carried out at the Institut für Informatik of the Technical University of Munich. Therefore, I would like to thank my former colleagues of the Munich CIP group (Computer-aided Intuition-guided Programming). In particular I wish to thank Prof. F.L. Bauer, Prof. M. Broy, Dr. W. Dosch, Dr. B. Möller, and especially Dr. H. Wössner for their support during my stay in Munich.

References

[1] J. Arsac: "Foundations of Programming"; London: Academic Press 1985, APIC Studies in Data Processing 23

[2] J. Backus: "Can Programming Be Liberated from the von Neumann Style? A Functional Style and Its Algebra of Programs", Comm. ACM 21:8, Aug. 1978, 613-641

[3] F. L. Bauer et al. (CIP Language Group): "The Munich Project CIP - Volume I: The Wide Spectrum Language CIP-L"; Berlin: Springer 1985, Lect. Notes in Comp. Sci 183

[4] M. Broy: "Fixed Point Theory for Communication and Concurrency", in: IFIP TC 2 Working Conference on "Formal Description of Programming Concepts II", Garmisch-Partenkirchen, June 1982

[5] M. Broy: "Semantics of Communicating Processes", Information and Control, 1983

[6] M. Broy: "Denotational Semantics of Concurrent Programs with Shared Memory", in: M. Fontet, K. Mehlhorn (eds.): "Symposium on Theoretical Aspects of Computer Science 1984", Paris, 11-13 Apr. 1984; Berlin: Springer 1984, Lect. Notes i Comp. Sci. 166, 163-173

[7] R. Bryant: "A Switch-Level Simulation Model for Integrated Logic Circuits", Lab. Computer Science, M.I.T., Ph. D. Thesis, Tech. Rep. MIT/LCS/TR-259, 1981

[8] W. Burge: "Stream Processing Functions", IBM J. Res. Devel. 19, 1975, 12-25

[9] C. Delgado Kloos: "Towards a Formalization of Digital Circuit Design", Fakultät für Mathematik und Informatik, Technische Universität München, Ph.D. Thesis Tech. Rep. TUM-I8604, Feb. 1986 (to appear in Lect. Notes in Comp. Sci., Berlin Springer)

[10] C. Delgado Kloos, W. Dosch, B. Möller: "On the Algebraic Specification of a Language for Describing Communicacting Agents", ÖGI/ÖCG Conference, Passau, Feb 1986, 53-73

[11] C. Delgado Kloos, W. Dosch: "Transformational Development of Digital Circuit Descriptions: A Case Study", in: W. Proebster (ed.): "CompEuro 87", Hamburg, 11-15 May 1987 (to appear)

[12] J. B. Dennis: "First Version of a Data Flow Procedure Language", in: B. Robinet (ed.): "Programming Symposium", Paris, 9-11 Apr. 1974; Berlin: Springer 1974 Lect. Notes in Comp. Sci. 19, 362-376

[13] D. L. Dietmeyer: "Logic Design of Digital Systems", Boston, MA: Allyn and Bacon 1978

[14] E. B. Eichelberger: "Hazard Detection in Combinational and Sequential Switching Circuits", IBM J. Res. Devel. 9, Mar. 1965, 90-99

[15] B. Möller, W. Dosch: "On the Algebraic Specification of Domains", in: H.-J. Kreowski (ed.): "Recent Trends in Data Type Specification", 3rd Workshop on Theory and Application of Abstract Data Types"; Berlin: Springer 1986, Informatik Fachberichte 116, 178-195

[16] W. Wadge, E. Ashcroft: "LUCID, the Dataflow Programming Language"; London: Academic Press 1985

A Fully Abstract Semantics for Data Flow Nets

Joost N. Kok

Centre for Mathematics and Computer Science
P.O. Box 4079, 1009 AB Amsterdam, The Netherlands

Two semantic models for data flow nets are given.
The first model is an intuitive, operational model. This model has an important draw-back: it is not compositional. An example given in [Brock & Ackerman 1981] shows the non-compositionality of our model. There exist two nets that have the same semantics, but when they are placed in a specific context, the semantics of the resulting nets differ.

The second one is obtained by adding information to the first model. The amount of information is enough to make it compositional. Moreover, we show that we have added the minimal amount of information to make the model compositional: the second model is fully abstract with respect to the equivalence generated by the first model.

To be more specific: the first model describes the semantics a data flow net as a function from (tuples of) sequences of tokens to sets of (tuples of) sequences of tokens. The second one maps a data flow net to a function from (tuples of) infinite sequences of finite words to sets of (tuples of) infinite sequences of finite words.

Note: This work has been carried out in the context of LPC : the dutch National Con-currency Project , supported by the Netherlands Organization for the Advancement of Pure Research (Z.W.O.), grant 125-20-04.

1. INTRODUCTION

In 1974 Kahn [KAHN 1974] gave a semantics for a certain class of data flow nets. His model is based on histories: he uses sequences of tokens. The nodes have to behave deterministically and should be continuous with respect to the prefix ordering on the sequences of tokens. Ever since that time researchers have tried to extend his ideas to more general classes of networks. Examples can be found in [KELLER 1978], [BROCK & ACKERMAN 1981], [ARNOLD 1981], [BOUSSINOT 1982], [PARK 1983], [STAPLES & NGUYEN 1985]. A straightforward extension of Kahn's framework does not work for all kinds of nodes and networks.

One of the problems was first shown in [BROCK & ACKERMAN 1981]. They showed that a seman-tics where a network is modeled as a function from tuples of words of tokens to sets of tuples of words of tokens, is not sufficient to obtain a compositional model. (We use sequences and words synonymously.) They give two networks t_1 and t_2 that have the same semantics: $[t_1] = [t_2]$. They construct a context $C()$ such that $[C(t_1)] \neq [C(t_2)]$. We give this example. Consider the two nets of figure 1.1.

We have three kinds of nodes in the nets t_1 and t_2. The node *dup* is a node which duplicates each token it receives, and sends both to the output line, *merge* is a node which merges its two inputs and *2 buffer* is a node which waits for a second token if it has received one, and then outputs both tokens. It is clear that any semantics which describes these two networks as a function from a tuple of sequences of tokens to a set of sequences of tokens should assign the same meaning to t_1 and t_2. The difference between the two nets is masked by the duplicate nodes. Consider the con-text of figure 1.2.

When we place t_1 and t_2 in this context, the resulting nets have a different semantics. If we plug

352

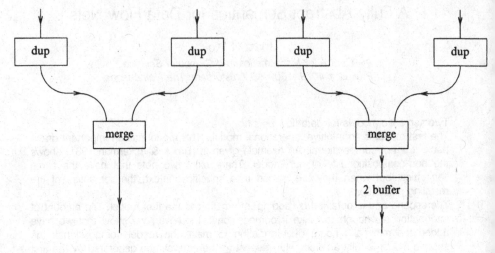

FIGURE 1.1

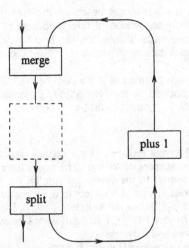

FIGURE 1.2

the nets in the context, we connect one of the input lines and the output line. Hence we obtain a net with one input and one output. The resulting nets have a different semantics. For example, in $[\![C(t_1)]\!](1)$ we have a sequence which starts with 12. In $[\![C(t_2)]\!](1)$ all sequences start with 11. In t_1 we can have that a token can spend some time between the *dup* node and the *merge* node. A second token can go around the feed back loop and pass before the token that is waiting between the two nodes. In t_2 this is impossible: the *2 buffer* pulls the second token down.

The semantics is not fine enough: it can not make all the distinctions necessary. A solution is to add some (time) information to the words. The scenarios as proposed by Brock & Ackerman are an example of this addition of information.

The main difficulty with adding information is that we can add too much information. A criterion to test if we have the right amount of information is to see whether or not the semantics is fully abstract. We define an equivalence relation $\equiv_\theta$ with the help of an operational semantics. The equivalence relation $\equiv_\theta$ on data flow nets is defined by: $t_1\equiv_\theta t_2$ iff $\theta[\![\,t_1\,]\!] = \theta[\![\,t_2\,]\!]$. Two nets are related by $\equiv_\theta$ iff they have the same input/output behavior in terms of words. A semantics $\mathcal{D}$ for data flow nets is called fully abstract with respect to this equivalence relation $\equiv_\theta$ if for all nets

t_1 and t_2 we have $\mathfrak{D}[\![\,t_1\,]\!] = \mathfrak{D}[\![\,t_2\,]\!]$ iff $C(t_1)\equiv_\theta C(t_2)$ holds for every context $C()$.
In this paper we give a denotational semantics that is fully abstract with respect to $\equiv_\theta$. It models a net by giving a function that maps a (tuple of) infinite sequences of finite words to a set of (tuples of) infinite sequences of finite words.

The outline of the rest of this paper is as follows: in section 2 we give the operational semantics, in section 3 the denotational semantics, section 4 relates the two, section 5 gives the fully abstractness result, and we conclude with section 6 where we compare our framework with other frameworks.

2. OPERATIONAL SEMANTICS

Assume that there is given a set of nodes *Node*. Let d be a typical member of this set of nodes. The set $Node^{n:m}$ is the set of nodes with n inputs and m outputs. We construct an automaton for every node $d \in Node$. This automaton can write and read words from tapes. Such an automaton has, in general, an internal state. Let S be the set of states and let s be a typical element. The automaton starts working in an initial state. The behavior of a node $d \in Node^{n:m}$ is specified by a function

$$\delta : (A^*)^n \times S \to P(S \times (A^*)^m)$$

The P denotes "subsets of". Note that the empty set is allowed. This function is called its specification. We assume for each node that such a specification is given. The intuitive meaning of a node

$$(\tilde{s},(\tilde{x}_1,\tilde{x}_2)) \in \delta((x_1,x_2),s)$$

is: given that the node is in state s and it has read (x_1,x_2) on its input lines, the node can "fire" and write $(\tilde{x}_1,\tilde{x}_2)$ on its output lines and, moreover, the automaton comes in a new state $\tilde{s}$.

Data flow nets are data driven. Our model has to capture this. We put a restriction on our automata. It should not be possible for a automaton to neglect some input.

Restriction: whenever there is more input available on a tape from which an automaton reads, it will read this information and use it to fire in a *finite* time.

The next step is the definition of the operational semantics. First we introduce the syntax of a data flow net

Definition 2.1. (Syntax of data flow nets)

$$t ::= \langle d_1,\ldots,d_k\rangle\{i_1{:}j_1,\ldots,i_n{:}j_n\} : k \geqslant 1, n \geqslant 0$$

A net consists of a number of basic nodes. The input lines of the nodes are numbered from left to right. The same applies to the output lines. Lines can be connected. This is indicated by the integers between the braces. As an example: $\{1{:}2,3{:}4\}$ means that the first input line is connected to the second output line and the third input line to the fourth output line. Without loss of generality we require that an input line is at most connected to one output line and that an output line is at most connected to one input line. If we have such a data flow net we can distinguish three kinds of lines:

1. input lines of nodes that are not connected to any output lines,
2. input lines of nodes that are connected to output lines,
3. output lines of nodes that are not connected.

In the context of a net, the first kind of lines are called the input lines of a net, the second kind the feed back lines and the third kind are called the output lines of a net.

This definition of the syntax of data flow nets may be to restrictive at first sight. The restriction that only one input line can be connected to one output line is no real restriction. We can use split nodes: nodes with one input which copy all incoming tokens to all output lines. We can use nodes with zero outputs to hide some lines from the outside world. The syntax is not compositional. We use here this syntax because it is easy to associate automata with this kind of networks. In section 3 we will use a different syntax. The nets we use here will be the normal forms of the nets of section 3.

Given a net, we associate a tape with each channel in the network. For every node in the network we have an automaton. These automata will work on the tapes. With each input line of the network a read only tape is associated, and with each output line a write only tape. On the tapes which correspond with feed back lines both reading and writing is possible. It is impossible to read something before it has been written. Stated in a different manner: a read head on a feed back tape is always behind a write head on the same tape. So the execution of a net

$$t \equiv <d_1, \ldots, d_k>\{i_1:j_1, \ldots, i_n:j_n\}$$

can be viewed as the k-automata $d_1, \ldots, d_k$ working simultaneously on tapes.

Example 2.1: The net

$$t \equiv <merge, split, plus\,1>\{2:4, 3:1, 4:3\}$$

as pictured in figure 2.2,

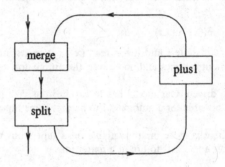

FIGURE 2.2

can be given an operational intuition by considering it as 3 automata, writing and reading on 5 different tapes, as is shown in figure 2.3.

The operational semantics Θ describes the behavior of a network as a function. This function takes as input a tuple of words. This tuple represents the input on the tapes which are associated with the input lines of the network. The words can be infinite. The operational semantics maps this tuple to a set of tuples of words. Each tuple represents a possible output on the output tapes after a run of the automata. Such a run can be infinite. We can obtain several alternatives because our nodes can be nondeterministic. Note that the operational semantics does not deliver the contents of the feed back tapes. If a network t has n inputs and m outputs then

$$\Theta(t) \in (A^{\infty})^n \to \mathcal{P}((A^{\infty})^m).$$

3. DENOTATIONAL SEMANTICS

In this section we define a denotational semantics for data flow nets. This semantics should be compositional. In the previous section we showed that the operational semantics was not compositional. The easiest way to obtain a compositional semantics is to define it in a compositional way. We introduce again data flow nets, but in a different way. They are build up in a compositional way:

Definition 3.1. (Syntax of data flow nets)
Let t be a typical element of the set Net of data flow nets, which is defined with the following BNF grammar:

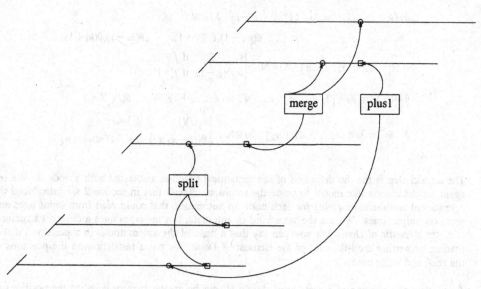

FIGURE 2.3

$$t ::= \quad d : d \in Node$$

$$| <t_1, \ldots, t_n> : n \geqslant 1$$

$$| \ t_1 \ \{i_1:j_1, \ldots, i_n:j_n \ \} : n \geqslant 1$$

Each net t has a normal form $NF(t)$. This normal form is an element of

$$\bigcup_{n,m} \{ \ <d_1, \ldots, d_n>\{i_1:j_1, \ldots, i_m:j_m\} : d_1, \ldots, d_n \in Node \ \}.$$

This normal form relates the "compositional" nets with the nets as defined in section 2. A formal definition of the normal form of a net will be given in section 4. In that section we look how the operational and denotational semantics are related.

With the help of this compositional definition of nets we define the denotational semantics. This definition consists of four steps:
1. introduction of the semantic domains,
2. giving a meaning to basic nodes d,
3. defining the semantical equivalent of the tupling operator,
4. and the modeling of feed back loops.

We start by giving the semantic domains.

Definition 3.2. (Semantic Domains)
Let Dom be the set of infinite sequences of finite words of tokens. An element $<x_1, x_2, x_3, \ldots >$ of Dom can be considered as a function which is an element of $\mathbf{N} \to A^*$. The integer i is mapped to z_i.
Let, for each $n \in \{0,1,2, \ldots \}$, Dom^n be the set of n tuples of elements of Dom. Let θ, Γ, Ψ be typical elements of these sets. An element θ of Dom^n can be seen as a function in $\{1, \ldots, n\} \to \mathbf{N} \to A^*$.
Let, for each $n,m \in \{0,1,2, \ldots \}$, $Dom^{n:m}$ be the set $Dom^n \to \mathscr{P}(Dom^m)$, where $\mathscr{P}(\ )$ denotes "subset of", and let ϕ be a typical element of these sets.

We introduce five operations on elements of Dom.
$$\theta\downarrow\{k_1, \ldots, k_l\} = \lambda i \in \{1, \ldots, l\} . \lambda j \in \mathbf{N} . \theta(k_i)(j)$$

$$\theta\uparrow\{k_1,\ldots,k_l\} = \lambda i \in \{1,\ldots,n-l\} . \lambda j \in \mathbf{N} .$$
$$< \ldots, \theta(k_1-1), \theta(k_1+1), \ldots, \theta(k_l-1), \theta(k_l+1), \ldots >$$

$$\epsilon\Box\theta = \lambda i \in \{1,\ldots,n\} . \lambda j \in \mathbf{N} . \begin{cases} \epsilon & \text{if } j=1 \\ \theta(i)(j-1) & \text{if } j>1 \end{cases}$$

$$\theta\hookleftarrow(\alpha_i)_i = \lambda i \in \{1,\ldots,n\} . \lambda j \in \mathbf{N} . \theta(i)(\sum_{l<j} \alpha_l +1) \cdots \theta(i)(\sum_{l \leq j} \alpha_l)$$

$$\theta_1\cdot\cdot\theta_2 = \lambda i \in \{1,\ldots,n_1+n_2\} . \lambda j \in \mathbf{N} . \begin{cases} \theta_1(i)(j) & \text{if } 1 \leq i \leq n_1 \\ \theta_2(i-n_1)(j) & \text{if } n_1 < i \leq n_1+n_2 \end{cases}$$

The second step is the the definition of the semantical function associated with a node d. We use again an automaton like model to guide the intuition. Recall that in section 2 we introduced the operational semantics by giving for each node an automaton that could read from input lines and write on output lines. We use the same kind of automata, but the tapes have a different structure: they are elements of *Dom*. We now can say that a head of the automaton is in a position i if it is reading or writing the i-th word of the element of *Dom*. We put a restriction on the positions of the read and write heads.

Restriction: the position of a write head should always be greater than or equal to the positions of all read heads.

A automaton associated with a node with two inputs and two outputs is shown in figure 3.3. The read heads have circles and the write heads squares.

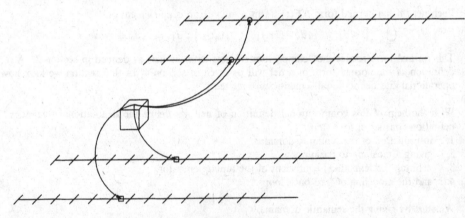

FIGURE 3.3

It is not the case that our automata should write exactly the words of an element of *Dom*. For example, if $<1,1,\ldots>$ is the content of a tape, it is possible that our automaton has written the word 111 an infinite number of times. The boundaries are artificial, and are only used for technical reasons. Note also that it is possible for a read or write head to move on without reading or writing. This is indicated by the "reading" or "writing" of the empty word.

We define for each node d a function ϕ_d by defining $\bar{\theta} \in \phi_d(\theta)$ if and only if there exist a run of automaton d on input tapes with contents θ, such that it writes $\bar{\theta}$ on its output tapes.

The third step is to find the semantical equivalent of the tupling operator.

Definition 3.4. (Semantic tupling)

$$:: : Dom^{n_1:m_1} \times Dom^{n_2:m_2} \to Dom^{n_1+n_2:m_1+m_2}$$

$$\phi_1 :: \phi_2 = \lambda\theta . \phi_1 \left[\lambda i \in \{1, \ldots, n_1\} . \lambda j \in \mathbf{N} . \theta(i)(j) \right]$$

$$\hat{\cdot}$$

$$\phi_2 \left[\lambda i \in \{1, \ldots, n_2\} . \lambda j \in \mathbf{N} . \theta(n_1+i)(j) \right]$$

where $\hat{\cdot}$ is the extension of concatenation to sets defined by

$$X_1 \hat{\cdot} X_2 = \bigcup \{x_1 \cdot x_2 : x_1 \in X_1 \wedge x_2 \in X_2 \}.$$

The fourth step is the modeling of the feed back loop. In the definition we required that on a feed back line the read head was not as far as the write head. We would like to use the structure of elements of *Dom* to formulate such a restriction.

A first guess would be that $\bar{\theta}$ is the result of input θ iff we have a run of our automaton on input θ that delivers $\bar{\theta}$ on its output lines, and, moreover, where on all feed back lines we have that the position of a write head is always greater than the position of a read head.

This guess turns out to be to restrictive. It should be the case that there exist finer partitions of θ and $\bar{\theta}$ such that we have a run of the automaton on these partitions in which the condition above is satisfied.

We have to be a bit more careful when we start the computation. When we start our automaton on a feed back line we first put the write head on the tape, and only after it has left the first position we place the read head on the tape. In the definition of $\mathcal{D}$ this restriction is formulated with the help of the $\epsilon\square$ operator. Suppose there exist a run of automata where we have two tapes with contents θ_1 and θ_2 that satisfy $\theta_1 = \epsilon\square\theta_2$. Assume that the first tape is write only and the second tape is read only. In a run of the automata we have that the the positions of the write heads are always greater or equal to the positions of every read head. If we place the two heads on one tape, we can get as contents θ_1 and by our ϵ shift it is guaranteed that the position of the read head is always less than the position of the write head.

A typical situation of a network with one node, one input line, one output line and one feed back line is shown in figure 3.5.

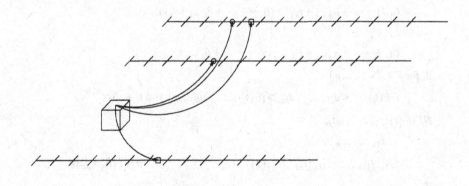

FIGURE 3.5

Now we are prepared to give the definition of the denotational semantics.

Definition 3.6 (Compositional Semantics)
Let

$$\mathcal{D} : Net \to \bigcup \{Dom^{n:m} : n.m \in \{0, 1, 2, \ldots\}\}$$

be recursively defined by

$$D(d) = \phi_d$$

$$D(< t_1, \ldots, t_n >) = D(t_1) :: \cdots :: D(t_n)$$

$$D(t \{i_1:j_1, \ldots, i_n:j_n\}) =$$

$$\lambda\theta . \{\bar{\theta} : \exists\dot{\theta} : \theta \uparrow \{j_1, \ldots, j_n\} = \bar{\theta} [$$

$$\exists\theta'\bar{\theta}'(\alpha_i)_i : \theta' \leftrightarrow (\alpha_i)_i = \theta \wedge$$

$$\bar{\theta}' \leftrightarrow (\alpha_i)_i = \dot{\theta} [$$

$$\exists\tilde{\theta} : \tilde{\theta}\downarrow \{i_1, \ldots, i_n\} = \epsilon \,\Box\, (\bar{\theta}' \downarrow \{j_1, \ldots, j_n\}) \wedge$$

$$(\tilde{\theta}\uparrow \{i_1, \ldots, i_n\}) = \theta' [$$

$$\bar{\theta}' \in D(t)(\tilde{\theta})]]] \}$$

4. RELATION BETWEEN OPERATIONAL AND DENOTATIONAL SEMANTICS

In this section we investigate the relation between the semantics of nets which where given in section 2 and 3. The operational semantics was defined on nets of a different form. First we define the normal form of nets which where given in section 3. We show that the denotational semantics of a net and its normal form are the same. In the last part of this section we give an abstraction operator α. This operator relates the two semantics: $\mathcal{O}(t) = \alpha(\mathcal{D}(t))$ for nets t which are in normal form.

Definition 4.1 (Normal Form)
Define the normal from a net recursively as follows:
1. $NF(d) = d$
2. $NF(< t_1, \ldots, t_n >) =$

$$<d_{11}, \ldots, d_{1m_1}, \ldots, d_{n1}, \ldots, d_{nm_n}>$$

$$\{i_{11}:j_{11}, \ldots, i_{1k_1}:j_{1k_1},$$

$$(\alpha_1 + i_{21}) : (\beta_1 + j_{21}), \ldots, (\alpha_1 + i_{2k_2}) : (\beta_1 + j_{2k_2})$$

$$, \ldots,$$

$$(\alpha_1 + \cdots + \alpha_{n-1} + i_{n1}) : (\beta_1 + \cdots + \beta_{n-1} + j_{n1})$$

$$, \ldots,$$

$$(\alpha_1 + \cdots + \alpha_{n-1} + i_{nk_n}) : (\beta_1 + \cdots + \beta_{n-1} + j_{nk_n})\}$$

if, for $l \in \{1, \ldots, n\}$

$$NF(t_l) = <d_{l1}, \ldots, d_{lm_l}>\{i_{11}:j_{11}, \ldots, i_{lk_l}:j_{lk_l}\} \text{ and } t_l \in Net^{\alpha_l : \beta_l}.$$

3. $NF(t \{i_1:j_1, \ldots, i_n:j_n\}) =$

$$<d_1, \ldots, d_{n_1}>$$

$$\{i_{11}:j_{11}, \ldots, i_{1k_1}:j_{1k_1}, (\alpha_1 + i_1) : (\beta_1 + j_1), \ldots, (\alpha_n + i_n) : (\beta_n + j_n)\}$$

if

$$NF(t) = <d_1, \ldots, d_{n_1}>\{i_{11}:j_{11}, \ldots, i_{1k_1}:j_{1k_1}\}$$

where, for $l \in \{1, \ldots, n\}$

$$\alpha_l = \#\{i : i \in \{i_{11}, \ldots, i_{1k_1}\} \wedge i \leq i_l\},$$

$$\beta_l = \#\{j : j \in \{j_{11}, \ldots, j_{1k_1}\} \land j \leqslant j_l\}.$$

Example: $NF((d\{1{:}1\})\{1{:}1\}) = d\{1{:}1,2{:}2\}$.

We give two properties of our denotational semantics. We use the two properties in the proof of $\mathfrak{D}(t) = \mathfrak{D}(NF(t))$. The first property states that, if a $\bar{\theta}$ is a possible tuple of outputs on input θ, we can add empty words (ϵ) at corresponding places in both θ and $\bar{\theta}$.

Lemma 4.2.

$\forall n,m \in \{1,2,3, \ldots\} \; \forall t \in Net^{n:m} \; \forall \theta, \theta' \in Dom^n \; \forall \bar{\theta}, \bar{\theta}' \in Dom^m \; \forall k \in \{0,1,2, \ldots\} \; [$

$\qquad \bar{\theta} \in \mathfrak{D}(t)(\theta)$

$\qquad \land$

$\qquad \theta' = \lambda i . \lambda j . \begin{cases} \theta(i)(j) & \text{if } j<k \\ \epsilon & \text{if } j=k \\ \theta(i)(j-1) & \text{if } j>k \end{cases}$

$\qquad \land$

$\qquad \bar{\theta}' = \lambda i . \lambda j . \begin{cases} \bar{\theta}(i)(j) & \text{if } j<k \\ \epsilon & \text{if } j=k \\ \bar{\theta}(i)(j-1) & \text{if } j>k \end{cases}$

$\qquad \Rightarrow$

$\qquad \bar{\theta}' \in \mathfrak{D}(t)(\theta') \;]$

The second property is about what happens if we take words together in both input and output. If we do it in the same place, we obtain that the new output is a possible behavior on the new input.

Lemma 4.3.

$\forall n,m \in \{1,2,3, \ldots\} \; \forall t \in Net^{n:m} \; \forall \theta \in Dom^n \; \forall \bar{\theta} \in Dom^m \; \forall k \in \{1,2, \ldots\} \; [$

$\qquad \bar{\theta} \in \mathfrak{D}(t)(\theta)$

$\qquad \land$

$\qquad \theta' = \lambda i . \lambda j . \begin{cases} \theta(i)(j) & \text{if } j<k \\ \theta(i)(k) \cdot \theta(i)(k+1) & \text{if } j=k \\ \theta(i)(j+1) & \text{if } j>k \end{cases}$

$\qquad \land$

$\qquad \bar{\theta}' = \lambda i . \lambda j . \begin{cases} \bar{\theta}(i)(j) & \text{if } j<k \\ \bar{\theta}(i)(k) \cdot \bar{\theta}(i)(k+1) & \text{if } j=k \\ \bar{\theta}(i)(j+1) & \text{if } j>k \end{cases}$

$\qquad \Rightarrow$

$\qquad \bar{\theta}' \in \mathfrak{D}(t)(\theta')$

Proofs: With our automata in mind, it is not difficult to see that these two properties hold. For example, if we consider the second lemma, we have to find splitting of the words on all the tapes, such that it is guaranteed that on feed back lines the read head is always behind the write head. It suffices to take the splitting which is used to obtain that $\bar{\theta} \in \mathcal{D}(t)(\theta)$. $\square$

Generalizations of lemma 4.2 and lemma 4.3 also hold. For example, it is possible to take at an infinite number of places words together or to add epsilons.

Before we compare $\mathcal{D}(t)$ and $\mathcal{D}(NF(t))$, we state the following property:

Lemma 4.4

Let n be an integer and t a data flow net. Take any run of this net on some input. Associate with each line in the net an integer. These integers should be such that for some moment in the run all these integers satisfy are equal to the position of the write head on the line and greater or equal to the position of the read head on a feed back line and equal to position of the write head on an output line and greater or equal to a position of a read head on a feed back line. This condition should hold for all integers simultaneously: the moment in the run is for all integers the same.

If we change the contents of as described below, then there exist also a run of the system on the new contents of the lines.

Change:

If a line has as content the infinite sequence of finite words $<x_1, x_2, \ldots >$ and associated integer α, then we change the contents into $<x_1, x_2, \ldots, x_\alpha, \epsilon, \ldots, \epsilon, x_{\alpha+1}, x_{\alpha+2}, \ldots >$ with n epsilons added.

Proof: omitted. $\square$

Theorem 4.5.

$\forall t \in Net\ [\mathcal{D}(t) = \mathcal{D}(NF(t))\ ]$

Proof: Proof is by induction to the structural complexity of t.

$(t \equiv d)$: The normal form $NF(d)$ equals d, so trivially $\mathcal{D}(t) = \mathcal{D}(NF(t))$.

$(t \equiv <t_1, \ldots, t_n>)$: By the definition of the denotational semantics and the induction hypothesis we have

$$\mathcal{D}(<t_1, \ldots, t_n>) = \mathcal{D}(t_1) :: \cdots :: \mathcal{D}(t_n) = \mathcal{D}(NF(t_1)) :: \cdots :: \mathcal{D}(NF(t_n)).$$

Suppose that $\bar{\theta} \in \mathcal{D}(<t_1, \ldots, t_n>)(\theta)$. This implies, by the definition of the normal form,

$$\exists \theta_1, \ldots, \theta_n, \bar{\theta}_1, \ldots, \bar{\theta}_n : \theta = \theta_1 (\cdots) \cdots (\cdots) \theta_n \wedge \bar{\theta} = \bar{\theta}_1 (\cdots) \cdots (\cdots) \bar{\theta}_n\ [$$

$$\forall i \in \{1, \ldots, n\}[$$

$$\bar{\theta}_i \in \mathcal{D}(NF(t_i))(\theta_i)]].$$

Choose such $\theta_1, \ldots, \theta_n, \bar{\theta}_1, \ldots, \bar{\theta}_n$. For each θ_i and $\bar{\theta}_i$ we can find Ψ_i and $\bar{\Psi}_i$ and a sequence of integers $(z_{ij})_j$ such that

$$\Psi_i \leftrightarrow (z_{ij})_j = \theta_i \wedge \bar{\Psi}_i \leftrightarrow (z_{ij})_j = \bar{\theta}_i .$$

and there exist, for each $i \in \{1, \ldots, n\}$, a run of the system $NF(t_i)$ on input Ψ_i that delivers as output $\bar{\Psi}_i$. In such a run, the write head on a feed back line is always at least one word further. Define

$$(z_j)_j = (\max_{i \in \{1, \ldots, n\}} z_{ij})_j.$$

Now we add both in Ψ_i and $\bar{\Psi}_i$ empty words, as in lemma 4.2, and we obtain Ψ_i' and $\bar{\Psi}_i'$, which satisfy

$$\Psi_i' \leftrightarrow (z_j)_j = \theta_i \wedge \bar{\Psi}_i' \leftrightarrow (z_j)_j = \bar{\theta}_i.$$

While $\bar{\Psi}_i' \in \mathcal{D}(t_i)(\Psi_i')$, we have, by the definition of $\mathcal{D}$, $\bar{\theta} \in \mathcal{D}(t)(\theta)$.

Next we prove the other implication. Suppose that $\bar{\theta} \in \mathcal{D}(NF(t))(\theta)$. This implies that there exist $\theta_1, \ldots, \theta_n, \bar{\theta}_1, \ldots, \bar{\theta}_n$ such that

$$\forall i \in \{1, \ldots, n\}[\bar{\theta}_i \in \mathcal{D}(NF(t_i))(\theta_i)] \wedge$$

$$\theta = \theta_1(\cdot\cdot) \cdots (\cdot\cdot)\theta_n \wedge \bar{\theta} = \bar{\theta}_1(\cdot\cdot) \cdots (\cdot\cdot)\bar{\theta}_n$$

Moreover, there exist a sequence $(z_i)_i$ and $\Psi_1, \ldots, \Psi_n, \bar{\Psi}_1, \ldots, \bar{\Psi}_n$ such that

$$\forall i \in \{1, \ldots, n\}[\Psi_i \leftrightarrow (z_i)_i = \theta_i \wedge \bar{\Psi}_i \leftrightarrow (z_i)_i = \bar{\theta}_i]$$

and that we have a run of the system $NF(t_i)$, which reads from tapes with contents Ψ_i and writes $\bar{\Psi}_i$ on output tapes. By induction $\bar{\Psi}_i \in \mathcal{D}(t_i)(\Psi_i)$ for $i \in \{1, \ldots, n\}$, and by the definition of $\mathcal{D}$

$$\bar{\Psi}_1(\cdot\cdot) \cdots (\cdot\cdot)\bar{\Psi}_n \in \mathcal{D}(<t_1, \ldots, t_n>)(\Psi_1(\cdot\cdot) \cdots (\cdot\cdot)\Psi_n)$$

and hence, by lemma 4.3,

$$\bar{\theta} \in \mathcal{D}(t)(\theta).$$

$(t \equiv t_1\{i_1 : j_1, \ldots, i_n : j_n\})$: Suppose $\bar{\theta} \in \mathcal{D}(t_1\{i_1 : j_1, \ldots, i_n : j_n\})(\theta)$. This implies by the definition of the denotational semantics

$$\exists \Psi : \Psi \uparrow \{j_1, \ldots, j_n\} = \bar{\theta}[$$

$$\exists \Psi' \theta'(z_i)_i : \Psi' \leftrightarrow (z_i)_i = \Psi \wedge \theta' \leftrightarrow (z_i)_i = \theta [$$

$$\exists \Gamma' : \Gamma' \downarrow \{i_1, \ldots, i_n\} = \epsilon \square (\Psi' \downarrow \{j_1, \ldots, j_n\}) \wedge \Gamma' \uparrow \{i_1, \ldots, i_n\} = \theta' [$$

$$\Psi' \in \mathcal{D}(t_1)(\Gamma')]]]$$

Take such $\Psi, \Psi', \theta', \Gamma'$. By the induction hypothesis we have

$$\Psi' \in \mathcal{D}(t_1)(\Gamma') \Rightarrow \Psi' \in \mathcal{D}(NF(t_1))(\Gamma').$$

Suppose that

$$NF(t_1) = <d_1, \ldots, d_k>\{\alpha_1, \beta_1, \ldots, \alpha_m : \beta_m\}.$$

For this normal form we can use the intuition of the automata. If

$$\Psi' \in \mathcal{D}(<d_1, \ldots, d_k>\{\alpha_1, \beta_1, \ldots, \alpha_n : \beta_n\})(\Gamma')$$

then we know that there exist a system of automata $d_1, \ldots, d_k$. For this system it is possible to make a run on input Ψ'', which is a refinement of Ψ', such that this run results in output Γ''. The tuple Γ'' is a refinement of Γ', and moreover, in the same way as Ψ'' is a refinement of Ψ': there exist a sequence of integers $(\bar{z}_i)_i$, all greater that zero, such that $\Psi'' \leftrightarrow (\bar{z}_i)_i = \Psi'$ and $\Gamma'' \leftrightarrow (\bar{z}_i)_i = \Gamma'$. Recall that

$$\Gamma' \downarrow \{i_1, \ldots, i_n\} = \epsilon \square (\Psi' \downarrow \{j_1, \ldots, j_n\}). \qquad (*)$$

Assume for simplicity that $n = 1$. We have, by (*), that if we concatenate some words of tape i_1, this corresponds to a word that is obtained by putting together some words on line j_1:

$$\Gamma''(i_1)(\bar{z}_1+1) \cdot \cdots \cdot \Gamma''(i_1)(\bar{z}_2) = \Psi''(j_1)(1) \cdot \cdots \cdot \Psi''(j_1)(\bar{z}_1)$$

$$\Gamma''(i_1)(\bar{z}_2+1) \cdot \cdots \cdot \Gamma''(i_1)(\bar{z}_3) = \Psi''(j_1)(\bar{z}_1+1) \cdot \cdots \cdot \Psi''(j_1)(\bar{z}_2)$$

$$\cdots$$

It is possible to replace the tape associated with i_1 by

$$\lambda j. \begin{cases} \epsilon & \text{if } j = 1 \\ \Psi''(j_1)(j-1) & \text{if } j > 1 \end{cases}$$

The reading on tape i_1 is slowed down. But now we can conclude that we can connect i_1 to j_1 and we obtain the desired result.

For the other implication, suppose $\bar{\theta} \in \mathcal{D}(NF(t_1\{i_1:j_1,\ldots,i_n:j_n\}))(\theta)$. We have a run of the system $NF(t)$, such that Ψ is input on the input tapes and $\bar{\Psi}$ is written on the output tapes. There is also a sequence $(z_i)_i$ such that $\theta = \Psi \leftarrow (z_i)_i$ and $\bar{\theta} = \bar{\Psi} \leftarrow (z_i)_i$. We break the connections $i_1:j_1,\ldots,i_n:j_n$, by the addition of n new input and n new output lines. We know that there exist a run of the system t_1 on these tapes. In this run the contents of output j_l are the contents of input i_l with one shift to right (one empty word added at the beginning). By induction, applied to t_1, we know that $\mathcal{D}(NF(t_1)) = \mathcal{D}(t_1)$. By definition of $\mathcal{D}$

$$\bar{\Psi} \in \mathcal{D}(t)(\Psi)$$

and by lemma 4.3

$$\bar{\theta} \in \mathcal{D}(t)(\theta).\ \square$$

We continue with the definition of our abstraction operator.

Definition 4.6: *Let $\theta \in Dom^n$ and let $\phi \in Dom^{n:m}$. We define*

$$\theta[j] = \lambda i \in \{1,\ldots,n\}\ .\ \theta(i)(1)\cdot\ \cdots\ \cdot\theta(i)(j)$$

$$\theta[\infty] = \lim_{j \to \infty} \theta[j]$$

and

$$\alpha : Dom^{n:m} \to ((A^\infty)^n \to \mathcal{P}((A^\infty)^m))$$

by

$$\alpha(\phi) = \lambda <y_1,\ldots,y_n>\ .\ \bigcup \{\overline{\theta}[\infty] : \exists\theta\,[\,\theta[\infty] = <y_1,\ldots,y_n> \wedge \bar{\theta} \in \phi(\theta)\,]\,\}$$

Theorem 4.7. $\forall t \in Net[\mathcal{O}(NF(t)) = \alpha(\mathcal{D}(NF(t))\,)]$

Proof: consider a run of the automaton on tapes which have contents in Dom. An element of Dom can be seen as a word which is cut in finite pieces. These pieces do not influence what can be written on or read of tapes. If we abstract from this timing information, it is clear that we get a run of automata which work on tapes with contents in A^∞. $\square$

5. FULLY ABSTRACTNESS OF THE DENOTATIONAL SEMANTICS

In this section we show that the denotational semantics is fully abstract with respect to the equivalence generated by the operational semantics. First we define the notion of a context. A context is a data flow net with a hole in it. In this hole we can put a net.

Definition 5.1. (Context)

$$C() ::= d : d \in Node$$
$$|\ 0$$
$$|\ <t_1,\ldots,t_k,C(),t_{k+1},\ldots,t_n>\ :\ n \geqslant 1,\ k \geqslant 0$$
$$|\ C()\{i_1:j_1,\ldots,i_n:j_n\}\ :\ n \geqslant 1$$

With $Net^{n:m}$ we denote the subset of Net of nets with n inputs and m outputs. With $Context^{n:m}$ we denote the subset of $Context$ of all contexts for nets with n inputs and m outputs. With the help of the notion of context we can formulate the fully abstractness condition.

Definition 5.2. (Fully Abstract)

$$\forall n,m \in \{1,2,3, \dots \}[$$
$$\forall t_1,t_2 \in Net^{n:m}[\mathfrak{D}(t_1) = \mathfrak{D}(t_2) \Leftrightarrow \forall C() \in Context^{n:m}[\Theta(C(t_1)) = \Theta(C(t_2))]]]$$

We prove that this condition holds in two steps. Theorem 5.3 and 5.4 together imply that the fully abstract condition holds.

Theorem 5.3.

$$\forall n,m \in \{1,2,3, \dots \}[$$
$$\forall t_1,t_2 \in Net^{n:m}[\mathfrak{D}(t_1) = \mathfrak{D}(t_2) \Rightarrow \forall C() \in Context^{n:m}[\Theta(C(t_1)) = \Theta(C(t_2))]]]$$

Proof: if $\mathfrak{D}(t_1) = \mathfrak{D}(t_2)$, then also, by the compositionality of $\mathfrak{D}$, $\mathfrak{D}(C(t_1)) = \mathfrak{D}(C(t_2))$. We have that $\Theta = \alpha \circ \mathfrak{D}$, and hence $\Theta(C(t_1)) = \Theta(C(t_2))$. $\square$

Theorem 5.4.

$$\forall n,m \in \{1,2,3, \dots \}[$$
$$\forall t_1,t_2 \in Net^{n:m}[\mathfrak{D}(t_1) \neq \mathfrak{D}(t_2) \Rightarrow \exists C() \in Context^{n:m}[\Theta(C(t_1)) \neq \Theta(C(t_2))]]]$$

Proof: If $\mathfrak{D}(t_1) \neq \mathfrak{D}(t_2)$ then we may assume that we can find θ and $\bar{\theta}$ such that

$$\bar{\theta} \in \mathfrak{D}(t_1)(\theta) \wedge \bar{\theta} \notin \mathfrak{D}(t_2)(\theta).$$

If we can not find such θ and $\bar{\theta}$ we reverse the role of t_1 and t_2.
In the rest of the proof we take $n = m = 1$. It is not difficult to extend the proof for nets with more inputs and/or outputs.
If $n = 1$ then $\theta \in \{1\} \to \{1,2,3, \dots \} \to A^*$ and if $m = 1$ then $\bar{\theta} \in \{1\} \to \{1,2,3, \dots \} \to A^*$. Define the context $C()$ to be $<t,()>\{2:3,3:2\}$, where t is the net pictured in figure 5.5.

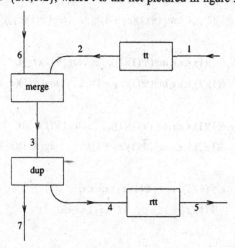

FIGURE 5.5

In the net t we find the following nodes:
merge: a node that merges its two inputs,
split: a node that, when it receives a token, copies it and outputs the two identical tokens, one on each output line,
tt: a node that tags tokens with a color, such that the difference between a tagged token and a non tagged token can be observed,
rtt: when it receives a tagged token, it outputs nothing, and when it receives a non tagged token, it will output it.

Define

$$\tilde{\theta} : \{1\} \rightarrow \{1,2,3, \dots \} \rightarrow A^*$$

by

$$\tilde{\theta}(1)(i) = \theta(1)(i) \cdot tag(\bar{\theta}(1)(i)).$$

and the following (possible) infinite words

$$\begin{cases} y = \theta(1)(1) \cdot \theta(1)(2) \cdot \theta(1)(3) \cdot \dots \\ \bar{y} = \bar{\theta}(1)(1) \cdot \bar{\theta}(1)(2) \cdot \bar{\theta}(1)(3) \cdot \dots \\ \tilde{y} = \tilde{\theta}(1)(1) \cdot \tilde{\theta}(1)(2) \cdot \tilde{\theta}(1)(3) \cdot \dots \end{cases}$$

We show

(i) $\tilde{y} \in \mathcal{O}(C(t_1))(y)$

(ii) $\tilde{y} \notin \mathcal{O}(C(t_2))(y)$

(i) We know that $\bar{\theta} \in \mathcal{D}(t_1)$. From the definition of $\mathcal{D}$ we conclude that there exist Ψ and $\bar{\Psi}$ such that there exist a run of the system t_1 on input Ψ which delivers as output $\bar{\Psi}$. There exists also a sequence $(z_i)_i$ such that $\theta \Leftrightarrow (z_i)_i = \Psi$ and $\bar{\theta} \Leftrightarrow (z_i)_i = \bar{\Psi}$. We number the channels of $C(t_1)$ as is indicated in figure 5.5. It is not difficult to see that there is a run of the system $C(t_1)$ possible when these channels have the following contents:

$6 : \;<\theta(1)(1),\epsilon, \dots ,\epsilon, (\,3+z_1 \; epsilons\,)$

$\qquad \theta(1)(2),\epsilon, \dots ,\epsilon,(\,3+z_2 \; epsilons\,)$

$\qquad \theta(1)(3),\epsilon, \dots ,\epsilon,$

$\qquad \dots >$

$3 : \;<\epsilon,\theta(1)(1),\epsilon,\epsilon,\epsilon,tag(\bar{\Psi}(1)(1)),, \dots ,tag(\bar{\Psi}(1)(z_1)),$

$\qquad \theta(1)(2),\epsilon,\epsilon,\epsilon,tag(\bar{\Psi}(1)(z_1+1)), \dots ,tag(\bar{\Psi}(1)(z_2)),$

$\qquad \dots >$

$7 : \;<\epsilon,\epsilon,\theta(1)(1),\epsilon,\epsilon,\epsilon,tag(\bar{\Psi}(1)(1)), \dots ,tag(\bar{\Psi}(1)(z_1)),$

$\qquad \theta(1)(2),\epsilon,\epsilon,\epsilon,tag(\bar{\Psi}(1)(z_1+1)), \dots ,tag(\bar{\Psi}(1)(z_2)),$

$\qquad \dots >$

$4 : \;<\epsilon,\epsilon,\theta(1)(1),\epsilon,\epsilon,\epsilon,tag(\bar{\Psi}(1)(1)), \dots ,tag(\bar{\Psi}(1)(z_1)),$

$\qquad \theta(1)(2),\epsilon,\epsilon,\epsilon,tag(\bar{\Psi}(1)(z_1+1)), \dots ,tag(\bar{\Psi}(1)(z_2)),$

$\qquad \dots >$

$5 : \;<\epsilon,\epsilon,\epsilon,\Psi(1)(1), \dots ,\Psi(1)(z_1),\epsilon,\epsilon,\epsilon,\epsilon,$

$\qquad \Psi(1)(z_1+1), \dots ,\bar{\Psi}(1)(z_2),\epsilon,\epsilon,\epsilon,\epsilon,$

$\qquad \dots >$

$1 : \;<\epsilon,\epsilon,\epsilon,\bar{\Psi}(1)(1), \dots ,\bar{\Psi}(1)(z_1),\epsilon,\epsilon,\epsilon,\epsilon,$

$\qquad \bar{\Psi}(1)(z_1+1), \dots ,\bar{\Psi}(1)(z_2),\epsilon,\epsilon,\epsilon,\epsilon,$

$\qquad \dots >$

$2 : \;<\epsilon,\epsilon,\epsilon,\epsilon,tag(\bar{\Psi}(1)(1)), \dots ,tag(\bar{\Psi}(1)(z_1)),\epsilon,\epsilon,\epsilon,\epsilon,$

$\qquad tag(\bar{\Psi}(1)(z_1+1)), \dots ,tag(\bar{\Psi}(1)(z_2)),\epsilon,\epsilon,\epsilon,\epsilon,$

... >

From $\theta = \alpha \circ \mathcal{D}$ we derive $\tilde{y} \in \mathcal{O}(C(t_1))$.

(ii) Suppose $\tilde{y} \in \mathcal{O}(C(t_2))(y)$. While $\theta = \alpha \circ \mathcal{D}$, there exist Ψ_1 and Ψ_2 such that $\Psi_1[\infty] = y$, $\Psi_2[\infty] = \tilde{y}$, $\Psi_2 \in \mathcal{D}(C(t_2))(\Psi_1)$ and there exist a run of the system $C(t_2)$ on input Ψ_1 such that Ψ_2 is delivered as output.

In this run of the system $C(t_2)$ all internal lines get contents. We take the numbering of the lines as in figure 5.5 and associate with lines $\{1,2,3,4,5\}$ a content $\Gamma_i \in \{1\} \rightarrow \{1,2,3,\ldots\} \rightarrow A^*$. Because $\Psi_1[\infty] = y$ and $\Psi_2[\infty] = \tilde{y}$ we know that

$$\Gamma_1[\infty] = \tilde{y},$$

$$\Gamma_2[\infty] = tag(\tilde{y}),$$

$$\Gamma_3[\infty] = \tilde{y},$$

$$\Gamma_4[\infty] = \tilde{y},$$

$$\Gamma_5[\infty] = y.$$

We define five infinite sequences of integers: $(k_i)_i$, $(l_i)_i$, $(m_i)_i$, $(n_i)_i$, $(o_i)_i$.

$$\Gamma_1[k_i-1] < \bar{\theta}[i] \leqslant \Gamma_1[k_i]$$

$$\Gamma_2[l_i-1] < tag(\bar{\theta}(i]) \leqslant \Gamma_2[l_i]$$

$$\Gamma_3[m_i-1] < \tilde{\theta}[i] \leqslant \Gamma_3[m_i]$$

$$\Gamma_4[n_i-1] < \tilde{\theta}[i] \leqslant \Gamma_4[n_i]$$

$$\Gamma_5[o_i] \leqslant \theta[i] < \Gamma_5[o_i+1]$$

Remark that the condition on $(o_i)_i$ is somewhat different from the other four.

Remark that $\forall i[k_i \leqslant o_i]$, Without loss of generality we may assume that $\forall i[k_i = o_i]$: we can always speed up the input line. Observe also that $\Gamma_2 \in \mathcal{D}(t_2)(\Gamma_1)$ and that there exist a run of the system t_2 on input Γ_1 that delivers Γ_2. We show that the following property holds for this run of t_2:

if the write head on line 1 is in position k_i, then the read head on line 5 has not yet reached position l_i.

Suppose the write head on line 5 is in position k_i. This implies that the read head on line 5 is in a position which is smaller than k_i. So this read head has not yet consumed all of $\bar{\theta}(1)(i)$.

This implies that the write head on line 4 is at most in position l_i, and hence the read head has not reached this position, i.e. it has not yet seen all of $tag(\bar{\theta}[i])$.

From this we derive that the write head on line 3 can be in m_i, but not further, and that the read head on line 3 is not yet in m_i.

The same applies to line 4, with m_i replaced by n_i.

If the read head on line four has not seen all of $\theta[i]$, it certainly has not seen the beginning of $\theta(1)(i+1)$, and hence the write head on line 5 can be in position o_i, but not in a position which is greater than o_i. From this we conclude that the read head on tape 5 is not in position o_i.

Define

$$\gamma_i = \#\{k_j : k_j = i\}$$

and

$$\Gamma_1' = <\epsilon, \ldots, \epsilon, \ (\gamma_1 \text{ epsilons})$$

$$\Gamma_1(1)(1),$$

$$\epsilon, \ldots, \epsilon, \ (\gamma_2 \text{ epsilons})$$

$$\Gamma_1(1)(2), \dots >$$

and

$$\Gamma_2' = <\Gamma_1(1)(1),$$
$$\epsilon, \dots, \epsilon, \, (\, \gamma_1 \text{ epsilons})$$
$$\Gamma_1(1)(2),$$
$$\epsilon, \dots, \epsilon, \, (\, \gamma_2 \text{ epsilons}) \dots >$$

We know that

$$\Gamma_2' \in \mathfrak{D}(t_2)(\Gamma_1')$$

by lemma 4.2. Define for $x_1, x_2 \in A^*$, $x_1 - x_2$ to be the difference of the two words. For example $1234 - 123 = 4$. Note that the difference $x_1 - x_2$ is only defined if x_2 is a prefix of x_1. Define

$$\Gamma_1'' = <\theta(1)(1), \dots, \theta(1)(\gamma_1), \Gamma_1(1)(1) - (\theta(1)(1) \cdots \theta(1)(\gamma_1)),$$
$$\theta(1)(\gamma_1 + 1) - (\Gamma_1(1)(1) - (\theta(1)(1) \cdots \theta(1)(\gamma_1))),$$
$$\theta(1)(\gamma_1 + 2), \dots >$$
$$\Gamma_2'' = <\bar\theta(1)(1), \dots, \bar\theta(1)(\gamma_1), \Gamma_2(1)(1) - (\bar\theta(1)(1) \cdots \bar\theta(1)(\gamma_1)),$$
$$\bar\theta(1)(\gamma_1 + 1) - (\Gamma_2(1)(1) - (\bar\theta(1)(1) \cdots \bar\theta(1)(\gamma_1))),$$
$$\bar\theta(1)(\gamma_1 + 2), \dots >$$

We have that

$$\Gamma_2'' \in \mathfrak{D}(t_2)(\Gamma_1'')$$

and hence, by lemma 4.4,

$$\bar\theta \in \mathfrak{D}(t_2)(\theta)$$

Contradiction $\square$.

6. CONCLUSION

The denotational framework presented in this paper is fully abstract with respect to the operational semantics. Our semantics can handle all nodes that can be described by the specification functions. This set of nodes includes some kinds of fair merge nodes. In section 2 we required that we can not forget any input and we can use (as internal states of nodes) oracles. One of the advantages of our model is, in our opinion, that we have on the one hand an intuitive model based on automata and on the other hand a formal calculus. On the calculus side we have domains, operations on them (like the ϵ shift) and it is possible to model the feed back loop by a fixed point of a higher order function. This approach was taken in [Kok 1986]. The framework presented there is compositional, but not fully abstract. It is possible to present the system of this paper in a similar style, without the intuition of automata. On the other hand, the automata theoretic approach simplifies proofs and provides insights into the model. The difficulty is that it applies directly only to nets in normal form.

The problems with finding a compositional semantics for nondeterministic data flow were first discussed in [Brock & Ackerman 1981]. The non-compositionality of a semantics based on words of tokens is often called the Brock-Ackerman anomaly. In the same paper they propose a compositional semantics. This semantics is based on scenarios. A scenario is a graph like structure. Such structures contain enough information for the compositionality. This framework is not fully abstract.

A different approach, for example taken by [Broy 1984,1985] and [Park 1983], is the use of oracles.

An oracle tells a nondeterministic node which choices it has to make. Given an oracle, a node behaves deterministically. It is possible to apply Kahn's method to a net, given oracles for all nondeterministic nodes. To obtain the semantics of a net take the union over all possible oracles. The frameworks based on oracles often use more sophisticated orderings on histories than just the prefix order. In this way it is possible to obtain a compositional semantics.
Algebraic treatments of nondeterministic nets are given in [Back & Mannila 1982] and in [Bergstra & Klop 1983].
In [Staples & Nguyen 1985] it is claimed that all of the models they know of are not fully abstract.

Acknowledgements: first of all, we would like to thank Jaco de Bakker, for the support and the guidance during the writing of this paper. A paper of him ([de Bakker et al 1985]) served as a starting point for our investigation. Some of the notation is borrowed from that paper, and an equivalent of theorem 4.5 (in an order theoretic context) can be found there. The careful reading of the various drafts of this paper and the suggestions to improve them are gratefully acknowledged. Next we would like to thank professor Rozenberg, who suggested the automata-theoretic interpretation of our model, and the other members of LPC kerngroep: professor de Roever, professor de Bakker, Ron Koymans and Iko Keesmaat for their patience and useful suggestions. We are also grateful to the concurrency group on the CWI (Jaco de Bakker, Frank de Boer, Jan Rutten, John-Jules Meyer and Erik de Vink) for their discussions on the contents of this paper.

REFERENCES

1. [ABRAMSKY 1983], S. Abramsky, *On Semantic Foundations for Applicative Multiprogramming*, in Proc. 10th ICALP (J. DIAZ ed.), LNCS 154, Springer, 1983, pp. 1-14.
2. [ABRAMSKY 1984], S. Abramsky, *Reasoning About Concurrent Systems*, in Distributed Computing (F.B. CHAMBERS, D.A. DUCE, G.P. JONES eds.), 1984.
3. [ARNOLD 1981], A. Arnold, *Semantique des Processus Communicants*, RAIRO 15 (2), 1981, pp. 103-109.
4. [BACK & MANNILA 1982], R.J. Back, N. Mannila, *A Refinement of Kahn's Semantics to Handle Nondeterminism and Communication*, in Proc. ACM Symp. on Distributed Comp., Ottawa, 1982, pp.111-120.
5. [DE BAKKER ET AL 1985], J.W. de Bakker, J.-J.Ch. Meyer, J. Zucker, *Bringing Color into the Semantics of Nondeterministic Data Flow*, Preprint, Centre for Mathematics and Computer Science, 1985.
6. [BERGSTRA & KLOP 1983], J. Bergstra, J.W. Klop, *Process Algebra for the Operational Semantics of Static Data Flow Networks*, Techn. Report Mathematical Centre IW 222/83, Amsterdam, 1983.
7. [BOUSSINOT 1982], Boussinot, *Proposition de semantique denotationelle pour des reseaux de processus avec operateur de melange equitable*, TCS 18, 1982, pp. 173-206.
8. [BROCK & ACKERMAN 1981], J.D. Brock, W.B. Ackerman, *Scenarios : A Model of Nondeterminate Computation*, in Proc. Formalization of Programming Concepts (J. DIAZ, J. RAMOS eds.), LNCS 107, Springer, 1981, pp.252-259.
9. [BROY 1983], M. Broy, *Fixed Point Theory for Communication and Concurrency*, in Formal Description of Programming Concepts-II (D. BJØRNER ed.), North-Holland, Amsterdam, 1983, pp. 125-148.
10. [BROY 1984], M. Broy, *Nondeterministic Data Flow Programs : How to avoid the Merge Anomaly*, preprint, Fakultät für Mathematik und Informatik, Universität Passau, 1984.
11. [BROY 1985], M. Broy, *Extensional Behavior of Concurrent, Nondeterministic, Communicating Systems*, in Control Flow and Data Flow : Concepts of Distributed Programming (M. BROY ed.), pp. 229-277.
12. [FAUSTINI 1982], A.A. Faustini, *An Operational Semantics for Pure Dataflow*, in Proc. 9th ICALP (M. NIELSEN, E.M. SCHMIDT, eds.), LNCS 140, Springer, 1982, pp. 212-224.
13. [KAHN 1974], G. Kahn, *The Semantics of a Simple Language for Parallel Programming*, in Proc. IFIP74, North-Holland, Amsterdam, 1977, pp. 993-998.

14. [KAHN & MACQUEEN 1977], G. Kahn, D.B. MacQueen, *Coroutines and Networks of Parallel Processes,* in Proc. IFIP 1977, North-Holland, Amsterdam, 1977, pp. 993-998.
15. [KELLER 1978], R.M. Keller, *Denotational Models for Parallel Programs with Indeterminate Operators,* in Formal Description of Programming Concepts (E.J. NEUHOLD ed.), North-Holland, Amsterdam, 1977, pp. 337-366.
16. [KELLER & PANANGADEN 1985], R.M. Keller, P. Panangaden, *Semantics of Networks Containing Indeterminate Operators,* in Seminar on Concurrency, Carnegie-Mellon University (S.D. BROOKES, A.W. ROSCOE, G. WINSKEL eds.), LNCS 197, Springer, 1985, pp. 479-496.
17. [KOK 1986], J.N. Kok, *Denotational Semantics of Nets with Nondeterminism,* in Proceedings ESOP 1986, LNCS 213, Springer, pp. 237-250.
18. [KOSINSKI 1978], P.R. Kosinski, *A Straightforward Denotational Semantics for Nondeterminate Data Flow Programs,* in Proc. 5th ACM POPL, 1978, pp. 214-221.
19. [NADLER 1970], S.B. Nadler, *Some Results on Multi-Valued Contraction Mappings,* in Set-Valued Mappings, Selections and Topological Properties of 2^X (W.M. FLEISCHMAN ed.), Lecture Notes in Mathematics, pp. 64-69, 1970.
20. [PARK 1983], D. Park, *The Fairness Problem and Nondeterministic Computing Networks,* in Foundations of Computer Science IV .2 (J.W. DE BAKKER, J. VAN LEEUWEN eds.), Mathematical Centre Tracts 159, Amsterdam, 1983, pp. 133-161.
21. [STAPLES & NGUYEN 1985], J.Staples, V.L. Nguyen, *A Fixpoint Semantics for Nondeterministic Dataflow,* Journal of the ACM, 32 (2), 1985, pp. 411-445.

The Concurrent Assignment Representation of Synchronous Systems

A R Martin and J V Tucker

Centre for Theoretical Computer Science
and
Department of Computer Studies
University of Leeds
Leeds LS2 9JT
England

Introduction

They have been at a great feast of languages, and stolen the scraps.

William Shakespeare
Love's Labour's Lost

We will present some simple programming language constructs for the theoretical and experimental analysis of synchronous parallel algorithms, continuously processing streams of data over time. We will describe new tools to formally specify the input-output behaviour of algorithms on streams of data; to program and simulate the algorithms; and to test algorithms against their formal specifications.

By a *synchronous parallel algorithm* we mean a network of modules or processors computing and communicating in parallel, and synchronised by some global clock. We suppose that at various times new data are received at the input modules, and that the network inputs and outputs infinite *streams* of data over time. Synchronous algorithms, such as systolic algorithms, with regular structure and short communication channels are suited to hardware implementation; it is this aspect that prompts our interest.

The constructs for representing synchronous parallel algorithms are *abstract data types*, *clocks*, *function routines* and *concurrent assignments*. Together they form a programming language notation that is easy to define formally, and simple to apply to a wide variety of algorithms (including the elegant, but complex *toroidal networks*). Moreover, the concurrent assignment construct is easy to implement and hence leads to software tools that are practically useful for the design and testing of synchronous systems. The language also allows proof systems for the formal verification of programs and, via the abstract data types, the formalisation of the process of top-down design by stepwise refinement. However, in this paper we will concentrate on the programming and testing of algorithms, and emphasise the practical application of the constructs.

The ideas behind the main constructs are, of course, well known. In particular, the concurrent assignment statement, often written

$$x_1, ..., x_n := e_1, ..., e_n$$

where x_i is a variable and e_i an expression for $1 \le i \le n$, has been used in Barron et al [1963], Dijkstra [1976], Gries [1978], Andrews [1982], Welch [1983] and Hoare [1985]. Our own application of the construct to synchronous parallelism is connected with our work on constructs for a functional language for defining synchronous parallel algorithms and, in particular, for verifying that they meet specifications (see Thompson and Tucker [1985] and Thompson [1987]). The language based on the concurrent assignment is *computationally equivalent* to the functional language, and is intended as a complementary language for simulation and testing.

Independently, in Chandy and Misra [1986a], the concurrent assignment has been used for the representation of systolic algorithms with the aim of verifying programs as they are developed (using ideas about invariants). (This is part of their general theory of concurrent program development : see also Chandy and Misra [1985] and Chandy and Misra [1986b].) Thus the material here complements and extends in a practical way some of the theoretical ideas in their work.

The structure of the paper is as follows. In the first section, we describe in more detail the informal model of synchronous computation and explain how the constructs can be used to formalise networks and algorithms; we treat the case of a toroidal network as an illustration. In Section 2, we give a detailed analysis of the formal specification and concurrent assignment representation of a linear systolic algorithm for convolution from Kung [1982]. Section 3 is devoted to a discussion of the practical use of the constructs, and presents a methodology for the concurrent assignment representation of a certain class of synchronous algorithms. Finally, in Section 4, we discuss a proposal to make a language *CARESS* based upon the four constructs; in addition, we comment on the relationship between the functional approach to a language for synchronous algorithms, and we suggest how they may be unified in the idea of a multirepresentational software environment for the design of synchronous systems.

We wish to thank the following people for discussions related to the subject matter of this paper. First and foremost we are indebted to B. C. Thompson. His work on the formal definition of a concurrent assignment language and a functional language; on the proof of their computational equivalence; and on the formal theory of top-down design for the functional language is an essential foundation for the language proposals of Section 4. Secondly, we thank N. A. Harman and C. Jervis for discussions on streams and function routines respectively. We thank J. van der Snepscheut for drawing our attention to the work of Chandy and Misra. Finally, one of the authors (A. R. Martin) thanks the Science and Engineering Research Council and Mullards Ltd. for their financial support.

1. Synchronous systems and the concurrent assignment

In this section we discuss a model of *synchronous parallel computation* and the use of the *concurrent assignment* for the representation and simulation of synchronous parallel algorithms.

1.1 What is a synchronous system?

We consider a synchronous parallel algorithm to be a network of processors or *modules* communicating and computing in parallel, with data from a set A.

The modules in the network are capable of some specific internal processing and are connected with other modules in the network via *channels*. Their behaviour is governed by a single *clock*. In each clock cycle, data is passed between connected modules and there follows some processing at every module. The time cycle is long enough to allow each module to complete both its external data communication and its internal processing. On completion of a cycle, the clock delivers a signal to each processor in the network simultaneously, signifying that communication and processing should once more proceed. New data can be read into the system from the *source* modules and, after a number of clock cycles, the desired result will be available for output by the *sink* modules.

The operation of the system is maintained by the *repeated* loading of new data from an infinite input stream $x = x(0), x(1), \cdots$ into the source modules. The number of time cycles required between accepting one set of input data and accepting the next is known as the *input period* of the system. In return the algorithm delivers an infinite stream output $y = y(0), y(1), \cdots$ of results at the sink modules.

For example, consider the network depicted in Figure 1.1.1. Each pair of processors p_i, p_j for $i = so, 1, ..., n$ and $j = 1, ..., n, si$, are connected together via channel $c_{i,j}$ and are synchronised by the clock via *enable* channels $e_1, ..., e_n$.

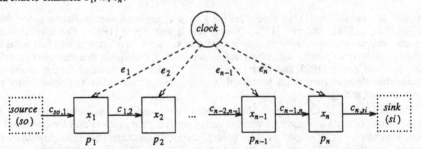

Figure 1.1.1: Linear network of processors synchronised by global clock

During each clock cycle, every module passes data to its neighbour, with p_1 obtaining a new element from the source module, and p_n passing its datum to the sink module for output. Once the datum has been transmitted along the channel, processing takes place and the result of this processing is ready for output the end of the cycle. The computation by module p_i can be defined by some *functional specification* $f_i : A \rightarrow A$, and the value it computes is stored in a local register x_i.

We are interested in *synchronous* rather than *asynchronous* systems because the concept of a single system-wide clock signal occurs naturally in hardware design; the clock signal serves two purposes: a *sequencing* reference, serving the *logical* purpose of defining the order with which system state changes may occur, and a *timing* reference serving the *physical* purpose of accounting for element and wiring delays in the paths from the input to output (see Mead and Conway [1980]).

To represent such a synchronised parallel network it is convenient and useful to choose an abstraction mechanism that facilitates clear, concise descriptions of the modules and clock, but which does not enter into unnecessary detail concerning communication or the enabling process that controls synchronisation. In the next section we will briefly explain why the concurrent assignment accomplishes this task and give an example of its use in Section 2.

1.2 The representation of synchronous systems

To represent a synchronous algorithm we must consider in turn its components:

Data. First we define the data and clock used in the algorithm. For simplicity we denote the set of data by A and denote the set of time cycles by $T = \{0, 1, \cdots \}$. In the examples studied in this paper, A will be the domain of a ring or a linearly ordered set; more generally A will be the domain of an *abstract data type* (see for example, Liskov and Zilles [1975] and Goguen et al [1978]).

Network. Next we establish a method of uniquely labelling individual processors and the local registers at each processor. For the linear networks in this paper we will label processors and stores from left to right (or top to bottom) using single subscripted variables; for example, we let x_i represent a register associated with module p_i. For two and three dimensional networks we will use two and three dimensional cartesian coordinates, for example p_{ij}, x_{ij} and p_{ijk}, x_{ijk}, where x_{ij} represents a register associated with module p_{ij}, and similarly for x_{ijk} and p_{ijk}. In general, networks are represented using graphs.

Module. We must establish a method of functionally specifying the module p_i by means of a function $f_i : A^m \rightarrow A$.

Algorithm. To represent the *parallel* operation of n modules in the network we will use a concurrent assignment of the form (we assume, for notational simplicity, that all modules compute functions requiring m arguments)

$$x_1, ..., x_n := f_1(x_{\lambda_{11}}, ..., x_{\lambda_{1m}}), ..., f_n(x_{\lambda_{n1}}, ..., x_{\lambda_{nm}})$$

wherein the variables $x_1, ..., x_n$ represent the registers holding the results of the simultaneous operation of the modules $p_1, ..., p_n$, the functions $f_1, ..., f_n : A^m \rightarrow A$ represent the functional behaviour of the modules, and $1 \leq \lambda_{ij} \leq n$.

Notice that the notation allows the *communication topology* of the network to be determined from the variable dependencies in the concurrent assignment. That is, the module p_i associated with $x_i := f_i(x_{\lambda_{i1}}, ..., x_{\lambda_{im}})$ in the concurrent assignment will have incoming communication links from modules $p_{\lambda_{i1}}, ..., p_{\lambda_{im}}$.

In several examples computation by a module p_i is dependent on time and hence the module specification has the form $f_i : T \times A^m \rightarrow A$. In such cases the concurrent assignment representation is

$$x_1, ..., x_n := f_1(t, x_{\lambda_{11}}, ..., x_{\lambda_{1m}}), ..., f_n(t, x_{\lambda_{n1}}, ..., x_{\lambda_{nm}}).$$

Top-down design. The set A of data together with the functions $f_1, ..., f_n$ specifying the modules constitute an abstract data type D over which the algorithm is a simple concurrent assignment statement. In practice, we must equip the set A of data with basic operations over which we can program the functions f_i. Thus we construct an abstract data type D' to underpin the formalisation of the algorithm. The operations of D' will be chosen so that the functional behaviour f_i of a module p_i is definable by an appropriate *function routine* g_i over the data type D', i.e. for $f_i : A^m \rightarrow A$ and g_i a function routine over D'

$$f_i(a) = g_i(a)$$

for all $a \in A^m$, where $g_i(a)$ is the result of executing g_i on a. In this way the algorithm formulated over D is implemented over D'.

In the case that the modules are dependent on time the functions have the form $f_i : T \times A^m \to A$ and hence the function routines must invoke operations on the time set T. We define a *clock* T to be an algebra with domain $\{0,1,...\}$, constant 0, and successor operation $t + 1$. A clock is the simplest abstract data type we can devise to formalise time, and turns out to have important properties for the theory of synchronous systems (see Harman and Tucker [1987]).

Ideally, and certainly in all our technical work, a *function routine* is understood to be a program that computes a function without side effects in every context of its execution. In many cases the function routines are simply expressions made by composing basic operations of the data type D'.

Implementing the functional specification f_i by constructing function routine g_i from the set of basic operations of the data type D' (and clock T) is a natural step, of course. But since we may *vary* the choice of the basic operators of D', and systematically implement them in terms of function routines based on simpler operations, and simpler abstract data types D'', the mechanism is the basis for a formalisation of a top-down design process which we will not describe here.

As we have seen in discussing these five topics the constructs needed for representing algorithms are: abstract data types and clocks to establish a level of data, time and module abstraction; function routines to analyse computation by modules; and concurrent assignments to represent the synchronised parallel execution of modules in networks. In concentrating on the practical use of these ideas, and on their application to examples, we will not do justice to the technical merits of working with function routines and abstract data types and using them to perform top-down design.

1.3 Toroidal networks

As as example, consider the two-dimensional network shown in Figure 1.3.1 which is known as a *bidirectional mesh-connected array* (with $n=3$ in this case). The functional specification f_{ij} of module p_{ij} has variable dependencies of the form:

$$f_{ij}(x_{i,j}, x_{i,j+1 \bmod n}, x_{i+1 \bmod n,j}, x_{i,j-1 \bmod n}, x_{i-1 \bmod n,j})$$

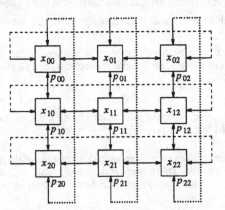

Figure 1.3.1: Communication topology of a bidirectional mesh-connected array

and the network can be represented by the concurrent assignment:

$x_{00},$ $x_{01},$ $x_{02},$
$x_{10},$ $x_{11},$ $x_{12},$
$x_{20},$ $x_{21},$ x_{22}
$:=$
$f_{00}(x_{00},x_{01},x_{10},x_{02},x_{20}),$ $f_{01}(x_{01},x_{02},x_{11},x_{00},x_{21}),$ $f_{02}(x_{02},x_{00},x_{12},x_{01},x_{22}),$
$f_{10}(x_{10},x_{11},x_{20},x_{12},x_{00}),$ $f_{11}(x_{11},x_{12},x_{21},x_{10},x_{01}),$ $f_{12}(x_{12},x_{10},x_{22},x_{11},x_{02}),$
$f_{20}(x_{20},x_{21},x_{00},x_{22},x_{10}),$ $f_{21}(x_{21},x_{22},x_{01},x_{20},x_{11}),$ $f_{22}(x_{22},x_{20},x_{02},x_{21},x_{12}),$

In the concurrent assignment program notice how each local register x_{ij} at module p_{ij} is dependent upon its own value, and the values of external registers at its four nearest neighbouring modules $p_{i,j+1 \bmod n}, p_{i+1 \bmod n,j}, p_{i,j-1 \bmod n}, p_{i-1 \bmod n,j}$.

Such a connected mesh array is best visualised as a *toroidal* network as shown in Figure 1.3.2.

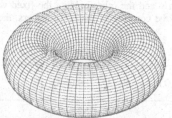

Figure 1.3.2: Communication topology of a torus

A number of toroidal networks and algorithms have been proposed (see for example, the papers on general toroidal architectures Fiat and Shamir [1984], Martin [1981] and Sequin [1981], and those on graph theoretic algorithms Van Scoy [1980] and Dewangan and Rangan [1983]). Using traditional techniques it is extremely difficult to program and simulate such networks due to the complex communication paths involved, however with a *concurrent assignment scheme* we can readily simulate algorithms utilising a toroidal architecture. Different algorithms are implemented by simply choosing different modules and substituting different functional specifications.

In conclusion, we note that the concurrent assignment specifies the operations of the registers of each module in a network rather than the message and data flows between modules; that is, it is *operation* based and not *communication* based. Naturally, all of the relevant communication and synchronisation details are present within the assignment, but they are abstracted away within the semantics of the construct.

Thus, the concurrent assignment provides a precise, simple and elegant high-level notation for the representation of synchronous systems.

2. A case study - systolic convolution

The term *systolic algorithm* was first used by H. T. Kung to refer to certain synchronous parallel algorithms typically consisting of a small number of basic modules repeated many times throughout a network, with communication between neighbouring modules along which data is regularly pumped as dictated by a global clock. Due to their regular structure and localised communications these systolic systems are particularly suited for implementation using VLSI technology (see Kung [1982]).

Such algorithms are normally described in a semi-formal way, using text and diagrams rather like that of Figure 1.1.1. The diagrams are of two types: those representing the communication topology of a system and those representing each module within a network, together with (an attempt at) the functional specification of its behaviour, as discussed in Section 1.2. The constructs provide a simple language to formalise these descriptions.

Simple and representative examples of many systolic systems are those implementing *convolution*. Convolution is a fundamental process in digital system processing: see Blahut [1985]. We will first consider a convolver as a black box and give it a formal specification from the point of view of a user; and then we will describe a systolic algorithm (from Kung [1982]) that implements it.

USER SPECIFICATION

2.1 Informal specification of the user level

Convolution involves the calculation of the *inner product* of two vectors $r = r_1, ..., r_n$, $x = x_1, ..., x_n$ over a ring R, such as the ring Z of integers or $Z[X]$ of polynomials over Z, and is informally defined as follows:

Let R be a ring. Given the fixed weights $r_1, r_2, ..., r_n \in R$ and the stream $x = x(0), x(1), \cdots$ of data from R, compute the stream of results $y = y(0), y(1), \cdots$ defined by

$$y(t) = r_1 x(t) + r_2 x(t+1) + \cdots + r_n x(t+n-1),$$

with $y(t) \in R$.

The convolver can be depicted as in Figure 2.1.1. It consists of two registers of length n: one holding elements from the data stream x and the other holding the fixed weights $r_1, ..., r_n$; and a core module to compute the inner product of the contents of the two registers, the output from which forms the results stream y.

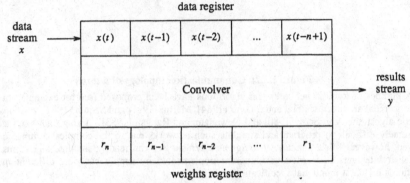

data register

data stream x

| $x(t)$ | $x(t-1)$ | $x(t-2)$ | ... | $x(t-n+1)$ |

Convolver

results stream y

| r_n | r_{n-1} | r_{n-2} | ... | r_1 |

weights register

Figure 2.1.1: Diagram of a convolver

The system is initialised by loading $r_1, ..., r_n$ into the weights register, and loading $x(0), ..., x(n-1)$ into the data register. Once initialised, when the processor is operating normally, the following takes place during time cycle t: the contents of the data register are updated by shifting the data one place to the right, with the leftmost location of the data register obtaining a new value from the data stream x and the rightmost location of the data register discarding its old value; the contents of both registers are passed to the module for the computation of the inner product; and lastly the inner product is output, forming the results stream y. Thus within each cycle we *input, compute* and *output*.

We will now formulate the convolution problem more rigorously.

2.2 Formal specification at the user level

Following the study of correlation in Harman and Tucker [1987], the process of convolution can formally be defined as a *stream transformation*. Let $T = \{0, 1, \cdots \}$ be the set of discrete timepoints or cycles. We define a sequence or *stream* of data from the ring R, to be a map $x : T \rightarrow R$ and we denote the *set of streams* by $[T \rightarrow R]$.

The convolution process is based upon a function $conv : R^n \times R^n \rightarrow R$ defined by

$$conv\ (\mathbf{r}, \mathbf{x}) = r_1 x_1 + \cdots + r_n x_n$$

where $\mathbf{r} = r_1, \cdots, r_n$ and $\mathbf{x} = x_1, \cdots, x_n$.

In our formalisation of the system, we will take the r_i's to be fixed and the x_i's to be elements of the infinite data stream x. A formal definition of convolution at the user level can be given as a stream transformation $CONV_U$ of the following general form:

$$CONV_U : [T \rightarrow R] \rightarrow [T \rightarrow R \cup \{u\}]$$

$$CONV_U\ (x)\ (t) = \begin{cases} u & \text{if } \neg S\ (t)\ or\ \neg R\ (t) \\ conv\ (r_1, \cdots, r_n, x(\delta_1(t)), \cdots, x(\delta_n(t))) & \text{if } S\ (t)\ and\ R\ (t), \end{cases}$$

Here u is a distinguished element not in R, indicating undefined or invalid data. The *set-up predicate* $S : T \rightarrow B$ determines when the system is *first* able to begin computing valid results, for example when it has loaded the weights and the first n elements from the data stream x necessary for a convolution. The *ready predicate* $R : T \rightarrow B$ determines when a valid result has been computed and is ready for output; and the *scheduling functions* $\delta_i : T \rightarrow T$ determine which elements from the data stream x are to be selected for input to the system.

Often the ready predicate R is based upon an *output period* λ for the system, i.e. a *constant* rate at which *valid* results are output from the system; and the scheduling functions δ_i depend upon an *input period* π for the system, i.e. a *constant* rate at which data is loaded into the system.

In this example, the *set-up predicate* $S : T \rightarrow B$ is defined by

$$S(t) = \begin{cases} f\!f & \text{if } t < s \\ t\!t & \text{if } t \geq s, \end{cases}$$

where $s = n-1$ indicating that n clock cycles are required to read in the weights and the first n-element vector from stream x. The *ready predicate* $R : T \rightarrow B$ is defined by

$$R(t) = \begin{cases} f\!f & \text{if } t < s + k \\ t\!t & \text{if } t \geq s + k, \end{cases}$$

where $k \geq 0$ is the *constant* number of cycles required to compute the function *conv*. In the specification $CONV_U$ we assume for simplicity that the function *conv* is computed within a single time cycle, i.e. we will aim to implement a specification with $k = 0$. The output period λ is 1, since after the set-up time s, valid results are ready in every time cycle. The *scheduling functions* $\delta_i : T \rightarrow T$ are defined by

$$\delta_i(t) = t - (s + k) + i - 1 \quad \text{for } i = 1, ..., n$$

The input period π is 1, since we input new values in every time cycle.

In Table 2.2.1 the output stream of $CONV_U(x)(t)$ is shown (note that $s = n-1$ and $k = 0$).

t	$CONV_U(x)(t)$
0	u
$\vdots$	$\vdots$
$n-2$	u
$n-1$	$conv(r_1, \cdots, r_n, x(0), \cdots, x(n-1))$
n	$conv(r_1, \cdots, r_n, x(1), \cdots, x(n))$
$\vdots$	
t	$conv(r_1, \cdots, r_n, x(t-n+1), \cdots, x(t))$
$\vdots$	$\vdots$

Table 2.2.1

Let us consider the model of time at work in this specification.

2.3 The model of time used in our analysis

The set T labels time cycles as shown in Figure 2.3.1.

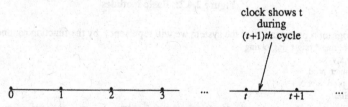

Figure 2.3.1: Model of time

Within each cycle, values are input (if required), a computation takes place, and resulting values are output. Thus, registers typically change their value within a cycle. In tracing data through the system we must consistently choose to record the contents of the register either before or after computation. We will choose to record the value after the computation, at the end of the cycle.

For example, in the trace in Table 2.2.1 in the *nth* cycle when the clock shows $n - 1$, we record the end of cycle value which is the first valid output.

Having specified the convolution problem at the user level let us look at a particular implementation, and specify its behaviour as a stream transformation to formally compare the user specification and the implementation.

IMPLEMENTATION SPECIFICATION

2.4 Informal specification of the implementation

Let the convolution network N_{CONV} be as depicted in Figure 2.4.1.

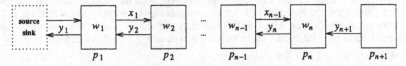

Figure 2.4.1: Communication topology for convolution

Informally, N_{CONV} describes the flow of data in stream x from cell to cell towards the right and the flow of results forming the stream y from cell to cell towards the left. The variables $w_1, ..., w_n$ are registers holding the weights $r_n, ..., r_1$; the variables $x_1, ..., x_n$ are registers holding elements from the data stream x; and the variables $y_1, ..., y_n$ are registers holding intermediate values in the computation of the output stream y.

We will now functionally specify each module in the system. The modules $p_1, ..., p_{n+1}$ are of three kinds: an input/output module where elements from the data stream x are input and elements from the results stream y are output; an inner-product module, for calculating the basic inner product step; and a zero module, for resetting the system. The functionality of p_1 is that of p_{io} in Figure 2.4.2. The functionality of p_i for $i = 2, ..., n$ is that of module p_{inner_prod} in Figure 2.4.2, which is given using our concurrent assignment notation and the function $f : R \times R \times R \to R$ defined by

$$f(w, x, y) = w \times x + y.$$

The functionality of p_{n+1} is that of p_{zero} in Figure 2.4.2.

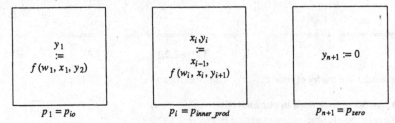

$$p_1 = p_{io} \qquad p_i = p_{inner\_prod} \qquad p_{n+1} = p_{zero}$$

Figure 2.4.2: Basic modules

In the program representation of the system we will represent f by the function routine:

```
function f : ring * ring * ring -> ring
invars w,x,y
outvars inner_prod
    inner_prod := w*x + y
endfunction
```

Network input and output: a single element from the data stream x is input every cycle ($\pi = 1$) register x_1 at module p_1, and a single element for the results stream y is output every cycle from register y at module p_1.

In the implementation we have chosen, a weight is pre-loaded into register w_i of module p_i, for $i = 1, ..., n$. The contents of the registers x_i and y_i are passed between *neighbouring* cells in opposite directions; p_i passes the contents of its register x_i to module p_{i+1} for $i = 1, ..., n-1$, and it passes the contents of its y_i register to module p_{i-1} for $i = 2, ..., n$. At each new cycle, the contents of x_i at module p_i is multiplied with its pre-loaded weight in register w_i and added to the contents of the incoming y_{i+1}. A the values flow through the system, the inner product is computed in stages, with partial results for module p_i being accumulated in register y_i.

From Figure 2.4.2 the contents of x_i is set to the contents of x_{i-1} for $i = 2$, ..., n and the contents of y_i is set to the value of $y_{i+1} + x_i w_i$ for $i = 1$, ..., n. The contents of register y_{n+1} at module p_{n+1} is always set to 0 so that the accumulating results collecting at y_n are initialised to 0.

To compute convolution with this algorithm we first load the weights r_1, ..., r_n into the weight registers w_1, $\cdots$, w_n in reverse order (that is r_i is placed in register w_{n-i+1}). To ensure correct interaction of the x's with the y's we need to pad each element in the x stream with 0's. After $2(n-1)$ cycles the first result appears at the *sink* module, followed by a new result every *two* cycles.

Let us now formulate a concurrent assignment program for the representation of this algorithm.

2.5 Concurrent assignment program for the implementation

To represent the data flow and processing in the system we need to define the values assigned to each local register x_i, y_i at module p_i (where appropriate) for $i = 1$, ..., $n+1$.

From the informal discussion above the value assigned to x_i at module p_i is given by

$$x_i = x_{i-1} \quad \text{for } i = 2, ..., n,$$

with x_1 obtaining its value from the data stream x. As a concurrent assignment we have (for n=3, say):

(A)   x2, x3 := x1, x2

Similarly, the value assigned to y_i at module p_i is given by

$$y_i = \begin{cases} f\ (w_1, x_1, y_2) & \text{for } i = 1 \\ f\ (w_i, x_i, y_{i+1}) & \text{for } i = 2, ..., n \\ 0 & \text{for } i = n+1. \end{cases}$$

As a concurrent assignment we thus have (for n=3, say):

(B)   y1, y2, y3, y4 := f(w1,x1,y2), f(w2,x2,y3), f(w3,x3,y4), 0

So, by enclosing (A) and (B) in a **repeat-forever** statement, to maintain the operation of the system over time, and adding data read and write statements as specified above, we arrive at the concurrent assignment program P_{CONV} (omitting variable and function declarations):

```
t := 0;  -- initialise system clock
read (w1,w2,w3);  -- input constant weights
repeat
    read (x1); -- input new data elements every cycle
    x2,x3,y1,y2,y3,y4 := x1,x2,f(w1,x1,y2),f(w2,x2,y3),f(w3,x3,y4),0;
    write (y1); -- output results every cycle
    t := t + 1 -- increment system clock
forever
```

2.6 Stream scheduling and weight loading for the implementation

For P_{CONV} to operate correctly it must be delivered specific data. The weights r_1, ..., r_n must be loaded correctly into the system and the data stream x must be re-scheduled so that its elements reach the system at the desired time.

As mentioned above the weights r_1, ..., r_n are loaded into modules p_1, ..., p_n in reverse order, that is register w_i holds the weight r_{n-i+1}.

The input data stream $x : T \rightarrow R$ is embedded in a new stream x' with new *system clock* T'; we define $x' : T' \rightarrow R$ by

$$x'(t) = \begin{cases} 0 & \text{if } odd(t) \\ x(t\ div\ 2) & \text{if } even(t). \end{cases}$$

Each time cycle of T is divided into two time cycles of T'. In Table 2.6.1 the relation between the input and output streams and values of the registers of P_{CONV} at each time cycle of T' are shown (for $n = 3$).

Time	Register Contents								
t	so	si	x_1	y_1	x_2	y_2	x_3	y_3	y_4
0	$x(0)$	$x(0)r_3$	$x(0)$	$x(0)r_3$	0	0	0	0	0
1	0	0	0	0	$x(0)$	$x(0)r_2$	0	0	0
2	$x(1)$	$x(1)r_3+x(0)r_2$	$x(1)$	$x(1)r_3+x(0)r_2$	0	0	$x(0)$	$x(0)r_1$	0
3	0	0	0	0	$x(1)$	$x(1)r_2+x(0)r_1$	0	0	0
$4=2(n-1)$	$x(2)$	$y(0)$	$x(2)$	$x(2)r_3+x(1)r_2+x(0)r_1$	0	0	$x(1)$	$x(1)r_1$	0
5	0	0	0	0	$x(2)$	$x(2)r_2+x(1)r_1$	0	0	0
6	$x(3)$	$y(1)$	$x(3)$	$x(3)r_3+x(2)r_2+x(1)r_1$	0	0	$x(2)$	$x(2)r_1$	0
7	0	0	0	0	$x(3)$	$x(3)r_2+x(2)r_1$	0	0	0
8	$x(4)$	$y(2)$	$x(4)$	$x(4)r_3+x(3)r_2+x(2)r_1$	0	0	$x(3)$	$x(3)r_1$	0
9	0	0	0	0	$x(4)$	$x(4)r_2+x(3)r_1$	0	0	0
$\vdots$	$\vdots$	$\vdots$	$\vdots$	$\vdots$	$\vdots$	$\vdots$	$\vdots$	$\vdots$	$\vdots$

Table 2.6.1

Notice that we do not have any controlling information in P_{CONV} for ensuring that only valid results are output, since at this stage we assume the output values are all valid. Clearly, from Table 2.6.1 we can see that the results are meaningless until $t=2(n-1)$, after which valid results are produced every 2 cycles. Below we will formally specify the system and state which results are valid and invalid from the user's viewpoint.

2.7 Formal specification of the implementation

A formal definition of convolution at the implementation level can now be given as the stream transformation $CONV_I$ defined by

$$CONV_I : [T' \to R] \to [T' \to R \cup \{u\}]$$

$$CONV_I\,(x')\,(t) = \begin{cases} u & \text{if } \neg S\,(t)\text{ or }\neg R\,(t) \\ conv\,(r_1, \cdots, r_n, x'(\delta_1(t)), \cdots, x'(\delta_n(t))) & \text{if } S\,(t)\text{ and } R\,(t), \end{cases}$$

The *set-up predicate* $S : T \to B$ is defined as above but with $s = 2(n-1)$. The *ready predicate* $R : T \to B$ is defined by

$$R\,(t) = \begin{cases} f\!f & \text{if } (t-(s+k))\bmod \lambda \neq 0\text{ or }t < s+k \\ tt & \text{if } (t-(s+k))\bmod \lambda = 0\text{ and }t \geq s+k, \end{cases}$$

The output period λ is 2, since after the set-up time s, valid results are ready in every *two* time cycles. The *scheduling functions* $\delta_i : T \to T$ are defined by

$$\delta_i\,(t) = t-(s+k)+i-1 \quad \text{for } i = 1, ..., n$$

The input period π is 1, since we input new values in every time cycle.

RECONCILIATION AND TESTING

2.8 Reconciliation of the user and implementation level specifications

It is now necessary to reconcile the implementation-level specification $CONV_I$ with the user level specification $CONV_U$ and to verify that they are consistent.

On inspection of the two specifications, $CONV_U$ and $CONV_I$, it can be seen that they are essentially equivalent, the only differences being that

(a) the set-up time s of $CONV_I$ is $2(n-1)$ (and not $n-1$ as in $CONV_U$), due to the necessary embedding of the data stream x within the data stream x', which has alternate zero elements for padding;

(b) the output period λ of $CONV_I$ is 2 (and not 1 as in $CONV_U$), again due to the differences between the two streams x and x'.

These differences are reconciled if we consider that the clock T' of $CONV_I$ is simply a clock that is *retimed* to run at twice the speed of the clock T of $CONV_U$. Theoretical tools for formalising the equivalence of stream transformations up to such retimings can be found in Harman and Tucker [1987].

Thus to establish that the systolic convolution algorithm, as represented by the program P_{CONV}, is a correct implementation of $CONV_U$ we have only to establish that it is a correct implementation of $CONV_I$.

2.9 Verification and testing

We are now in a position to test P_{CONV} against its formal specification $CONV_I$. Traditionally, we would need to execute P_{CONV} upon an appropriate file of test data streams and then compare the results produced with those produced by hand simulation of the specification $CONV_I$.

However, thanks to the formalisms we have developed, and in particular the fact that $CONV_I$ is a formal specification, it is possible to automate this process. A software toolset can be developed to:

(a) automatically generate the test streams,
(b) automatically execute the program P_{CONV} upon these test streams, and also animate its specification $CONV_I$; and
(c) automatically give an analysis of the equivalence of the specification and its implementation.

We will return to these points in the next section.

3. Practical observations

In this section we will discuss some practical problems that arise when building algorithms using the proposed language constructs. We will then formulate a methodology for the construction of concurrent assignment programs for a general class of synchronous systems, including the one for convolution studied in this paper.

3.1 Concurrent assignment programs

The use of abstract data types, clocks and function routines are fairly well covered in the literature, and we do not discuss them in any more detail here. However, from a practical viewpoint, the concurrent assignment is little used and not as well understood and so we will discuss it in more detail.

Concurrent assignment programs as we have described them suffer from two principal difficulties:

They are inflexible. Any concurrent assignment program will describe a network for a *fixed* number n of modules; to alter the network size it is necessary to re-specify the concurrent assignment program. We do not want to completely rewrite a program, adding new variables and so on, every time we alter n. Ideally n, and any other parameters of the system, should only be changed once (for example, at the head of the program) to effect the desired change.

They can be incomprehensible. If n is large then, due to the long concurrent assignments, it is more difficult to comprehend the program and its construction is therefore more error prone.

To solve these problems we need to introduce suitable software tools into the user's programming environment: to ease the writing of concurrent assignment programs, and to allow changes to be made automatically. A number of approaches suggest themselves:

(a) augment our programming language with higher-level constructs;
(b) produce an independent pre-processing language that allows parameterisations and a translator for this language that maps on to the simpler basic concurrent assignment language;
(c) input concurrent assignments under the control of a syntax-directed editor, which has the ability to automatically expand a simple notation into concurrent assignments; or
(d) use an interactive graphics system that permits the specification of networks and modules graphically, rather than textually, so that the diagrams can then be converted automatically into concurrent assignment programs. An example of a system that gives the user the ability to interactively specify networks and concurrent systems graphically is the Hearts system (see Snyder [1986] and Snyder [1984]).

We are against increasing the size of the base language as in approach (a) because, by keeping the language small, the formal specification of the syntax and semantics of the language is easy, and the production of faster, neater and more reliable compilers is simple. Approaches (b), (c) and (d) are preferable since they allow us to establish the simple concurrent assignment language as a *kernel language*, upon which the many other tools within the programming environment can base their output (see Section 4).

A typical aid to concurrent assignment program construction, such as the pre-processor, would operate as shown in Figure 3.1.1.

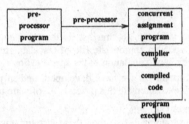

Figure 3.1.1: The interaction of the pre-processor with the compiler

The simplest approach is (b) and we have built a prototype pre-processor for the prototype kernel language. In addition, we are currently developing an interactive graphics interface as mentioned in (d). We will design a syntax-directed editor at a later stage.

Having constructed in our language an executable implementation of a network using the tools above, it is necessary to exercise it upon streams of data. We will now discuss aspects of generating streams for such purposes.

3.2 Stream scheduling or compilation

A characteristic of the synchronous algorithms we are interested in is that they work upon infinite data streams. These streams tend to be more simple at the user level than at the algorithm or network level.

For example, in the elementary case of convolution in Section 2, the user specification $CONV_U$ operates upon the x data stream

$$x = x(0), x(1), \cdots$$

whereas the program P_{CONV} operates upon a suitably translated data stream x' where elements from the stream x are padded with alternate 0's,

$$x' = x(0), 0, x(1), 0, \cdots$$

This mapping between user level and network level streams we will call *stream scheduling* or *stream compilation*. This is a subject for independent theoretical investigation but we may still raise the question of how to handle the input and output of these streams in our programs.

One approach for dealing with streams in a network is to incorporate any necessary translations within the program implementation of the network itself. This is achieved through the use of a special source routine or module which takes a user level stream and transforms it into a network level stream, and a special sink routine or module which transforms the network level stream back to a user level stream. Hence, in this approach not only does the program have to implement the network, it also has the task of transforming data streams between different levels. In some cases these transformations can be as complex as the system algorithm. As a result the implementation of a system becomes far more complex than is necessary because we are trying to solve two problems at once: implementation of the network and translation of the streams.

For this reason, we feel it is necessary to abstract details concerning stream scheduling or stream compilation away from the details of a system; the source and sink modules, and the network modules should be separate sections of code. To do this an independent *stream specification and translating language* is necessary, to write specifications that generate files of data, and to write algorithms that map between the different stream levels. Thus, in this language we define the sets of streams to be input at the user level and the algorithms, called *protocols* or *schedules*, that load the streams into the network. In essence our configuration will look like that in Figure 3.2.1.

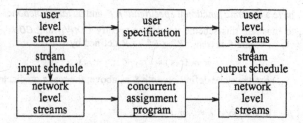

Figure 3.2.1: Compilation of streams between user and network levels

The user will enter a stream at one level, this will be compiled into a lower level to be operated upon by the concurrent assignment implementation of the network, the output from which will be re-compiled back to the user level for eventual display to the user.

The process of reconciliation described after the convolution example in Section 2 becomes the matter of compiler correctness for schedules in the general situation. Some simple formal tools for analysing scheduling by means of clock retimings after the fashion of Section 1 are contained in Harman and Tucker [1987]. A very general theoretical analysis has been undertaken by our colleague K. Meinke (see Meinke [1987]). Upon these theoretical foundations a stream compiler will be designed.

3.3 A practical programming methodology

Although some of the tools mentioned above aid the construction of large concurrent assignment programs, they do not significantly aid the transition from an informal algorithm specification to an executable program, i.e. given a user specification and a collection of semi-formal systolic pictures we have no way of routinely or mechanically constructing a concurrent assignment program.

We will give a general scheme for user specifications that applies to a class of synchronous systems we are interested in, and then develop a programming methodology based around formal specifications of that special class. The specification allows simple stream generation and compilation, and a parameterisation suitable for a preprocessing tool for the language. Following Harman and Tucker [1987] we will define a very simple general scheme for data independent stream transformers.

3.4 The general scheme of type I

Let $C_1, ..., C_r, A_1, ..., A_s$ be non-empty sets of data.
Let $f : T \times C_{c_1} \times \cdots \times C_{c_k} \times A_{\lambda_1} \times \cdots \times A_{\lambda_n} \to A_{\mu_1} \times \cdots \times A_{\mu_m}$ where $c_1, ..., c_k \in \{1, ..., r\}$, $\lambda_1, ..., \lambda_n \in \{1, ..., s\}$ and $\mu_1, ..., \mu_m \in \{1, ..., s\}$ be the functional specification of a processor.
Let the *set-up predicate* $S : T \to B$ be defined by

$$S(t) = \begin{cases} ff & \text{if } t < s \\ tt & \text{if } t \geq s, \end{cases}$$

where s is the *set-up time* of the system. Let the *ready predicate* $R : T \to B$ be defined by

$$R(t) = \begin{cases} ff & \text{if } (t-s) \bmod \lambda \neq 0 \text{ or } t < s \\ tt & \text{if } (t-s) \bmod \lambda = 0 \text{ and } t \geq s, \end{cases}$$

where λ is the *output period* and s is the set-up time. Finally, let the *scheduling functions* $\delta_i : T \to T$ be defined by

$$\delta_i(t) = ((t-s) \ div \ \pi) + i - 1 \quad \text{for } i = 1, ..., n,$$

where π is the *input period*.

We say *stream transformation* $F : [T \to A_{\lambda_1}] \times \cdots \times [T \to A_{\lambda_n}] \to [T \to A_{\mu_1}^{\mu}] \times \cdots \times [T \to A_{\mu_m}^{\mu}]$ is defined from function f by a *data independent scheme of type I* if for S, R and $\delta_1, ..., \delta_n$ as above and parameters $a_i \in C_{c_i}$

$$F(x_1, ..., x_n)(t) = \begin{cases} u & \text{if } \neg S(t) \text{ or } \neg R(t) \\ f(t, a_1, ..., a_k, x_1(\delta_1(t)), ..., x_n(\delta_n(t))) & \text{if } S(t) \text{ and } R(t) \end{cases}$$

Here $A_i^{\mu} = A_i \cup \{u\}$ for u a distinguished element not in A_i, indicating undefined or invalid data. This processor is said to have a *dynamic functional specification* F and a *static functional specification* f.

For example, to illustrate this scheme we will re-specify $CONV_U$ and $CONV_I$ from Section 2. Here $C_i = A_i = R$ for $i = 1, ..., n$; and f is $conv : R^n \times R^n \to R$ defined by

$$conv(\mathbf{r}, \mathbf{x}) = r_1 x_1 + \cdots + r_n x_n;$$

the set-up predicate $S(t)$ has the same definition with S as above; the ready predicate $R : T \to B$ is defined by

$$R(t) = \begin{cases} ff & \text{if } (t-s) \bmod \lambda \neq 0 \text{ or } t < s \\ tt & \text{if } (t-s) \bmod \lambda = 0 \text{ and } t \geq s, \end{cases}$$

and replacing λ by its value, 1 in $CONV_U$ we have:

$$R(t) = \begin{cases} ff & \text{if } ff \text{ or } t < s \quad i.e \text{ if } t < s \\ tt & \text{if } tt \text{ and } t \geq s \quad i.e. \text{ if } t \geq s; \end{cases}$$

and finally, the scheduling functions $\delta_i : T \to T$ are defined by

$$\delta_i(t) = ((t-s) \ div \ \pi) + i - 1 \quad \text{for } i = 1, ..., n$$
$$= t - s + i - 1 \quad \text{for } i = 1, ..., n.$$

where π is replaced by its value 1 in $CONV_U$. Thus we have $F = CONV_U : [T \to R] \to [T \to R]$ defined by

$$CONV_U(x)(t) = \begin{cases} u & \text{if } \neg S(t) \text{ or } \neg R(t) \\ conv(r_1, \cdots, r_n, x(\delta_1(t)), \cdots, x(\delta_n(t))) & \text{if } S(t) \text{ and } R(t), \end{cases}$$

i.e. $CONV_U$ is a stream transformer of type I.

Having shown that $CONV_U$ is a stream transformer of type I, by referring back to Section 2 we also notice that $CONV_I$ is of exactly the same form as $CONV_U$ when we set $s = 2(n-1)$, $\lambda = 2$ and $\pi = 1$; hence $CONV_I$ is also a stream transformer of type I.

What is now necessary is to devise a programming methodology and supporting software tools that can realistically be applied to this general scheme to produce concurrent assignment algorithms.

3.5 A methodology for the construction of concurrent assignment programs

A systematic approach to the construction of concurrent assignment programs is necessary. If we do not have a methodology for their construction then, as algorithms and networks get increasingly complex (for example, algorithms based on the toroidal networks of Section 1), we will soon be dealing with large concurrent assignment programs that are not only difficult to prove correct, but also bear little or no resemblance to their original algorithm description.

In consequence, we need a *high level pre-processing language* that is tailored to the construction of implementations of a set of algorithms (for example algorithms that conform to a general scheme such as that of type I); facilitates the automatic generation of arbitrary large concurrent assignments; and retains the structure of the original informal algorithm description.

The programs in this paper have the following general form:

---

variable declaration -- *omitted for reasons of space.*
function definition -- *define function routines.*
variable initialisation -- *initialise variables where necessary and read in system constants*
repeat -- *execute our input, compute, output cycle continually*
    conditional read statement; -- *read new data every πth cycle.*
    concurrent assignment; -- *execute network.*
    write statement; -- *write data every cycle.*
    t := t + 1 -- *increment system clock.*
forever

Notice that the input, compute, output model of cycle activity of Section 2.3 is explicit in the program structure; i.e. each cycle we input data if required according to the input period; compute on the data; and output the results for tracing and analysis.

We need to isolate the parameters and functions that differ between individual specifications and the implementations and develop a suitable notation to represent them. From the type I scheme and the example programs, the significant differences between programs are: the dimensions of the system; the definition of the network N (i.e. the concurrent assignment implementation of the function f in the general scheme); the input period π when it is not 1 since we need to know when to input new values; constant values occurring in the system; and the registers at which stream input and output occur for the system.

We want N to be a single concurrent assignment constructed from the systolic diagrams of our algorithm description. However, we do not specify one large concurrent assignment, since this would re-introduce the problems of bulk and inflexibility, but instead we specify a collection of different *basic cells* or *modules* and function routines (taken directly from our informal algorithm description) together with their correct placement in the network from which we can generate a concurrent assignment of any desired size.

3.6 An introduction to a high level pre-processor

To illustrate our pre-processor we will re-implement P_{CONV} directly from its original specification in Section 2. We will then compare the new high level program H_{CONV} and the kernel level concurrent assignment program P_{CONV2} it generates.

3.6.1 Convolution

We need to specify the dimensions of the particular network we wish to create, any function routines used by the program, a description of the basic cells that form the network, and the registers at which stream input and output occur for the system,

Consider H_{CONV} in Figure 3.6.1. An account of the main features and constructs of this program is presented below:

The **const** block (1) specifies the constants parametrising the algorithm; in this case the size n of the network. The **var** block (2) declares the variables used in the network. The *var<expr>* notation (3) signifies that the evaluated expression *expr* will be concatenated to the variable *var*, for example "y<0>,y<n+1>" will be replaced by "y0,y4" and "w<i>,x<i>,y<i> **where** i := 1 **to** n" will be replaced by "w1,x1,y1,w2,x2,y2,w3,x3,y3" (in the case where n is 3). We use the **where** notation to specify repetition. Repetition statements can be combined using a ',' to specify multi-dimensional variables. For example, the statement:

"x<i><j> **where** i := 1 **to** 3, j := 1 **to** 3"

would generate the following string in the kernel level program:

"x11, x12, x13, x21, x22, x23, x31, x32, x33".

The **algorithm** construct (4) denotes the start of the algorithm. The notation "*ring* ^ n" is a shorthand for the n-fold sequence "*ring* * *ring* * .... * *ring*". We use "[...]" to enclose the type and number of those values that are expected as stream elements. Thus algorithm *conv* requires a vector of n constants, and a single input stream of values; and outputs a single stream of values.

The **constvars** construct (5) determines which values are to be input as constants to the kernel level program.

The **instream** construct (6) determines which registers will hold new input values in the kernel level program when they are received from the input stream.

The **outstream** construct (7) determines which registers will be used for output in the kernel level program when data for the results stream is ready.

The **function** construct (8) defines a function routine in the obvious way.

The **cell** construct (9) defines the functionality and placement of particular cells or modules within the system.

The construction of the complete concurrent assignment for the kernel level program is achieved by expanding the left and right hand side of each concurrent assignment within each cell and then combining them together into one single concurrent assignment.

Stream input occurs before the concurrent assignment is executed during every πth cycle. If the *input period* π is not specified then it is assumed to be 1, i.e. we input data every cycle. Stream output always occurs after the concurrent assignment is executed.

Constant value input statements are generated automatically before the central **repeat-forever** body commences. An optional initialisation section is also permitted before the central body for variable initialisation; though this feature is not used in this example.

The predefined time variable t is incremented after the read, compute, write operations have all been completed; thus, the length of a single time cycle includes input and output as well as the execution of the concurrent assignment.

The high level concurrent assignment program H_{CONV} (with dimension $n = 3$) will generate the kernel level concurrent assignment program P_{CONV2} given in Figure 3.6.2

The structure of P_{CONV2} is the same as that of the previous program P_{CONV}, however its high level description is far clearer; and its construction simpler and quicker. We do not have large concurrent assignments in our high level program; and can easily alter the size of the ones generated simply by changing a single constant n in H_{CONV}.

```
(1)     const
                n is 3  -- size for which the algorithm should be constructed.
(2)     var  -- declare variables used by the system
(3)             w<i>, x<i>, y<i> : ring where i := 1 to n;
                y<0>, y<n+1>   : ring
(4)     algorithm conv : ring^n * [ring] -> [ring]  -- the algorithm itself
(5)     constvars    w<i>  where i := 1 to n  -- constant values
(6)     instream     x<1>  -- register to store incoming stream elements.
(7)     outstream    y<1>  -- register to store outgoing stream elements.
        network conv  -- beginning of the network description
(8)             function f : ring^3 -> ring  -- definition of function routine
                invars w, x, y  -- input arguments
                outvars inner_prod  -- return value
                    inner_prod := w * x + y
                endfunction
(9)             cell io  -- define a cell called io
                    y<1> := f(w<1>, x<1>, y<2>)
                endcell
                cell inner_prod  -- define a cell called inner_prod
                    x<i>, y<i> := x<i-1>, f(w<i>, x<i>, y<i+1>) where i := 2 to n
                endcell
                cell zero  -- define a cell called zero
                    y<n+1> := 0
                endcell
        endnetwork  -- end of the network description
```

Figure 3.6.1: Pre-processor program H_{CONV}

```
var
        t : time;  -- predefined variable for time
        w1,x1,y1,w2,x2,y2,w3,x3,y3 : ring;
        y0,y4 : ring
function f : ring * ring * ring -> ring  -- from high level program.
invars w,x,y;
outvars inner_prod;
        inner_prod := w * x + y
endfunction
t := 0;  -- initialise system clock.
read (w1, w2, w3);  -- read in constant weights
repeat  -- continually repeat execution of the system
        read (x1);  -- read in new values every cycle
        y1,x2,y2,x3,y3,y4 := f(w1,x1,y2),x1,f(w2,x2,y3),x2,f(w3,x3,y4),0;
        write (y1);  -- write out result every cycle
        t := t + 1  -- increment the system clock
forever
```

Figure 3.6.2: Concurrent assignment program P_{CONV2}

3.7 Conclusion

The generation of the kernel level program P_{CONV2} using the pre-processor was very simple. All th information contained in the high level program H_{CONV} was *gained directly from the stream specificatic and the systolic diagrams.*

The new notation is independent of size, input and output periods and set-up time; it clearly reflects the structure of the original systolic design and does not contain large or complex concurrent assignments. In addition, because the generation of the kernel level programs is automatic, inconsistencies in algorithm designs are easier to spot.

Pre-processors for various commonly occurring classes of synchronous algorithms can be created and optimised as our classification theory of synchronous algorithms develops.

4. A proposal for a language

We propose to specify and implement a language based on the four constructs: abstract data types; clocks; function routines; and concurrent assignments. The language will be called *CARESS* (for Concurrent Assignment REpresentation of Synchronous Systems). A prototype language and compiler exist without the feature of user-defined abstract data types; a programmer's toolset involving ideas explained in Section 3 is being developed.

The language promises to be a satisfactory tool for analysing synchronous concurrent systems in the algorithmic stages of their design, both theoretically and experimentally.

From the point of view of its formal definition, and the specification and verification of its programs, the language benefits *in the short term* from its use of stores and assignments, since the semantics, and Floyd-Hoare verification theory, of elementary von Neumann constructs is well understood (see Apt [1981], de Bakker [1980] and Tucker and Zucker [1987]). Such work is a good foundation for studies of function routines which play an essential role in using abstract data type modules (a substantial study of this topic is Jervis [1987]). However, in the case of verification there is an alternative longer term strategy that we will explain shortly.

In this paper we have concentrated on some basic ideas involved in programming, simulating, and testing designs for algorithms with a language like *CARESS*. Note that the formal specification of synchronous systems, by means of stream transformers, is essential in order to give us a theoretical foundation for testing that allows us to *automatically* simulate and test our synchronous designs.

The ideas on formal specification we have used have been studied in detail independently of their application to *CARESS* in Harman and Tucker [1987]. The formulation of user specifications and implementation specifications is an interesting activity in its own right and requires its own software tools to create files of streams and to execute or *animate* specifications on such test data. Practical work on such a stream specification simulator is in progress as part of the project on the stream specification and translation language discussed in 3.2.

The language *CARESS* coupled to a stream specification simulator is intended to form the basis of a software environment for the design of synchronous algorithms.

To this basic environment can be added a functional language based upon abstract data types, clocks, and recursive functions. This language will be used to represent algorithms based on the synchronous model of Section 1 with a view to *formally proving* function programs representing synchronous algorithms meet specifications. It is important to think of this second collection of constructs as forming an independent language; an introduction to the constructs can be found in Thompson and Tucker [1985]; a detailed account of a prototype language, together with more complex algorithms and verifications, is contained in Thompson [1987]. This language we intend to call *DEDEKIND*, after Richard Dedekind who introduced the primitive recursive functions in 1888.

However, the idea behind adding the functional language *DEDEKIND* is to provide a second language, which is suited to verification, and is *computationally equivalent* to *CARESS*, which is suited to simulation and testing. The detailed study of the proofs of equivalence of constructs, and intertranslation of programs, has been undertaken by B. C. Thompson, who has also shown that the functional language is very well suited to formalising top-down design: see Thompson [1987].

In our prototype multirepresentational environment we propose to compile *DEDEKIND* programs to *CARESS* programs for their execution.

References
Andrews [1982].
Gregory R. Andrews, "The Distributed Programming Language SR - Mechanisms, Design and Implementation," *Software - Practice and Experience*, vol. 12, pp. 719-753, 1982.
Apt [1981].
K. R. Apt, "Ten years of Hoare logic. A survey - part 1," *ACM Trans. on Programming Languages and Systems*, vol. 3, pp. 431-483,

1981.

de Bakker [1980].
    Jaco de Bakker, *Mathematical Theory of Program Correctness*, Prentice-Hall International, 1980.

Barron et al [1963].
    D. W. Barron, J. N. Buxton, D. F. Hartley, E. Nixon, and C. Strachey, "The Main Features of CPL," *The Computer Journal*, vol. 6, pp. 134-143, 1963.

Blahut [1985].
    R. E. Blahut, *Fast Algorithms for Digital Signal Processing*, Addison-Wesley, 1985.

Chandy and Misra [1985].
    K. Mani Chandy and Jayadev Misra, *Parallelism and Programming: The Proper Perspective*, Computer Studies Departmental report, University of Texas at Austin, 1985.

Chandy and Misra [1986a].
    K. Mani Chandy and J. Misra, "Systolic Algorithms as Programs," in *Distributed Computing*, vol. 1, Springer-Verlag, 1986.

Chandy and Misra [1986b].
    M. Chandy and J. Misra, "An example of stepwise refinement of distributed programs: quiescence detection," *ACM Trans. on Programming Languages and Systems*, vol. 8, pp. 326-343, 1986.

Dewangan and Rangan [1983].
    Ramesh Dewangan and C. Pandu Rangan, *A Simple Implementation of Warshall's Algorithm on a VLSI Chip*, Dept. of Computer Science and Engineering, Indian Institute of Technology, 1983.

Dijkstra [1976].
    Edsgar W. Dijkstra, *A Discipline of Programming*, Prentice-Hall, 1976.

Fiat and Shamir [1984].
    Amos Fiat and Adi Shamir, "Polymorphic Arrays: A novel VLSI layout for Systolic Computers," in *25th FOCS*, pp. 37-45, IEEE, 1984.

Goguen et al [1978].
    J. A. Goguen, J. W. Thatcher, E. G. Wagner, and J. B. Wright, "An Initial Algebra approach to the Specification, Correctness and Implementation of Abstract Data Types," in *Current trends in Programming Methodology*, ed. R. T. Yeh, vol. IV Data Structuring, pp. 80-149, Prentice-Hall, 1978.

Gries [1978].
    D. Gries, "The Multiple Assignment Statement," *IEEE Transactions on Software Engineering*, vol. SE-4, pp. 89-93, 1978.

Harman and Tucker [1987].
    N. A. Harman and J. V. Tucker, *The Formal Specification of a Digital Correlator I : User Specification*, Centre for Theoretical Computer Science Report, The University of Leeds, 1987.

Hoare [1985].
    C. A. R. Hoare, *Communicating Sequential Processes*, Prentice-Hall International, 1985.

Jervis [1987].
    C. Jervis, *On the Specification, Implementation and Verification of Data Types*, PhD Thesis, Department of Computer Studies, The University of Leeds, to appear, 1987.

Kung [1982].
    H. T. Kung, "Why Systolic Architectures?," *Computer*, vol. 15, no. 1, pp. 37-46, 1982.

Liskov and Zilles [1975].
    Barbara H. Liskov and Stephen N. Zilles, "Specification Techniques for Data Abstraction," *IEEE Transactions on Software Engineering*, vol. SE-1, no. 1, pp. 7-19, March 1975.

Martin [1981].
    A. J. Martin, "The Torus: An Exercise in Constructing a Processing Surface," in *Caltech Conference on VLSI*, 1981.

Mead and Conway [1980].
    C. Mead and L. Conway, *Introduction to VLSI Systems*, Addison-Wesley, 1980.

Meinke [1987].
    K. Meinke, *A Mathematical Theory of Computation for Synchronous Circuits*, PhD Thesis, Department of Computer Studies, The University of Leeds, to appear, 1987.

Van Scoy [1980].
    Frances L. Van Scoy, "The Parallel Recognition of Classes of Graphs," *IEEE Trans. on Computers*, vol. C-29, no. 7, pp. 363-370, July 1980.

Sequin [1981].
    C. H. Sequin, "Doubly Twisted Torus Networks for VLSI Processor Arrays," in *Eigth Annual Symposium on Computer Architecture*, Minneapolis, Minnesota., 1981.

Snyder [1984].
    Lawrence Snyder, "Parallel Programming and the Poker Programming Environment," *Computer*, vol. 17, no. 7, pp. 27-36, July, 1984.

Snyder [1986].
    Lawrence Snyder, "Hearts: A Dialect of the Poker Programming Environment specialized to Systolic Computation," in *Proc. of the International Workshop on Systolic Arrays at The University of Oxford*, July 1986.

Thompson [1987].
    Ben Thompson, *Foundation of Compilation for VLSI Systems*, PhD Thesis, Department of Computer Studies, The University of Leeds, to appear, 1987.

Thompson and Tucker [1985].
    B. C. Thompson and J. V. Tucker, "Theoretical Considerations in Algorithm design," in *Fundamental algorithms for computer graphics*, ed. R. A. Earnshaw, pp. 855-878, Springer-Verlag, 1985.

Tucker and Zucker [1987].
    J. V. Tucker and J. Zucker, in *Program correctness over abstract data types, with error state semantics*, North-Holland, to appear, 1987.

Welch [1983].
    P. H. Welch, "Parallel Assignment Revisited," *Software - Practice and Experience*, vol. 13, pp. 1175-1180, 1983.

A New and Efficient Implementation of Multiprocess Synchronization

S.Ramesh
Department of Computer Science and Engineering
Indian Institute of Technology
Bombay - 400076,INDIA

1. Background and Motivation

With the widespread popularity of distributed processing, many high level notations/languages for expressing distributed programs have been proposed, which include Hoare's CSP[Ho] and ADA[Do]. A basic feature of all these language proposals is the use of message passing mechanisms as the means of process interaction. An important property of these mechanisms is that process interaction involves exactly two processes : one process sends a message while another process receives the message.

Recently, a few new mechanisms have been suggested for process communication that are symmetric and generalizations of the above two-process mechanisms. They are Shared Actions[RM] and Joint Actions[BK1]. These new mechanisms allow not only two but also an arbitrary number of processes to communicate simultaneously with each other. The communication is effected by permitting the concerned processes to collectively execute a piece of sequential code that accesses and updates the variables of the different processes involved.

This paper is concerned with the problem of implementation of such multi-process communication mechanisms. This problem is essentially the multiprocess generalization of the implementation of two-process mechanisms. The main task in the implementation of two-process as well as the multiprocess primitives is the implementation of global nondeterministic selection. Global nondeterminism is an important feature of all the high level langauges suggested for distributed programming; it is an extension of local nondeterminism[Di], first employed by Hoare[Ho]. During the execution of such programs, a process may be confronted with more than one choice of 'paths' to take, one of which is selected nondeterministically by the process. In local nondeterminism, the selection is purely decided by the process making the selection. Whereas in the other case, the selection is determined by similar selections by other processes. That is, a process selects a particular path provided there are many more processes (one more process in the case of two-process mechanism) each of which selects a corresponding path in its execution. It may be noted that this problem is essentially an agree-ment problem: making two or more processes agree over their selections.

Providing an efficient decentralized solution to this problem is a nontrivial task. Many unsuccessful attempts were made before an efficient implementation was given by Buckley and Silberschatz[BS]. They formulated four criteria to be satisfied by any efficient decentralized implementation and gave a solution (henceforth, referred to as BS - protocol or BS - algorithm) satisfying all these criteria. BS - algorithm is a two-phase algorithm which has been improved later by Back et al. [BEK] to get a single phase algorithm, that is more efficient and fair. Other solutions to this problem have been given in[Sb,Sc,Si]; they do not satisfy one or more of the above four criteria.

1.1 Our Contribution :

All these solutions offered in [BS,BEK,Sb,Sc,Si] are for the case of two-process mechanisms. We present, in this paper, a solution for the multiprocess mechanisms. Specifically, we give an implementation of the programs that use shared actions[RM]. The main contribution of this paper is to provide a new efficient solution, to the implementation problem of global nondeterminism in the general case of multiprocess synchronization that satisfies all the four criteria (more precisely, the criteria naturally extended to the case of multiprocess mechanisms) of Buckley and Silberschatz. It has also been that this new solution can be extended directly to one that is fair(more precisely that is just) with respect to processes and actions.

Other important features of our solution are: it is a single phase algorithm; when reduced to the two-process case, it gives rise to a new efficient solution different from all the existing solutions given for the same problem.

1.2 Related Works and Comparision :

A few solutions have been offered for the implementation of multiprocess mechanisms [BK2, BHK, Ek]. But all the implementations given in [BK2,BHK] make an assumption about the underlying network, entirely different from our assumptions. They assume that processes (more precisely, processors) in the underlying network communicate via a broadcasting facility. Whereas our solution assumes a general network, in which no such facility is available; the only way in which processes communicate is via point to point links that connect pairs of processes.

The implementation outlined by Eklund[Ek], however, assumes a point-to-point communication network. But our implementation is different and better than Eklund´s solution because of the following reasons : (1) Not all four criteria of Buckley and Silberschatz are satisfied by his implementation: the criterion, that among all processes that can participate in any handshake, atleast one will participate within a finite time, in a handshake (not necessarily the same one), is not satisfied by his implementation. This condition is guaranteed only for the processes that can participate in the lowest ordered handshake. Even with a dynamic ordering of the handshakes that ensures that each handshake is eventually ordered lowest, the above criterion will not be satisfied. This is because even before a handshake is ordered lowest, all the participating processes may go to the passive waiting state. (2) There is no need, in our implementation, to order (either statically or dynamically) the handshakes nor to work out a directed cycle of processes participating in the same handshake required by Eklund's implementation.(3) our solution can be extended to satisfy fairness. (4) The communication complexity of our implementation is of the same order as that of his solution.

1.3 Organization of the Paper :

The rest of the paper is organised as follows: Section 2 briefly gives an overview of PPSAs, the programs that employ shared actions; more detailed discussion can be found in [RM,Ra1]. The problem of implementation is taken up in Section 3. The correctness and the complexity of the implementation are discussed in Section 4. Finally, the paper concludes with Section 5 in which certain possible extensions to the present implementation are discussed.

2. PPSAs - Programs with Processes Involving Shared Actions

A PPSA is a high level distributed program consisting of a fixed number of processes. Each process has its own set of variables (disjoint from those of other processes) and a process code. Each process code may involve four kinds of actions : <u>Simple shared actions</u>, <u>boolean shared ac tions</u>, <u>alternate actions</u> and <u>iterative actions</u>. A simple shared action involves a command in GCL(the Guarded Command Language due to Dijkstra[Di]) while a boolean shared action involves a boolean expression. A shared action (simple or boolean) may occur in the process codes of more than one process and is said to be <u>shared by</u> all those processes in whose process codes it occurs; trivially the set of processes sharing an action could be a singleton. A shared action <u>may involve</u> the variables of a process that shares it. Also whenever a variable of a process occurs in a shared action, the action should be shared by that process.

An alternate action (iterative action) is of the form if $ga_1 \, \square \, \cdots \, \square \; ga_k$ fi (**do** $ga_1 \, \square \, \cdots \, \square \; ga_k$ **od**) where for each i $\in k = \{1,\ldots,k\}$, ga_i is a <u>guarded action</u> of the form g --> S; g is a guard and S is a sequence of actions involving simple shared/alternate/iterative actions. The general form of g is b;b´ where b is a boolean shared action shared by <u>only one process</u> and b´ is a boolean shared action shared by <u>more than one process</u>. The actions b and b´ are respectively called the <u>local</u> and <u>nonlocal compo</u> nents of g. The guard g can have only a local or nonlocal component and must have at least one such component.

Syntactically, a PPSA, say PP, consists of a declaration followed by a list of shared actions and a list of processes. The declaration defines a set of variables of PP. Each shared action in the shared action list has a name, a list of names of processes that share it and a <u>body</u>. The body is a GCL command or a boolean expression. Similarly each process in the process list has a name, a list of its variables and process code. The set of variables listed in a process is disjoint from the set of variables listed in any other process in the list and union of all these sets is the set of variables declared at the head of PP. The process code of a process is an action list consisting of names of simple shared/alternate/iterative actions. The names of processes and shared actions should be disjoint.

The following is an example of a PPSA:

```
PP ::  /*list of variables of PP*/
       var x₁,x₁´,x₂,x₂´,x₃,x₃´:integer;
       /* list of shared actions of PP */
       init₁: shared by P₁:
              x₁ := k₁
       end ;
         .
         .
         .
       init₃ : shared by P₃:
               x₃ := k₃
       end;
       exchange₁ : shared by P₁,P₂:
                   x₁´ := x₂ ;
                   if x₁ > x₁´ ---> x₁,x₁´:= x₁´,x₁
                   □  x₁ ≯ x₁´ ---> skip
                   fi ; x₂ := x₁´
       end;
       exchange₂: shared by P₂,P₃:
                  x₂´ : = x₃;
                  if x₂ > x₂´ ---> x₂,x₂´: = x₂´,x₂
                  □ x₂ ≯ x₂´ ---> skip
                  fi ; x₃ := x₂´
       end ;
       unsorted: shared by  P₁,P₂,P₃:
                 (x₁ > x₂) V (x₂ > x₃)
       end ;
       /* list of processes of PP */
       [P₁:: var x₁,x₁´;   /* variables of P₁ */
            init₁;
            do unsorted ---> exchange₁ od        /* process code of P₁ */
       || P₂:: var x₂,x₂´;  /* variables of P₂ */
            init₂;
            do unsorted ---> exchange₁; exchange₂ od   /* process code of P₂ */
       || P₃:: var x₃,x₃´;
            init₃;
            do unsorted ---> exchange₂ od
       ]
```

It may be noted that $init_1,\ldots,init_3$, $exchange_1$ and $exchange_2$ are simple shared actions while ´unsorted´ is a boolean shared action of PP; k1,...k3 are fixed integers. The shared actions $init_2$ is not shown above, as it can be obtained from

init_1 by replacing the subscript 1 of k, x and P, by 2.

2.1 Model of Execution

The execution of a PPSA involves the concurrent execution of its processes. Each process is executed by an agent (processor). The execution of a process consists of executing the actions in its process code (in the order specified). The execution of an action <u>succeeds</u> or <u>fails</u> (for the ease of presentation, we ignore trivial modes of failures like arithmetic overflow, division by zero etc.). The execution of a shared action in a process fails if one of the processes sharing that action has terminated. Otherwise, the execution of the action is delayed until all processes sharing that action reach the stage of executing the action in their respective process codes. The action is then <u>collectively</u> executed by all these processes.

In the case of simple shared action, such a collective execution may result in a change of values of the variables involved in the action. This change is the same as that would be produced when the body of the shared action is executed in accordance with GCL semantics. On the other hand, such a collective execution of a boolean shared action makes the processes know the value of the body which is nothing but a boolean expression. It may be noted that the effect of collective execution of a shared action shared by only one process can be produced by simply executing/evaluating the body of the shared action.

The collective execution of a simple shared action succeeds iff the execution of its body, in accordance with GCL semantics, succeeds whereas that of a boolean shared action succeeds iff the body evaluates to true.

The execution of an alternate action consists of selecting(the selection is nondeterministic) a guarded action, with a successfully executable guard, and executing it; if no guarded action has a successfully executable guard, the execution of the alternate action fails. The execution of a guarded action consists of executing its guard first and then the action list following the guard. A guard is executed by executing its constituent components from left to right. The guard succeeds iff the execution of its constituent component(s) succeed(s). The execution of an iterative action similarly consists of repeatedly performing the following action until all of its guards fail : select non-deterministically a guarded action, with a successfully executable guard, and execute it.

The execution of a process terminates successfully when all the actions executed during the execution have been successfully executed while that of a PPSA terminates successfully when all of its processes have been successfully executed. The execution of a PPSA fails whenever the execution of at least one of its processes fails or a deadlock occurs. A deadlock occurs when there is a set of processes each of which is ready to execute a shared action but is waiting for one or more processes (in the set) to reach the stage of executing the shared action.

As an illustration of this model of executing, consider the execution of

PP(the PPSA given earlier). Concurrent execution of P_1, P_2 and P_3 constitutes the execution of PP. The execution of each process P_i, $i = 1, \ldots, 3$, involves first executing $init_i$ and then repeatedly executing the only guarded action in the iterative action, that follows $init_i$, until ´unsorted´ fails. Each $init_i$ is shared by only one process and hence does not require any synchronization; it initializes x_i to k_i. The action ´unsorted´ is shared by all the processes and hence involves synchronization of all the four processes. Each $exchange_i$, $i = 1, 2$, exchanges the value of x_i and x_{i+1}, if $x_i > x_{i+1}$. Consequently repeated execution of the guarded actions of the iterative actions, eventually makes ´unsorted´ fail thereby sorting $x_1, \ldots, x_3$.

Remark 2.1 : It is evident from the execution model of PPSAs that shared actions are (like CSP primitives [Ho]) the means of process interactions. However, they differ from CSP primitives in one important aspect : shared actions are a multi-process generalization of two-process CSP primitives, as they can allow an arbitrary number of processes to synchronize and communicate with each other.

Remark 2.2 : The execution of an alternate/iterative action involves selection and execution of guarded actions. Since the execution of a guarded action involves executing the nonlocal component, it requires that each of the processes sharing the component to select a corresponding guarded action(that has the same nonlocal component). Thus the selection process is the generalization of the corresponding selection problem in CSP-like languages where only two processes will have to agree over the selection of guarded actions.

We shall now discuss the main problem of the paper, the implementation of PPSAs, especially the implementation of the selection process.

3. Implementation

The implementation of PPSAs requires a network of processes (more precisely, processors) that are connected to each other via point-to-point communication links. The processes are indexed by natural numbers, so that they are totally ordered by their indices. The point-to-point links are bidirectional and they neither corrupt, lose nor change the order in which messages are communicated among them. Any process can communicate with any other via these links, either directly or through one or more processes.

We have seen that the process codes of a PPSA involve simple shared actions, alternate actions and iterative actions. Hence, the implemenation of a PPSA consists of implementing each of these actions.

The implementation of simple shared action is straightforward and hence we do not discuss this here; for details of this implementation one can refer to [Ral].

The execution of an alternate(iterative) action(by a process) involves the following steps: (i) Selection of a guarded action whose local component evaluate to true,(ii) evaluating the nonlocal component and if the evaluation yields the value true then executing the action list following the guard and (iii) detecting whether the condition for failure (termination) of the action holds or not. Of all these steps, the nontrivial step is the selection step; the implementation of steps (ii) and (iii) are straightforward and we do not discuss this here. Consider the selection by a process P_i of an action, say, b_i; $b \text{--}> S_i$, where b_i and b are the local and nonlocal components and S_i is the list of actions; This selection requires that any P_j, sharing b should also select (at the same time) a b-action (a guarded action having b as the nonlocal component). As noted earlier, this is essentially a problem of agreement among a collection of processes and is the multiprocess generalization of the guard selection problem in the implementation of CSP with output guards. We shall now provide an efficient algorithm to solve this problem.

3.1 Distributed Selection Of Guarded Actions

As mentioned in the introduction, we give an algorithm for this problem that satisfy all the four criteria of Buckley and Silberschatz[BS]. Let b_i; $b \text{--}> S_i$ be a guarded action to be selected by a process P_i. Then the four criteria can be rephrased in the context of multiprocess synchronization as follows: (1) the number of processes that should be involved in the selection of b_i;$b \text{--}> S_i$ should be as small as possible, the minimum number being the total number of processes that share b, (2) the amount of system information that each of these processes know should also be minimum; only the states of those processes sharing b, be known to each of them, (3) when all the processes sharing b are ready to select b-actions, then atleast one of them will select an action (not necessarily the b-action) within a finite time and (4) the number of messages exchanged for making a selection by any process is bounded.

In order to get an algorithm that satisfies all these four criteria, we follow the same general outline of BS-algorithm. That is, each process is allowed to make a finite number of attempts to make any selection, during which time it exchanges a finite number of messages with other processes; and if it fails in all its attempts then it is allowed to go to a state (called W-state) in which it no longer makes any attempt to select but ready to agree over any acceptable selection made by other processes. More precisely, any process is modelled to be in one of the following states : E-state, W-state and a few intermediate states. In state E, a process is not attempting any selection but busy executing some action. A process is in one of the intermediate states when it is attempting to make a selection. Any process transits from E-state to one of the intermediate states, when it is required to make a selection. It then transits among the intermediate states for a finite number of times after which it goes either to E-state or W-state. In BS-algorithm, four intermediate states are required with two states per phase. Our algorithm involves only one phase and require just two states which we call Q1 and Q2.

The basic idea behind the algorithm is as follows. Any process P_i, when it encounters an alternate/iterative action during the execution, transits from E-state to Q1-state. In Q1-state, it chooses one of the actions, say, b_i;$b \text{--}> S_i$ with b_i

evaluating to true. Then it transits to Q2 and proceeds to get the agreement from all the processes, including itself(!), that share b. It should be noted that the fact P_i attempts to select an action does not mean that it has agreed to the selection; this is because when it is in the process of getting the agreement from other processes, it may give its consent to another process for the selection of another action. This happens since the process of getting agreement is asynchronous and follows the discipline given below.

We shall say that P_j is captured by P_i, whenever the former gives its consent to the latter to select an action. Thus, in order to select an action, P_i should capture itself and other processes sharing b. The following discipline is adopted in capturing processes:

(1) A process can capture itself, only if it is free(not captured by anyone).

(2) A procss can capture another process for the selection of a b-action, only if the latter process is free and is ready to select a b-action.

(3) When a process is captured by another, no other process can capture it; any process attempting to capture it is delayed.

(4) the capturing of different processes is done in steps and in the strict ordering of the process indices, i.e., if P_j and P_k are two processes to be captured by P_i, then the attempt to capture P_k is not made until P_j is captured by P_i, for any $j < k$.

If P_i succeeds in capturing all the processes sharing b, then the selection process is complete and it goes over to E-state directing all the captured processes to go to E-state. However, it is delayed when it tries to capture a process P_j (P_j may be P_i itself) that is already captured by some other process. P_i will eventually get a response saying that its attempt to capture P_j is successful or not depending upon whether P_j is freed by its captor or P_j makes the transition to E-state. If P_is attempt fails then it frees all the already captured processes and makes a fresh attempt to select another action, if any. If all the actions have been tried for selection in vain, then P_i transits to W-state.

It may be noted that, since only the capturing conditions (1), (2), (3) and (4), given above are to be satisfied for any process to be captured, P_i may be captured by another process, when it(P_i) is attempting to capture some process. It may also be noted that any request to capture a process is definitely answered eventually. Hence there is no need for more than one phase of computation as employed in BS-algorithm. The definite answer is got thanks to the capturing condition (3) which states that capturing is done in strict sequencing. This avoids the formation of circular chain of delayed processes waiting for each other's response.

We shall now describe the algorithm in more precise terms.

The following messages are exchanged among processes attempting selections.

req(b,i,j) - The request message from P_i to P_j in order to capture the latter for selecting a b-action yes(b,j,i) - The consent message from P_j to P_i that signals that P_j is captured by P_i.

no(b,j,i) - The no message from P_j to P_i that indicates that P_j is not ready to be captured by P_i

abort(b,i,j) - The message from P_i to P_j signalling that P_j is freed on account of P_i not being able to capture all the required processes.

success(b,i,j) - This is also a message from P_i to P_j that indicates that P_i's attempts to capture all the concerned processes is successful and that P_j can go to E-state, selecting a b-action.

The details of the different states in which any process P_i can be found are:

E-state - Execution state, in which P_i is executing and not attempting any selection

Q1-state - In this state, P_i is attempting to make a selection of a b-action

Q2-state - In this state, P_i has made a selection and is trying to capture all the relevant processes

W-state - Wait state, in which P_i passively waits for other processes to capture it.

The protocol requires each process P_i to maintain the following variables:

guard : It is an array variable whose index set is the set of all nonlocal components and range set is {untried, closed, rejected}. For any nonlocal component b, guard(b) can take one of these three values as follows:

        guard(b) = closed, if P_i does not want to select the b-action

               = untried, if P_i is ready to select the b-action but not yet made the attempt to select.

               = rejected, when P_i made an unsuccessful attempt to select the b-action.

captured : It is a boolean variable which is true, if P_i is captured by some process.

delay : It is a set variable, which at any time contains the indices of those processes whose request to capture P_i have been delayed.

List : It is a list variable containing, at any time, a sequence of indices in increasing order of those processes which P_i is yet to send its request for capturing them.

In addition to these variables, a function ´partners´ is used. Given a nonlocal component b, partners(b) is the sequence of the indices of all those processes that share b. The indices occur in increasing order.

We can now describe the protocol. Table 1 gives the details of the protocol, by giving the behaviour of any process P_i. Si and Si´s denote the state of P_i before and after an event occurs. The event may be receiving a message given under

Msgin, or/and sending a message - given under Msgout - or/and doing some local action - given under local action done.

In this table, for the sake of uniformity, P_i is shown to send (receive) message to (from) itself. Actually, these communications should be treated as appropriate local actions on the variables of P_i. In the table, $|list|$, h(list) and t(list) respectively denote the number of elements in ´list´, the head element of ´list´ and the tail of ´list´; a sequence having ´j´ as the head and ´s´ as the tail, will be denoted by j.s. ¬ and & denote logical negation and conjunction; $\emptyset$, U and - denote the empty set, set union and set difference operations respectively. Furthermore, i,j and k are indices of distinct processes and b,b´ and b˝ are distinct nonlocal components.

Si	Msgin	Si´	Local Action	Msgout
E	req(b,j,i)	E	---	no(b,i,j)
E	---	Q1	delay:=$\emptyset$,for each enabled b-action do guard(b):=untried	---
Q1&guard(b)=untried &partners(b)=j.s	---	Q2	list:=partners(b)	req(b,i,j)
Q1 & ¬ captured & guard(b)≠closed	req(b,j,i)	Q1	captured:=true	yes(b,i,j)
Q1 & captured & guard(b)≠closed	req(b,j,i)	Q1	delay:=delay U {j}	---
Q1 & captured & guard(b)=closed	req(b,j,i)	Q1	---	no(b,i,j)
Q1 & captured	success(b,j,i)	E	---	no(b´,i,k),for each k∈delay
Q1 & captured & delay=$\emptyset$	abort(b,j,i)	Q1	captured:=false	---
Q1 & captured & delay=A U {k} for some set A	abort(b,j,i)	Q1	delay:=delay-{k}	yes(b´,i,k)
Q1&guard(b)≠untried for each b	---	W	---	---
Q2 & ¬ captured guard(b)≠closed	req(b,j,i)	Q2	captured:=true	yes(b,i,j)
Q2 & captured & guard(b)≠closed	req(b,j,i)	Q2	delay:=delay U {j}	---
Q2 & captured & guard(b)=closed	req(b,j,i)	Q2	---	no(b,i,j)
Q2 & $|list|$>1	yes(b,j,i)	Q2	list:=t(list)	req(b,i,k),for k=h(list)
Q2 & $|list|$=1	yes(b,j,i)	E	---	success(b,i,k) for each P_k sharing b, no(b´,i,j) for each j∈delay
Q2 & $|list|$≥1	no(b,j,i)	Q1	guard(b):=rejected	abort(b,i,k),for each k captured by i
Q2 & captured & delay=$\emptyset$	abort(b,j,i)	Q2	captured:=false	---
Q2 & captured & delay=A U {k} for some set A	abort(b,j,i)	Q2	delay:=delay-{k}	yes(b´,i,k)

Q2 & captured	success(b,j,i)	E	captured:=false	abort(b´,i,k),for each k captured by i, no(b´´,i,k),for each kЄdelay.
W & ¬ captured & guard(b)≠closed	req(b,j,i)	W	captured:=true	yes(b,i,j)
W & captured & guard(b)≠closed	req(b,j,i)	W	delay:=delay U {j}	---
W & guard(b)=closed	req(b,j,i)	W	---	no(b,i,j)
W & captured & delay=∅	abort(b,j,i)	W	captured:=false	---
W & captured & delay=A U {k}	abort(b,j,i)	W	delay:=delay - {k}	yes(b´,i,k)
W & captured	success(b,j,i)	E	captured:=false	no(b´,i,k),for each kЄdelay.

We shall establish the correctness of the algorithm and analyse its complexity, in the next section.

4.Analysis of the Algorithm

4.1 Logical Analysis of the Algorithm:

The following theorems state the important properties of the algorithm.

Theorem 1: Any process which is in Q1-state will within a finite time enter either the W-state or E-state.

Theorem 2: Whenever a process, say, P_i goes over to E-state as a result of successful selection of a b-action, then all the other processes sharing b also go over to E-state selecting b-actions; furthermore, in such a case, the local components, if any, of all these selected actions evaluate to true.

Theorem 3: When a process P_i enters W-state then for every enabled b-action in P_i, it is not the case that all the processes sharing b are in the W-state.

Theorem 1 asserts that no process will spend an unbounded amount of time in trying to select a guarded action. Theorem 2 is a sort of soundness condition that guarantees that whenever a process selects a b-action all the processes sharing b also select b-actions with all the corresponding local components evaluating to true. Theorem 3 ensures deadlock freedom. Since W-state is a passive state, any process entering it, will not attempt, on its own, any selection. Hence, to avoid deadlocking, atleast one of the processes should be ´outside´ the W-state to ´awaken´ the other processes, if any, that have gone into the W-state.

It can be easily seen that these theorems state the results that are multiprocess generalizations of the corresponding results proved in [BS,BEK]. Hence, it follows from these theorems that the given selection algorithm satisfies the generalised criteria (3) and (4) stated in Section 3.1; it is obvious to infer from the algorithm that the other two criteria are also satisfied.

Theorem 1 follows from the following facts: (1) any process P_i starting from Q1-state, before going to E-state or W-state, flips over from Q1 to Q2 atmost as many number of times as there are guarded actions that P_i is willing to select and

(2) a process in Q2-state jumps back to Q1-state after a finite amount of time. Fact (1) is easy to prove. Fact (2) is a consequence of the discipline followed in capturing processes. The discipline of capturing processes, one after another in the increasing order of their indices ensures that there cannot be a set S of processes, each of which is delayed to capture a process (which may be itself) in S which is already captured by another process in S; existence of such a set contradicts that the indices of the processes are totally ordered.

Theorem 2 is straightforward to prove.

Theorem 3 can be proved by contradiction. Suppose that for a nonlocal component b, all P_i sharing b are in W-state at some time. Any of these processes, say, P_{i1} must have gone to W-state(without going to E-state), after receiving a ´no´ message from some other process, say, P_{i2} that shares b. P_{i2} cannot be in W-state at that time, since it can send a ´no´ message only when it is in or is about to enter E-state. Hence P_{i2} must have gone to W-state, only after receiving a ´no´ message from P_{i3} different from P_{i1}. P_{i3}, in turn, should have received a ´no´ message from P_{i4}, different from both P_{i1} and P_{i2}, in order to go to W-state. Continuing this argument, we get a sequence of processes $P_{i1}, P_{i2}, \ldots$, each of which went to W-state after receiving a ´no´ from the process next in the sequence. But there is only a finite number of processes that share b. Hence there will be a process P_j in the above sequence for which there is no process that is in E-state (or about to enter E-state) to say ´no´. This contradicts the fact that P_j has entered the W-state.

4.2 Complexity Analysis of the Algorithm: We shall evaluate the efficiency of the algorithm in terms of the message load caused by any process. We shall calculate the worst case message load. The worst case message load caused by any process P_i is the sum of the maximum number of messages P_i sends out on its own and the maximum number of messages it receives in response.

Let m_i be the maximum number of guarded actions in any alternate/iterative action in P_i); further, let k be the maximum number of processes that can share any action in the PPSA(note that $2 \leq k \leq n$). P_i, starting from Q1-state, goes finally to either E-state or W-state, within which period, it sends messages and receives responses.

Case(i): P_i goes to E-state eventually: In this case, P_i sends out the maximum number of messages, when it succeeds in selecting an action, after attempting in vain to select (m_i-1) actions. The maximum number of messages exchanged then are, $m_i(k-1)$ request messages, $m_i(k-1)$ yes/no messages, $(m_i-1)(k-1)$ aborts and $(k-1)$ successes. Note that, of the k-processes to be captured, P_i is also included. The communication performed to capture itself is essentially a local action and hence not included in the message count.

Thus the total message load in this case is $3(k-1)m_i$.

Case(ii): P_i goes eventually to W-state: In this case, all the attempts by P_i to select any one of the m_i actions are in vain. Hence the total number of messages are $m_i(k-1)$ requests, $m_i(k-1)$ yes/no messages and $m_i(k-1)$ aborts. Hence the total count is $3(k-1)m_i$.

Thus the maximum message load caused by a single process is $3(k-1)m_i$. It may be noted that this maximum load is caused by that process P_i for which the indices of all the processes participating with P_i for selections are less than i. For other processes, the maximum load will be less than the above by atmost m_i; this is because, for each guarded actions the maximum number of ´abort´ messages sent is reduced by one message.

This maximum load can be compared with the message load in Eklund´s algorithm[Ek], which is $(2km_i-m_i+1)$. $(2km_i-m_i+1)$ is less than $3(k-1)m_i$ for all values of k>2; for k=2 they are equal. However, both are of the same order. It may be mentioned that the load caused by a process in Eklund´s algorithm is always fixed and the same for all processes, wheras the load of $3(k-1)m_i$ in our case is the worst case load.

Consider the special case of k=2. In this case, the mechanism is a two-process mechanism and the message load due to a process has been shown in[Ra2] to be $2m_i + q_i$, where q_i is the maximum number of processes, with indices less than i, that are referred in the guards of any alternate/iterative action. Compare this with the message loads of BS-algorithm and the two algorithms due to Back et al.[BEK]; they are respectively $2m_i+3q_i$, $4m_i-2q_i$ and $4m_i-3q_i$. In the worst case, the values of q_i are m_i, 0, 0 respectively. Consequently, the worst case message loads are $5m_i$, $4m_i$ and $4m_i$ respectively all being greater than $3m_i$, which is the worst case value of our algorithm.

Given the maximum load of $3(k-1)m_i$, the maximum number of system messages associated with a successful selection is $3k(k-1)m_i$; in the special case of k=2, this is $4m_i + 2q_i$.

5. Improvements and Future Work:

The algorithm proposed in Section 3, suffers from one disadvantage, namely, it is not fair with respect to either processes nor actions as can be seen from the following argument: Suppose P_i is a process which goes to W-state, after attempting in vain to select any action. Let b;b´ --> S be any one of these actions and b´ be the action shared by P_i and P_j only, where i<j. It may happen that after P_i had gone to W-state, P_j may be infinitely often be ready (and even attempt) to select the b´action but may not succeed at all. This is because of the following reason:in order to select the b´-action, P_j has to capture P_i before capturing itself,since i<j. While P_j waits for the capture of P_i, it may get captured by another process P_k for the selection of another action which may be successful. Consequently, P_j may infinitely often go to E-state without selecting the b´-action and hence P_i may starve indefinitely.

We shall show that the proposed algorithm can be easily modified to get a solution that satisfies the following fairness requirement:

Theorem 4:   If a process has got an action that is infinitely often <u>continuously</u> enabled, then it will eventually go to E-state.

By continuous enabling of a b-action, we mean that, whenever a process sharing b is outside E-state, it is ready to select the b-action.

The modification essentially involves changing the response of processes to capturing requests. In the original algorithm, any capturing request made by a process P_i to another process P_j (in order to select a b-action) is greeted with a ´yes´, iff P_j is free and ready to select the b-action; the request is rejected otherwise. In order to get a fair solution, the algorithm is so modified that P_i´s request is rejected iff P_j is free but not ready to select the b-action; if P_j is not free(i.e., it is either in E-state or captured) then P_i´s request is queued up in a queue, at P_j, that contains all the requests made by other processes to capture P_j. P_j, whenever it becomes free, checks the queue and removes all those requests for which it is not ready and sends ´no´ messages to the corresponding processes. P_j, then, removes the first request, if any, from the queue and sends a ´yes´ to the corresponding process.   Thus any process requesting to capture P_j for the selection of a b-action is delayed in the queue, till its turn comes, as long as P_j is willing to select the b-action.   Excepting for this modification , the other aspects of the algorithm (like the number of states, the types of messages exchanged and the conditions under which state transitions occur) remain the same.

It can be easily shown, along the same lines, that the modified algorithm satisfies Theorems (1) - (3) of Section 4.

What Theorem 4 guarantees is referred in the literature as weak fairness or justice with respect to the processes. Weak fairness with respect to actions, can also be achieved by making each process follow a fair selection policy while selecting b-actions for execution; this fair selection policy should ensure that no process that flips over from Q1 to Q2 state infinitely often, avoids selecting any particular b-action that can be selected(i.e that has a local component which evaluates to true). Note that action fairness ensures that whenever an action is infinitely often enabled <u>continuously,</u> it will be eventually be executed.

It may be noted that the complexity analysis carried out in Section 4, directly applies to the above modifications. Due to space limitations, we are not going into the detailed discussion on the improvements, their correctness and their complexity; we will report these in a future paper.

In[Ra2], we have presented another way of modifying the algorithm of Section 3 to get a solution that satisfy process fairness, in the special case of two-process communication primitives.

It is interesting to see how the proposed algorithm can be modified to get an algorithm that satisfies the stronger fairness requirement that guarantees that whenever an action is enabled infinitely often(not necessarily continuously), it is executed eventually. Currently work is in progress to get such a fair solution.

Acknowledgements: The author wishes to thank I.I.T. Bombay especially Prof.Mehndiratta for the financial support given during the period of this work. Also many thanks are due to Prof.Eklund for furnishing the author with his paper and to Radhakrishnan, Ravindran and the referees for their useful comments, which improved the presentation of this paper.

References

[BK1]   Back,R.J.R. and Kurki-Suonia,R., Decentralization of process nets with centralized control, Proc. of 2nd ACM Conf. on PODC, Montreal, August 1983.

[BK2]   Back,R.J.R. and Kurki-Suonia,R., Cooperation in distributed system using symmetric multiprocess handshaking, Tech.Report, Ser.A, No.34, Abo Akademi, Finland, 1984.

[BEK]   Back,R.J.R., Eklund.P. and Kurki-Suonia,R., A fair and efficient implementation of CSP with output guards, Tech.Report, Ser.A, No.38,Abo Akademi, Finland, 1984.

[BHK]   Back,R.J.R.,Hartikainen, E. and Kurki-Suonio,R., Multiprocess Handshaking on broadcasting networks, Tech.Report, Dept. of Computer Science, Ser.A, No.42, Abo Akademi, Finland, 1985.

[BS]   Buckley,G.N. and Silberschatz,A., An effective implementation for the generalized input-output construct of CSP, ACM TOPLAS, Vol.5, No.2, 1983.

[Di]   Dijkstra,E.W.D., A discipline of programming, Prentice-Hall, Englewood Cliffs, 1976.

[Do]   U.S.DOD., Programming language ADA: Reference manual, LNCS 106, Springer-Verlag, Berlin, 1981.

[Ek]   Eklund,P., Synchronizing Multiple Processes in common handshakes, Tech. Report, Ser.A, No.39, Dept. of Computer Science, Abo Akademi, Finland, 1984.

[Ho]   Hoare,C.A.R., Communicating sequential processes, Communication of the ACM, Vol.21, No.8, 1978.

[RM]   Ramesh,S. and Mehndiratta,S.L., A new class of high level programs for distributed computing systems, Proc. of 5th Conf. on FST-TCS, LNCS 206, Springer-Verlag, Berlin, 1985.

[Ra1]   Ramesh,S., Programming with Shared Actions: A methodology for developing distributed programs, Ph.D thesis submitted to I.I.T., Bombay, June 1986.

[Ra2]   Ramesh,S., A new efficient implementation of CSP with output guards, Submitted for Publication.

[Sb]   Silberschatz,A.,Communication and synchronization in distributed systems, IEEE-TSE, Vol.SE-5, No.6, 1979.

[Sc]   Schwartz,J.S., Distributed synchronization of communicating sequential processes, Tech. Report, DAI TR 56, Department of A.I., University of Edinburgh.

[Si]   Sistla,A.P., Distributed algorithms for ensuring fair interprocess communication, Proc. of the ACM Conf. on PODC, Vancouver, 1984.

Rewriting techniques for the temporal analysis of communicating processes[*]

Ph. Schnoebelen[†]

Laboratoire d'Informatique Fondamentale
et d'Intelligence Artificielle
Grenoble - FRANCE

Abstract

State transitions systems are the most commonly used model for the static analysis of the dynamic behaviour of parallel programs. One difficulty for implementing such analyzers is the lack of structure of the set of states. As a consequence, only finite state systems are considered as analyzable. We present a method based on term rewriting, which permits to mechanically deal with transition systems having an infinite number of states, and show how it can be applied to the FP2 programming language where communicating processes are described through rewrite rules.

1 Introduction

State transition systems [Kel76] are at the basis of almost every model of parallel computation, and indeed they have proved to be suited for the formal analysis of the behaviour of distributed systems [Sif82].

It is with such considerations in mind that the FP2 language [Jor86] has been devised. In FP2, one can define parallel communicating processes and combine them. These processes are defined with (some kind of) rewrite rules which directly translate into labelled state transition systems. In addition, the uniform use of terms and rewrite rules throughout the language gives some algebraic structure to the set of states and to the transition relation. This structure may be used to build a tool for automatically analysing the behaviour of FP2 processes, for, in general, it is the lack of such a structure that prevents the formal methods developed around transition systems from being actually implemented, and usually only finite state systems are mechanically handled (with protocol analysis as a typical target application).

In this paper, we investigate the term rewriting aspects of FP2 and show that they allow us to represent and manipulate the sets of states (i.e. predicates) which appear while analysing the behaviour of processes. These results are obtained as an application of the *anti-unification* algorithm of H. Comon [Com86b,Com86c].

We first recall the necessary definitions and results about transition systems. Then we present the subset of FP2 which will be considered in the following. The third section describes the representation we propose for predicates and explains how it can be used. Then we consider, as an example application, a one-place buffer for which several properties are proved.

---

[*]This work has been supported, in part, by ESPRIT Project 415 and by CNRS Project C3.

[†]Author's address: LIFIA-IMAG, BP 68, 38402 St Martin d'Heres CEDEX, FRANCE. UUCP: mcvax!imag!lifia!phs

2 Transition systems

The reader can find a complete presentation of the material of this section in, for example, [Sif82].

A transition system is a couple $S = (Q, \rightarrow)$ where Q is a countable set of *states* and $\rightarrow \subseteq Q \times Q$ is a *transition relation* on the states of Q. If $(q, q') \in \rightarrow$, noted $q \rightarrow q'$, we say that $q \rightarrow q'$ is a *transition* of S, that q' *can be reached (is reachable)* from q, or that q' is a *possible successor* of q. A state which has no possible successor is a *blocked* state (or a *sink* state) and we write $SINK$ for the subset of all blocked states.

A transition is intended to model an *indivisible step* of the system. Moreover, nothing prevents $\rightarrow$ from being a non-functional relation, i.e. there may exist states with *several* possible successors. Transition systems are *sequential, non-deterministic* models.

A sequence $w = q_0, q_1, \ldots$ of states such that $q_i \rightarrow q_{i+1}$ for all i is a *computation*, having q_0 as initial state. A computation may be finite only if its last state is a blocked state. We note $q \xrightarrow{*} q'$ if q' belongs to a computation starting from q. $\xrightarrow{*}$ is the reflexive and transitive closure of $\rightarrow$. If $q \xrightarrow{*} q'$, we also say that q' is reachable from q.

2.1 Predicates and predicate transformers

Given $S = (Q, \rightarrow)$ a transition system, we consider $P(Q)$, the powerset of Q. $P(Q)$ can be given a boolean algebra structure $\mathcal{L} = (P(Q), \cup, \cap, -, Q, \emptyset)$ (see [Grä79]) which is isomorphic to the algebra of unary predicates on Q (i.e. one-place functions from Q to $\{$true, false$\}$), if we associate to the predicate $\mathbf{P}$ the subset $P \subseteq Q = \{q \in Q \mid \mathbf{P}(q) = \textbf{true}\}$. The lattice $(P(Q), \cup, \cap)$ is a distributive complete lattice with Q and $\emptyset$ as, respectively, top and bottom elements.

Let $\mathcal{F}$ be the set of unary functions mapping $P(Q)$ into $P(Q)$. An element of $\mathcal{F}$ is a *predicate transformer*. We define on $\mathcal{F}$ the operations $\vee, \wedge, \neg, \tilde{}, {}^*$ and $^\times$ by:

$$(\mathbf{F} \vee \mathbf{G})(P) = \mathbf{F}(P) \cup \mathbf{G}(P)$$

$$(\mathbf{F} \wedge \mathbf{G})(P) = \mathbf{F}(P) \cap \mathbf{G}(P)$$

$$(\neg\mathbf{F})(P) = \overline{\mathbf{F}(P)}$$

$$\tilde{\mathbf{F}}(P) = \overline{\mathbf{F}(\overline{P})}$$

$$\mathbf{F}^*(P) = P \cup \mathbf{F}(P) \cup \mathbf{F}^2(P) \ldots$$

$$\mathbf{F}^\times(P) = P \cap \mathbf{F}(P) \cap \mathbf{F}^2(P) \ldots$$

for all $\mathbf{F}, \mathbf{G} \in \mathcal{F}$, $P \subseteq Q$, with the usual $\mathbf{F}^{n+1} = \mathbf{F}.\mathbf{F}^n$ and $\mathbf{F}^0 = I$, the identity function on $P(Q)$. $\tilde{\mathbf{F}}$ is called the *dual* of $\mathbf{F}$, $\mathbf{F}^*$ and $\mathbf{F}^\times$ are $\mathbf{F}$*starred* and $\mathbf{F}$*crossed*.

We also define two special predicate transformers: $pre[\rightarrow]$ and $post[\rightarrow]$, written pre and $post$ when $\rightarrow$ is clear from the context, by:

$$pre(P) = \{q \in Q \mid \exists q' \in P, q \rightarrow q'\}$$

$$post(P) = \{q \in Q \mid \exists q' \in P, q' \rightarrow q\}$$

Informally, $pre(P)$ is the set of states from which P can be reached in one step, $post(P)$ is the set of states which can be reached in one step, coming from P. From these definitions, it appears that $pre(A \cup B) = pre(A) \cup pre(B)$, pre and $post$ are *distributive* (and then they are monotonic). We may also remark that $pre[\rightarrow] = post[\rightarrow^{-1}]$.

We can form the dual of *pre* and *post*: $\widetilde{post}(P)$ is the set of states that cannot be reached (in one step) from a state not in P, that is, the states which can be reached only from states of P, or which cannot be reached at all. Similarly, $\widetilde{pre}(P)$ is the set of states from which we cannot go outside P (in one step), that is, the states from which we can go only to P, or from which we are blocked, and then we see that $SINK = \widetilde{pre}(\emptyset)$.

2.2 Temporal modalities as predicate transformers

It is now possible to define the four well-known modal operators of branching-time temporal logic (see [Lam80,AH86])[1]:

- $q \in \mathbf{POT}\ P$ iff a state of P can be reached from q:

$$\mathbf{POT}\ P = \{q \in Q \mid \exists q' \in P, q \xrightarrow{*} q'\} = pre^*(P)$$

- $q \in \mathbf{ALL}\ P$ iff all states reachable from q are in P:

$$\mathbf{ALL}\ P = \{q \in Q \mid \forall q' \in Q, q \xrightarrow{*} q' \Rightarrow q' \in P\} = \widetilde{pre}^{\times}(P)$$

- $q \in \mathbf{INEV}\ P$ iff any computation starting from q contains a state of P:

$$\mathbf{INEV}\ P = \{q \in Q \mid \forall w = q_0(=q) \to q_1 \to q_2 \to \ldots\ \exists i \in N, q_i \in P\}$$

$$\mathbf{INEV}\ P = (I \vee pre \wedge \widetilde{pre})^*(P)$$

- $q \in \mathbf{SOME}\ P$ if there is a computation starting from q, containing only states of P:

$$\mathbf{SOME}\ P = \{q \in Q \mid \exists w = q_0(=q) \to q_1 \to q_2 \to \ldots\ \forall i \in N, q_i \in P\}$$

$$\mathbf{SOME}\ P = (I \wedge (pre \vee \widetilde{pre}))^{\times}(P)$$

We have $\mathbf{ALL} = \widetilde{\mathbf{POT}}$ and $\mathbf{SOME} = \widetilde{\mathbf{INEV}}$

2.3 Temporal analysis of transition systems

In this framework it is possible to express some properties we would like to prove about a transition system $S = (Q, \to)$.

For example, $\neg\mathbf{POT}\ SINK$ is the set of states from which it is not possible to reach $SINK$, that is, to reach a blocked state. S *will not* deadlock if it is initialized in a state of $\neg\mathbf{POT}\ SINK = \neg pre^*(SINK)$. S *will* deadlock if it is in a state of $\mathbf{INEV}\ SINK = (I \vee pre \wedge \widetilde{pre})^*(SINK)$. S *may* deadlock if it is in a state of $\mathbf{POT}\ SINK$. S *will always have the possibility* to deadlock in the future it it is initialized in $\mathbf{ALL\,POT}\ SINK$. Note that this is different from $\mathbf{POT}\ SINK$ because when S is in $\mathbf{POT}\ SINK$, it is possible to leave $\mathbf{POT}\ SINK$ and then to reach a state where no future deadlock is possible, while if S is in $\mathbf{ALL\,POT}\ SINK$, no matter which transitions are chosen, it will always be possible to reach $SINK$.

If we want to use this approach in a tool for the analysis of transition systems, we have to find a way to compute such predicates. This is possible because of the monotonicity of our basic predicate transformers and because $\vee$, $\wedge$

---

[1] Classically $\mathbf{POT}$, $\mathbf{ALL}$ and $\mathbf{INEV}$ are written $\Diamond, \Box$ and $\leadsto$. Our notation appeared in [QS82].

and $\widetilde{}$ preserve monotonicity. Indeed, in order to compute $\mathbf{F}^*(P)$ (with $\mathbf{F}$ monotonic), one just computes $\mathbf{F}^0(P), \mathbf{F}^1(P), \mathbf{F}^2(P) \ldots$ until $\mathbf{F}^{n+1}(P) \subseteq \mathbf{F}^n(P)$ for some $n \in N$ (until $\mathbf{F}^{n+1}(P) \supseteq \mathbf{F}^n(P)$ if we are looking for $\mathbf{F}^\times(P)$) in which case $\mathbf{F}^*(P)$ is simply $\bigcup_{i=0\ldots n} \mathbf{F}^i(P)$. If $\mathbf{F}$ is also distributive, the halting criterion is $\mathbf{F}^{n+1}(P) \subseteq \bigcup_{i \leq n} \mathbf{F}^i(P)$ (note that we do not need to make any assumption about the continuity of $\mathbf{F}$, and that, in general, *pre* and *post* are not continuous).

Of course, this procedure may fail to terminate (computing **INEV** $SINK$ is solving the halting problem for a specific system), but it gives us a semi-decision criterion. One particular case where it always terminates is when Q is finite and, indeed, some systems have already been developped to analyze finite transition systems: see [Que81,QS82].

We may summarize this section by saying that we are now able to analyze the temporal behaviour of transition systems provided that we have a sufficiently rich set of elementary predicates, that we can form the unions, intersections and complements of predicates, that we can compute the *pre* and *post* functions and, last but not least, that we can decide the equivalence of two given predicates, which amounts to be able to check for emptiness of a predicate if we know how to do the other operations.

An important point is that the other methods used for the analysis of transition systems essentially use the same building blocks, so that the techniques we present in the remaining sections could be used with another temporal logic (e.g. [GS85]), or in the algorithms defined in the "observational equivalence" approach [Mil80].

3   The FP2 programming language

FP2 is a *parallel* programming language based on term rewriting. We shall shortly present a subset of the language on which we shall prove temporal assertions. A more complete description of the language may be found in [Jor86].

The main feature of FP2 we want to use is the possibility of defining communicating processes through rewrite systems, which are extremely well suited for formal manipulations. This will allow us to represent and compute with predicates in a very smooth way.

3.1   Types and terms

In FP2, types are defined as term algebras on sets of constructor names. This follows the now well-established theory of algebraic specifications for abstract data types [GHM78,GH78]. Functions on these types are defined through equations, which give an operational semantics built on pattern matching and term rewriting. Types and functions may be *generic*, i.e. parameterized by other types and functions in the sense of [Ehr82,EKT*84], but we shall not consider these features in this paper. The interested reader should refer to [Jor86] or look at other languages with the same features [GM85,BE86].

Formally, the types are defined as the initial algebra T_Σ of an heterogenous (i.e. many-sorted) signature $\Sigma = (S, \Sigma_{s \in S})$ where S is a set of *sorts* and Σ_s is a set of *constructor names* for the sort s, given with an arity function $\rho_s : \Sigma_s \to S^*$ [Grä79]. S^* is the set of finite strings over S and we use ϵ to denote the empty string.

For example, we could have $S = \{Bool, Nat\}$, $\Sigma_{Bool} = \{true, false\}$, $\Sigma_{Nat} = \{O, succ\}$, $\rho_{Bool}(true) = \rho_{Bool}(false) = \rho_{Nat}(O) = \epsilon$ and $\rho_{Nat}(succ) = (Nat)$, which means that $true$ and $false$ are boolean constants, O is a integer constant and $succ$ is a one place constructor having an integer as argument.

In the FP2 syntax, such a signature is entered by:

$$
\begin{array}{ll}
type\ Bool\ is & type\ Nat\ is \\
\quad true & \quad succ(Nat) \\
\quad false & \quad 0 \\
end & end
\end{array}
$$

3.2 Communicating processes

In FP2, one can define and use *communicating processes*. An FP2 process is a transition system whose states are ground terms and whose transitions are described by rewrite rules. The transitions are labelled by *events* which are communication actions with the external environment[2].

Formally, an FP2 process has a set of (typed) *connectors* (i.e. ports through which it sends and receives messages). The transmission of a value v along a connector C is a *communication*, written $C(v)$. An event is a possibly empty set of communications occurring within one transition. The states of a process are terms built on a set of *state constructors* (given with their arity), so that the states of a process really form another abstract data type. The possible transitions are defined by *transition rules*. A transition rule is a rewrite rule (for the state) with an event part. The process also has *initial rules* which specify possible initial states.

Here is an example process: ADD is initialized in state X, then it repeatedly receives two natural numbers along its A and B connectors, computes their sum and sends it along its C connector before going back to its initial state.

$$
\begin{array}{rcll}
\textbf{proc}\ ADD\ \textbf{is} & & & \\
 & & ==> & X \\
X & : & A(n)\ B(m) \quad ==> & Y(n,m) \\
Y(0,n) & : & C(n) \quad ==> & X \\
Y(succ(n),m) & : & ==> & Y(n,succ(m)) \\
\textbf{end} & & &
\end{array}
$$

After the inputs $A(3)$ and $B(4)$ (say), ADD is in state $Y(3,4)$ and then the only possible transitions are $Y(3,4) \rightarrow Y(2,5) \rightarrow Y(1,6) \rightarrow Y(0,7)$. In state $Y(0,7)$, the output $C(7)$ will occur.

These transition rules define an operational semantics: at initialisation, the process non-deterministically chooses one of its initial rules and then computes its initial state. Then, a rule is *preapplicable* if its left hand side matches the current state, it is *applicable* if the environment agrees with the communications of the event part (*internal rules*, i.e. rules having an empty event, are always applicable if they are preapplicable). The process eventually chooses (non-deterministically) an applicable rule and applies it: the event occurs and the current state of the process is rewritten. We see that the process exhibits *global nondeterminism* as the environment may forbid the application of a preapplicable rule, in which case another rule will eventually be chosen.

In the full FP2 language, processes may also use user-defined functions instead of just constructors. We do not consider this possibility in this paper, in fact constructors are sufficient to define a process for any computable function [Per84].

Term rewriting is a very popular topic and it has proven to be well suited for the formal analysis of programs. Indeed, in the next section we shall apply some successful

---

[2]Transition systems are often defined as a couple $(Q, (\xrightarrow{a})_{a \in A})$ where A is a set of *actions* which provide the labelling [Sif82,Kel76]. And then $\rightarrow = \bigcup_{a \in A} \rightarrow_a$.

methods from that field. However, it should be clear that our problems are different from those usually studied in the rewriting community (see [HO80]): for example, we are not interested in Church-Rosser properties but, for process transitions, the consequences of *fair rewriting* could be studied. Also our transition rules always apply at the top of the terms and not on a subterm: such rewriting systems have been called *term transition systems* in [Per84] and *head-rewriting systems* in [DL86]. Another recent example of an exotic treatment of rewriting systems is [Kap86].

3.3 Networks of processes

It is possible to combine FP2 processes using a set of process combining operators. One specific feature of FP2 is that the networks obtained by applying these operators can be described as elementary processes: they have connectors, state constructors, initial rules and their behaviour is described by transition rules. From the ten operators of [Jor86], we shall only present the most basic three:

- if P and Q are two processes, then $P\|Q$ ("P in parallel with Q") is just P and Q together, considered as a single system. A state of $P\|Q$ is a couple of a state of P and a state of Q. A transition of $P\|Q$ is a transition of P, or a transition of Q, or a transition of P together with a transition of Q^3.

- if P is a process, A and B two of its connectors, then $P + A.B$ ("A connected to B in P") is a process whose states and connectors are those of P. $P + A.B$ has all transitions of P but, in addition, if P has the transition $q \xrightarrow{A(v)\,B(v)\cdots} q'$ then $P + A.B$ has the transition $q \xrightarrow{} q'$. In this transition, the value v transmitted along A and the v transmitted along B are no longer exchanged with the environment: instead, v is *exchanged* between A and B. This makes use of a specific feature of FP2: the possibility of having several communications in a same event. Let us note that a variant of this operation yields $q \xrightarrow{A.B(v)\cdots} q'$, $A.B$ being an internal connector whose actions are visible from outside, although not dependent on outside actions. Practically, the rules of $P + A.B$ are obtained from the rules of P by an application of the unification algorithm.

- if P is a process and A one of its connectors, then $P - A$ ("A hidden in P") is the process P where the A connector has been removed. The transitions of $P - A$ are all transitions of P which do not mention A in their event part. If A has been previously connected to a B connector, then the exchanges between A and B are still allowed as they do not mention A any longer. This feature is used so often that the shorthand $P + +A.B$, for $P + A.B - A - B$, has been developped.

4 Temporal analysis of FP2 processes

We now describe how it is possible to take advantage of the term rewriting features of FP2 to apply the methods of section 2.3. Our goal is to mechanically analyze processes having (possibly) an *infinite set of states*.

4.1 Predicates as state terms with variables

In order to manipulate infinite sets of states, the first idea is to use state terms with *variables* to denote the set of all their possible instantiations. Classically we introduce

---

^{3}This operator, combining synchrony and asynchrony, is similar to the $\|$ operator of Meije [AB84,Bou85], a calculus close to Milner's SCCS [Mil83], but it is as old as [Jor82].

some infinite sets $X = (X_s)_{s \in S}$ of variables of sort s and note $T_\Sigma(X)$ the set of well-typed terms with variables. We note $Var(t)$ the set of variables occurring in t.

As a first example, $Y(0, succ(n))$, where $n \in X_{Nat}$, could denote the set of all states $Y(i, j)$ where $i = 0$ and $j > 0$, what we could write :

$$\|Y(0, succ(n))\| = \{Y(0, 1), Y(0, 2), \ldots\}$$

and more generally, assuming correct typing of terms and variables:

$$\|t\| = \{\sigma t \mid \sigma \text{ is a ground substitution}\}$$

We may now compute the intersection of two predicates denoted by terms with variables:

$$\|t_1\| \cap \|t_2\| = \|g(t_1)\| = \|g(t_2)\|$$

where g is the *most general unifier* of t_1 and t_2, written mgu_{t_1,t_2}. This is true if t_1 and t_2 have no variables in common. If they share some variables, it is always possible to rename the variables in one of the two terms. We shall write $t_1 \wedge t_2$ for $mgu_{t_1,t_2}(t_1)$ ($= mgu_{t_1,t_2}(t_2)$) when it exists (and assume that $t_1 \wedge t_2$ takes care of the renaming problems). If $t_1 \wedge t_2$ does not exist, then $\|t_1\| \cap \|t_2\| = \emptyset$. Note that this is only possible because we are working inside an initial term algebra (as in Prolog) and do not consider any kind of equational congruence.

It is also possible to apply *pre* and *post* on such predicates if the transition is described by an FP2 transition rule "$t_1 \Rightarrow t_2$", in which case *pre* and *post* are just rewriting functions :

$$post[t_1 \Rightarrow t_2](\|t\|) = \|mgu_{t,t_1}(t_2)\|$$

(if $t \wedge t_1$ exists), and if R is the set of transition rules describing an FP2 process then :

$$post[R](\|t\|) = \bigcup_{r \in R} post[r](\|t\|)$$

with similar results for *pre*.

Here a first difficulty appears. The union of predicates denoted by terms is not always denotable with a term[4]. We may overcome this difficulty by allowing predicates denoted by a (finite) set of terms with variables, and we may introduce the notation :

$$\|t_1, t_2, \ldots t_n\| = \bigcup_{i=1 \ldots n} \|t_i\|$$

It is still possible to compute intersections and unions of predicates :

$$\|t_1 \ldots t_n\| \cap \|t'_1 \ldots t'_{n'}\| = \bigcup_{i \le n, j \le n'} \|t_i \wedge t'_j\| = \|t_i \wedge t'_j\|_{i,j}$$

$$\|t_1 \ldots t_n\| \cup \|t'_1 \ldots t'_{n'}\| = \|t_1 \ldots t_n, t'_1 \ldots t'_{n'}\|$$

and the *pre* and *post* functions :

$$post(\|t_1 \ldots t_n\|) = \bigcup_{i=1 \ldots n} post(\|t_i\|)$$

---

[4]But some problems do not require to compute unions of predicates, for example the halting problem for processes having only one transition rule [Per86].

However, this representation has some flaws. For example, one would like to be able to check if two predicates are equal as sets (remember the stabilization criterion of the iterative computation of section 2.3). But it is not easy to see if $\|t_1 \ldots t_n\|$ and $\|t'_1 \ldots t'_{n'}\|$ denote the same set of states. Of course, if (say) t_2 *filters* t_1 (i.e. there exists σ such that $\sigma t_2 = t_1$) then $\|t_1, t_2 \ldots\| = \|t_2 \ldots\|$. But some examples are more complicated, consider :

$$\|X(true, false), X(b, b)\| = \|X(true, b), X(false, false)\| \quad (b \in X_{Bool})$$

However, the main drawback of this representation, studied in [PR85], is that it does not handle the negation of predicates, that is, there may exists some t such that $\overline{\|t\|}$ cannot be a *finite* union $\bigcup_i \|t_i\|$[5]. For instance, with $n \in X_{Nat}$:

$$\overline{\|Y(n, n)\|} = \|Y(succ^i(0), succ^{i+1}(n)), Y(succ^{i+1}(n), succ^i(0))\|_{i \in N}$$

4.2 Constrained terms

We now describe a method allowing us to (finitely) represent the predicates we have to manipulate, to form their union, intersection and negation, to apply the *pre* and *post* functions (given a finite set of transition rules) and, finally, to test two predicates for equivalence. This method entirely relies upon the *anti-unification* algorithm of [Com86c,Com86b].

First of all, some definitions are required:

- An *inequation* is a pair of terms, written $t \# t'$. It denotes the set of all ground substitutions σ such that $\sigma t \neq \sigma t'$.

- A *constrained term* is a term t together with a finite sequence c of *inequations* "$t_i \# t'_i$". The constrained term "t & $(t_i \# t'_i)_{i=1 \ldots n}$" denotes the set of ground terms :

$$\{\sigma t \mid \forall i = 1 \ldots n, \sigma t_i \neq \sigma t'_i\}$$

These constrained terms allow us to handle the problem of negating a predicate, for example $\overline{\|Y(n, n)\|}$ is simply $\|Y(n, m)$ & $n \# m\|$.

- A constraint $(t_i \# t'_i)_i$ is *normalized* iff :

$$t_i \text{ is a variable} : \forall i, t_i = x_i \in X_{s_i} \qquad (i)$$
$$x_i \in Var(t'_j) \Rightarrow i > j \qquad (ii)$$

This technical point is important[Com86c,Com86b]. For our problem, it allows us to decide if a given constrained predicate denotes an empty set. For example, consider the predicate:

$$\|X(n, m, p) \text{ & } n \# succ(p) ; n \# succ(m) ; m \# p\|$$

This predicate is not empty : we may choose any value for p, say 0. When we substitute with $[p \leftarrow 0]$, we get:

$$\|X(n, m, 0) \text{ & } n \# 1 ; n \# succ(m) ; m \# 0\|$$

where m is still free (has not been substituted), this is the whole point of condition (ii). So we may just pick any value for m, provided it is different from 0, say 1, and the third inequation is satisfied. Using $[m \leftarrow 1]$ we get:

$$\|X(n, 1, 0) \text{ & } n \# 1 ; n \# 2 ; 1 \# 0\|$$

---

[5]But this problem only appear with terms where a variable occurs twice (a *non-linear* term).

Then, thanks to (*ii*), n is still free and we may choose a value different from 1 and 2, say 0. That way, we have built a term belonging to the predicate, $X(0,1,0)$, which therefore cannot be empty[6].

4.3 Normalization of constraints

We must now show how it is possible to compute with constrained terms. The first problem we need to solve is to be able to always reduce a constrained term to a finite set of terms with normalized constraints. The complete proof that this is indeed possible is given in [Com86a] but we cannot afford to go through all its intricacies here. We shall just work out an example which, we hope, is explanatory enough to convince the reader.

Suppose we are given the signature $\Sigma = \{f, h\}$ where f is a binary function and h a constant, together with the constrained term:

$$\|X(x, y, z, u, v) \ \& \ f(h, z) \# f(h, f(y, h)) \ ; \ f(y, f(f(z, h), y)) \# f(u, f(u, f(v, h)))\|$$

- We begin with the first inequation :

$$f(h, z) \# f(h, f(y, h))$$

and begin by checking if, at a given occurrence, the functions names are different in the two terms, what we call a *function clash*. In such a case the inequation is always satisfied and we just drop it. If there is no function clash (that is the case here), then we may remove all functions names which are corresponding, what we call *flattening* the terms:

$$f(h, z) \# f(h, f(y, h)) \ \Rightarrow \ < h, z > \# < h, f(y, h) >$$

What we obtained is a *multi-inequation*. It is satisfied if two corresponding terms in a pair are different, while with sequence of inequations (i.e. constraints), all inequations must be satisfied simultaneously. This corresponds to the multi-equations of [MM82].

In our case, after a second flattening, we immediately obtain the normalized:

$$z \# f(y, h)$$

- We now flatten the second inequation:

$$f(y, f(f(z, h), y)) \# f(u, f(u, f(v, h)))$$
$$\Rightarrow \ < y, f(f(z, h), y) > \# < u, f(u, f(v, h)) >$$
$$\Rightarrow \ < y, f(z, h), y > \# < u, u, f(v, h) >$$

We are allowed to exchange terms from one side to the other:

$$\Rightarrow \ < y, u, y > \# < u, f(z, h), f(v, h) >$$

which, combined with flattening, always allows us to have one side with only variables.

We may also change the order of the terms in the multi-ineqation:

$$\Rightarrow \ < y, y, u > \# < u, f(v, h), f(z, h) >$$

---

[6]Generally, a normalized constrained predicate is never empty if no x_i is ranging over a *finite* type. In the other case, it is possible to look for a substitution by considering every possible values for x_i.

- What we try to obtain with this reordering of the variables is a multi-inequation $< x_1, x_2, \ldots > \# < t_1, t_2, \ldots >$ where equal x_i's have been collected together, that is:

$$x_i = x_j \Rightarrow \forall k, i \leq k \leq j : x_i = x_k$$

and where no x_i appears in a t_j with $i \leq j$. Of course, if $t_i = x_i$ then the pair must be removed.

If this condition cannot be met, it means that the two sides of the multi-inequation *cannot be unified* because there is a circular inclusion of variables into terms[MM82], and we may just drop the inequation.

- In the case of $< y, y, u > \# < u, f(v, h), f(z, h) >$, this condition is satisfied. We now take the last variable (u) and consider two cases: whether u is different from $f(z, h)$, which gives us the normalized:

$$\|X(x, y, z, u, v) \ \& \ u\#f(z, h) \ ; \ z\#f(y, h)\|$$

- or else we may apply the substitution $[u \leftarrow f(z, h)]$, which yields:

$$< y, y, f(z, h) > \# < f(z, h), f(v, h), f(z, h) >$$

$$\Rightarrow < y, y > \# < f(z, h), f(v, h) >$$

Of course, the substitution must also be applied to $X(x, y, z, u, v)$, and from now on we shall be dealing with $X(x, y, z, f(z, h), v)$.

- When we substituted u, the fact that it appeared only once ensured that substituting it would simplify the expression, possibly after some flattening. Now the variable we are considering (y) is present more than once. The method we apply in this case will reduce the number of occurrences of such a variable. We consider two possibilities: whether $f(z, h)$ and $f(v, h)$ are "different", in which case the inequation is satisfied, or they are equal. In the first case, we obtain $f(z, h)\#f(v, h)$ which reduces to $z\#v$ and we return the normalized:

$$\|X(x, y, z, f(z, h), v) \ \& \ z\#f(y, h) \ ; \ z\#v\|$$

- In the second case, we unify $f(z, h)$ and $f(v, h)$, which gives $[v \leftarrow z]$ and we apply this substitution to our terms:

$$\Rightarrow < y, y > \# < f(z, h), f(z, h) > \Rightarrow < y > \# < f(z, h) >$$

This inequation considered with the result of the first one does not give a normalized constraint:

$$z\#f(y, h) \ ; \ y\#f(z, h)$$

- In such a situation, we consider the several possible forms a term may have and substitute a variable with them, what we call *splitting* the variable[7]. In our case,

---

[7]This idea of considering the several possible forms to compute the complement of a set of terms has already been used in [Thi84], but without the use of constraints, it could only handle linear terms.

a term may have the forms h or $f(y_1, y_2)$ where y_1 and y_2 are fresh variables. We may now split y: if we apply $[y \leftarrow h]$, we get:

$$z \# f(h, h) \; ; \; h \# f(z, h)$$

where there is a function clash in the second pair, and we may return the normalized:

$$\|X(x, h, z, f(z, h), z) \; \& \; z \# f(h, h)\|$$

- while with $[y \leftarrow f(y_1, y_2)]$, we get:

$$z \# f(f(y_1, y_2), h) \; ; \; f(y_1, y_2) \# f(z, h)$$

$$\Rightarrow z \# f(f(y_1, y_2), h) \; ; \; < y_1, y_2 > \# < z, h >$$

and now, the second multi-inequation is satisfied if $y_1 \neq z$:

$$\|X(x, f(y_1, y_2), z, f(z, h), z) \; \& \; z \# f(f(y_1, y_2), h) \; ; \; z \# y_1\|$$

- or, when $y_1 = z$, if:

$$z \# f(f(z, y_2), h) \; ; \; y_2 \# h$$

which amounts to $y_2 \# h$ because z appears in both sides of the first inequation, which is therefore always satisfied, and we may return:

$$\|X(x, f(z, y_2), z, f(z, h), z) \; \& \; y_2 \# h\|$$

We are finally done: we obtained a set of disjoint normalized constrained terms, that we may now gather:

$$\|X(x, y, z, u, v) \; \& \; u \# f(z, h) \; ; \; z \# f(y, h)\|$$

$$\|X(x, y, z, f(z, h), v) \; \& \; z \# f(y, h) \; ; \; z \# v\|$$

$$\|X(x, h, z, f(z, h), z) \; \& \; z \# f(h, h)\|$$

$$\|X(x, f(y_1, y_2), z, f(z, h), z) \; \& \; z \# f(f(y_1, y_2), h) \; ; \; z \# y_1\|$$

$$\|X(x, f(z, y_2), z, f(z, h), z) \; \& \; y_2 \# h\|$$

4.4 Computing with constrained predicates

We may now compute the union, intersection, ...of predicates. These operations are described as applying on disjoint sets of normalized predicates and returning constrained predicates which we may normalize as we have seen in the previous subsection.

- The easiest problem is the intersection:

$$\|t \; \& \; c\| \cap \|t' \; \& \; c'\| = \|t \wedge t' \; \& \; mgu_{t, t'}(c; c')\|$$

where the result remains to be normalized.

Of course the intersection of disjoint predicates distributes into a set of disjoint intersections.

- The negation of a constrained predicate is more involved. For example, in order to compute the complement of $\|t \ \ \& \ \ (x_1 \# u_1, \ldots)\|$, we may first take the complement of $\|t\|$, using the methods we saw in the previous subsection[8]. The remaining solutions contain terms of $\|t\|$ that do not satisfy the first inequation:

$$\|t[x_1 \leftarrow u_1]\|$$

and the terms of $\|t \ \& \ x_1 \# u_1\|$ that do not satisfy the second inequation:

$$\|t[x_2 \leftarrow u_2] \ \& \ x_1[x_2 \leftarrow u_2] \# u_1[x_2 \leftarrow u_2]\|$$

and so on. What we obtain are *disjoint* predicates (which must be normalized). Of course, the negation of a set of constrained predicates is the intersection of the several individual complements.

- Union is not simply reduced to juxtaposition of the sets of predicates because we want a set of *disjoint* predicates, but we may ressort to rules like $P \cup P' = P \cup (P' \cap \overline{P})$ which generate a disjoint union.

- Computing the *pre* and *post* function is easy:

$$post[t_1 \Rightarrow t_2](\|t \ \& \ c\|) = \|mgu_{t,t_1} t_2 \ \& \ mgu_{t,t_1} c\|$$

Of course, when we have several transition rules and several constrained predicates, we distribute everything, and then normalize the union of the results.

- Finally, testing predicates for equivalence (i.e. set-theoretic equality) reduces to checking emptiness (because $P = P' \Leftrightarrow P - P' = P' - P = \emptyset$), which is possible as explained in section 4.2.

The complete machinery may be now be applied on realistic examples, where it appears that the full complexity of anti-unification is seldom really required, most of the computations being done with unconstrained terms.

Let us end this section by noting that term inequations have been introduced in [Col84] and have been studied more deeply in [LMM86]. However, these papers considered only infinite signatures (even more, [Col84] considered signatures with an infinite set of distinct constants). In this framework, which does not apply to our problem, it is easier to solve inequations. The main difference is that a variable cannot be covered by a finite set of non variable terms, thus one does not have to (and cannot anyway) "split" variables.

5 Analysis of an example process

We shall now test these methods on a simple FP2 process : a one-place buffer. Such a simple choice is motivated by the obligation of doing every computation by hand and explaining every single step, but the same results could be proven about any complicated FP2 network which is "externally equivalent" to a one-place buffer because, in our approach, we shall never make any specific assumption about the internal details of the buffer.

---

[8]Rigorously, we have not seen how to compute the "complement of a term", but this is exactly what is done in [Com86a], and the reader who understood how to normalize constraints should now have a clear intuition of how this may be done. Just note that $\|\overline{t}\|$ is not simply $\|z \ \& \ z \# t\|$ where z does not appear in t.

In FP2, the buffer is written:

$$proc\ BUFF1\ is$$
$$==> X$$
$$X\ :\ I(x)\ ==> Y(x)$$
$$Y(x)\ :\ O(x)\ ==> X$$
$$end$$

X is the state where $BUFF1$ is empty and waiting for an input along I, and $Y(x)$ the state where it is storing the value x, awaiting the opportunity to send it along O.

5.1 Safety properties

As a first result, it is possible to prove that $BUFF1$ is deadlock-free. Of course, this is evident from its definition but this simple property will be a first example of how to use our method mechanically.

In general, a process is deadlock-free if it cannot reach $SINK$, that is, if:

$$INIT \cap \mathbf{POT}\ SINK = \emptyset$$

In our case:

$$
\begin{aligned}
SINK &= \widetilde{pre}(\emptyset) \\
&= \neg pre(\overline{\emptyset}) \\
&= \neg pre(\|X, Y(x)\|) \\
&= \neg pre(\|X\|) \cap \neg pre(\|Y(x)\|) \\
&= \overline{pre(\|X\|)} \cap \overline{pre(\|Y(x)\|)} \\
&= \overline{\|Y(x)\|} \cap \overline{\|X\|} \\
&= \|X\| \cap \|Y(x)\| \\
&= \emptyset
\end{aligned}
$$

And now, $SINK = \emptyset \Rightarrow \mathbf{POT}\,SINK = \mathbf{POT}\,\emptyset = \emptyset \Rightarrow INIT \cap \mathbf{POT}\,SINK = \emptyset$, which implies that $BUFF1$ is deadlock-free.

The next property we shall prove about $BUFF1$ is that it is divergence-free. We say that a process is *diverging* if it is engaged in an infinite sequence of internal, silent transitions, i.e. transitions with an empty set as occurring event, and we write τ for this empty event, like in [Mil80]. We say that a process is *divergence-free* if it cannot diverge.

A process which is both deadlock-free and divergence-free will always be (eventually) ready for a communication with the external environment.

In order to prove this property, we shall split the transition relation $\rightarrow$ into different parts corresponding to the different events which may occur in a transition. In the case of $BUFF1$, we consider $\rightarrow\ =\ \xrightarrow{I} \cup \xrightarrow{O} \cup \xrightarrow{\tau}$, where $\xrightarrow{I}$ accounts for all transitions involving an I communication, $\xrightarrow{O}$ accounts for all transitions containing an O communication and $\xrightarrow{\tau}$ accounts for all "silent" or "internal" transitions. In the following, we shall index our operators $(pre, \mathbf{POT}, \ldots)$ with the transition relation upon which they are built.

In FP2, it is easy to construct these different transition relations because each transition rule of a given process accounts for transitions having the same kind of event (i.e the values of the message may change but the connectors involved in the event are always the same), thus splitting $\rightarrow$ in different parts is just partitioning the set of transition rules.

In the case of divergence, a diverging computation is just an *infinite* computation involving only $\overset{\tau}{\to}$ transitions. Thus a process may diverge immediately if it is in a state of $\mathbf{SOME}_{\overset{\tau}{\to}}\overline{SINK_{\overset{\tau}{\to}}}$, it may diverge in the future if it is in a state of $\mathbf{POT}_{\to}(\mathbf{SOME}_{\overset{\tau}{\to}}\overline{SINK_{\overset{\tau}{\to}}})$ and it is divergence-free if $INIT \cap \mathbf{POT}_{\to}(\mathbf{SOME}_{\overset{\tau}{\to}}\overline{SINK_{\overset{\tau}{\to}}}) = \emptyset$.

$BUFF1$ has no rules corresponding to a τ event, thus $\overset{\tau}{\to}$ is empty and then $SINK_{\overset{\tau}{\to}}$ is the set of all states: $\|X, Y(x)\|$, and then $\overline{SINK_{\overset{\tau}{\to}}} = \emptyset$. Then, because $\mathbf{SOME}\,\emptyset = \emptyset$ and $\mathbf{POT}\,\emptyset = \emptyset$ for every transition relation, then we do have $INIT \cap \mathbf{POT}_{\to}(\mathbf{SOME}_{\overset{\tau}{\to}}\overline{SINK_{\overset{\tau}{\to}}}) = \emptyset$.

5.2 Properties about communications

Our next step will be to prove a more complicated property about the input-output behaviour of $BUFF1$, that: "it may only wait for an input along I, then send a value along O, and then wait for a new input and so on". In most formalisms, this property cannot even be expressed by a finite formula! In CCS[Mil80], this behaviour is written $\mu P.I \to O \to P$.

This property is explicitly referring to the communications a process may or may not, will or will not, generate. There exist theoretical frameworks, based upon the approach we presented in section 2, which can deal with explicit reference to communications in the temporal analysis of transition systems.

However, we had no place to develop these results in the short recalls of section 2 and, in our next examples, we shall use another method that we call "observation of processes".

Basically, we shall insert $BUFF1$ in a network which will reach different states depending on the communicating behaviour of $BUFF1$. The surrounding network is an ad-hoc process we define in the sole purpose of observing the behaviour of $BUFF1$. This is possible because an FP2 network is just an FP2 process, on which the methods of section 4 may be applied.

The subject of this paper is not to present a systematic way of designing an observing process for every temporal property (we have not even presented a formal language for expressing these temporal properties). In our example, it will always be obvious that the observing process we propose does indeed observe the considered property.

Thus, in order to prove this "IO" property, we shall insert $BUFF1$ in a network which will observe it. The surrounding network will always allow any communications, thus $BUFF1$ is left free of its moves (though they are observed), but if it has not the required behaviour, then the observing process will immediately reach a specific state:

$$\text{proc } OBSERV \text{ is}$$

$$
\begin{array}{lll}
 & & ==> X \\
X & : \quad I'(x) & ==> Y \\
Y & : \quad O'(x) & ==> X \\
X & : \quad O'(x) & ==> K \\
X & : \quad O'(x)\ I'(y) & ==> K \\
Y & : \quad I'(x) & ==> K \\
Y & : \quad O'(x)\ I'(y) & ==> K \\
\end{array}
$$

$$end$$

The first two rules do the observing. The four following rules are just there in order to always allow any communications from $BUFF1$, and if they are used $OBSERV$ reaches the (blocked) K state.

The network is simply:

$$proc\ IOBUFF1\ is\ BUFF1\|OBSERV\ ++I.I'\ ++O.O'$$

Its rules are computed according to the definitions of [Jor86]:

$$proc\ IOBUFF1\ is$$

$$
\begin{array}{rcl}
& & ==> XX \\
XX & : & ==> YY(x) \\
XY & : & ==> YK(x) \\
YX(x) & : & ==> XK \\
YY(x) & : & ==> XX
\end{array}
$$

$$end$$

Now $BUFF1$ has the correct "IO" behaviour if $OBSERV$ *cannot* reach its K state, i.e. if the network cannot reach the states of $\|XK, YK(x)\|$, that is if:

$$INIT \cap \mathbf{POT}\,\|XK, YK(x)\| = \emptyset$$

Let us compute $\mathbf{POT}\,\|XK, YK(x)\|$ using the definition $\mathbf{POT} = pre^*$ from section 2.2:

$$pre\|XK, YK(x)\| = pre\|XK\| \cup pre\|YK(x)\| = \|YX(x)\| \cup \|XK\|$$

and then we have finished because we have found some n (here $n = 0$) such that $pre^{n+1}\|XK, YK(x)\| \subseteq pre^n\|XK, YK(x)\|$. Then $\mathbf{POT}\,\|XK, YK(x)\| \cap INIT = \emptyset$ and $IOBUFF1$ cannot reach its "K" states, which proves that $BUFF1$ has the required behaviour.

5.3 Properties involving the values of messages

When we proved that $BUFF1$ had an alternated I and O behaviour, we said nothing about the values transmitted in these communications. We shall now prove that the value x sent along the O connector is always the same x that had previously been entered along the I connector.

The observer process for this property is:

$$proc\ OBSERV2\ is$$

$$
\begin{array}{rcl}
& & ==> X \\
X\ :\ I'(x) & & ==> Y(x) \\
Y(x)\ :\ O'(x) & & ==> X \\
Y(x)\ :\ O'(y) & & ==> K
\end{array}
$$

$$end$$

This process is simplified because it is possible to assume the already proven fact that $BUFF1$ repeatedly engages in I then O communications. The third rule of $OBSERV2$ will always admit any value from O, even a value y different from the x previously entered along I, but then $OBSERV2$ will deadlock. In contrast, it is possible to use the second rule of $OBSERV2$ *only if* the value output by $BUFF1$ is the same value that has just been entered along I, and then $OBSERV2$ does not deadlock.

As a consequence, if we define the network:

$$proc\ VALBUFF1\ is\ BUFF1\|OBSERV2\ ++I.I'\ ++O.O'$$

it *will always deadlock* if an $I(x)$ communication of $BUFF1$ is followed by an $O(y)$ communication with $y \neq x$, while it *may avoid deadlock* (but may also deadlock) if the y in $O(y)$ is always equal to the x of the immediately preceding $I(x)$[9].

The rules of $VALBUFF1$ are:

proc $VALBUFF1$ is

$$
\begin{array}{rcl}
 & ==> & XX \\
XX : & ==> & YY(x,x) \\
YY(x,x) : & ==> & XX \\
YY(x,y) : & ==> & XK
\end{array}
$$

end

and we must prove that $VALBUFF1$ may avoid to reach a state XK or YK, which is a "K" state for $OBSERV2$.

Formally, this property is:

$$INIT \cap \mathbf{SOME} \; \overline{\|XK,YK(x)\|} \neq \emptyset$$

$$\Leftrightarrow \; INIT \cap \neg \mathbf{INEV} \; \|XK,YK(x)\| \neq \emptyset$$

using $\mathbf{INEV} = (I \vee pre \wedge \widetilde{pre})^*$, we have:

$$pre\|XK,YK(x)\| = \|YY(x,y)\|$$

$$
\begin{aligned}
\widetilde{pre}\|XK,YK(x)\| &= \neg pre \overline{\|XK,YK(x)\|} \\
&= \neg pre \|XX,XY(x),YX(x),YY(x,y)\| \\
&= \overline{\|YY(x,x),XX\|} \\
&= \|XY(x),XK,YX(x),YK(x),YY(x,y) \; \& \; x{\#}y\|
\end{aligned}
$$

$$(pre \wedge \widetilde{pre})\|XK,YK(x)\| = \|YY(x,y) \; \& \; x{\#}y\|$$

$$(I \vee pre \wedge \widetilde{pre})\|XK,YK(x)\| = \|XK,YK(x),YY(x,y) \; \& \; x{\#}y\|$$

$$pre\|XK,YK(x),YY(x,y) \; \& \; x{\#}y\| = \|YY(x,y)\|$$

$$
\begin{aligned}
\widetilde{pre}&\|XK,YK(x),YY(x,y) \; \& \; x{\#}y\| \\
&= \neg pre \overline{\|XK,YK(x),YY(x,y) \; \& \; x{\#}y\|} \\
&= \neg pre \|XX,XY(x),YX(x),YY(x,x)\| \\
&= \overline{\|YY(x,x),XX\|} \\
&= \|XY(x),XK,YX(x),YK(x),YY(x,y) \; \& \; x{\#}y\|
\end{aligned}
$$

$$
\begin{aligned}
(I \vee pre \wedge \widetilde{pre})&\|XK,YK(x),YY(x,y) \; \& \; x{\#}y\| \\
&= \|XK,YK(x),YY(x,y) \; \& \; x{\#}y\|
\end{aligned}
$$

We have reached the stabilization point of our iteration:

$$\mathbf{INEV} \; \|XK,YK(x)\| = \|XK,YK(x),YY(x,y) \; \& \; x{\#}y\|$$

$$\Leftrightarrow \neg \mathbf{INEV} \; \|XK,YK(x)\| = \|XX,XY(x),YX(x),YY(x,x)\|$$

---

[9] Thus this process *will* catch any "bad" behaviour from $BUFF1$, but it cannot force it and it would be possible that $BUFF1$ chooses to exhibit the correct behaviour and remains undetected while clearly failing the specification. But for this special $BUFF1$ process the observer is still correct because $BUFF1$ is deterministic with regards to the values it sends out (the value sent along O is given by the actual state of the process).

and with $INIT = \|XX\|$:

$$INIT \cap \neg\mathbf{INEV}\,\|XK, YK(x)\| = \|XX\| \neq \emptyset$$

which proves that $VALBUFF1$ may avoid deadlock, and then complete our proof.

6 Conclusion

We have seen how the anti-unification algorithm allowed us to effectively represent and manipulate the predicates which appear in the formal analysis of transition systems. However this paper has raised several problems that remain to be studied:

- A language should be defined for the expression of temporal properties of FP2 processes. There already exist such formalisms and it should be possible to devise one which takes into account the specific features of FP2: events made out of several communications, state terms as elementary predicates, ...

- A systematic method for deriving an observer process from a temporal assertion involving communications should be developed. This could have some feedback on the definition of the language for temporal assertions.

- The iterative computation of some predicates may well not terminate. Of course, the problem is undecidable in general, but sometimes the result may be found (and proven correct) using induction. It should be possible to combine some heuristics and the formal treatment of inductive properties in rewrite systems to obtain a tool with more potential applications.

References

[AB84]   D. Austry and G. Boudol. Algebre de processus et synchronisation. *Theoretical Computer Science*, 30(1), 1984.

[AH86]   E. Allen Emerson and J. Y. Halpern. "Sometimes" and "Not Never" revisited: on branching versus linear time temporal logic. *Journal of the ACM*, 33(1):151–178, 1986.

[BE86]   D. Bert and R. Echahed. Design and implementation of a generic, logic and functional programming language. In *Proc. ESOP 86, Saarbrucken, LNCS 213*, Springer-Verlag, March 1986.

[Bou85] G. Boudol. *Notes on Algebraic Calculi of Processes*. Research Report 395, INRIA, April 1985.

[Col84] A. Colmerauer. Equations and inequations on finite and infinite trees. In *FGCS'84 Proceedings*, November 1984.

[Com86a] H. Comon. About disequations simplification. 1987. Not yet published.

[Com86b] H. Comon. *An Anti-Unification Approach to Decide the Sufficient Completeness of Algebraic Specifications*. Research Report Lifia 50 Imag 619, Univ. Grenoble, July 1986. To appear in J. Comp. Sys. Sci.

[Com86c] H. Comon. Sufficient completeness, term rewriting systems and anti-unification. In *8th Conf. on Automated Deduction, Oxford, LNCS 230*, Springer-Verlag, 1986.

[DL86]   Ph. Devienne and P. Lebegue. Weighted graphs: a tool for logic programming. In *Proc. CAAP 86, Nice, LNCS 214*, Springer-Verlag, March 1986.

[Ehr82] H.-D. Ehrich. On the theory of specification, implementation and parametrization of abstract data types. *Journal of the ACM*, 29(1):206–227, 1982.

[EKT*84] H. Ehrig, H.-J. Kreowski, J. Thatcher, E. Wagner, and J. Wright. Parameter passing in algebraic specification languages. *Theoretical Computer Science*, 28, 1984.

[GH78] J. V. Guttag and J. J. Horning. The algebraic specification of abstract data types. *Acta Informatica*, 10, 1978.

[GHM78] Guttag, Horowitz, and Musser. Abstract data types and software validation. *Communications of the ACM*, 21(12), 1978.

[GM85] J. Goguen and J. Meseguer. EQLOG: equality, types, and generic modules for logic programming. In DeGroot and Lindstrom, editors, *Functional and Logic Programming*, Prentice Hall Int., 1985.

[Grä79] G. Grätzer. *Universal Algebra*. Springer-Verlag, second edition, 1979.

[GS85] S. Graf and J. Sifakis. From Synchronization Tree Logic to Acceptance Model Logic. In *Logics of Programs. Proceedings, LNCS 193*, Springer-Verlag, 1985.

[HO80] G. Huet and D. Oppen. Equations and rewrite rules: a survey. In *Formal Language Theory. Perspectives and Open Problems*, Academic Press, 1980.

[Jor82] Ph. Jorrand. Specification of communicating processes and process implementation correctness. In *Int. Symp. on Programming, LNCS 137*, Springer-Verlag, 1982.

[Jor86] Ph. Jorrand. Term rewriting as a basis for the design of a functional and parallel programming language. A case study: the language FP2. In *Fundamentals of Artificial Intelligence, LNCS 232*, Springer-Verlag, 1986.

[Kap86] S. Kaplan. Rewriting with a non-deterministic choice operator: from algebra to proofs. In *Proc. ESOP 86, Saarbrucken, LNCS 213*, Springer-Verlag, March 1986.

[Kel76] R. M. Keller. Formal verification of parallel programs. *Communications of the ACM*, 19(7):371–384, 1976.

[Lam80] L. Lamport. "Sometimes" is sometimes "Not Never". In *Proc. ACM Symp. Principles of Programming Languages*, January 1980.

[LMM86] J.L. Lassez, M.J. Maher, and K.G. Marriot. *Unification Revisited*. Research Report RC 12394, IBM. T.J. Watson Research Center, November 1986.

[Mil80] R. Milner. *A Calculus of Communicating Systems*. Volume LNCS 92, Springer-Verlag, 1980.

[Mil83] R. Milner. Calculi for synchrony and asynchrony. *Theoretical Computer Science*, 23, 1983.

[MM82] A. Martelli and U. Montanari. An efficient unification algorithm. *ACM Transactions on Programming Languages and Systems*, 4:258–282, 1982.

[Per84] J. M. Pereira. *Processus communicants ; un langage formel et ses modèles. Problèmes d'analyse*. Thèse de 3eme cycle, Univ. Grenoble, 1984.

[Per86] J. M. Pereira. *Noetherian functions and termination of head rewriting rules : a tool for the halting problem in programming languages*. Research Report, Univ. Grenoble, July 1986.

[PR85] J. M. Pereira and C. Rodriguez. *The reachability analysis in communicating processes founded in term transition system*. Research Report Lifia 37 Imag 567, Univ. Grenoble, December 1985.

[QS82] J. P. Queille and J. Sifakis. Specification and verifications of concurrent systems in CESAR. In *Int. Symp. on Programming, LNCS 137*, Springer-Verlag, 1982.

[Que81] J. P. Queille. The CESAR system: an aided design and certification system for distributed applications. In *Proc. of the 2nd Int. Conf. on Distributed Computing Systems*, pages 149–161, Computer Society Press, 1981.

[Sif82] J. Sifakis. A unified approach for studying the properties of transitions systems. *Theoretical Computer Science*, 18, 1982.

[Thi84] J.J. Thiel. Stop loosing sleep over incomplete specifications. In *Proc. ACM Symp. Principles of Programming Languages*, 1984.

Optimistic And-Parallelism in Prolog

Hans Tebra

Dept. of Mathematics and Computer Science
Vrije Universiteit
P.O. Box 7161
Amsterdam

ABSTRACT

The principle of stream-parallelism is used to discuss a general method for AND-parallelism in executing logic programs written in Prolog. The method is entirely transparent, it delivers solutions in the same order as Prolog, but tries to achieve a higher degree of parallelism than other dynamic methods for clauses containing shared variables.

1. Introduction

The demand for higher performance of Prolog implementations has resulted in a growing effort of research activities in recent years. A major direction of research is devoted to *compilation* of Prolog clauses to an intermediate code, that is emulated on a common sequential general-purpose computer. This approach was initiated with the DEC-10 Prolog compiler[13] and later refined to the Warren Abstract Machine (WAM) which became a standard for efficient translations[6]. The compilation approach proved that efficient implementations were possible with current sequential computer systems. Further efforts in this direction are the design of micro-coded and pipelined special-purpose processors to execute this WAM code directly in hardware. Both the Japanese Sequential Inference Machine PSI[7] and the Pipelined Prolog Processor[11] are examples of research in the direction of faster hardware processors. The expected or observed performance of this approach is currently around 10^5 logical inferences per second.

Another direction of research for faster Prolog implementations attempts to exploit the parallelism that exists in the logic program. Here two different aspects can be identified; first the problem of dividing the activities of a sequential implementation into different processes that are expected to run in parallel, and second, the assignment of these processes to an efficient multi-processor computer system.

Where several researchers have proposed new logic programming languages that can offer a high degree of parallelism[9, 12], this paper opts for the second direction, the parallel approach, to achieve better performance of a Prolog implementation. Although Prolog is strictly sequential from the programmers point of view, this paper shows that there is some potential for parallelism, to be accomplished "below the surface". Chapter 2 contains an overview of existing methods to divide activities among processes and how to maintain a correct order of execution between parallel processes. It shows different control methods, ranging from highly static to pure dynamic analysis and reveals how a popular programming technique, based on the notion of *streams* is overlooked by these methods. Chapter 3 then introduces a new method for dynamic control of process activities, called the *optimistic binding control* method, that supports a higher degree of parallel execution of stream-based logic programs. Finally, chapter 4 gives an impression of the proposed multi-processing system, a software simulation of which is currently being constructed.

2. AND-parallelism

The major cost of executing a logic program comes from the retrieval of clauses and their subsequent unification with a given goal. An obvious way to distribute the work is to assign each goal to a separate process and have each process find clauses and unify in parallel. Two main categories of management of the parallel processes can be identified, based on the moment when the parallel goal solving processes are created.

The first method, called *OR*-parallelism, creates as many processes as there are clauses that potentially unify with the given goal. For the new goals that are made when a goal reduces to the body of a clause, the processes are evaluated sequentially. The second, *AND*-parallel, method acts in the opposite way, it creates only a single process to select a clause and perform unification, but it creates new processes for all goals in the body simultaneously.

The AND-parallel method will be studied in this paper because of the requirement to produce results in the order as imposed by the behaviour of sequential Prolog. For non-deterministic programs, OR-parallel methods would demand expensive overhead to maintain the imposed order of results. On the other hand, the main problem of AND-parallelism is to control access to a shared variable; by concurrent access from different processes that are attempting to bind it, it must be prevented that conflicting values are generated. For example, in the goal statement

$$\leftarrow a(X), b(X)$$

processes are created for a and b and each of them attempts, in a unify operation, to bind the variable X to some value. When the first clause found by a has the form

$$a(1) \leftarrow \cdots$$

the variable X is bound to 1. A clause

$$b(2) \leftarrow \cdots$$

found by b would cause X to be bound to 2 and the binding conflict is born.

2.1. Goal Ordering Methods

Static analysis methods attempt to detect the cases where different processes are involved in unifications with some shared variable. In these cases, processes for each of the goals are not started in parallel, but are executed sequentially. Besides the obvious case given above, the method must be able to detect cases where shared variables occur as a result of a particular method of using the containing clause. In the following clause for p,

$$p(X,Y) \leftarrow a(X), b(Y).$$

two distinct variables are used. For goals like $p(1,2)$ and $p(A,B)$, the formal variables X and Y either became instantiated or are true distinct variables. The difficult cases occurs with the goal $p(S,S)$ where X and Y are replaced by the same actual variable S, shared between the two new goals $a(S)$ and $b(S)$.

To detect whether this use of the predicate actually occurs, an expensive static analysis of the entire program must take place and it remains to be seen if all possible occurrences of goals can be foreseen[5]. Disadvantages of the method are the complex analysis, generating large numbers of different cases to examine. When the analysis is unable to investigate all possible conditions this method must decide to execute the processes sequentially under all circumstances for reasons of security.

When the analysis is split between an *intra-clause* analysis, performed in advance, and an *argument typing test* done when the clause is actually called at run-time, the total cost of the static analysis is considerable reduced and many cases of parallel execution are preserved. This method, called *Restricted And-Parallelism*[4] translates the clauses to *conditional graph expressions* that result from the static analysis, and employs simple tests to check for independence of variables.

The third method, pure dynamic examination, attempts to find parallel execution paths for a clause after its head has been unified to the goal. It continuously reexamines the set of goals that are delayed to see if some more parallel execution is possible after earlier goals have been satisfied[2, 3]. Dynamic methods require much run-time overhead to examine the collection of delayed processes and check the dependencies.

2.2. Stream Parallelism

All three methods of the previous section ignored parallelism in stream-based programs. The stream variable is treated like any other shared variable; the goal ordering methods allow only one of the processes containing a shared variable to proceed and forces all other processes with access to the variable to wait until the first process terminates.

For variables that are used for assignments to elementary values, this scheme is the best that can be achieved. In streams however, the construction and assignment of a value to a variable is no single, atomic operation. The stream is likely to be constructed in a number of simpler operations; each contributing to the construction of the stream by adding a single element to it.

The following program shows an application of streams; it consists of the *squares* (N,L) predicate that makes a list L of the first N squares†. The *sum* (L,T) predicate sums the numbers in a list L and leaves the answer in T.

> squares(N,[P|L]) ← N>0, P is N*N, N1 is N-1, squares(N1,L).
> squares(0,[]).

> sum([E|L],S) ← sum(L,S1), S is S1+E.
> sum([],0).

The goal statement

$$←squares(10,X), sum(X,S), write(S). \tag{2.1}$$

calculates the expression $\sum_{k=1}^{10} k^2$ and prints the result.

Goal ordering methods would be unable to detect the parallelism that is inherent to the

---

† The list is constructed in reversed order.

processing of the shared list S in statement (2.1). After the *squares* process has calculated the first square and put it in the list, this value is available to the *sum* process. Meanwhile, the *squares* process proceeds with the second element, thereby allowing overlapped activity of a producer of list elements and a consumer of the elements.

This kind of parallelism is fully exploited in the parallel logic languages Parlog[1] and Concurrent Prolog[9]. To apply this kind of parallelism in sequential Prolog, it must be noted that by means of the general backtracking mechanism, the producer may decide to invalidate parts of the list that is has just made and try to make another result. When the consumer processes have seen some of the invalidated values, the consumer has to be backed out accordingly. As the parallel logic languages do not offer backtracking, their management of parallel producers and consumers is easier. For a stream-parallel mechanism in Prolog, to be discussed in the next chapter, this situation must be adequately treated.

3. Optimistic method

In the stream-parallel approach, the collection of goals that share a stream variable in one of their arguments is not necessarily executed serially. Some authority is still needed to obtain correct assignments and provide a consistent way of backtracking. In the *optimistic binding method* presented in this chapter, the responsibility to control assignments to variables is entirely in the processes themselves. The method is more general, it not only allows stream-sharing processes to run in parallel, but treats all other shared variables in the same way.

3.1. Overview of the validation scheme

While a process is performing a unification, it may encounter variable-bindings that have been made out of order and are not strictly allowed. It will correct these bindings to new values that reflect the sequentially imposed behaviour of the program. This means that processes are truly running in parallel and use a priority-based mechanism to *validate* the bindings that are encountered in the unification.

As an example, consider the goal statement

$$\leftarrow a(X), b(X), c(X). \tag{3.1}$$

where processes are created to solve the goals a, b and c. As all three processes will start immediately, it is not guaranteed that it is process a that first binds the variable to some value. When c wins this contest, it may bind X to some value, say β. The process for b may accept this binding when its first clause is something like

$$b(\beta) \leftarrow \cdots \tag{3.2}$$

When the first clause used by a has the form

$$a(\beta) \leftarrow \cdots$$

the binding β for X is accepted and no conflicts have arisen. The parallel execution succeeds at the highest speed possible. The processes b and a, after detection of a binding made by a right-neighbor process like c, always validate this binding and have permission to replace it by another one, which automatically has higher priority because these processes are closer to a sequential order of evaluation. When process a first has found the clause

$$a(\alpha) \leftarrow \cdots \tag{3.3}$$

the binding of X to β must be replaced by a binding to α. Subsequently, the processes b and c must be instructed to resatisfy their goals.

The synchronization method is optimistic because each of the processes hopes that its binding, although perhaps out of sequential order, will be the correct one that is likely to be chosen by the other processes if they would bind it. In the example above, the optimism of c was confirmed by the action of b, though the action of a invalidated the unifications done by b and c.

3.2. Proof diagrams for a stream example

The general structure of a program that contains a stream producer and a stream consumer, like the *squares* and *sum* predicates mentioned in the previous chapter, is given by the following program. The *make* predicate, based on the $m(E)$ predicate to generate new values for successive elements E of the stream, acts as the producer and *eat* is used to consume each of these elements. For each of the clauses the diagram is given, this is the building block for a graphical representation of the execution performed by a collection of parallel processes.

make([E|L]):- m(E),make(L).

make([]).

eat([E|L]):- e(E),eat(L).

eat([]).

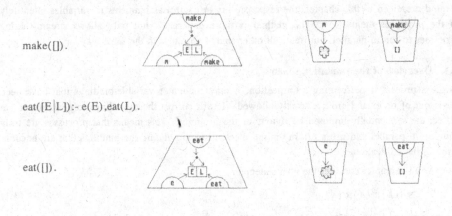

Fig. 1. Clauses and the corresponding building blocks.

The goal statement

$\leftarrow make(X),eat(X)$.

gives rise to a tree-shaped collection of processes, each of which unifies the head of a clause to a goal received by its parent. One such tree, obtained by the alternating sequence of *make* and *eat* unifications, is given by the proof diagram of Fig. 2. The stream is constructed in a sequence of *make* steps each of which adds an element E to the datastructure. In Fig. 3, another proof diagram is made for a schedule where the *eat* step is done before the corresponding *make* step takes place. This is remarkable, because the *eat* steps, obviously intended to be consumers, now seem to play the role of producers of the shared datastructure. It must be noted however that the real productions are still done by *make* processes, because they are responsible for

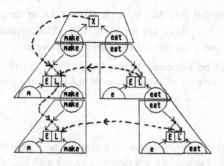

Fig. 2. Proof diagram for the goal statement *make*(*X*),*eat*(*X*) is constructed by the alternating sequence *make*, *eat*, *make*, *eat*.

making the elements *E* of the list. The *eat* processes produce the framework of the stream, not the actual contents itself.

Here the optimism of the method is again demonstrated; in this example the extension of the list can be done by either the *make* or the *eat* predicate, they will both unify to the list *dot* functor.

The example demonstrates that no strict order of execution is needed to build and access a shared structure. Where Prolog would make the left-most tree of *make* steps first, the optimistic method imposes no strict order, and is shown to work properly in the example where the second tree is grows ahead of the tree to the left of it.

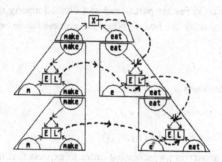

Fig. 3. Proof diagram for the goal statement *make*(*X*),*eat*(*X*) is constructed when *eat* precedes *make* in the alternating sequence.

3.3. Precedence Intervals

The validation mechanism is based on a comparison of the priority of the current process and the priority of the process that has made a binding to a shared variable. Each process receives a priority, called the *precedence*, from its parent. The precedence reflects the sequence of process in a sequential interpreter. Every process has a precedence interval $[B_l, B_r)$ which is a subset of the real numbers. The left boundary B_l is the actual value of the precedence of the process during unification of the first clause for the given goal. The remaining values of the interval are available to the child processes that are created by this process.

The interval will be partioned in two ways. First, it will be partioned for each of the clauses, and second, for each of these clauses it will be further partitioned for each of the terms in the clause.

3.3.1. Or-partition

In general a predicate definition consists of c clauses and during the unification of the goal with the k-th clause the process uses the sub-interval $[p_l, p_r)$ with bounds defined by

$$p_l = B_l + (c-k) \times \frac{B_r - B_l}{c}$$

$$(k = 1, \ldots, c) \tag{3.4}$$

$$p_r = B_l + (c-k+1) \times \frac{B_r - B_l}{c}$$

The sequence of interval boundaries is generated in *reverse* order to support a simple *undo mechanism* that is needed to erase effects made by unifications performed in one clause when the clause is rejected and the next alternative must be evaluated. Details of this operation are discussed in the next section.

3.3.2. And-partition

If unification of the goal with some clause head succeeds, the interval obtained from the corresponding or-partition is further partitioned and divided among the children that are possible created by the process to solve the body. When the process has selected a rule with n terms, the clause

$$head \leftarrow t_1, t_2, \ldots, t_n \tag{3.5}$$

defines a sequence of numbers p_i such that

$$p_l = p_0 < p_1 < \cdots < p_n < p_{n+1} = p_r \tag{3.6}$$

and each child t_i receives the interval $[p_i, p_{i+1})$.

The and-partition generates an increasing order to express that the leftmost goal has priority over goals to the right of it when bindings to shared variables are made. An initial interval is determined for the goal that has been issued by the user, new intervals are made by division of the interval of the parent process in smaller pieces. An example of the interval partition is given in Fig. 4.

3.4. Validation

When an uninstantiated variable receives a binding in the course of unification, the precedence of the process performing the unification is recorded in the area of the variable. If this variable is again referred to in another unification, it is obvious that its binding is inspected. In the sequential implementations, difference between the structures accessible through this binding would immediately lead to failure. The parallel implementation however must compare the

$$a(X) \leftarrow b(P)$$
$$a(X) \leftarrow c(Q),d(Q),e(R).$$
$$a(X) \leftarrow f(Z).$$

Fig 4. The process representing goal a(Q) receives values $B_l=0$ and $B_r=60$, the interval [0,60). It is divided in three parts for each of the three clauses of predicate a. The first clause gets interval [40,60) assigned. When the second clause is selected, the interval for a is [20,40). It is further split in 4 parts, and the interval [30,35) is given to the process assigned to solve goal d. The last clause for a receives the interval [0,20).

precedence of the recorded binding p_b with the precedence of the current process p_t upon conflict. If $p_t > p_b$, the existing binding is maintained and the current unification must fail. On the other hand, if $p_t < p_b$, the binding that the current process intends to make has priority over the existing value. The old binding is overwritten, the precedence p_t is recorded at the variable and the process that made that binding must be restarted. Other processes that have seen the old contents of the variable must also be restarted. To identify these processes, the variable not only maintains the precedence of the process that has made the binding, but collects the precedence values of all processes that have accessed the variable and have agreed on its current, but now invalid, state. The precedence of a process can be used to localize it in the set of active processes.

As all the processes that relied on the old value are treated similar in the conflict resolution, it is sufficient to maintain for each variable a set of precedence values of processes, called the *access set*, that have either bound or inspected the contents.

More precisely formulated, the conditions for access and conflict resolution as follows. Let a process T with precedence p_T unify a term τ with an instantiated variable X which has an access set A_X.

- When the unification succeeds p_T is added to A_X.
- The unification fails due to the current binding of X.

As X is instantiated, set A_X is non-empty and there is a minimal precedence m_X. If $p_T < m_X$, a new binding is made to τ and all process whose precedence is in set A_X have to be restarted. If $p_T > m_X$, the old binding survives and the unification performed by T will fail.

Each process that is backed out at the resolution of the conflict is likely to have made more bindings which are no longer valid. When these bindings are made to variables in the *environment* of the process (the caller of the goal, of one of its ancestors), these bindings must be erased if no other process has used them. A common technique for sequential implementations is to keep a list of variables that are scanned on failure to reset these variables.

In the optimistic method, it is not necessary to remember the variables which it has accessed during its unification; the validation scheme can be used to detect illegal contents of variables. When the current clause cannot be used to solve the given goal, possible bindings made to the environment are left as they are. The next alternative clause may possibly access these bindings. It will replace them if needed because it has a precedence interval with lower values.

3.5. Permission required for backtracking

The precedence information maintained by a process and stored in the access sets of variables is used to resolve conflicting bindings that are made as a result of parallel unifications. It is natural to expect that a process, when it is backed out after such a conflict, rejects the current clause and immediately attempts to unify its goal against the next clause, in order to achieve the best performance possible. In some conditions this may result in a loss of valid solutions which will be found in the sequential evaluation however. An example is given in Fig. 5.

a(X,Y):- b(X),c(X,Y).

b(1):-fail.
b(2).

c(2,1).
c(1,2).

Fig 5. The sequential evaluation of goal $a(P,Q)$ gives the solution $P=2,Q=1$. A parallel evaluation executed in the following way does not find a solution at all. Assume that it first tries to solve subgoal $c(X,Y)$, this gives the bindings $P=2$ and $Q=1$. Then goal $b(X)$, with lower precedence, overwrites the binding of P with $P=1$ and preempts process c. If process c tries the second clause, the binding of P is accepted and Q is bound to 2. Now process b has evaluated the body and will fail. It erases the binding of P, detects the access to P by process c and preempts c again. Process c cannot find another clause and reports a failure to the parent, process a.

The example demonstrates that a process cannot skip the first clause and try another unification if the shared variables involved in the conflict have not yet received a binding that can be relied on. In the figure, process c rejected its binding for variable P while process b was still not sure whether it found a solution.

Loss of valid solutions is avoided when process can only select another clause for unification if they have explicit permission to do so. The permission is given when all instantiated variables that may receive bindings from process with lower precedence have a *stable* contents, i.e. they are no longer subject to erase of contents. An implementation is by means of a *capability token* that is passed from the user-supplied goal to the processes that are created in the course of the evaluation. When the token arrives in a process for the first time, the process has selected the first clause for its goal. Usually some time has passed between the moment when this process has initiated a unification on the head of the first clause and the moment when the token arrives. So usually the outcome of the unification is known, either a success, a failure, or even a preemption caused by another process which has a lower precedence. Evidence for both of the failures has possibly disappeared, so the unification has to be done over in that case. If successful, the body of the clause causes the generation of new goals that are sent to new process. The token is sent to the leftmost of these process. If the clause happens to be a fact, the token is immediately passed to the parent.

The token will be used to carry information on the outcome of a solved goal to the parent; the $F-token$ carries a failure-message and the $S-token$ carries the success of solving the goal. In the other direction, requests for answers are passed; either the first attempt, or retry to generate another result, this is called the $N-token$ (for *new* or *next*).

During successful reductions, the route of the token is based on a strictly increasing value of the precedence of the process, this reflects the order of unifications exactly. When the token is

result of	current clause is a	
unification	fact	rule
success	S-token is passed back to the parent	new process have been created for sub-goals and the leftmost process receives the N-token
failure	the next clause, if any, is selected for unification, otherwise the F-token is passed back to the parent	

Fig. 6. Summary of token manipulations

in a process, failure to find another clause causes the process to pass the F-token back to its parent.

4. A multiprocessor system

In a multiprocessor system equipped with shared memory, a new binding is immediately visible to all tasks. Here the validation can take place in the unification algorithm when a conflicting value is encountered. The shared memory often forms the bottleneck of the system; when more processing elements (PE's) are added, the overall performance only increases up to some level. All multiprocessing architectures with some central unit will suffer from this behaviour. Scalable architectures do not have this property; the overall performance is a linear function of the number of processing elements. For these systems the processing elements have their own memory and use messages to communicate with processes that are located in other PE's[8].

In these systems, the goal solving processes must make the bindings in local storage and pass them to other processes explicitly, by sending a message. It assumes that the goals, handed out by a parent process to its children, contain copies of variables, not references to the variables in the goal frame of the parent directly. When the child makes a binding from a goal variable to a head structure, the new value for the goal variable is copied back in the area of the parent.

The optimistic parallel Prolog interpreter described in the previous chapter is currently being written. It depends on a network of message-passing processors. A simulated version of a rectangular network of processors, each of which is connected to at most 4 neighbours, is implemented with the task facility of C++[10]. The network simulator can easily be adapted to construct rectangular networks of arbitrary size by changing some compile-time constants in the program. The total number of (simulated) processors in the network is only constrained by the total amount of memory used by these processors; the simulation runs as a single process under the UNIX† system and must face some limit on the size of the memory occupied by this process. Currently, a rectangle of 4 × 4 processors is used during the development of the system. a unification procedure was written to implement the optimistic binding method, the topology of which is given in Fig. 7.

The system is capable of loading a Prolog program and distributing the clause definitions over different processors. The upper-left processor, called the *control* node, can be instructed to

---

† UNIX is a Registered Trademark of AT&T Bell Laboratories.

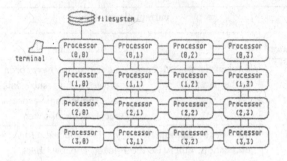

Fig. 7. Example of a 4×4 rectangular layout. The upper-left processor is attached to a file system and terminal.

load the parts of programs (all clauses for a single predicate) in certain nodes. Each of the processors has a small memory for storage of clauses. They also have an index of all the predicates that are loaded in the entire rectangle; clauses that are not stored locally can thus be requested from the nearest node with the definitions.

The control node reads a goal from the terminal and sends a message to a designated node in the network. This node consults its index and retrieves the predicate definitions, either from the local memory or from the nearest node. When clauses are retrieved from another node, the new location of the predicate to its neighbour nodes which may adapt their index.

The implementation of this multi-processor simulator was completed in April 1987. Experiments will be carried out to determine the cost of this dynamic control method.

5. Summary

The optimistic method for AND-parallelism discussed in this paper is designed with the parallel manipulation of streams in mind, and implements the general AND-parallelism instantaneously. This is an advantage over other methods which either concentrate on the traditional AND-parallelism, or provide parallel execution of streams only.

Validation, the essential issue for a consistent operation of the parallel unification processes, is implemented by means of precedence values. The precedence is a real number that is associated to the processes and the instantiated variables and reflects the priority of one parallel process over the other. Variables must keep a precedence values for the processes that has accessed the variable. In this way redo-messages can be send to all processes that have to be restarted when a failure is detected. Backtracking is only allowed when a process has received the special token, this forces the system to do backtracking sequentially, but precludes that results are lost.

A rectangular network of message passing PE's is being developed to examine the behaviour of the optimistic method. It must provide insight in the wasted resources caused by binding conflicts and the overhead that is involved to maintain consistent operation.

6. References

1. Clark, K. and S. Gregory, "PARLOG: Parallel Programming in Logic," *ACM Transactions on Programming Languages and Systems* 8(1), pp. 1-49 (January 1986).

2. Conery, J.S., "The AND/OR Process Model for Parallel Interpretation of Logic Programs," Technical Report 204, University of California Irvine (1983).

3. Conery, J.S. and D.F. Kibler, "AND Parallelism and Nondeterminism in Logic Programs," *New Generation Computing* 3, pp. 43-70 (1985).

4. DeGroot, D., "Restricted And-Parallelism," *Proceedings of the International Conference on Fifth Generation Computer Systems*, pp. 471-478 (1984).

5. DeGroot, D. and Jung-Herng Chang, "A Comparison of two And-Parallel Execution Models," *Hardware and Software Components and Architecture for the 5th Generation*, AFCET informatique (1985).

6. Goto, A. and D.H.D. Warren, "An Abstract Prolog Instruction Set," Techincal Note 309, SRI International, Menlo Parc, CA (October 1983).

7. Nakajima, K., "Evaluation of PSI Micro-interpreter," ICOT Technical Report 142 (1986).

8. Seitz, Charles L., "The Cosmic Cube," *Communications of the ACM* 28(1), pp. 22-33 (1985).

9. Shapiro, E.Y., "A Subset of Concurrent Prolog and Its Interpreter," ICOT Technical Report TR-003, Institute for New Generation Computer Technology, Tokyo (February, 1983).

10. Stroustrup, B., "A Set of C Classes for Co-routine Style Programming," Bell Laboratories Computing Science Technical Report No 90 (July,1982).

11. Tick, E. and D.H.D. Warren, "Towards a Pipelined Prolog Processor," *Proc. of the 1984 International Symposium on Logic Programming*, pp. 29-42 (February 6-9,1984).

12. Ueda, K., "Guarded Horn Clauses," ICOT Technical Report 103 (1985).

13. Warren, D.H.D., "Implementing Prolog - compiling predicate logic programs," D.A.I. Research Report No. 39 & 40 (May, 1977).

AN EFFICIENT GARBAGE COLLECTION SCHEME FOR PARALLEL COMPUTER ARCHITECTURES.

Paul Watson and Ian Watson

Dept. of Computer Science, The University

Oxford Road, Manchester M13 9PL

England

1 Introduction

A large amount of work has been undertaken in recent years on the design of garbage collection schemes for parallel computers. This has been largely driven by the need for an efficient scheme to reclaim the redundant parts of the computational graphs produced when programs written in Declarative Languages [DARL83] are evaluated by graph reduction [WATS86][KELL84][KIEB85]. Garbage Collection is especially important in implementations of declarative languages, as they tend to consume new storage locations at a much higher rate than do conventional programming languages. In conventional languages, computation is performed by repeatedly changing the 'state' of the computation, as represented by the contents of fixed storage locations (variables). In Declarative languages there is no concept of state, and any re-use of storage locations must be achieved by garbage collection, rather than by the program itself. Without an efficient scheme to allow the re-use of store locations holding redundant parts of the computational graph, the amount of storage required to run programs would be unacceptably high.

Parallel computers add to the problem of Garbage Collection, usually by introducing the need for synchronisation in the Garbage Collection schemes. This can have a major effect on the efficiency of Garbage Collection.

The paper examines the problems of garbage collection on parallel machines, and proposes a new scheme which has been implemented on the Flagship parallel machine architecture [WATS87]. It is efficient because it requires no synchronisation.

2 Garbage Collection on a Parallel Machine

All the proposed Garbage Collection algorithms are based on one of two schemes [COHE81]: Reference Counting and Mark-Scan. Each of these will be considered in turn.

2.1 Reference Count Garbage Collection

In the standard Reference Count Garbage Collection scheme, each node in the computational graph contains an extra field which is used to hold a count of the number of arcs pointing to it in the graph. As arcs are created or destroyed, the value of the reference count field is updated accordingly. When it reaches

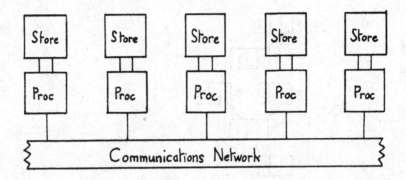

Figure 1: The Physical Architecture of the Flagship Machine

zero, there can be no arcs pointing to the node, and so it is no longer a part of the computational graph. Therefore, the storage space the node occupies can be reclaimed. The main disadvantage of the scheme is that it cannot reclaim cyclic graphs. Some extensions to the basic scheme have been proposed to deal with cyclic structures [HUGH84] [BROW85], however they do have a significant computational overhead.

Another serious problem is that Reference Count Garbage Collection requires synchronisation if it is to work correctly in most distributed systems. In order to illustrate this point, a fragment of the evaluation of part of a declarative program in the Flagship Machine will be examined. The physical architecture of the machine is shown in Figure 1. It consists of a set of closely coupled processor store pairs connected together by a high performance communication network. The computational graph is spread over the stores of all the processors, each of which can directly access only that part of the store to which it is closely coupled. All accesses of a non-local store must be achieved by sending a request to the processor coupled to that store. Each processor simplifies those reducible sub-graphs contained in its local store. The intention behind employing this form of physical structure is that the vast majority of store-processor interactions will take place between a processor and its local store, across a very high bandwidth link. The nodes of the graph are stored as packets. A packet has a number of fields which can hold atomic constants or packet addresses (called pointers), allowing graphs of packets to be represented.

Reference Count garbage collection requires synchronisation if it is to work correctly in the Flagship machine. This will be illustrated by a simple example.

Figure 2 shows three 'snap-shots' in the life of a packet P (in these figures, for clarity, a packet is drawn

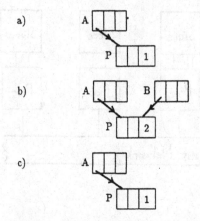

Figure 2: Snapshots of Part of a Computational Graph in a Single Processor.

as consisting of 2 pointer fields, plus a reference count field). It is assumed that this packet is part of a computational graph in the store of a single processor.

In Figure 2a, packet P has a Reference Count of 1, as there is only one pointer to it (in the first field of packet A). In Figure 2b, another packet (B) has copied the pointer to P from A, and so the reference count of P has been incremented to 2. In Figure 2c, packet B has been garbage collected and so the pointer from B has been destroyed, reducing the reference count of P to 1 again.

Figure 3 shows what could happen if this same sequence of events occurred in a parallel computer, such as the Flagship machine. The initial graph is as in Figure 2, except that packet A is in Processor 1, and packet P in Processor 2. When cell B is created, containing a copy of the pointer to P from A, as packet P is in another processor it cannot be accessed directly by Processor 1, and so a message is sent to Processor 2, telling it to increment the reference count of P. Figure 3b shows the state of the graph when B has copied the pointer to P, but the message to increment the reference count of P has not yet been carried out by Processor 2 (perhaps because it is still in transit). Similarly, when B is Garbage Collected, a message is sent to decrement the reference count of P. Both these messages will take a finite time to reach Processor 2, and Figure 3c shows the graph which results if the second message (to decrement the reference count of P) is carried out before the first. Packet P has a reference count of 0 until the message to increment the reference count is processed, after which the state is shown in Figure 3d. P ends up with the correct reference count, but a problem occurs if P is reclaimed when its reference count is 0 (Figure 3c). The address of P could be added to the list of free addresses at this point, leading to P being overwritten by a new packet. The computational graph would then be incorrect.

This problem can occur in distributed systems because conventional Reference Count schemes only work so long as the reference count of a packet is at all times equal to the number of pointers to that

435

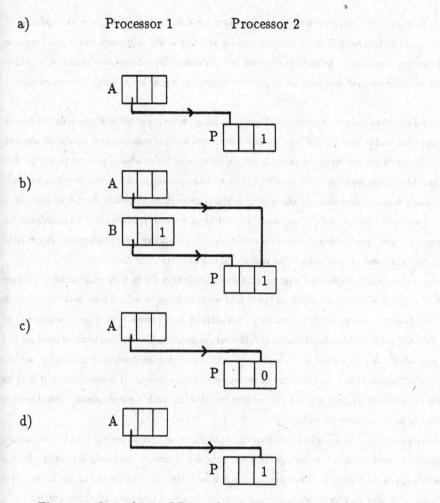

Figure 3: Snapshots of Part of a Computational Graph in Two Processors

packet. In a single serial computer in which the processor has direct access to the store, the updating of reference counts can be made indivisible with the creation and destruction of pointers, and so this invariant holds. Therefore, a packet can be garbage collected and reallocated if its Reference Count is 0, at which time it can be safely assumed that there are no pointers to it and so it is no longer part of the computational graph.

In many distributed systems (such as the Flagship machine), reference count field manipulation cannot be performed indivisibly with pointer creation and destruction because remote stores cannot be accessed directly, and so the reference count of a packet is not always equal to the number of pointers to that packet.

The synchronisation problem could be solved if all message passing in the system was time ordered, but this would impose constraints on the communications network and degrade the performance of a distributed machine. Alternatively, a two way synchronisation message protocol could be introduced for all garbage collection updates to ensure that the correct ordering is achieved, but this considerably reduces the computational speed of the machine (the reasons for this are detailed in Section 8).

Another problem with Reference Count garbage collection is that if it is to be guaranteed to produce the correct result in all cases, the reference count field must be large enough to cope with the situation where every field in every packet in the entire packet store of each processor contains a pointer to one packet. This will require a large reference count field when, in practice, the reference count of most packets will be very small. A compromise is to decide on a maximum reference count, and modify the scheme slightly so that the count in a packet is not decremented when a pointer to it is destroyed, if it is at its maximum value. Unfortunately, this has the consequence that any packet whose reference count reaches the maximum value can never be reclaimed.

Despite its problems, Reference Count garbage collection has several properties which make it attractive. It distributes the work expended on garbage collection naturally in time, as the manipulations of reference count fields happen continually as the expression graph is evaluated. This makes it suitable for real-time applications. It is also very localised: only those parts of the graph being evaluated are affected by it. In a two-level storage system, as the store accesses required to execute processes and perform reference count manipulation will be concentrated in the same part of the graph, Reference Count garbage collection should not cause the number of page faults to increase significantly.

2.2 Mark-Scan Garbage Collection

In conventional Mark-Scan Garbage Collection, an extra bit is required in each packet: the Mark Bit. Garbage collection occurs in two phases, with the Mark Bit reset in all packets before the first begins. Phase 1 (the Mark phase) consists of setting the Mark Bit of every packet which is a node in the computational graph. This is achieved by starting from a packet, or group of packets, known to be in the graph, setting their Mark Bits, and then tracing through the rest of the graph by following the addresses in the packets fields, setting the Mark Bit of each packet encountered.

Phase 2, the Scan phase, consists of examining each packet in the entire store. If a packet's Mark Bit is not set, then it is not part of the expression graph, and so it can be reclaimed.

The advantages of Mark-Scan garbage collection are that it can reclaim cyclic structures, and only one extra bit is required per packet. There is however a major problem with the basic scheme: all computation must stop while the two phases of garbage collection take place. Consequently it is not distributed in time, which prevents its use in real-time applications.

In recent years, interest in the design of LISP computers has led to research into modifications to the basic Mark-Scan scheme to make it more evenly distributed in time. In most of these variants, the garbage collection and computational work are performed in alternate, short time-slots, making the scheme suitable for real time applications [BAKE78] [LIEB83]. Most such schemes appear to be very inefficient in practise, and severely degrade the speed of evaluation of the user program. As a consequence, many users of LISP machines run programs with the garbage collector switched off, only turning it on when the computer runs out of store. Some of the inefficiencies are caused because real-time Mark-Scan garbage collectors are not localised in the same way as Reference Count schemes. The garbage collector is often working in a completely different area of store from that in which the computation is taking place, which causes page faults in a two-level store.

One efficient distributed Mark-Scan garbage collector, designed by Moon [MOON84], makes use of the fact that most packets are short-lived, and so the packet store is divided into regions by age. The youngest regions are garbage collected more frequently than the older ones, as they are likely to contain more redundant packets.

There are very few proposals for Mark-Scan garbage collectors designed to run on distributed computers. The synchronisation needed between processors is difficult to achieve without a considerable overhead in both computation and storage. One of the most interesting proposals is that of Keller and Hudak [HUDA82], which is able to delete unwanted processes, as well as redundant packets.

3 Reference Count versus Mark-Scan Garbage Collection

There is a division of opinion in the literature as to which type of garbage collection is the most efficient. The fundamental difference between the two basic types of garbage collection is that Reference Counting is localised to those parts of the graph affected by the computation, while Mark-Scan must trace through all the accessible packets, eliminating them from being candidates for the free address list. This gives Reference Counting an advantage, because in a two level store, the performance of a computation can be degraded by a Mark-Scan collector which must access parts of the packet store not required by the computation, in order to trace the accessible packets. This can reduce the amount of primary store available to hold the part of the graph required by the processor to perform the computation, and so cause page faults.

Another advantage of Reference Counting is that packets are reclaimed immediately they become disconnected from the expression graph. This allows the longer lived packets to be concentrated in the store, because locations vacated by short-lived redundant packets can be re-used immediately. In fact the Moon Mark-Scan collector described above attempts to emulate this natural property of Reference Count garbage collection by concentrating its efforts on recently created packets.

While Reference Count garbage collection has many desirable properties, there are still the problems of synchronisation in a distributed machine, and reclaiming cyclic graphs, which would need to be overcome if it was to be suitable for use in parallel machines. The rest of this paper describes a modified form of Reference Count garbage collection which removes the need for synchronisation, and gives greater locality of store accessing. This makes it attractive for parallel machines, but does not overcome the problem of reclaiming circular structures. The solution adopted for the Flagship machine is to implement the modified Reference Count scheme, and also implement a secondary Mark-Scan collector to remove circular structures (which are rarely created in this machine). Because it is not the main method of garbage collection, the efficiency of the Mark-Scan collector is not so critical, and its overheads, for example synchronisation costs, can be more readily tolerated.

4   Weighted Reference Count Garbage Collection.

This section describes a modified form of Reference Count garbage collection which differs from the conventional scheme as each pointer in the computational graph has an integer stored with it. This will be called the **weight** of the pointer. The crux of Weighted Reference Counting is that all operations must preserve the invariant that:

The sum of the weights of the pointers to a packet is equal to the reference count of that packet.

If the weight of all pointers was fixed at 1, then this would reduce to the conventional Reference Count scheme, however by updating pointer weights, as well as reference counts, a scheme can be devised which will work without synchronisation on a distributed machine in which reference count field manipulation cannot be done indivisibly with pointer creation and destruction.

The scheme is as follows. When a packet is created, its reference count is set to a non-zero integer, and the sum of the weights of all the pointers to it is made equal to that reference count. When a pointer to a packet is destroyed, the weight of the pointer is subtracted from the reference count of the packet being pointed to. However, when a pointer is copied, rather than increase the reference count of the pointed to packet, the weights of the copied pointer and the new copy are chosen so that their sum is equal to the original weight of the copied pointer, with the constraint that neither is set to zero. For example, if a pointer with a weight of 75 is copied, then the weights of the old and new pointers could be set to 38 and 37. The scheme works in a distributed system because the reference count of a packet is only ever reduced.

As it is never increased, there is no possibility that reference count updates performed in the wrong order will cause the count to reach 0 prematurely. Therefore, when it does reach 0, there can be no pointers to it.

5 A Practical Embodiment of the Scheme.

The first description of the above scheme in the literature appears to have been given by Weng [WENG79]. Unfortunately, as it stands it is not practical because each pointer must now have an extra field to contain its weight. This field must be the same width as a packets reference count field, and so the size of a packet would be increased so much that the scheme becomes impractical. In this section, a solution to this problem, which minimises the amount of extra memory required, is described.

The scheme uses logarithmic compression to reduce the size of the weight fields. When a packet is created, its reference count is made equal to the largest power of two that will fit into the reference count field. The weights of all the pointers to it are also set to be powers of 2. When a pointer is copied, its weight is halved and stored back in itself, and in the new pointers weight field. This restricts the weights of all pointers to powers of two.

Figure 4 shows the example of Figure 3, but with the Weighted Reference Count scheme. Each packet's reference count field is assumed to be 8 bits wide, and so the reference count of a newly created packet is 128. Thus, in Figure 4a, if P has just been created it will have a reference count of 128, and so the pointer to P in processor A has a weight of 128 (in the figure, pointer weights are shown in brackets).

When B copies the pointer to P from A, the weight of the copied pointer is halved (128/2=64) and stored back in itself and also in the weight field of the new pointer (Figure 4b). Now, when B is Garbage Collected, a message is sent to Processor 2 so that the Reference Count of P is reduced by the weight of the destroyed pointer (64). Therefore, in Figure 4c, P has had its Reference Count reduced by 64 to 64.

The importance of this particular embodiment of the scheme is that because pointer weights are always powers of two, they can be stored as their logarithm to the base 2. When a weight is to be subtracted from the Reference Count of a packet because a pointer has been destroyed, the anti-logarithm of the weight must be taken before the subtraction is performed. This could be implemented by shifting 1 left in a register n times, where n is the logarithm, or by using a look-up table stored in ROM. When a pointer is copied, halving the weight requires its logarithmic representation to be decremented.

The compressed representation for weights allows the size of the weight fields in packets to be small. If the weight field is n bits wide, then the largest value it can represent is $2^n - 1$. This corresponds to a maximum Reference Count weight of 2^{2^n-1}. Therefore, if the reference count field in a packet is 8 bits wide, only a 3 bit weight field is needed for each pointer.

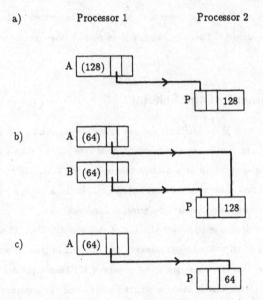

Figure 4: Snapshots of Part of an Evaluation Graph in Two Processors (using Weighted Pointers)

6 Copying a Pointer whose Weight is One.

There is a major problem with the scheme as described so far. When a pointer with a weight of 1 is copied, the weight cannot be split into two non-zero integers. This is analogous to the problem in the conventional reference counting scheme of what should be done when the reference count field of a packet is at its maximum value, but must be incremented, as another pointer to it has been created.

Figure 5 shows a solution to this problem which involves inserting a special indirection packet into the computational graph. Figure 5a shows a graph in which packet A contains a pointer to packet P with a weight of 1. Packet P has a reference count of rc. Another packet, B, is to be created holding a copy of the pointer to P in A, but the pointer's weight is 1 and so it cannot be halved. To solve the problem, an indirection packet, N, is created, and the fields in packets A and B are set to point to it (Figure 5b). The new packet, N, points to P with a weight of 1, but as N is newly created, it has the maximum reference count (128), which can be halved, giving 64 as the weights of the pointers in packets A and B.

In order to reduce the number of extra store accesses incurred by having indirection nodes in the computational graph, in the Flagship machine, when a graph headed by an indirection node is evaluated the indirection node is overwritten with the result of the evaluation. Therefore all subsequent accesses do not have to trace through the indirection.

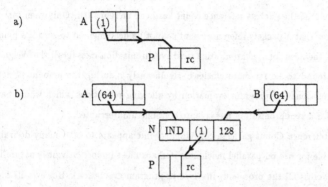

Figure 5: The use of an Indirection Packet to Copy a Pointer whose Weight is 1.

7   Increased Locality due to the Weighted Reference Count Scheme

The scheme increases the locality of store accesses in Reference Count garbage collection because when a pointer is copied, unlike in the conventional scheme, the reference count field of the pointed to packet is not changed. Consequently, that packet need not be accessed. This can give more benefit than just preventing a single store access. If this packet is in secondary store, a page fault is saved, while if it is in another processor, a message through the communication network need not be sent. The former benefit could also make the scheme attractive in serial computer systems. It is only when a pointer is destroyed that the pointed to packet need be accessed. Therefore the number of packets accessed by the Weighted Reference Count scheme is approximately half that of the conventional scheme (the need to create indirection packets prevents it from being exactly a half).

8   Experimental Results and Conclusions

The Weighted Reference Count garbage collection scheme has been implemented in software simulators of the Flagship machine for over two years. During that time the evaluation of many different functional programs has been studied. The scheme has proved to be very efficient: the amount of time spent on garbage collection is only a small fraction of that spent on actual computation. Also, in no programs has the number of indirection packets created risen to more than 0.1% of the total number of packets created during an evaluation. This is true, even for programs in which shared structures are heavily accessed.

Experiments have been conducted in which the conventional Reference Count scheme with two way synchronisation messages, and the Weighted Reference Count scheme have been implemented in two otherwise identical graph reduction models of computation, running on the Flagship machine software simulator [JEBS85]. In the two way message scheme, when during a reduction a pointer to a packet held in a remote store is copied, that reduction process is suspended until a message has been received back from the remote processor to indicate that the packets reference count has been incremented. Only then can the reduction proceed. This ensures that a packets reference count cannot be decremented to zero if a pointer to it still exists. By removing the need for synchronisation (and synchronisation messages), the Weighted Reference Count scheme was found to be far more efficient: significantly reducing the amount of network traffic, and increasing the efficiency of program evaluation by allowing reductions which would have had to be suspended waiting for a synchronisation message, to continue uninterrupted.

The Weighted Reference Count garbage collection scheme appears to offer many desirable properties which make it suitable for use on parallel machines. Perhaps most importantly, it is naturally distributed in time and space (across all the processors involved in program evaluation). However its high locality in terms of store accesses is also important in an environment where a remote store access is costly because a message must be sent through the network to a remote processor.

9 Acknowledgements

We would like to thank Tony Jebson of International Computers Limited for devising the Reference Count scheme with synchronising messages, as well as for writing the simulator and performing the experiments which allowed its performance to be compared with that of the Weighted Reference Count scheme. The authors would also like to thank Ursula Hayes who prepared the diagrams for the paper. The Flagship project is funded by the United Kingdom ALVEY programme, and International Computers Limited.

10 References

BAKE78 H.G. Baker, Actor Systems for Real Time Computation, MIT Laboratory for Computer Science MIT/LCS/TR-197,1978.

BROW85 D.R. Brownbridge, Cyclic Reference Counting for Combinator Machines, in Functional Programming Languages and Computer Architecture, Lecture Notes in Computer Science No. 101, Springer-Verlag, 1985.

COHE81 J. Cohen, Garbage Collection of Linked Data Structures, ACM Computer Surveys, Vol. 13 No. 3, 1981.

DARL83 J.Darlington, The New Programming: Functional and Logic Languages, in Proc. Distributed Computing- a Review for Industry, SERC, 1983.

HUDA82 P. Hudak & R.M. Keller, Garbage Collection and Task Deletion in Distributed Applicative Processing Systems, in Proc. Conf. on Lisp and Functional Programming, ACM, 1982.

HUGH84 R.J.M. Hughes, Reference Counting with Circular Structures in Virtual Memory Applicative Systems, Programming Research Group, Oxford University, 1984.

JEBS85 A. Jebson, Private Communication, 1985.

KELL84 R.M. Keller & C.H. Lin, The Performance of a Reduction Based Multiprocessor, IEEE Computer, Vol. 17 No. 7, 1984.

KIEB85 R.B. Kieburtz, The G-Machine: A fast Graph-Reduction Evaluator, Functional Programming Languages and Computer Architecture, Lecture Notes in Computer Science No. 101, Springer-Verlag, 1985.

LIEB83 H. Lieberman & C. Hewitt, A Real-Time Garbage Collector Based on the Lifetimes of Objects, Communications of the ACM, Vol. 26, No. 6, 1983.

MOON84 D. Moon, Garbage Collection in a large LISP system, Proceedings of the 1984 ACM Conference on Functional Languages.

WATS86 I. Watson, P. Watson & J.V. Woods, Parallel Data-Driven Graph Reduction, in Fifth Generation Computer Architectures, North-Holland, 1986.

WATS87 I. Watson, J.Sargeant, P.Watson & J.V. Woods, Flagship Computational Models and Machine Architecture, International Computers Limited, Technical Journal, May 1987.

WENG79 K-S. Weng, An Abstract Implementation for a Generalized Dataflow Language, MIT Laboratory for Computer Science MIT/LCS/TR-228.

Task Sequencing Language
for
Specifying Distributed Ada Systems

TSL-1

D.C. Luckham
D.P. Helmbold
D.L. Bryan
M.A. Haberler

Program Analysis and Verification Group
Computer Systems Laboratory
Stanford University
Stanford, California 94305

Abstract

TSL-1 is a language for specifying sequences of tasking events occuring in the execution of distributed Ada[1] programs. TSL-1 specifications are included in an Ada program as formal comments. They express constraints to be satisfied by the sequences of actual tasking events that can occur. An Ada program is consistent with its TSL-1 specifications if its runtime behavior satisfies them. This paper presents an overview of TSL-1. The features of the language are described informally, and examples illustrating the use of TSL-1, both for debugging and for specification of tasking programs, are given. Some important constructs, as well as topics related to uncertainty of observation of distributed programs, are dealt with in other papers. In the future, constructs for defining abstract units will be added to TSL-1, forming a new language TSL-2 for the specification of distributed systems prior to their implementation in any programming language.

1. Introduction

Previously, we have studied techniques for automatically detecting tasking errors in Ada programs by runtime monitoring [7]. We demonstrated that classical kinds of errors such as deadlock and global blocking can be detected by our methods when the errors result from misuse of task rendezous. We also concluded that specifications expressing the intended order and synchronization of interactions between tasks could also be monitored at runtime by similar techniques. Such specifications are necessary in order to detect task communication errors generally when tasks communicate by means of global variables or ways other than the "preferred" Ada rendezvous. These specifications would be expressed in a suitable language, and supplied by the programmer with the program.

Task Sequencing Language, TSL, is an outgrowth of our previous work [8]. It provides three kinds of facility for specifying distributed systems. The first kind are *actions*. Actions specify *events* in the system which are significant and are to be included in the history of events whenever they occur during a computation. The second kind are specifications of *sequences* of events that should (or should not) occur in the history of events. The third kind are definitions of *properties* of entities in the system, where the properties depend on the history of events and may change their values as new sequences of events happen.

TSL declarations and specifications are placed in the text of an Ada program — called the

---

[1]Ada is a registered trademark of the U.S. Government.

underlying Ada program. They appear as Ada comments and therefore have no effect when processed by standard Ada tools. They are recognized by a TSL compiler, which transforms them into Ada data structures and calls to the TSL runtime monitor. At runtime the declared events and specifications (in their compiled data structure form) are passed to the TSL monitor as the scopes in which they occur are elaborated and executed. The resulting history of events is ordered linearly, and will henceforth be called the *stream of events* (or *event stream*). The *stream of events* that occurs during the execution of the underlying Ada program is monitored for consistency with the TSL specifications. The TSL runtime monitor is implemented using techniques generalizing those presented in [5, 6]. We will refer to the TSL compiler and monitor together as the TSL system.

This paper gives an overview of the current version of TSL (called TSL-1) which is intended for use primarily to test and debug tasking behavior. A restricted form of TSL (without pattern variables) is described first, and then the description of the general form is based on that. Section 3 is the overview; Section 4 gives examples, and touches on the use of TSL to hide irrelevant details of tasking activity. The TSL-1 report [13] includes a syntax definition, an "informal" semantics, and deals with expressing *safety* and *liveness* in TSL.

A fundamental concept in TSL specifications is *order* of events. However, the order in which events from an underlying distributed Ada system appear in the event stream, as viewed by the TSL monitor, is not always significant. That one event preceeds another in the stream of events passing by an observer may often tell that observer nothing. This uncertainty is a consequence of Ada semantics and the freedom accorded to implementations of Ada. It is unavoidable in any practical distributed system which permits many processors to operate independently. Fortunately, certain pairs of events do occur in the underlying Ada system in a definite order, and it can be assumed that their order in the event stream is the same. These are called *connected* events. Methods of constructing *robust* TSL specifications using connected events that are independent of uncertain sequences of events are described in [13].

TSL-1 is envisaged as the basic part of TSL for specifying behavior of distributed Ada systems. The language design presented here is preliminary. The constructs in TSL-1 have been chosen not only to express useful properties, but also so that monitoring of specifications at runtime is implementable. More powerful constructs are being considered for an extended language called TSL-2. New constructs will provide an ability to define hierarchies of abstract processes and actions, and to specify temporal connections between sets of actions. TSL-1 will continue to provide the basic facilities for specifying behavior at any given level in the TSL-2 design.

The ultimate goal of this work is to develop a specification language for concurrent systems that is independent of any implementation language. It will allow a simulation of a system at a given level of abstraction to be monitored for consistency with behavioral specifications referring to the actions defined at that level. An Ada tasking program is viewed as representing a distributed system at a particular level of detail in a TSL-2 design. Rendezvous constructs, for example, would be represented as actions satisfying standard Ada connection specifications at that level.

Acknowledgement

We are indebted to Sigurd Meldal, who is presently colaborating on the design of TSL-2, for many improvements to this present paper.

2. Illustrative Problems

This introduction to TSL will draw on two simple Ada tasking programs to give examples illustrating various points. The programs are described informally below. The reader will be able to follow the illustrations from the descriptions. Later on we will give Ada text for the programs.

2.1 Automated Gas Station

The Ada program simulates an automated gas station [7]. The gas station contains tasks representing the station operator, the customers, and the pumps. A customer arrives at the station, prepays the operator, pumps gas, receives change from the operator, and leaves. The operator accepts prepayments, activates pumps, computes charges and gives customers their change. The pumps are used by the customers, and report the amount pumped to the operator.

2.2 Reliable Soldiers Problem

The Ada program represents a General and a number of soldiers as tasks. The General sends an order to each soldier, either "advance" or "retreat". Each soldier subsequently sends an message to each of his comrades, which is supposedly the order he received, but he might lie sometimes. When each soldier has received a copy of all of his comrades orders, he takes an action, which is to obey the order he has been told most often. A soldier is *reliable* if he sends the order that he received from the General to everyone [11]. The problem is to specify that all reliable soldiers take the same action.

3. Overview of TSL

The semantics of TSL are based on a model of observing the computation of an Ada program whereby events occuring during the computation are organized into an ordered linear sequence. An event may signify something in the computation of a single thread of control, or it may signify something involving more than one thread of control, such as the start of a rendezvous between two tasks. This sequence of events is called the *event stream*.

The threads of control may be executing on many processors. It is assumed that the events occuring in a single thread of control appear in the stream in the order in which they were executed. When two events occur in separate threads of control, only a weak assumption is made regarding their order in the event stream. Namely, only those pairs of events that are *connected* – to be defined later – are assumed to occur in the event stream in the order in which they occur in the computation of the underlying program. For example, if A and B are tasks, "A **calls** B" and "B **accepts** A" are always connected events and must occur in this order both in the Ada computation and in the stream. On the other hand, "A **calls** B **at** E" and "B **accepting** E" need not be connected events, depending on the Ada program executing them, and their order in the event stream may or may not be significant. Under the assumption that only pairs of connected events are required to have the same order in the event stream as their order of execution in the Ada program, the event stream can be implemented in a practical and efficient manner.

TSL provides three simple capabilities: (1) declaration of events called *actions*, and *perform* statements which insert those declared events into the event stream, (2) declaration of constraints on the event stream, called *specifications*, and (3) definition of simple kinds of *properties* associated with entities in the underlying program, the values of which depend on the event stream, and *update* statements for computing the values of properties.

TSL also provides predefined events and properties relating to the basic tasking constructs of Ada. The predefined events denote such actions as accepting an entry, issuing an entry call, and activating a task. For example, "the OPERATOR task is **accepting** entries PRE_PAY and CHARGE" is a predefined event occuring when the OPERATOR task executes a select statement with open accept alternatives for those entries. The predefined properties include whether or not a task is running, blocked, or terminated, if an entry of a task is open, and so on. For example, "BLOCKED (OPERATOR)" is a boolean-valued property that is TRUE at certain points in the event stream – e.g., if the most recent event in the stream signifies that the OPERATOR has executed an accept statement and previous events signify that no task has both executed a call to the corresponding entry and is waiting for the call to terminate; it will remain true until new events signifying calls to the operator appear in the event stream.

TSL declarations and statements appear as comments in the *underlying* Ada program. These comments are prefaced by the TSL comment symbols, "--+" indicating that they are to be processed by the TSL compiler. A TSL declaration is placed in a declarative part of the Ada program. It is transformed into an Ada data structure by the TSL compiler, and is passed to the TSL monitor when the Ada declarative region is elaborated. TSL declarations are action declarations, specifications (including macros), property declarations, and property bodies (specifying how to compute property values). A TSL *perform* statement corresponding to an action, is placed in a sequence of statements of the Ada program within the scope of the action declaration; it is compiled into Ada text that sends a structure representing an event to the TSL monitor.

To give a brief overview of how TSL interacts with the Ada program, consider the case of TSL *specifications*. First of all, the event stream, representing activity in the underlying program, is generated by Ada statements inserted into the underlying program by the TSL compiler. A TSL specification contains a pattern that can match many different sequences of events, and it expresses whether its pattern is required or forbidden to occur in the event stream of the program. That is, informally, a TSL specification has the semantics: "a subsequence of the underlying event stream between such and such events must or must not match the pattern". Specifications usually cannot be checked immediately like an assertion. Instead, they must be monitored over a period of time by the TSL monitor.

A TSL specification is *elaborated* by the TSL monitor when the declarative region containing the specification is elaborated. If the declarative region is elaborated more than once, a new instance of the specification is passed to the monitor by each elaborating thread of control. A copy of an elaborated specification may be *activated* by the TSL monitor when an appropriate subsequence of events occurs in the event stream. It will remain active until its *terminating* events occur, in which case it is either *satisfied* or *violated*. When an elaborating thread of control leaves a declarative region, all TSL specifications declared in that region which were elaborated by that thread become inactive. Any activated copies of these specifications are treated as if their terminating events had occurred.

Different kinds of error situations may arise in a TSL computation. For example, a specification may be violated, indicating an inconsistency with the underlying Ada program. Other kinds of errors such as type mismatches may also occur. No specific action is required in error situations. Implementations of TSL are free to take any action, including aborting the TSL monitor and issuing error messages. Normally, such actions would be diagnostic in nature and would not disturb the computation of the underlying Ada program.

Terminology and Conventions:

Events are expressions in TSL and also components of the stream of events representing activity in the underlying program. We will use the term *event* to refer to events in TSL specifications, and *stream event* to refer to an event in the underlying event stream.

Reserved words in TSL are written in lowercase boldface. Names of TSL predefined types and properties are in uppercase. Identifiers in TSL may be written either all capitalized or only the first letters capitalized.

3.1 Types, Expressions, and Basic Events

There are no type declarations in TSL. The standard types of TSL are (1) the TSL types TASK, ENTRY, TASK_TYPE, ACTION, and (2) the Ada types INTEGER, BOOLEAN, and the Ada discrete types. These types define domains of values and operations on those values. Values of type TASK are the task identifiers (abbreviation: *ids*) uniquely associated by TSL with each activated thread of control during a computation. (The domain of values of task ids depends on the TSL implementation – in many cases ids will be implemented as integers.) The names of task objects in the underlying Ada program are constants of the TSL type, TASK, so a task name may be used in TSL expressions to designate its task id value. The constant, **main** always refers to the main program and **self** always denotes the task id of the executing task.

The sets of values of the types ENTRY, TASK_TYPE, and ACTION are unique *ids* associated with names of task entries, and task types in the underlying Ada program, and with TSL actions. Entry names, task type names, and action names may be used as literals in a TSL specification whenever they are visible in the Ada program; they must be fully expanded according to Ada rules, if necessary, to avoid ambiguity. The only operations on the TASK, ENTRY, TASK_TYPE, and ACTION types are the equality and inequality operations, and assignment. In addition, there is a literal **null** in each of these TSL types that denotes a null value.

The types INTEGER, BOOLEAN, and the discrete types are the standard Ada types – i.e., in TSL expressions the standard Ada operations associated with those types are allowed. (Note that the syntax summary lists only a subset of the Ada operations on these types; this reflects a restriction in the present TSL monitor implementation.)

A task type declared in the Ada program defines a subtype of the TASK type in TSL. This subtype has the same name in TSL as the Ada task type, and consists of those TSL task ids associated with objects of the Ada task type.

TSL contains two kinds of expressions, *primary expressions* denoting values, and *events*. Primary expressions are composed according to well known composition rules from literals, TSL variables (called placeholders, described later), TSL operators (a subset of Ada operators), and TSL properties (which obey the same composition rules in expressions as Ada functions). Events in TSL are built up from *basic events*.

A *basic event* denotes the occurrence of an *action* in the underlying program. There are six predefined classes of basic events (see syntax summary). The six predefined event classes denote Ada tasking actions. Each predefined class of event implies a particular TSL type for each of its constituent expressions; these types are indicated in the syntax definition of an event class by the italic prefix of the names. For example, the start of rendezvous is a predefined event class. The TSL syntax,

start_rendezvous ::= *task*_name **accepts** *task*_name **at** *entry*_name

indicates the types of the three constituent names. An example of a start rendezvous event is

OPERATOR **accepts** CUSTOMERS(5) **at** PRE_PAY

which specifies an event in which the operator starts a pre-pay rendezvous with the fifth customer task in the array of customers.

It is assumed that type mismatches never can occur in the event stream. Type mismatches may occur during a TSL computation as described later, either in the matching process or in the evaluation of expressions. Generally such mismatches will be detectable only at runtime. Whenever a TSL type mismatch occurs, the TSL computation is erroneous. No specific action is required in erroneous situations.

Each kind of basic event is said to be *generated* by one of the tasks that appear in the event. For example a **calls** event, T1 **calls** T2 **at** E is generated by T1.

3.2 User-Defined Events

Execution of tasking statements in the underlying Ada program results in corresponding predefined TSL events being entered into the event stream. These predefined events often do not include all of the significant events in a computation that are needed to specify the correct behavior. This is particularly true, for example, when tasks can communicate by means of shared data. TSL therefore provides a facility allowing declaration of other events that should be entered into the event stream.

New classes of basic events are declared by *action* declarations. An action declaration may be placed in the position of either an Ada entry declaration in a task, or an Ada basic declaration. For example, suppose we wish to define as an event, the activity whereby the General sends an order to a soldier. An *action* declaration,

action Order(M : Order_Type; S : TASK);

can be made either as a basic declaration in the Ada program, or else as an action of the General task; in the latter case, it is placed in the position of a task entry. Here, Order_Type is a discrete type in the Ada program, and TASK is the TSL standard task identifier type. The task type SOLDIER in the underlying program can also be used in the action declaration if it is visible at that point:

action Order(M : Order_Type; S : SOLDIER).

SOLDIER defines a subtype of the TASK type in TSL.

This action declaration declares a new class of basic events of the form,

T **performs** Order(M1, S1)

where T is the task id of the thread of control performing the action, and the types of constituent expressions in the event are those declared in the parameter list of the corresponding *action* declaration. In this example, M1 is of type Order_Type, and S1 is a task id of a task of type, SOLDIER (i.e., a member of the subtype of TASK defined by the type, SOLDIER). T is said to *generate* the performs event.

TSL provides *perform* statements corresponding to user-declared actions. These are statements that may be placed in the underlying Ada program to indicate when, in the course of a computation, that action is actually performed. If the action is in the position of a basic declaration, then corresponding perform statements may be placed in the position of an Ada statement within the scope of the action declaration. If the action declaration is in the position of an entry in a task declaration, corresponding perform statements may be placed in the body of the task, but only where Ada **accept** statements for such an entry could be placed. This restriction ensures that an action in a task specification can only be performed by the task itself, and not by subordinate tasks.

Perform statements are executed when an Ada statement in the same position would be executed, and result in a basic event of the event class corresponding to the action being placed in the stream. Therefore, the user, having declared an action, can place *perform* statements appropriately to define the meaning of that action in relation to other events taking place in the Ada program.

Example: An action declaration and perform statement.

```
        task General is
--+         action Order(X : Move; S : Task);
        end;

        task body General is
            M : Move := Decide(Advance);
        begin
            for I in 1 .. Max_Soldiers loop
--+             perform Order(M, Soldiers(I));
                Mailboxes(I) := M;
            end loop;
        end General;
```

Commentary

In this example the action is defined by the **perform** statement as occuring when the General places an order in the soldier's mailbox. An event,

General_Id **performs** Order(M, Soldiers(I))

will enter the event stream when the assignment statement is executed. In more complex simulations of the Byzantine General's problem the Ada activity denoted by the action might involve a sequence of events such as the activation and use of messenger tasks to communicate the order to a soldier. In such cases, it may be necessary to declare other actions such as Start_Order and Complete_Order to correctly represent the relationship between this event and other events in the program.

The formal parameters in action declarations have the Ada parameter modes, **in, out,** and **in out.** The expressions in the corresponding perform statements must obey the Ada rules for actual parameters of procedure calls regarding **modes.**

Note that the predefined basic events are equivalent to user-defined actions when corresponding perform statements are placed in each program in appropriate positions in relationship to Ada tasking statements (which is what the TSL compiler does).

3.3 Matching

In TSL *matching* is the fundamental operation on events, analagous to evaluation of expressions. A TSL event *matches* an event from the underlying stream if the stream event is of the same class and has the same constituent values. The event,

OPERATOR **accepts** CUSTOMERS(5) **at** PRE_PAY

would *match* all of the start rendezvous stream events where the OPERATOR has accepted CUSTOMERS(5) at entry PRE_PAY. (Note that an instance of a TSL event may occur in the stream many times as distinct stream events.)

We also use the concept of an event matching an interval. An *interval* of the event stream is a contiguous section of the event stream containing one or more stream events. A TSL event matches an interval of the event stream if it matches a stream event in the interval.

3.4 Compound Events

There are four classes of compound events: *one_of, all_of, sequence,* and *iterative* events. They are constructed from finite sets of two or more events connected together by **or, and, =>,** and ↑ respectively. The constituent events of a compound event may be compound events.

A *one_of* compound event matches an interval of the event stream if any of its constituent events matches the interval. An *all_of* compound event matches an interval of the event stream if there is a one – one association between its constituent events and disjoint subintervals of the interval such that each constituent event matches the subinterval associated with it. A *sequence* of N events matches an interval of the event stream if the interval can be partitioned into N disjoint subintervals such that each event matches the corresponding subinterval and the correspondence preserves order (i.e. the first event in the sequence matches the first subinterval, etc.). An iterative even, A↑N, matches an interval if A matches N disjoint subintervals of the interval.

Note that when matching compound events: *(1)* non-matching stream events may occur between matching ones, and *(2)* constituent events must be matched by non-overlapping intervals. Also, an iterative event matches whenever its constituent event matches a positive integer number of times; if the integer exponent is not positive, the event matches every interval.

Examples of compound events and matching.

A one_of event:
    OPERATOR **accepting** PRE_PAY **or** OPERATOR **calls** CUSTOMERS(1) **at** CHANGE

An all_of event:
    OPERATOR **calls** CUSTOMERS(1) **at** CHANGE **and** CUSTOMERS(1) **accepting** CHANGE

A sequence event:
    (CUSTOMERS(1) **calls** OPERATOR **at** PRE_PAY   =>
     CUSTOMERS(1) **calls** PUMPS(1) **at** START_PUMPING =>
     CUSTOMERS(2) **calls** PUMPS(1) **at** START_PUMPING)

An iterative event:
    (OPERATOR **accepting** PRE_PAY)↑5

Matching compound events:
    if the event stream is: ... , A, C, B, D, A, E, B, ...
        the TSL event, A **and** B *matches the subintervals:*
            [A, C, B], [B, D, A], [A, E, B]
        the TSL event, A => B *matches subintervals:*
            [A, C, B], [A, E, B]
        the TSL event: (A **and** D) => (A **and** B) *matches interval:*
            [A, C, B, D, A, E, B].
        the TSL event, A↑2 *matches the subinterval:*
            [A, C, B, D, A].
In all cases the subintervals are the minimal matching intervals; intervals containing them also match

The definition of matching implies certain equivalences between compound events. For example,

    (A and B)

matches an interval I if and only if (A => B) **or** (B => A) matches I.

3.5 Specifications

A TSL *specification* consists of three events in the following order: an *activating* event, a *specified* event (or *body*), and a *terminating* event. The activator begins with the keyword, **when**, and the terminator begins with one of the keywords, **before** or **until**. The specified event may be *negated*, in which case it is preceeded by negation, **not**; the activating and terminating cannot be negated. A specification is either *positive* or *negative* depending whether the specified event is not, or is, negated.

It should be noted that all three component events in a specification may be compound events, although it is normal for the activator and terminator to be only basic events.

The semantics of a positive specification may be described informally as follows:

    "whenever the activating event matches a stream interval, the specification is *activated*. For that activation, both the specified event and the terminator simultaneously begin matching intervals of the event stream, starting at the next event in the stream and continuing until one of them matches an interval. Whenever the specified or terminating events match, that activation of the specification is completed. If the specified event matches before the terminator, the specification is *satisfied*. If the terminator matches before the specified event, the specification is *violated*. If they both match the same (shortest) interval, the specification is *satisfied* if the terminator begins with **until** and is *violated* if it begins with **before**. Finally, if the scope of an active specification is exited, any activation is treated as if the terminating event had matched."

Example: Satisfaction and violation of positive specifications.

in the event stream interval: ... , A, C, B, D, A, E, B, ...
    the following TSL specification is satisfied:
        when A
          then   (C => D)
          before (B => A);

    the following TSL specification is violated:
        when (A => B)
          then   (C => D)
          before (D => A);

If the specification is negated, the meanings of satisfaction and violation are reversed. The activator event specifies *when* the specification becomes active. A **before** terminator specifies that the specified event must match *before* the terminator, whereas an **until** terminator specifies that the specified event must match by the time the terminator matches.

Example: Specification of a gas pump's protocol.

```
when PUMP accepts OPERATOR at TURN_ON
    then (PUMP accepts CUSTOMER at START_PUMPING  =>
          PUMP accepts CUSTOMER at FINISH_PUMPING =>
          PUMP calls OPERATOR at CHARGE)
    before OPERATOR calls PUMP at TURN_ON;
```

Commentary

The specification is enabled whenever the declarative region of the Ada program in which it occurs, is elaborated. It is then activated whenever an event occurs in the stream signifying that the PUMP accepts a rendezvous with the OPERATOR at its TURN_ON entry. As a result of such an event, an activation of the specification is created. For each activation, the specification requires that the PUMP must execute the three actions in the sequence (body of the specification) *before* the OPERATOR calls the PUMP at TURN_ON again (terminating event). So the pump must continually satisfy its protocol.

Example: Specification denying one race condition for a pump.

```
when OPERATOR accepts CUSTOMERS(1) at PRE_PAY
    then not (OPERATOR accepts CUSTOMERS(2) at PRE_PAY         =>
              PUMPS(1) accepts CUSTOMERS(2) at START_PUMPING =>
              PUMPS(1) accepts CUSTOMERS(1) at START_PUMPING)
    before PUMPS(2) accepts CUSTOMERS(1) at START_PUMPING;
```

Commentary:

This specification will be passed to the TSL monitor whenever an Ada declaration in its position would be elaborated. After elaboration, it is activated each time the OPERATOR accepts a prepayment from the first customer task, CUSTOMERS(1). The sequence (in the body of the specification) will match any subsequent stream interval where the OPERATOR accepts a prepayment from CUSTOMER(2), who then gets ahead to use PUMP(1) before CUSTOMER(1). This describes a *race* between customers one and two for the first pump. Since the specification is negated it will be violated every time this particular race condition occurs.

The termination event for this specification is CUSTOMER(1) starting PUMP(2). If this happens *before* the sequence matches, the specification is *satisfied* since it is negated. Notice that the body and terminator cannot complete their matching at the same stream event, so replacing **before** by **until** does not change the meaning of the specification. It may happen that after activation neither the body nor the terminator match. This will be the case, for example, if CUSTOMERS(1) uses PUMPS(3). When the declarative region of the specification is exited, the terminator is assumed to match, leading to satisfaction in this example.

When a TSL specification is elaborated its Ada names are replaced by the corresponding TSL ids, and it is then passed to the TSL monitor.

3.6 Placeholders and General Matching

The examples given so far of events and specifications clearly lack generality. The basic events must in fact be identical with the stream events in order to match. What is most often required is an ability to specify a set of stream events that differ at their component values. For example, we may wish to specify a TSL event that will match any stream event in which the OPERATOR accepts a customer at PRE_PAY.

Variable parts of a basic event, compound event, or specification are indicated by identifiers beginning with the question mark symbol, "?". They are called *"placeholders"* since they indicate a position for any *value* of their type. There is no explicit placeholder declaration

The type of a placeholder is determined by its position in an event according to the syntax for that class of event if it is predefined, or according to the formal parameter list of the action declaration if it is user-defined. There is also a special wild-card placeholder, **any**, for each TSL type, which obeys different matching rules from normal placeholders.

Examples: Basic events with placeholders.

```
GENERAL performs ORDER(Move => Advance, Soldier => ?S);
OPERATOR releases ?C from PRE_PAY(PUMP_ID => ?P);
```

Commentary

Intuitively, the first event will match any event where the general orders any soldier, ?S, to advance (the named form of parameter bindings is used in the ORDER action). The second event will match any event where the operator completes a rendezvous at its PRE_PAY entry with any task, ?C, for any pump, ?P.

The meaning of basic and compound events containing placeholders is defined by a more general concept of matching, which in turn depends on the concept of instantiaton.

Instantiation.

A TSL event or specification may be *instantiated* if there is an association of a unique value with each placeholder and with each position of **any**. The instantiation is the event or specification that results when each placeholder is replaced by the associated value at all of its positions, and **any** is replaced at each of its positions by the value associated with that position.

Matching.

A TSL event or specification *matches* a stream event or interval if there is an instantiation of it which matches that stream event or interval according to the previous matching rules.

For example, the TSL event:

```
OPERATOR accepts ?T at ?E
```

matches all stream events where the OPERATOR starts a rendezvous with any calling task at any entry.

The instantiation rules require a placeholder to be associated with the same value at all positions, whereas **any** may have a different value at each position. Thus the stream interval

```
..., OPERATOR accepts CUSTOMER at PRE_PAY, OPERATOR accepts PUMP atCHANGE, ...
```

does not match

```
OPERATOR accepts ?T1 at ?E and OPERATOR accepts ?T2 at ?E
```

because ?E cannot be instantiated to different entry names at different positions. However, it does match each of the following events:

```
(1)   OPERATOR accepts ?T1 at any and OPERATOR accepts ?T2 at any;
(2)   OPERATOR accepts ?T1 at ?E1 and OPERATOR accepts ?T2 at ?E2;
```

The semantics of specifications with placeholders is defined from the semantics for the previously discussed ground cases when there are no placeholders.

1. A specification is activated when there is an instantiation of its activation event which matches an interval of the stream.

2. This instantiation is applied to both the *specified* and *terminator* events. The resulting events are the constituent specified and terminator events for that activation. They may be *partially instantiated* in that only some of the placeholders have been assigned values.

3. The specified and terminator events from step 2 are both matched concurrently against subsequent intervals of the event stream. The smallest interval following the activating interval which matches (an instance of) one or both of these events is found. At this point the satisfaction or violation of the specification is determined from the definition for ground specifications without placeholders.

Specifications containing placeholders must obey one restriction to maintain the independence of the specified and terminator events:

If a placeholder occur in *both* the specified and terminator events then it must also occur in the activation event.

As a result of this restriction, such a placeholder will be bound by the matching of the activator event.

The previous example of a specification may now be stated in a more useful form.

Example: Specification denying all instances of a race condition.

```
when OPERATOR accepts ?C1 at PRE_PAY
     then not (OPERATOR accepts ?C2 at PRE_PAY    =>
               ?P1 accepts ?C2 at START_PUMPING   =>
               ?P1 accepts ?C1 at START_PUMPING)
     until ?P2 accepts ?C1 at START_PUMPING
```

Commentary

This specification will be activated each time the OPERATOR accepts a prepayment from any customer. The sequence in the body will then match any subsequent stream interval where the OPERATOR accepts a prepayment from a (later) customer who then gets ahead to use the pump to be used by the first customer. Since the specification is negated it will be satisfied if the first customer gets to use any pump *before* the specified sequence matches. If the second customer uses a pump before the first customer, then a race is averted if the first customer uses a different pump. If however, the first customer uses the same pump, after the second customer, a race has occurred in which the first customer lost. In this case the body and terminator both match an interval ending at the same event — ?P1 and ?P2 represent the same pump. To exclude this case, **until** must be used. The negated specification expresses "the body must not match before the terminator nor simultaneously with it".

Type mismatches may occur during the matching of a specification. For example, an instantiation may associate a value with a placeholder that matches the type required at one position of the placeholder but not at another position. Such situations are errors in the TSL computation, and may indicate an inconsistency with the underlying Ada program.

3.7 Properties

Properties may be associated with entities in the underlying Ada program by TSL property declarations. The types to which the property applies are specified in the declaration; all entities of those types then have the property. Properties may be viewed as user-defined dynamic attributes, analogous to standard attributes provided by Ada such as E'COUNT and T'CALLABLE. For example, we can declare a property of pumps at the Gas Station called In Use.

Example: A property declaration.

```
property In_Use(PUMP) : BOOLEAN := FALSE;
```

The *values* of properties are functions of the event stream. These values are computed by *update* statements.

Update statements behave as concurrent processes which match specifications against intervals in the event stream, and update property values whenever the matching process is successful. An update statement contains an *activator* event, a *specified* event, and an assignment to a property. The assignment part is prefaced by the reserved word, **set**. Whenever the activating event matches, the update statement is activated. Subsequently, whenever the specified event matches, the assignment is executed, and that activation completes. The update may be re-activated by another matching of its activator.

The update statements for a property are included in a body associated with the property declaration. A property and its body may be declared separately in the same Ada declarative region. This is similar to Ada subprograms, but also includes task specifications and bodies. Mutually recursive properties are allowed but should be used with caution (see below).

Example: In_Use property declaration and body.

```
property In_Use(PUMP) : BOOLEAN := FALSE
is
    when ?X accepts any at START_PUMPING
        set In_Use(?X) := TRUE;
    when ?X accepts any at FINISH_PUMPING
        then OPERATOR releases ?X from CHARGE
        set In_Use(?X) := FALSE;
  end In_Use;
```

Commentary

The specification part declares a boolean valued property of every value of the subtype, PUMP, of the TSL type TASK. It has an initial value, FALSE. The following body contains a sequence of *update* statements. After the property definition is elaborated, the update statements are all matched concurrently against the event stream. In this example, whenever the first update matches, the property for that value of the placeholder, ?X, is set to TRUE; concurrently, whenever the second update matches, it is set to FALSE. Consequently, the In_Use property for each pump changes its value when the pump accepts its START_PUMPING entry, and when it accepts FINISH_PUMPING and then finishes a rendezvous with the OPERATOR at CHARGE.

Example: A task's most recent action.

```
property Last_Done(TASK) : ACTION := null
is
    when ?T performs ?A
        set Last_Done(?T) := ?A;
  end Last_Done;
```

Commentary

Last_Done is a property of tasks yielding values of the ACTION type. Initially the property has the null value. Each time a task performs an action, including a TSL predefined action, the value of the property for that task is updated to this most recent action. Note (see below) that basic events signifying predefined actions have equivalent forms as performs events that match the activator in Last_Done.

Property declarations and bodies are passed to the TSL monitor when their declarative region in the Ada program is elaborated.

The value of a property may be referenced in a TSL expression by a notation similar to a standard Ada function call. The property name is followed by a list of values of types corresponding to the list of TSL types in the property declaration. Such an expression always denotes the *current* value of the property. For example, we can declare a global count of all active tasks. The definition uses the current value of the count property, as well as the predefined events, **activates** and **terminates**:

Example: The number of active tasks.

```
property ACTIVE_COUNT : INTEGER := 1
is
    when any activates
```

```
                set ACTIVE_COUNT := ACTIVE_COUNT + 1;
        when any terminates
                set ACTIVE_COUNT := ACTIVE_COUNT - 1;
    end ACTIVE_COUNT;
```

The ACTIVE_COUNT expression on the right side of the assignments denotes the current value of the property.

TSL provides predefined properties describing the status of Ada tasks, such as, **Running**, **Calling**, **Accepting**, and so on. Nearly all of the predefined properties can be defined by property declarations and bodies using the predefined basic events. (This is not possible in some cases because the set of TSL predefined events is inadequate.)

Example: Definition of a predefined property.

```
    property Calling(TASK) : BOOLEAN := FALSE is
        when ?T calls any then
            set Calling(?T) : TRUE;
        when any releases ?T then
            set Calling(?T) := FALSE;
    end Calling;
```

If more than one **set** assignment to the same property is executed at the same event in the event stream, the TSL computation is erroneous. The resulting value of the property will be one of the assigned values, but which one is not specified by TSL. Similarly, if mutually dependent properties are **set** at the same event, their values may depend on the order of execution of the assignments. Such situations are erroneous and the resulting values are not specified. If a type mismatch occurs during the execution of a **set** assignment, the TSL computation is erroneous and the assignment is not executed.

3.8 Guards

Often the occurrence of a stream event is important only in certain contexts. TSL provides *guards* to specify context. A guard is a boolean condition built up from expressions (especially properties) using relational operators and boolean connectives. A guard is bound to a basic event by the reserved word **where** to form a *guarded event*. A Guarded event can match a stream event only when the guard condition is true.

Examples: Guarded events.

```
    OPERATOR calls CUSTOMERS(1) at CHANGE
        where not (TERMINATED(CUSTOMERS(1))

    ?C calls ?P at START_PUMPING where not In_Use(?P)

    ?X activates any where ACTIVE_COUNT < 1000
```

Basic events are the only kind of events that can be guarded. Compound events and specifications are built up from guarded basic events, but may not be guarded themselves.

A guard denotes the value of a boolean expression at each stream event. Since a guard may change value as a new stream events occur, it is important to define an order in which matching and execution of updates are performed.

Whenever a new stream event is considered in attempting to match a guarded event, an order of matching of specifications and executing **set** assignments is defined as follows:

1. possible matching instantiations of guarded events are computed using the current values of properties to evaluate guards. This includes guarded events in specifications and in updates.
2. **set** assignments resulting from step 1 are executed in some order that is not specified.

In the last example above, if the next stream event is an activation, and the current value of ACTIVE_COUNT is 999, the guarded event will be matched first — successfully. Then the value of ACTIVE_COUNT will be set to 1000.

During evaluation of a guard, Ada subexpressions are evaluated according to Ada rules. In particular, a placeholder in an expression must be replaced by a value associated with it in a (partially complete) matching before the expression is evaluated. If a placeholder is unbound by the matching, evaluation of the expression results in an erroneous TSL computation. There is one exception to this rule. If an unbound placeholder occurs as an operand of an equality operator during guard evaluation, say, ?P = E, then the value of E is associated with the placeholder ?P and the guard is true. If both operands of an equality expression are unbound placeholders, the result is also an error.

3.9 Parameter Bindings

The optional parameter binding in basic events (the *call, accept, start_rendezvous, end rendezvous,* and *performs* categories) is given in the Ada named parameter form. The formal parameters of the Ada entry declarations or TSL action declarations are used as parameter names. Only those parameters of interest need be named in the binding part of a basic event.

For example,

```
OPERATOR accepts ?C1 at PRE_PAY(AMOUNT => ?X1)
```

will match stream events in which the operator accepts prepayment from a task (in actuality, any customer), and ?X1 will be associated with the actual amount in each such event (AMOUNT is a formal parameter of PRE_PAY).

This extra context is sometimes important in specifying events accurately and reducing unwanted matching. We can change the race condition specification (Section 3.6) by adding an entry binding:

```
when OPERATOR accepts ?C1 at PRE_PAY(AMOUNT => ?X1)
    then not (OPERATOR accepts ?C2 at PRE_PAY(AMOUNT => ?X2)    =>
             ?P1 accepts ?C2 at START_PUMPING where(?X2 < ?X1) =>
             ?P1 accepts ?C1 at START_PUMPING)
    until ?P2 accepts ?C1 at START_PUMPING;
```

This specification will be violated only if a customer who has paid less beats an earlier customer to the pump.

4. Examples

4.1 Simulation of an Automated Gas Station

This example illustrates the use of TSL to specify task interactions in a completed Ada Program. Only predefined TSL events are used, so there are no user-defined actions. The basic Ada declarations and some of the TSL specifications are shown. The corresponding Ada bodies, which do not contain any TSL statements, are omitted.

The gas station contains tasks representing the station operator, the customers, and the pumps. A customer arrives at the station, prepays the operator, pumps gas, receives change from the operator, and leaves. The operator accepts prepayments, computes charges and gives customers their change. The pumps are used by the customers, and report the amount pumped to the operator.

```
procedure GAS_STATION is

    task OPERATOR is
        entry PRE_PAY(AMOUNT      : in INTEGER;
                      PUMP_ID     : in INTEGER;
                      CUSTOMER_ID : in INTEGER);
```

```
              entry CHARGE(AMOUNT   : in INTEGER;
                          PUMP_ID : in INTEGER);
        end OPERATOR;

        task type CUSTOMER is
            entry GET_CUSTOMER_ID(NUMBER : in INTEGER);
            entry CHANGE(AMOUNT : in INTEGER);
        end CUSTOMER;

        task type PUMP is
            entry GET_PUMP_ID(NUMBER : in INTEGER);
            entry ACTIVATE(LIMIT : in INTEGER);
            entry START_PUMPING;
            entry FINISH_PUMPING(AMOUNT_CHARGED : out INTEGER);
        end PUMP;

--  1. specification of constraints on customers.
    --+ property HAS_PAID(CUSTOMER, PUMP) : BOOLEAN := FALSE
    --+ is
    --+     when OPERATOR releases ?C from PRE_PAY(PUMP_ID => ?P)
    --+         set HAS_PAID(?C, ?P) := TRUE;
    --+     when ?C calls ?P at FINISH_PUMPING
    --+         set HAS_PAID(?C, ?P) := FALSE;
    --+ end HAS_PAID;

    --+     not (?C calls ?P at START_PUMPING where not HAS_PAID(?C, ?P));

--  A customer's protocol.
    --+ when ?C calls OPERATOR at PRE_PAY
    --+     then (?C calls ?P at START_PUMPING =>
    --+           ?C calls ?P at FINISH_PUMPING =>
    --+           ?C accepting CHANGE)
    --+     before ?C accepts OPERATOR at CHANGE;

--  2. specification of a pump's protocol.
    --+ when ?P accepts OPERATOR at ACTIVATE
    --+     then (?P accepts ?C at START_PUMPING  =>
    --+           ?P accepts ?C at FINISH_PUMPING =>
    --+           ?P calls OPERATOR at CHARGE)
    --+     before OPERATOR calls ?P at ACTIVATE;

--  3. constraint on the operator.
    --+ when OPERATOR accepts ?P at CHARGE
    --+     then (OPERATOR calls ?C at CHANGE)
    --+     before OPERATOR accepting;

--  4. specification guarding against races for a pump.
    --+ when OPERATOR accepts ?C1 at PRE_PAY
    --+     then not (OPERATOR accepts ?C2 at PRE_PAY    =>
    --+               ?P1 accepts ?C2 at START_PUMPING  =>
    --+               ?P1 accepts ?C1 at START_PUMPING)
    --+     before ?P2 accepts ?C1 at START_PUMPING;
            ...
    --  Ada bodies and arrays of customers and pumps.
end GAS_STATION;
```

4.2 A Byzantine General's Problem

This example illustrates the use of action declarations and TSL specifications to specify task communications at a level of abstraction which hides the actual details of how the communication takes place. The Ada program is divided informally into two parts, a *top level design* and a *simulation*, to distinguish between the abstract actions and one of many possible implementations.

The top level design shows the abstract program in which actions are not implemented by Ada text. Connections between actions are specified in TSL, and the main behavioral requirement of the program is also specified. At this level, a designer may wish to write a "quick simulation" (or "rapid prototype") to establish if the specifications can be satisfied.

The *simulation* contains the rest of the Ada program. It represents a very simple way of implementing the General, the Soldiers, and the actions; it may not be the final implementation of choice. Each action is interpreted in this implementation by TSL **perform** statements that indicate when the action is executed.

It should be noted that the TSL specifications are incomplete. Protocols for Soldiers, for example, are ommitted. Only those specifications dealing with connections and reliability are shown here.

-- *Top level actions and specifications.*

```
generic
    Max_Soldiers : Positive;
procedure Byzantine;

procedure Byzantine is

    type Move is (Advance, Retreat);

    task General is
--+     action Order(X : Move; S : Task);
    end;

    task type Soldier is
        entry Receive_Identity(I : Integer);
--+     action Receive_Order(X : out Move);
--+     action Send_Copy(A : Move; L : Soldier);
--+     action Act(X : Move);
    end Soldier;
```

-- *Specification of connections between actions*

```
--+     property Ready(Soldier) return Boolean := False
--+     is
--+     when General performs General.Order(X => ?Y, S => ?L)
--+         then set Ready(?L) := True;
--+     when ?L performs Soldier.Receive_Order(X => ?Y)
--+         then set Ready(?L) := False;
--+     end;

--+     not ?L performs Soldier.Receive_Order(X => ?Y)
--+     where not Ready(?L);

--+     not (?L2 performs Soldier.Act =>
--+         ?L1 performs Soldier.Send_Copy(A => ?M, L => ?L2));
```

```
--    Specification of Reliability and Agreement.

--+       property Reliable(Soldier) : BOOLEAN := TRUE is
--+           when ?L performs Soldier.Receive_Order(X => ?M)
--+               then ?L performs Soldier.Send_Copy(A => ?M1) where
--+                                                              ?M1 /= ?M
--+                   set Reliable(?L) := FALSE;
--+       end Reliable;

--+  << AGREEMENT >>
--+       not (?L1 performs Soldier.Act(A => ?M1) where Reliable(?L1) =>
--+            ?L2 performs Soldier.Act(A => ?M2) where (Reliable(?L2) and
--+                                                      ?M2 /= ?M1));

--    Simulation of top level specification.
             type Army is array (Positive range <>) of Soldier;
             type Mail is array (Positive range <>) of Move;
             Soldiers            : Army(1 .. Max_Soldiers);
             Mailboxes, Actions : Mail(1 .. Max_Soldiers);
             Communications : array(1 .. Max_Soldiers) of
                                             Mail(1 .. Max_Soldiers);

             function Decide(X : Move) return Move is ... end;
             function Summarize(X : Mail) return Move is ... end;

--    Byzantine bodies.
             task body General is
                 M : Move := Decide(Advance);
             begin
                 for I in 1 .. Max_Soldiers loop
--+                  perform Order(M, Soldiers(I));
                     Mailboxes(I) := M;
                 end loop;
             end General;

             task body Soldier is
                 My_Id : Integer;
                 A, Copy : Move;
             begin
                 accept Receive_Identity(I : Integer) do
                     My_Id := I;
                 end;
                 delay 5.0;
--+              perform Receive_Order(A);
                 A := Mailboxes(My_Id);
                 for J in 1 .. Max_Soldiers loop
                     if J /= My_Id then
                         Copy := Decide(A);
--+                      perform Send_Copy(Copy, Soldiers(J));
                         Communications(J)(My_Id) := Copy;
                     end if;
                 end loop;
                 delay 5.0;
--+              perform Act( Decide(Summarize(Communications(My_Id))));
                 Actions(My_Id) := Decide(Summarize(Communications(My_Id)));
```

```
    end Soldier;

begin

    for J in 1 .. Max_Soldiers loop
        Soldiers(J).Receive_Identity(J);
    end loop;

    end Byzantine;
```

Commentary

At the top level, the actions define communication between the declared tasks. The General, for example, is specified to perform Order actions. Soldiers are specified to perform three actions, receiving an order, sending copies of orders, and acting. The TSL specifications constrain performance of these actions.

The property, Ready, defines a *correspondence* between pairs of Order and Receive_Order actions performed by the General and the Soldiers respectively. Two stream events *correspond* under this property if they match the two activators in a single instantiation of the property body, and if in addition, they are the earliest events in their respective local streams that do not already correspond to other events under the property. Thus, the *correspondence* is defined inductively over the event stream. The first TSL specification constrains an Order action to be performed *before* a corresponding Receive_Order action. Since all event streams must satisfy this, the corresponding pairs of actions are *connected* — they must always be observed in this order. This specification defines a flow of data between *actors* since the placeholder, ?Y, is an **in** mode parameter in the Order action and an **out** mode parameter in the Receive_Order action.

The second specification is a typical *safety* requirement: a soldier must not act before all buddies have sent their copies to him. A *liveness* protocol requiring soldiers to send copies of their orders to comrades is not given here, but it would be expressed similarly to protocols in the Gas Station.

Reliability is defined as a property possessed by Soldiers. It is set to true initially — all soldiers are assumed reliable until their actions prove otherwise. *Agreement* between reliable soldiers is expressed by a very simple specification that will be violated if there is a single event of a reliable Soldier performing an act, followed by a single event in which a reliable Soldier performs a different act.

The TSL specifications are all placed in the top level declarative region. They are activated on scope entry and remain active, unless violated, until scope exit.

The remainder of the Ada program is informally called a *simulation*. It implements the actors (General and Soldiers) and the actions. The task bodies carry out actions according to simple protocols which were not specified here. More important is the use of TSL **perform** statements to express a correspondence between the actions and the simulation. A **perform** statement is placed so as to assert when an action is being performed. Delay statements are included as a crude way to satisfy the specifications that connect some of the pairs of **perform** events.

The Byzantine procedure may be instantiated in a simple test program. If this program is processed by the TSL compiler and then compiled (by an Ada compiler) and executed, it will generate a stream of events. This stream will consist mainly of **performs** events for user-defined actions. It will be monitored for consistency with the TSL specifications.

A possible initial interval of an event stream for this program is:

```
    main activates General,
    main activates Soldiers(2),
    main activates Soldiers(1),
        . . .           -- activation of all other tasks.
```

```
main calls Soldiers(1) at Receive_Identity(I => 1),
General performs Order(Advance, Soldiers(1)),
Soldiers(1) accepts main at Receive_Identity(I => 1),
Soldiers(1) releases main from Receive_Identity(I => 1),
main calls Soldiers(2) at Receive_Identity(I => 2),
General performs Order(Advance, Soldiers(2)),
Soldiers(2) accepts main at Receive_Identity(I => 2),
Soldiers(2) releases main from Receive_Identity(I => 2),
Soldiers(2) performs Receive_Order(Advance),
Soldiers(2) performs Send_Copy(Advance, Soldiers(1)),
Soldiers(2) performs Send_Copy(Advance, Soldiers(3)),
Soldiers(1) performs Receive_Order(Advance),
Soldiers(1) performs Send_Copy(Advance, Soldiers(2)),
main calls Soldiers(3) at Receive_Identity(I => 3),
...
```

It is possible to use **perform** statements to express the correspondence between actions and implementation because the simulation in this example is very simple. In general, actions may involve other observable events so that their execution leads to overlapping sequences of events. In TSL-2 a more powerful action body construct will be provided to deal with such cases.

If this simulation satisfies the TSL specifications, the designer may choose to continue developing the program in several ways: (1) a more sophisticated implementation may be needed for the actions so there is no shared data between tasks, (2) further specifications may be imposed, (3) a module such as the General may be expanded in detail that does not affect communication with the army, such as a "joint chiefs of staff" that debate internally. TSL-2 will contain constructs to support these kinds of refinements within a structured discipline so that consistency between design and simulation, when established at one level, is not lost in further development.

5. Relationship to Other Work

Some of the concepts in TSL have appeared in one form or another in earlier papers on specifying both the sequential and concurrent aspects of programs. We mention briefly some important related works. First, sequences and recursive macros in TSL specifications are closely related to path expressions for defining execution sequences to synchronize processes [2]. Secondly, the idea of using sequences to specify concurrent processing has often been proposed in the research literature, Early pioneering examples being Gilles Kahn [10], and Ole-Johan Dahl [4]. Similar ideas have also been applied more recently in the event description language, EDL described by Bates and Wileden in [1]. The query aspects of TSL, as embodied in the concept of matching, has something of the flavor of Carl Hewitt's Planner [9], and later generalizations of Planner such as Prolog [3]. Application of Prolog to checking for deadlock errors in the history of Ada tasking program has been investigated by Carol LeDoux in [12]. Finally, an operational semantics for TSL can be given by mapping the constructs into event/token graphs, and defining the matching process in terms of operations on those graphs. Event/token graphs are closely related to Petri nets [14]. We did not investigate the use of Petri nets directly in defining TSL semantics.

References

[1]   Bates, P.C. and Wileden, J.C.
        EDL: A Basis for Distributed System Debugging Tools. In *Proceedings of Hawaii International Conference on System Sciences*, pages 86-93. Hawaii International Conference on System Sciences, Honolulu, Hawaii, January, 1982.

[2]   Campbell,R.H. and Habermann, A.N.
        The Specification of Process Synchronization by Path-Expressions. *Lecture Notes in Computer Science*, 16, 1974.

[3]   Clocksin, W.F., and Mellish, C.S.
        Programming in Prolog. Springer-Velag, 1981.

[4]   Dahl, O.-J.
        Time Sequences as a Tool For Describing Program Behaviour Research Report in Informatics 48, University of Oslo, August, 1979.

[5]   Helmbold, D.P. and Luckham, D.C.
        Debugging Ada Tasking Programs In *Proceedings of the IEEE Computer Society 1984 Conference on Ada Applications and Environments*, pages 96-110. IEEE, St. Paul, Minnesota, October 15-18, 1984. Also published, Stanford University Computer Systems Laboratory TR 84-262, July, 1984, Program Analysis and Verification Group Report 25.

[6]   Helmbold, D.P., and Luckham, D.C.
        Runtime Detection and Description of Deadness Errors in Ada Tasking. CSL Technical Report 83-249, Stanford University, November, 1983. Program Analysis and Verification Group Report 22.

[7]   Helmbold, D.P., and Luckham, D.C.
        Debugging Ada Tasking Programs. *IEEE Software* 2(2):47-57, March, 1985. In Proceedings of the IEEE Computer Society 1984 Conference on Ada Applications and Environments, pp.96-110. IEEE, St. Paul, Minnesota, October 15-18, 1984. Also published as Stanford University CSL TR.84-263, July, 1984.

[8]   Helmbold, D.P., and Luckham, D.C.
        TSL: Task Sequencing Language. In *Proceedings of the 1985 SIGAda International Conference*, pages 255-274, ACM, Paris, France, May, 1985. Also published in a special edition of *Ada Letters*, Vol.V, Issue 2, September-October 1985.

[9]   Hewitt, C.
        Planner: A Language for Proving Theorems and Manipulating Models in a Robot. Massachusetts Institute of Technology, January, 1971.

[10]   Kahn, G. and MacQueen, D.
        Coroutines and Networks of Parallel Processes. In *Proceedings of IFIP Congress '77*, pages 993-998, North-Holland Publishing Company, Amsterdam, August, 1977.

[11]   Lamport, L., Shostak, R., and Pease, M.
        The Byzantine Generals Problem. *Transactions of Programming Languages and Systems*, 4(3):382-401, July, 1982.

[12]   Ledoux, C., and Parker, D.S.
        Saving Traces for Ada Debugging. In *Proceedings of the Ada International Conference'85*, pages 97-108, Cambridge University Press, 1985.

[13]   Luckham, D.C., Helmbold, D.P., Bryan, D.L., and Meldal, S.
        Task Sequencing Language for Specifying Distributed Ada Systems: TSL-1. Forthcoming CSL Technical Report, 1987.

[14]   Peterson, J.L.
        Petri Nets. *Computing Surveys*, 9(3), September, 1977.

Authors Index Volume II

Vol. 219: Advances in Cryptology – EUROCRYPT '85. Proceedings, 1985. Edited by F. Pichler. IX, 281 pages. 1986.

Vol. 220: RIMS Symposia on Software Science and Engineering II. Proceedings, 1983 and 1984. Edited by E. Goto, K. Araki and T. Yuasa. XI, 323 pages. 1986.

Vol. 221: Logic Programming '85. Proceedings, 1985. Edited by E. Wada. IX, 311 pages. 1986.

Vol. 222: Advances in Petri Nets 1985. Edited by G. Rozenberg. VI, 498 pages. 1986.

Vol. 223: Structure in Complexity Theory. Proceedings, 1986. Edited by A.L. Selman. VI, 401 pages. 1986.

Vol. 224: Current Trends in Concurrency. Overviews and Tutorials. Edited by J.W. de Bakker, W.-P. de Roever and G. Rozenberg. XII, 716 pages. 1986.

Vol. 225: Third International Conference on Logic Programming. Proceedings, 1986. Edited by E. Shapiro. IX, 720 pages. 1986.

Vol. 226: Automata, Languages and Programming. Proceedings, 1986. Edited by L. Kott. IX, 474 pages. 1986.

Vol. 227: VLSI Algorithms and Architectures – AWOC 86. Proceedings, 1986. Edited by F. Makedon, K. Mehlhorn, T. Papatheodorou and P. Spirakis. VIII, 328 pages. 1986.

Vol. 228: Applied Algebra, Algorithmics and Error-Correcting Codes. AAECC-2. Proceedings, 1984. Edited by A. Poli. VI, 265 pages. 1986.

Vol. 229: Algebraic Algorithms and Error-Correcting Codes. AAECC-3. Proceedings, 1985. Edited by J. Calmet. VII, 416 pages. 1986.

Vol. 230: 8th International Conference on Automated Deduction. Proceedings, 1986. Edited by J.H. Siekmann. X, 708 pages. 1986.

Vol. 231: R. Hausser, NEWCAT: Parsing Natural Language Using Left-Associative Grammar. II, 540 pages. 1986.

Vol. 232: Fundamentals of Artificial Intelligence. Edited by W. Bibel and Ph. Jorrand. VII, 313 pages. 1986.

Vol. 233: Mathematical Foundations of Computer Science 1986. Proceedings, 1986. Edited by J. Gruska, B. Rovan and J. Wiedermann. IX, 650 pages. 1986.

Vol. 234: Concepts in User Interfaces: A Reference Model for Command and Response Languages. By Members of IFIP Working Group 2.7. Edited by D. Beech. X, 116 pages. 1986.

Vol. 235: Accurate Scientific Computations. Proceedings, 1985. Edited by W.L. Miranker and R.A. Toupin. XIII, 205 pages. 1986.

Vol. 236: TEX for Scientific Documentation. Proceedings, 1986. Edited by J. Désarménien. VI, 204 pages. 1986.

Vol. 237: CONPAR 86. Proceedings, 1986. Edited by W. Händler, D. Haupt, R. Jeltsch, W. Juling and O. Lange. X, 418 pages. 1986.

Vol. 238: L. Naish, Negation and Control in Prolog. IX, 119 pages. 1986.

Vol. 239: Mathematical Foundations of Programming Semantics. Proceedings, 1985. Edited by A. Melton. VI, 395 pages. 1986.

Vol. 240: Category Theory and Computer Programming. Proceedings, 1985. Edited by D. Pitt, S. Abramsky, A. Poigné and D. Rydeheard. VII, 519 pages. 1986.

Vol. 241: Foundations of Software Technology and Theoretical Computer Science. Proceedings, 1986. Edited by K.V. Nori. XII, 519 pages. 1986.

Vol. 242: Combinators and Functional Programming Languages. Proceedings, 1985. Edited by G. Cousineau, P.-L. Curien and B. Robinet. V, 208 pages. 1986.

Vol. 243: ICDT '86. Proceedings, 1986. Edited by G. Ausiello and P. Atzeni. VI, 444 pages. 1986.

Vol. 244: Advanced Programming Environments. Proceedings, 1986. Edited by R. Conradi, T.M. Didriksen and D.H. Wanvik. VII, 604 pages. 1986

Vol. 245: H.F. de Groote, Lectures on the Complexity of Bilinear Problems. V, 135 pages. 1987.

Vol. 246: Graph-Theoretic Concepts in Computer Science. Proceedings, 1986. Edited by G. Tinhofer and G. Schmidt. VII, 307 pages. 1987.

Vol. 247: STACS 87. Proceedings, 1987. Edited by F.J. Brandenburg, G. Vidal-Naquet and M. Wirsing. X, 484 pages. 1987.

Vol. 248: Networking in Open Systems. Proceedings, 1986. Edited by G. Müller and R.P. Blanc. VI, 441 pages. 1987.

Vol. 249: TAPSOFT '87. Volume 1. Proceedings, 1987. Edited by H. Ehrig, R. Kowalski, G. Levi and U. Montanari. XIV, 289 pages. 1987.

Vol. 250: TAPSOFT '87. Volume 2. Proceedings, 1987. Edited by H. Ehrig, R. Kowalski, G. Levi and U. Montanari. XIV, 336 pages. 1987.

Vol. 251: V. Akman, Unobstructed Shortest Paths in Polyhedral Environments. VII, 103 pages. 1987.

Vol. 252: VDM '87. VDM – A Formal Method at Work. Proceedings, 1987. Edited by D. Bjørner, C.B. Jones, M. Mac an Airchinnigh and E.J. Neuhold. IX, 422 pages. 1987.

Vol. 254: Petri Nets: Central Models and Their Properties. Advances in Petri Nets 1986, Part I. Proceedings, 1986. Edited by W. Brauer, W. Reisig and G. Rozenberg. X, 480 pages. 1987.

Vol. 255: Petri Nets: Applications and Relationships to Other Models of Concurrency. Advances in Petri Nets 1986, Part II. Proceedings, 1986. Edited by W. Brauer, W. Reisig and G. Rozenberg. X, 516 pages. 1987.

Vol. 256: Rewriting Techniques and Applications. Proceedings, 1987. Edited by P. Lescanne. VI, 285 pages. 1987.

Vol. 257: Database Machine Performance: Modeling Methodologies and Evaluation Strategies. Edited by F. Cesarini and S. Salza. IX, 250 pages. 1987.

Vol. 258: PARLE, Parallel Architectures and Languages Europe. Volume I. Proceedings, 1987. Edited by J.W. de Bakker, A.J. Nijman and P.C. Treleaven. XII, 480 pages. 1987.

Vol. 259: PARLE, Parallel Architectures and Languages Europe. Volume II. Proceedings, 1987. Edited by J.W. de Bakker, A.J. Nijman and P.C. Treleaven. XII, 464 pages. 1987.